THE FRED JONES JR. MUSEUM OF ART
AT THE UNIVERSITY OF OKLAHOMA

Selected Works

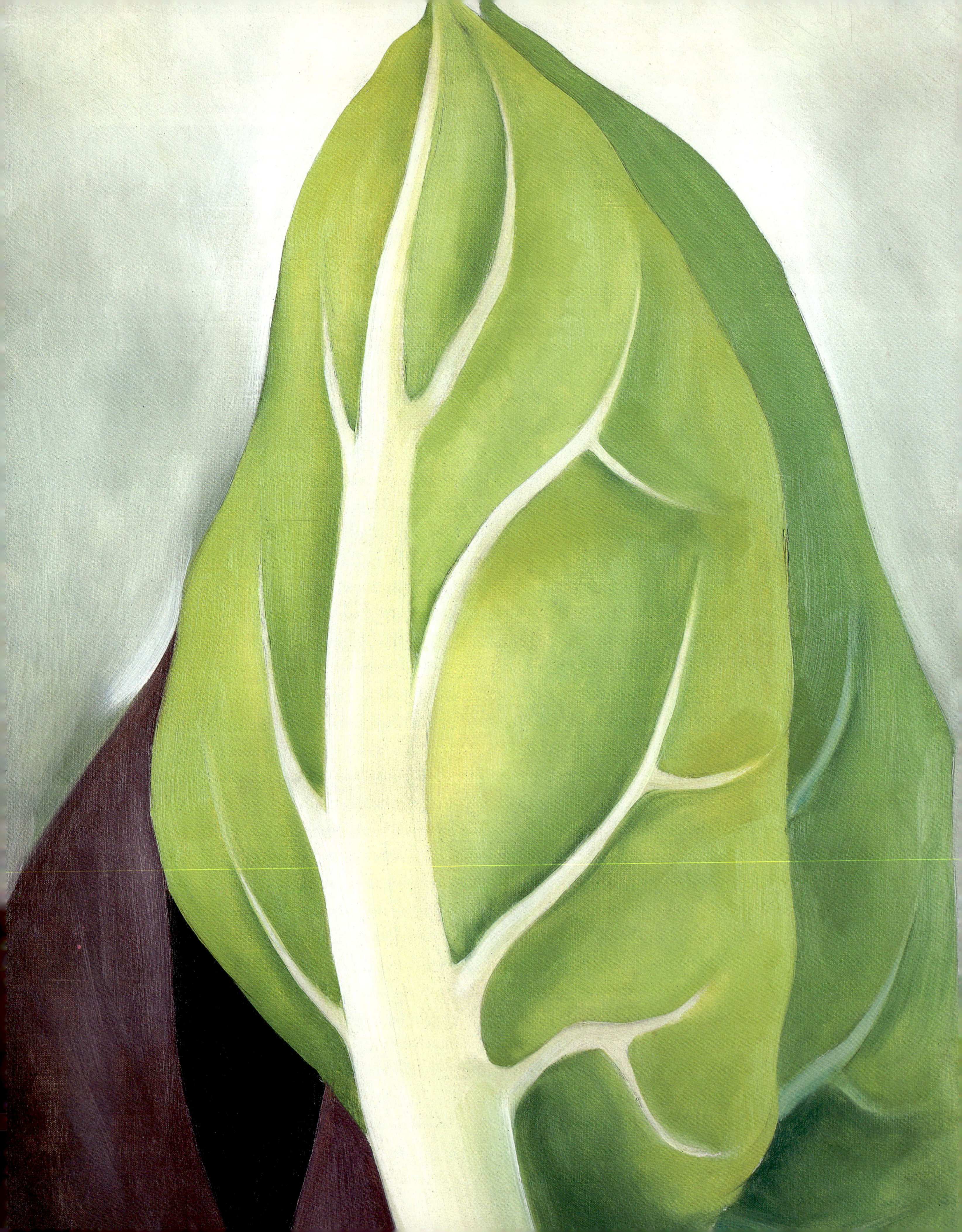

Eric McCauley Lee
Rima Canaan

THE FRED JONES JR. MUSEUM OF ART
AT THE UNIVERSITY OF OKLAHOMA

Selected Works

University of Oklahoma Press
Norman

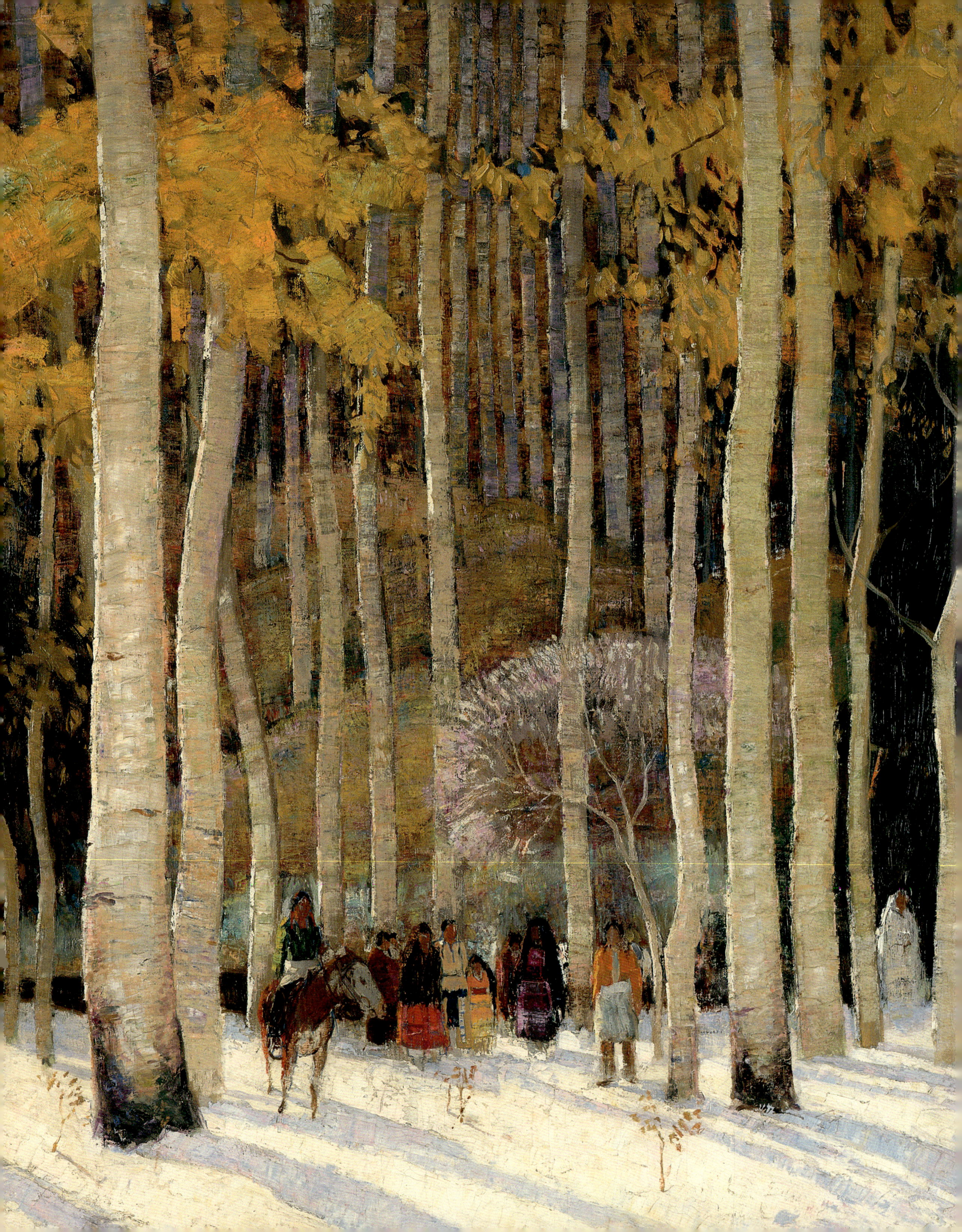

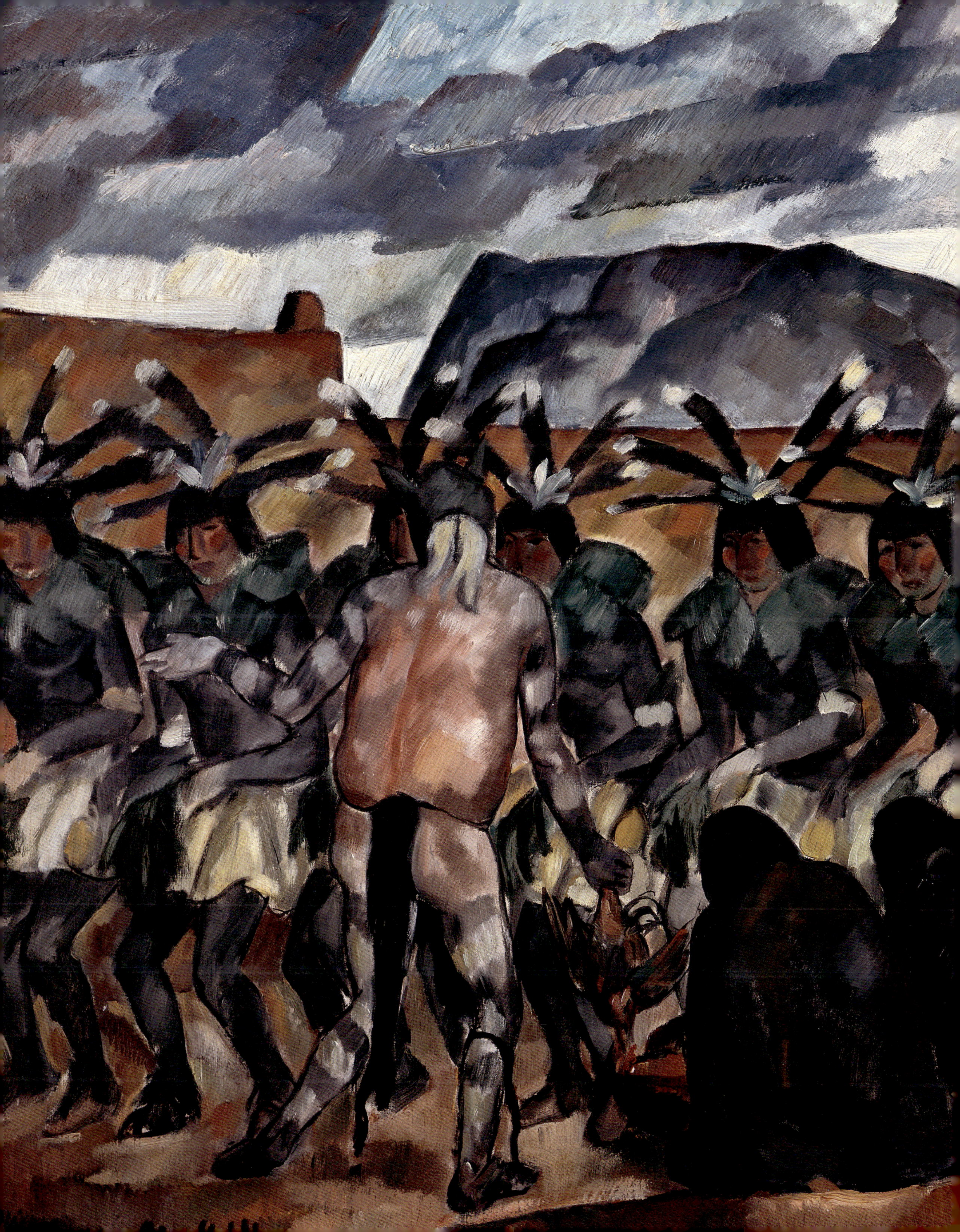

Joseph Tate of Tulsa; William H. Thams of Midland, Texas, in memory of his wife, Roxanne Thams; J. Donald Walp of Dallas; and Wanda Otey Westheimer and the late Jerry Westheimer.

At the University of Oklahoma, people who have aided with the catalogue include Provost Nancy Mergler; David Maloney, J. P. Audas, Robyn Tower, and Charlotte Gay of the Office of Development; and Catherine Bishop and Jerri Culpepper of the Office of Public Affairs. In the School of Art, I am grateful to Director Andrew Phelan as well as to art historians Alan Atkinson, Susan Caldwell, Victor Koshkin-Youritzin, and Mary Jo Watson. Byron Price, director of the School of Art's Charles M. Russell Center for the Study of Art of the American West, has also been helpful.

I am thankful to the museum's Board of Visitors and to the Museum of Art Association, which have both been steadfast in their support. I also wish to acknowledge the museum staff, in particular Jane Aebersold, Susan Baley, Ross Cotts, Joyce Cummins, Anita Hanley, Quinn Johnson, Lynette Lobban, Sandra Milligan, Stacey Myers, Mary Jane Rutherford, Susan Slepka Squires, and Becky Zurcher. Gail Kana Anderson has worked long hours in coordinating the illustrations for the catalogue.

At the University of Oklahoma Press, I am thankful to Director John Drayton, Chuck Rankin, and Patsy Willcox. At Marquand Books, many thanks go to Ed Marquand, as well as to Jennifer Harris, Zach Hooker, John Hubbard, Linda McDougall, John Trombold, Jennifer Sugden, and Marie Weiler.

I have deep appreciation and admiration for my coauthor, Rima Canaan, whose hard work made this book a reality.

Finally, my gratitude extends to the family of the late Fred Sr. and Mary Eddy Jones, especially their daughter, Marylin Jones Upsher, and grandsons, Fred Hall, Brooks Hall, and Kirkland Hall. Their continued support of the museum has made this catalogue possible.

Eric McCauley Lee
Director
The Fred Jones Jr. Museum of Art
The University of Oklahoma

Foreword

A museum cannot flourish and fulfill its mission to society without the vision and generosity of countless people. At this critical moment in the history of the University of Oklahoma's Fred Jones Jr. Museum of Art, with the opening of the Mary and Howard Lester Wing designed by the architect Hugh Newell Jacobsen, I would like to thank all who have contributed to making the museum one of the most distinguished of any American university.

The Lester Wing could not have been realized without the unprecedented, extraordinary support of University of Oklahoma President David L. Boren and First Lady Molly Shi Boren. The expansion is concrete evidence of their love of art and their recognition of the importance of museums within a university education.

My utmost gratitude goes to the many donors who contributed to the new addition built to house the Aaron M. and Clara Weitzenhoffer Bequest and other works from the permanent collection. The lead gift came from Mary and Howard Lester of San Francisco, in whose honor the wing is named. The Sarkeys Foundation of Norman, Oklahoma, made a major donation, as did the Helmerich Foundation of Tulsa; the Fred and Mary Eddy Jones Foundation of Oklahoma City; the McCasland Foundation of Duncan, Oklahoma; the University of Oklahoma Foundation, Inc.; and the Anne and Henry Zarrow Foundation of Tulsa. Additional benefactors to the building campaign were Nancy and George Records of Oklahoma City, Ellen and Richard Sandor of Chicago, and Dee Dee and Jon Stuart of Tulsa. Gifts were also made by Natalie and Paul Buckthal of Amarillo, Texas; Elaine and Gene Edwards of Amarillo; Mary and Dick Clements of Oklahoma City; Lissa and Cy Wagner of Midland, Texas; and ConocoPhillips Petroleum. Other donors to the new building include Molly Shi and David L. Boren of Norman; Melinda and Gerry Cater of London; Tripp Hall and Rudy Hymer of Norman, in honor of Nikki, Owen, and Ayako Takahashi Weitzenhoffer; the Helmerich Trust of Tulsa; the Fred Jones Jr. Museum of Art Association; LaVona and William J. Rushton of Birmingham, Alabama; Bill Saxon of Dallas and the late Wylodean Saxon; Suzi Sugarman of Norman; Bob Tuttle and Maria Hummer of Los Angeles; Max Weitzenhoffer of Norman; and Wanda Otey Westheimer of Ardmore, Oklahoma, and the late Jerry Westheimer. Oklahoma State Senator Cal Hobson's leadership also helped fund the project.

Over the years, numerous benefactors have contributed to forming the museum's permanent collection, and I am ever grateful to these individuals, some of whose names appear in the catalogue's introduction and in the captions of illustrations. These people have established a legacy that will be enjoyed by generations of students and visitors to the museum. In addition to Clara and Aaron Weitzenhoffer, the following have made recent important gifts: Peggy and Frank Ladd of Amarillo, Texas; Rita and Simon Levit of Tulsa; R. E. Mansfield; Russell Ruby of Muskogee, Oklahoma; Ellen and Richard Sandor; the late Patrick Sutherland of Norman; Priscilla C. and

Contents

Foreword 8

Introduction 11

Permanent Collection 19

Notes 288

Index of Artists 290

Library of Congress Cataloging-in-Publication Data
Lee, Eric McCauley.
The Fred Jones Jr. Museum of Art at the University of Oklahoma: selected works / Eric McCauley Lee, Rima Canaan.
p. cm.
Includes index.
ISBN 0-8061-3673-1 (hc : alk. paper)
ISBN 0-8061-3680-4 (sc : alk. paper)
1. Fred Jones Jr. Museum of Art—Catalogs. 2. Art—Oklahoma—Norman—Catalogs. I. Lee, Eric McCauley. II. Canaan, Rima. III. Fred Jones Jr. Museum of Art. IV. Title.
N627.4.F74C36 2004
708.166'37—dc22 2004055395

Designed by John Hubbard with assistance by Zach Hooker
Edited by Jennifer Harris
Proofread by Sherri Schultz
Color separations by iocolor, Seattle
Produced by Marquand Books, Inc., Seattle
www.marquand.com
Printed and bound by CS Graphics Pte., Ltd., Singapore

DETAILS

Front cover: Vincent van Gogh, *Portrait of Alexander Reid* (cat. no. 16)
Back cover: Ernest L. Blumenschein, *Haystack, Taos* (cat. no. 39)
Frontispiece: Georgia O'Keeffe, *Cos Cob* (cat. no. 65)
Page 4: Irving K. Manoir, *Aspen and Snow* (cat. no. 48)
Page 10: B. J. O. Nordfeldt, *Thunder Dance* (cat. no. 55)
Pages 18–19: Paul Signac, *Coast Scene* (cat. no. 17)

Dedicated to the memory of
Fred and Mary Eddy Jones

Mr. and Mrs. Jones built the museum's original facility in 1971 as a memorial to their son, Fred Jones Jr., who died in an airplane crash during his senior year at the University of Oklahoma.

This book was made possible through a gift from their daughter, Marylin Jones Upsher, and grandsons, Fred Jones Hall, Brooks Hall, and Kirkland Hall, who continue the family's legacy of generosity to the university.

ERIC McCAULEY LEE

Introduction

This catalogue features, in roughly chronological and thematic sequence, 101 works in the collection of the Fred Jones Jr. Museum of Art at the University of Oklahoma. Deciding which objects to include out of the museum's eight thousand was difficult. The final selection presents a different artist in each entry and focuses on the criteria of quality and representativeness. Each entry highlights only a single work of art, but related works in the collection appear as accompanying illustrations.

THE MUSEUM'S EARLY DECADES

The origins of the Fred Jones Jr. Museum of Art date to the 1920s, when Oscar Brousse Jacobson (1882–1966) began to collect art for the University of Oklahoma even before the establishment of its art museum. Jacobson, himself a painter, had been director of the university's School of Art since 1915 and strongly believed that firsthand encounters with original works of art were an important component of art instruction and of every well-rounded education.

In 1936, the University of Oklahoma officially founded its art museum with the acquisition of a collection of Asian art, the gift of Louis Haines "Lew" Wentz (1877–1949) and Richard Gordon Matzene (1880–1950), both of Ponca City, Oklahoma. The Wentz-Matzene Collection of 758 objects featured Gandharan sculpture, Persian miniatures, Nepalese and Tibetan art, and Chinese ceramics, bronzes, and paintings. Matzene was an English-born professional photographer and adventurer who spent many years traveling through Asia and collecting art before settling in Oklahoma in the mid-1920s. Oilman Lew Wentz financed Matzene's additional art-buying trips to Asia until the two men donated the resulting collection to the University of Oklahoma.

The university appointed Jacobson as director of the fledgling Museum of Art in conjunction with his duties as director of the School of Art. Until his retirement in 1950, the founding director continued to acquire works for the museum, such as photographs by Edward Weston. Jacobson is noted for his involvement with American Indian art and artists, especially the Kiowa Five artists, who studied at the university; while director, he purchased for the museum nearly 250 American Indian paintings, pots, and textiles. When he supervised the Oklahoma branch of the Federal Art Project of the Works Progress Administration (W.P.A.), one of the U.S. government's Depression-era art programs, Jacobson arranged for the university to acquire from the W.P.A. over 150 paintings, watercolors, prints, and sculptures, including American Indian paintings and an important canvas by Stuart Davis.

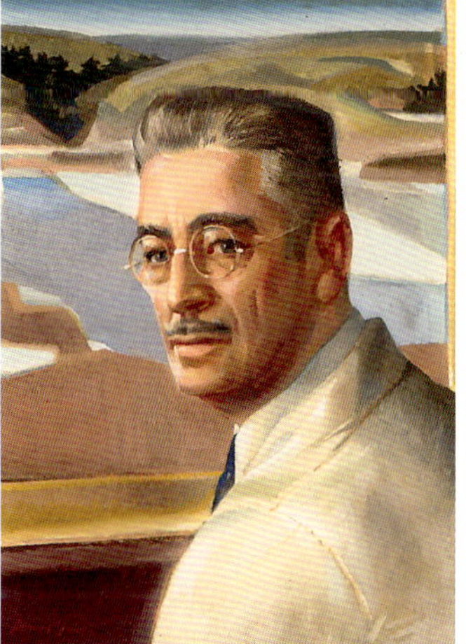

Oscar B. Jacobson, as painted by Leonard Good (1907–2000), 1947, oil on canvas, 23 × 17 in. Gift of Cedric and Daisy Marks, 1984

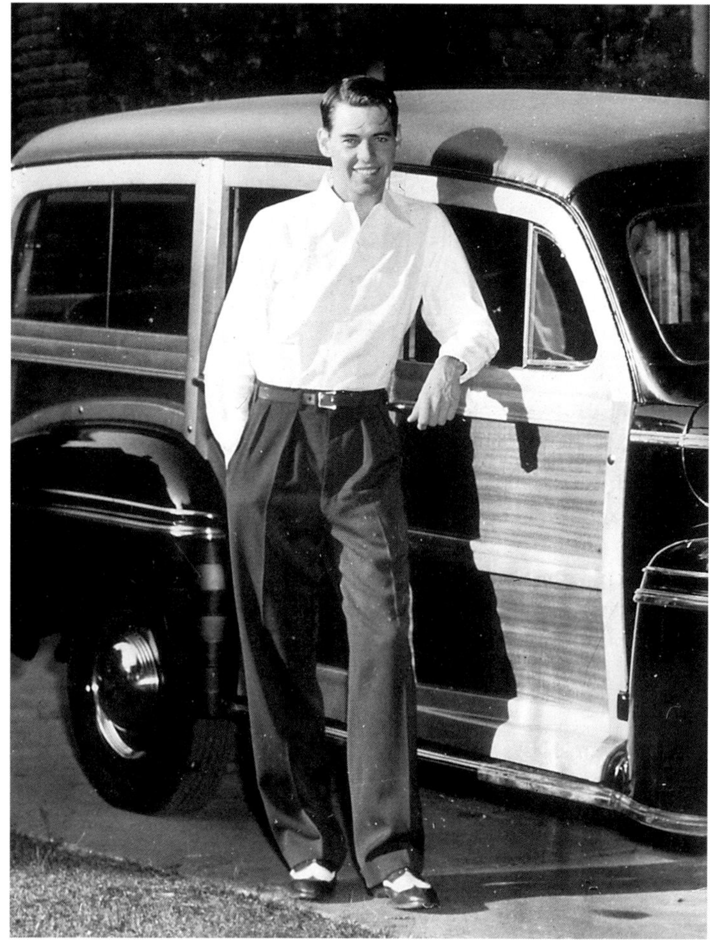

Fred Jones Jr.

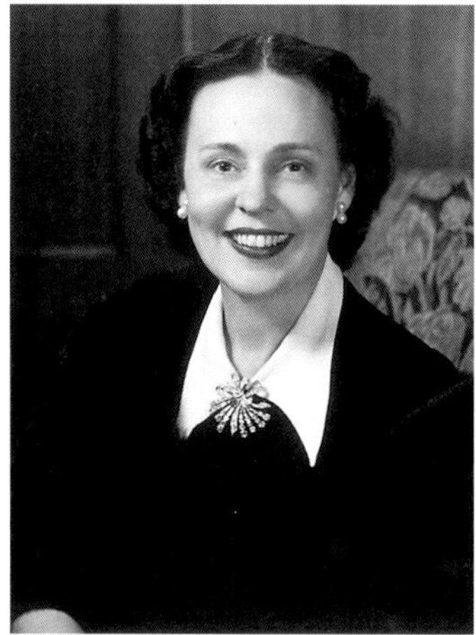

Mary Eddy Jones

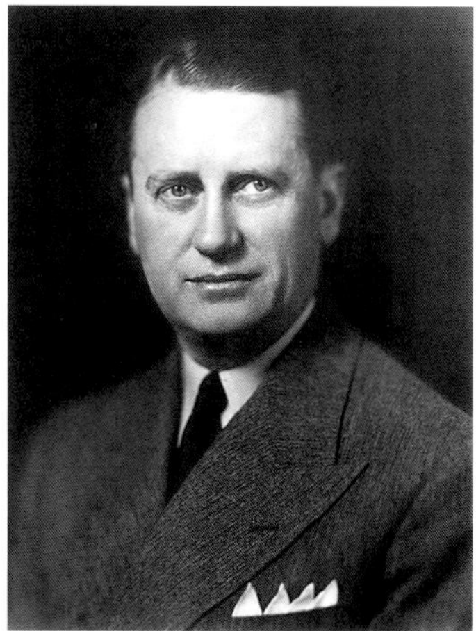

Fred Jones Sr.

In 1948, Jacobson made what would today be considered his most significant acquisition for the museum when he oversaw the purchase of 36 out of the 117 American paintings and watercolors comprising the controversial exhibition "Advancing American Art." The Office of International Information and Cultural Affairs of the U.S. Department of State had organized this exhibition to tour internationally and demonstrate the best in American art. After premiering in its entirety at the Metropolitan Museum of Art, New York, in 1946, the show was divided into two smaller exhibitions: one traveled to Latin America (Havana and Port-au-Prince, Haiti), and one traveled to Europe (Paris and Prague). Politicians, journalists, and embittered, disenfranchised artists attacked the left-wing sympathies and Modernism of some of the exhibition's artists as un-American and questioned the use of taxpayers' money for funding the show. Magazines and newspapers ballyhooed the resulting controversy, and Congress eventually held hearings to investigate the State Department's art program. The State Department dismantled the exhibition and sold the works of art in mid-1948 as war surplus. Through Jacobson's initiative, the University of Oklahoma's art museum purchased almost one-third of the show at the ninety-five percent discount that the State Department gave to educational institutions. As a result, the museum paid $50 for Georgia O'Keeffe's *Cos Cob,* for which the State Department had paid $1,000. In addition to the O'Keeffe painting, the museum also acquired works by William Baziotes, Romare Bearden, Adolph Gottlieb, Edward Hopper, Jack Levine, George L. K. Morris, Ben Shahn, Max Weber, and others. This group of paintings has become known as the museum's State Department Collection.

From his personal collection, Jacobson gave the museum prints by Paul Cézanne, Henri Matisse, Pierre-Auguste Renoir, and others, as well as a painting by B. J. O. Nordfeldt. Jacobson also bequeathed to the museum a painting and prints by Birger Sandzén, who had been his art teacher and mentor at Bethany College, in Lindsborg, Kansas, before Jacobson attended graduate school in art at Yale University.

For several years after Jacobson's retirement in 1950, the position of director was shared among School of Art professors. In 1956, the museum's budget was separated from the School of Art. (The museum now reports directly to the university's provost and is formally independent of the School of Art and College of Fine Arts.)

Sam Olkinetzky, the museum's longest-serving and first full-time director, led the museum from 1958 until 1984. During Olkinetsky's tenure, the collection grew steadily, especially in the fields of contemporary art and photography. Prices for photographs were low at that time because the market was still nascent, and the museum acquired—with the guidance of Edwin J. Deighton, the museum's assistant director and himself a photographer—significant examples by major photographers from the nineteenth and twentieth centuries. In 1972, the Museum of Art Association formed as an adjunct support group funding acquisitions, conservation, opening receptions, awards at the annual student exhibitions, an educational travel program, and other activities.

Originally, the museum occupied two rooms of the Art Building (now the university's Visitor Center, called Jacobson Hall) but eventually expanded into the entire building. In 1971, the museum moved into a permanent home, when Mr. and Mrs. Fred Jones of Oklahoma City donated to the university the museum portion of a new fine arts building in memory of their son, Fred Jones Jr.

During his senior year at the University of Oklahoma, Fred Jones Jr. had died in an airplane crash while traveling to the 1950 Sugar Bowl. His parents had originally planned to build a nondenominational chapel as a memorial and had commissioned the maverick architect Bruce Goff, then the dean of the university's architecture school, to design the structure. *Architectural Forum* published the plans, which received much attention, but the chapel was never built. The Joneses later visited Frank Lloyd Wright at Taliesin West in Arizona to discuss the possibility of Wright's designing a chapel, but they eventually decided to focus instead on an arts-related building.

The Joneses funded the construction of the 27,000-square-foot museum portion of the Fred Jones Jr. Memorial Art Center, designed by the Oklahoma City architecture firm of Howard and Samis. (The School of Art and the administrative offices of the College of Fine Arts occupy the rest of the building.) This museum building contains over 15,000 square feet of gallery space.

The Jones family has continued its generosity to the museum through gifts supporting the endowment, operations, and the acquisition of art. In recognition of the Jones family's long history of support, the university in 1992 renamed the University of Oklahoma Museum of Art as the Fred Jones Jr. Museum of Art.

Succeeding Olkinetzky, Thomas R. Toperzer was director from 1984 until 1997. Under Toperzer's leadership, the museum renovated

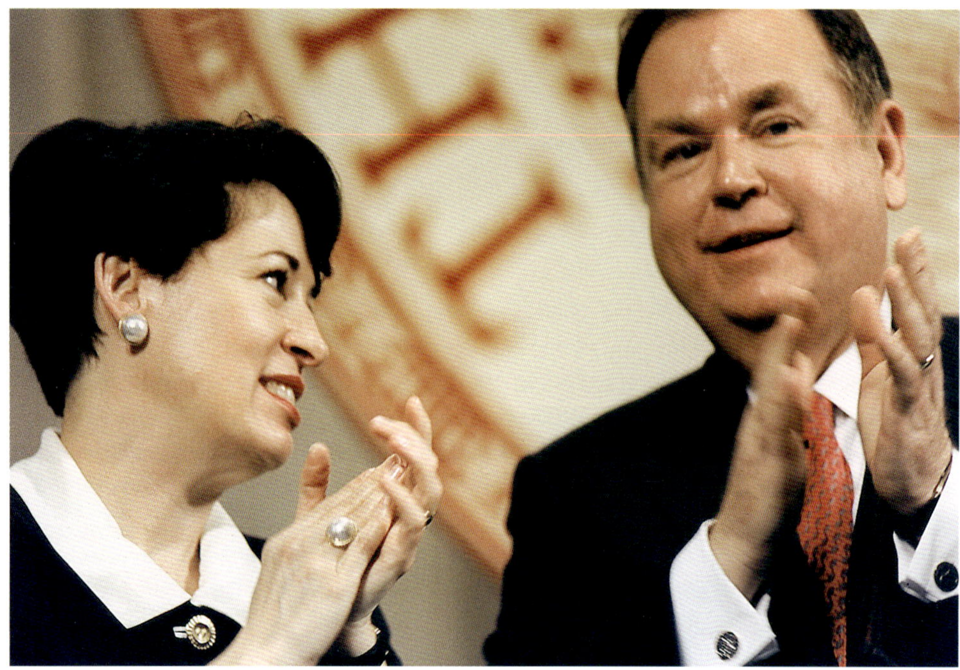

President David L. Boren and First Lady Molly Shi Boren

its galleries, mounted a number of ambitious exhibitions, and in 1985 inaugurated the Board of Visitors, which has continued to provide critical support for the museum's programs. Toperzer oversaw the acquisition of watercolors by John Marin, as well as many works of contemporary art.

THE BOREN YEARS

In 1994, David L. Boren retired from the U.S. Senate to become president of the University of Oklahoma. President Boren and First Lady Molly Shi Boren, themselves art collectors (focusing especially on American Indian art) and donors to the museum, have given the museum exceptional support. In 1996, the Borens spearheaded a successful fundraising campaign, with Mrs. Fred Jones Sr. as the lead donor, that enabled the museum to acquire the important collection of the late Richard H. and Adeline J. Fleischaker, who had lived in Oklahoma City. Composed primarily of American Indian and Southwestern art (especially the art of Taos and Santa Fe), this collection of over four hundred works elevated the museum to a new level and introduced a period of tremendous growth for the institution.

After the museum acquired the Fleischaker Collection, it received two additional private collections of primarily Taos art. In 2003, William H. Thams of Midland, Texas, in memory of his wife, Roxanne, gave the museum thirty major paintings by Taos artists such as Ernest L. Blumenschein, E. Irving Couse, Nicolai Fechin, Leon Gaspard, E. Martin Hennings, Bert Geer Phillips, and Joseph Henry Sharp. Following this extraordinary donation came the 2004 gift from Priscilla C. and Joseph Tate, of Tulsa, of a collection of twelve works by the members of the Taos Society of Artists. Together, the Fleischaker, Tate, and Thams collections give the Fred Jones Jr. Museum of Art one of the finest representations of Southwestern art in any museum.

The American Indian collection, which Oscar Jacobson initially developed and which had received a tremendous boost with the acquisition of the Fleischaker Collection, greatly expanded yet again with the 2003 gift of the R. E. Mansfield Collection. Especially strong in pottery and works by contemporary American Indian artists, the Mansfield Collection of over one thousand objects was split evenly between the Fred Jones Jr. Museum of Art and the Smithsonian's National Museum of the American Indian in Washington, D.C.

Wanda and Jerome Westheimer of Ardmore, Oklahoma, have made numerous contributions, including works by Sam Francis, Luis Jiménez, and Maurice B. Prendergast, which continue the tradition of major donations that the Westheimer family began in the 1970s. J. Donald Walp of Dallas has made many gifts of art ranging from Pre-Columbian and Inuit art to twentieth-century U.S. and Mexican prints.

Well-known photography collectors Ellen and Richard Sandor of Chicago have presented the museum with over fifty works by some of the most significant figures in the history of photography, including Bill Brandt, Edward S. Curtis, André Kertész, W. Eugene Smith, James Van Der Zee, and Garry Winogrand. The Sandors also made a financial contribution to establish a permanent photography gallery that displays rotations from the museum's important photography collection, which has now grown to over 1,200 prints. In recognition of the Sandors' generosity, the museum has named its photography gallery the Ellen and Richard L. Sandor Gallery.

Scores of other donors have contributed major works of art over the years. Most recently, Rita and Dr. Simon Levit of Tulsa joined this list with the donation of *The Sacrifice of Isaac,* a large-scale Cor-Ten steel sculpture by Menashe Kadishman (b. 1932), one of Israel's leading artists. This work will be installed on the grounds of the museum.

The Weitzenhoffer Bequest

In 2000, the museum received a transformative bequest of French Impressionist art by Clara Rosenthal Weitzenhoffer of Oklahoma City and La Jolla, California. Mrs. Weitzenhoffer (1912–2000), a native of Olney, Illinois, was the daugher of pioneering oil developer Henry Rosenthal and his wife, Irma Rosenthal. Mrs. Weitzenhoffer attended Wellesley College and the University of Wichita. In 1938, she married Aaron Max Weitzenhoffer (1895–1960), a founder of the Davon Oil Company, whose family had settled in Oklahoma in 1888. Aaron and Clara Weitzenhoffer became noted leaders in philanthropic, cultural, and educational organizations in Oklahoma City and enthusiastic patrons of the University of Oklahoma, from which their only child, Max, graduated in 1962.

The Weitzenhoffer gift was the largest donation of French Impressionist art ever made to a public university in the United States and the largest single donation ever made to the University of Oklahoma. According to Max Weitzenhoffer, "My parents' good fortune made it possible for my mother to acquire these works of art, which gave her so much pleasure during her lifetime. For her, this bequest was a way of giving something back to Oklahoma and its people, a way of saying thank you. My mother could also see what a strong new commitment to the arts the university was making, and wanted to advance it in this very special and important way."

A Tony Award–winning Broadway producer, Max Weitzenhoffer himself has been a longtime major donor to the museum; he has given over thirty works of art, including Alan Davie's *Big Solid Sender,* paintings by Oscar Schlemmer and Patrick Heron, and Barbara Hepworth's *Two Figures,* installed at the entrance of the museum. (In honor of the Weitzenhoffer family's decades of support for the arts at the University of Oklahoma, the university in 2004 renamed the College of Fine Arts as the Weitzenhoffer Family College of Fine Arts.)

The Mary and Howard Lester Wing

In 1971, after Mary Eddy Jones first toured the museum building that she and her husband had funded in memory of their son, she wrote about the architecture to F. Donald Clark, dean of the College of Fine Arts: "It more than exceeded our expectations for beauty, functionalism, and that simplicity which is so often so very difficult to attain. Yet, it also contains some drama. . . ." These same words apply to the museum's new addition, designed by acclaimed architect Hugh Newell Jacobsen of Washington, D.C. Named in honor of Mary and Howard Lester of San Francisco, the wing adds more than 34,000 square feet

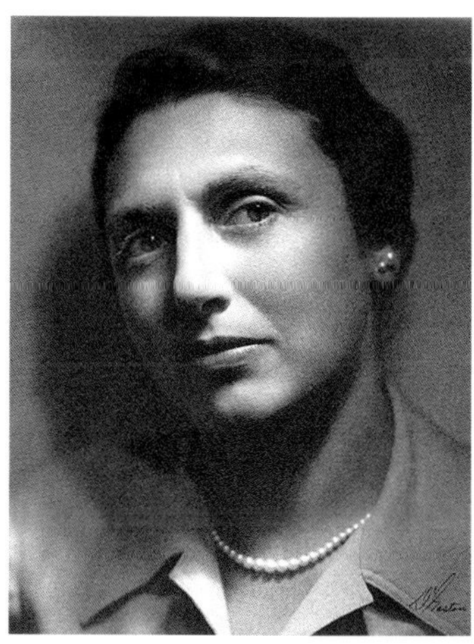

Clara Weitzenhoffer

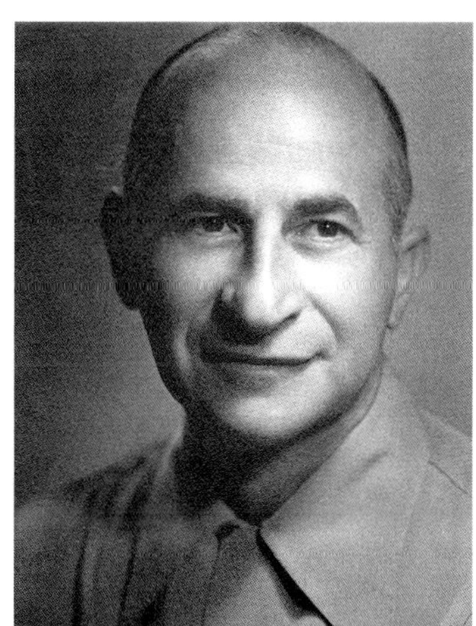

Aaron Weitzenhoffer

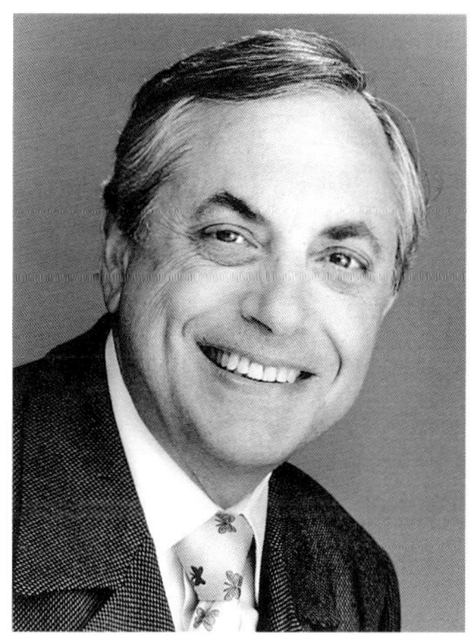

Max Weitzenhoffer

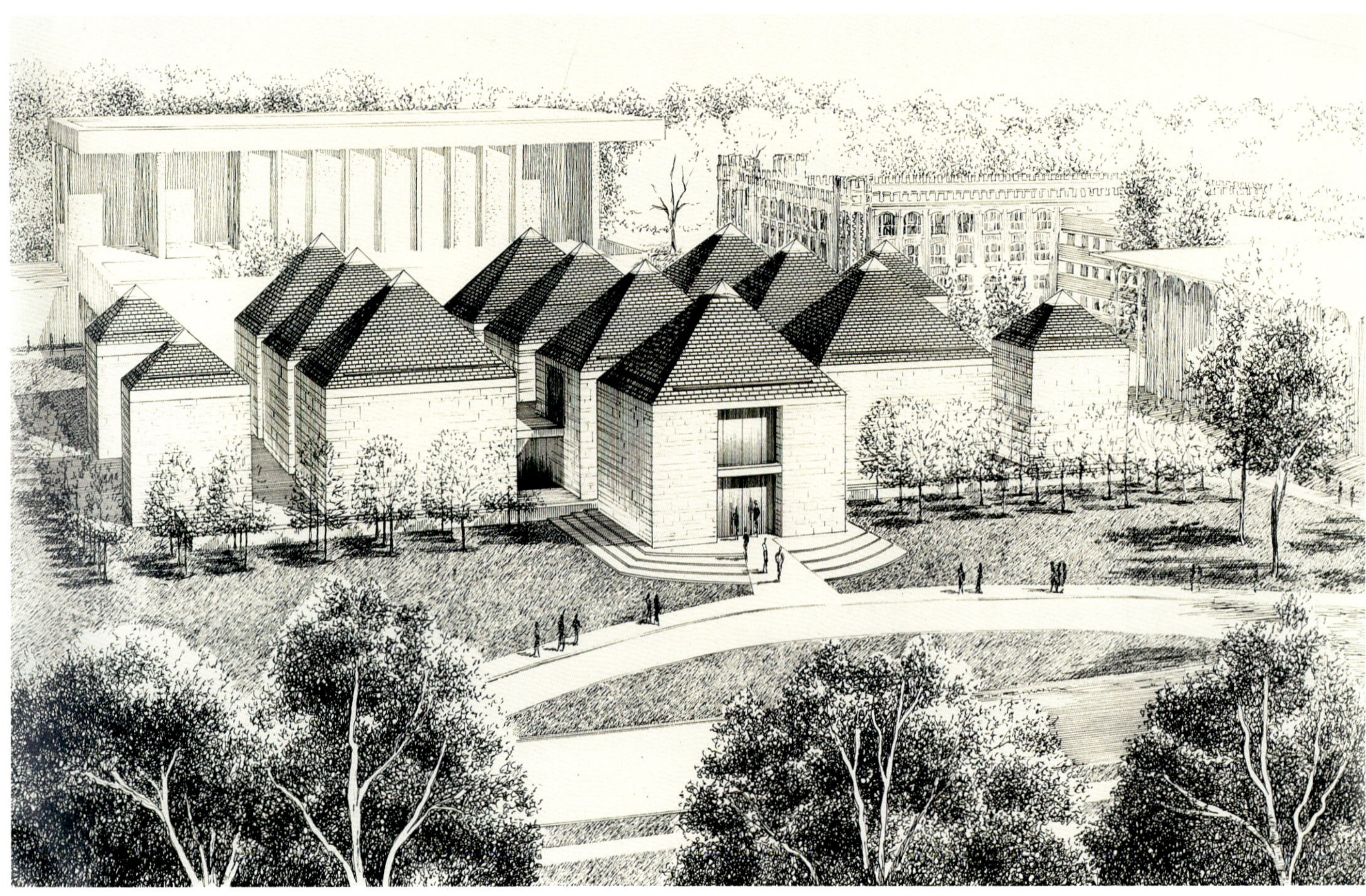

Drawing of the Fred Jones Jr. Museum of Art's Mary and Howard Lester Wing, designed by architect Hugh Newell Jacobsen

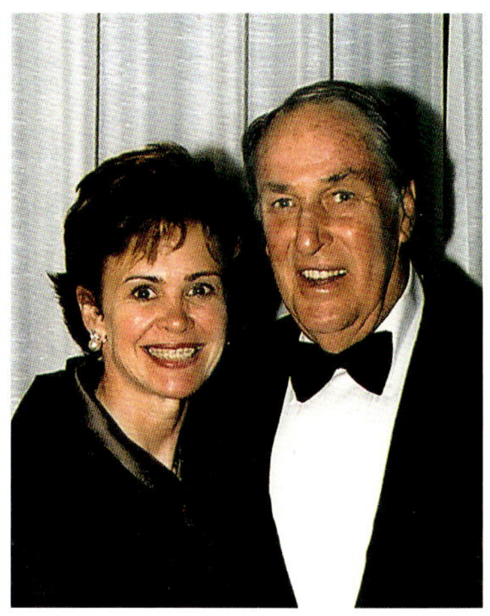

Mary and Howard Lester

Menashe Kadishman
Israel, b. 1932
The Sacrifice of Isaac, 1985,
Cor-Ten steel,
H. 15 ft. 1 in.
Gift of Dr. and Mrs. Simon A. Levit and family, 2003

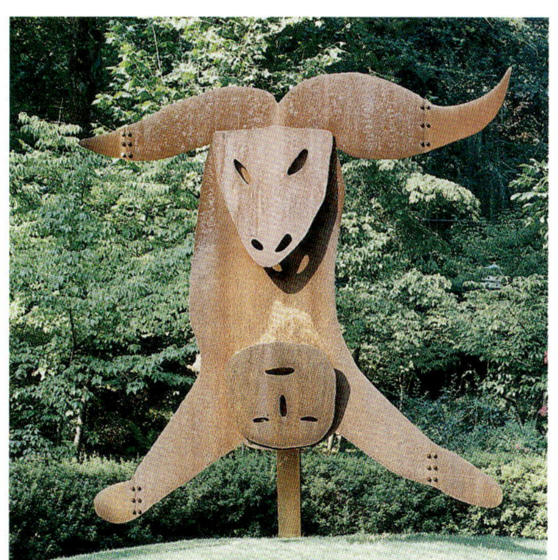

to the earlier museum building. The Lester Wing features galleries for the Weitzenhoffer Collection, additional galleries, a 150-seat auditorium, an orientation room, a classroom, a museum store, and a new main entrance. Jacobsen designed the Lester Wing as a sequence of limestone pavilions having pyramidal slate roofs with glass skylights at their apexes. The building features an abundance of natural light, pure geometries, clarity of plan, and well-proportioned, top-lighted galleries that have an intimate, human scale. The resulting serene, contemplative spaces put the visitor in the proper frame of mind for viewing works of art.

The interior and exterior of the building are in dialogue. The interior repeats the same use of materials as the exterior: limestone, slate, glass, and bronze. Inside the museum, the many large walls of glass afford glimpses of the outside world. Outside, these same windows allow passersby to see into the museum.

The Lester Wing is an heir to the architecture of Louis I. Kahn, who designed the Kimbell Museum in Fort Worth and who taught Jacobsen at Yale. The pyramid-covered pavilions of the Lester Wing recall in particular Kahn's Trenton Bathhouse in New Jersey.

The Weitzenhoffer Collection will be installed in galleries that replicate the collection's original setting in the Weitzenhoffers' Oklahoma City home, including the eighteenth-century English furniture and Chinese export porcelain that was part of Clara Weitzenhoffer's bequest. These galleries will evoke the private house museums that flourished from around 1890 to 1940, such as the Frick Collection in New York or the Phillips Collection in Washington, D.C.

Coinciding with the opening of the Lester Wing, this catalogue celebrates the extraordinary development of the Fred Jones Jr. Museum of Art's collection over nearly three-quarters of a century. The catalogue also looks forward to the new era that the Lester Wing heralds.

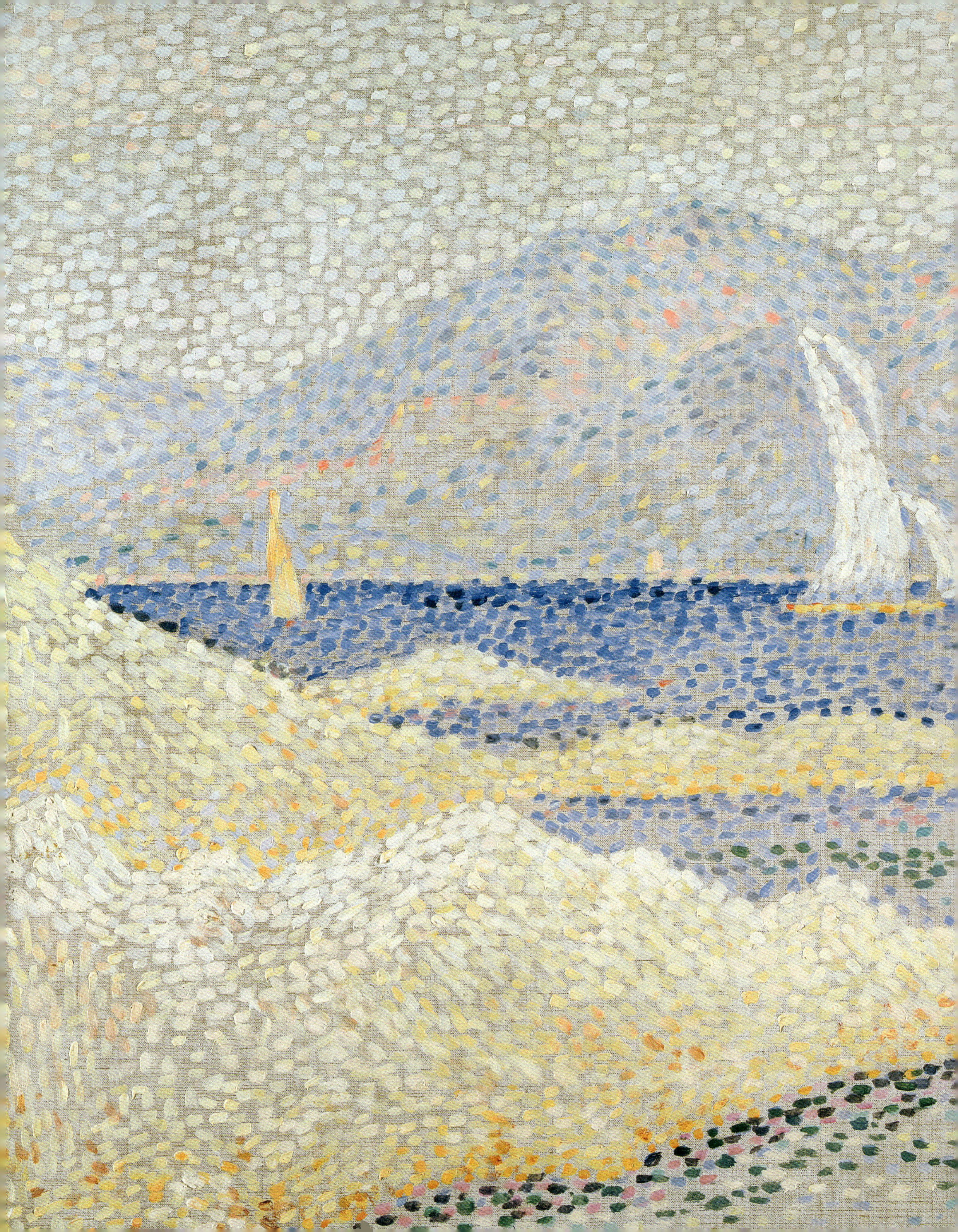

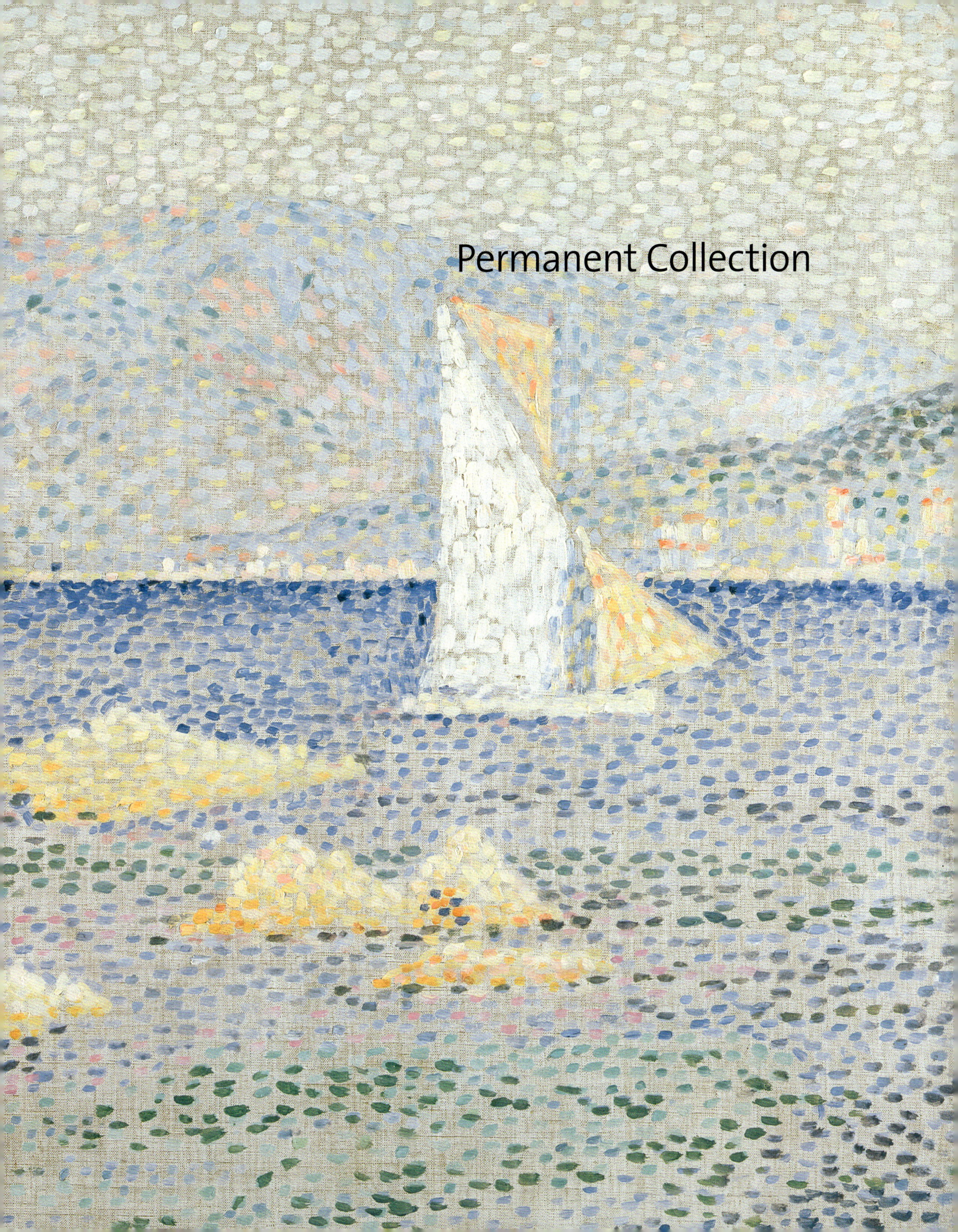

Permanent Collection

1 Unknown

India, Gandhara

Buddha, Trajanic period, A.D. 100–200
Schist
H. 17½ in.
Gift, Wentz-Matzene Collection, 1936

The museum's Wentz-Matzene Collection includes 115 sculptures in stucco and schist from ancient Gandhara. Between the first and fifth centuries A.D., Gandhara was a thriving Buddhist region in the northern area of the Indus River valley, in what is present-day Pakistan and western Afghanistan. Gordon Matzene acquired the museum's Gandharan sculptures during his travels, probably from dealers in Peshawar or elsewhere in the Punjab. The sculptures are most likely from the Buddhist monasteries or shrines (*stupas*) at Hadda and from monasteries such as Takht-i-Bahi in the Swat Valley north of Peshawar.

Most Gandharan art was produced during the Kushan dynasty, founded by nomadic people who had migrated from western China. The works in the museum's collection were made as architectural relief decorations that aided worshippers. Gandhara was one of the first cultures to depict the Buddha in human form instead of through symbols.

An Indian prince who became the Buddha, or Enlightened One, Siddhartha Gautama founded Buddhism in the sixth century B.C. He taught that salvation and nirvana are attainable through righteous conduct, meditation, knowledge, and renunciation of materialism.

The present sculpture, about one-third life-size and probably originally the upper portion of a seated figure, depicts the Buddha in meditation. As is typical, the Buddha appears frontally in rigid form. Also characteristically, the robed Buddha wears his hair in a topknot, or *usnisa* (peak), and has elongated ears, the result of the heavy earrings he had worn as a prince before his enlightenment.

Gandharan art displays Greco-Roman and Persian elements melded with Indian Buddhism. In the present work, the Greco-Roman style appears in the robe, with heavy folds that suggest a body underneath, and in the naturalism of the Buddha's head, which resembles the Greek and Roman god Apollo. Scholars once thought that Classical influences in Gandharan art derived from the fourth-century B.C. conquest of the region by Alexander the Great. More recently, experts have come to believe that the Greco-Roman influences were transmitted later, through trade routes and by artisans from the eastern parts of the Roman empire who worked at the Kushan court.

Many of the stucco works in the museum's Gandharan collection retain traces of their original paint. Unlike the schist sculptures, the stucco ones were often cast from molds.

The Taliban regime that formerly ruled Afghanistan destroyed much Gandharan art, including in 2001 the colossal Buddhas of Bamiyan.

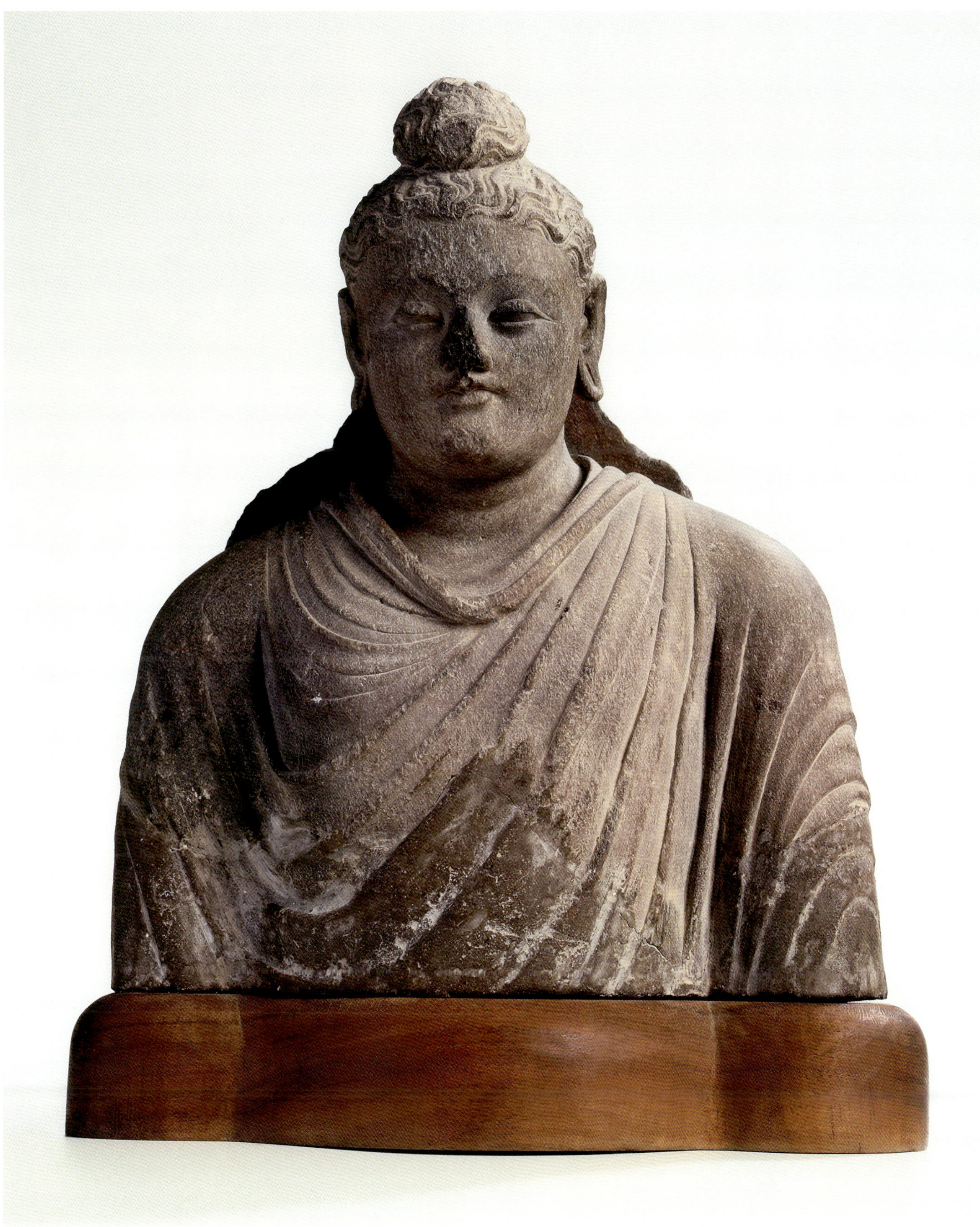

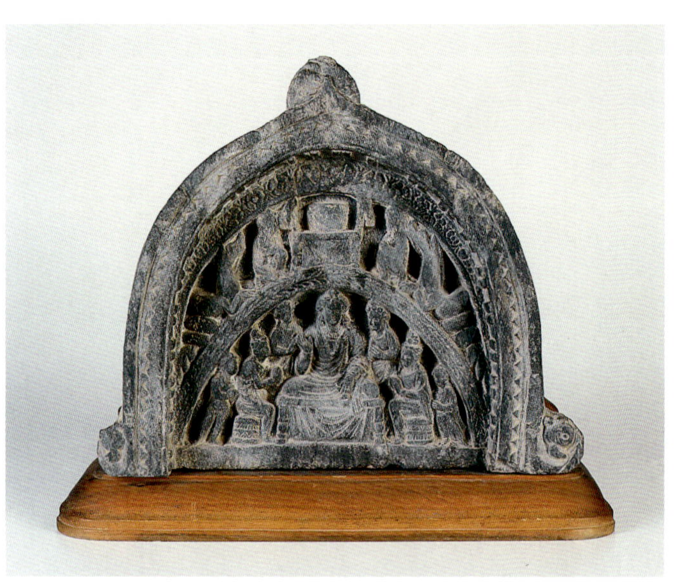

Unknown
India, Gandhara
Education of Buddha, Trajanic period, A.D. 100–200, schist, H. 16 in.
Gift, Wentz-Matzene Collection, 1936

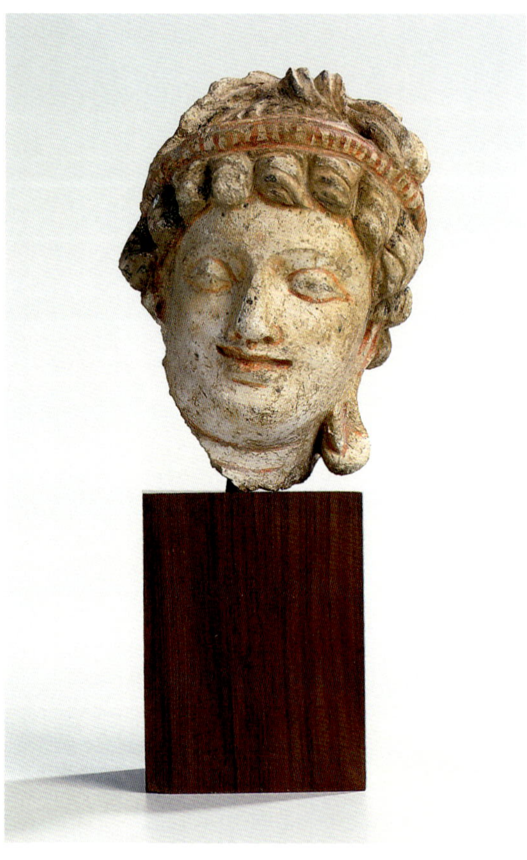

Unknown
India, Gandhara
Bodhisattva, Trajanic period, A.D. 100–200, stucco, H. 6¾ in.
Gift, Wentz-Matzene Collection, 1936

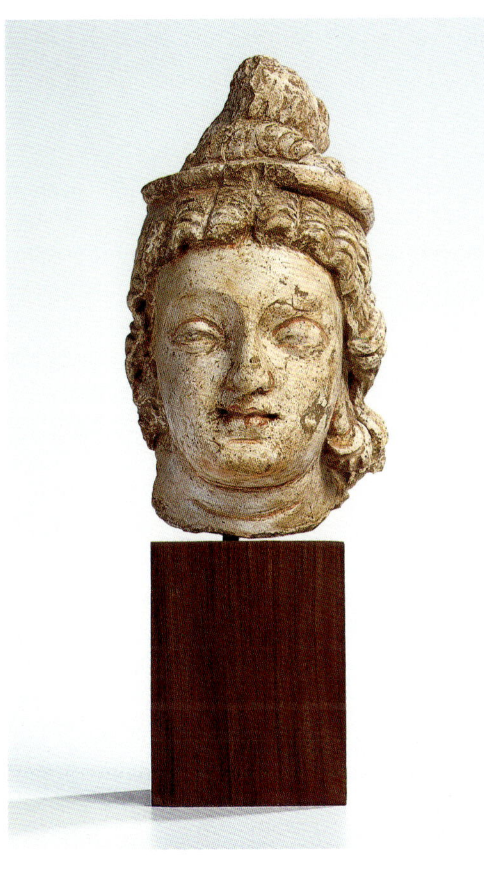

Unknown
India, Gandhara
Bodhisattva, Trajanic period, A.D. 100–200, stucco, H. 8⅛ in.
Gift, Wentz-Matzene Collection, 1936

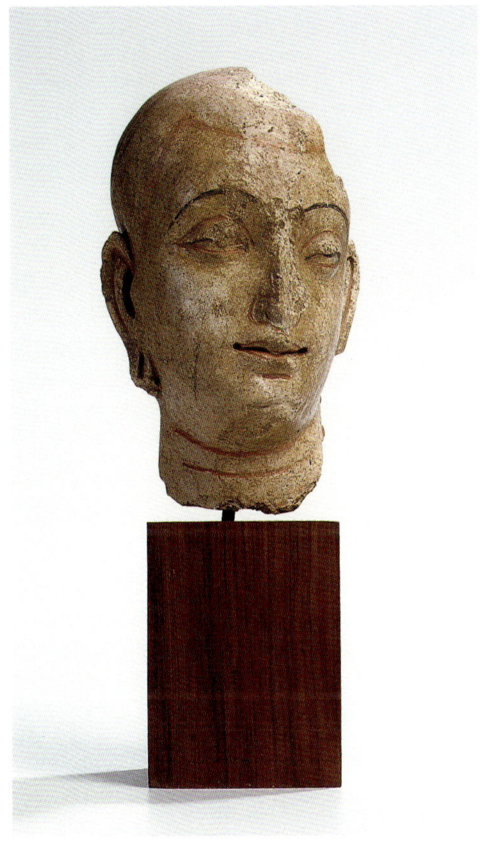

Unknown
India, Gandhara
Monk, Trajanic period, A.D. 100–200, stucco, H. 8 in.
Gift, Wentz-Matzene Collection, 1936

2 Unknown

China

Horse, Tang dynasty, A.D. 618–906
Ceramic
H. 19 in.
Gift of the Lon B. Turk Family, 1994

The arts flourished during the Tang dynasty, which united China as a single empire for a long period of prosperity and splendor. The Tang capital, Chang'an (today Xi'an), was the largest city in the world. Under the Tang, the Silk Route experienced its greatest era, and foreign influences flowed into China from India and western Asia. Buddhism was the dominant religion of the Tang dynasty.

As in earlier dynasties, during the Tang period, figures of people, animals, houses, furniture, and tools were placed in tombs to accompany and protect the dead in the afterlife. These figures were called *ming ch'i,* or "spirit articles." Generally, the higher the status of the deceased, the greater the number of *ming ch'i*. The figures of people represented, among others, foreigners, musicians, servants, civil servants, warrior guardians, and ladies of the court. Some figures even depicted men on horseback, playing polo.

Horses, introduced into China from central Asia, were symbols of high rank both in life and as tomb figures. Other animals made into *ming ch'i* included goats, oxen, sheep, camels, dogs, and ducks. Some of the figures were half human, half animal.

Funerals during the Tang dynasty were often extravagant affairs, occasionally leading to financial disaster for the surviving relatives. Mourners carried the tomb figures in funeral processions. In A.D. 742, the government set a limit (based on the deceased's rank) on the number of *ming ch'i* that could be included in a tomb.

Ming ch'i were made of fine, low-fire earthenware, usually finished with a lead glaze in colors such as amber yellow (as in the present work), brown, green, and occasionally cobalt blue. The colors typically used in Tang ceramics are called *sancai* (meaning "three-color"), although the color range was much greater.

Craftsmen applied the colored glazes by splashing and by painting. They sometimes used glaze-resistant wax on areas they wanted to remain unglazed. Such a method was probably used on the unglazed portions of the present horse, including the saddle and base. The red paint on the horse's saddle was added after firing.

The majority of Tang lead-glazed figures were produced around the metropolitan areas of Chang'an and Luoyang. Production mostly ended after a rebellion in A.D. 756 and the Tibetan invasion of China in A.D. 763. Following the Tang dynasty, Chinese ceramics no longer used *sancai* lead glazes.

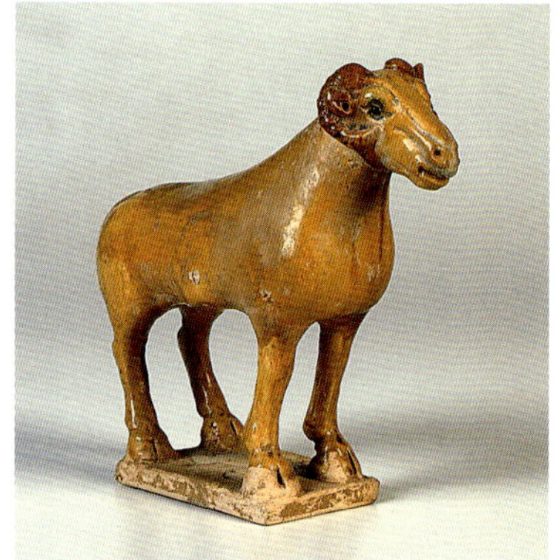

Unknown
China
Tomb Figure (Goat with Brown Horns), Tang dynasty, A.D. 618–906, ceramic, H. 6½ in.
Gift, Wentz-Matzene Collection, 1936

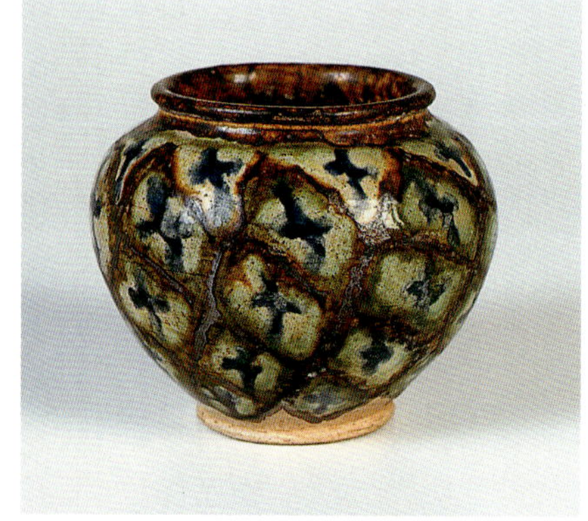

Unknown
China
Jar, Tang dynasty, A.D. 618–906, porcelain, H. 6 in. Gift, Wentz-Matzene Collection, 1936

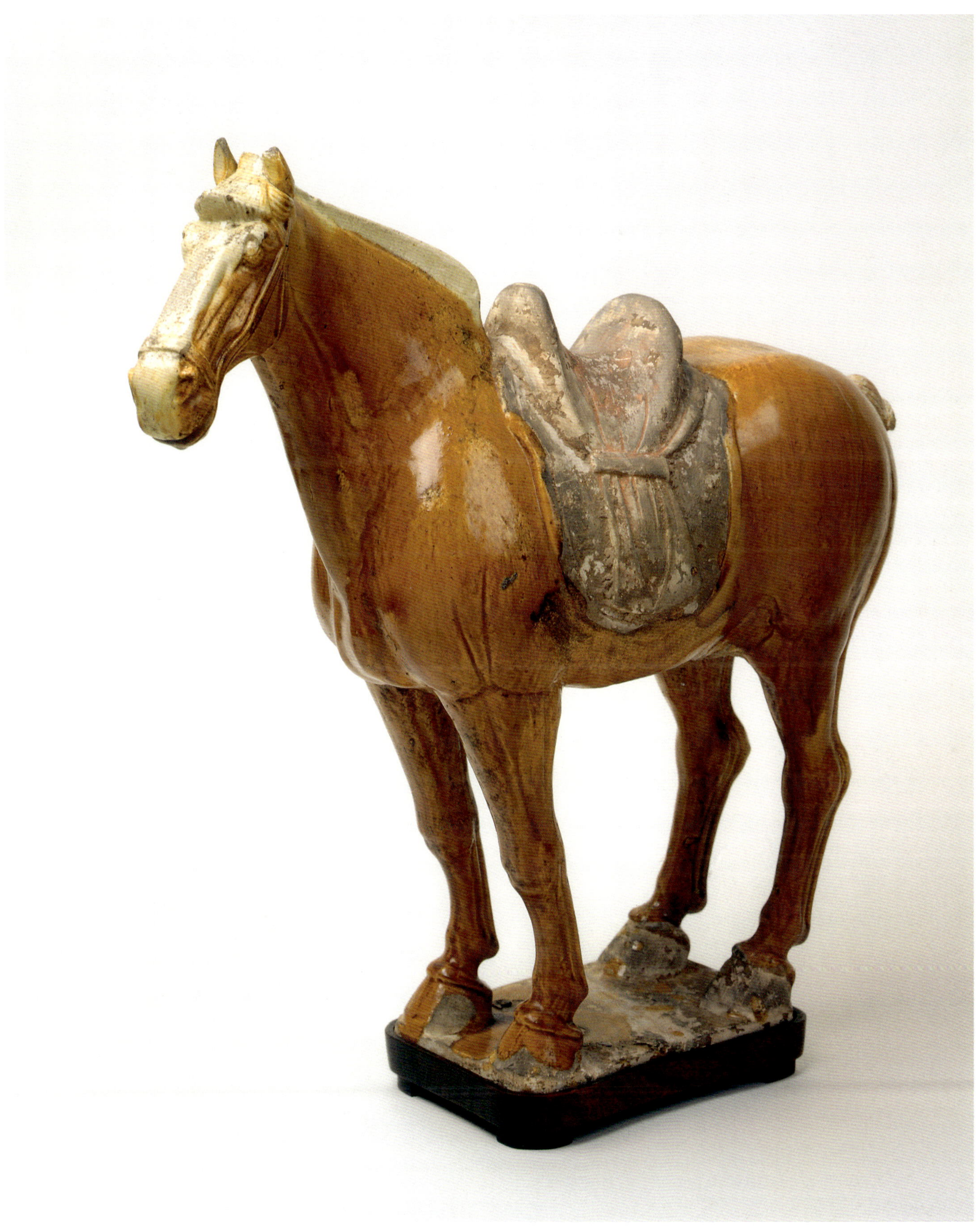

3 Unknown

Persia

Shahnama: Isfandiyar in His Armored Car Encounters the Simurgh, c. 1600
Tempera on paper
11 × 7 in.
Gift, Wentz-Matzene Collection, 1936

This illuminated sheet depicts a scene from the most famous work of Persian (Iranian) literature, the *Shahnama,* or *Book of Kings,* which is an epic poem consisting of approximately sixty thousand lines of rhyming couplets. The poem tells the stories of heroes such as Rustam, a legendary warrior who in early Persia fought in the service of his king. The poet Firdausi (c. A.D. 934–1020) completed the *Shahnama* in A.D. 1010, after more than thirty years of setting to verse tales that he had gathered from all over Persia. Firdausi relates the history and traditions of the Persians, from their mythological origins at the creation of the world to the downfall of the Sasanid empire in the mid-seventh century A.D. His poem became one of the most popular books in the Middle East. The earliest known illustrated manuscripts of the *Shahnama* date from the fourteenth century.

The *Shahnama* breaks down the history of Iran into four main sections corresponding to dynasties. The museum owns twenty sheets from a richly illustrated manuscript of the *Shahnama;* these sheets depict scenes from the Kayanian dynasty and show the heroes Rustam and Isfandiyar, who fight Persia's supernatural enemies, including witches, dragons, and demons, and its human foes, the rulers of Turan.

In the *Shahnama,* Isfandiyar is a king's son who proves himself a warrior through seven challenges, or "courses." In the fifth course, he kills the Simurgh, a fantastical bird strong enough to lift an elephant in its talons. The bird is so old that it has seen the world destroyed three times and has accumulated enough learning to possess all the knowledge of the ages. In the present sheet, Isfandiyar has just spotted the bird he is about to kill.

Later in the epic, after many intrigues and battles, Isfandiyar and Rustam fight one another. Rustam kills Isfandiyar by shooting into Isfandiyar's eye a magic arrow that the Simurgh had given Rustam.

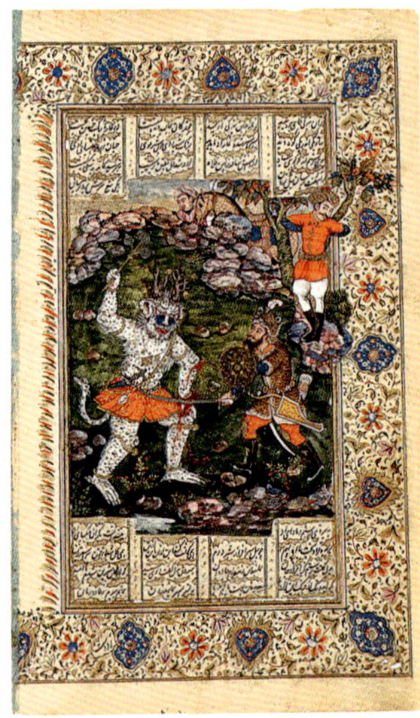

Unknown
Persia
Shahnama: Rustam and the White Demon. Rustam's Seventh Course: He Slays the White Demon, c. 1600, tempera on paper, 11 × 7 in.
Gift, Wentz-Matzene Collection, 1936

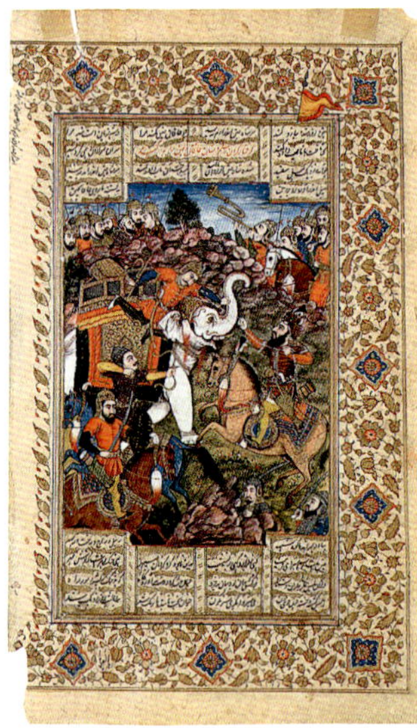

Unknown
Persia
Shahnama: Rustam Capturing the Emperor of China, c. 1600, tempera on paper, 11 × 7 in.
Gift, Wentz-Matzene Collection, 1936

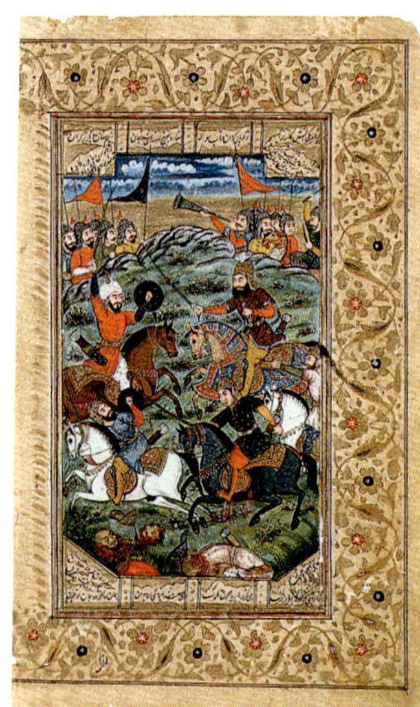

Unknown
Persia
Shahnama: Rustam and Isfandiyar Begin Their Combat, c. 1600, tempera on paper, 11 × 7 in.
Gift, Wentz-Matzene Collection, 1936

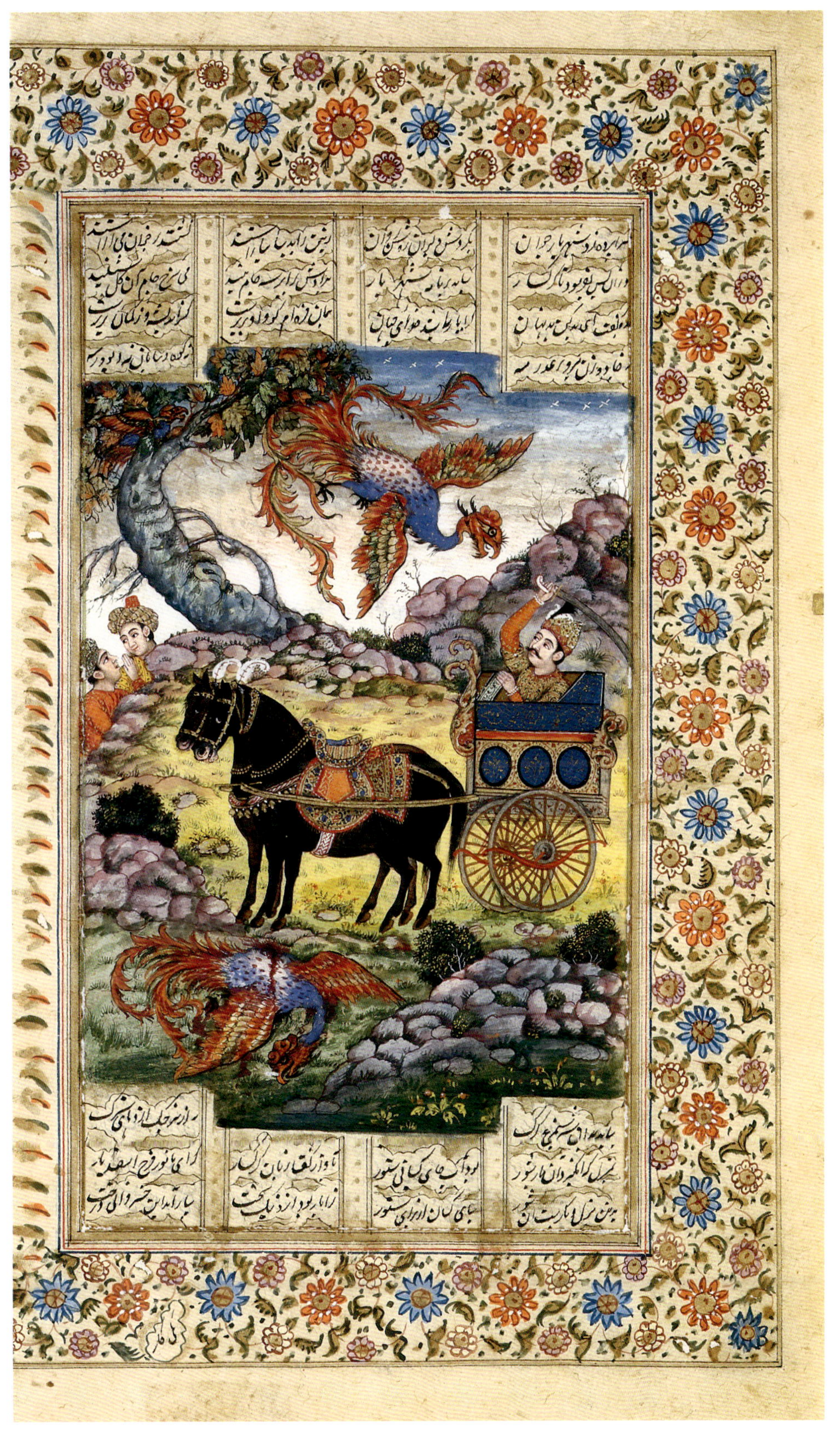

4 Attributed to Fakeye Family

Yoruba, Nigeria

Oshe Shango, prior to 1950
Wood
H. 29½ in.
Fred Jones Jr. Memorial Fund Purchase, 1983

The Yoruba people live in present-day Nigeria and Benin in western Africa. Their city-states, including Oyo and Ife, date back over 1,000 years, and their ancient art traditions have continued into the present day. After the Oyo-Yoruba empire collapsed in the late eighteenth century, a long period of unrest and warfare ensued. Many Yoruba people were dispersed to Brazil, Haiti, and Trinidad, where traces of Yoruba culture persist, as well as to cities in the United States.

The Yoruba believe in a dual existence: the tangible world of the living and a spiritual world inhabited by the supreme creator (Olodumare), deified ancestors (*orisha*), other ancestors, and spirits. According to the Yoruba, the earthly life is only a transitory state before people move on to their true homes in the next world.

The present figure is from a dance wand (*oshe*) used to honor Shango, the god of thunder and lightning, who was the deified fourth king of Oyo. As king, Shango was greatly feared; he had magical powers and emitted fire from his mouth when he spoke.

The dance wand's headdress, in the form of a double-headed ax, embodies power and is the symbol of Shango. The form derives from the shape of celts (prehistoric stone axes) that appear on the ground following storms, after the rain has washed away the soil covering them. The Yoruba believe that Shango casts these celts to the ground during storms. In the dance wand, the female figure is a devotee of Shango. The ax emerges out of her head, suggesting a union, during a possession trance dance, of the devotee and the god.

In Yoruba culture, only men carve. The figures, made of wood or ivory, typically have large heads in relation to their bodies. The eyes and other facial features are also oversized.

The present work has been attributed to a member of the Fakeye family, which has produced several leading Yoruba master carvers.

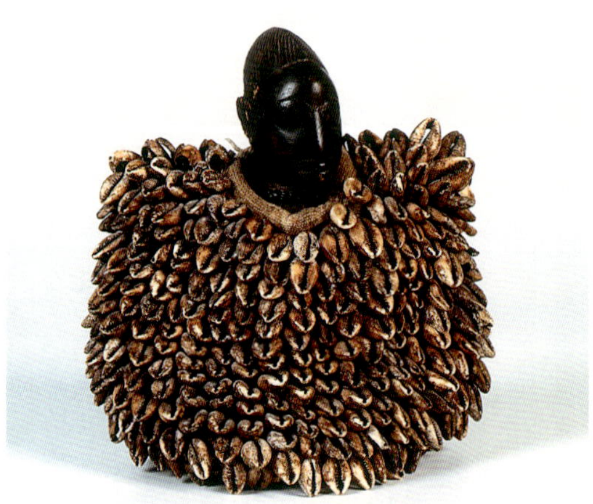

Unknown
Yoruba, Nigeria
Royal Female Ibeji (Twin) Figure, late nineteenth or early twentieth century, wood and cowrie shells, H. 9 in. Museum purchase, 1980

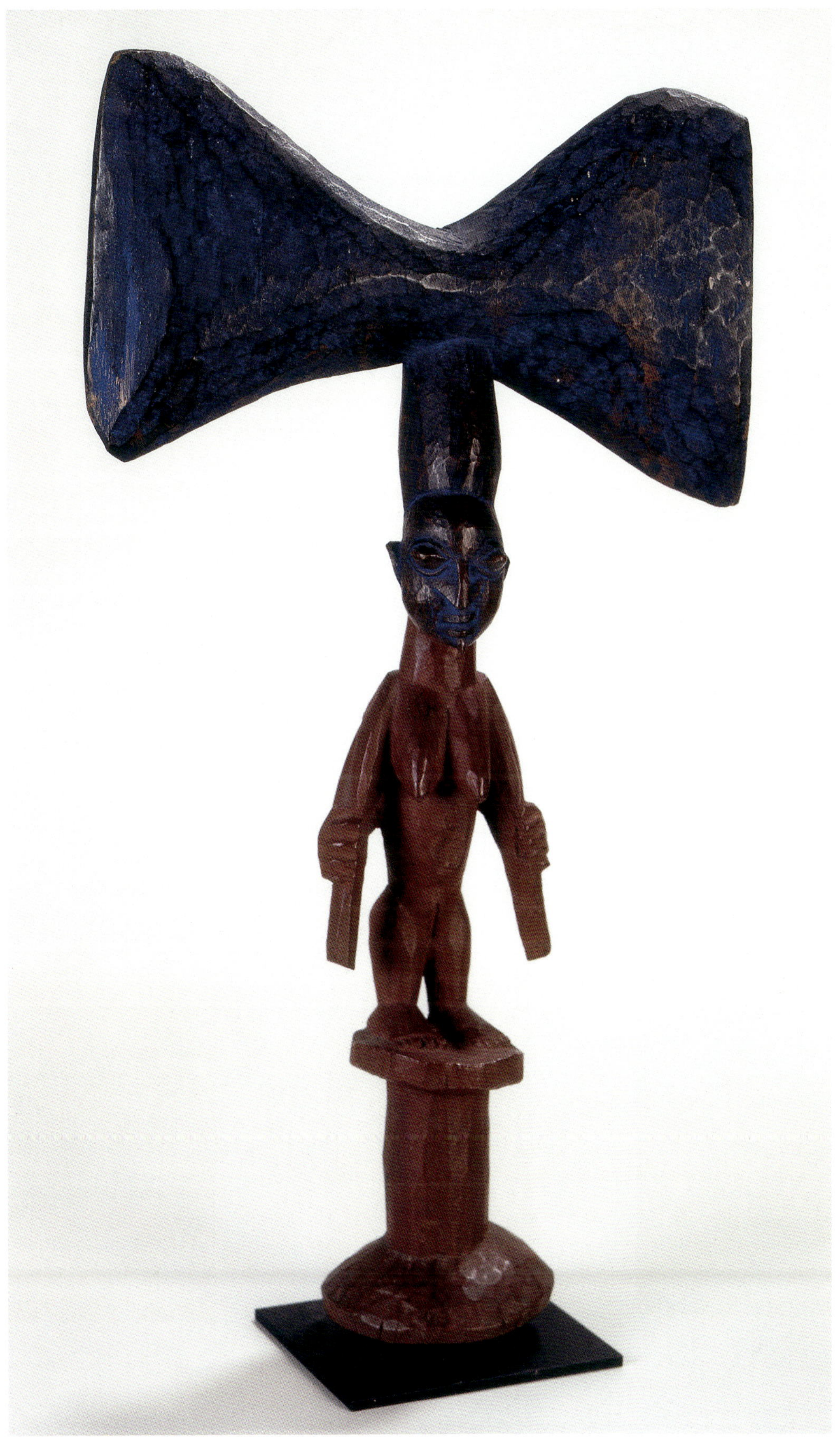

5 Unknown

Greece

Baptism of Christ on the River Jordan, mid-sixteenth century
Tempera on panel
13 × 9⅜ in.
Gift of Ambassador George Crews and Cecilia DeGolyer McGhee, 1998

"Icon" derives from the Greek word *eikon,* meaning "image." Depicting holy persons or biblical scenes, icons are devotional paintings that serve in the Eastern Orthodox Church as visual aids for religious instruction and as objects of veneration. They are a legacy of Byzantine art. The production of icons, as much an exercise of faith as of creativity, requires conformity to the Church's traditional guidelines on subject matter, form, and composition. Icons are made both for private worship in the home and for inclusion in large altar screens (iconostases) in churches.

The present icon depicts the narrative of Christ's baptism. Christ stands nude in the blue, stylized water of the River Jordan, which teems with fish. On the left, John the Baptist leans over the riverbank to baptize Christ, while on the right, four angels wait in attendance with Christ's robes. As is customary in depictions of the baptism of Christ, a personification of the sea appears in the water on the lower left, and a smaller personification of the River Jordan on the lower right.

According to the New Testament, at the moment of baptism, Christ "saw the heavens opened, and the Spirit like a dove descending upon him: And there came a voice from heaven, *saying,* Thou art my beloved Son, in whom I am well pleased" (Mark 1:10–11). In the icon, above Christ's head, the sky opens in a half circle and the Holy Spirit descends in the form of a dove. The rearmost angel looks up at the Holy Spirit.

Diagonals made by the converging river and land and a vertical made by the body of Christ and the descent of the Holy Spirit all direct the viewer's eye to the area above Christ's head. The upper, heavenly realm of the icon and all nimbi (halolike radiances) are gilt. Worshippers considered the light reflected by such gilding in icons as an earthly manifestation of the divine.

This icon bears strong stylistic affinities with earlier Italian art, such as works by the Sienese painter Duccio di Boninsegna (c. 1255–1319), who was greatly influenced by Byzantine icon painting. However, whereas Italian art evolved from the early fourteenth century on and allowed for greater freedom of artistic expression, icon painting remained static because its artists were bound by the traditions and rules of image making.

This icon is one of forty-one given to the museum by Ambassador George Crews McGhee and his wife, Cecilia DeGolyer McGhee. The icons are from Greece, Russia, Romania, and Asia Minor, and date from the sixteenth through the nineteenth centuries. Ambassador McGhee graduated from the University of Oklahoma in 1933 and was a Rhodes Scholar at Oxford University. After a career in the petroleum industry, he served the U.S. government in a number of prominent posts, including the ambassadorship to the Federal Republic of Germany from 1963 until 1968. McGhee began collecting icons in the early 1950s, during his tenure as U.S. ambassador to Turkey.

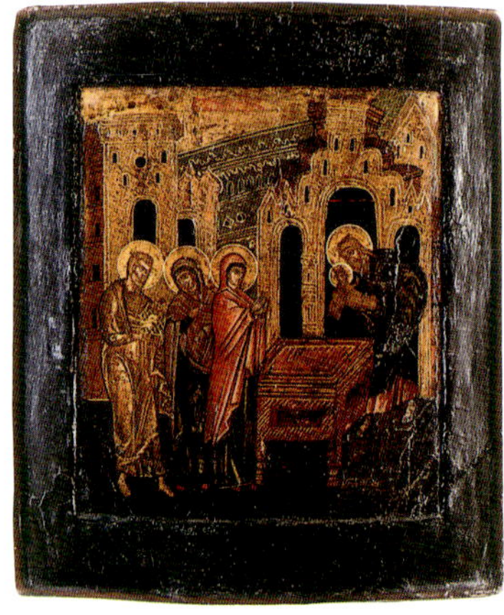

Moscow School
Russia
The Presentation of Christ in the Temple, c. 1600, tempera on panel, 12¼ × 10½ in. Gift of Ambassador George Crews and Cecilia DeGolyer McGhee, 1998

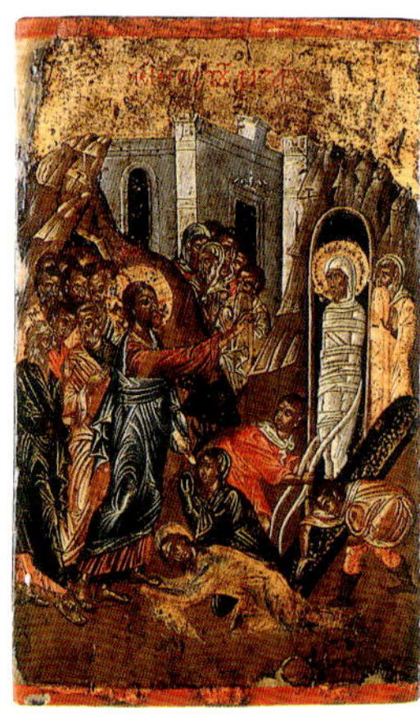

Unknown
Greece
Christ Raising Lazarus from the Dead, sixteenth to seventeenth centuries, tempera on panel, 17½ × 11⅛ in. Gift of Ambassador George Crews and Cecilia DeGolyer McGhee, 1998

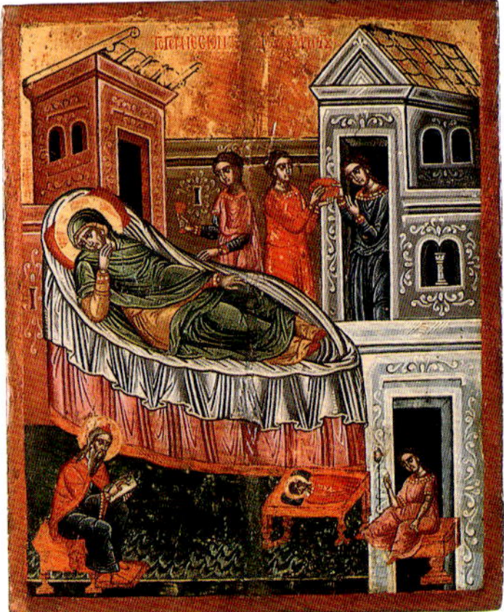

Unknown
Greece
The Birth of John the Baptist, late seventeenth century, tempera on panel, 13⅛ × 10⅞ in. Gift of Ambassador George Crews and Cecilia DeGolyer McGhee, 1998

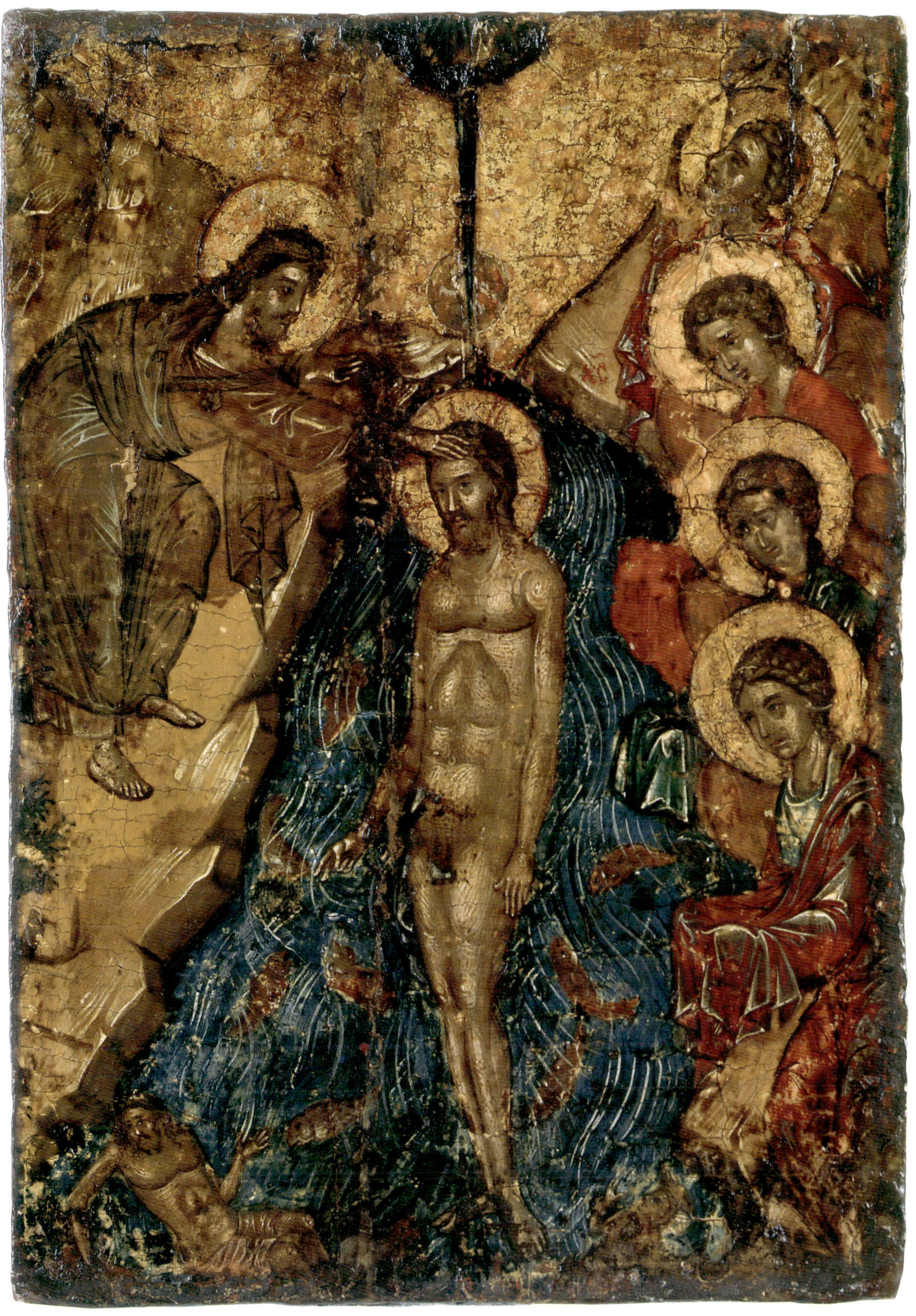

6 Jean-Baptiste-Camille Corot

France, 1796–1875

Cowherd Resting at the Foot of Cool Hills (Le Repos du vacher au pied des fraîches collines), c. 1855–65
Oil on canvas
19¾ × 24⅛ in.
Aaron M. and Clara Weitzenhoffer Bequest, 2000

This poetic landscape is typical of Jean-Baptiste-Camille Corot's late, atmospheric style, with the common motifs of hills, water, and trees with diaphanous foliage, all depicted in a limited color range of grays mixed with greens, ochres, and whites.

Born in Paris to a bourgeois family, Corot decided to devote himself full-time to art at age twenty-six. He studied landscape painting in Paris, after which he traveled in Italy for over two and a half years, starting in late 1825. Italy became an integral part of the artist's education—he made outdoor sketches of Rome and its environs, which he used as studies and exercises for larger exhibition paintings produced in the studio. Throughout his life, Corot traveled often during the summers, including not only to Italy, but also to Switzerland and around France. On these trips, he gathered source material for the exhibition canvases painted in Paris during the winters.

Corot had steady success and showed often at the Paris Salon, the prestigious annual government-sponsored exhibition. Until the mid-1840s, however, he did not receive much critical attention. In 1845, the poet and art critic Charles Baudelaire called Corot the leader of the modern school of landscape painting. Corot was elected to the Salon jury in 1849, and by the early 1850s, his reputation was established and his art heralded.

Cowherd Resting at the Foot of Cool Hills does not represent an actual site, but the round tower in the distance is reminiscent of a castle overlooking Lake Nemi. This famous lake in the Alban Hills near Rome had classical associations and had been a popular subject for landscape painters since the seventeenth century. Corot had painted the site during visits to Italy. A red-hatted cowherd, for whom the painting is named, lies below the trees near the water in which two cows are standing.

A master of light, Corot greatly influenced Impressionist artists such as Claude Monet and Camille Pissarro, who often painted alongside him in the forest of Fontainebleau, outside Paris.

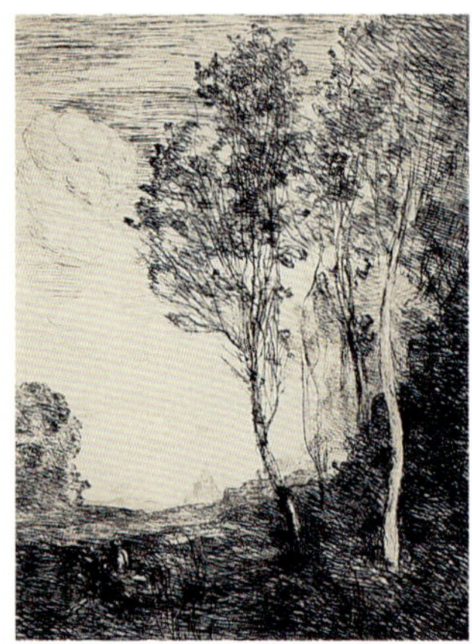

Jean-Baptiste-Camille Corot
France, 1796–1875
Souvenir d'Italie, 1863, etching on paper, 11½ × 8¾ in. Gift of J. Donald Walp, 1998

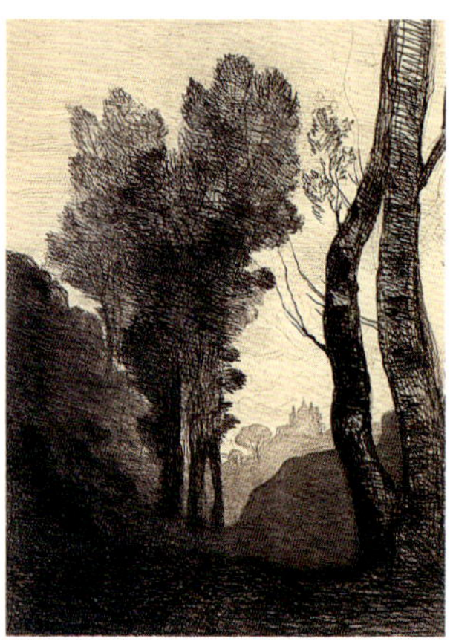

Jean-Baptiste-Camille Corot
France, 1796–1875
Environs de Rome, 1866, etching, 11⅜ × 8⅜ in. Gift of the Carnegie Corporation, prior to 1932

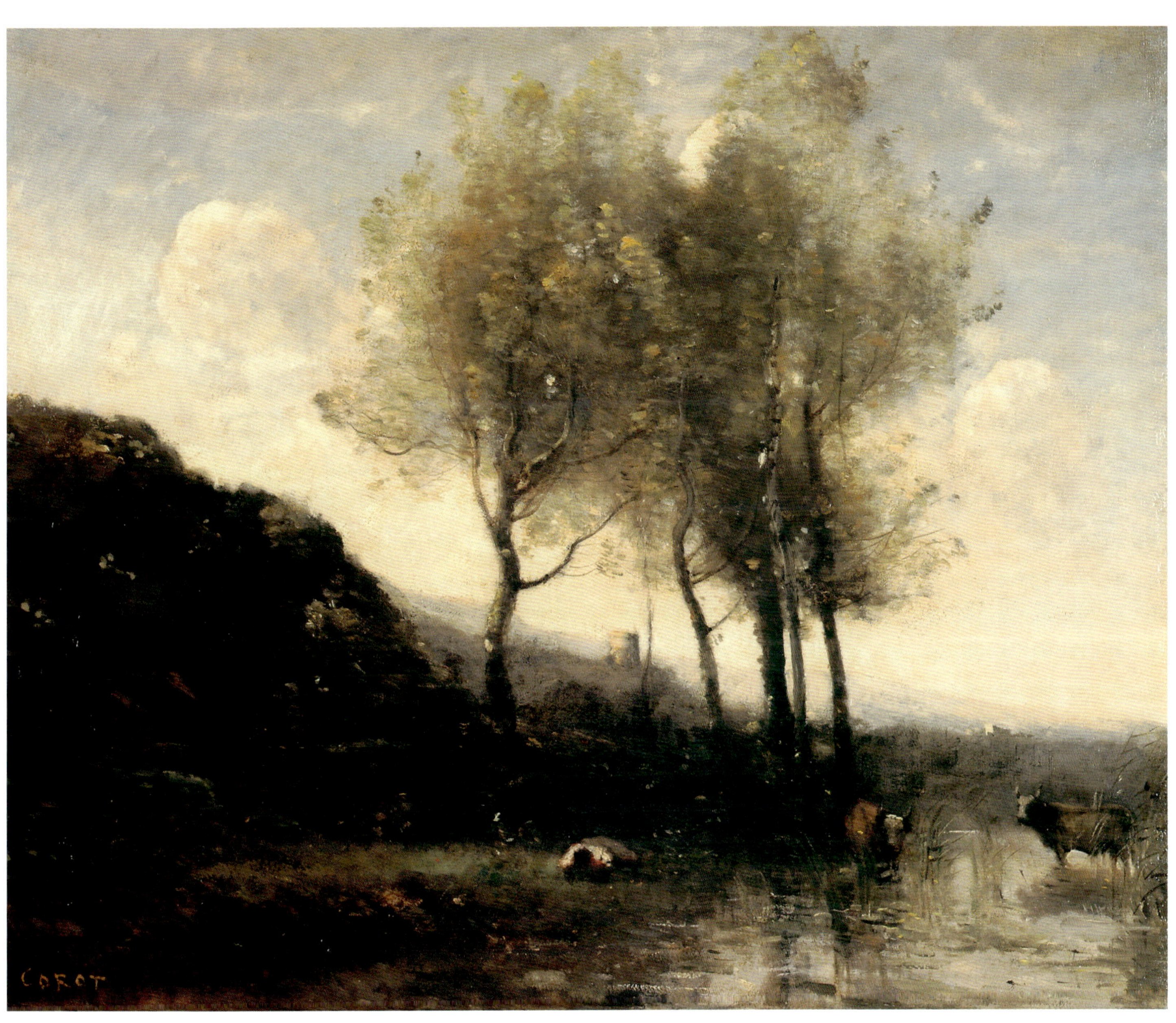
COROT

7 Eugène Boudin

France, 1824–1898

Figures on the Beach, Trouville (Personnages sur la plage, Trouville), 1866
Watercolor and pencil on paper
5⅝ × 10⅞ in.
Aaron M. and Clara Weitzenhoffer Bequest, 2000

The son of a mariner, Eugène Boudin was born in Honfleur, a picturesque fishing village on the coast of Normandy. Boudin decided to become a professional artist in 1847 and went to Paris, where he was inspired by the seventeenth-century Dutch school, in which marine painting figured prominently, and by the contemporary French Barbizon painters, who often worked outdoors in the forest of Fontainebleau near the village of Barbizon, painting naturalistic landscapes.

Boudin became best known for paintings depicting the aristocracy and bourgeoisie vacationing on the beaches of Trouville and neighboring Deauville. In Normandy, on the English Channel, Trouville and Deauville were two former fishing villages that became fashionable resorts and developed rapidly in the mid-nineteenth century. Often, artists and writers were the first to discover such towns, which became popular especially with Parisian and English vacationers. Trouville was called the "jewel" or "queen" of the Channel. Like many of these resorts, Trouville had a casino and was visited and painted by several artists in the 1860s, from Gustave Courbet to Boudin's younger close friend, Claude Monet.

Figures on the Beach, Trouville is a quickly painted study on which Boudin included a few annotations for color—for example, some dresses are inscribed "bleu." Well-dressed vacationers are depicted on the beach, observing and being observed. International flags, including the French tricolor, appear to the right, beyond the vacationers. These flags flew along the beach in front of major hotels, such as the Hôtel des Roches Noires, the grandest hotel in Trouville.

The Impressionists greatly admired Boudin's seascapes and beach scenes; they liked his depiction of atmosphere and light as well as his recording of contemporary life. With their images of bourgeois leisure, Boudin's beach scenes prefigured the Impressionists' paintings of the modern world. Boudin exhibited regularly at the Paris Salon and showed in the first Impressionist exhibition, in 1874.

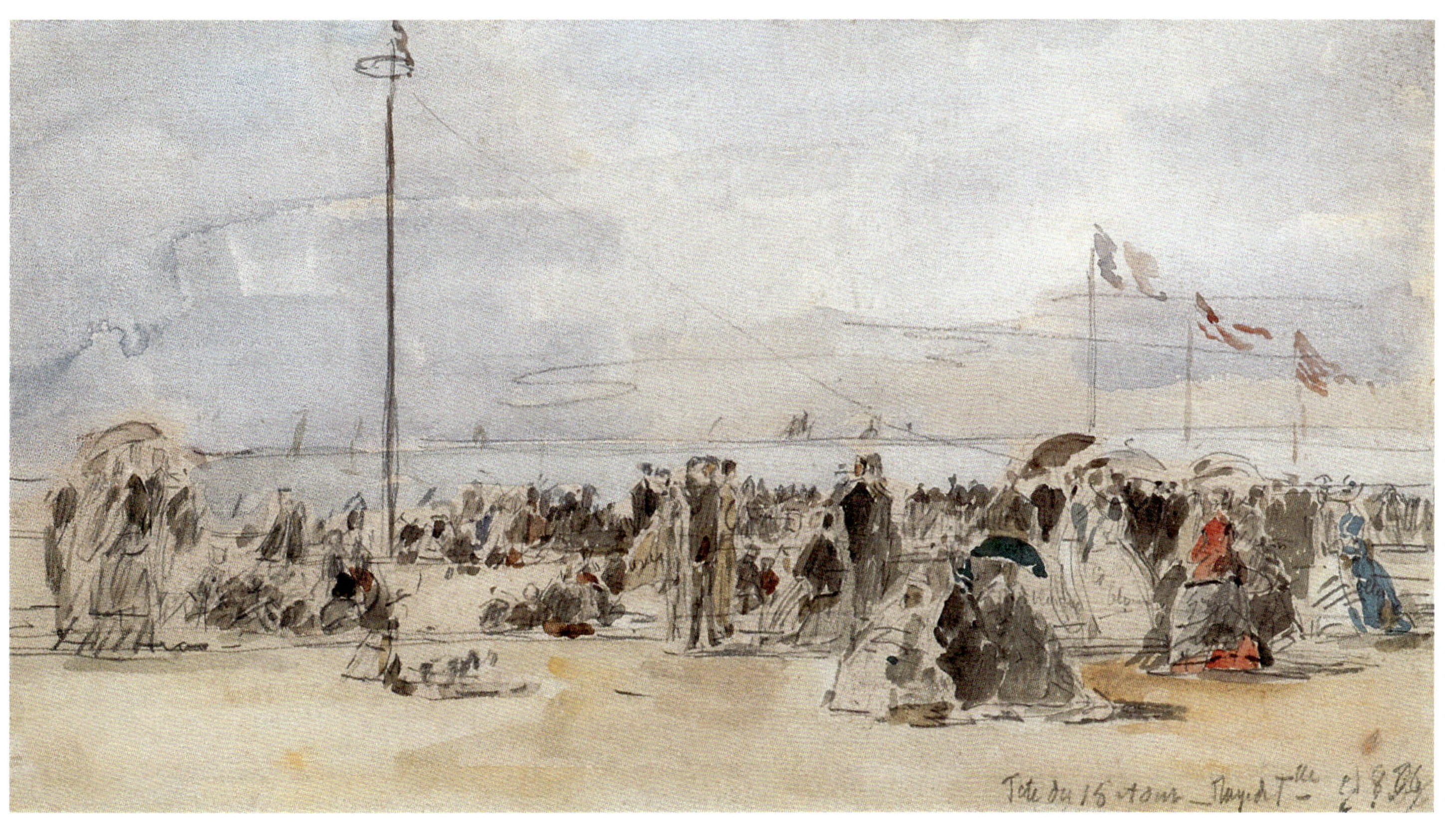

8 Claude Monet

France, 1840–1926

Riverbank at Lavacourt (La Berge à Lavacourt), 1879
Oil on canvas
$23\frac{1}{2} \times 35\frac{1}{4}$ in.
Aaron M. and Clara Weitzenhoffer Bequest, 2000

The term "Impressionism" was coined by hostile critics in 1874 in reaction to the title of a painting by Claude Monet, *Impression, Sunrise,* which depicted the harbor of Le Havre under fog. By 1876, the word was being used in a neutral way, and the artists—among them Pierre-Auguste Renoir, Edgar Degas, Camille Pissarro, and Alfred Sisley—soon began to call themselves Impressionists.

The Impressionists emphasized *observed* nature. They depicted contemporary, nonnarrative subjects and captured fleeting moments of light and atmosphere, usually with a bright palette rendered with fragmented, flickering brushstrokes on canvases that were nonhierarchical (meaning that no one part of the canvas was given more emphasis than another). The artists showed the life around them, often one of bourgeois leisure. In a review of the first Impressionist show, in 1874, the art critic Jules-Antoine Castagnary wrote: "They are Impressionists in the sense that they render not the landscape but the sensation produced by the landscape."

The Impressionists held an antiacademic stance, although most had formal training. In accordance with their antiacademic views, they organized exhibitions that, unlike the official Salon, were independent, nonjuried, and not government-sanctioned. Artists were invited to participate under the condition that they would not show at the official Salon. The group organized eight exhibitions, held between 1874 and 1886.

In 1864, Monet painted in the forest of Fontainebleau with Renoir, Sisley, and Jean-Frédéric Bazille. They painted outdoors for the rest of the 1860s, often depicting figures in a landscape. Between 1872 and 1878, Monet lived in Argenteuil, where other Impressionists also worked, including Renoir, Sisley, Edouard Manet, and Gustave Caillebotte. About twenty minutes from Paris by train, Argenteuil was a fast-changing Parisian suburb and a weekend riverside resort known for its boating on the Seine. In 1878, Monet moved from Argenteuil to Vétheuil, a small rural village farther downriver on the Seine.

Vétheuil seemed untouched by industrialism and the modern age, even though Paris was less than forty miles away. Monet and his family lived there until 1881. Unlike the paintings of Monet's Argenteuil period, which depict the fusion of nature with modern life, the paintings of the Vétheuil period are agrarian, representing a countryside that had remained unchanged for centuries. Often painting outdoors, Monet scrutinized a concentrated area surrounding the town in various seasons and weather.

One of Monet's favorite subjects during this time was quaint Lavacourt, a hamlet on the left bank of the Seine, opposite Vétheuil. In *Riverbank at Lavacourt,* the present work, Monet painted the towpath alongside the river.

Monet's Vétheuil period was among the most productive in his career, but it was a difficult time for him personally. The artist suffered financial hardship and felt discouraged about his work, which critics attacked for its lack of finish. Above all, during 1879 (the year of the present work), his wife, Camille, was bedridden with an illness, probably cancer, and she died in early September, at age thirty-two.

Monet had lived in the Vétheuil house with his wife and two sons —one born in March 1878—as well as close friends Alice and Ernest Hoschedé and their children. The Hoschedés had been wealthy early collectors of Impressionism with a lavish lifestyle, but they lost their fortune and, along with their six children, moved in with Monet and his family (twelve in all!). Ernest Hoschedé soon took a job in Paris with a newspaper but left his family in Vétheuil because of the cheaper rent.

At some point, the relationship between Monet and Alice Hoschedé became romantic. They moved together to Poissy in 1881 and to Giverny in 1883, and they married in 1892, after the death of Ernest. Monet lived in Giverny for the rest of his life.

In his later works, Monet produced series of paintings that focused on a single image, such as haystacks or the façade of Rouen Cathedral; he depicted the same image in different seasons and at different times of the day. He also increasingly focused on painting his garden, with its water lilies and Japanese footbridge.

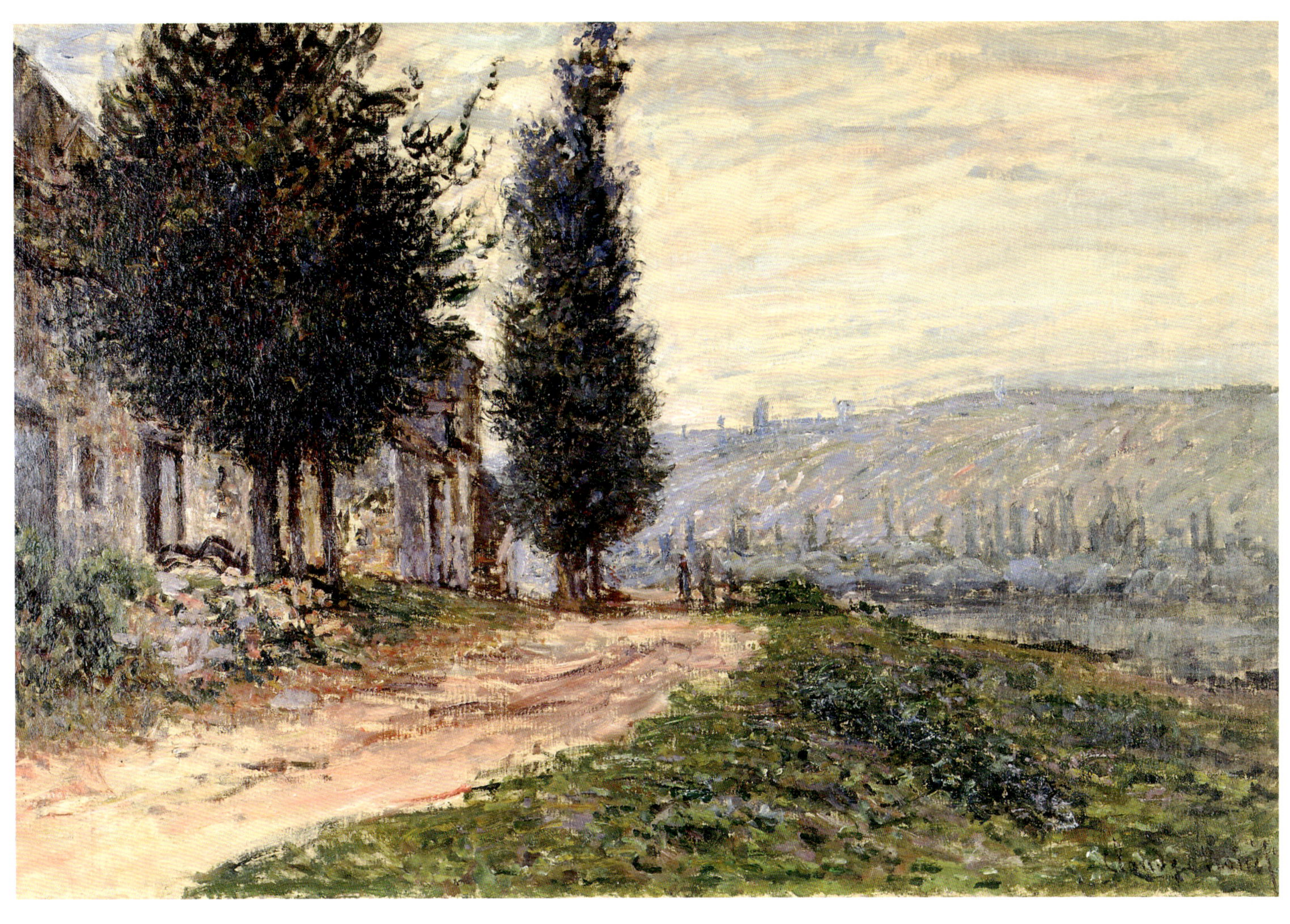

9 Pierre-Auguste Renoir

France, 1841–1919

Roses, 1878
Oil on canvas
16⅜ × 13¼ in.
Aaron M. and Clara Weitzenhoffer Bequest, 2000

Pierre-Auguste Renoir was, along with Claude Monet, one of the great colorists of the core Impressionist group. Renoir was born in Limoges, the son of a tailor and dressmaker. The family moved to Paris in 1844, and in his teens, Renoir worked as a porcelain decorator. Renoir began to copy Old Masters in the Louvre in 1860, and the following year became a frequent visitor to the studio of the artist Charles Gleyre, where he met Monet, Jean-Frédéric Bazille, and Alfred Sisley, young artists who would all become Impressionists. Renoir studied at the Ecole des Beaux-Arts from 1862 through 1864, and probably began at that time to paint outdoors, which he often did in the forest of Fontainebleau with Monet, Bazille, and his closest friend, Sisley.

From the mid-1860s until the opening of the first Impressionist exhibition in 1874, Renoir had some works accepted by the Salon and many others rejected. These were nudes, portraits, and genre paintings, often inspired by the artists Gustave Courbet or Eugène Delacroix.

Renoir's submissions to the first Impressionist exhibition, in 1874, showed a lighter palette and sensuous, fluid brushwork. The paintings Renoir produced during the rest of the 1870s—when *Roses* and the Weitzenhoffer Collection's *Young Woman in the Country* were created—are examples of classic Impressionism, such as the Musée d'Orsay's *Ball at the Moulin de la Galette,* which captures the light, color, and leisure of modern, bourgeois Paris.

But Renoir broke from the Impressionist group and began to exhibit at the Salon in 1878, the year *Roses* was painted. After the third Impressionist exhibition (1877), he submitted no other works to an Impressionist exhibition. By the end of the 1870s, a bleak period personally and financially for some other Impressionists such as Monet, Renoir had become a successful and fashionable painter.

During the 1880s, Renoir modified his painting style, reining in his natural propensity toward color in favor of more emphasis on composition and linear drawing, through which he hoped to give his art a greater sense of permanence. From the 1890s on, Renoir returned to his softer, coloristic style, as is seen in two additional works in the Weitzenhoffer Collection: *Chrysanthemums* and a portrait of his third son, *Coco (Claude).*

In *Roses,* the flowers themselves are painted wet-on-wet with oil paint thinned with turpentine, as is typical of Renoir's work of the 1870s. After painting the flowers, Renoir, using a sable brush that accentuated the softness of his brushstrokes, painted the light-dappled table with the bluish shadows cast by the flowers, and the thickly applied, multihued brownish background.

Roses once belonged to the Prince de Wagram, one of Renoir's most important early collectors.

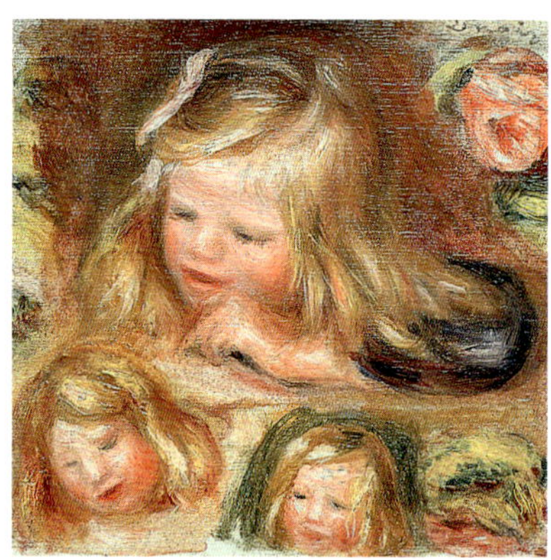

Pierre-Auguste Renoir
France, 1841–1919
Coco (Claude), c. 1905, oil on canvas, 9½ × 10 in. Aaron M. and Clara Weitzenhoffer Bequest, 2000

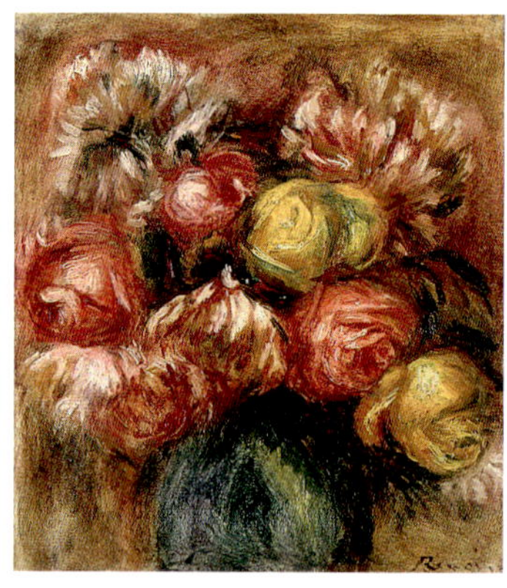

Pierre-Auguste Renoir
France, 1841–1919
Chrysanthemums, n.d., oil on canvas, 11 × 10 in. Aaron M. and Clara Weitzenhoffer Bequest, 2000

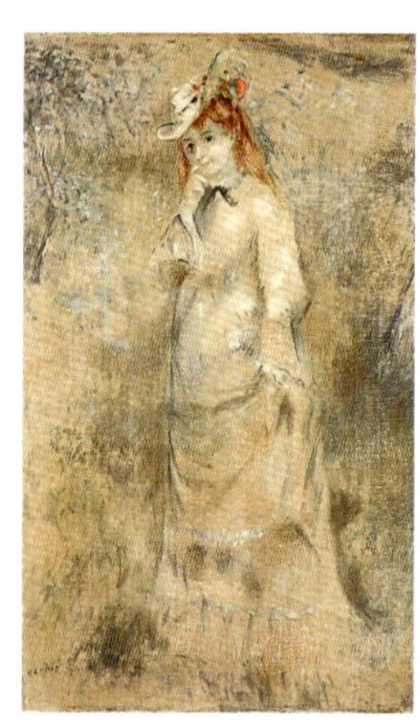

Pierre-Auguste Renoir
France, 1841–1919
Young Woman in the Country: Portrait of Madame Henriot, the Actress (Jeune femme dans les champs), 1877, oil on canvas, 28⅝ × 16⅞ in. Aaron M. and Clara Weitzenhoffer Bequest, 2000

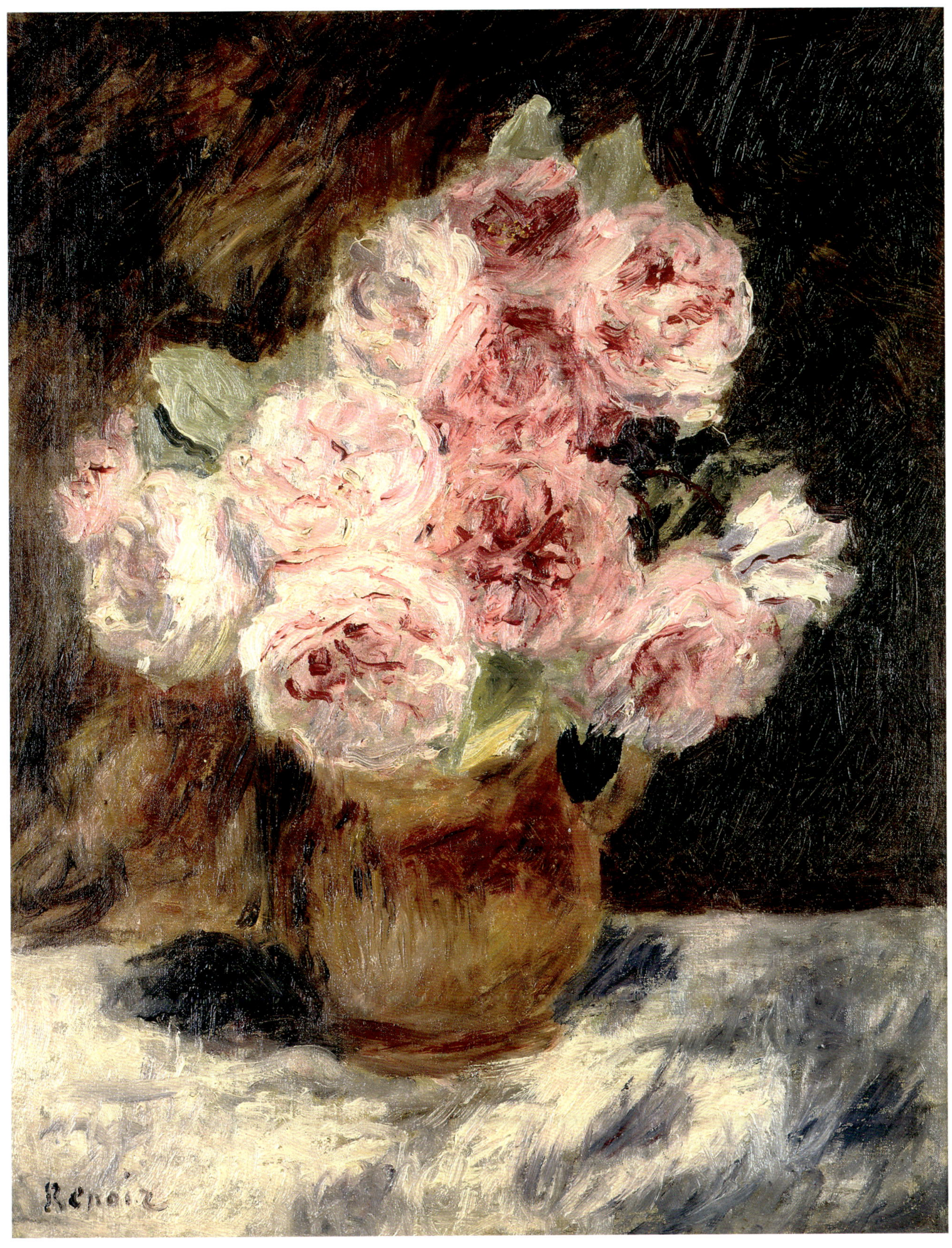
Renoir

10 Edgar Degas

France, 1834–1917

Dancer at the Bar (Danseuse à la barre),
c. 1885
Charcoal with pastel and white chalk on paper
12¼ × 9½ in.
Aaron M. and Clara Weitzenhoffer Bequest, 2000

Distinctive among the Impressionists for his emphasis on drawing and the human figure, Degas is perhaps best known for his depictions of ballerinas. The artist portrayed dancers more often in rehearsal, backstage, or at rest, rather than in performances on stage. Basing his art on rigorous observation, he never idealized ballerinas, and he made clear that dancers, like artists, achieve their seemingly effortless grace through hard work. Nevertheless, Degas claimed that "the dancer has been for me no more than a pretext to paint pretty materials and render movements."

Dancer at the Bar is among a group of over 100 life drawings of ballerinas at practice, which were most likely created during the early to mid-1880s. Rather than studies for finished works, these quick sketches probably served as exercises for the artist. They often show vestiges of Degas's revisions of particular gestures and include Degas's notes to himself, such as in the present drawing "plus croisée [noir?] la jambe" (more crossed [black?] the leg).

Degas kept many drawings and studies in his studio; they were dispersed in a large sale the year after his death. These works have studio-stamped signatures in red, as seen in the bottom left of *Dancer at the Bar.*

Degas sometimes made charcoal tracings of his drawings. Such a tracing exists of *Dancer at the Bar.*

The Impressionists came from diverse social backgrounds. Unlike Pierre-Auguste Renoir or Armand Guillaumin, who were from the working class, Degas, like Edouard Manet, was from the well-to-do haute bourgeoisie. Similarly, the Impressionists were of diverse political persuasions, from Degas's conservatism to Camille Pissarro's anarchist sympathies.

Degas, who is famous for his sometimes voyeuristic depictions of women, never married. He originally planned to become a lawyer but decided to study art instead. He trained in the studio of a former pupil of Jean-Auguste-Dominique Ingres and later at the Ecole des Beaux-Arts, where he received a traditional art education that emphasized the importance of drawing. Steeped in the classical tradition and in academic rigor, Degas became a painter of modern life and one of the core figures of Impressionism, although he preferred to call himself a Realist or Naturalist.

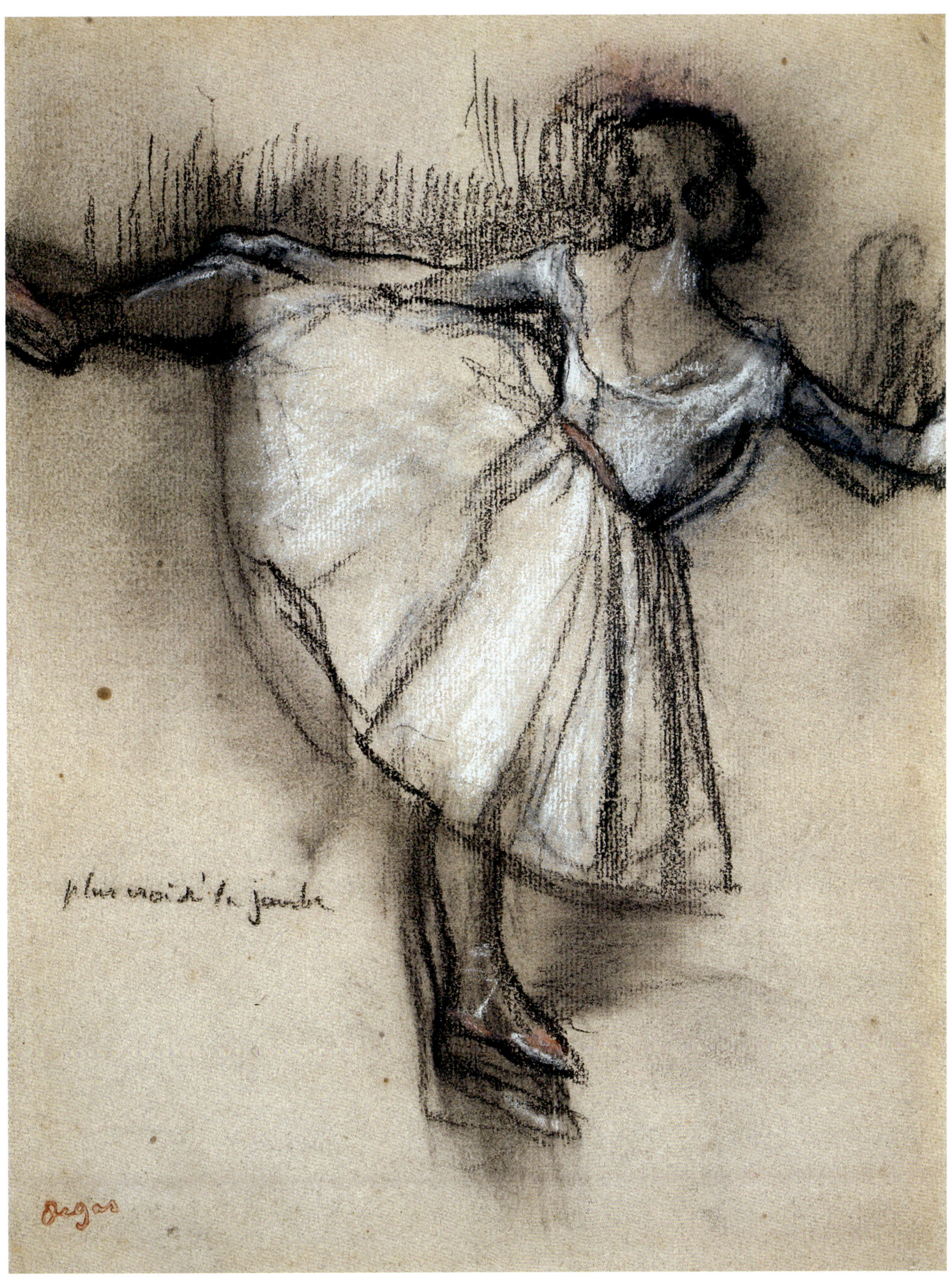
plus croisé la jambe
Degas

11 Jean-Louis Forain

France, 1852–1931

The Dressing Room (La Loge), c. 1890
Pastel and gouache on paper
18⅞ × 11¾ in.
Aaron M. and Clara Weitzenhoffer Bequest, 2000

In late-nineteenth-century Paris, Jean-Louis Forain was famous as a satiric illustrator with a biting wit, but he also exhibited in four of the eight Impressionist shows. Born in Reims, Forain moved to Paris with his family around 1860. He studied art under Jean-Baptiste Carpeaux.

In 1879, Forain's close friend Edgar Degas invited him to exhibit in the fourth Impressionist exhibition, the same show that Degas had invited Mary Cassatt to join. Degas was Forain's strongest influence, and the two often worked from the same models. Forain met regularly with the Impressionists, who discussed art in Montmartre at the Café Guerbois and later at the Café de la Nouvelle Athène. (Forain is known, too, for his friendships with the poets Paul Verlaine and Arthur Rimbaud.)

Following the Impressionists, Forain brightened his palette and paid more attention to light, as is seen in *The Dressing Room,* in which light flows through the door hidden by the screen and illuminates the figures, the back wall, and part of the floor. Forain's subject matter, too, was inspired by the Impressionists, and he depicted scenes from contemporary Paris. Degas's impact is evident in the theme of the present work, which shows a ballerina and her suitor in a dressing room at the Opéra, with the ballerina's assistant looking on. The assistant, perhaps the dancer's mother or a procuress, is a reminder of the ravaging effects time will have on the young woman.

The man in *The Dressing Room* is both haughty, as indicated by his pose and upright head, and lecherous, as indicated by his stare. Wealthy, powerful men who subscribed to the boxes at the Opéra had access to the backstage, including the foyer, dressing rooms, and the dancers themselves. Dancers in the nineteenth century were strictly from the lower class, and they endured long hours of hard work from a young age. Often, they would be seduced by "protectors," who would offer them gifts and attention. By the end of the century, however, the stardom achieved by some ballerinas began to attract dancers from other classes, and some of the stars married into the upper class.

In the present work, Forain placed great attention on the dancer's legs, which at the time were among the most eroticized parts of a woman's body, rarely seen under the long, bustled skirts of the period.

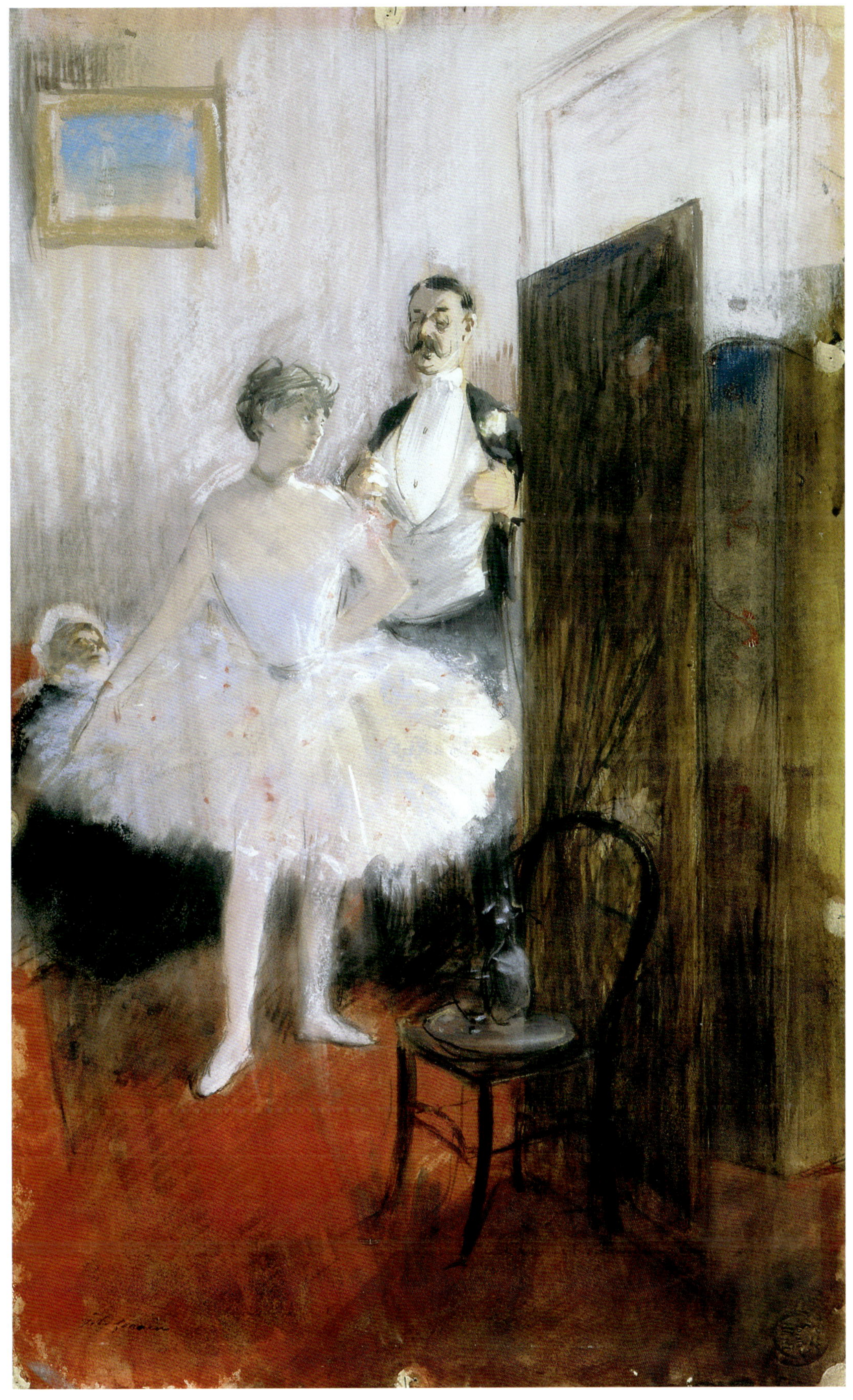

12 Mary Cassatt

U.S., 1844–1926

Sara in a Dark Bonnet Tied under Her Chin, c. 1901
Pastel on paper
21 × 16¼ in.
Aaron M. and Clara Weitzenhoffer Bequest, 2000

Mary Cassatt was the only American to be included in the Impressionist exhibitions in Paris. Artists and critics alike accepted her as a full-fledged member of the Impressionist group.

Born the daughter of a banker in Pittsburgh, then known as Allegheny City, Cassatt spent most of her adult life in France, while maintaining strong ties with the United States. She lived abroad as a child, from 1851 until 1855. In 1860, she began classes at the Pennsylvania Academy of the Fine Arts but left again for Europe in 1866 to study for four years in Paris, Rome, and elsewhere with, among others, Jean-Léon Gérôme and Thomas Couture. After sixteen months in the United States during 1870 and 1871, she returned to Europe, traveling widely and studying art in museums. She was attracted to the great colorists of the past, such as Diego Velázquez and Peter Paul Rubens, whose vibrant, sketchy style she would assimilate into her own. She finally settled in Paris in 1874. Three years later, her parents and sister moved to Paris, and Cassatt's two brothers and their families became frequent visitors.

After Cassatt settled in Paris, she met and befriended at the Louvre Edgar Degas, who introduced her to the other Impressionists and invited her to show in the fourth Impressionist exhibition, of 1879. She subsequently exhibited in the Impressionist shows of 1880 and 1881 and the final one, of 1886. Cassatt had already shown in the Paris Salon for several years. She had successful solo exhibitions in the 1890s in Paris and New York. From the sale of her art, she was able to buy in 1894 a château in the country, after which she divided her time between the château and Paris, with visits to the south of France.

Although Cassatt never married or had children, she became most heralded for her portrayals of the mother-and-child theme and of little girls, as in *Sara in a Dark Bonnet Tied under Her Chin,* subjects she increasingly concentrated on, starting in the late 1880s.

Especially after 1900, Cassatt often painted girls in large bonnets or hats decorated with ribbons and flowers, as in the present pastel. When Cassatt found a favorite model, she would make numerous studies. Around 1901, she sketched and painted Sara, then five or six years old and the granddaughter of Emile-François Loubet, a former president of the French Republic, over fifty times. Cassatt is said to have admired the little girl's disposition and expressive face.

The present work is in greater focus in the most important part of the composition, the girl's face, where the pastel is blended to establish smooth tonal gradations. Sara's body is loosely sketched. Pastel is perfectly suited for sketching, and together the pastel and sketch produce a sense of speed and immediacy, which gives the impression of capturing life. In *Sara in a Dark Bonnet Tied under Her Chin,* the pastel and sketch elements combine to create a vibrant portrait that captures the spirit of childhood. A superb draftsman, Cassatt had always used pastels for sketching purposes, but she did not use them for finished works until she met the consummate pastelist Degas and became associated with the Impressionists in the late 1870s.

Sara in a Dark Bonnet Tied under Her Chin is both a sketch and a finished composition. In the early years of Impressionism, critics, most of whom still maintained a sharp distinction between a sketch and a finished work, attacked the Impressionists' works for being too sketchy and therefore unfinished. By the time the present work was created, however, tastes had shifted and caught up with the Impressionists, and Cassatt's pastels such as this one were extremely popular among collectors.

Cassatt advised several pioneering American collectors of Impressionism, including her friends Bertha Honoré Palmer and Louisine Havemeyer, the great benefactors of, respectively, the Art Institute of Chicago and the Metropolitan Museum of Art.

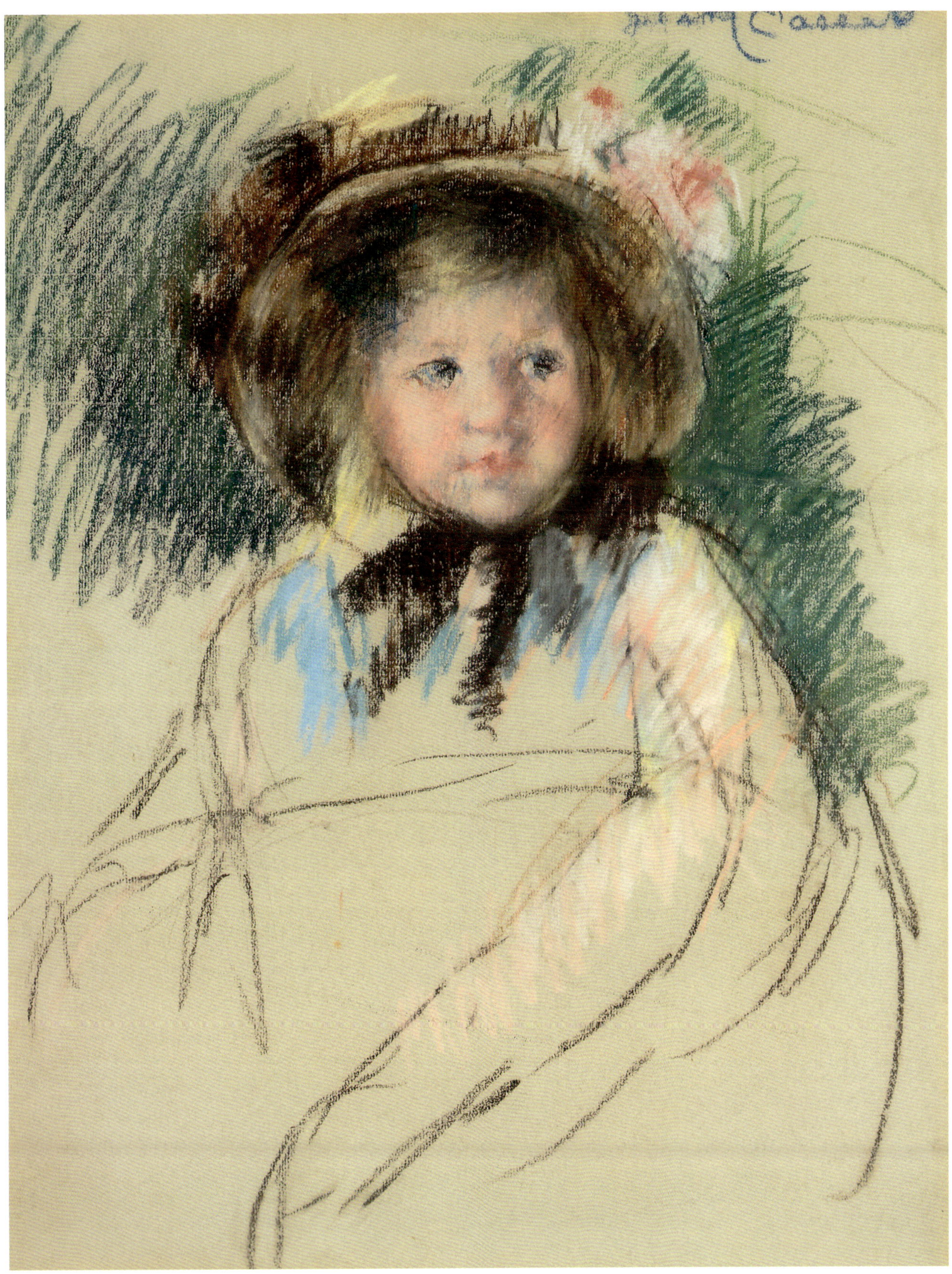

13 Camille Pissarro

France, 1830–1903

Shepherdess Bringing in Sheep (Bergère rentrant des moutons), 1886
Oil on canvas
18¼ × 15 in.
Aaron M. and Clara Weitzenhoffer Bequest, 2000

Camille Pissarro was born in the Virgin Islands to French-Jewish parents who were of Portuguese descent. In the 1840s, he attended school in France. He spent over a year working as an artist in Venezuela before moving permanently to France in 1855.

The only artist to show in all eight Impressionist exhibitions and the oldest member of the Impressionist group, Pissarro was always receptive to younger artists and new ideas. Among the Impressionists, he was known as the teacher, advising, for instance, the early careers of Paul Cézanne and Paul Gauguin. Mary Cassatt reportedly said that Pissarro was such a teacher "that he could have taught stones how to draw correctly."

Many of the Impressionists were opposed to art schools, although most had received considerable formal training. Pissarro, however, was essentially self-taught as an artist. He did attend private classes at the Ecole des Beaux-Arts in Paris in 1856, and starting in 1859, he studied at the Académie Suisse in Paris, where he met Cézanne, Armand Guillaumin, and Claude Monet. (At the Académie Suisse, students could work from a model but received no instruction.) During the 1860s, Pissarro exhibited in the official Salon, but he began to associate with the artists from the Académie Suisse, who later formed the Impressionist group.

During the 1870s, Pissarro painted in an Impressionist style, in which he tried to capture what he called his "sensations" before nature, with a lightened palette and fragmented brushstrokes. Long interested in peasant life, he was distinctive from the other Impressionists (except, perhaps, Alfred Sisley) in his preference for rustic themes such as those painted by his hero Jean-François Millet.

In London in 1871, Pissarro married a woman who worked for his family, and together they had eight children. From 1872 until 1882, the couple lived in Pontoise, a small town northeast of Paris, where the artist painted peasants and scenes of country life and worked alongside Cézanne, who lived nearby at Auvers.

Around 1880, a "crisis of Impressionism" occurred when many Impressionists such as Pierre-Auguste Renoir reevaluated their art and altered their styles after they had not received the expected success and recognition. Pissarro had already modified his style in the late 1870s, painting with smaller, more regular brushstrokes and building up the surface of the canvas in layers, as is seen in *Shepherdess Bringing in Sheep.*

The present painting is one of many images of peasants, usually women, going about their daily routines, that Pissarro produced in the 1880s, when he paid increasing attention to figures. Pissarro's peasants are often absorbed in thought and painted in an unsentimentalized manner. He identified with peasants and admired their hard work, which he likened to the work of a painter.

In 1884, Pissarro moved to Eragny-sur-Epte, a village in Normandy approximately sixty miles north of Paris, where the artist would be based for the rest of his life. The following year, in the Paris studio of Guillaumin, Pissarro met Paul Signac, who in turn introduced Pissarro

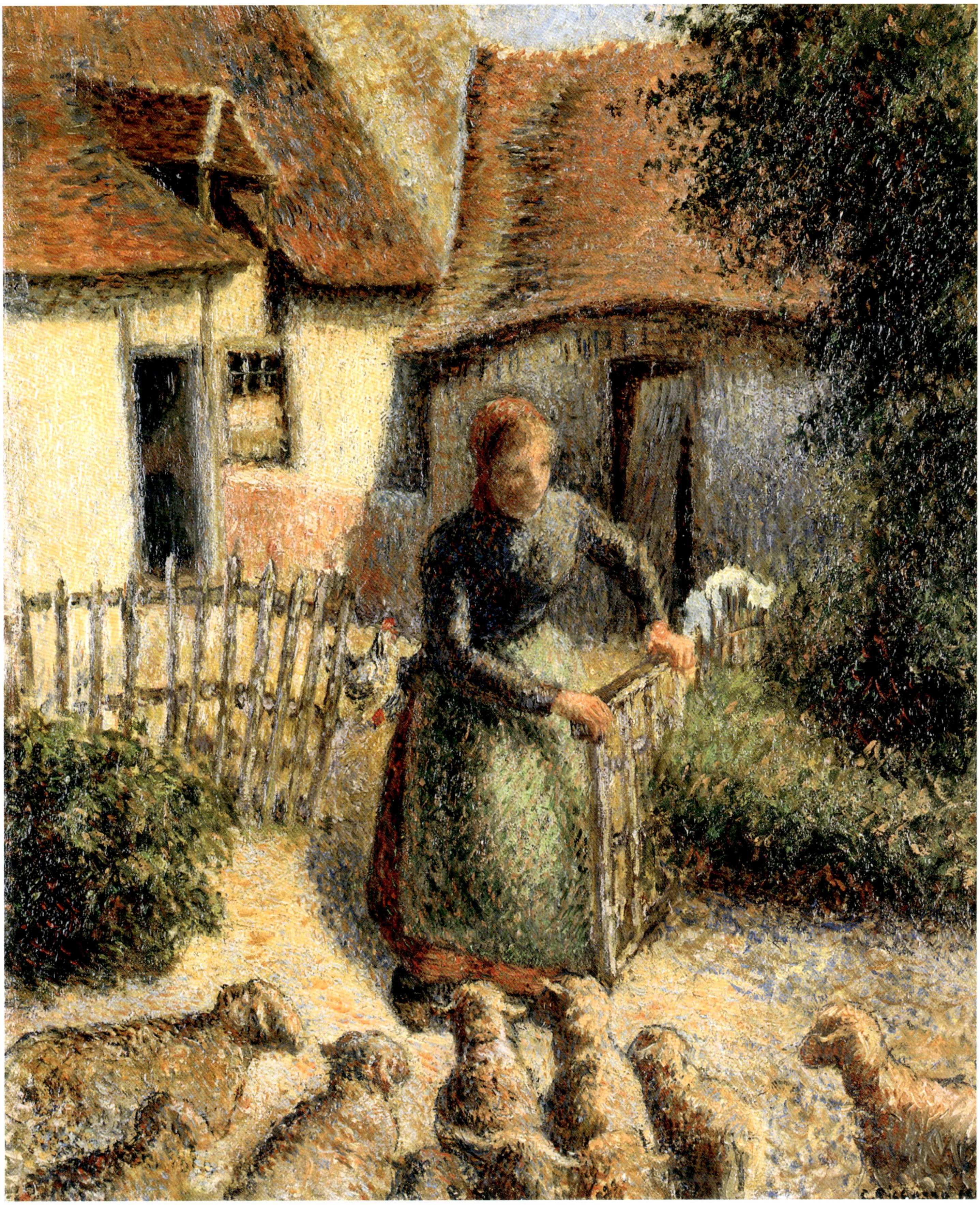

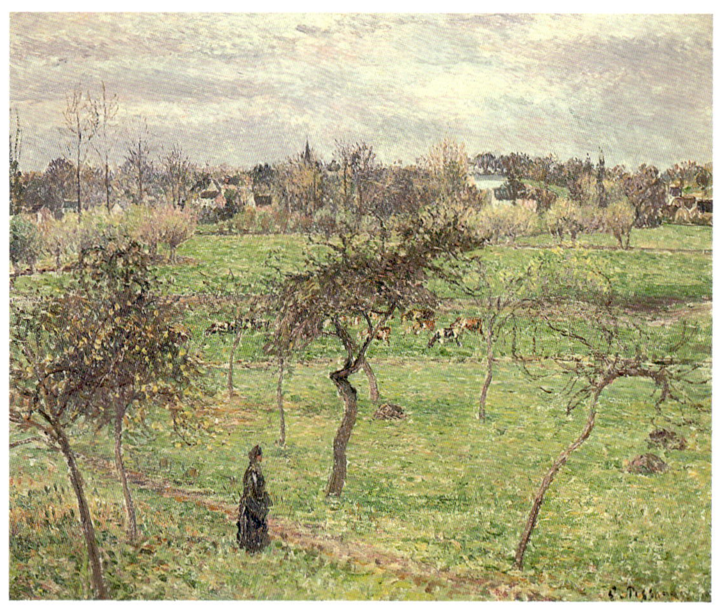

Camille Pissarro
France, 1830–1903
Meadow at Eragny (Le Pré à Eragny), 1894, oil on canvas, 25⅜ × 32 in. Aaron M. and Clara Weitzenhoffer Bequest, 2000

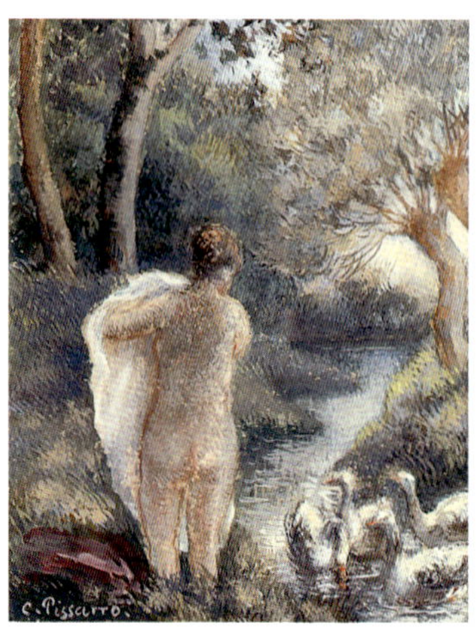

Camille Pissarro
France, 1830–1903
Nude with Swans, c. 1895, gouache on paper, 8½ × 6½ in. Aaron M. and Clara Weitzenhoffer Bequest, 2000

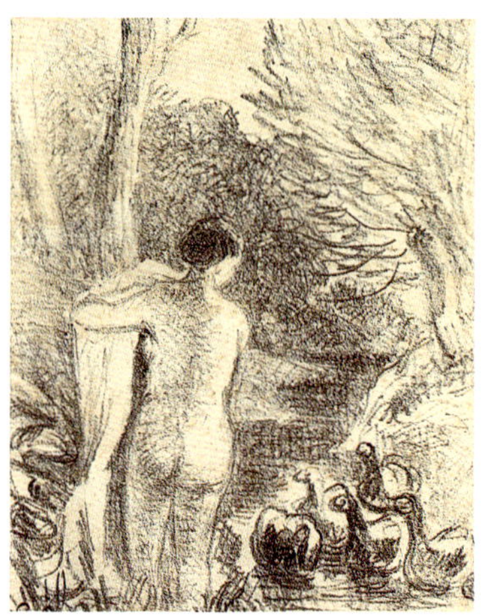

Camille Pissarro
France, 1830–1903
Nude with Swans, c. 1895, lithograph, 6½ × 5¼ in. Aaron M. and Clara Weitzenhoffer Bequest, 2000

to Georges Seurat. Signac and Seurat were interested in developing a new, scientific approach to painting (as opposed to the more intuitive Impressionist approach) that was based on the rules of color contrasts as laid out by color theorists such as Eugène Chevreul and the American Ogden Rood. Having questioned the tenets of Impressionism for several years, Pissarro banded with these young avant-garde painters to form a new movement, with Seurat as its leader, which would soon be labeled Neo-Impressionism. At the final Impressionist exhibition, in 1886—the year of *Shepherdess Bringing in Sheep*—the Neo-Impressionists exhibited together in a separate room, the centerpiece being Seurat's famous *Sunday Afternoon on the Island of La Grande Jatte,* now at the Art Institute of Chicago.

In a letter to his dealer, Pissarro summarized the goals of Neo-Impressionism, which is characterized by the technique of Pointillism: "To seek a modern synthesis of methods based on science. . . . To substitute optical mixture for mixture of pigments. In other words: the breaking up of tones into their constituents. For optical mixture stirs up more intense luminosities than does mixture of pigments." (For more on Pointillism, see cat. no. 17.) So in separating color into its basic components of small brushstrokes (or dots) and juxtaposing them with their complements, the Neo-Impressionists hoped their paintings would achieve greater brilliance.

The present work is an early example of Pissarro's practice of Neo-Impressionism, as is seen in the many flecks (and larger blocks) of contrasting colors. Neo-Impressionism interested the artist for the next few years, even though his works rarely display a pure form of Pointillism such as that found in Signac's *Coast Scene,* in the Weitzenhoffer Collection.

The Philadelphia Museum of Art owns a charcoal sketch for *Shepherdess Bringing in Sheep.* A related painting, executed before Pissarro's conversion to Neo-Impressionism, depicts the same farm buildings, near his home in Eragny-sur-Epte, without the figure.

Throughout the 1890s and up until his death in 1903, Pissarro returned to an Impressionist style, creating numerous city views of Paris, Rouen, and elsewhere, as well as country scenes such as the museum's *Meadow at Eragny,* which depicts the view from the artist's studio (located in a converted barn), including the neighboring village of Bazincourt on a hillside less than two miles away. Additionally in the 1890s, Pissarro painted female nudes in a manner reminiscent of Millet, as in the Weitzenhoffer Collection's *Nude with Swans.* (The Weitzenhoffer Collection also includes a Pissarro lithograph based on *Nude with Swans.*)

14 Armand Guillaumin

France, 1841–1927

Still Life (Nature morte), c. 1885
Oil on canvas
7½ × 9½ in.
Aaron M. and Clara Weitzenhoffer Bequest, 2000

Armand Guillaumin grew up in Moulins, France, and moved to Paris at sixteen in search of work. Against the wishes of his family, he became an artist, attending the Académie Suisse in Paris in the early 1860s while supporting himself with government jobs. (He could not devote himself full-time to painting until he won a state lottery in 1891.) At the Académie Suisse, he met Camille Pissarro, Claude Monet, and Paul Cézanne.

In 1863, Guillaumin exhibited in the famous Salon des Refusés, which featured paintings that had been rejected by the official Salon—for example, Edouard Manet's *Déjeuner sur l'herbe*. Guillaumin associated with the painters who would form the Impressionist group, regularly meeting them at cafés. He participated in six of the eight Impressionist exhibitions.

While working for the Paris-Orléans Railway, Guillaumin painted outdoors around Paris and became especially noted for his depictions of life along the Seine. Like Pissarro, he identified with the working class, from which he came, and his paintings of industrial settings influenced Paul Signac, Georges Seurat, and their Neo-Impressionist followers.

Guillaumin's works of the 1870s show the high-keyed, bright palette of the Impressionists, and in that decade, he painted landscapes alongside Pissarro at Pontoise and Cézanne at neighboring Auvers. During the 1880s, Guillaumin intensified the brilliance of his colors and emphasized contrasting complementary colors, as seen in *Still Life* with its blues and oranges, and reds and greens.

Guillaumin remained one of Cézanne's few lasting artist friends, and Cézanne's influence is apparent in *Still Life*, which depicts a Cézannesque subject. Apples, which Cézanne began to paint in the 1870s, are now considered one of Cézanne's iconic motifs, but when Guillaumin painted *Still Life* in the 1880s, Cézanne was known only to a few artists and writers; he had not exhibited in Paris since the 1870s and spent most of his time in Aix-en-Provence, in the south of France. Cézanne was not "discovered" by Parisians until an exhibition of 1895, at which time he was described by the critic Thadée Natanson as the "painter of apples." Cézanne's influence is also seen in the execution of *Still Life*, with its slow, methodical, constructive brushstrokes.

Guillaumin's dealer in the 1880s was Vincent van Gogh's brother, Theo. Vincent and Guillaumin became friends when Vincent lived in Paris from 1886 until 1887. Guillaumin lived on the ground floor at 54 rue Lepic in Montmartre, while Vincent and Theo shared an apartment on the third floor. The Van Gogh apartment appears in the museum's *Portrait of Alexander Reid*, by Vincent van Gogh (see cat. no. 16).

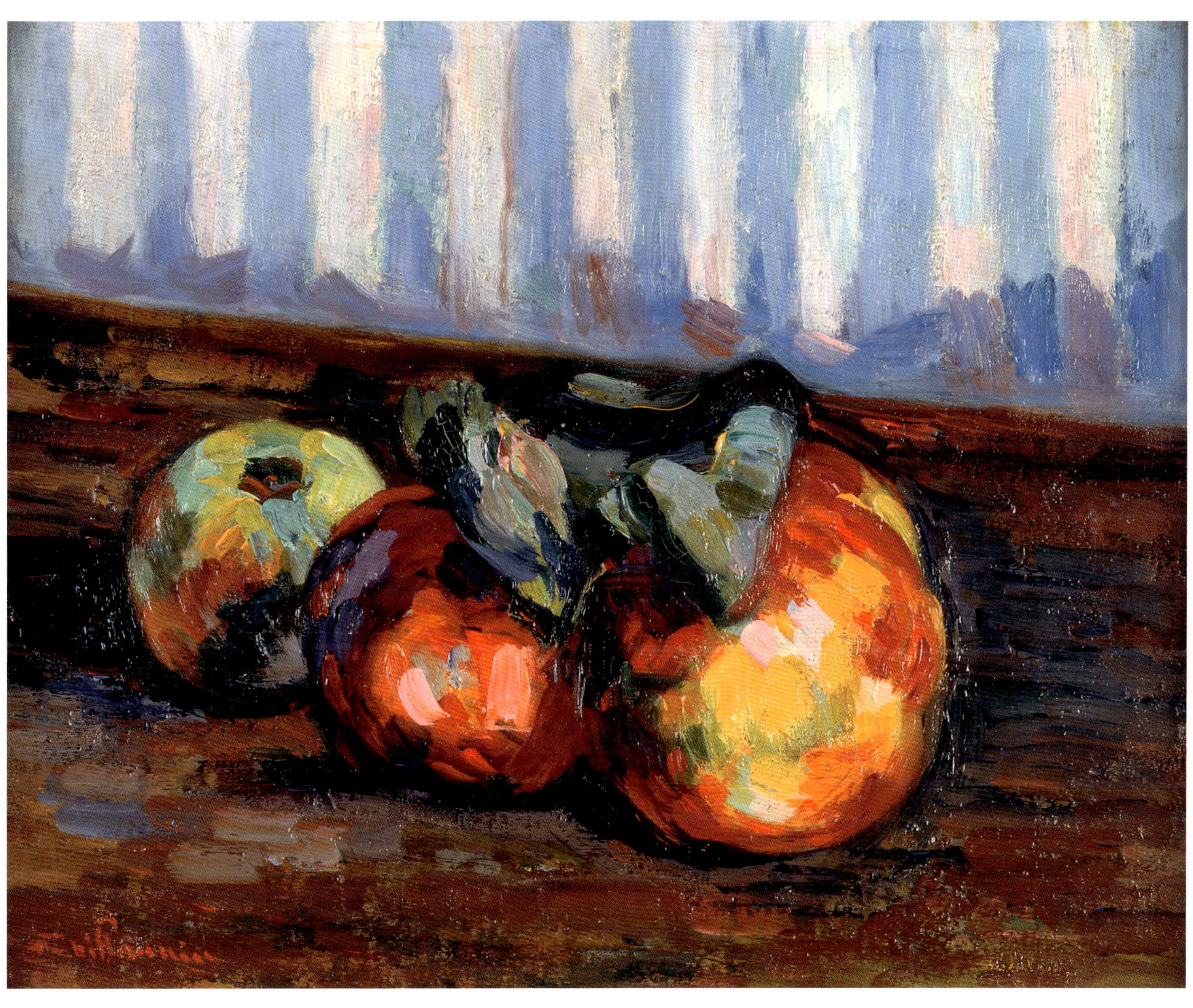

15 Paul Gauguin

France, 1848–1903

Winter Day, 1886
Oil on canvas
28¼ × 22 in.
Aaron M. and Clara Weitzenhoffer Bequest, 2000

While working as a stockbroker, Paul Gauguin began to paint in the early 1870s. He became a pupil and close associate of Camille Pissarro, who inspired Gauguin to adopt an Impressionist style, with short brushstrokes and an emphasis on light and color. Gauguin showed in the fourth Impressionist exhibition, in 1879, and in subsequent Impressionist exhibitions through the eighth and final one, which took place in 1886, a few months after this snow scene was painted. The present work is possibly the *Winter Landscape* that Gauguin exhibited in the eighth Impressionist exhibition.

Gauguin struggled financially after losing his job as a stockbroker following the 1882 market crash. In 1873, he had married a Danish woman, Mette Gad, and in late 1884, he moved with his family to Copenhagen, where his in-laws lived. However, the Danes were not receptive to his art, and in June 1885, Gauguin returned to France with one son, leaving his wife and other children in Denmark.

Gauguin's wife, Mette, amassed a large collection of works by her estranged husband, including *Winter Day.* Sometime before 1917, Mette gave *Winter Day* to her friend and lawyer in Copenhagen, Konrad Levysohn. Underneath *Winter Day,* nailed to the same stretcher, Levysohn found another work by Gauguin—*Sweet Dreams,* a painting of 1881 that tenderly depicts one of Gauguin's children sleeping. Levysohn returned *Sweet Dreams* to Mette, and it now hangs in the Ordrupgaard Museum in Denmark. *Winter Day* remained in Levysohn's family until around 1948.

Winter Day was once known, probably erroneously, as *Copenhagen.* The painting is dated 1886, but Gauguin was not in Copenhagen that year. Unless it was painted from sketches or memory (which the artist sometimes did during this time), the painting most likely depicts a suburb of Paris or a nearby village such as Pontoise, where Gauguin had lived near Pissarro a few years earlier. Pontoise, like many towns around Paris, had a towering smokestack similar to the one in the painting, but the buildings in *Winter Day* do not appear to be specifically French or Danish. The painting was exhibited in Copenhagen in 1917 with the title *Winter Day;* a new title of *Copenhagen* was attached to it later, before it was acquired by the Weitzenhoffers. In the absence of additional evidence definitively identifying the setting, the 1917 title *Winter Day* is more appropriate.

Compositionally, *Winter Day* resembles Paul Cézanne's *House of Dr. Gachet* (1873), now in the Musée d'Orsay, Paris. During Gauguin's Impressionist period, he sometimes painted with Cézanne, a fellow disciple of Pissarro, and Cézanne's compositions inspired Gauguin, who before his financial troubles was an early Cézanne collector.

In the years after painting *Winter Day,* Gauguin departed from an Impressionist style during travels to the village of Pont-Aven in Brittany, to Arles in the south of France (where he lived with an increasingly unstable Vincent van Gogh), and to Tahiti. Gauguin's influential later work, for which he is best known, depicts the "primitive" cultures of Tahiti with expressive color and line, and with mystical overtones.

The Impressionists, especially Claude Monet, Pissarro, and Alfred Sisley, often painted winter landscapes or, as they called them, *effets de neige* (effects of snow).

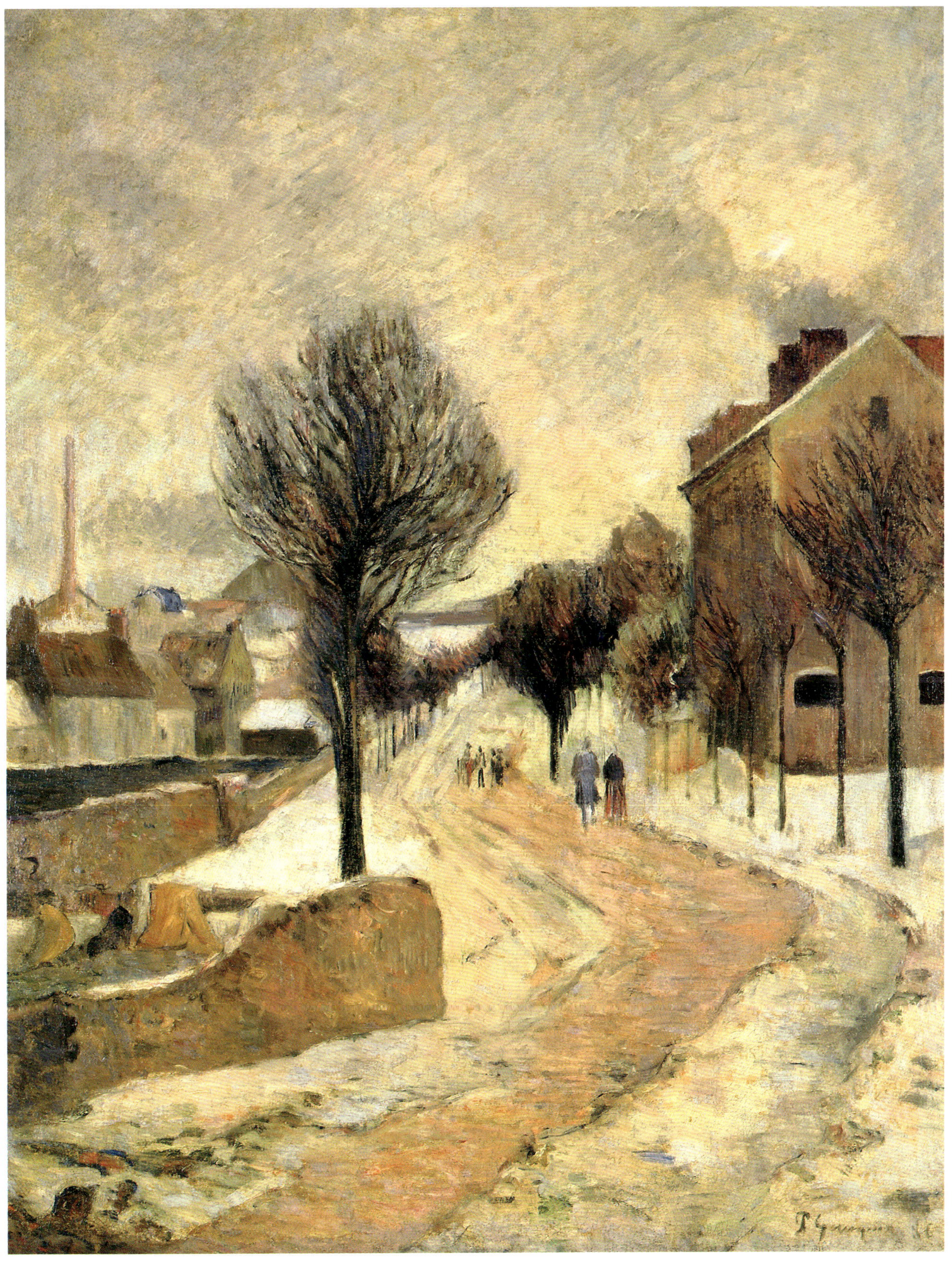

16 Vincent van Gogh

Netherlands, 1853–1890

Portrait of Alexander Reid, c. 1887
Oil on panel
16½ × 13¼ in.
Aaron M. and Clara Weitzenhoffer Bequest, 2000

Alexander Reid (1854–1928), the Scottish subject of this portrait by Vincent van Gogh, was the son of a successful art dealer in Glasgow. Not wanting to join his father's business, Reid became an artist but eventually began to show and sell work by other artists. He befriended Van Gogh in London during the 1870s, when Reid worked for the international art-dealing firm Goupil & Cie. In 1886, Reid moved to Paris to work for the same firm, which also employed Vincent's brother, Theo van Gogh. From the fall of 1886 through the winter of 1887, Reid lived with the Van Gogh brothers in their Paris apartment, where Van Gogh painted this portrait of Reid. (Legend has it that Reid hastily moved out of the Van Gogh apartment after Vincent suggested a suicide pact one night.)

Reid was almost the same age as Van Gogh, and his features are curiously similar to Van Gogh's own, as is also revealed in another portrait of Reid by Van Gogh, now at the Kelvingrove Art Gallery, Glasgow. A Scottish man who in 1887 knew both men wrote of their resemblance: "The likeness was so marked that they might have been twins. I have often hesitated, until I got close, as to which of them I was meeting. They even dressed somewhat similarly, though I doubt if Vincent ever possessed anything like the Harris tweeds Reid usually wore." In fact, this painting and the one in Glasgow were once considered Van Gogh self-portraits instead of portraits of Reid.

Reid's large hands in the present painting resemble the powerful hands of Louis-François Bertin in Jean-Auguste-Dominique Ingres's portrait of Bertin. (Although it was in a private collection until it entered the Louvre in 1897, the portrait of Bertin was already well-known when Van Gogh painted Reid.) Reid's loosely painted shoes echo the still lifes of shoes and boots that Van Gogh painted in Paris.

Portrait of Alexander Reid could be called a painting about friendship. Not only is it of Van Gogh's friend, Reid, but it may also be the actual painting that Vincent gave to Reid in a gesture of friendship. Moreover, two of the three paintings in the background have been identified as works by Van Gogh's friend Frank Myers Boggs, an American artist who lived in France; Boggs had given Van Gogh these paintings as gifts. One of the background paintings depicts *Coal Barges on the Thames,* and the other *Honfleur Harbor.* (The painting between the two works by Boggs is one of several portraits of peasant women that Van Gogh painted in the mid-1880s.) The two paintings by Boggs are now in the Van Gogh Museum in Amsterdam, and they are inscribed prominently in the lower-left corner of each canvas: "à son ami Vincent/BOGGS" (To his friend Vincent/BOGGS) and "A l'ami Vincent/Boggs" (To the friend Vincent/Boggs).

Van Gogh was volatile and had problems with most relationships. He idealized his friendships and longed to form strong bonds

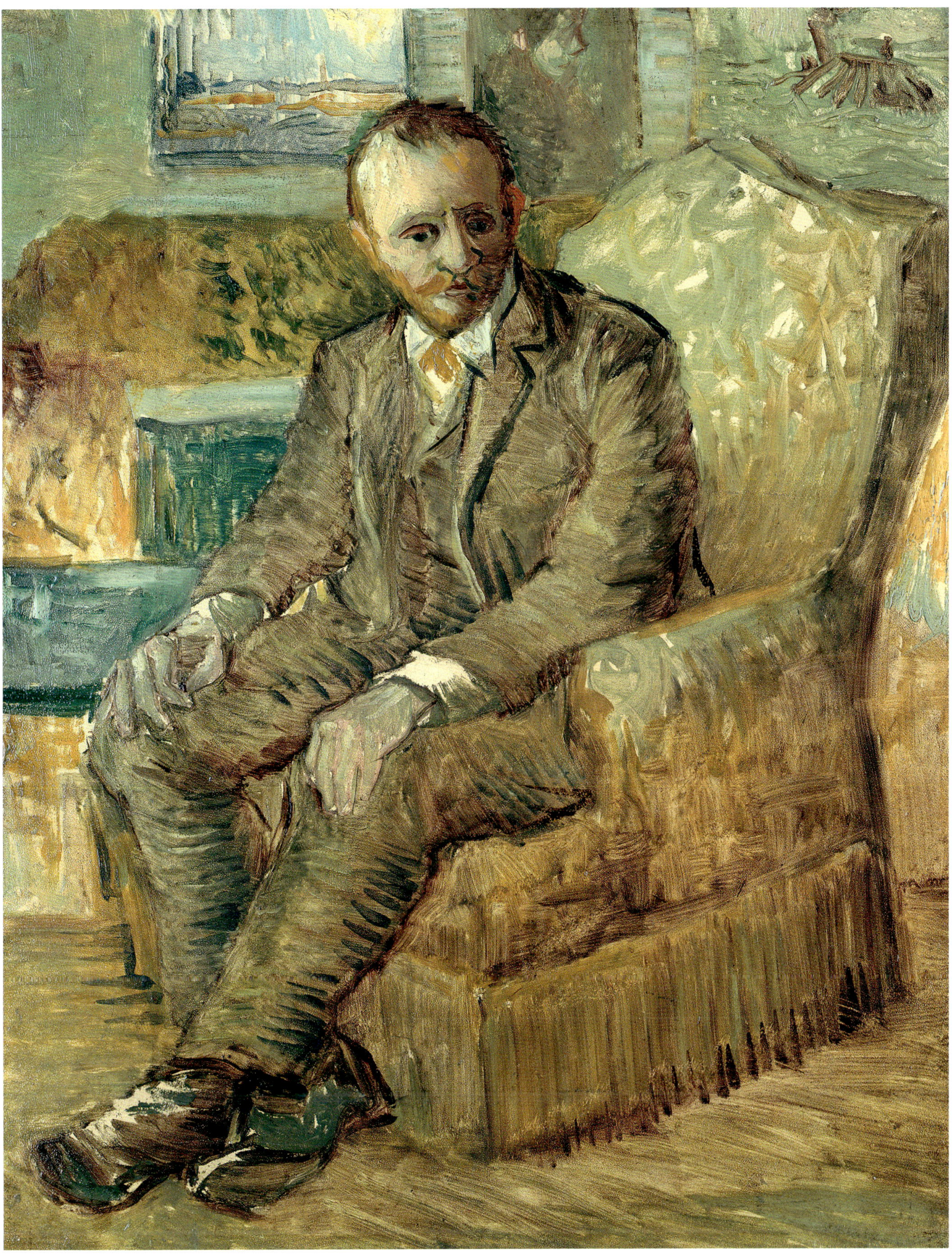

with artists, such as Paul Gauguin, but Van Gogh inevitably fell out with them. This happened with Alexander Reid, with whom Van Gogh eventually quarreled.

In his letters, Vincent often mentioned Alexander Reid, and these letters offer clues about the quarrel, which seems to have been about Reid's reluctance, in part for financial reasons, to arrange for an Impressionist exhibition in London. In an 1888 letter to Theo, Van Gogh wrote that Alexander Reid "made a foolish mistake in loving dead pictures [paintings by dead artists, which Reid believed were more profitable] and completely neglecting living artists," such as the Impressionists. And in another letter of the same year, Van Gogh wrote about the cause of the argument: "that Reid was ambitious, and that, being short of money like all of us, he was beside himself when it was a question of making money."

In other letters, Van Gogh wrote that Reid was "very nervous" and had an "overwrought nervous system." This is interesting, since Reid looks anxious in the present portrait.

Despite his criticisms of Reid, Vincent wrote somewhat remorsefully to Theo in the summer of 1889: "How often I think of Reid when I am reading Shakespeare, and how often I have thought of him while I was worse than I am now. Thinking that I was far, far too hard on him and too discouraging when I claimed that it was better to care for the painters than the pictures."

Portrait of Alexander Reid is historically important as the only surviving record of the Paris apartment that Van Gogh shared with his brother between 1886 and 1887. The apartment, to which Vincent and Theo moved in June 1886, was at 54 rue Lepic in Montmartre, the street where Henri de Toulouse-Lautrec also lived.

Vincent van Gogh was born in Zundert, the Netherlands. After a stint as an art dealer in The Hague, and after working as a teacher and an evangelist, Van Gogh took up painting. He was largely self-taught as an artist. He was an avid reader of English and French literature, and he studied the works of other artists, learning, for instance, from the paintings of Eugène Delacroix to articulate form through color and modeling rather than line.

When Van Gogh arrived in Paris in February 1886, he hoped to join the avant-garde, and he met many of the Impressionists through his brother Theo, who sold their works. In Paris, Van Gogh befriended Gauguin and was greatly influenced by the Neo-Impressionist works that he saw in 1886 at the last Impressionist exhibition. The Impressionist and Neo-Impressionist artists inspired Van Gogh to brighten his palette and use contrasting colors, which henceforth figured prominently in his work. Like many other artists during the period, he also became interested in Japanese prints, which with their non-Western perspective and flat areas of saturated color were novel to Europeans.

In February 1888, Van Gogh moved to Arles, in southern France, where his paintings became more expressionistic and his colors intensified. In Arles, he attempted to start an artists' colony, a brotherhood of artists that he called "The Studio of the South." He and Theo convinced Gauguin to move to Arles in October 1888, but Gauguin fled at Christmas, after Van Gogh cut off his own ear following an argument. While in Arles, Van Gogh experienced several bouts with mental illness. For a year, from May 1889 to May 1890, he institutionalized himself in nearby St-Rémy, continuing to make drawings and paintings, including *Starry Night,* now at the Museum of Modern Art, New York. Van Gogh then moved to Auvers-sur-Oise, a small town north of Paris, where he was under the care of Dr. Paul Gachet and where he continued to paint.

In July 1890, Van Gogh shot himself; he died two days afterward at age thirty-seven. Six months later, his brother Theo also died.

Van Gogh has become one of the most popular and influential artists of all time. Having sold only one work while he was alive, he has also become an archetype of the genius who is misunderstood during his lifetime.

17 Paul Signac

France, 1863–1935

Coast Scene, 1893
Oil on canvas
18½ × 22 in.
Aaron M. and Clara Weitzenhoffer Bequest, 2000

Born in Paris, Paul Signac decided to become an artist after visiting a Claude Monet exhibition in 1880, and his early works were in an Impressionist style. Together with Georges Seurat and Camille Pissarro, Signac forged the Neo-Impressionist movement.

Neo-Impressionism, also known as Pointillism or Divisionism, was based on scientific principles of color separation, whereas Impressionism had been intuitive. Signac used the term "Divisionism" to describe the Neo-Impressionist separation of color into dots or patches of pure hues, as seen in *Coast Scene.* "Pointillism" refers specifically to the use of dots. (For more on Neo-Impressionism, see Camille Pissarro, *Shepherdess Bringing in Sheep,* cat. no. 13.)

When Signac met Seurat in 1884, the latter was exhibiting *Bathers at Asnières* (now at the National Gallery, London), a painting in which some of the principles of Divisionism, but not Pointillist brushstrokes, are already evident. Signac, however, was still painting in an Impressionist style. Seurat and Signac began to collaborate on the development of a new, supposedly scientific painting technique, and by 1886, they were both using Pointillist brushstrokes. Signac painted in a Neo-Impressionist style for the rest of his life.

In 1891, Seurat died, and in 1899, Signac wrote *From Delacroix to Neo-Impressionism,* a defense of Neo-Impressionism and a book that greatly influenced German Expressionist artists, the Italian Futurists, and the French Fauves. (For more on the Fauves, see Raoul Dufy, *The Beach of Sainte-Adresse,* cat. no. 23.)

An avid sailor, Signac moved in 1892 from Paris to St. Tropez, in the south of France on the Riviera. During his many sailboat cruises along the Riviera and elsewhere, he made drawings and watercolors, which he used as studies for works painted in the studio, such as the sun-drenched *Coast Scene.*

Signac methodically constructed *Coast Scene* with isolated, parallel brushstrokes of pure color that give the sensation of shimmering light.

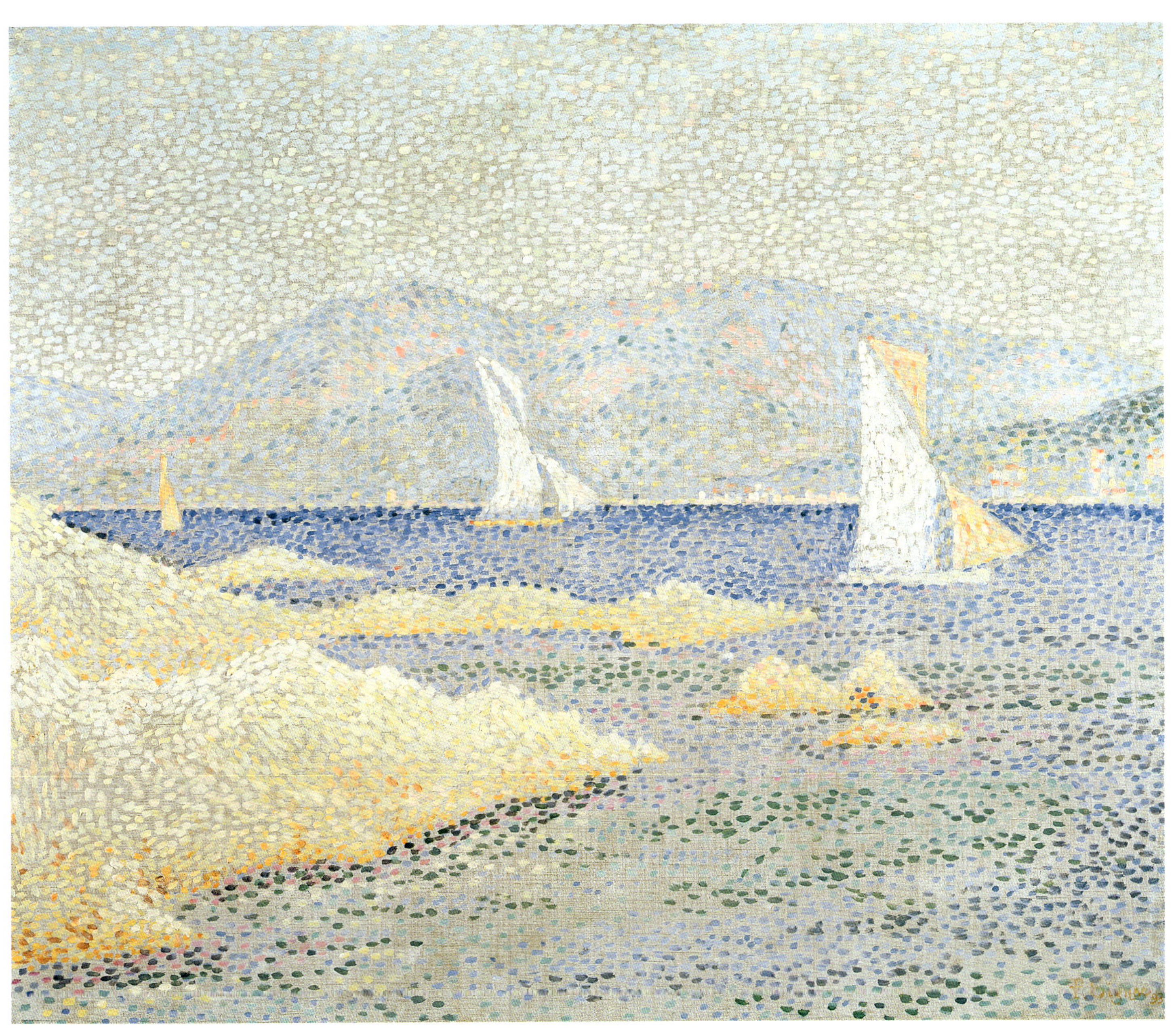

18 Paul Cézanne

France, 1839–1906

Bathers (Les Baigneurs), c. 1896
Lithograph
9 × 11 in.
Gift of Oscar B. Jacobson, before 1949

A seminal figure in the history of Modern art, Paul Cézanne was a native of Aix-en-Provence, in the south of France. (Aix was also the hometown of the artist's writer-friend Emile Zola.) Cézanne's father persuaded him to study law at the Université d'Aix, but in 1861, Cézanne quit his legal training and went to Paris to become an artist. Thereafter, he moved back and forth between the north, including Paris and the nearby towns of Pontoise and Auvers, and the south, including Aix and L'Estaque, where his mother owned a house.

Cézanne's works of the 1860s are turbulent, sometimes even violent, in their paint handling and subject matter. The official Salon repeatedly rejected his submissions. During the 1870s, Cézanne went through an Impressionist phase, with Camille Pissarro as his mentor. When Cézanne participated in the first (1874) and third (1877) Impressionist exhibitions, critics ridiculed his work more than that of any other artist.

Cézanne agreed with the Impressionists that artists should study nature. However, unlike the Impressionists, he believed that art should not focus on capturing fleeting moments but should depict the order and structure underlying the visible world. He said that he wanted to make of Impressionism "something solid and enduring, like the art in museums." His mature work, the style of which he developed in the late 1870s and early 1880s, repeats favorite motifs, such as bathers, still lifes, or Mont-Sainte-Victoire, a mountain on the outskirts of Aix. Cézanne slowly and carefully painted with broad brushstrokes, making no attempt to disguise the fact that they were brushstrokes. He thus exploited the tension between the actual flat, two-dimensional canvas and the painting's illusion of depth. His paintings are as much about the artist's difficult process of depicting a subject as about the subject itself.

In the mid-1870s, Cézanne, following a long tradition in art, began to portray bathers—groups of males or females—in landscapes. He usually worked without models. He brought the theme to its apogee in three large canvases dating from 1895 through 1906, which are now in the National Gallery in London, the Philadelphia Museum of Art, and the Barnes Collection in Merion, Pennsylvania.

Cézanne made small prints in Auvers in 1873 but did not produce additional prints until the 1890s when he made three lithographs. Of these three prints, only the present one was published. It is also the only one for which Cézanne likely drew on the lithographic stone himself instead of having assistants transfer the image from a drawing. The dealer Ambroise Vollard published *Bathers* at the end of 1897, as part of an album of thirty-two prints by older artists, such as the Impressionists, and younger artists, such as Edouard Vuillard and Henri de Toulouse-Lautrec.

Already during the 1880s, Cézanne had begun to develop the composition ultimately used in this lithograph. The figure on the right probably derives from the Louvre's ancient sculpture of *Cincinnatus.* The figure with raised, bent arms—a pose that appears in many of Cézanne's paintings of male bathers—may derive from Michelangelo's *Dying Slave,* which Cézanne sketched in the Louvre.

Although the Impressionists were aware of his work, Cézanne received little public recognition until near the end of his life. In 1895, Vollard gave Cézanne his first solo show, after which Cézanne exhibited frequently and became a celebrated artist.

Especially after a 1907 posthumous retrospective held in Paris, Cézanne had an enormous impact on other artists, including Pablo Picasso and Georges Braque as they developed Cubism. A number of works that appear in this catalogue owe a debt to Cézanne, including paintings by Armand Guillaumin (cat. no. 14), Maurice de Vlaminck (cat. no. 24), Victor Higgins (cat. no. 44), Andrew Dasburg (cat. no. 50), B. J. O. Nordfeldt (cat. no. 55), and Jozef Bakos (cat. no. 56).

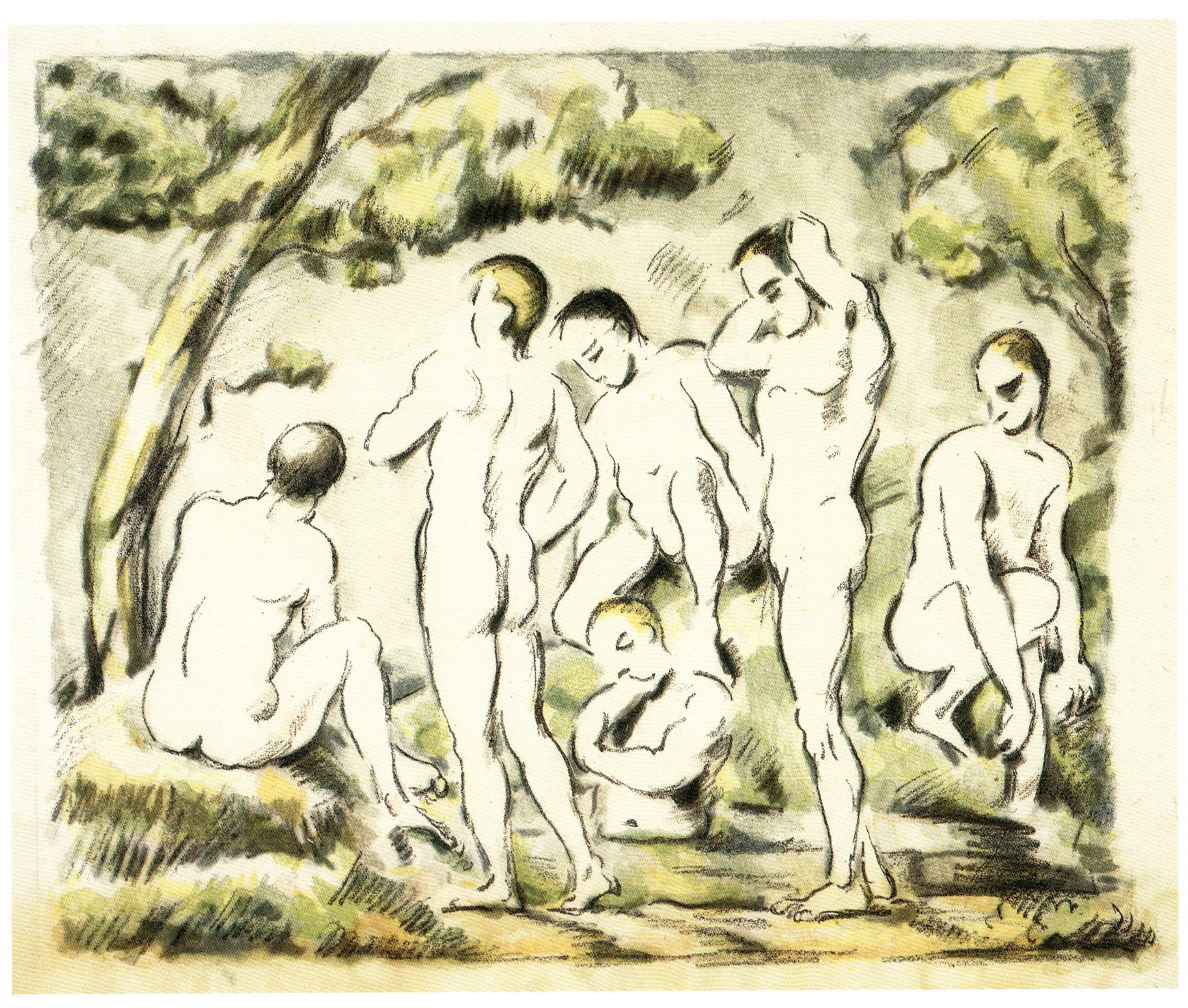

19 Odilon Redon

France, 1840–1916

Carnations (Les Oeillets), n.d.
Pastel on paper
23 × 20 in.
Aaron M. and Clara Weitzenhoffer Bequest, 2000

Born and educated in Bordeaux, Odilon Redon studied violin and tried, albeit unsuccessfully, to become an architect. In 1864, he briefly trained as an artist in the Paris studio of the painter Jean-Léon Gérôme, but then returned to Bordeaux. Only after having served as a soldier during the Franco-Prussian War of 1870–71 did Redon finally commit himself to a career in the visual arts. He settled in Paris, spending summers in Bordeaux, at Peyrelebade, his childhood home and father's estate, a place that inspired him and to which he returned frequently until it was sold in 1897.

In Paris, Redon produced a series of charcoal drawings called Noirs (Black Ones), which were haunting, mysterious fantasies, dreamlike and melancholy. From 1879 through the 1890s, he produced a large number of lithographs after the Noirs. (The museum has two.)

Redon began to exhibit in Paris in the 1880s, including at the final Impressionist exhibition, in 1886. The general public showed little interest in the Noirs, but the works attracted the attention of the literary avant-garde, which saw affinities with the poetry of Charles Baudelaire. Baudelaire follower Joris-Karl Huysmans mentions the Noirs in his famous novel *A rebours*. Redon was close friends with the Symbolist poet Stéphane Mallarmé and is sometimes called "the Mallarmé of painting"; Redon was considered a major Symbolist artist, although he distanced himself from such labels and groups.

Around 1890, Redon began to use colorful oils and pastels in works with subject matter related to the Noirs. Perhaps his second son, born in 1889, helped to inspire the more optimistic use of color. (His first son had died as an infant in 1886.) After 1900, Redon no longer created Noirs. His primary concern became the depiction of flowers, as in *Carnations*. These later works nevertheless retain the mysteriousness of the Noirs. For instance, the flowers and vase in *Carnations* do not sit on a surface, but seem to float, as though in a dream.

Henri Matisse admired Odilon Redon's paintings and pastel drawings of flowers, and the Surrealists regarded Redon as one of their precursors.

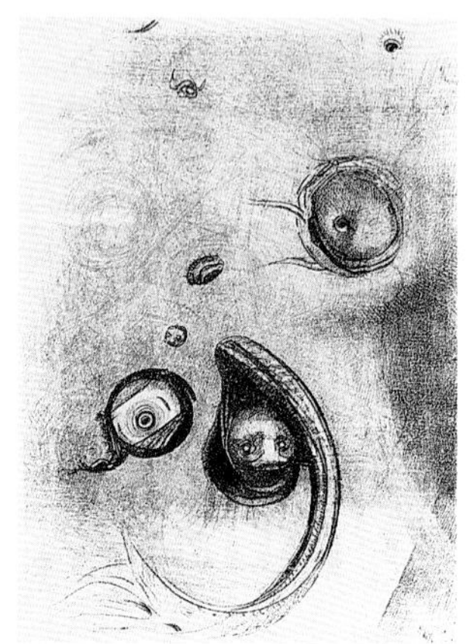

Odilon Redon
France, 1840–1916
And eyes without heads were floating like mollusks (Et que des yeux sans tête flottaient comme des mollusques), Plate XIII from *La Tentation de Saint-Antoine*, 1896 (2nd edition, 1938), lithograph, edition: 65/210, 12⅛ × 8¾ in. Museum purchase, 1966

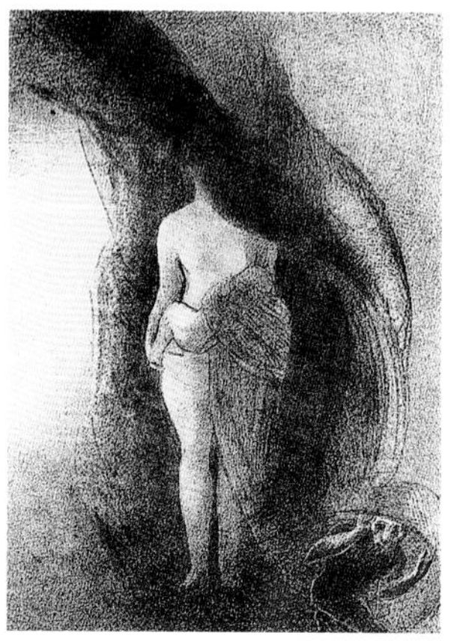

Odilon Redon
France, 1840–1916
I am still the great Isis! Nobody has ever lifted my veil! My offspring is the sun! (Je suis toujours la grande Isis! Nul n'a encore soulevé mon voile! Mon fruit est le soleil!), Plate XVI from *La Tentation de Saint-Antoine*, 1896 (2nd edition, 1938), lithograph, edition: 105/210, 11 × 8 in. Museum purchase, 1974

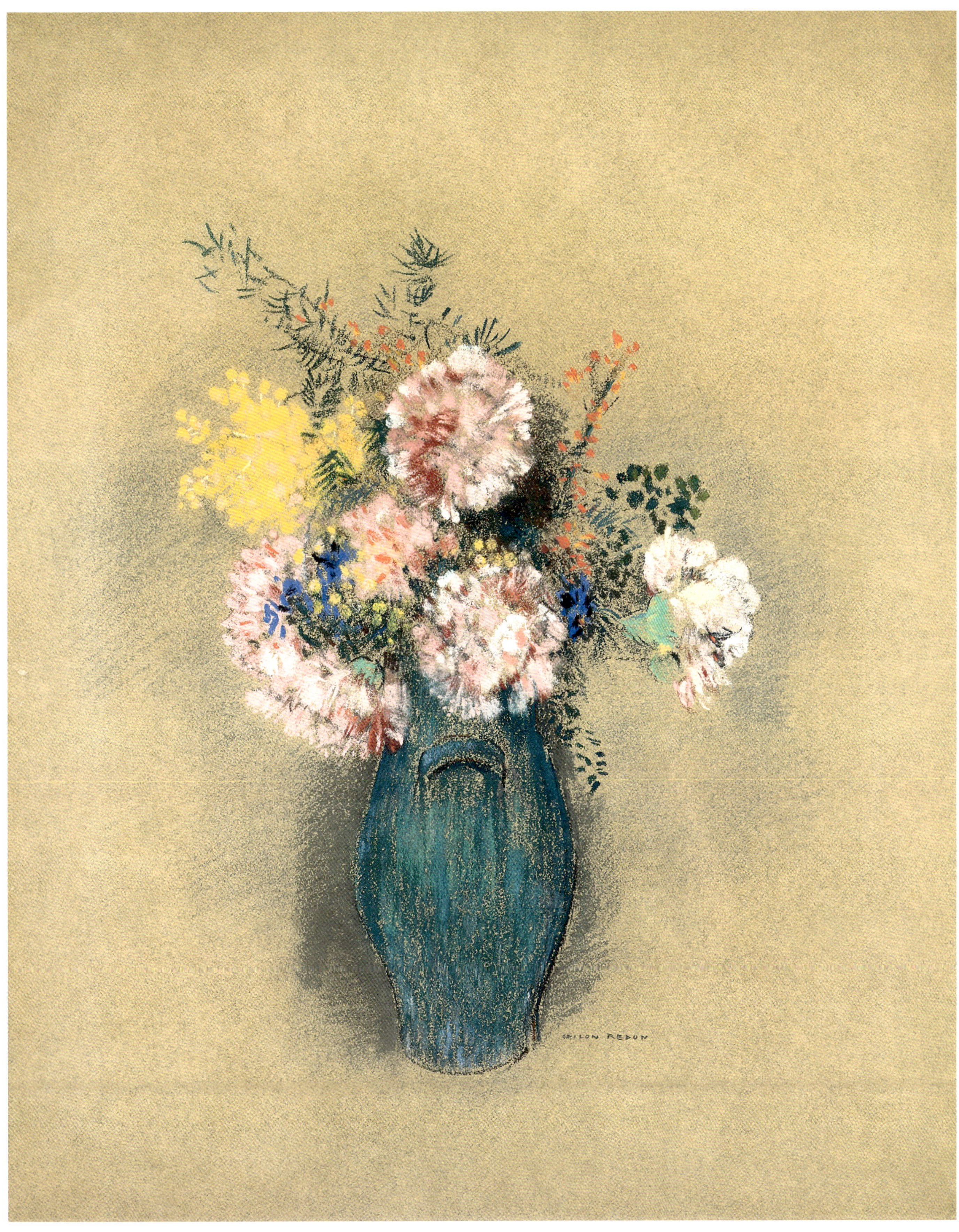
ODILON REDON

20 Henri de Toulouse-Lautrec

France, 1864–1901

Portrait of a Girl, 1892
Oil on canvas
$11^3/_8 \times 9^1/_2$ in.
Aaron M. and Clara Weitzenhoffer Bequest, 2000

Famous for his paintings and posters of the cabarets and demimonde of late-nineteenth-century Paris, Henri de Toulouse-Lautrec was born in Albi, in southwestern France, the son of wealthy aristocrats—a strong-willed, domineering mother and a flamboyantly eccentric, womanizing father. From them, Lautrec inherited a bone disease that made him a dwarf and, after many broken bones, disabled.

Lautrec learned to paint from his father and his uncle, both amateur artists, before moving to Paris to train for five years in the studio of Léon Bonnat and Fernand Cormon, where he met and befriended Vincent van Gogh. In 1884, Lautrec moved to the rue Lepic on the hill of Montmartre, then the poorest section of Paris and home to many artists. At the foot of the hill were many prostitutes and nightclubs, including the famous Moulin Rouge. In Montmartre, he lived *la vie de bohème,* much to the embarrassment of his family.

An alcoholic with erratic, disruptive behavior, Lautrec became a well-known presence in Montmartre, always carrying with him a sketchbook. He formed close friendships with a wide cross-section of society, from aristocrats to artists to prostitutes, whom Lautrec—who despised hypocrisy—often painted in a direct manner, with no sentimentality.

He achieved success and recognition with both the general public and the avant-garde, and he exhibited often, including in the Exposition du Petit Boulevard, organized by Van Gogh in 1887. In 1891, Lautrec became famous in Paris with his first poster, *Moulin Rouge, La Goulue.* Over the next decade, he received numerous commissions for other posters, illustrations, and advertisements.

In 1892, Lautrec received a commission to decorate a brothel in Paris on the rue d'Amboise. In the brothel's main salon, he painted imitations of eighteenth-century paneling, which were inset with eighteen medallion-shaped portraits, many in profile, of the prostitutes available on the premises. The present painting is one of those portraits.

Lautrec lived in brothels for short periods and was said to have contracted syphilis. In 1899, he was briefly institutionalized. He died of a stroke in 1901, at age thirty-seven.

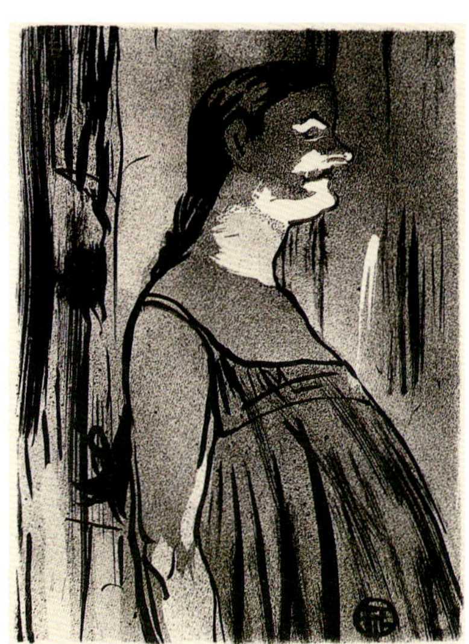

Henri de Toulouse-Lautrec
France, 1864–1901
Madame Abdala, 1893, lithograph, edition of 550, $10^1/_2 \times 7^7/_8$ in. Museum purchase, 1962

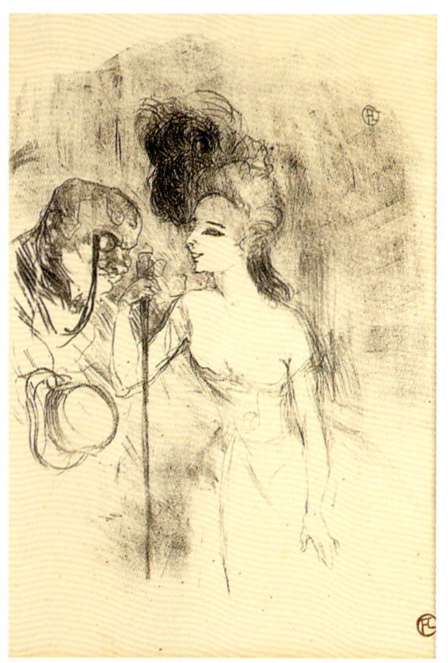

Henri de Toulouse-Lautrec
France, 1864–1901
Leaving the Theater (Sortie de théâtre), 1896, lithograph, edition of 25, $14 \times 9^3/_4$ in. Gift of Colleen McCullough, 1999

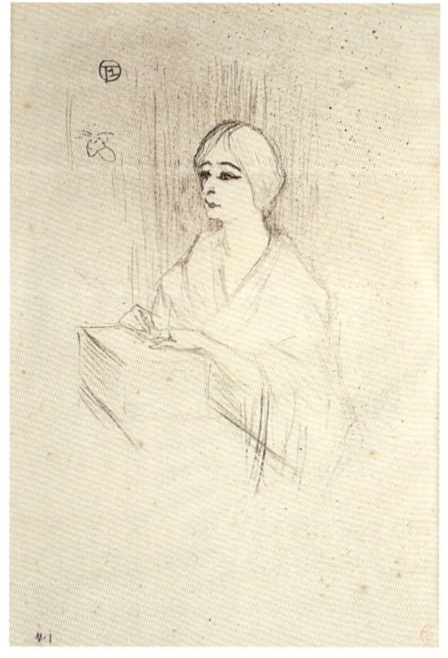

Henri de Toulouse-Lautrec
France, 1864–1901
Yahne in Her Box (Yahne dans sa loge), 1895, lithograph, edition of 25, $14 \times 9^3/_4$ in. Gift of Colleen McCullough, 1999

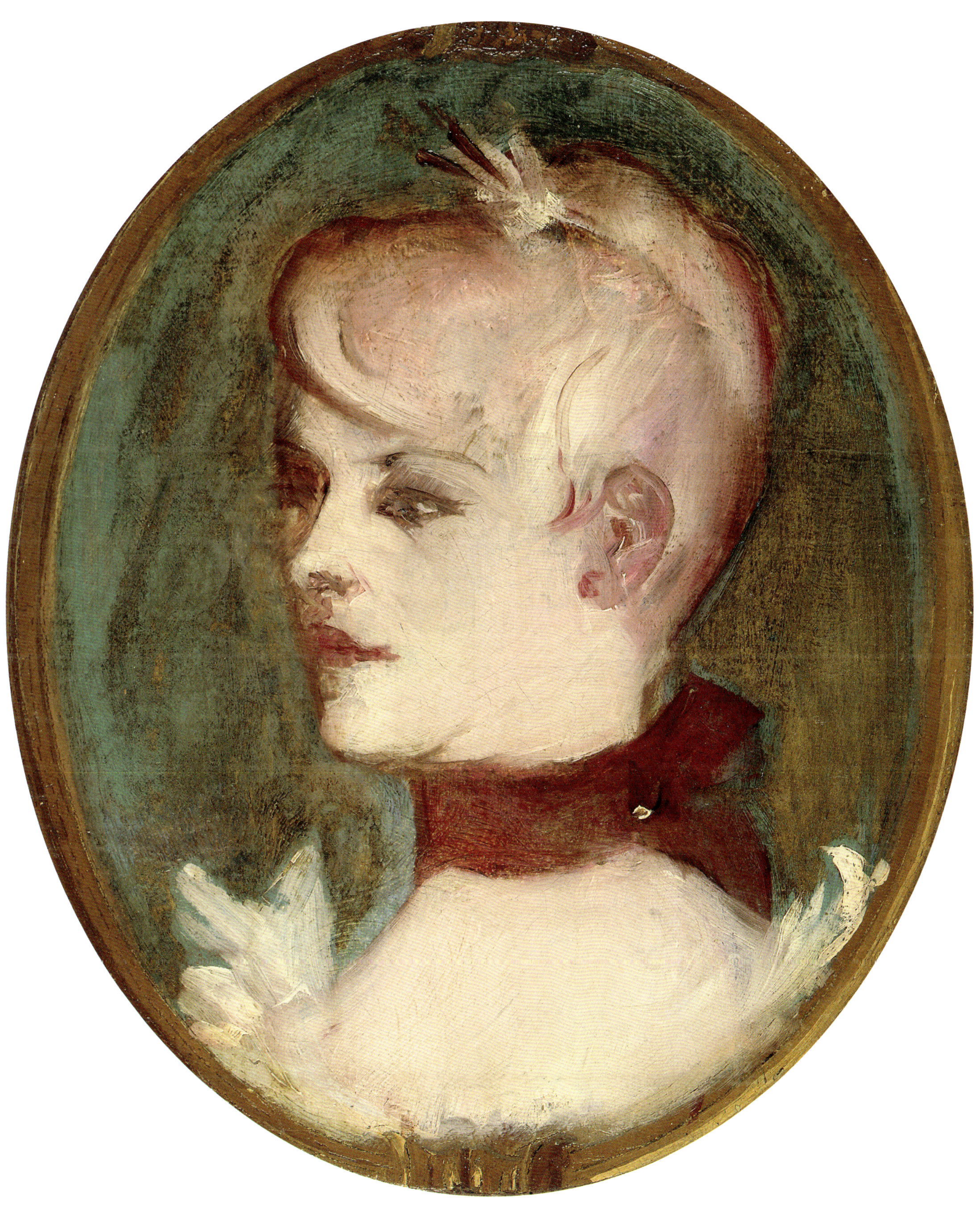

21 Edouard Vuillard

France, 1868–1940

Madame Hessel and Lulu in the Dining Room at the Château des Clayes (Madame Hessel et Lulu dans la salle à manger des Clayes), c. 1935–38
Pastel on paper
30⅝ × 31⅝ in.
Aaron M. and Clara Weitzenhoffer Bequest, 2000

Edouard Vuillard was a poet of the commonplace, transforming interiors into realms of mystery. He grew up in Paris, the son of a dressmaker. In 1886, he trained as an artist at the Académie Julian, and the following year attended the Ecole des Beaux Arts. As a student, he spent much time on his own studying Old Masters in the Louvre, especially the seventeenth-century Dutch artists and the eighteenth-century French painter Jean-Baptiste-Siméon Chardin.

During the late 1880s, Vuillard joined a group of disaffected young art students in Paris who formed a quasi-mystical brotherhood that they labeled the Nabis (Hebrew for "prophets") and that exhibited collectively through the next decade. The Nabis, whose greatest exponents were Vuillard and Pierre Bonnard, rejected the naturalism of their academic training. Instead, they embraced the revolutionary teachings of Paul Gauguin after he had departed from Impressionism. Gauguin's Synthetism, a branch of Post-Impressionism, emphasized the imagination and called for a synthesis of natural form and artistic feeling. Inspired by Gauguin and Japanese prints, the Nabis' paintings, usually small in scale (especially Vuillard's), concentrated on decorative qualities such as patterns, simplicity of design, and flat fields of vibrant color with bold contours. Three paintings from Vuillard's Nabi period are in the Weitzenhoffer Collection.

After 1900, Vuillard's works became larger and more luminous, with more conventional three-dimensional perspective, as in *Madame Hessel and Lulu in the Dining Room at the Château des Clayes.* The portraits and interiors of this period typically depict the private worlds of upper-middle-class French society. By this time, Vuillard had achieved financial security through his art, and the onetime avant-gardist settled into a comfortable, bourgeois life.

The daughter of a wealthy textile merchant, Lucy Hessel was the wife of Jos Hessel, a partner in the prominent Parisian art-dealing firm Bernheim-Jeune, which represented Vuillard. Throughout the artist's final four decades, Madame Hessel was his closest friend, confidante, and muse, and Vuillard portrayed her often. In the present work, Madame Hessel appears in a room of the Château des Clayes near Versailles, which the Hessels had acquired in 1925 and which Vuillard frequently visited. The figure in the background is Lulu, one of Lucy Hessel's daughters. Vuillard pays as much attention to the light shining through the window onto the window casement, floor, and back wall as to his models.

Although he remained a lifelong bachelor, Vuillard's figure paintings were mostly of women and children.

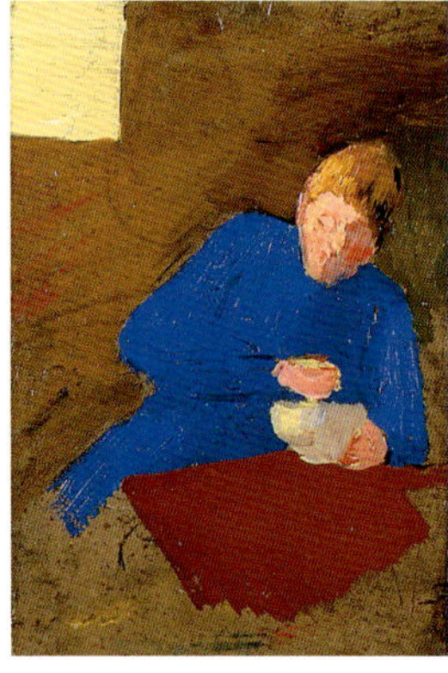

Edouard Vuillard
France, 1868–1940
Marie Holding a Bowl, c. 1891, oil on cardboard, 9⅜ × 6¾ in. Aaron M. and Clara Weitzenhoffer Bequest, 2000

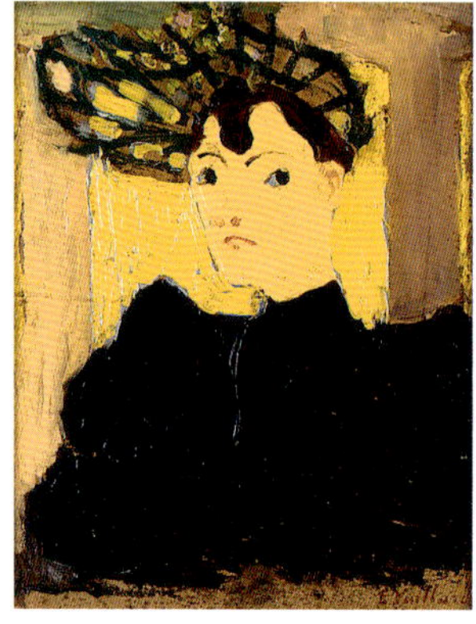

Edouard Vuillard
France, 1868–1940
Woman in a Green Hat, c. 1890, oil on cardboard, 8½ × 6⅞ in. Aaron M. and Clara Weitzenhoffer Bequest, 2000

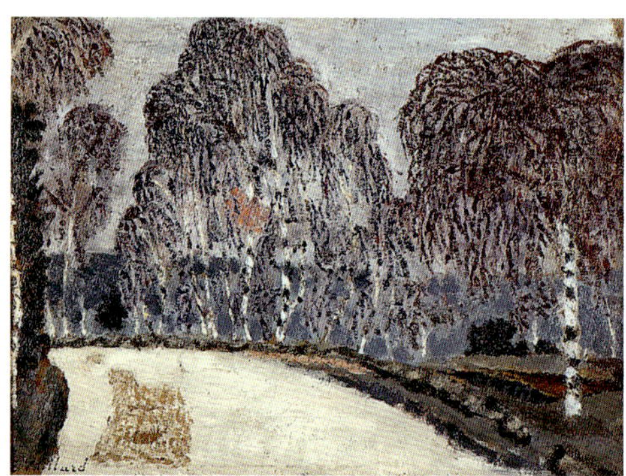

Edouard Vuillard
France, 1868–1940
Birches at l'Etang-la-Ville (Bouleaux à l'Etang-la-Ville), 1896, oil on cardboard, 7½ × 10 in. Aaron M. and Clara Weitzenhoffer Bequest, 2000

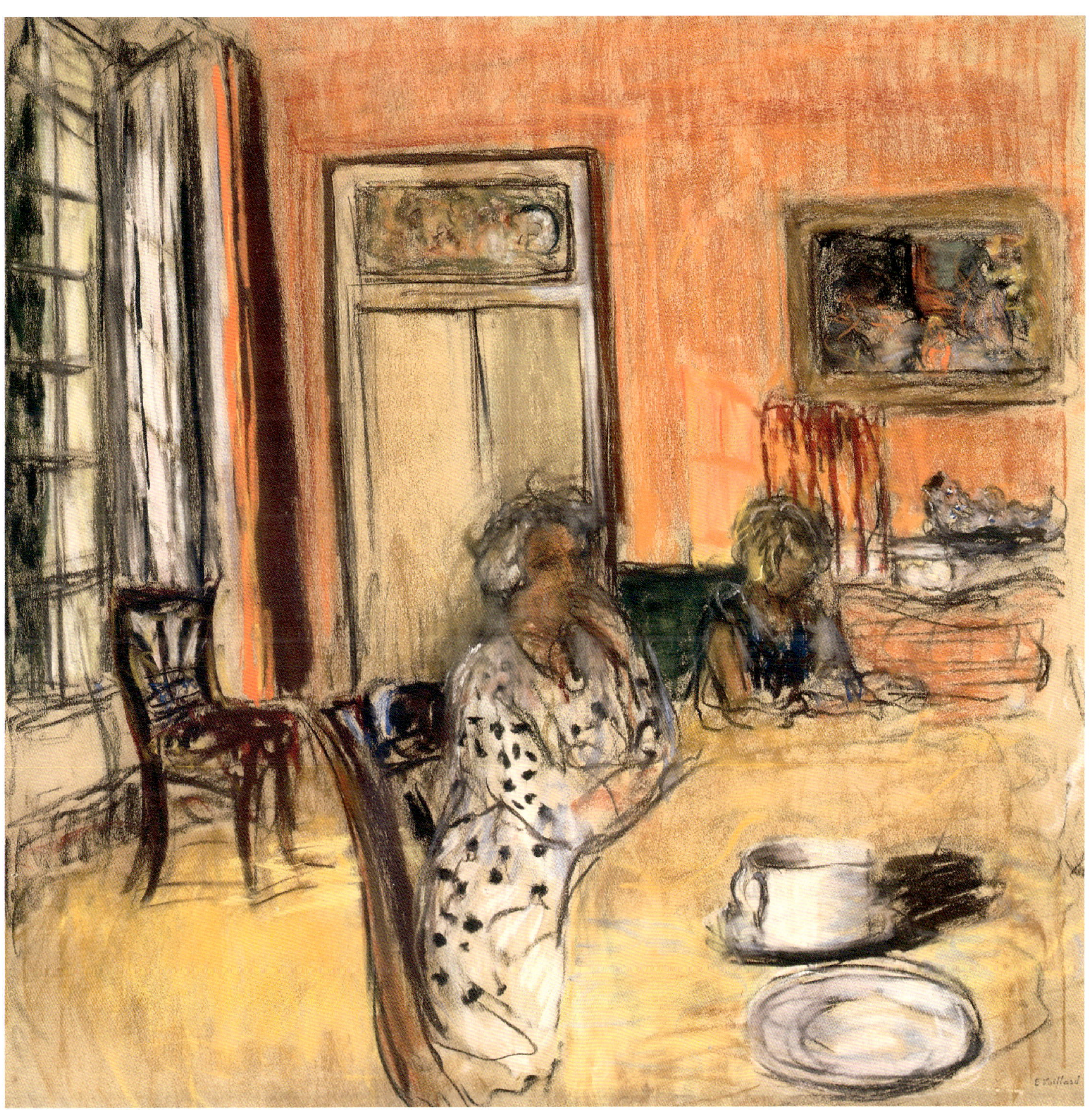
E Vuillard

22 Pierre Bonnard

France, 1867–1947

Still Life with Teapot (Nature morte à la théière), 1936–37
Oil on canvas
15¼ × 18¼ in.
Aaron M. and Clara Weitzenhoffer Bequest, 2002

To please his father, Pierre Bonnard became a lawyer in 1889. Already, however, he had been studying art for two years at the Académie Julian in Paris, where he met some of the artists who established with him the group that called itself the Nabis, the Hebrew word for "prophets." (For more on the Nabis, see cat. no. 21.) Bonnard became known as the "Japanese Nabi" because he was so enthusiastic about Japanese prints.

During the 1890s, Bonnard and fellow Nabi Vuillard were labeled "Intimistes" for their paintings of intimate interiors depicting everyday life. Also in the 1890s, Bonnard painted street scenes of Paris and, like Henri de Toulouse-Lautrec, produced set designs and posters for the theater, as well as illustrations for books, newspapers, and magazines.

The Nabi artists disbanded after the first years of the twentieth century, but Bonnard and Vuillard remained friends. In 1909, Bonnard made the first of what would become many long visits to the south of France, where the intense, shimmering light would be reflected in his paintings. In 1925, he bought, in the southern town of Le Cannet, a house that he named Le Bosquet.

Bonnard's later paintings, such as *Still Life with Teapot,* usually depict his private world—for example, rooms at Le Bosquet or the artist's wife, Marthe, in a bathtub. These works emphasize color, luminosity, and subjectivity, epitomizing the writer Emile Zola's definition of art as "a corner of nature seen through a temperament." Although created decades after the emergence of Fauvism and Cubism, Bonnard's later paintings seem closer in spirit to Impressionism than to the avant-garde movements of the twentieth century. Nevertheless, Bonnard stated that he wanted to go beyond Impressionism, with more expressive color and more rigorous structure.

Bonnard's sensuous paintings record what the artist called "the adventures of the optic nerve." Much looking is often required for the viewer to decipher what exactly is depicted. For instance, in the present work, what precisely is the orange strip on the right side of the painting? Is it the floor or a continuation of the table under a cloth? Bonnard often organized his compositions with strong verticals and horizontals taken from walls, doors, windows, or furniture; examples in *Still Life with Teapot* include the ambiguous strip along the painting's right border and the edge of the table at the painting's bottom. Objects appearing in the margins, such as the pitcher and the chair back, correspond to peripheral vision. Bonnard frequently used unconventional perspective, as in this still life's tabletop, which seems to tilt forward.

From 1920 on, the artist received critical recognition and commercial success. Pablo Picasso dismissed Bonnard's art as of the nineteenth century, but today Bonnard's late works are considered some of the great achievements in twentieth-century painting.

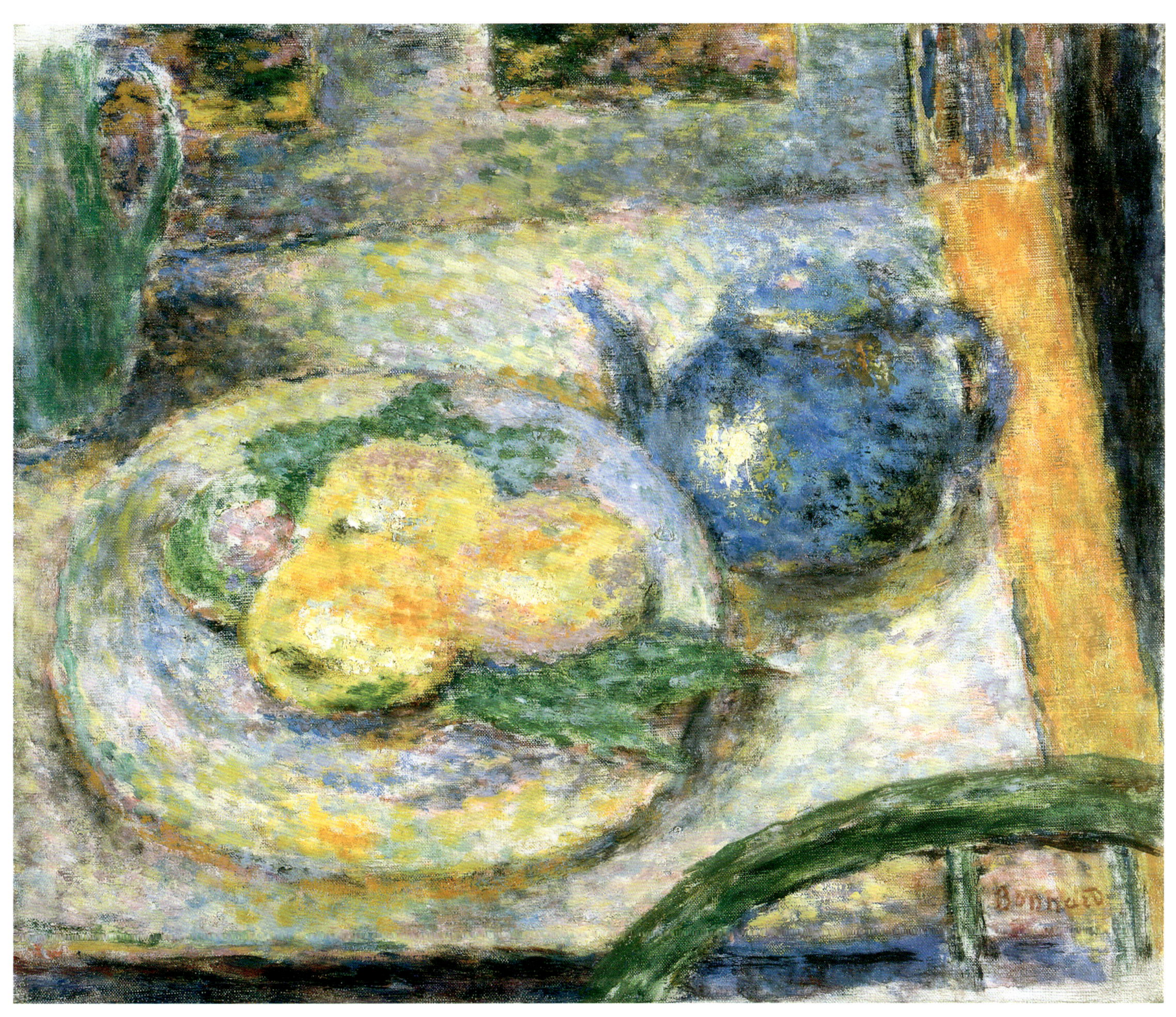
Bonnard

23 Raoul Dufy

France, 1877–1953

The Beach of Sainte-Adresse (La Plage de Sainte-Adresse), 1906
Oil on canvas
18⅛ × 21⅝ in.
Aaron M. and Clara Weitzenhoffer Bequest, 2000

In 1905, Henri Matisse, André Derain, and Maurice de Vlaminck unleashed a riot of color at the Salon d'Automne, Paris's fall exhibition of contemporary art. These artists, inspired by Vincent van Gogh, Paul Gauguin, and Paul Signac, simplified design and liberated color from its descriptive function, using it instead as an exuberant vehicle of expression and pictorial construction. A critic described the artists as *fauves* (wild beasts), and the label stuck for this first Modern art movement of the twentieth century.

Raoul Dufy, who had received traditional art training in his native Le Havre and then in Paris, was immediately and decisively affected by his encounter with the Fauves. At the Salon d'Automne of 1905, he was especially inspired by Matisse's painting *Luxe, calme, et volupté,* and in 1906, Dufy painted the present Fauvist work, which depicts the beach of Sainte-Adresse at Le Havre.

Dufy had already painted the beach of Sainte-Adresse numerous times: in 1901 and 1902 in the manner of Eugène Boudin (see cat. no. 7), whose beach scenes of Normandy Dufy discovered in the museum of Le Havre, and in 1904, in an Impressionist style. During his stay in Paris from 1900 until 1905, Dufy had increasingly worked like an Impressionist, painting nature as he saw it. In Paris, he encountered the works of the Impressionists at the gallery of Paul Durand-Ruel and the paintings of Van Gogh through the art dealers Bernheim-Jeune. Dufy studied Claude Monet (who had also painted Sainte-Adresse many times), Auguste Renoir, and especially Camille Pissarro.

Dufy described works such as *The Beach of Sainte-Adresse:*

> *Around 1905–1906, I was painting on the beach at Sainte-Adresse. I had previously painted beaches in the manner of the Impressionists, and had reached saturation point, realizing that this method of copying nature was leading me off into infinity, with its twists and turns and its most subtle and fleeting details. I myself was standing outside the picture. Having arrived at some beach subject or other, I would sit down and start looking at my tubes of paint and my brushes. How, using these things, could I succeed in conveying not what I see, but that which is, that which exists for me, my reality? . . . From that day onwards, I was unable to return to my barren struggles with the elements that were visible to my gaze. It was no longer possible to show them in their external form.*

In the present painting, figures appear in the lower-right corner, including a woman pushing a baby carriage. These figures are on the wide roadway, constructed in the 1880s, that led from Saint-Adresse to the center of Le Havre.

Until age twenty-three, Dufy lived in Le Havre, then a prosperous commercial port. Family financial difficulties required him to work, and he spent five years as a customs inspector of produce. A talented draftsman, he studied at the Ecole des Beaux-Arts in Le Havre, and in 1900, he won a scholarship to study for four years at the Ecole des

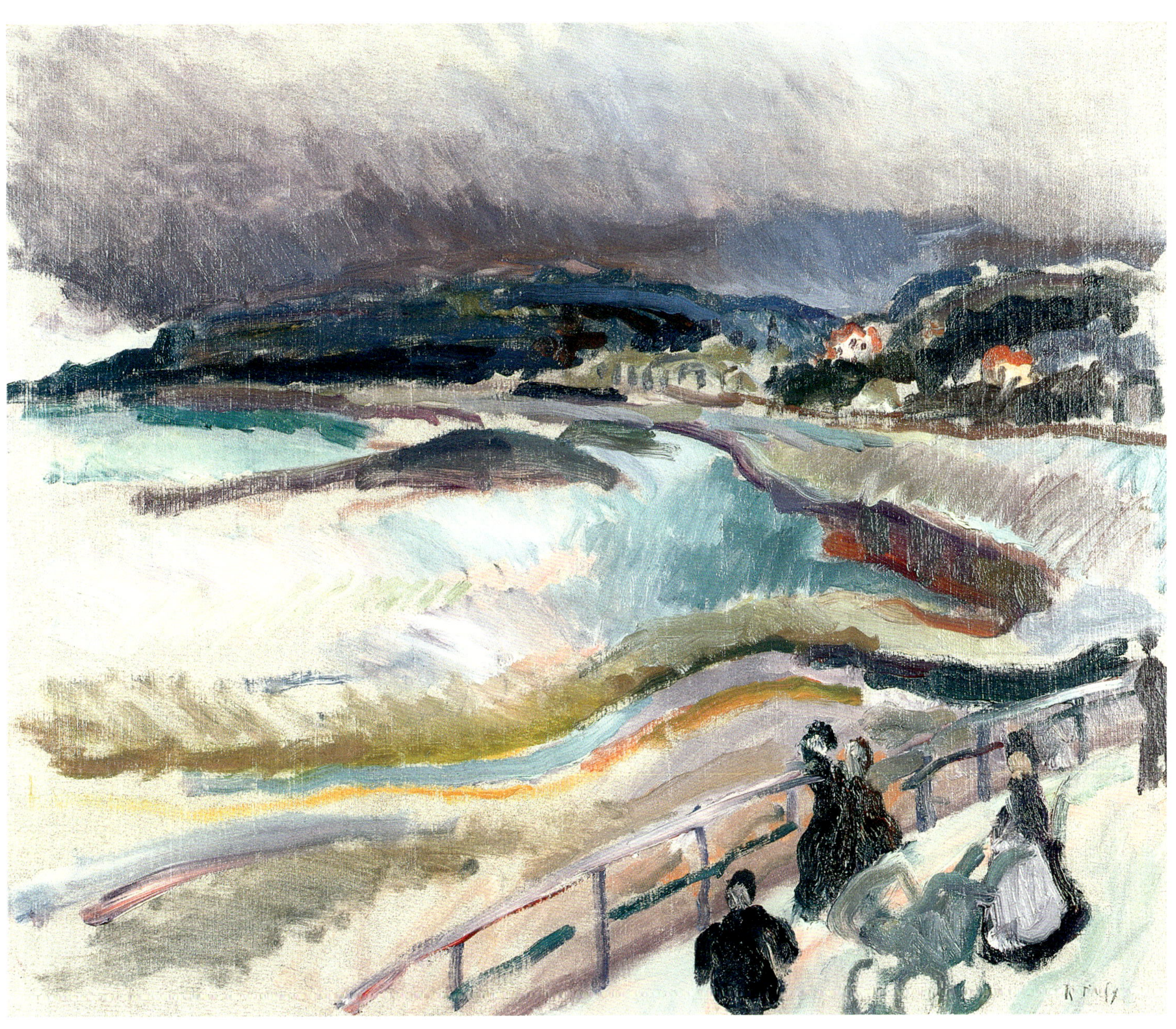

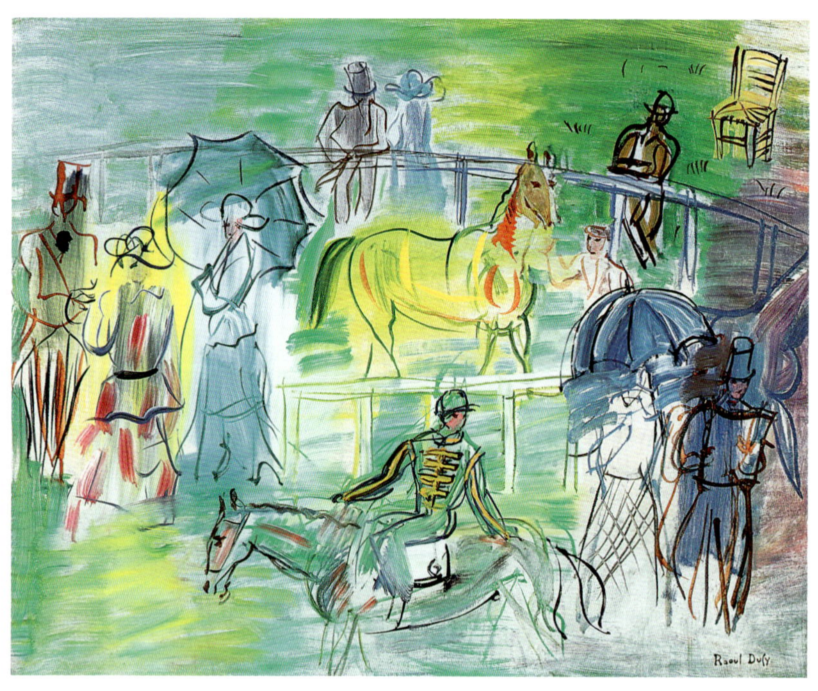

Raoul Dufy
France, 1877–1953
Paddock, n.d., oil on canvas, $23\frac{1}{2} \times 28\frac{3}{4}$ in. Aaron M. and Clara Weitzenhoffer Bequest, 2000

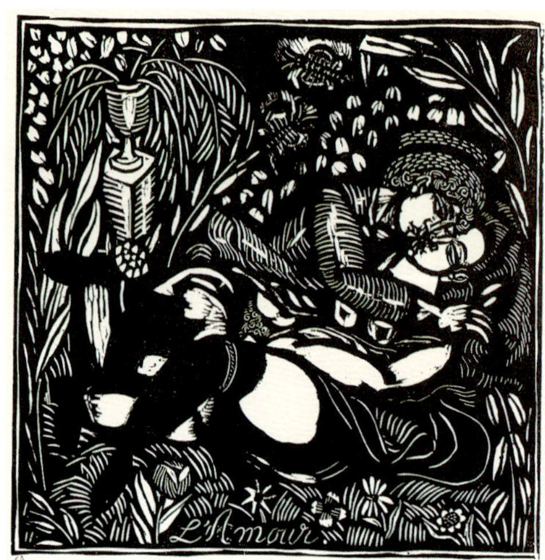

Raoul Dufy
France, 1877–1953
Love (L'Amour), 1910, woodcut, $12\frac{1}{8} \times 12\frac{1}{4}$ in.
Museum purchase, 1973

Beaux-Arts in Paris, where he could not adapt to the traditional academic training. In addition to painting, he produced fabric and stage sets. Dufy maintained a lifelong interest in seaside subjects, and he repeatedly referenced Le Havre and the bay of Sainte-Adresse in his images of shells, bathers, and regattas.

Dufy painted Fauvist works for only a brief period, but the brilliant, expressive colors of Fauvism and the paring down of an image to its essentials remained with him for the rest of his career. Dufy's best-known style was developed in the early 1920s, and is seen in the museum's *Paddock*. It is a decorative style full of energy and is characterized by emblematic, lyrical drawing that resembles linear arabesques, and an expressive, arbitrary use of color. In the 1920s and 1930s, Dufy painted a number of works dealing with horse racing.

24 Maurice de Vlaminck

France, 1876–1958

The Seine at Chatou (La Seine à Chatou),
1910
Oil on canvas
20¾ × 25¼ in.
Aaron M. and Clara Weitzenhoffer Bequest, 2000

Maurice de Vlaminck was born in Paris, the son of a mother who taught the piano and a father of Flemish descent who taught the violin. Vlaminck was a musician himself, playing the violin in orchestras and café-concerts around Paris. He spent part of his childhood at Chatou, the subject of the present painting. He became interested in painting in 1892, although he continued to work as a musician, as well as a mechanic and racing cyclist.

Near Paris on the west bank of the Seine, Chatou had been a village with major estates during the eighteenth century. After a railroad station only nine miles from central Paris opened in Chatou in the nineteenth century, the town became a popular riverside retreat for Parisians, and many pleasure villas were built. Rowing was a favorite activity at Chatou, and visitors could rent boats. The Impressionists often painted the leisure activities in towns along the Seine, such as Chatou and Argenteuil, which was three miles upstream. Pierre-Auguste Renoir is especially associated with Chatou, which is the setting for one of his most famous paintings, *The Luncheon of the Boating Party,* in the Phillips Collection, Washington, D.C.

Between 1900 and 1901, the self-taught painter Vlaminck shared a studio at Chatou with André Derain. Derain introduced him to Henri Matisse in 1901 in Paris, where Vlaminck also saw and was greatly affected by the expressionistic canvases of Vincent van Gogh. Vlaminck, Derain, and Matisse would become the original Fauves, artists who painted with brilliant, expressive, nonnaturalistic color. (For more on the Fauves, see cat. no. 23.)

Vlaminck modified his Fauvist style when he encountered the work of Paul Cézanne in 1907; he remained under Cézanne's spell until around 1910. Vlaminck especially admired Cézanne's emphasis on structure. Cézanne's influence appears in *The Seine at Chatou,* with its restrained palette and methodical, constructive brushstrokes. As is common in Cézanne's landscapes, Vlaminck bisected this canvas with a tree that accentuates the flat picture plane, establishes scale, and serves to define the space between the foreground and background.

Vlaminck's later expressionistic works, such as the Weitzenhoffer Collection's *Landscape,* often depict French roads with houses and dramatic skies.

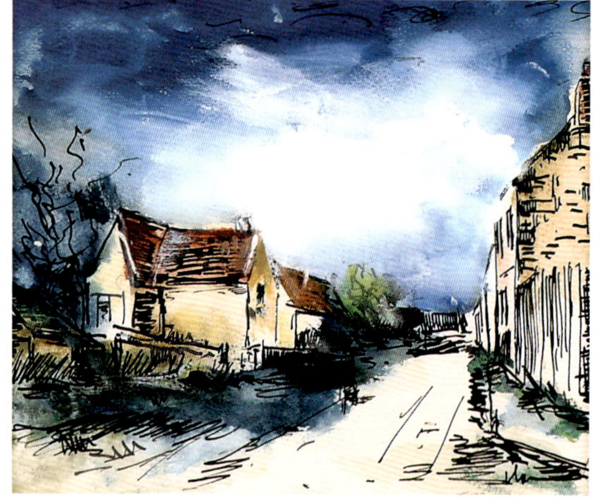

Maurice de Vlaminck
France, 1876–1958
Landscape, n.d., watercolor on paper, 21½ × 25½ in. Aaron M. and Clara Weitzenhoffer Bequest, 2000

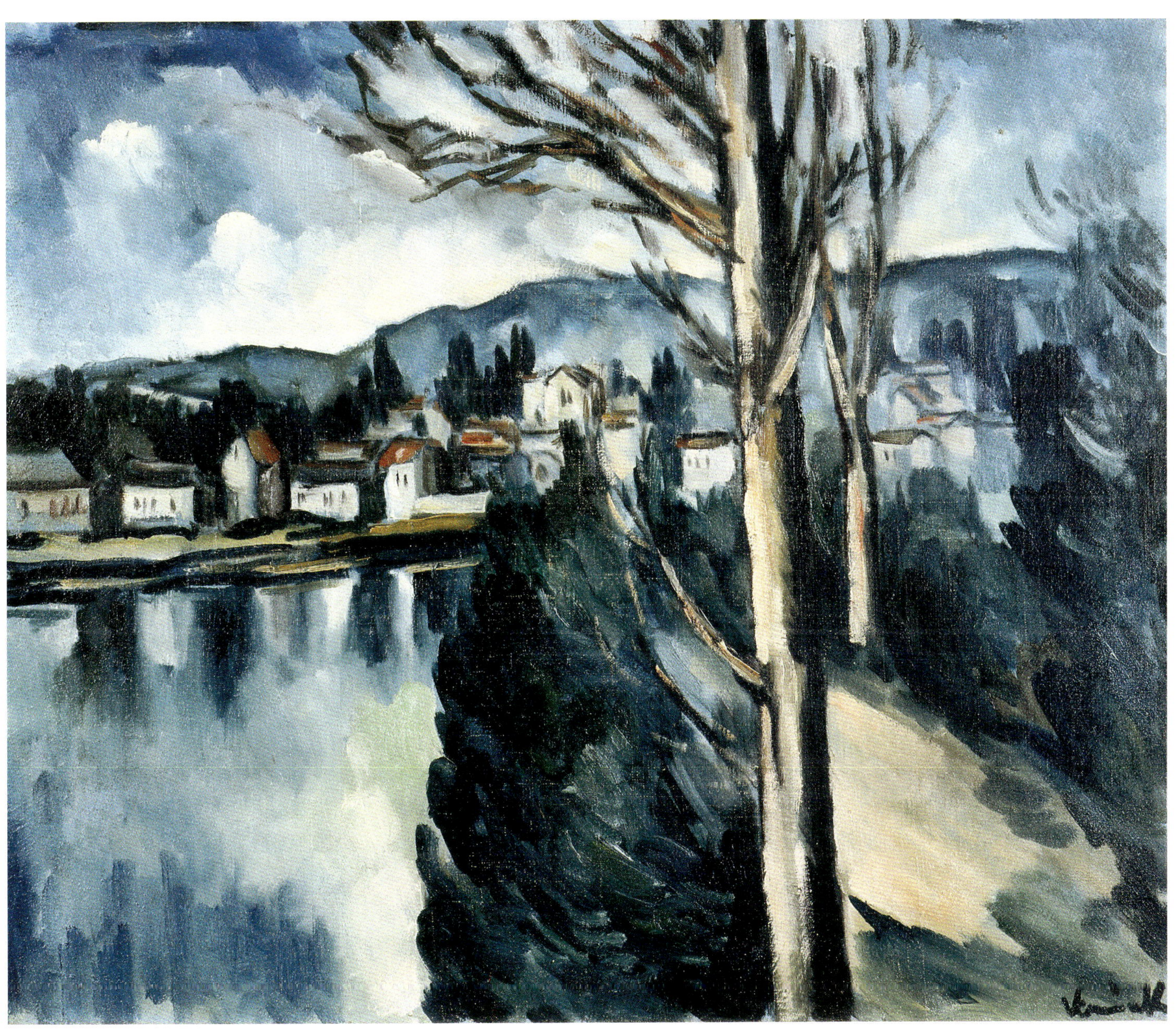

25 Henri Matisse

France, 1869–1954

Odalisque with a Bowl of Fruit (Odalisque à la coupe de fruits), 1925
Lithograph
Edition: 24/50
14 × 11 in.
Gift of Oscar B. Jacobson, prior to 1949

A towering figure of twentieth-century art, Henri Matisse decided to become an artist at a relatively late age. He grew up in the village of Bohain-en-Vermandois in northern France, where his father owned a grain business. At his family's urging, he studied law in Paris from 1887 until 1889, before returning to his hometown to work as a clerk in a law office. Matisse found this job boring, and he began to take drawing classes at a local school that trained primarily tapestry and textile designers.

While recovering from appendicitis in 1890, Matisse taught himself to paint and, a year later, abandoned law for art. In Paris, he studied with William-Adolphe Bouguereau at the Académie Julian, before leaving for the studio of Gustave Moreau, whose teaching emphasized color, feeling, and the imagination. Matisse later renounced his academic training, but from it he retained a belief in the importance of drawing the human figure.

In the mid-1890s, Matisse achieved some recognition and success with conventional paintings of still lifes and interiors in subdued colors. However, later in the decade, under the influence of Impressionism and especially his friend Camille Pissarro, he lightened his palette and loosened his brushwork. Paul Signac's writings on Neo-Impressionism further inspired Matisse.

At the turn of the twentieth century, Matisse resumed drawing classes at a number of Parisian academies, and he studied sculpture as well. He met the younger students André Derain and Maurice de Vlaminck, with whom Matisse would develop Fauvism, a style that emphasized an expressive, almost violent use of color. (For more on Fauvism, see cat. no. 23.)

After initial attacks, Matisse became celebrated as the avant-garde leader of the Fauves. Gertrude Stein and her brother, Leo, began to collect his work, and they introduced him to Pablo Picasso in 1906. Picasso would become Matisse's lifelong creative rival.

In 1908, Matisse published *Notes of a Painter,* in which he outlined his aesthetic goals, to which he adhered for the rest of his life. In an oft-repeated quotation, he wrote: "What I dream of is an art of balance, of purity and serenity, devoid of troubling or depressing subject-matter . . . a soothing, calming influence on the mind, something like a good armchair which provides relaxation from physical fatigue."

As Matisse grew more interested in Orientalist (North African, Middle Eastern, and Islamic) themes—which for well over a century had fascinated Western European artists, such as Eugène Delacroix and Matisse's own teacher, Moreau—he traveled in 1906 to North Africa. In 1910, Matisse saw an Islamic exhibition in Munich and then visited the Moorish cities in southern Spain. He spent the winters of 1912 and 1913 in Morocco. Matisse's travels, along with the challenge presented by Picasso and Georges Braque's Cubism and his exposure to the brilliant colors of Persian miniatures (see, for example, cat. no. 3), led to larger decorative compositions that were rich in color and exotic in subject matter.

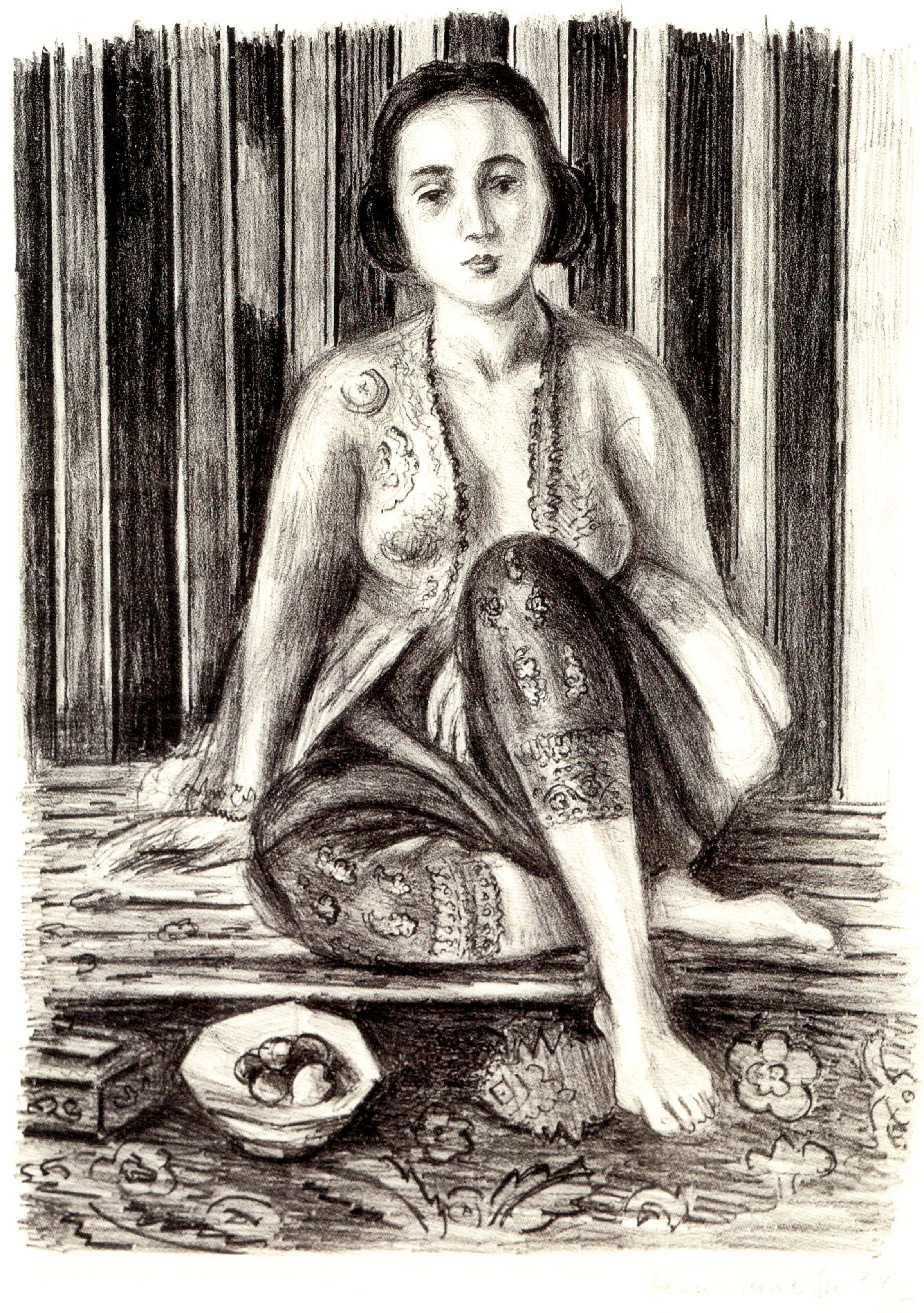

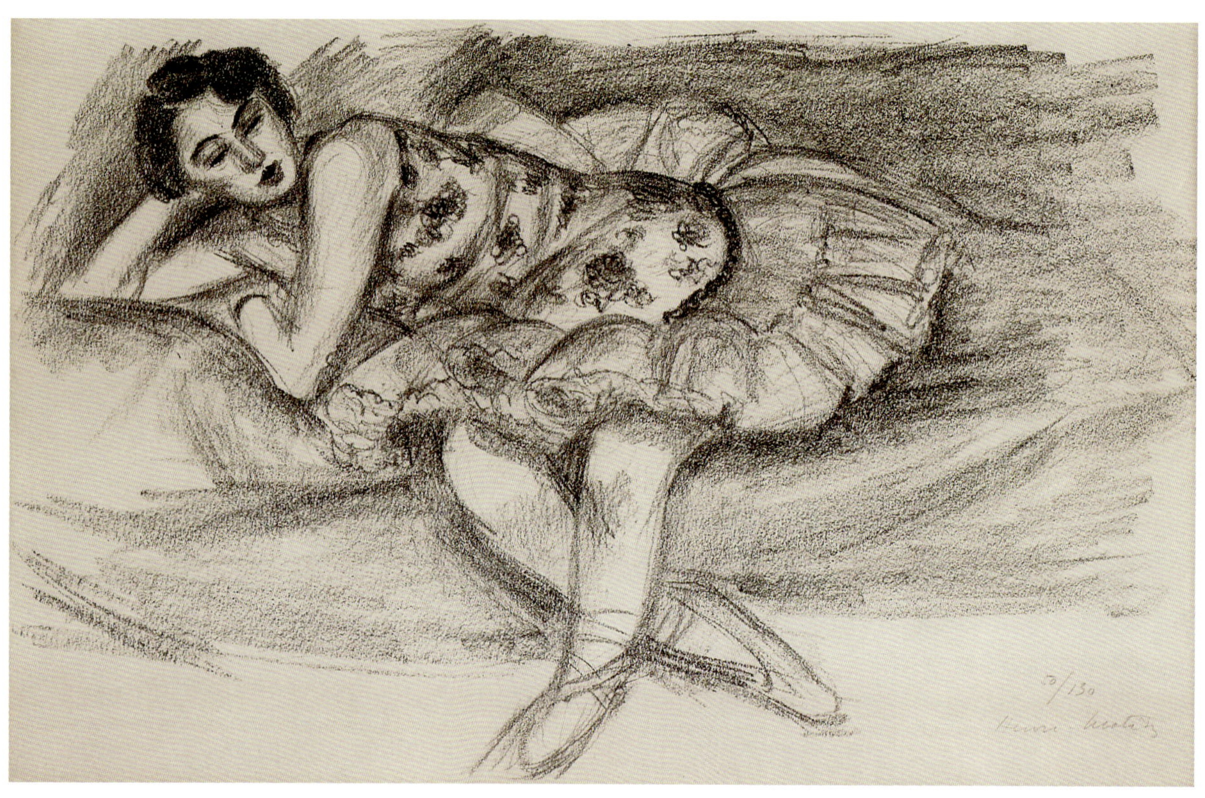

Henri Matisse
France, 1869–1954
Dancer on Couch, from *Ten Dancers (Danseuse au divan, pliée en deux, "Dix danseuses"),* 1927, lithograph, edition: 50/130, 11 × 18$\frac{1}{16}$ in. Purchase, Richard H. and Adeline J. Fleischaker Collection, 1966

At the end of 1917, Matisse visited Nice, where he would spend increasingly more time, away from his family, until he mostly lived there. Over the next decade, during which he created *Odalisque with a Bowl of Fruit,* Matisse retreated from large-scale, Modernist, decorative compositions to focus on greater naturalism. The female figure, interiors, landscapes, and still lifes were his primary subjects; light was a chief concern.

As the 1920s progressed, Matisse painted less but produced more sculptures, drawings, and prints. He had made his first prints in 1906 and in 1914 installed a hand press in his Paris studio. He used the press to make a variety of prints: etchings, drypoints, monotypes, and lithographs.

Matisse created fifty lithographs between 1922 and 1925, the year of the present work. *Odalisque with a Bowl of Fruit* depicts Henriette Darricarrère, a musician and former ballet dancer who was Matisse's companion and favorite model between 1920 and 1927. The lithograph shows some of Matisse's preferred motifs—decorative patterns and the female figure dressed in an Orientalist costume. For his depiction of light, Matisse utilized the whiteness of the paper. Instead of flattening the woman, he modeled her into three-dimensional form.

Other prints that Matisse created in the 1920s include a portfolio of ten lithographs featuring a tutu-clad ballet dancer who stands, sits, or reclines but never dances or practices. Sergey Diaghilev's Ballets Russes, with George Balanchine's choreography, probably inspired these prints; the museum owns one.

By the 1930s, Matisse had long been internationally famous, with exhibitions worldwide and many articles and books published about him. He traveled to Tahiti and the United States, where Albert C. Barnes commissioned him to paint a mural for the Barnes Foundation in Merion, Pennsylvania.

A 1941 operation for a tumor left Matisse confined to a wheelchair, but he continued to live and work on a hill above Nice. He developed his luminous, expansive late style in large paintings of interiors, the decoration of the Chapelle du Rosaire at Vence (1948–51), and a series of paper cutouts.

26 Pablo Picasso

Spain, 1881–1973

Seated Nude Crowned with Flowers
(Femme nue couronée de fleurs),
from the *Vollard Suite,* 1930
Etching
Edition: 310
12¼ × 8⅝ in.
Museum purchase, 1967

Born in Malaga, Spain, the son of an artist who also taught art, Pablo Picasso demonstrated extraordinary precociousness in drawing as a child. In 1891, the family moved to La Coruña, on the Atlantic coast, and in 1895, to Barcelona. Picasso studied art with his father, on his own, and intermittently at several art schools in Spain.

In 1900, Picasso traveled to Paris, where he sold a few paintings, and then moved back and forth between Paris and Spain until 1904. The 1901 suicide of his close friend, the painter Carles Casagemas, helped initiate Picasso's Blue Period, in which he created sentiment-laden images of people on the margins of society. During the Blue Period, Picasso produced his first important etching, *The Frugal Repast* (1904).

From 1904 on, Picasso made France his home. Later in 1904, he began his Rose Period, characterized by a brighter palette of pinks and flesh tones, coupled with delicate drawing. During Picasso's Rose Period, American expatriate siblings Leo and Gertrude Stein began to collect his paintings.

Primitivism—derived from African, Oceanic, and ancient Iberian sculpture—began to permeate Picasso's art in 1906, and led to the creation of *Les Demoiselles d'Avignon,* a painting of raw expressive power. This canvas broke down pictorial space into facets and planes, prefiguring the more intellectual Cubism, which Picasso, partly through the inspiration of Paul Cézanne, developed over the next decade alongside the artist Georges Braque. Cubism made Picasso famous and had a decisive impact on the course of twentieth-century art and culture.

During the 1920s, while still interested in Cubism, Picasso explored an ordered classical style, with an emphasis on line. Classicism considers line, rendered with simplicity, more significant than color, because line appeals to the mind and color to the less pure sense of vision. (Following World War I, many artists and even composers in France produced Classical-style works, a phenomenon Jean Cocteau described as a postwar *rappel à l'ordre* [call to order].)

Around 1925, Picasso became involved with Surrealism. He soon abandoned Classicism in his painting but continued to create Classical-style drawings and prints, such as *Seated Nude Crowned with Flowers.* In this etching, Picasso has absolute mastery over line and renders the model's appearance and mass with utmost clarity and economy of means.

Seated Nude Crowned with Flowers is from a series of 100 etchings, dating from 1930 to 1937, commissioned by Picasso's dealer, Ambroise Vollard. Called the *Vollard Suite,* the series ranks among the supreme achievements of printmaking. Most of the deeply personal prints are Classical in style. Their subjects include: life in a sculptor's studio, in which the sculptor, who is obsessed with his model, is an idealized self-portrait of Picasso; the Minotaur, a creature that is half-man and half-bull, with whom Picasso identified; Rembrandt; and the Battle of Love.

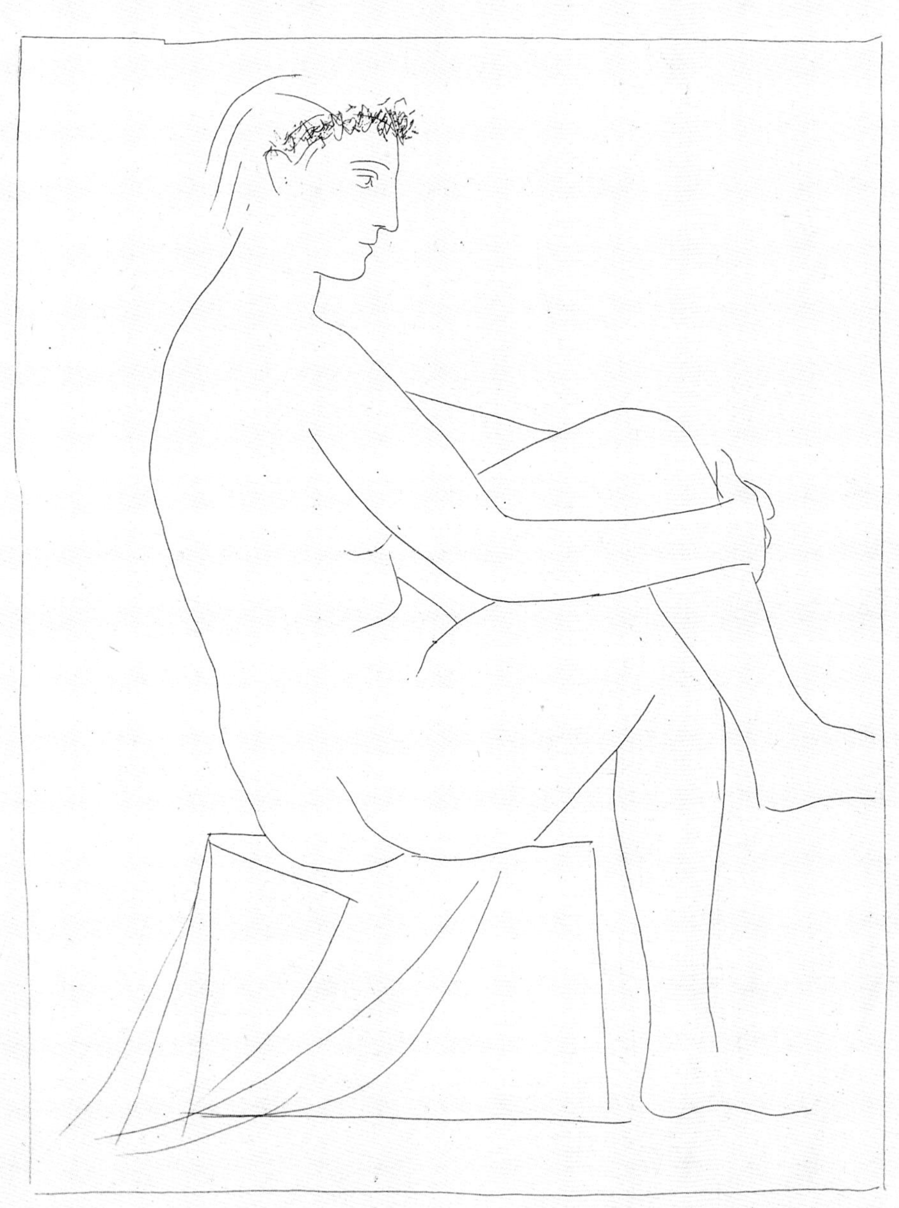

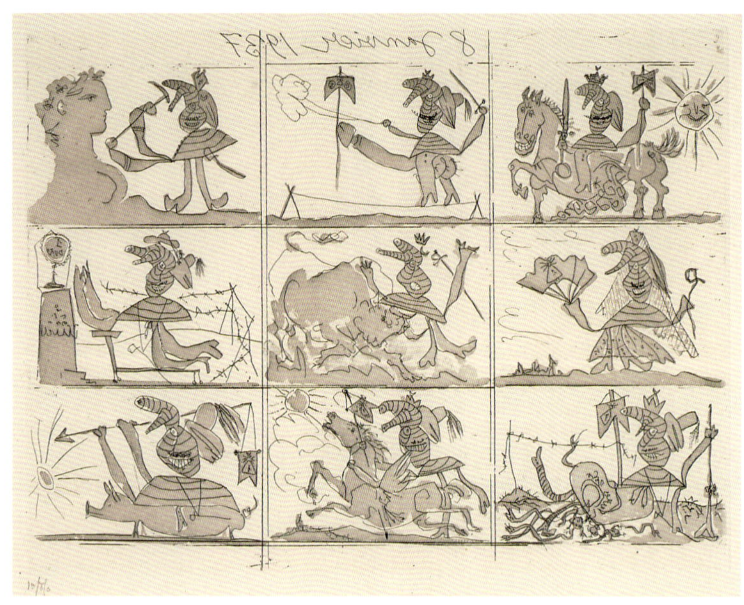

Pablo Picasso
Spain, 1881–1973
Dreams and Lies of Franco, 1937, etching, edition: 10/80, 14 × 17½ in. Museum purchase, 1967

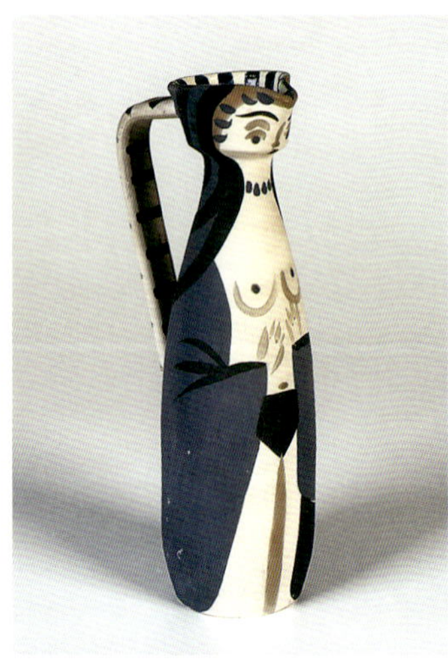

Pablo Picasso
Spain, 1881–1973
Woman (Femme), 1955
Ceramic pitcher, edition of 100, H. 13 in.
Gift of Professor Emeritus Roger Corsaw, 1976

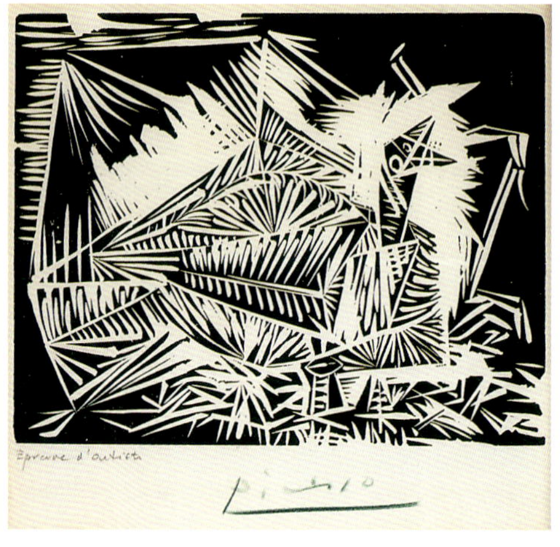

Pablo Picasso
Spain, 1881–1973
Young Pigeon, 1939, linocut, edition: Artist's Proof, 6 × 7 in. Purchase, Richard H. and Adeline J. Fleischaker Collection, 1996

Seated Nude Crowned with Flowers is the first plate of the *Vollard Suite,* but it does not fit into any of the above categories. The etching seems a serene, female version of Michelangelo's male nudes on the ceiling of the Sistine Chapel.

Ambroise Vollard, whose portraits appear in the *Vollard Suite,* had long promoted Picasso and had given the artist a solo exhibition as early as 1902, shortly after Picasso arrived in Paris. The dealer also promoted Cézanne, Paul Gauguin, Pierre-Auguste Renoir, and Vincent van Gogh, and published the Cézanne lithograph in the museum's collection (see cat. no. 18).

In 1937, the year Picasso completed the *Vollard Suite,* he produced two prints called *Dreams and Lies of Franco,* one of which is in the museum's collection. Picasso's first overtly political works, these prints attacked the Fascist regime of Francisco Franco in Spain and looked ahead to the artist's masterpiece, *Guernica,* painted later that year.

27 André Kertész

U.S., b. Hungary, 1894–1985

Piet Mondrian, Paris, 1926
Vintage gelatin silver print
9 × 7¼ in.
Gift, Ellen and Richard L. Sandor Collection, 2000

Born in Budapest, Hungary, André Kertész took his first photographs at age twelve. He was self-taught, and his early images depict peasants and idyllic Hungarian folk subjects. After working at the stock exchange in Budapest from 1912 until 1914, he served in the military during World War I, when he photographed the war and its aftermath; these photographs won awards and were published in magazines. After the war, he returned to the stock exchange job, which he disliked, but still took photographs during his free time. Following several friends who had left Hungary, Kertész moved to Paris in 1925.

Many of Kertész's early photographs in Paris were of tourist sites, such as the Eiffel Tower. Paris at the time was the center of the cultural avant-garde, and Kertész became acquainted with several major artists then living in the French capital, including the Dutch painter Piet Mondrian (1872–1944). Kertész made the present portrait of Mondrian in Paris in 1926, and the next year exhibited this actual print in his first exhibition, at the Galerie au Sacre Printemps. In the same exhibition, Kertész also premiered *Chez Mondrian,* a photograph depicting a corner of Mondrian's quiet, ordered studio, and an image that has become an icon in the history of photography.

Kertész became an acclaimed photographer in Paris. While there, he produced a series of nudes that were distorted to appear as if they were seen in a funhouse mirror.

In 1936, Kertész moved to New York, where he worked as a contract photographer for several magazines. After illness forced him to quit his magazine jobs in 1962, he resumed full-time photography of subjects of his own choice. The post-1962 pictures include photographs taken from New York windows; the museum owns one such photograph.

Piet Mondrian, Paris, a sepia-toned photograph, remained in Kertész's own collection for fifty years. Upon closer observation, the image emerges as a play of geometries, with ovals and strong diagonals.

A key figure in the Modernist movement, Piet Mondrian had one of the most recognizable styles of the twentieth century. Early works by this artist are naturalistic, but he experimented with various styles—such as Pointillism and, by 1911, Cubism—before developing his own abstract style between 1912 and 1914.

Mondrian spent World War I in the Netherlands. During this period, he reduced his palette to red, blue, yellow, black, and white squares and rectangles demarcated by black bands arranged strictly as horizontals and verticals. He called his style "Neoplasticism" and claimed that his works in this style were not purely abstract or nonobjective, but actually depicted the underlying structure and essence of the visible world.

In 1917, Mondrian became a founder of the De Stijl movement, which applied his type of abstraction to architecture and industrial design. In 1919, he moved to Paris. After publishing in the magazine *De Stijl* and exhibiting with other De Stijl members, Mondrian resigned from the group in 1925 (the year before Kertész photographed him), when De Stijl artist Theo van Doesburg started to use diagonals in his work.

In 1938, Mondrian moved to London. Two years later, like many artists, he fled war-torn Europe for New York, where he died in 1944.

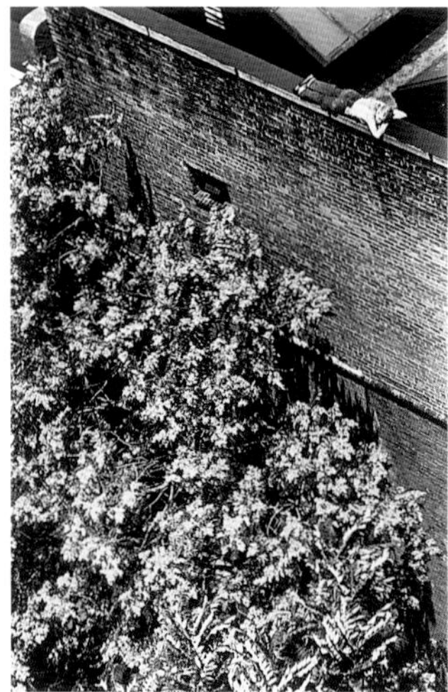

André Kertész
U.S., b. Hungary, 1894–1985
New York City, July 10, from the *Ten Photographs* portfolio, 1977, gelatin silver print, edition: 32/75, 9½ × 6¼ in. Purchased with funds from the Museum of Art Association Fund, 1978

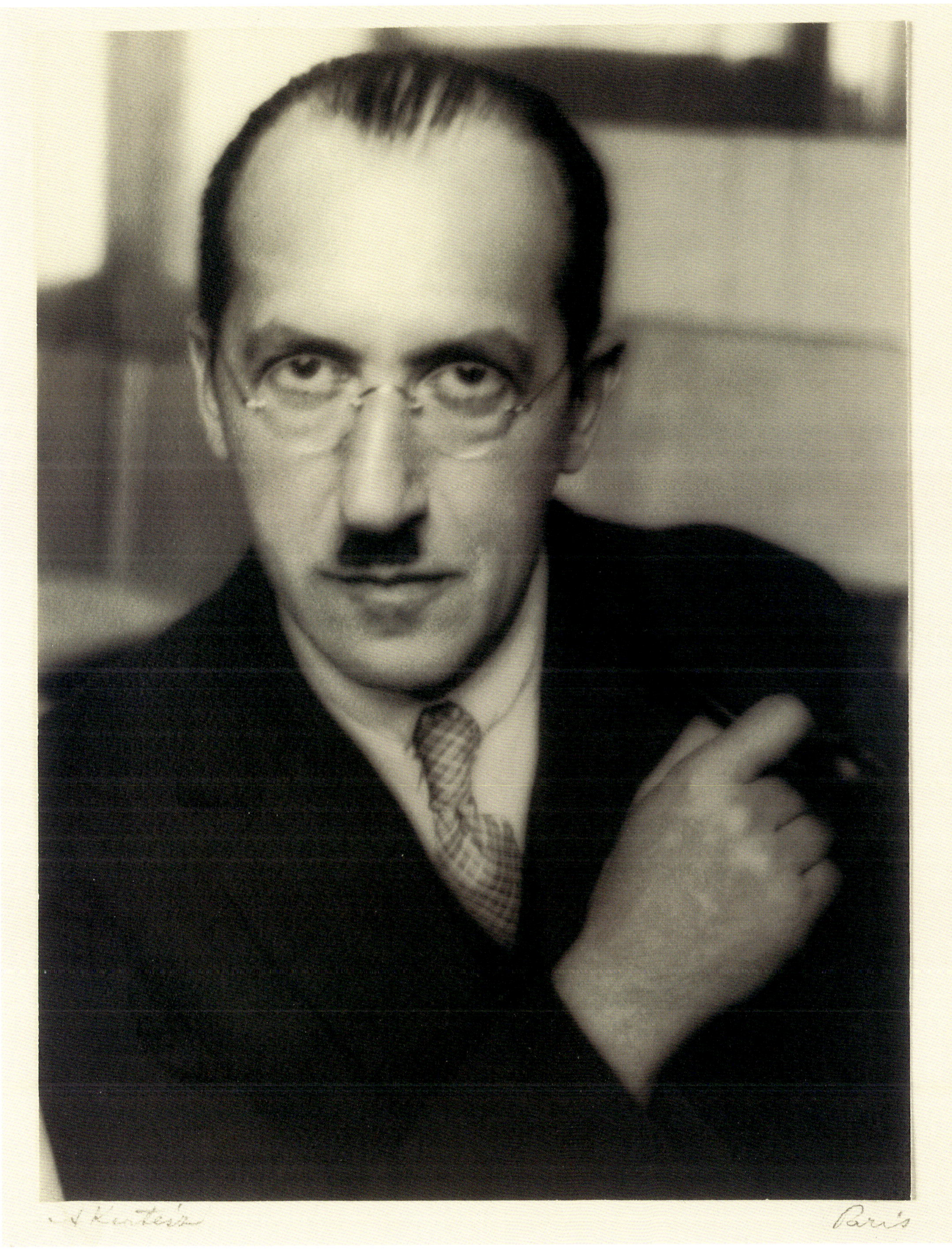
A Kertész
Paris

28 John Singleton Copley

U.S., 1738–1815

Portrait of Mrs. Jabez Bowen (Sara Brown), c. 1771–74
Oil on canvas
29 13/16 × 24 3/4 in.
Partial gift of Mr. and Mrs. Frank A. Ladd, 2002

John Singleton Copley is often considered the first great American-born painter. He grew up in Boston, the stepson of an engraver who exposed Copley to art and taught him the rudiments of printmaking. As a painter, Copley was largely self-taught, beginning his career as a portraitist in the mid-1750s and soon becoming the preeminent American portraitist of the colonial era. In 1774, he moved with his family to England, in part to prove himself in the larger arena of the London art world. After a year in Italy on the Grand Tour, he returned to London, where he continued to earn a living from portraits but received recognition for his modern-day history paintings, such as *Watson and the Shark* (1778), at the National Gallery of Art, Washington, D.C., and *The Death of Major Pierson* (1783), at the Tate Gallery, London.

Sara Brown (1742–1800) lived in Providence, Rhode Island, throughout her life. She was the daughter of shipping magnate Obadiah Brown. In 1762, she married Jabez Bowen (1739–1815), who became a prominent lawyer. From 1778 until 1786, Jabez Bowen was the deputy governor of Rhode Island, and from 1785 until his death three decades later, he was the chancellor of Brown University, which was named for one of Sara's relatives. Copley also painted a portrait of Jabez Bowen, now in a private collection, as a companion to the present picture. (The Townsend-Goddard family of Newport cabinetmakers created for Mr. and Mrs. Jabez Bowen a celebrated suite of furniture, now at the Winterthur Museum in Delaware.)

In *Portrait of Mrs. Jabez Bowen*, Copley depicted the sitter in a solemn, direct manner. She is strongly lit against a plain background, and the artist made no attempt to hide her double chin. However, Sara is richly attired. Gold braid, lace, and pearls adorn her rose-colored satin drapery and low-bodiced, blue velvet dress. Additional pearls, accentuating the light in Sara's eyes, decorate her hair, which is pulled back into a blue-and-gold turban, an example of the Turkish-style fancy dress ("turquerie") fashionable in eighteenth-century Europe and, in emulation, America. It has been suggested that Sara Bowen requested that Copley paint her in this dress and pose after seeing in the artist's Boston studio a similar portrait of Mrs. Moses Gill, painted in 1773 and now at the Museum of Art of the Rhode Island School of Design.

Copley created some of his greatest portraits at around the same time he painted Sara and Jabez Bowen.

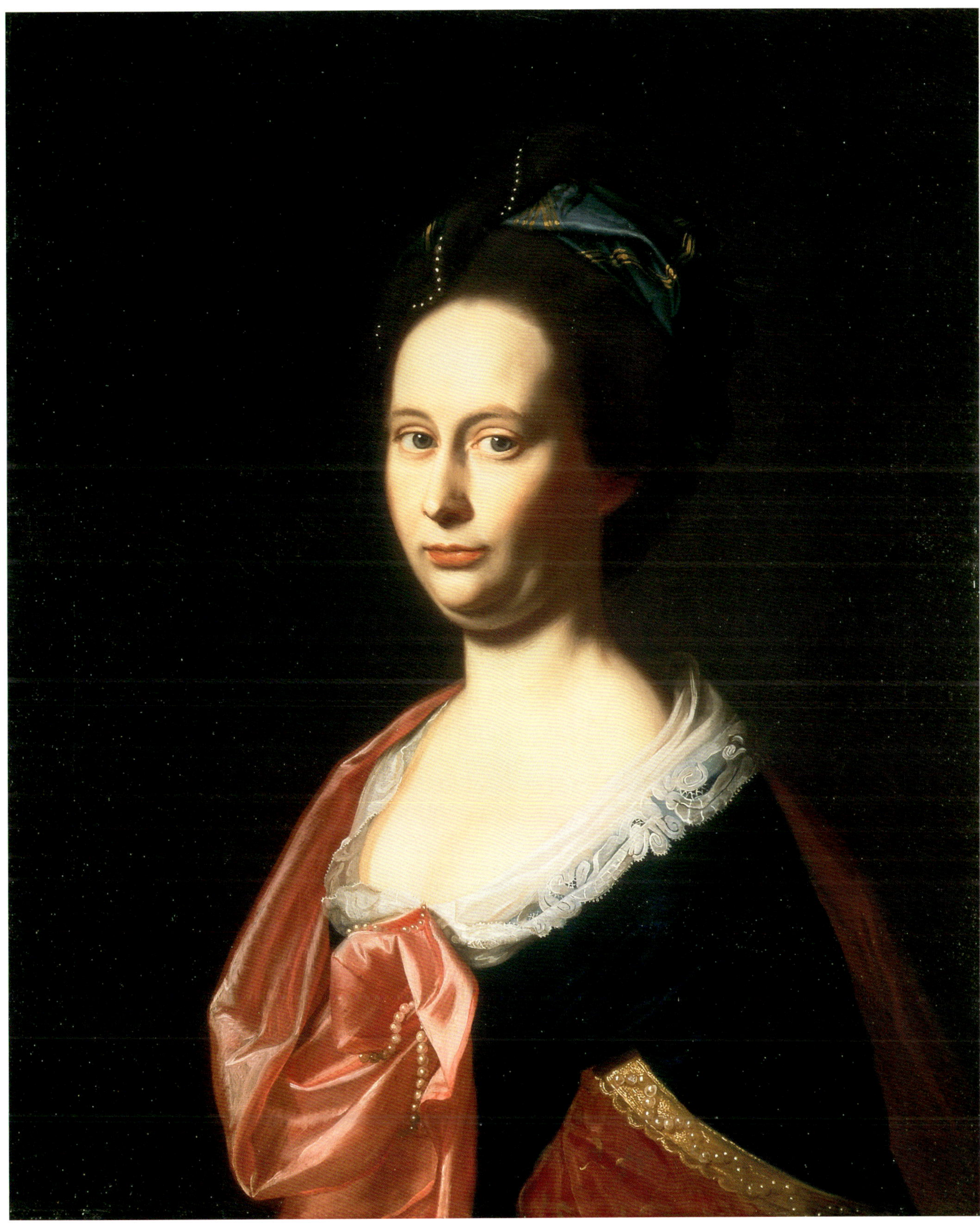

29 Albert Bierstadt

U.S., b. Germany, 1830–1902

Yosemite Valley, n.d.
Oil on paper mounted on canvas
16 × 20 in.
Purchase, Richard H. and Adeline J. Fleischaker Collection, 1996

When he was two, Albert Bierstadt emigrated with his family from Germany to New Bedford, Massachusetts, where he grew up. After working as an itinerant drawing master in New England, he studied at the renowned art academy in Düsseldorf, Germany. He remained in Europe for four years, traveling also to Switzerland and Italy.

In 1857, Bierstadt returned to New Bedford, and in the following year, he submitted a painting to the annual exhibition of the National Academy of Design. In 1859, he first went west, with Frederick W. Lander's Honey Road Survey Party. He traveled deep into the Rocky Mountains to South Pass, making sketches of the landscape and photographs of the American Indians and other people he saw.

Back in his Tenth Street studio in New York, Bierstadt used his sketches and photographs to create panoramic canvases of the American West, which made him famous. An example is the Metropolitan Museum of Art's *The Rocky Mountains, Lander's Peak* (1863), a vast painting that balances the sublimity of an Edenic landscape with American Indian figures in the foreground. This work sold to an English collector in 1865 for $25,000, at the time a huge sum for a painting.

In 1863, during the Civil War, Bierstadt traveled west again by stagecoach and on horseback. He went to San Francisco and continued on to Yosemite Valley, where the artist spent seven weeks sketching. After going north to the Columbia River in Oregon, Bierstadt headed back to New York, where he used his sketches to produce large paintings of the West, including canvases that capture the wonder and power of Yosemite. He revisited Yosemite and California in 1871, but there were now many tourists brought by the new transcontinental railroad, so Bierstadt focused on the more remote areas of the valley. He returned to New York in 1873.

Seeming to depict unspoiled nature, *Yosemite Valley* shows Cathedral Rock to the left, dramatically lit. Bierstadt painted this view a number of times in the 1860s and 1870s and probably sketched the present work outdoors in Yosemite. Most likely, this sketch served as preparation for the large-scale paintings produced in the studio in New York.

Bierstadt based the composition of *Yosemite Valley* on the structure of Classical landscape paintings, as developed by artists such as Claude Lorrain in the seventeenth century. For instance, Bierstadt used trees as framing devices on the painting's right. The viewer's eye is led along the river, through the darkened foreground, to the brilliant light illuminating the steep, jagged mountains in the distance.

Bierstadt's large-scale paintings fell out of favor by the mid-1870s, as more intimate works by other artists became popular. When interest in Bierstadt revived during the 1960s, it was the preparatory sketches rather than the panoramic works that first received attention.

The museum owns another Bierstadt *plein air* (outdoor) oil sketch, *Hastings on the Hudson River,* which depicts autumn foliage with light shining through the trees.

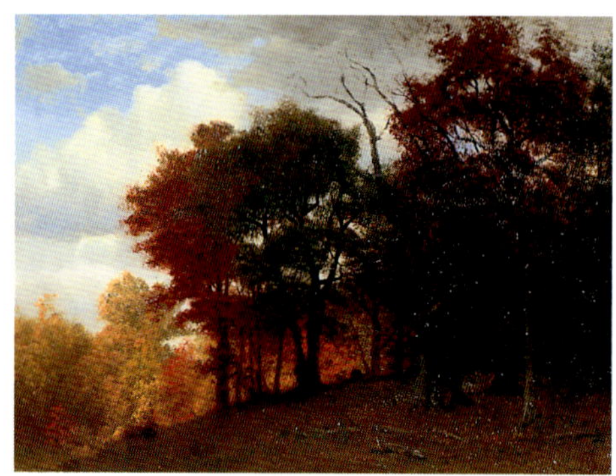

Albert Bierstadt
U.S., b. Germany, 1830–1902
Hastings on the Hudson River, 1865, oil on linen, 13 1/16 × 18 1/4 in. Gift of Marion K. and Lynn A. Cohenour, 1994

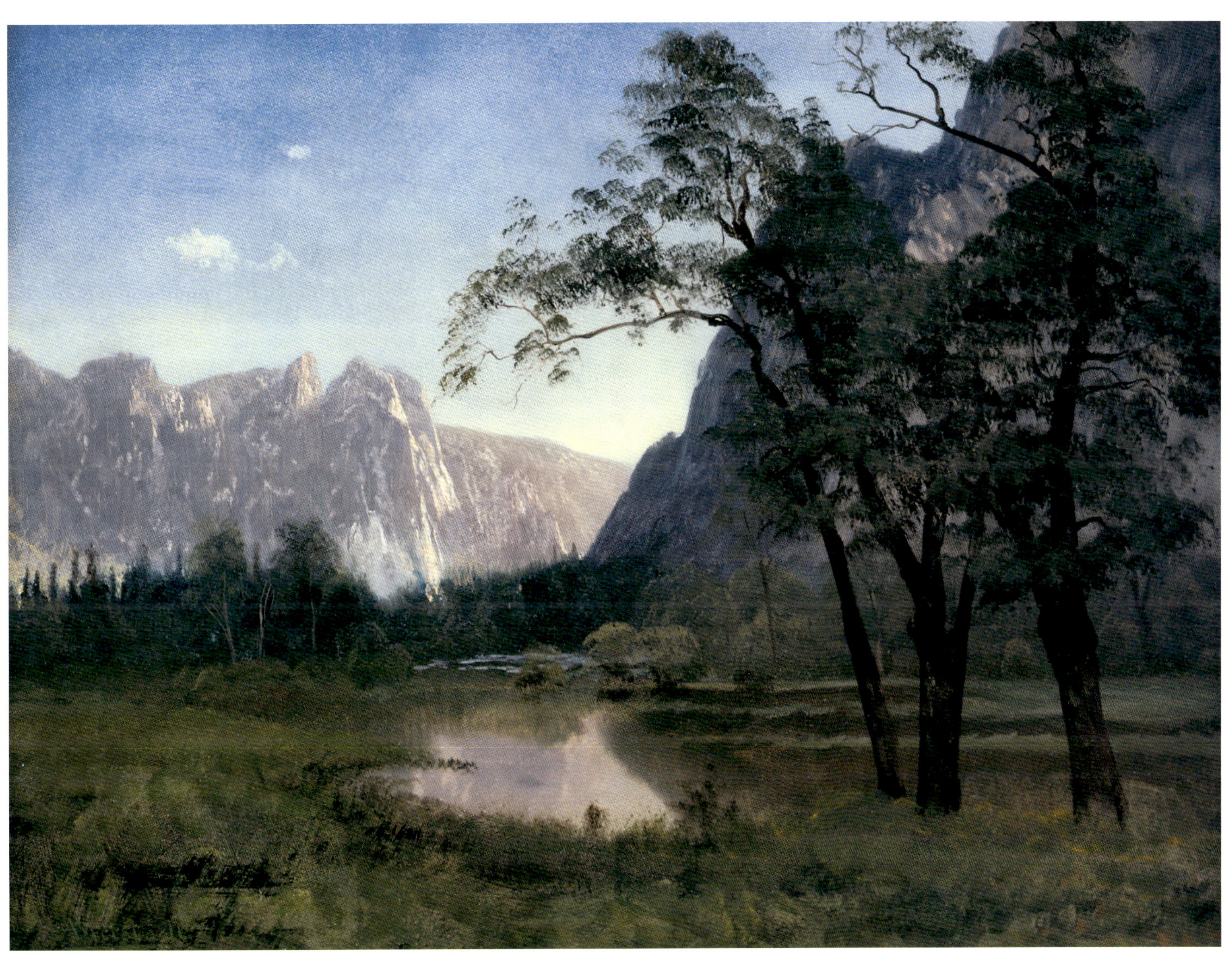

30 Thomas Moran

U.S., b. England, 1837–1926

Entrance to the Grand Canal, Venice, 1905
Oil on canvas
30 × 40 in.
Gift of Russell Ruby, Muskogee, Oklahoma, 2004

The present work is one of Thomas Moran's many views of Venice in the manner of the artist's hero, the great English Romantic landscape painter J. M. W. Turner (1775–1851). The painting depicts the mouth of the Grand Canal, with the domes of the Church of Santa Maria della Salute in the center and on the right the Campanile (bell tower), Doge's Palace, and barely visible domes of St. Mark's Basilica. Moran has taken liberties with topographical accuracy: the Venetian palaces on the left are fictional—the artist included them to anchor the composition. The painting's dominant feature is blazing light, which symbolizes the glory of Venice. This light is the product of a setting sun, which alludes to the notion current both in Turner's day and in Moran's that Venice was a sinking, dying city.

Born in Bolton, England, in 1837, the son of a weaver, Thomas Moran immigrated in 1844 with his family to Kensington, Pennsylvania, near Philadelphia. He apprenticed as an engraver and painted with his artist brother, Edward. By age twenty-one, Moran had exhibited an oil painting at the Pennsylvania Academy of the Fine Arts.

Through prints and engravings, Moran came to know the work of J. M. W. Turner. In 1862, Moran and his brother traveled to England to study the paintings of Turner firsthand. They made copies after Turner and visited the places that Turner had painted along the coast of England. Moran noted that Turner often departed from topographical accuracy in favor of pictorial, atmospheric, or dramatic effects, and this inspired Moran to do the same. Like Turner, Moran became a master of watercolor.

In 1866, Moran returned to Europe to continue studying European art and to exhibit his painting, *Children of the Mountain,* in Paris at the Exposition Universelle of 1867. The painting seemed to depict an actual Western landscape but was only an invention by an artist who had not yet traveled to the West.

In 1871, Moran was invited, along with the photographer William Henry Jackson, to join a U.S. Geological Survey expedition to Yellowstone. Within a year, Moran's drawings and watercolors of the trip, as well as Jackson's photographs, convinced Congress to preserve the area as a national park. In 1872, Congress purchased Moran's immense *Grand Canyon of the Yellowstone,* which became the first landscape painting to hang in the U.S. Capitol. Two years later, Congress bought Moran's *Chasm of the Colorado,* which depicts the Grand Canyon of the Colorado River. These vast canvases were intended to form a triptych with a third, *Mountain of the Holy Cross.* Moran had hoped to exhibit them together in Philadelphia at the Centennial Exposition of 1876, but Congress refused to lend its two paintings.

By the mid-1870s, Moran was signing his works with the initials "TYM," which stood for Thomas "Yellowstone" Moran. His reputation

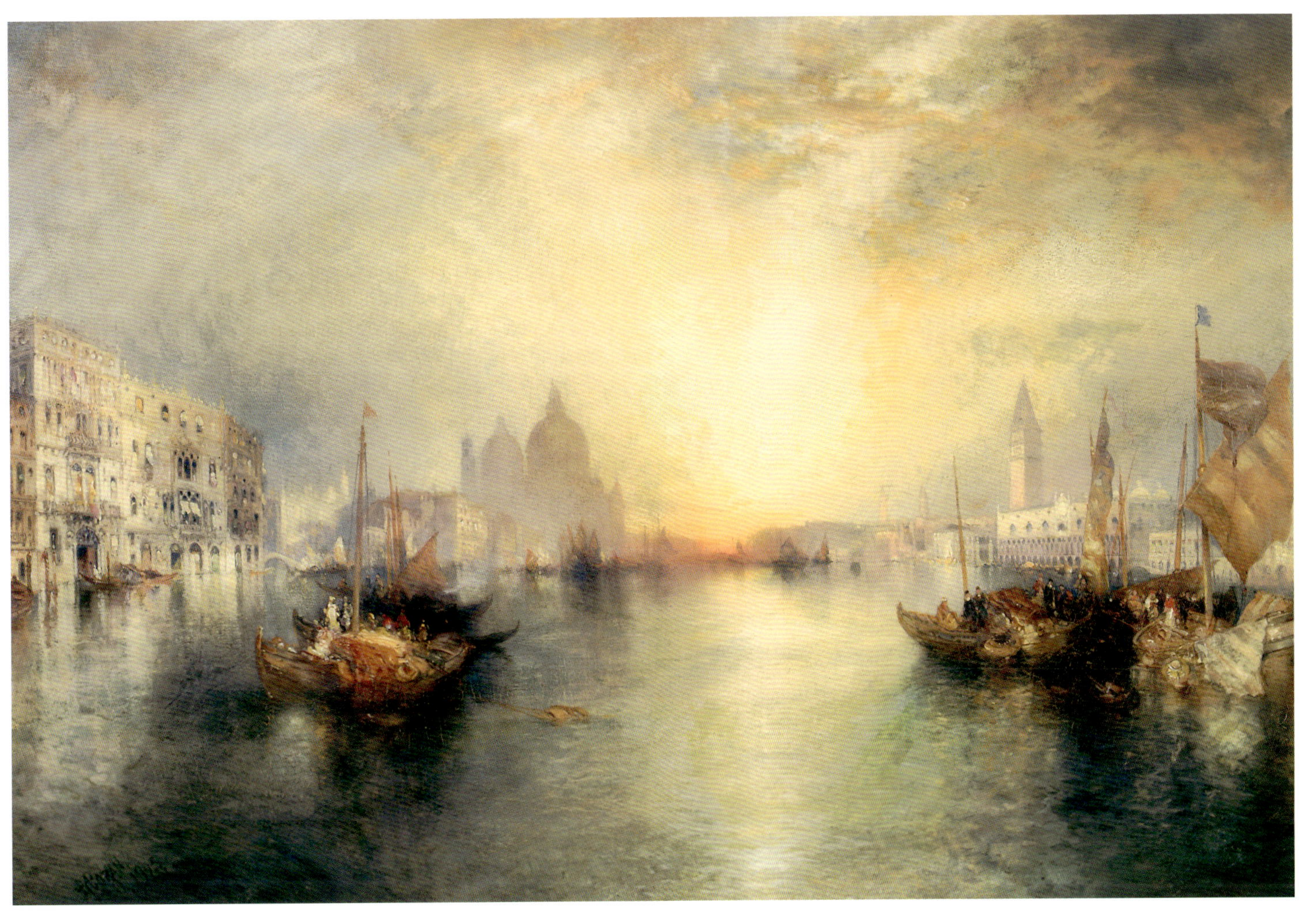

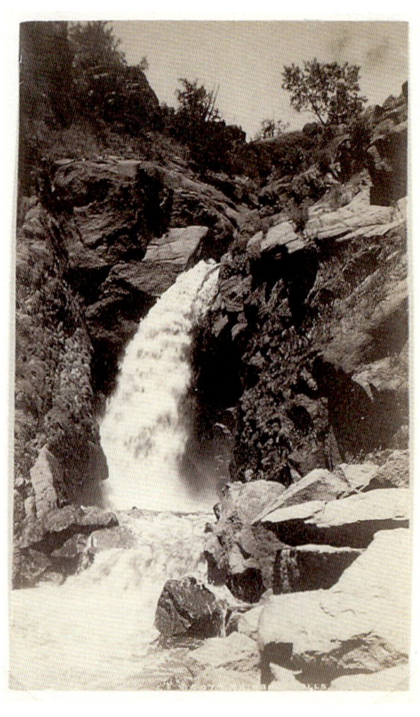

William Henry Jackson
U.S., 1843–1942
Rainbow Falls, c. 1880, albumen print,
7¼ × 4⅜ in. Museum purchase, 1983

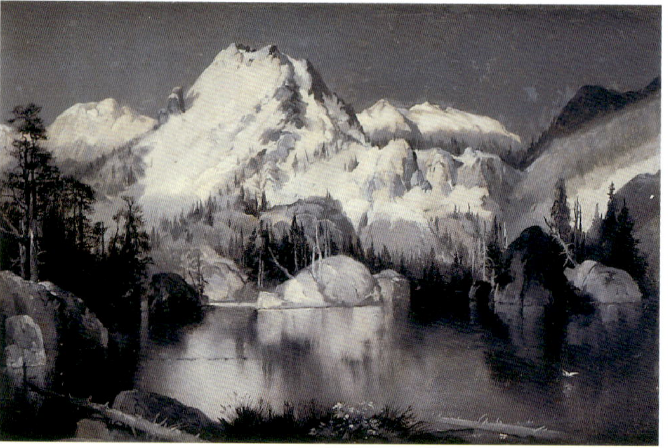

Thomas Moran
U.S., b. England, 1837–1926
Crystal Lake, 1895, oil on canvas board,
11 × 17 in. Purchase, Richard H. and
Adeline J. Fleischaker Collection, 1996

as a painter of panoramic Western landscapes now rivaled that of Albert Bierstadt (see cat. no. 29). (Like Bierstadt, Moran traveled extensively, to England, Italy, Mexico, and Cuba.)

In 1892, Moran returned to the West, revisiting the Grand Canyon, which he had first painted in the 1870s, and Yellowstone. His traveling companion was again the photographer William Henry Jackson.

Although best known for his sublime landscapes of the Rocky Mountains and the Southwest (especially the Grand Canyon), Moran painted other scenes, including industrial settings, seascapes, and landscapes of Long Island, where in East Hampton he settled and built a studio in 1884. Among his most popular works, in addition to his images of the West, were his views of Venice, which he painted in his Long Island studio for decades after his 1886 sojourn in that most dreamlike of cities.

Moran continued to paint into his final decade, but his panoramic landscapes had become outdated. In 1920, he moved from East Hampton to Santa Barbara, California, where he died in 1926.

31 Childe Hassam

U.S., 1859–1935

Good Harbor Beach, Gloucester, 1909
Watercolor and gouache on paper
8 7/16 × 11 7/16 in.
Aaron M. and Clara Weitzenhoffer Bequest, 2003

The son of a prosperous Boston merchant, the American Impressionist Childe Hassam began his career by apprenticing to an engraver and working from the late 1870s until the mid-1880s as an illustrator, especially for children's books. In the early 1880s, he studied at the Lowell Institute and the Boston Art Club and began to paint landscape watercolors, which he showed in solo exhibitions in Boston.

By the mid-1880s, Hassam was recognized as a painter of atmospheric urban street scenes. Beginning in 1886, he lived in Paris for three years. He studied drawing at the Académie Julian, and his work showed increasing awareness of the French Impressionists, with fragmented brushwork and a lightened palette. Although Hassam was considered an American Impressionist, he disliked the label and preferred to be called a painter of light and air.

Returning to the United States, Hassam moved to New York, where he continued to paint city scenes. During the summers, he painted New England coastal towns, many with art colonies, such as Gloucester, Massachusetts; Cos Cob and Old Lyme, Connecticut; and East Hampton, New York, where he bought a summer house in 1919.

During the 1890s, Hassam exhibited regularly and became one of the leading American artists. Visits to Europe in 1896 and 1897 exposed him to Post-Impressionism and led to stronger brushstrokes and an even more vivid palette. In both 1910 and 1911, he traveled to Europe, where he painted the Bastille Day celebrations in Paris. These works foreshadow his well-known World War I images of patriotic flag-draped parades down New York's Fifth Avenue.

The present work depicts a beach in Gloucester. Since the mid-nineteenth century, the scenery and light of this historic coastal town, on rugged Cape Ann in Massachusetts, had attracted artists such as Fitz Hugh Lane and Winslow Homer, who produced his early watercolors there. Artists continued to paint Gloucester well into the twentieth century, with, for example, Stuart Davis depicting it in his 1935 painting *Waterfront,* in the museum's collection (see cat. no. 71). Beginning in the early 1880s, Hassam visited Gloucester many times throughout his career.

Good Harbor was a popular beach, with white sand and tranquil green water ideal for wading at low tide. The present watercolor features a single bather and a small boardwalk leading to a row of boats. Other figures appear in the distance as little more than specks on the beach that wraps around the harbor.

Hassam was suspicious of Modern art, but much of his own art in the twentieth century focused on abstract qualities, as seen in the broad patches of paint that emphasize the work's flat surface in *Good Harbor Beach, Gloucester.* In this watercolor, Hassam used exposed, unpainted paper as part of the composition, as Maurice B. Prendergast had done in *South Side Hills* (see cat. no. 32) and Edward Hopper in *House in Provincetown* (see cat. no. 70).

Hassam designed his own frames, on which he incorporated the letter "H," representing his name. *Tree Landscape,* in the museum's Fleischaker Collection, retains its original Hassam frame.

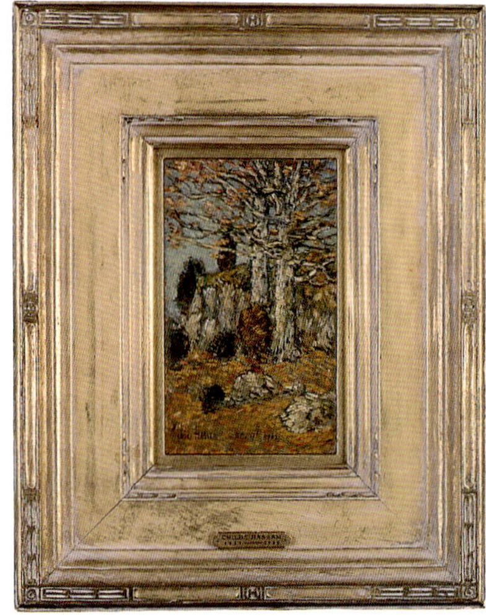

Childe Hassam
U.S., 1859–1935
Tree Landscape, 1903, oil on panel, 12 1/8 × 7 in. (excluding frame). Purchase, Richard H. and Adeline J. Fleischaker Collection, 1996

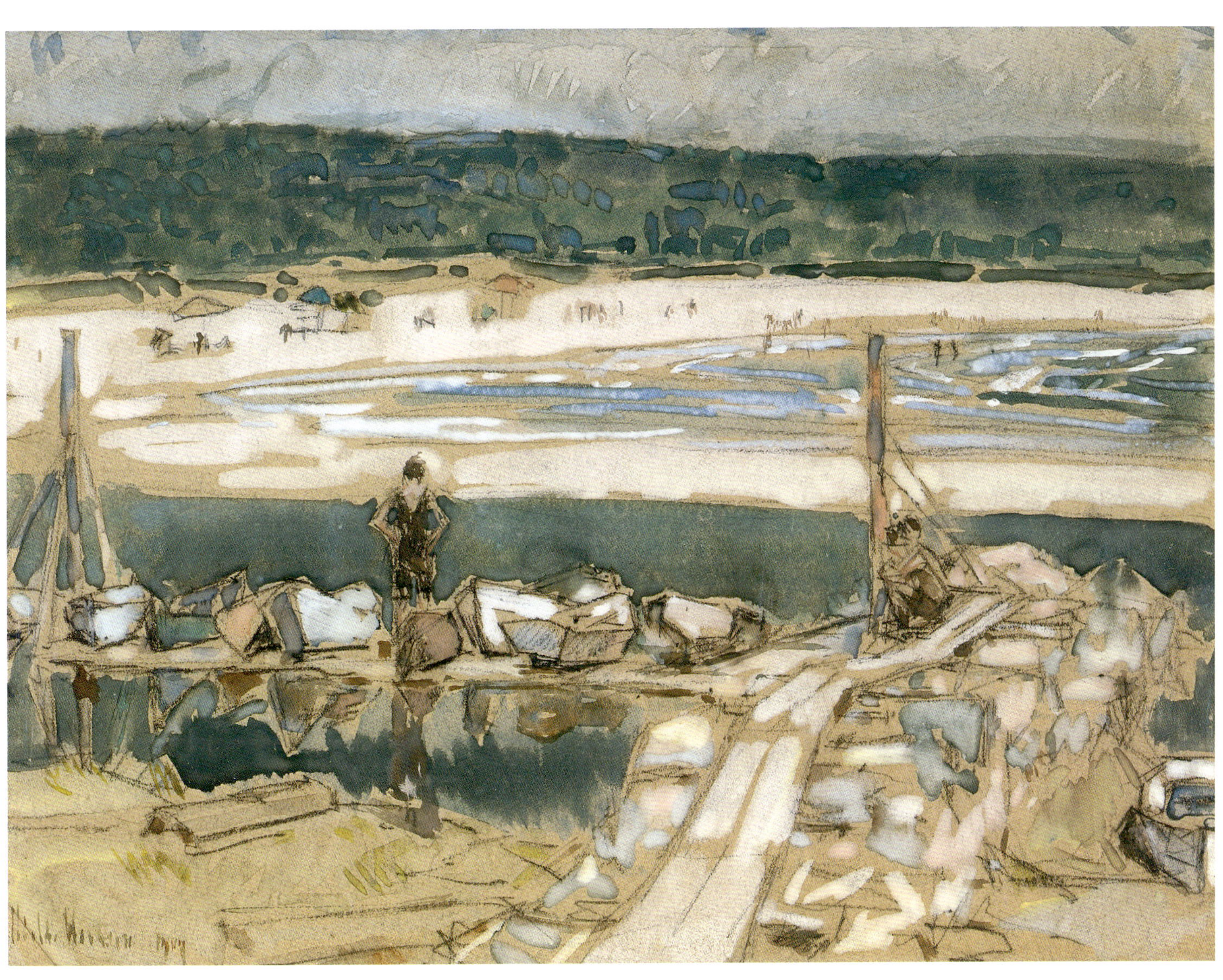

32 Maurice B. Prendergast

U.S., 1859–1924

South Side Hills, c. 1912–13
Watercolor on paper
13½ × 19½ in.
Gift of Jerome M. and Wanda Otey Westheimer, 1998

The Post-Impressionist Maurice B. Prendergast was born in Newfoundland, Canada, and at age ten moved with his family to Boston. After beginning his career as a commercial artist, Prendergast traveled to Paris in 1891 and studied at the Académie Colarossi and later at the Académie Julian. He disliked the discipline of the academies and sought his subject matter, like the French Impressionists before him, in the cafés and gardens of Paris and along the French coast. He was influenced by Nabi artists, such as Pierre Bonnard and Edouard Vuillard. (For more on the Nabis, see cat. no. 21.)

When Prendergast returned to Boston in 1898, he worked as an illustrator and exhibited watercolors of French and American coastal scenes peopled with an urban middle class. He spent 1898 and 1899 in Italy, where he painted watercolors depicting life in Venice and found inspiration in the rich color of early Renaissance frescoes. Back in the United States, Prendergast lived in New York, producing experimental watercolors and having his first solo exhibition in 1900.

Prendergast began to paint more often in oils following a 1907 trip to France, where he saw the art of Paul Signac (see cat. no. 17) and the Fauves and attended the major Paul Cézanne retrospective (see cat. no. 18). At the Macbeth Gallery in New York in 1908, Prendergast showed in the landmark exhibition of The Eight, which included the circle of Robert Henri. (For more on The Eight, see cat. no. 53.) In 1913, Prendergast's participation in the Armory Show—which he helped to organize and in which he exhibited three oils and four watercolors—reaffirmed his identification with the avant-garde.

South Side Hills dates from around the time of the Armory Show, when Prendergast was considered one of the most modern American artists. It depicts an area at the harbor of St. John's, Newfoundland, Prendergast's birthplace. Works such as *South Side Hills* have been compared to Byzantine mosaics, in which planes of pure, gemlike color create flat patterns across a surface. Like Edward Hopper in *House in Provincetown* (see cat. no. 70), Prendergast utilized the exposed, unpainted white paper to accentuate the light within the painting.

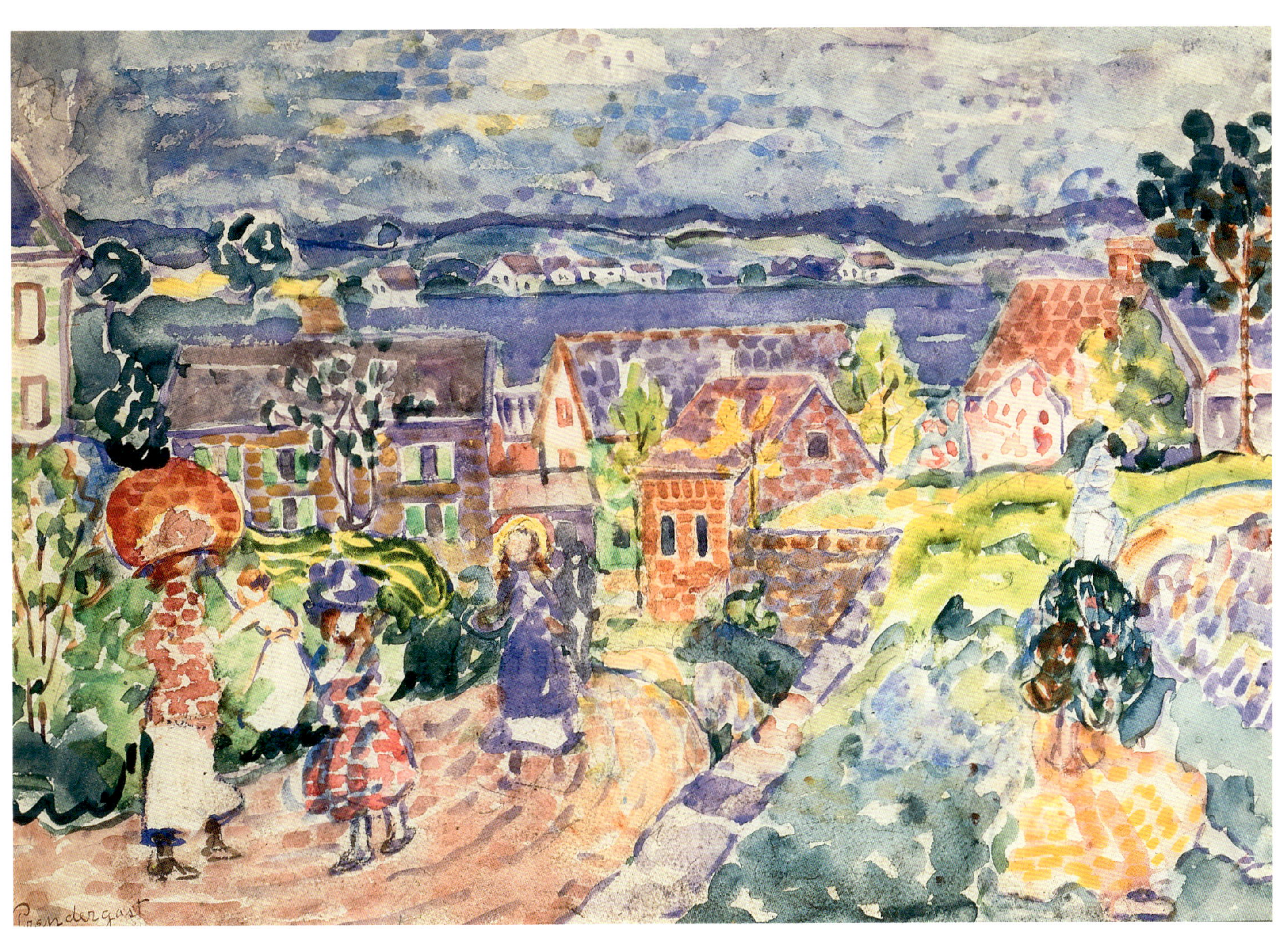

33 Unknown

Navajo

Second Phase Chief's Blanket, c. 1870s
Wool with vegetable dyes
54 × 64 in.
Museum purchase, 1937

Navajo Indians consider weaving a sacred activity and believe that the ancestor Spider Woman wove the universe itself out of cosmic materials. In the American Southwest, textile weaving dates back to around A.D. 700 and reached its zenith in the work of the Navajo Indians in the mid-nineteenth century. American Indian textiles were originally cotton, but wool became the favored material after the Spanish introduced sheep into North America. The Navajo initially learned the art of weaving, in both technique and style, from Pueblo Indians, probably in the late seventeenth century. The oldest known surviving Navajo weavings date to the late eighteenth century.

Early Navajo so-called First Phase Chief's blankets consist of parallel bands of blue-on-white or brown-on-white. The weaver arranged the stripes horizontally along an imaginary center line. Only men wore the blankets, which they wrapped around their bodies.

Around 1850, the First Phase pattern evolved into the Second Phase Chief's pattern with the introduction of nine red blocks, arranged symmetrically on the stripes, as in the present weaving. Oscar Jacobson acquired this Second Phase Chief's blanket for the museum one year after it opened.

Handspun weavings involved gathering wool, cleaning and carding it, and spinning it into yarn. The weaver then dyed the yarn and wove it on an upright loom. Traditionally, weaving was a woman's art, but occasionally men, such as the Navajo medicine man Hosteen Klah, also wove textiles.

The term "Chief's blanket" is inaccurate, because there were no chiefs among the Navajo. Any male member of the tribe could wear the blankets, although more important figures usually wore them. The blankets were also sold to other Indian groups and to Anglos.

The second half of the nineteenth century witnessed many changes in Navajo weaving. The Second Phase Chief's pattern evolved into the Third Phase when the red blocks along the bands became diamond-shaped. As a broader range of commercial dyes and ready-made yarn became available, weavers could focus their attention on increasingly complex and flamboyant designs. Furthermore, the expanded clientele, created by the arrival of the railroad, pressured weavers to adapt their designs to new tastes. The orientation of the weavings went from horizontal to vertical, and non-Indians began to use the weavings not as articles of clothing but as rugs and tapestries.

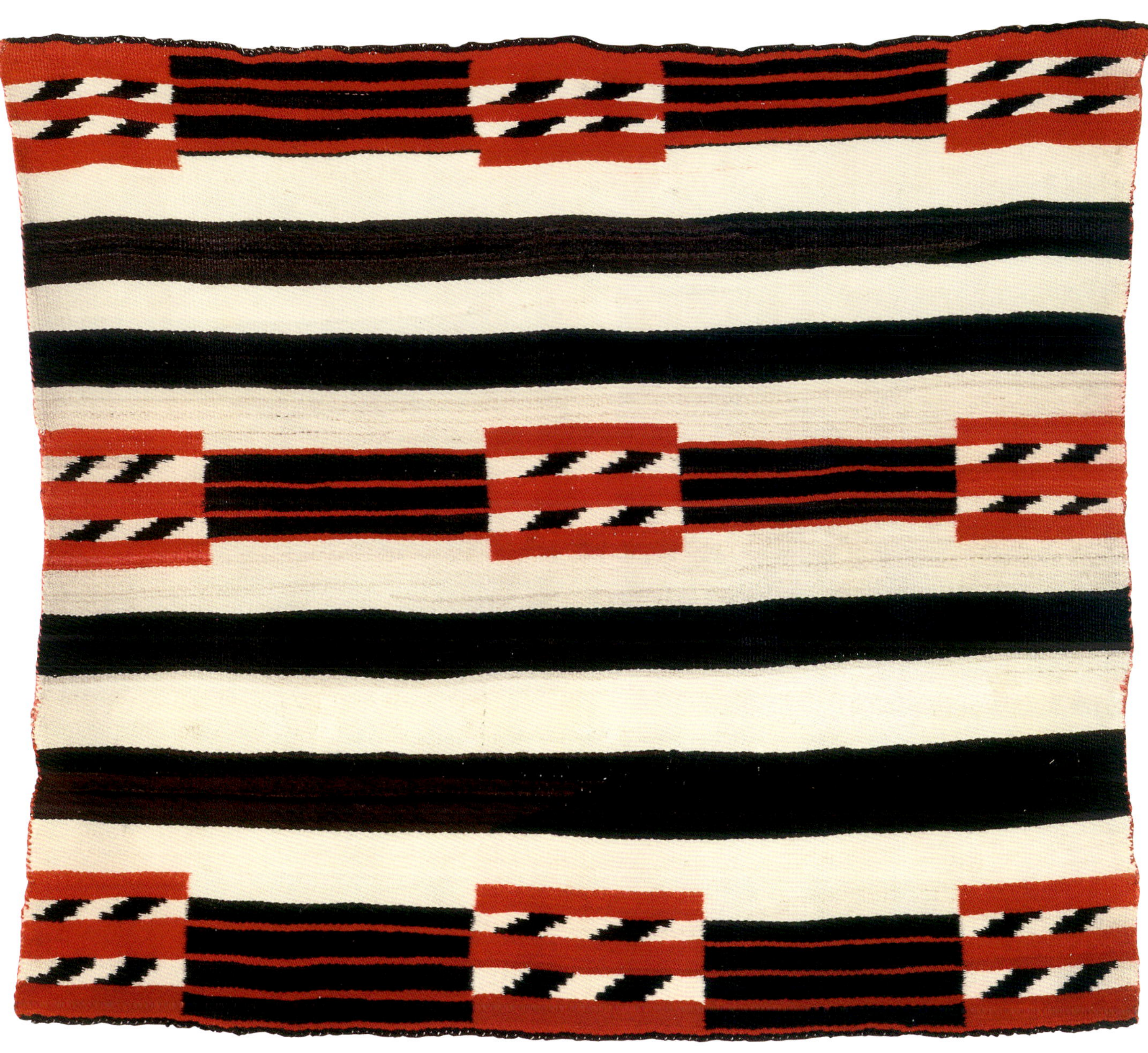

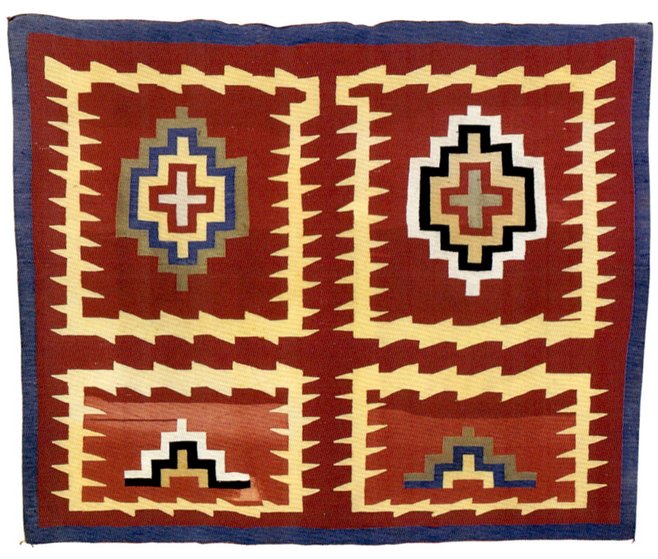

Unknown
Navajo
Blanket, c. 1870, wool, 55 × 68½ in. Gift of President and Mrs. David L. Boren, 2001

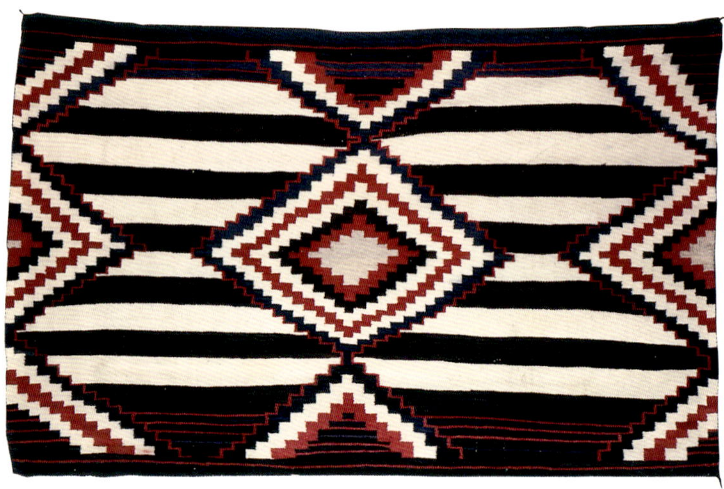

Unknown
Navajo
Third Phase Chief's Blanket, n.d., wool, 60 × 91½ in. Gift, R. E. Mansfield Collection, 2003

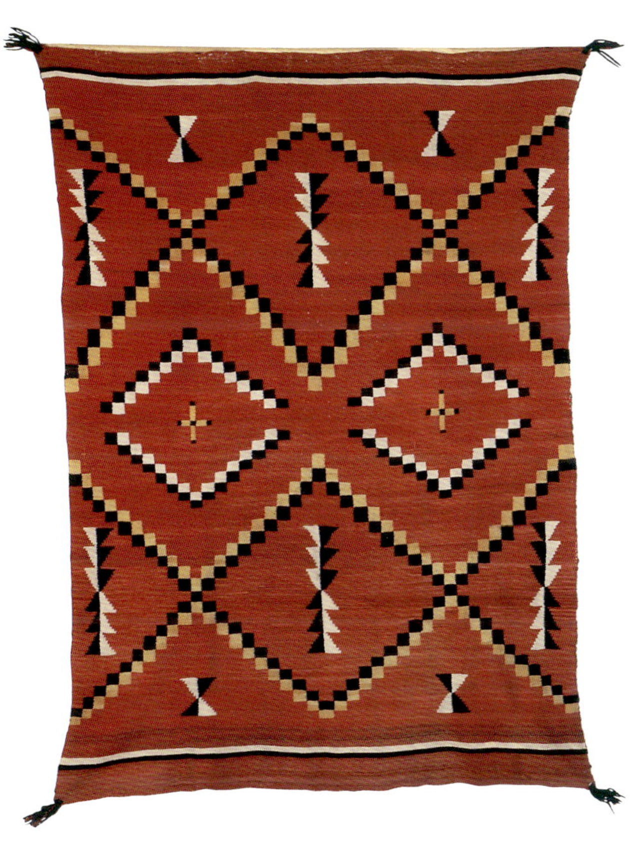

Unknown
Navajo
Man's Transitional Wearing Blanket, c. 1890, wool, 72 × 53 in. Gift, R. E. Mansfield Collection, 2003

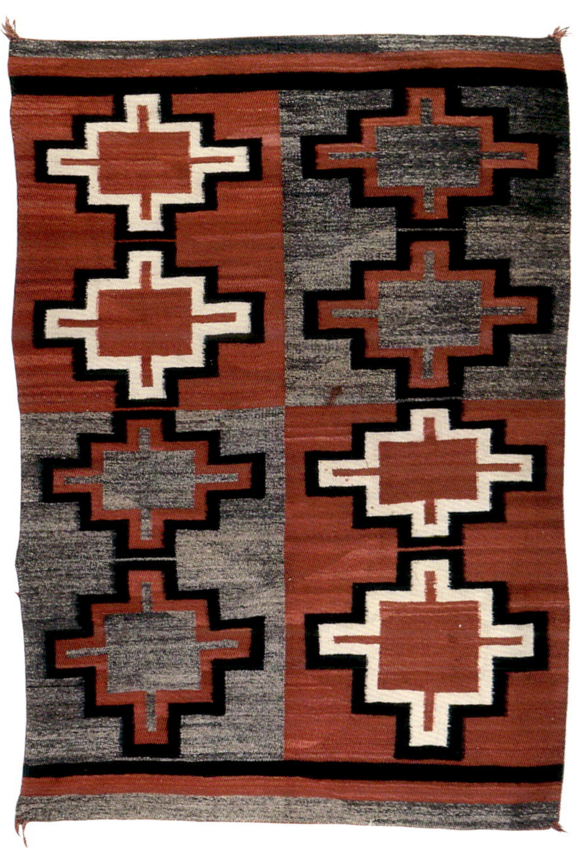

Unknown
Navajo
Blanket, n.d., wool, 72 × 56 in. Museum purchase, 1949

34 Unknown

Western Apache

Basket (Olla), 1890
Woven fibers
H. 12¾ in.
Purchase, Richard H. and Adeline J. Fleischaker Collection, 1996

Basketry dates back at least eight thousand years in North America. It is the best-known art form of the Apache Indians, a nomadic people forced onto reservations in the mid-nineteenth century.

The Western Apache inhabited the mountains of central Arizona and were organized into five subtribes. They relied on hunting and gathering as well as agriculture. They made little if any pottery; instead, they used baskets as serving dishes and for storing and transporting corn, seeds, and water. By the 1880s, the Western Apache were producing baskets for the Anglo trade.

Traditionally, only women wove Apache baskets. The weaver first selected the fibers, usually consisting of willow or cottonwood, for the basket's body. Then she prepared the fibers by debarking, scraping, and smoothing them to use as foundation rods. To make sewing splints, she split some of these rods into three thin strands. The weaver then formed the basket by coiling the sewing splints around the larger rods of warp. (The weft is what is visible on the basket, while the warp forms the underlying structure.) She coiled from right to left.

Against the basket's tan ground, the weaver made the decorative motifs using a prepared black fiber called "devil's claw." Devil's claw is hard, so in addition to the decorations, the weaver used it to reinforce the basket's rim and base, areas that would receive the most wear. A critical issue in the weaving was the relationship between the basket's three-dimensional form and its two-dimensional decoration.

Human figures, as seen on the featured *olla,* began to appear on Western Apache baskets in the mid-nineteenth century. Geometric forms predominate in Western Apache basketry, even in the depiction of animal and human figures. The vertical diamonds in the present work may be stylized representations of rattlesnakes.

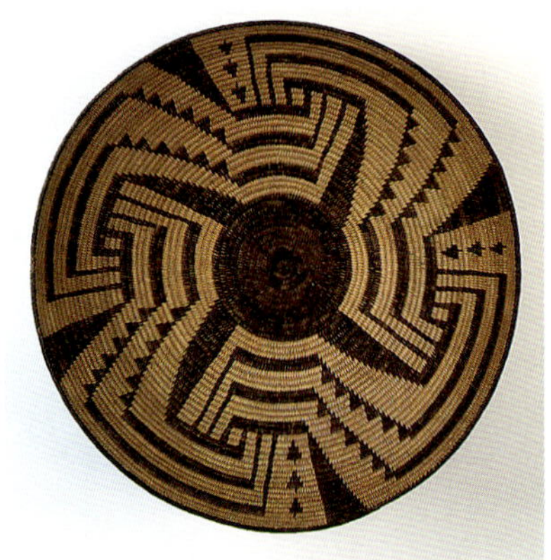

Unknown
Papago/Tohono O'odham
Basket Tray, c. 1910–20, grasses, yucca, and martynia, DIAM. 22 in. Purchase, Richard H. and Adeline J. Fleischaker Collection, 1996

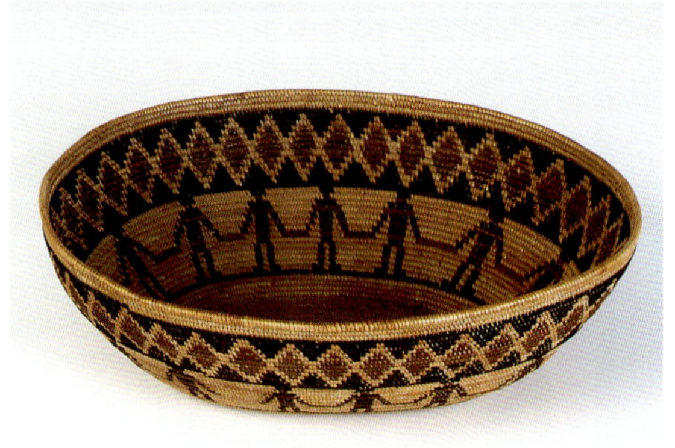

Unknown
Yokuts, California
Oval Basket, c. 1900–15, split willow rods, sedge root, bracken fern root, and redbud, 3½ × 10½ in. Purchase, Richard H. and Adeline J. Fleischaker Collection, 1996

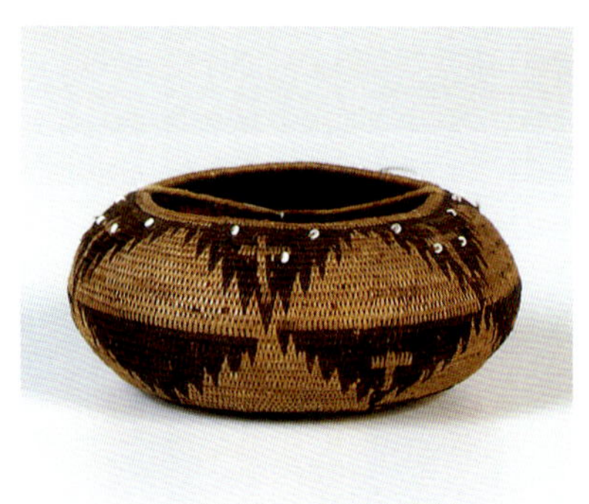

Unknown
Pomo, California
Miniature Basket, c. 1900, split rods, willow or wedge root, bracken fern root, and clamshell, DIAM. 3¾ in. Purchase, Richard H. and Adeline J. Fleischaker Collection, 1996

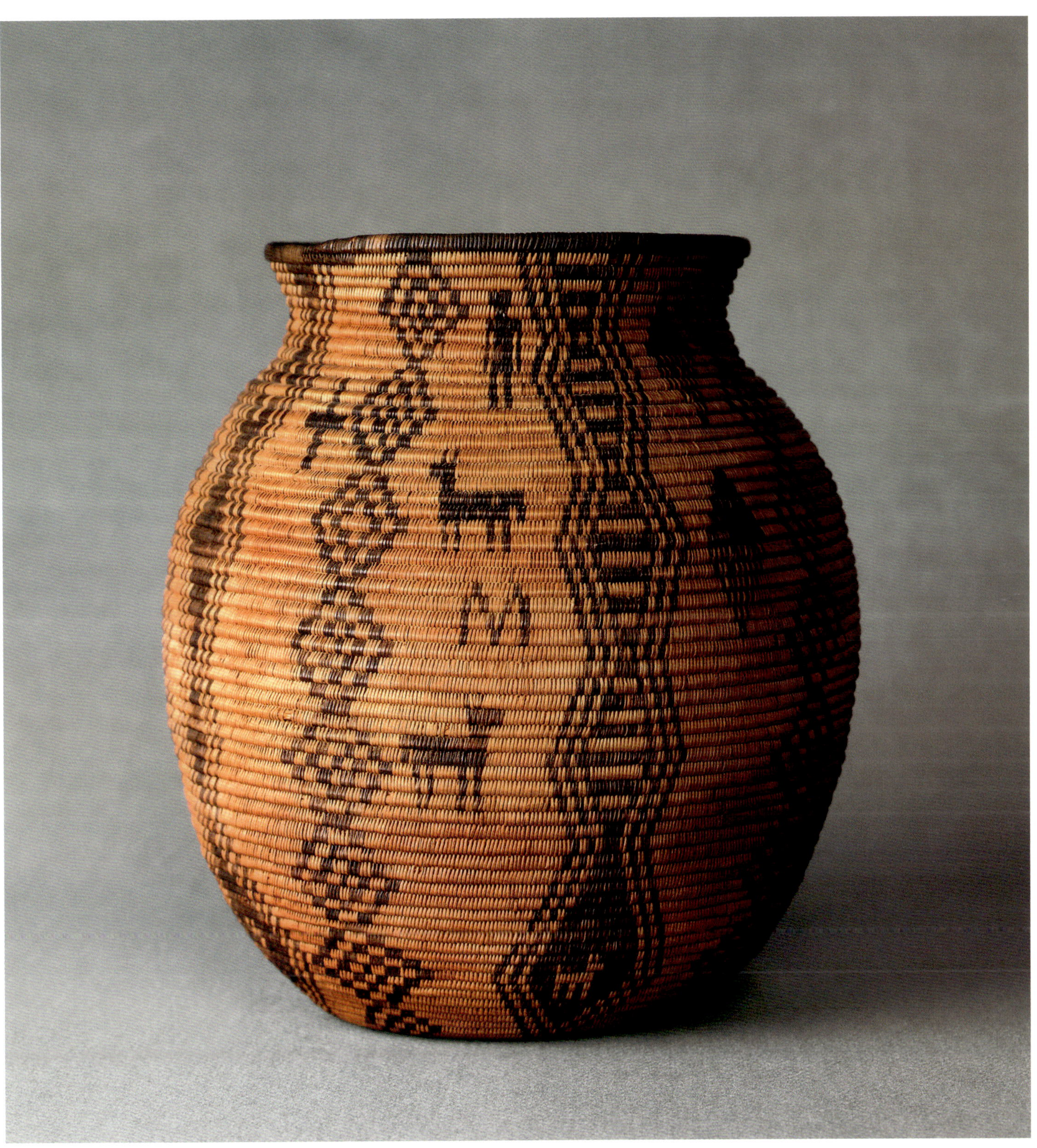

35 Henry Farny

U.S., b. France, 1847–1916

Suspense, 1890
Gouache on paper
14 × 10 in.
Purchase, Richard H. and Adeline J. Fleischaker Collection, 1996

Henry Farny was born in Ribeauville, France. He and his family immigrated to the United States in 1853, when Farny was six. They settled in western Pennsylvania, near an Indian reservation, where Farny was first introduced to American Indian life, which later became the primary subject of his art.

In 1859, Farny moved with his family to Cincinnati, where he apprenticed to a lithographer and worked as an illustrator for *Harper's,* before moving to New York in 1866 to continue working as an illustrator. From 1867 until 1870, he traveled through Europe, was a painter's assistant in Rome, and studied in Vienna and in Germany. He then returned to Cincinnati and resumed work as a commercial artist.

In 1881, Farny spent three months in the Dakota Territory sketching, taking photographs, and collecting American Indian artifacts. Back in Cincinnati, he used the materials that he had gathered in the West to paint American Indian subjects, especially the life of the Plains Indians, which would make him famous. A newspaper reporter wrote in 1881—before Frederic Remington and Charles M. Russell were known as artists—that Farny had "struck an artistic bonanza" with his Indian subjects, adding, "[Farny] draws Indians, he paints Indians, he sleeps with an Indian tomahawk near him, he lays greatest store by his Indian necklaces and Indian pipe, he talks Indian and he dreams of Indian warfare." After the trip to the Dakotas, Farny himself stated, "The plains, the buttes, the whole country and its people, are fuller of material for the artist than any country in Europe."

By 1893, Farny was able to give up illustration work to devote himself completely to painting. He traveled to the West at other times, but worked primarily from his studio in Cincinnati, where he would become the founder and director of the Cincinnati Art Students League.

Although he also painted larger oils, Farny is best known for his detailed, small-format paintings in gouache, such as *Suspense.* He attempted to depict American Indians in a realistic, unromanticized manner, although his paintings sometimes convey nostalgia for a vanishing way of life.

Suspense captures a dramatic moment. An American Indian holds a rifle and hides behind a rock, perhaps in ambush, while a white man on horseback, also carrying a rifle but as yet unaware of the Indian's presence, travels in his direction.

The painting could be said to represent the confrontation of American Indian and European cultures. Ironically, the Indian's gun, which visually serves to direct one's eye from the Indian to the man on horseback, is a product of white civilization.

Below Farny's signature in the painting's lower-right corner is his emblem of a dot inside a circle, which the artist inscribed on all his works after his 1881 trip to the Dakotas. The emblem represents "Wasitcha" (white face-maker chief), a name reputedly given to Farny by the Sioux tribe.

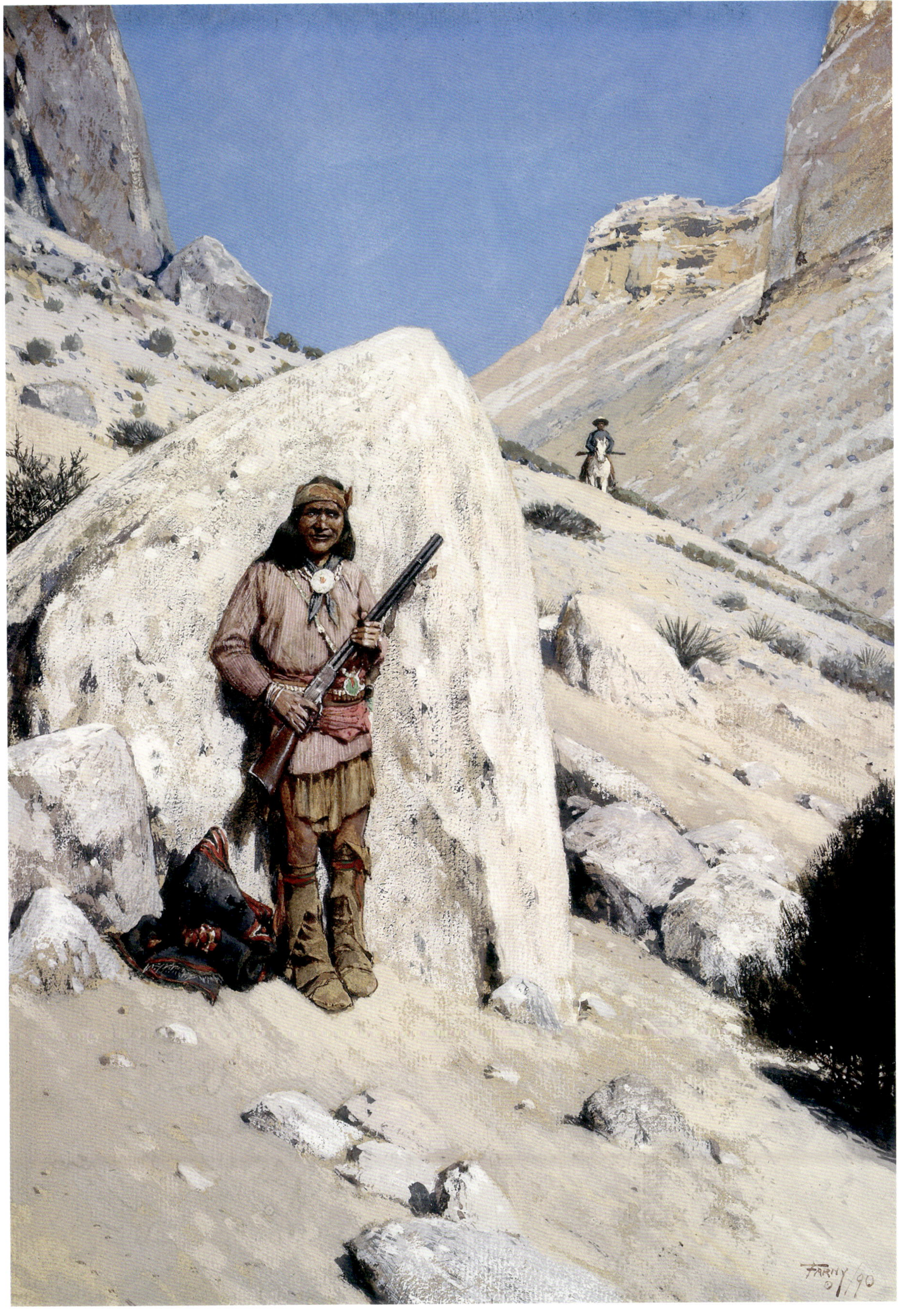
FARNY

36 Charles Schreyvogel

U.S., 1861–1912

Sioux Attacking a Stagecoach, 1909
Oil on board
4⅞ × 11⅞ in.
Purchase, Richard H. and Adeline J. Fleischaker Collection, 1996

Charles Schreyvogel became known for his images of the Indian wars that lasted from the 1860s through the Wounded Knee Massacre of 1890. He painted a heroic Wild West that had already passed, depicting soldiers and cavalrymen as heroes and Indians as stereotypes of violent savages. He portrayed the Sioux in particular as warlike inhabitants of the Northern Plains who resisted white settlement of their territories.

The son of German immigrants, Charles Schreyvogel was born in New York. After training in Munich and Düsseldorf, Germany, from 1887 through 1890, Schreyvogel returned to the United States, where the Wild West shows of "Buffalo Bill" Cody inspired him to paint Wild West subjects. Buffalo Bill himself encouraged the artist, and the show manager permitted Schreyvogel to sketch the cowboy and Indian performers.

Schreyvogel first traveled to the West in 1893, to the Ute reservation in southwestern Colorado. He afterward made frequent trips west to collect material for carefully researched paintings produced in his studio in Hoboken, New Jersey, across the river from Manhattan. When Schreyvogel met Theodore Roosevelt at the White House, the president granted him permission to visit any Indian reservation or military camp in the United States.

Schreyvogel exhibited a Western painting in 1900 in New York, at the National Academy of Design, where the picture won an award. His Western works remained highly acclaimed until his death.

In *Sioux Attacking a Stagecoach,* the stagecoach and Indians on horseback race across the plains, with the Rocky Mountains in the distance. The painting's horizontal format emphasizes the left-to-right movement, creating a cinematic effect. Indeed, the painting resembles a still from a Western film. As with most of his works, Schreyvogel composed his picture to maximize the drama.

Schreyvogel's output was limited, and his paintings are usually large. Although *Sioux Attacking a Stagecoach* is small, it packs all the action and excitement of the larger-scale works.

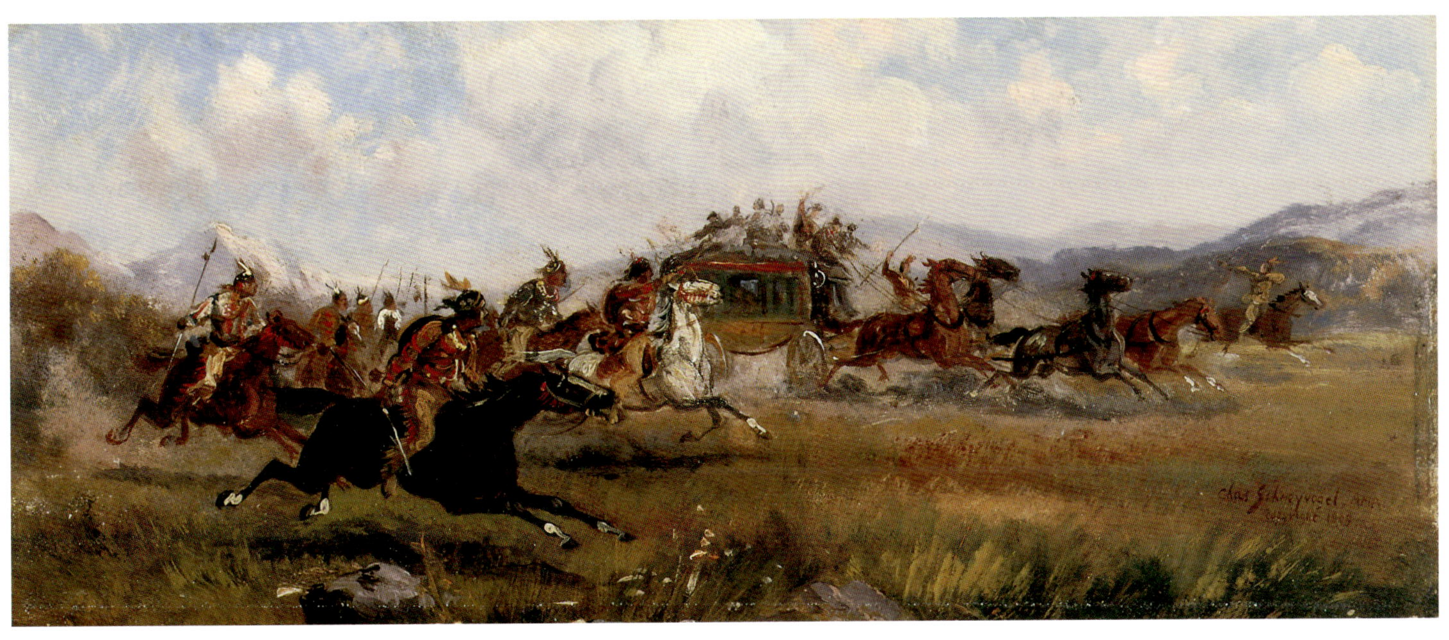

37 William Robinson Leigh

U.S., 1866–1955

Lullaby, 1918
Oil on canvas
28 × 22 in.
Purchase, Richard H. and Adeline J. Fleischaker Collection, 1996

William Robinson Leigh was a contemporary of Frederic Remington (1861–1909) and Charles M. Russell (1864–1926), although he substantially outlived them both. Best known for his paintings of American Indians, cowboys in the Old West, and Western landscapes such as the Grand Canyon, Leigh, like Russell, often depicted Indians as a great but vanishing people.

Born in Berkeley County, West Virginia, to a family ruined by the Civil War, Leigh showed an interest in art from childhood. His parents sent him to live with relatives in Baltimore when he was fourteen so that he could study at the Maryland Institute of Art. In 1883, with the support of wealthy relatives, Leigh traveled to Germany to study at the Royal Academy in Munich. When he returned to the United States at age thirty, he lived for a decade in New York, where he became an illustrator of books and magazines such as *Harper's, Scribner's,* and *Collier's.*

Leigh's lifelong relationship with the Southwest started in 1906, when the Southern Pacific Railroad commissioned him to paint Western landscapes and sent him to the Grand Canyon and New Mexico to paint the Zuni and Laguna Pueblos. Of this first trip to New Mexico, Leigh later wrote: "My entire horizon had now been revamped. . . . My field was the frontier West. From now on I knew I must return as often to that field as possible." Although he always maintained his New York studio, he henceforth spent his summers on painting trips, usually in the Southwest, but also occasionally in Wyoming.

In his autobiography, Leigh ascribed his love of Western subjects to a love of animals and the outdoors, a fascination with American Indians, and a belief that the West was the true America. (He also took pride in believing that he descended from the Indian princess Pocahontas, the alleged savior of Jamestown's Captain John Smith.)

Leigh created his paintings in the studio. First he would develop ideas for a painting with a series of drawings, until the final composition took shape in a master drawing. He would then reproduce this drawing in charcoal on a canvas. After fixing the charcoal so that it would not smear, he would paint directly over the charcoal. His style was conservative in an age of great experimentation in art, and he obsessively, perhaps even self-defensively, attacked Modernism as decadent.

In *Lullaby,* an Indian mother seated by a fire holds a cradleboard, as the Virgin might hold the Christ child in a traditional Nativity. The reflected firelight places emphasis on the cradleboard holding the infant, who is the promise for the future in this quiet, contemplative painting.

The Kiowa-style cradleboard shown in *Lullaby* was part of Leigh's studio collection of objects and is now at the Gilcrease Museum in Tulsa, Oklahoma. The Gilcrease owns the largest collection of this prolific artist's work, as well as the contents of Leigh's New York studio on the day he died.

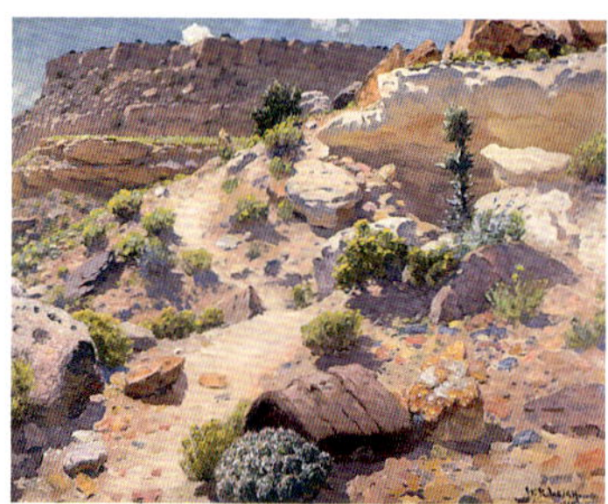

William Robinson Leigh
U.S., 1866–1955
The Crane Ranger Station, 1915, oil on canvas board, 13⅛ × 17 in. Purchase, Richard H. and Adeline J. Fleischaker Collection, 1996

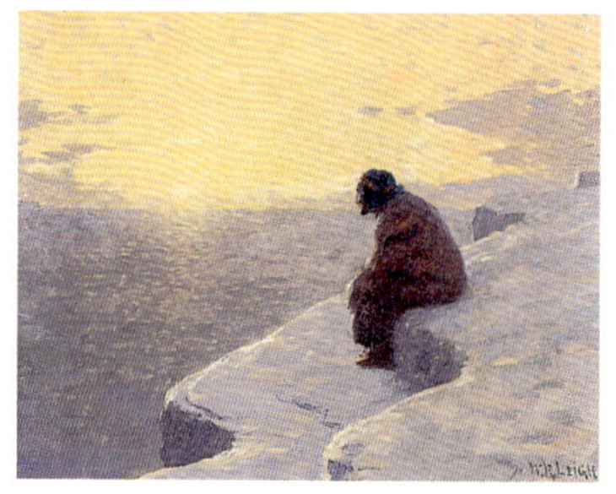

William Robinson Leigh
U.S., 1866–1955
The Vision Seeker, 1912, oil on canvas board, 8 × 10 in. Purchase, Richard H. and Adeline J. Fleischaker Collection, 1996

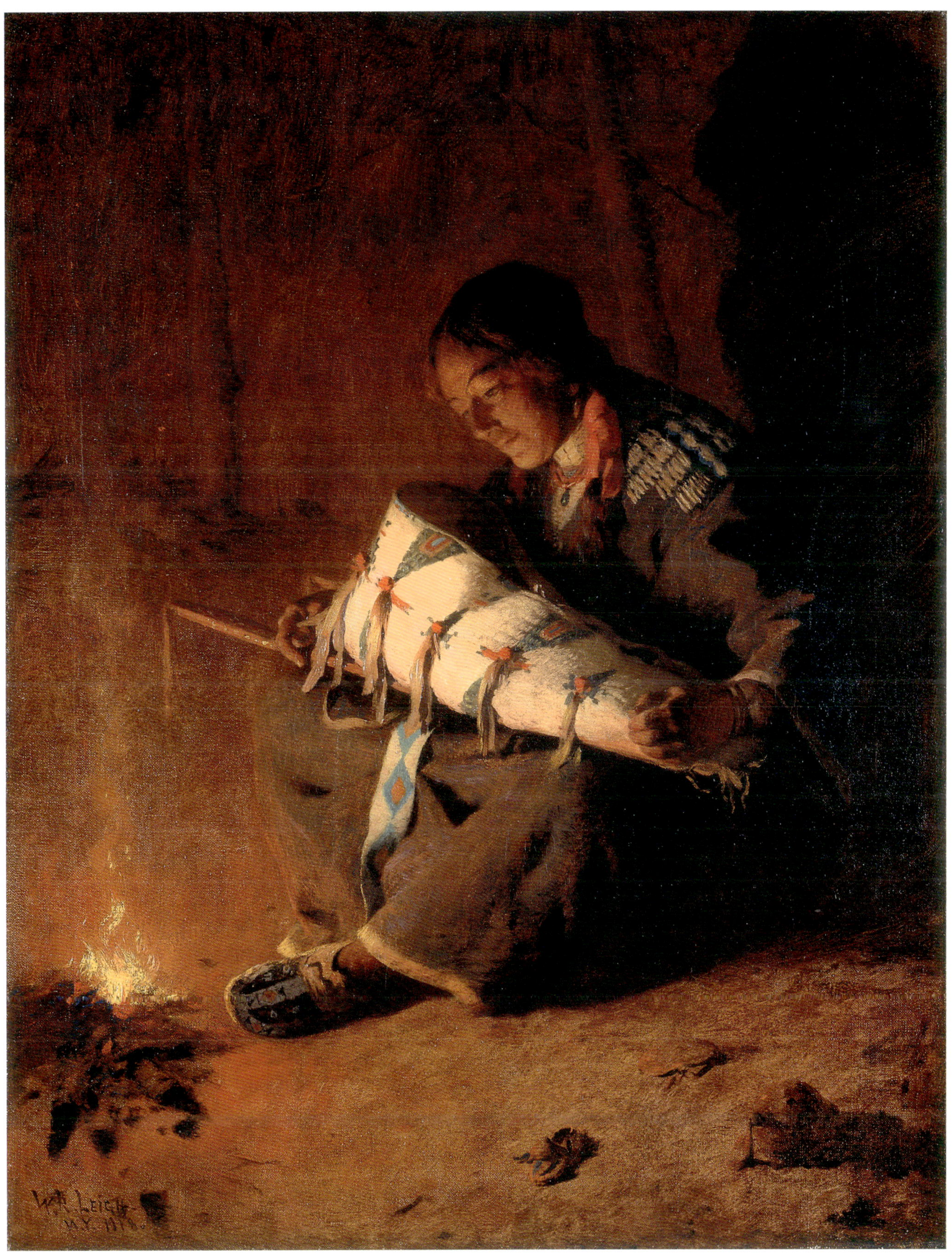

38 Joseph Henry Sharp

U.S., 1859–1953

Hunting Son, 1926
Oil on canvas
16 × 20 in.
Purchase, Richard H. and Adeline J. Fleischaker Collection, 1996

Joseph Henry Sharp was the oldest member of the Taos Society of Artists and the first to travel to Taos, where he spent part of the summer of 1893 making sketches for an illustration for *Harper's.* Taos greatly impressed Sharp, and in 1895, when he went to Paris to attend the Académie Julian, his enthusiastic stories about New Mexico encouraged fellow Americans and future Taos artists Ernest L. Blumenschein, Bert Geer Phillips, and E. Irving Couse to visit Taos also. Back in the United States in 1896, Sharp taught at the Cincinnati Art Academy and spent summers in Taos and cold winters among Montana's Northern Plains Indians, whose lifestyle he feared would disappear more quickly than that of the Southwestern Pueblo Indians. The artist established permanent residence in Taos in 1912.

Born in Bridgeport, Ohio, Sharp had a swimming accident as a child, which led to his eventual deafness. He attended Cincinnati's McMicken School of Design and the Cincinnati Art Academy before traveling to Europe in 1881 to study painting in Antwerp. In 1883, on the recommendation of fellow Cincinnati artist Henry Farny, Sharp traveled through the American Northwest and Southwest (although not Taos), painting American Indians. Sharp then returned to Europe, working in the Munich studio of Carl Marr and traveling with Cincinnati painter Frank Duveneck to Italy and Spain, where Sharp copied works by Diego Velázquez and Francisco Goya, who remained lasting inspirations. (*Hunting Son*'s somber tone, offset by the model's purple and green dress, may be said to reflect this Spanish influence.)

Although he also painted landscapes, Sharp's primary subjects were American Indians. In an interview, he discussed his lifelong fascination:

> *I was always interested, even as a small boy. I guess it was Fenimore Cooper who first attracted me to the Indian. It was the romance of youth, of boyhood I suppose. But boys always did like Indians. When I came to know them I liked them for themselves. Perhaps they attracted me as subjects to paint because of their important historical value as first Americans. . . . Then the color of their costumes and dances, this no less attracted me. Their color is glorious and so belongs to them and to their country.*

The other Taos artists called Sharp "The Anthropologist" because of his concern for accuracy in his portrayal of Indians and his belief that he was recording a disappearing culture. In 1902, Phoebe Hearst, the mother of William Randolph, bought eighty of Sharp's Indian portraits, not for an art museum but for the Museum of Anthropology at the University of California, Berkeley. This gave Sharp the financial freedom to leave his teaching post in Cincinnati to devote himself full-time to painting.

Sharp's first Southwestern model was Soaring Eagle, with whom Sharp became close friends. Soaring Eagle was a great hunter who trained his son, John Gomez, to become an equally talented hunter.

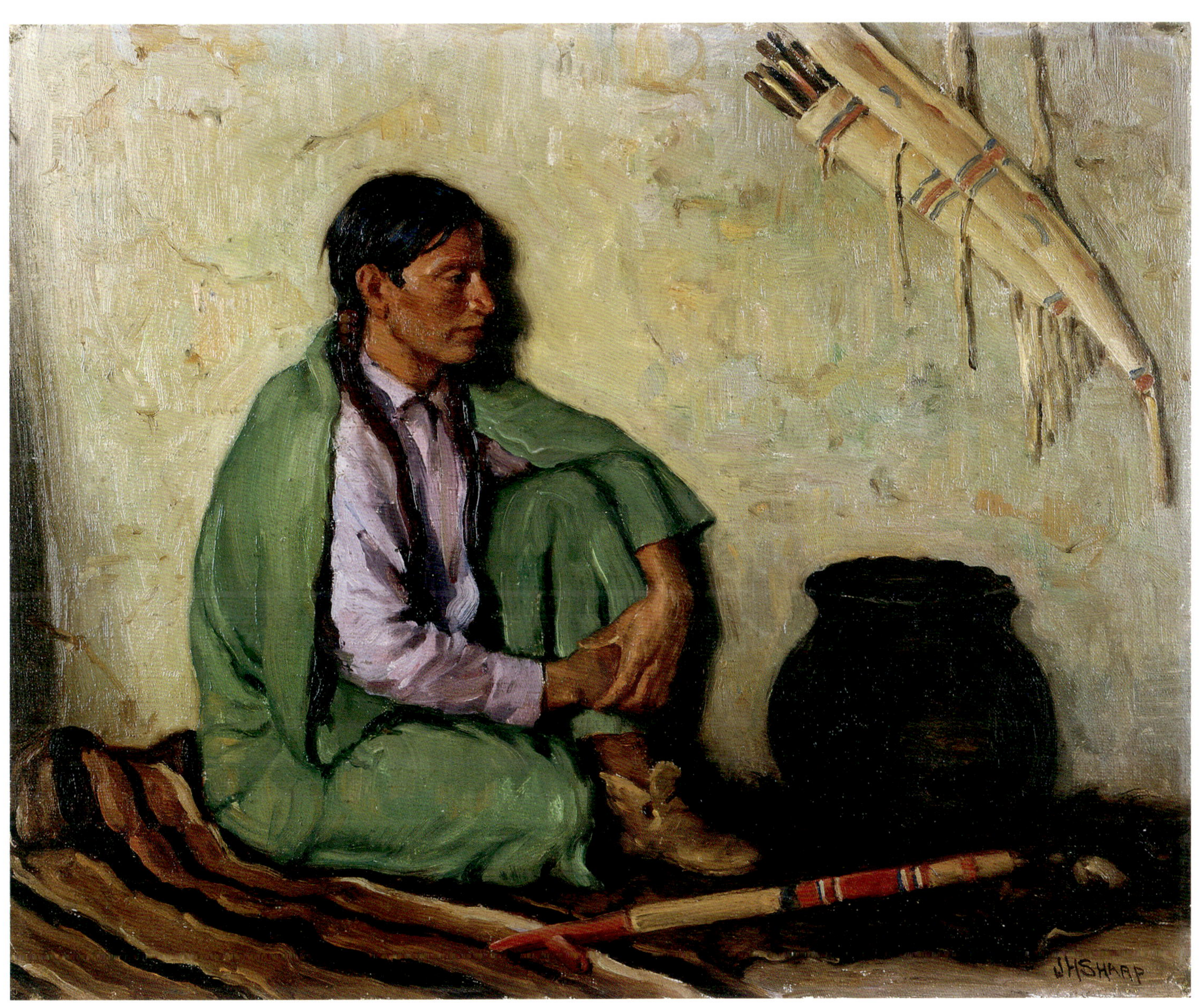
JHSHARP

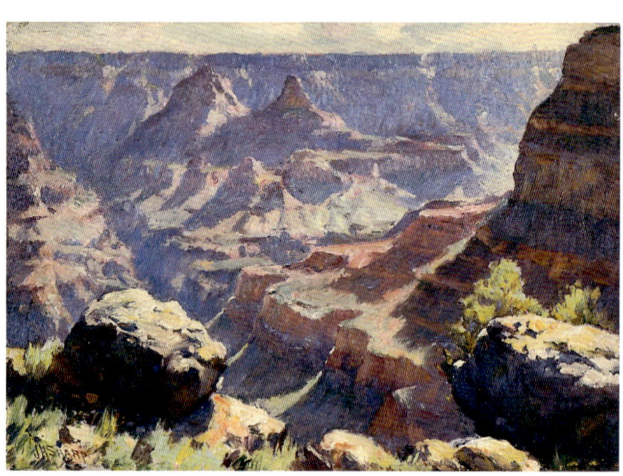

Joseph Henry Sharp
U.S., 1859–1953
Grand Canyon, n.d., oil on canvas, 10 × 14 in. Purchase, Richard H. and Adeline J. Fleischaker Collection, 1996

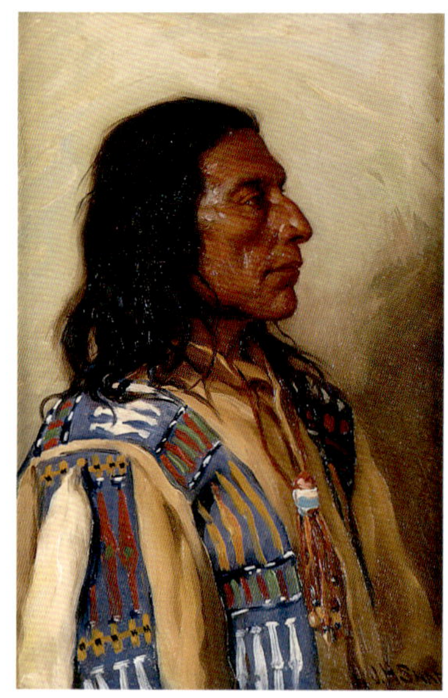

Joseph Henry Sharp
U.S., 1859–1953
Fine Bull, n.d., oil on canvas, 28 × 22¼ in. Gift of William H. Thams in memory of Roxanne P. Thams, 2003

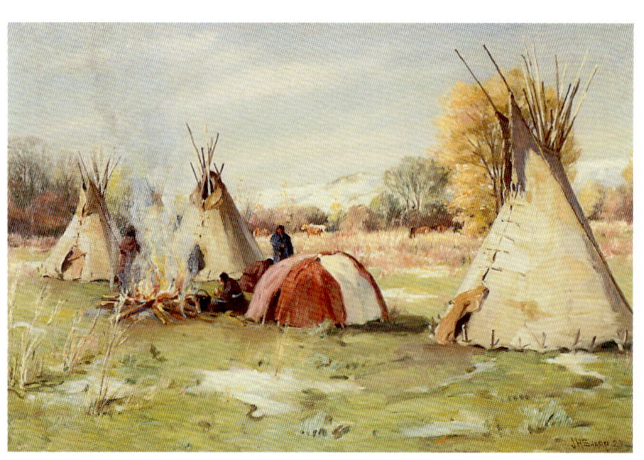

Joseph Henry Sharp
U.S., 1859–1953
Crow Reservation—Teepees and Indians (Sweat Lodge), 1920, oil on canvas, 20 × 30 in. Gift, Priscilla C. and Joseph N. Tate Collection, 2004

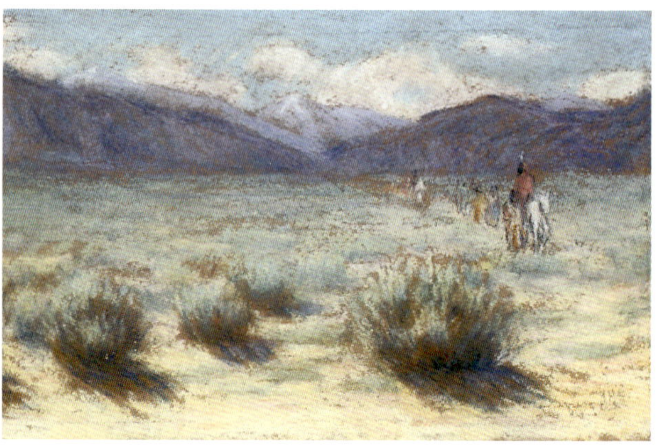

Joseph Henry Sharp
U.S., 1859–1953
Indians on Horses, n.d., pastel on paper, 4¼ × 6½ in. Purchase, Richard H. and Adeline J. Fleischaker Collection, 1996

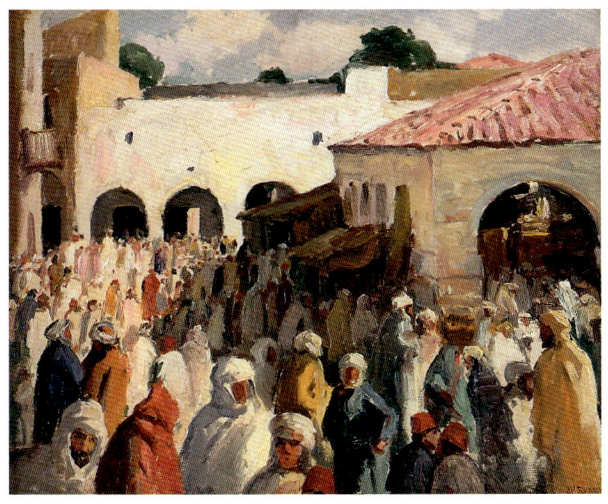

Joseph Henry Sharp
U.S., 1859–1953
Sidi-bou-Said (Tunisia), n.d., oil on masonite, 16 × 20 in. Gift of William H. Thams in memory of Roxanne P. Thams, 2003

Gomez became known as Hunting Son (Chúyah). Like his father, Hunting Son was one of Sharp's favorite models.

In the museum's painting, Hunting Son poses in Sharp's studio, surrounded by props chosen from the artist's extensive collection of American Indian artifacts, which was acquired in the 1950s by the artist's last major patron, Thomas Gilcrease of Tulsa. A shadow cast by firelight accentuates the seated figure and establishes the spatial relationship of Hunting Son to the studio wall. (Sharp built this studio, surrounded by a garden, behind the adobe home he purchased in 1909. The house included a former *morada,* or chapel, that had once belonged to a Penitente sect of flagellants, whose rites, it was said, had left permanent bloodstains on the adobe's interior.)

Sharp's first wife died in 1913, and he married her sister two years later. From the 1920s on, they divided their time between Taos and a winter home in Pasadena, California, with much travel, including a North African trip that resulted in a Tunisian painting in the museum's Thams Collection.

Throughout his career, Sharp remained true to his academic training. Although he lived through the emergence of Abstract Expressionism, his art was untouched by Modernism.

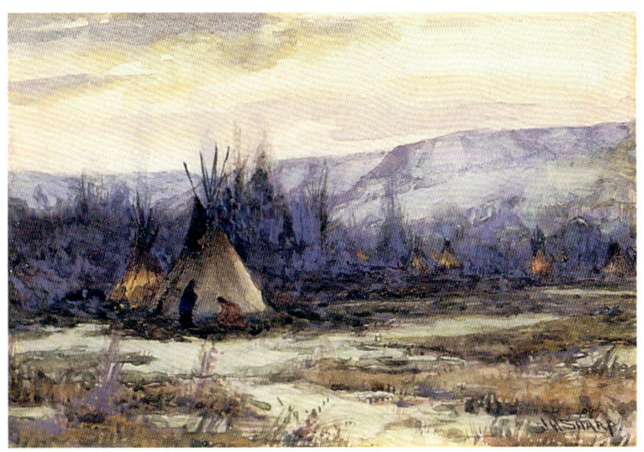

Joseph Henry Sharp
U.S., 1859–1953
Teepees at Dusk, n.d., watercolor on paper, 7 × 10½ in. Purchase, Richard H. and Adeline J. Fleischaker Collection, 1996

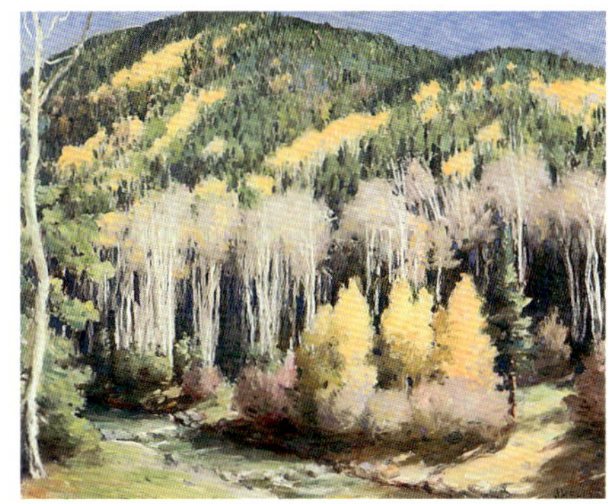

Joseph Henry Sharp
U.S., 1859–1953
Aspens–Hondo Canyon–Falling Leaves, 1941, oil on canvas, 16 × 20 in. Purchase, Richard H. and Adeline J. Fleischaker Collection, 1996

39 Ernest L. Blumenschein

U.S., 1874–1960

Haystack, Taos, before 1927
Oil on canvas
24 × 27 in.
Gift of William H. Thams in memory of Roxanne P. Thams, 2003

Ernest L. Blumenschein, or "Blumy," as he was often called, was born in Pittsburgh and raised in Dayton, Ohio, the son of a German musician father and an American mother with New England roots. The young Blumenschein played the violin and won a scholarship to the Cincinnati Conservatory of Music, but after a year, he decided to pursue his interest in art, studying at the Cincinnati Art Academy, at the Art Students League in New York, and from 1895 until 1896 at the Académie Julian in Paris. There he met fellow students Bert Geer Phillips and Joseph Henry Sharp. Sharp told Blumenschein and Phillips about the extraordinary town and environs of Taos, which he had visited in 1893. So it might be said that the Taos art colony originated in Paris.

When Blumenschein and Phillips returned to the United States, they shared a studio in New York. Two years later, they took a train to Denver, where they bought a wagon and horse with the idea of traveling south into Mexico, painting along the way. In what has become a legendary story, a wagon wheel broke when the artists were about twenty miles north of Taos. After a coin toss, it was decided that Blumenschein would make the journey to Taos, carrying the broken wheel to the nearest blacksmith for repairs, while Phillips remained behind to guard the wagon. Although Blumenschein's back ached from the heavy wheel, he was overwhelmed by the scenery of Taos. Years later, he recalled how he felt and what he saw, in words that could describe his painting *Haystack, Taos:*

> *At four p.m. on the third of September, 1898, I started down the mountain on what resulted in the most impressive journey of my life. . . .*
>
> *Vividly I recall the discomfort of lugging that unwieldy load with no relief in sight, no wagon going my way, no hope to ease sore muscles until I reached Taos, the dim picture of which I had made in imagination from Sharp's slight description.*
>
> *But Sharp had not painted for me the land or the mountains and plains and clouds. No artist had ever recorded the New Mexico I was seeing. No writer had ever written down the smell of this air or the feel of that morning's sky. I was receiving under rather painful circumstances, the first great unforgettable inspiration of my life. . . .*
>
> *The morning was sparkling and stimulating. The beautiful Sangre de Cristo range to my left was quite different in character from the Colorado mountains. . . . The sky was a clear, clean blue with sharp moving clouds. The color, the effective character of the landscape, the drama of the vast spaces, the superb beauty and serenity of the hills, stirred me deeply.*
>
> *I realized I was getting my own impressions from nature, seeing it for the first time with my own eyes, uninfluenced by the art of any man. Notwithstanding the painful handicap of the broken wheel I was carrying, New Mexico inspired me to a profound degree.*

By the time Blumenschein returned to the wagon, after a journey of two days and three nights, Phillips, too, was enchanted by northern New Mexico, and the two decided to stay in Taos. Blumenschein returned to New York a few months later, but Phillips remained, becoming

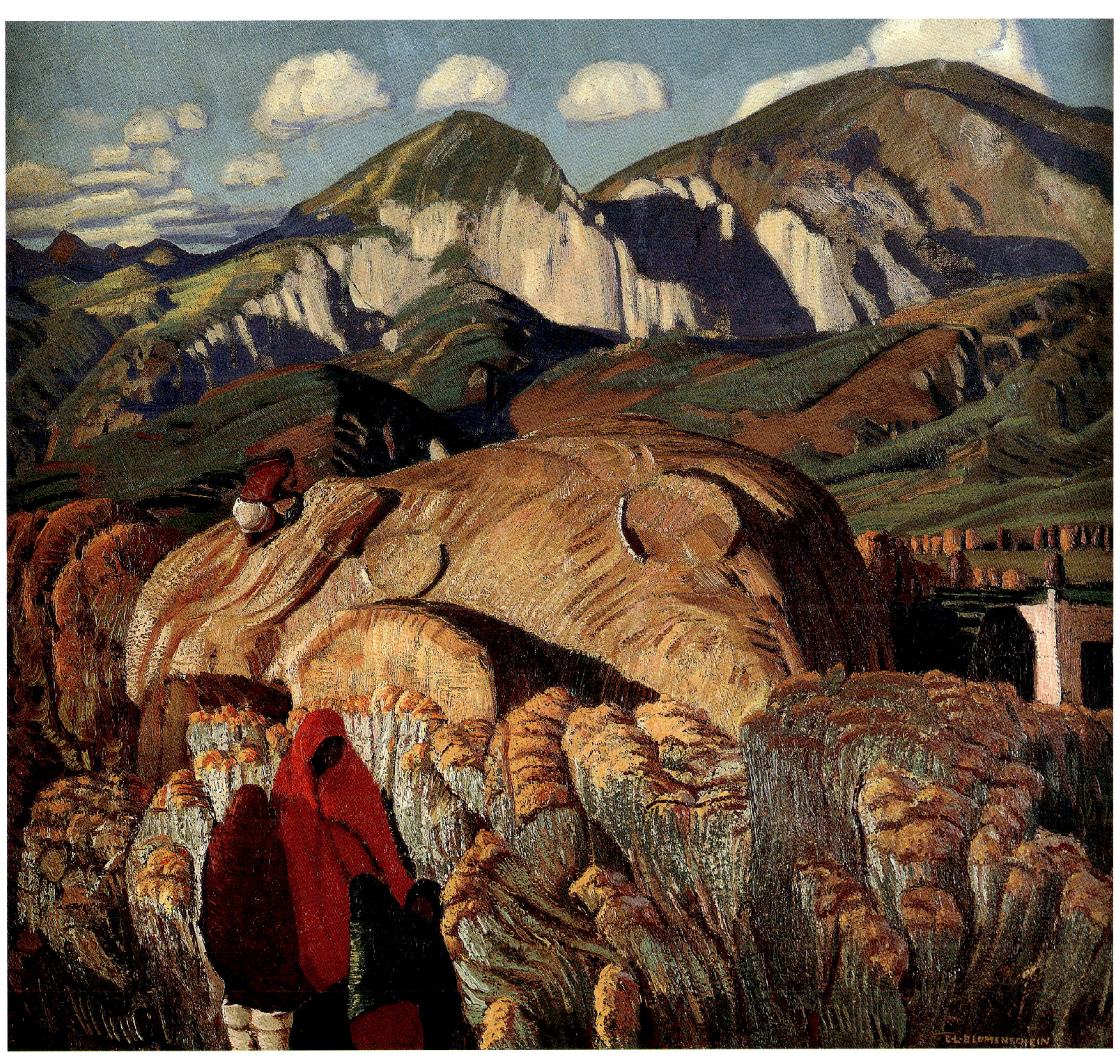
E.L. BLUMENSCHEIN

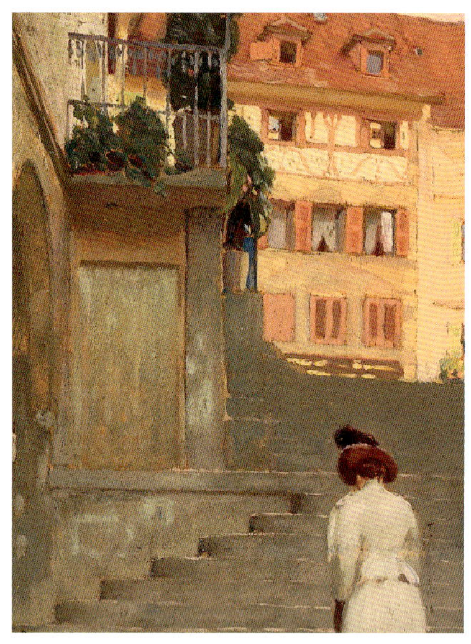

Ernest L. Blumenschein
U.S., 1874–1960
Paris Apartment, 1906–9, oil on panel, 10 × 8 in. Purchase, Richard H. and Adeline J. Fleischaker Collection, 1996

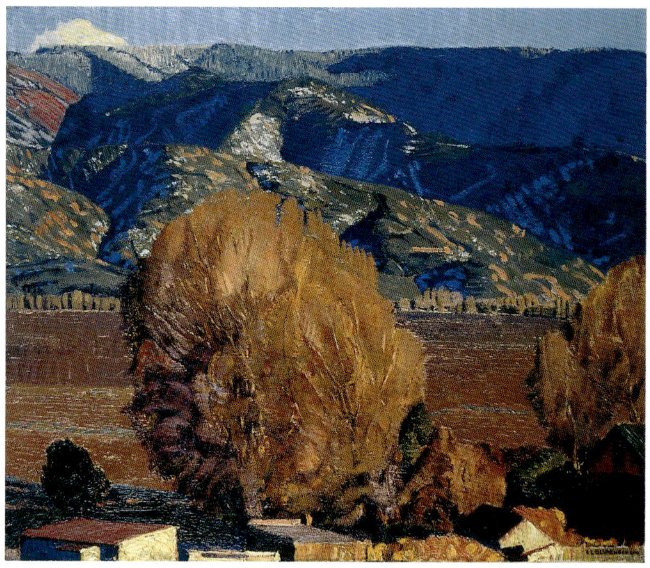

Ernest L. Blumenschein
U.S., 1874–1960
Taos Valley and Mountain, n.d., oil on canvas, 22 × 26 in. Purchase, Richard H. and Adeline J. Fleischaker Collection, 1996

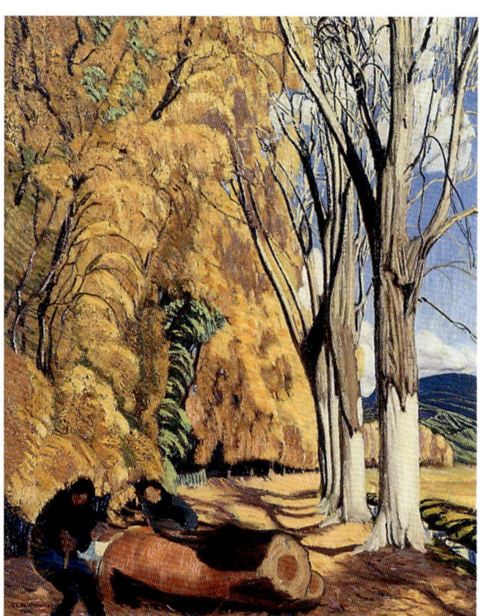

Ernest L. Blumenschein
U.S., 1874–1960
Yellow Cottonwoods, n.d., oil on canvas, 24 × 30 in. Gift, Priscilla C. and Joseph N. Tate Collection, 2004

the first permanent resident of Taos among those who would form the Taos Society of Artists in 1915.

In 1899, Blumenschein traveled again to Paris, where he remained until 1909, and where he married Mary Shepard Greene, who was a successful American artist living in Paris and at the time better known than he. A painting in the Fleischaker Collection depicts their apartment.

From 1910 through 1918, the couple and their young daughter spent summers in Taos and the rest of the year in New York, where Blumenschein taught at the Art Students League and worked as a commercial artist, producing illustrations for magazines such as *Scribner's* and *Harper's* and for books by, among others, Willa Cather, Joseph Conrad, Stephen Crane, and Jack London. After moving permanently to Taos in 1919, Blumenschein abandoned illustration work to focus exclusively on fine art, a change in direction made possible by the financial freedom derived from his wife's inheritance.

Although his solid academic education always remained the bedrock of his art, Blumenschein was interested in recent developments such as Post-Impressionism and was sympathetic to Modernism. He compared painting to music, with color likened to rhythm.

Blumenschein's typical working method involved making quick memory sketches to remind him of his original response to a subject. He would transfer the sketches to canvas, which he would sometimes work on for several months, even repainting the canvases after they had been exhibited.

An owner of *Haystack, Taos* wrote that the original owner, Mrs. K. F. Moore, had said that Blumenschein had given her the painting for teaching him to play bridge. *Haystack, Taos* captures an autumn harvest and the undulations of the Sangre de Cristo Mountains to the northwest of Taos. It is one of Blumenschein's finest landscapes.

40 Bert Geer Phillips

U.S., 1868–1956

Nar-Ah-Kig-Gee-Ah Tzur (Kit Carson's Apache Scout), c. 1900–1910
Oil on canvas
19 × 15 in.
Gift of William H. Thams in memory of Roxanne P. Thams, 2003

Like many painters of American Indian subjects, Bert Geer Phillips became interested in Indians when, as a boy, he read the frontier novels of James Fenimore Cooper. Phillips grew up in upstate New York, not far from the sites of Mohican battlegrounds. He studied art in New York City at the Art Students League and the National Academy of Design. After five years as an artist and illustrator in New York, he spent seven months in England and then traveled to Paris in 1895 to study at the Académie Julian, where Joseph Henry Sharp regaled Phillips and Ernest L. Blumenschein with recollections of a trip to Taos. Phillips eventually settled in Taos in 1898. (The famous broken wagon wheel story that prompted Phillips and Blumenschein to visit Taos is recounted in cat. no. 39.) In 1915, Phillips was a founding member of the Taos Society of Artists.

Phillips maintained close personal ties to the Indians of the Taos Pueblo. In his early years in New Mexico, he painted a number of Indian portraits, including *Nar-Ah-Kig-Gee-Ah Tzur.* In his portraits of Indians, Phillips depicted his sitters frontally, with directness, emphasizing their individuality and dignity. Initially, Phillips had trouble getting the Indians to pose, because they believed that capturing their images in portraits would weaken them, causing sickness or even death. Gradually, as the artist earned their trust, the Indians overcame these notions, and he often painted them in their homes.

In *Nar-Ah-Kig-Gee-Ah Tzur,* the sitter's folded arms create a stable base for the image; this composition ultimately derives from Renaissance prototypes, such as Leonardo da Vinci's *Mona Lisa.*

Phillips wrote that Nar-Ah-Kig-Gee-Ah Tzur was "an old Apache nearly ninety, who had been a scout under Kit Carson, [and who] could hold a pose longer than I could work at one time. I had to make him rest to get myself rested." In a letter to Blumenschein, Phillips noted that Nar-Ah-Kig-Gee-Ah Tzur, "meaning 'less two' got the name when a young buck . . . at a battle between the Apaches & Comanches in which the [Apaches] . . . killed all but two of their enemies."

The connection of the sitter to Kit Carson (1809–68) must have delighted Phillips, whose childhood hero had been this mythic Western figure who had made Taos his headquarters and who was buried there. When the U.S. government established a national forest in the mountains around Taos, it was Phillips who suggested the name: the Kit Carson National Forest. (For four years, Phillips served as the forest's first ranger.)

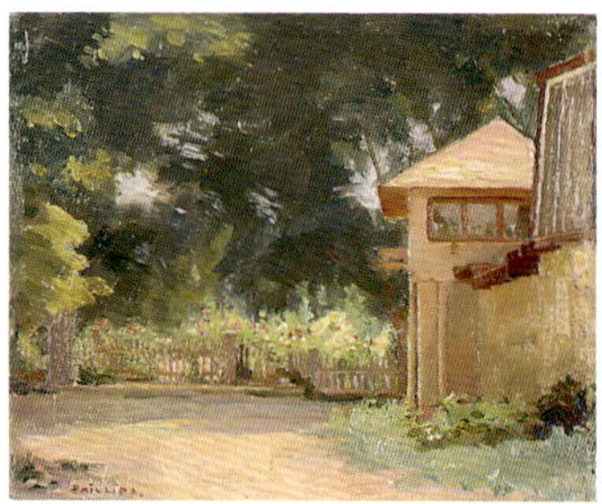

Bert Geer Phillips
U.S., 1868–1956
Back of Phillips's Studio in Taos, n.d., oil on artist board, 8 × 10 in. Purchase, Richard H. and Adeline J. Fleischaker Collection, 1996

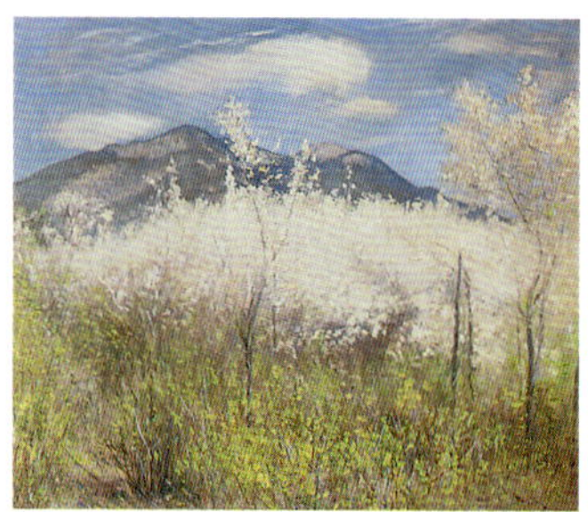

Bert Geer Phillips
U.S., 1868–1956
Wild Plum Blossoms, n.d., oil on board, 25 × 30 in. Gift, Priscilla C. and Joseph N. Tate Collection, 2004

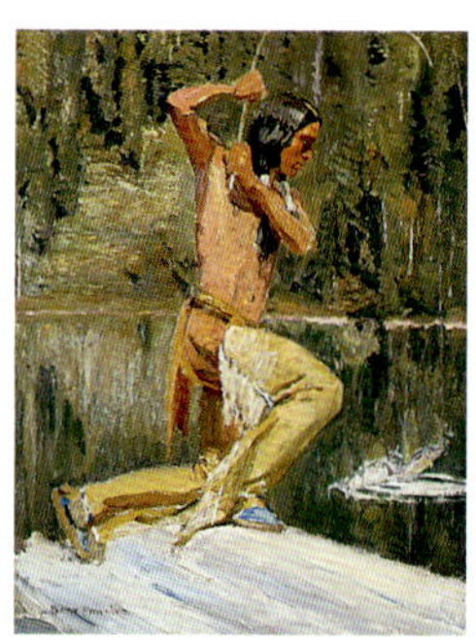

Bert Geer Phillips
U.S., 1868–1956
Indian Fishing, n.d., oil on canvas, 10½ × 8½ in. Gift, Priscilla C. and Joseph N. Tate Collection, 2004

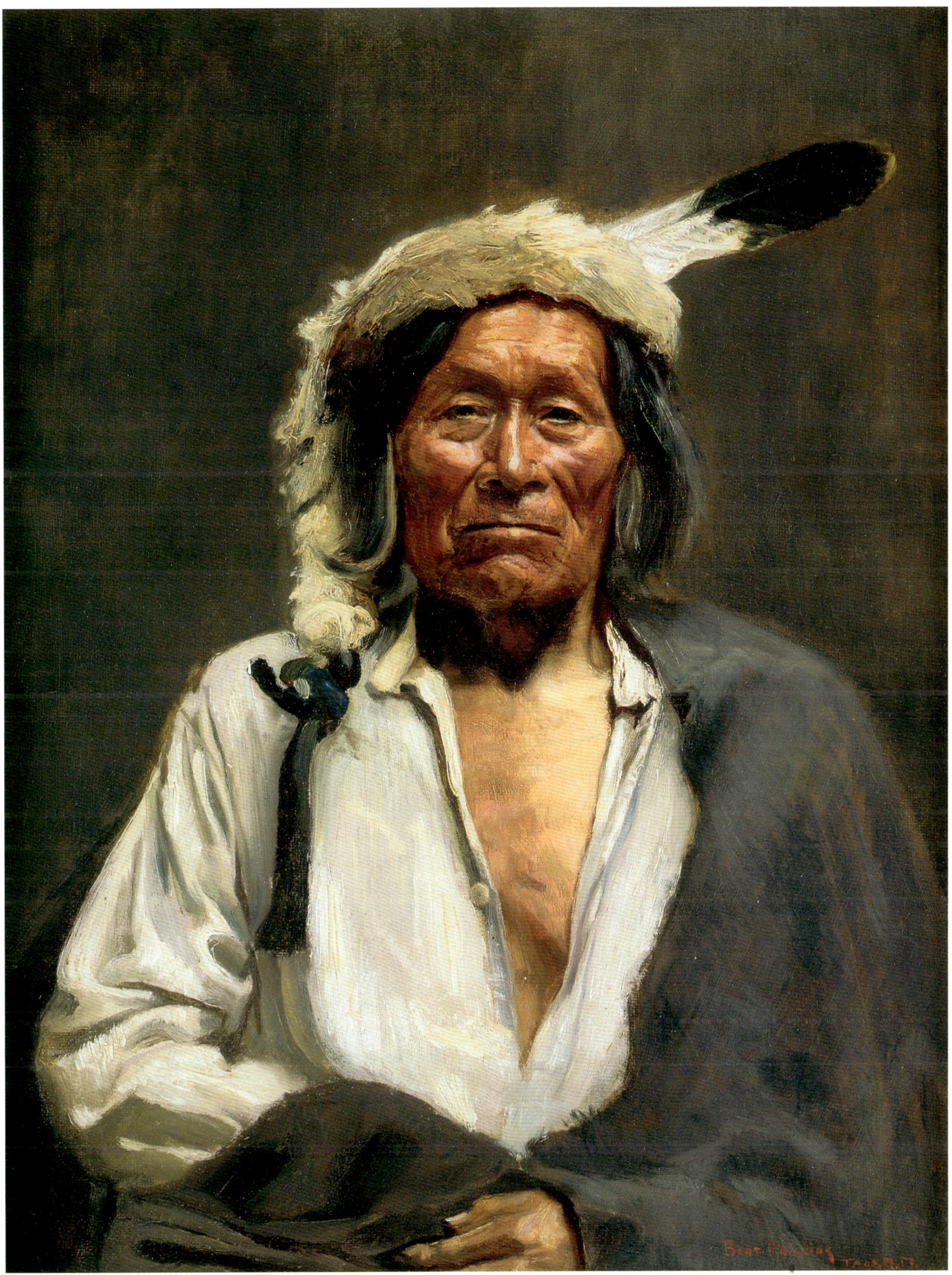
Bert Phillips
TAOS N.M.

41 Oscar E. Berninghaus

U.S. 1874–1952

Taos Indians on Mesa, n.d.
Oil on canvas
30 × 34 in.
Gift, Priscilla C. and Joseph N. Tate Collection, 2004

Of the original Taos artists, Oscar E. Berninghaus was unusual for being essentially self-taught (except for night classes in art at Washington University, St. Louis) and for never having studied in Europe. A native of St. Louis and the son of a lithograph salesman who had immigrated to the United States from Germany, Berninghaus was apprenticed to become a lithographer and commercial artist. He first visited Taos in 1899, when he was commissioned by the Denver and Rio Grande Railroad to travel through Colorado and New Mexico to paint watercolor sketches for travel brochures. Berninghaus spent a week in Taos, where, in his own words, he "became infected with the Taos germ." During his stay, he met the artist Bert Geer Phillips. Profoundly inspired by Taos and his encounter with Phillips, Berninghaus left determined to devote himself to a career in painting.

Berninghaus returned to Taos in 1900 for the summer. He continued to spend part of each year in New Mexico and the rest in St. Louis, until he moved permanently to Taos in 1925. (His studio in St. Louis was for a while next door to that of famed Western artist Charles M. Russell.) In 1915, Berninghaus became one of the founding members of the Taos Society of Artists, along with Ernest L. Blumenschein, E. Irving Couse, W. H. Dunton, Bert Geer Phillips, and Joseph Henry Sharp. He remained a dedicated member until the society dissolved in 1927. During his lifetime, he achieved considerable commercial success and critical recognition.

A masterful draftsman, Berninghaus painted the landscape around Taos, often with horses, and scenes of American Indian pageantry and daily life. He believed that from Taos would emerge a truly American art, "a distinctive art, something definitely American."

Taos Indians on Mesa shows the vast tableland west of Taos, with a view of the looming Sangre de Cristo Mountains. The canvas was painted in New Mexico, as indicated by the inscription "Taos–N.M." under Berninghaus's signature. In general, the paintings Berninghaus made in St. Louis tend to present romantic narratives of the Old West, while the works he created in Taos offer more objective depictions of contemporary New Mexico.

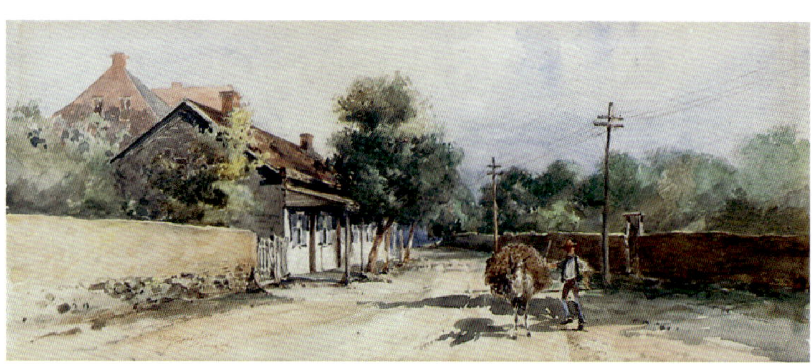

Oscar E. Berninghaus
U.S. 1874–1952
Santa Fe, 1899, watercolor, 4½ × 10 in.
Purchase, Richard H. and Adeline J. Fleischaker Collection, 1996

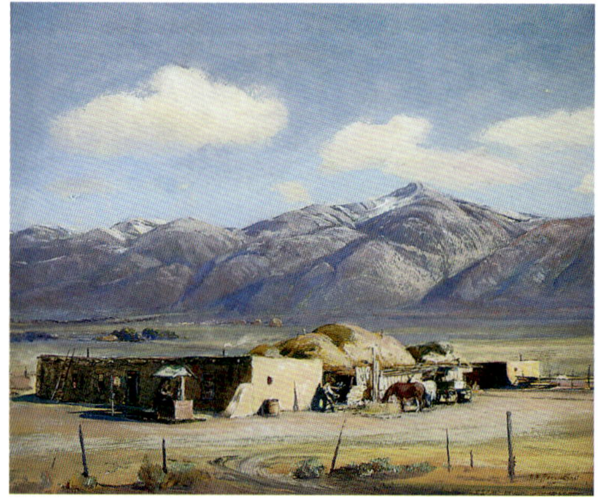

Oscar E. Berninghaus
U.S. 1874–1952
Adobe House, n.d., oil on board, 16 × 20 in. Purchase, Richard H. and Adeline J. Fleischaker Collection, 1996

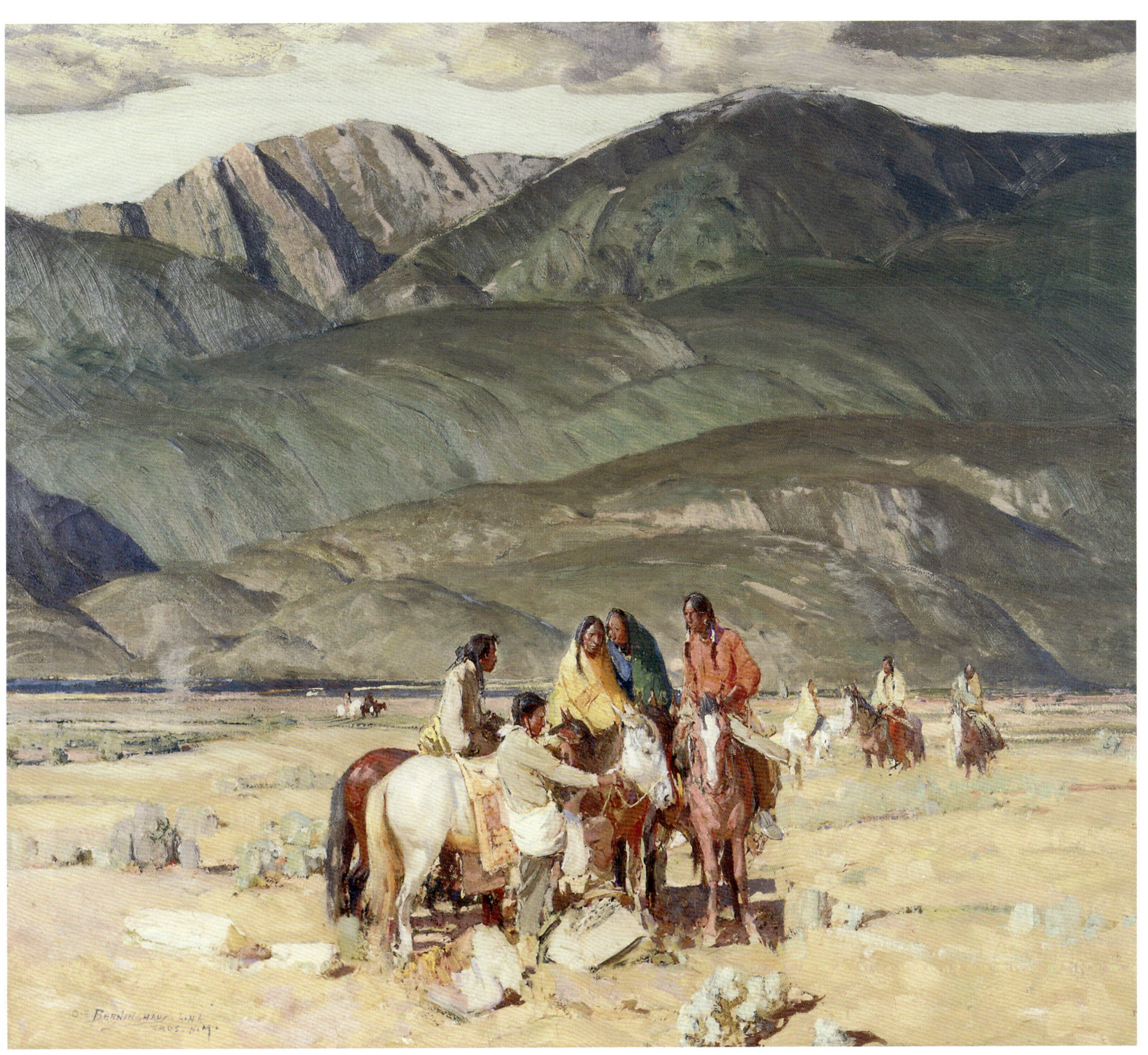

42 E. Irving Couse

U.S., 1866–1936

In Ambush, 1915–16
Oil on canvas
24 × 29 in.
Gift of William H. Thams in memory of Roxanne P. Thams, 2003

The first president of the Taos Society of Artists, E. Irving Couse was born in Saginaw, Michigan. He trained at the Art Institute of Chicago, at the National Academy of Design in New York, and beginning in 1886, for four years at the Académie Julian in Paris. From 1893 until 1896, Couse and his wife, a fellow American artist, lived in an art colony in northern France. Couse initially visited Taos in 1902, on the recommendation of fellow artists Ernest L. Blumenschein and Joseph Henry Sharp, whom he had met in Paris in 1896.

Before painting Taos Indians, Couse had spent time on his wife's family ranch in Washington State with plans to paint American Indians of the Northwest Coast, but he had been discouraged when most of them refused to pose, fearing that their souls would be transferred to their painted images. (A study of a Northwest Indian from the Umatilla tribe is in the Fleischaker Collection.) Blumenschein and Sharp encouraged Couse to spend a summer in Taos, where the Indians had become more willing to model. Starting in 1903, Couse spent summers in Taos while keeping his New York studio. In 1927, he became a permanent resident of Taos. The Taos Indians called him "Green Mountain" because of his girth and the green sweater he often wore.

Couse's paintings of American Indians became famous through reproductions in calendars published by the Santa Fe Railroad during the 1920s and 1930s. Unlike Sharp or Bert Geer Phillips, Couse was more concerned with idealized images than historical accuracy. In his paintings, Couse did not hesitate to use an object that might not be anthropologically correct if he thought it was called for pictorially. He followed the traditional working method of distinguishing the sketch from the finished work and always produced the finished works in the studio. Often, as with *In Ambush*, he would pose and photograph the models in New Mexico and then paint from the photographs in his New York studio. He usually completed the figure first and added the background later. He sometimes made color studies outdoors. (A few of these works are in the Fleischaker Collection.) Couse designed his own frames, and *Love Song*, another painting by Couse in the museum's collection, retains its original Couse-designed frame.

In Ambush is typical of the idealized paintings Couse became best known for and that he produced for over thirty years: a quiet, introspective painting of an Indian depicted as a noble, innocent, spiritual being. The Indian as "noble savage" had long been a common stereotype, a

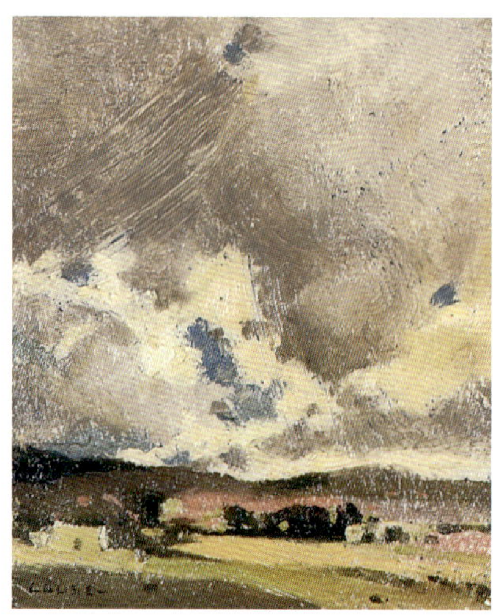

E. Irving Couse
U.S., 1866–1936
Couse Studio, Taos, New Mexico, n.d., oil on board, 6 × 5 in. Purchase, Richard H. and Adeline J. Fleischaker Collection, 1996

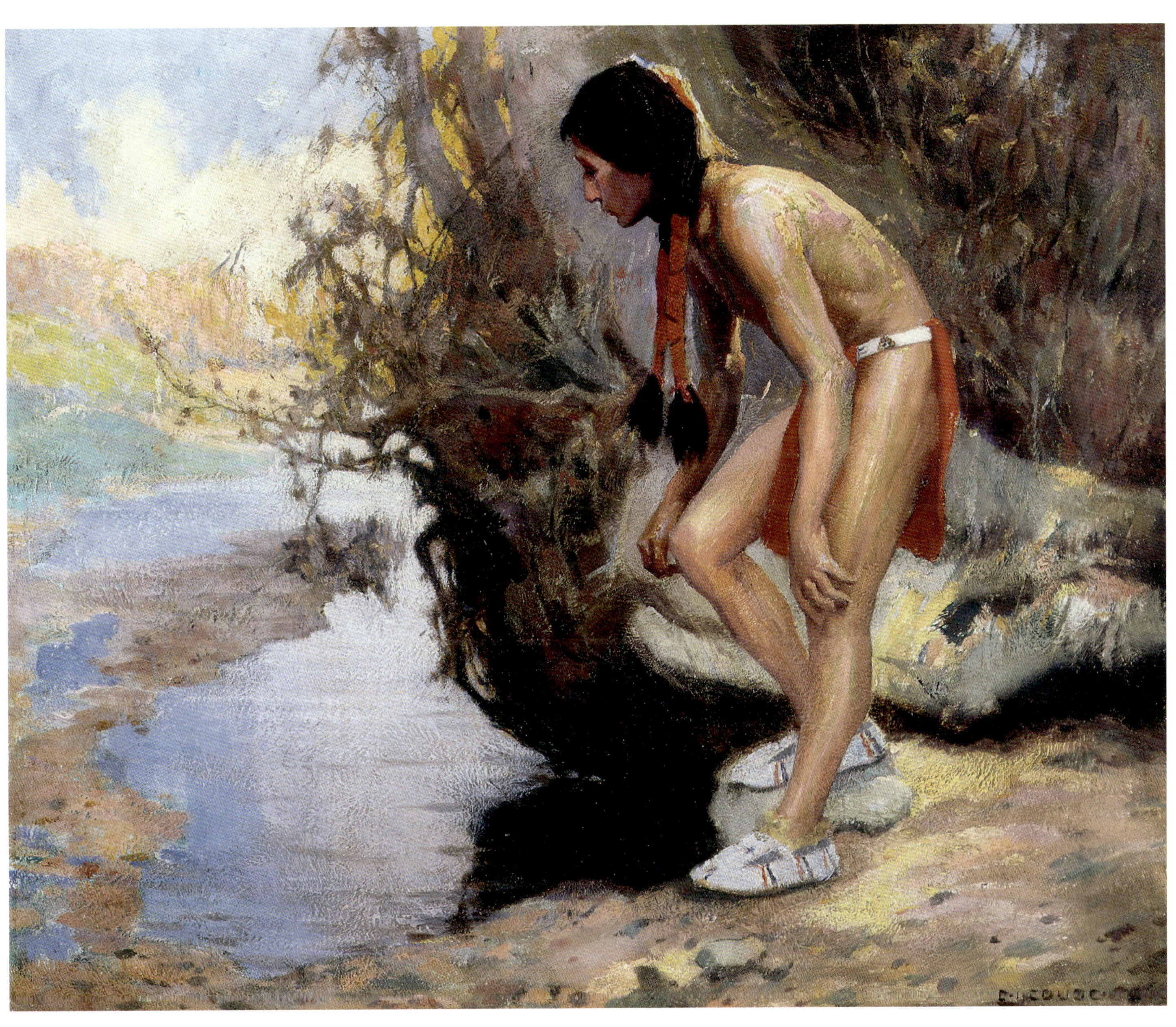

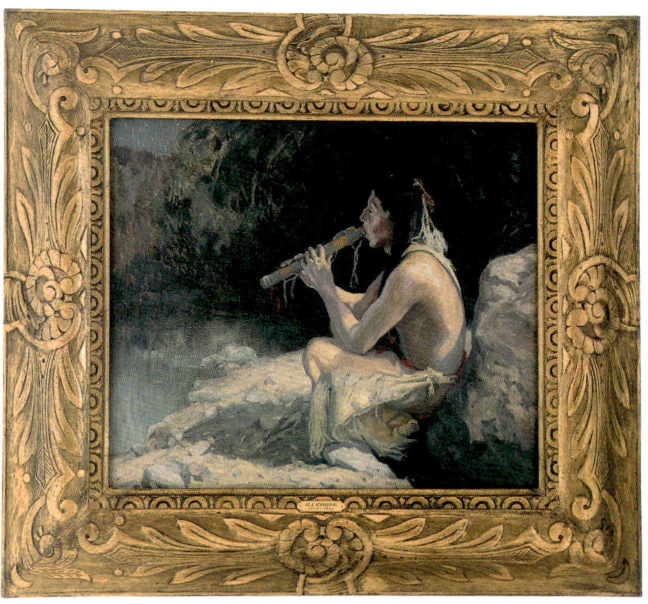

E. Irving Couse
U.S., 1866–1936
Love Song (Moonlight), n.d., oil on canvas, 20 × 24 in. (excluding frame). Gift of William H. Thams in memory of Roxanne P. Thams, 2003

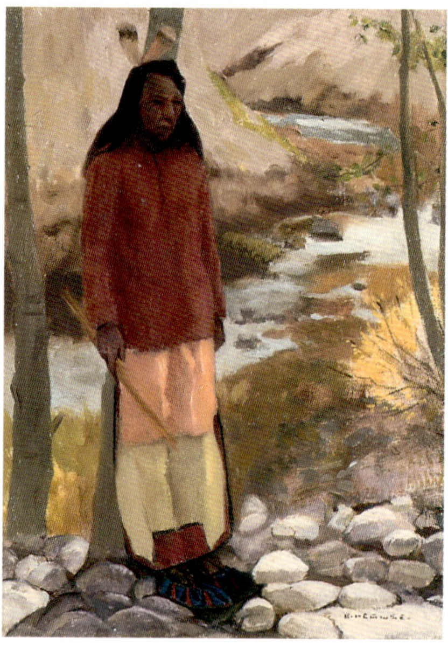

E. Irving Couse
U.S., 1866–1936
Study of Umatilla Indian, Columbia River, 1897, oil on canvas, 16 × 12 in. Purchase, Richard H. and Adeline J. Fleischaker Collection, 1996

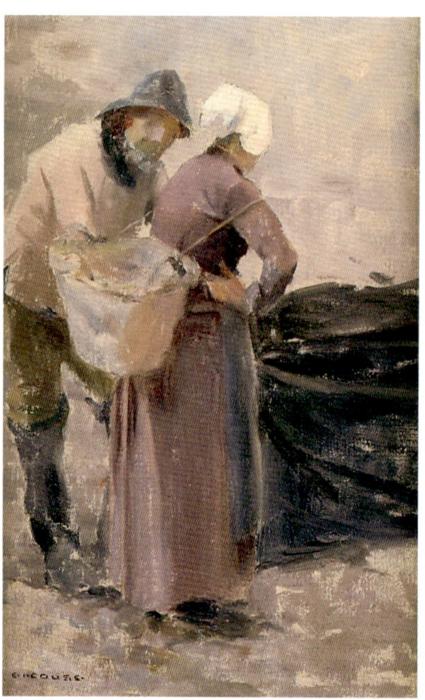

E. Irving Couse
U.S., 1866–1936
The Housewife Looking at the Fisherman's Catch, c. 1900, oil on canvas, 16⅛ × 10½ in. Gift of William H. Thams in memory of Roxanne P. Thams, 2003

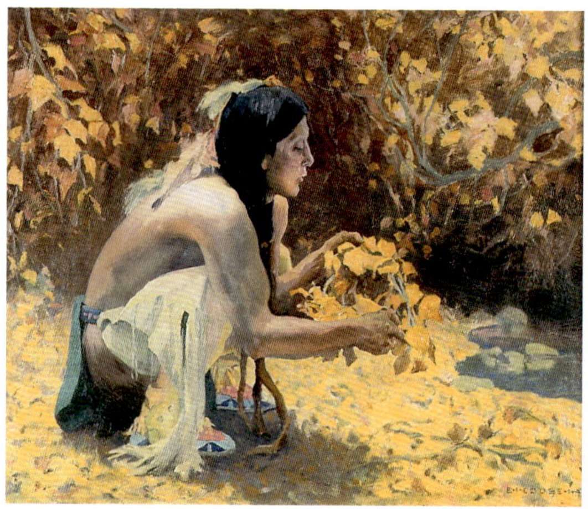

E. Irving Couse
U.S., 1866–1936
The Medicine Maker, n.d., oil on canvas, 23½ × 28½ in. Gift, Priscilla C. and Joseph N. Tate Collection, 2004

romanticization especially appealing as an antidote to the modern, industrialized world. In *In Ambush,* the Indian wears only moccasins, a loincloth, and decorated braids. He stands in front of a mass of tree roots that extend into the river. The background is broadly brushed and atmospheric.

Academic art theory considered rendering the nude figure the most difficult aspect of art. In painting a seminude Indian, Couse looked back to classical nudes and demonstrated his academic expertise. The sitter for *In Ambush* was probably Ben Lujan, one of Couse's favorite models from the Taos Pueblo. Lujan first posed for Couse at age twelve. In addition to serving as a frequent model, Lujan worked as the Couse family's gardener—he would pose in the morning and work in the garden in the afternoon.

Couse's granddaughter, Virginia Couse Leavitt, maintains that the title *In Ambush* does not seem appropriate and was probably not the original.

43 W. H. Dunton

U.S., 1878–1936

Indians of Taos, n.d.
Oil on canvas board
7¾ × 9⅞ in.
Gift, Priscilla C. and Joseph N. Tate Collection, 2004

W. H. "Buck" Dunton grew up in Augusta, Maine, the son of an amateur painter. At eighteen, he began to spend winters working as an illustrator or studying at the Cowles Art School in Boston and summers working as a hunter and ranch hand in various states in the West; he continued this routine for over fifteen years. In 1903, he moved to New York, where he became highly successful as an illustrator of Western literature, including the novels of Zane Grey.

Around 1911, Dunton enrolled at the Art Students League in New York, where one of his teachers was Ernest L. Blumenschein, who persuaded Dunton to visit Taos in 1912. Dunton was captivated by Taos, returning in 1913 for the summer and permanently settling there in 1914, the year his paintings began to be accepted in prestigious juried exhibitions in New York, Philadelphia, and Chicago.

Dunton became a founding member of the Taos Society of Artists in 1915; he resigned for unknown reasons in 1922. Afterward, he marketed his own work, organizing exhibitions in Oklahoma and Texas. During the Depression, when it was difficult to sell paintings, he made less expensive lithographs and portrait drawings. He died of cancer in 1936.

Dunton's typical subjects were rugged Western hunters and cowboys, whom he considered a vanishing breed. In 1925, he wrote:

> *The west has passed—more's the pity. In another twenty-five years, the old-time westerner will have gone too—gone with the buffalo and the antelope. I'm going to hand down to posterity a bit of unadulterated* real thing *if it's the last thing I do.*

He often painted Taos and its environs, and in an article titled "The Painters of Taos," in the August 1922 issue of the *American Magazine of Art,* Dunton described Taos's appeal:

> *[Taos was] remote from commercialism and the sordid, restful in its peaceful isolation, quiet along its crooked alleys, in the soft shadows of the adobe walls. The mountain rivers sang of happiness. The pines of the peaks breathed a lullaby of sleep.*

A serene painting, *Indians of Taos* depicts two Indians on horseback—one wears a traditional headdress and a brilliant red robe. They traverse an arid, sun-drenched, sagebrush-filled landscape, with mountains in the distance.

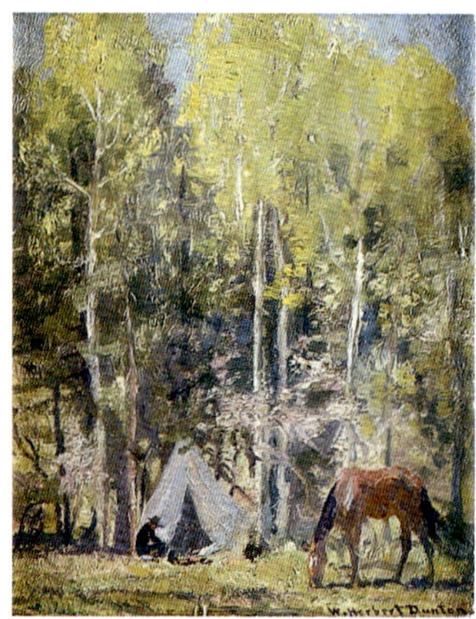

W. H. Dunton
U.S., 1878–1936
Hunter's Camp in Aspen Forest, 1920, oil on panel, 10 × 8 in. Purchase, Richard H. and Adeline J. Fleischaker Collection, 1996

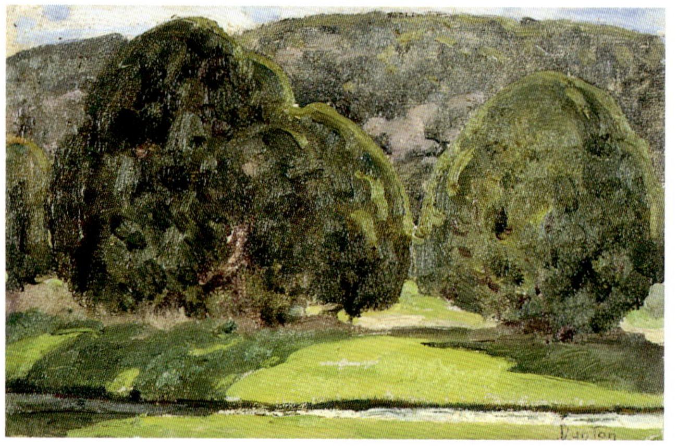

W. H. Dunton
U.S., 1878–1936
Sunlight and Cedars, c. 1933, oil on board, 5 × 7 in. Purchase, Richard H. and Adeline J. Fleischaker Collection, 1996

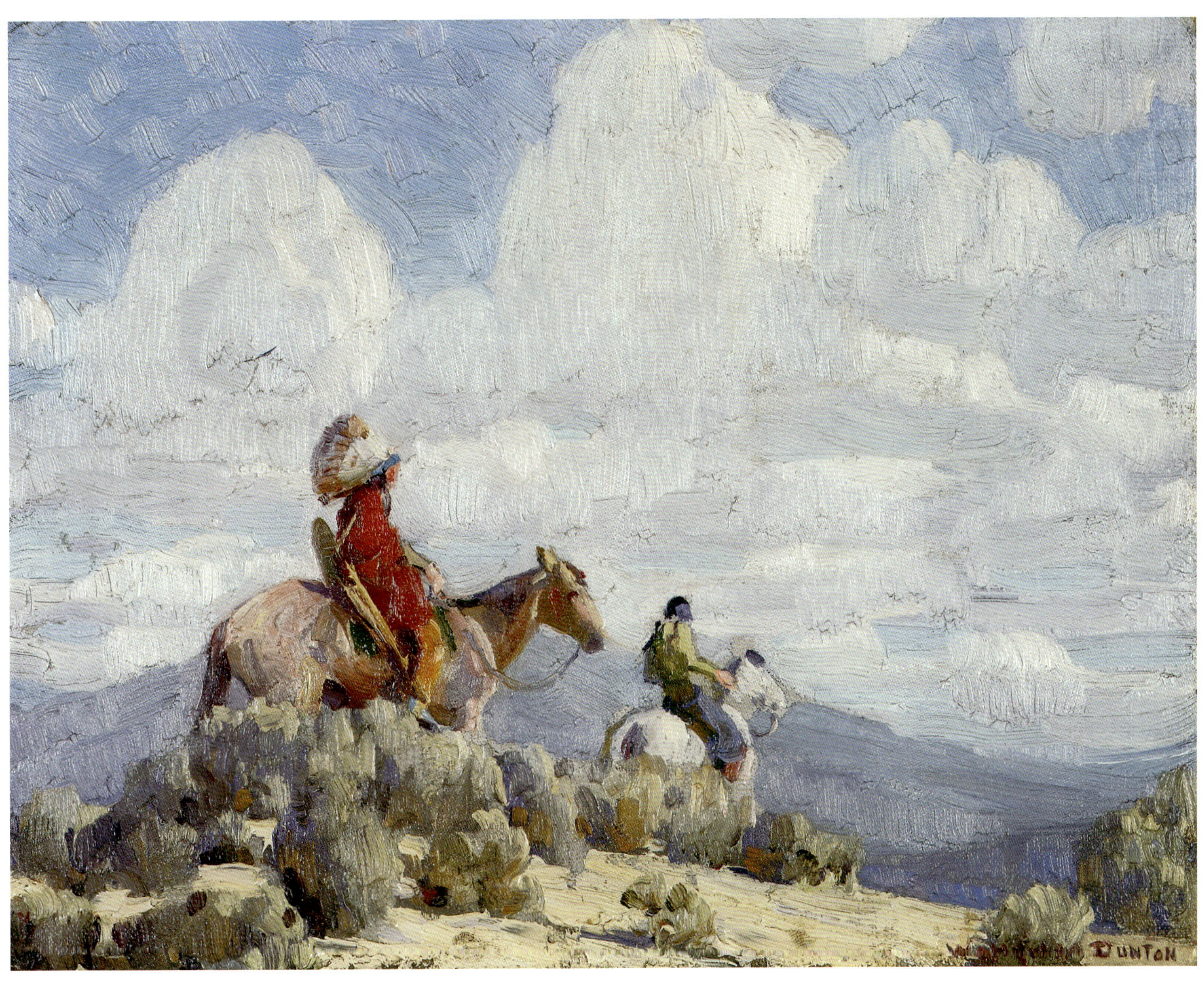
DUNTON

44 Victor Higgins

U.S., 1884–1949

Poplars and Young Fields, c. 1940s
Oil on canvas
30 × 22 in.
Gift, Priscilla C. and Joseph N. Tate Collection, 2004

Victor Higgins grew up on a farm in Indiana and enrolled at the Art Institute of Chicago at age fifteen. For two and a half years, starting in 1911, he traveled through Europe, where he studied art in Paris at the Académie de la Grande Chaumière and in Munich at the Royal Academy. Fellow students in Munich included Chicagoans and future Taos artists Walter Ufer and E. Martin Hennings. After Higgins returned to Chicago, former Chicago mayor Carter Harrison Jr. and his associates sponsored Higgins's trip to Taos in 1914 in return for paintings by the artist, as they would do shortly for Ufer and later for Hennings and Irving K. Manoir. Henceforth, Higgins divided his time between Taos and Chicago. He joined the Taos Society of Artists in 1917.

While in Europe, Higgins held fast to his traditional art training and was not influenced by avant-garde movements. In New Mexico, however, he became one of the more experimental members of the Taos Society of Artists. He occasionally painted American Indian models, but his typical subjects were still lifes and Southwestern landscapes; *Poplars and Young Fields* is one in a series of late paintings depicting Jeantette Lane in Taos under changing skies. In *Poplars and Young Fields,* Higgins conducted a Modernist exploration of light and color, with broad, parallel brushstrokes reminiscent of Paul Cézanne.

Another late painting by Higgins in the museum's collection is the freely executed *Taos,* most likely one of the small, spontaneous oil paintings produced in the 1940s, which Higgins called the Little Gems. In the Little Gems, Higgins simplified his subjects to their essences and painted quickly, outdoors, from a seat that he specifically made for the trunk of his car.

Higgins's second, brief marriage was to Marion Koogler McNay, whose house and art collections became San Antonio's McNay Art Museum.

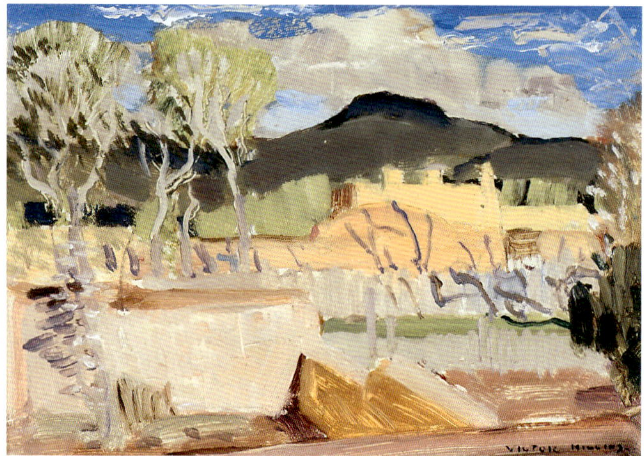

Victor Higgins
U.S., 1884–1949
Taos, c. 1940s, oil on board, 6½ × 9½ in.
Purchase, Richard H. and Adeline J. Fleischaker Collection, 1996

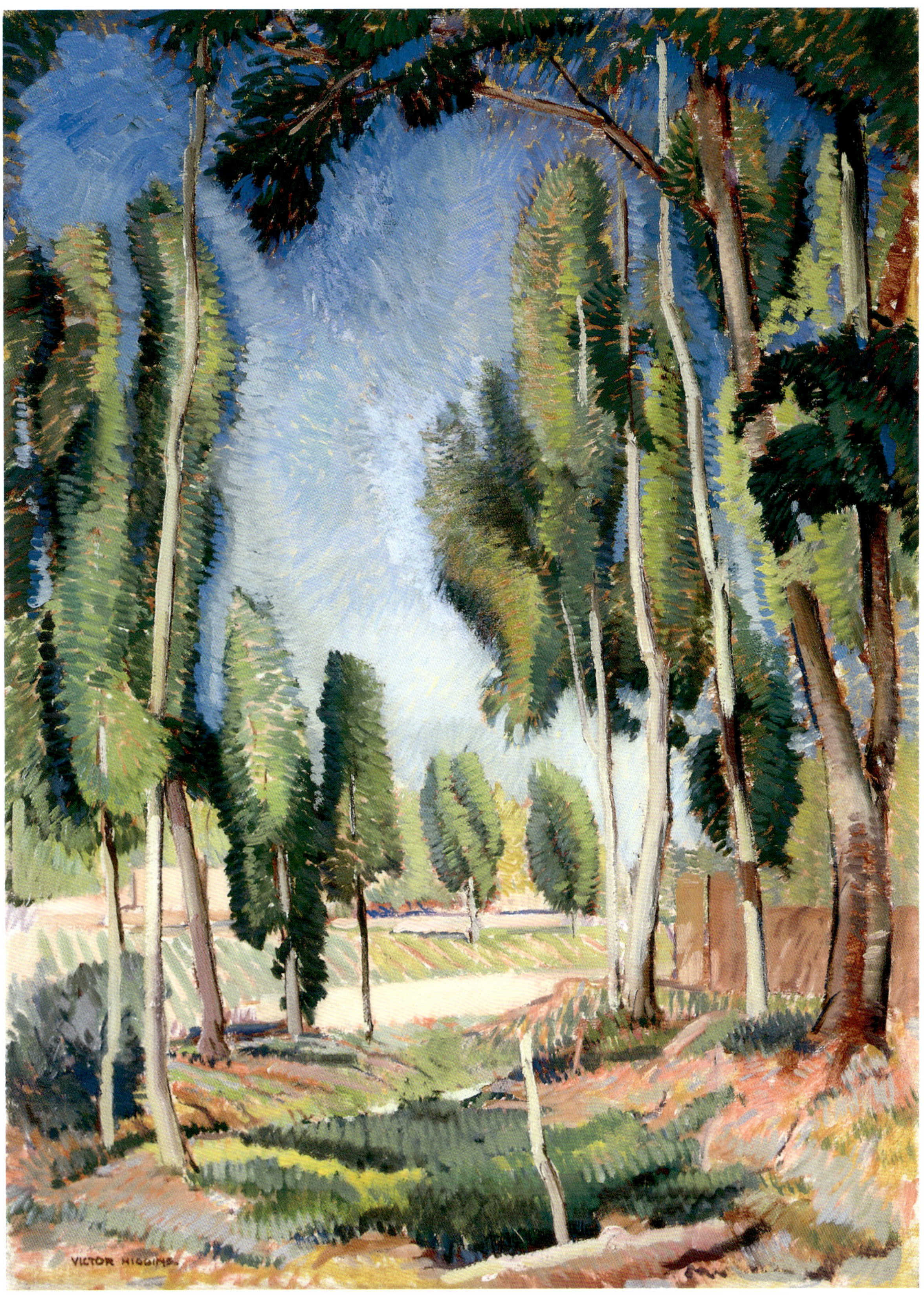
VICTOR HIGGINS

45 Walter Ufer

U.S., 1876–1936

Indian on Horseback with Colt, n.d.
Oil on canvas
16 × 20 in.
Purchase, Richard H. and Adeline J. Fleischaker Collection, 1996

When he arrived in Taos in 1914, Walter Ufer said: "God's country! I expect to live and die here." He returned to Taos the following two years, and in 1917 became a member of the Taos Society of Artists. During the 1920s, Ufer became one of the most recognized Taos artists.

Born in Germany, the son of a firearms engraver, Ufer and his family immigrated to Louisville, Kentucky, in 1880. He decided to become an artist after visiting the World's Columbian Exposition in Chicago in 1892. The following year, he traveled to Hamburg, Germany, where he worked as a lithographer for a few years, and then moved to Dresden to study at the Royal Academy. Upon returning to the United States, he established himself as a commercial artist and portrait painter in Chicago starting in 1900, but in 1911 he returned to Germany for two years of additional study in Munich. In 1914, former Chicago mayor Carter Harrison Jr., who had become enamored of Taos during an earlier visit, subsidized a trip to Taos for Ufer in return for paintings. Unlike most other Taos artists, Ufer was politically an ardent leftist, and it was even said that Leon Trotsky once visited him in Taos. Ufer squandered the considerable earnings he made from his paintings in the 1920s through a lavish lifestyle, and he was often in debt. He died of appendicitis in 1936.

Like many Taos artists, Ufer was eager for the United States to develop its own national art, and he stated:

> *I believe that if America gets a National Art it will come from the Southwest [rather] than from the Atlantic Board. Because we are really different from Europeans, and the farther away from European influence, the better for us. . . . The strong beauty that the Southwest holds . . . is what holds us out here.*

Ufer typically portrayed contemporary Indians engaged in everyday activities and wearing store-bought clothes, not their traditional costumes. The subject matter was suggested by Ufer's patron, Carter Harrison Jr., who wrote in a letter to the artist:

> *It seems to me that abundant artistic material could be found in painting the Indians as they are today—plowing with their scrubby Indian ponies, digging in the fields, on horseback, and lying around the pueblo. This phase of Indian life has not yet received artistic treatment. The hunting with bows and arrows, stalking game in the costumes of the past, etc., have been done to death by talented men.*

In Taos, Ufer brightened his palette and changed his working methods from painting in a studio to painting outdoors, without making preparatory sketches. In 1920, he wrote in an exhibition catalogue, "Studio work dulls the mind and the artist's palette."

A former pupil, Regina Tatum Cooke, recorded Ufer's painting methods. After drawing in the composition, he went over the drawing with a mixture of permanent blue, burnt sienna, and turpentine, with which he would also lay in the shadows. (He did not use black.) He next

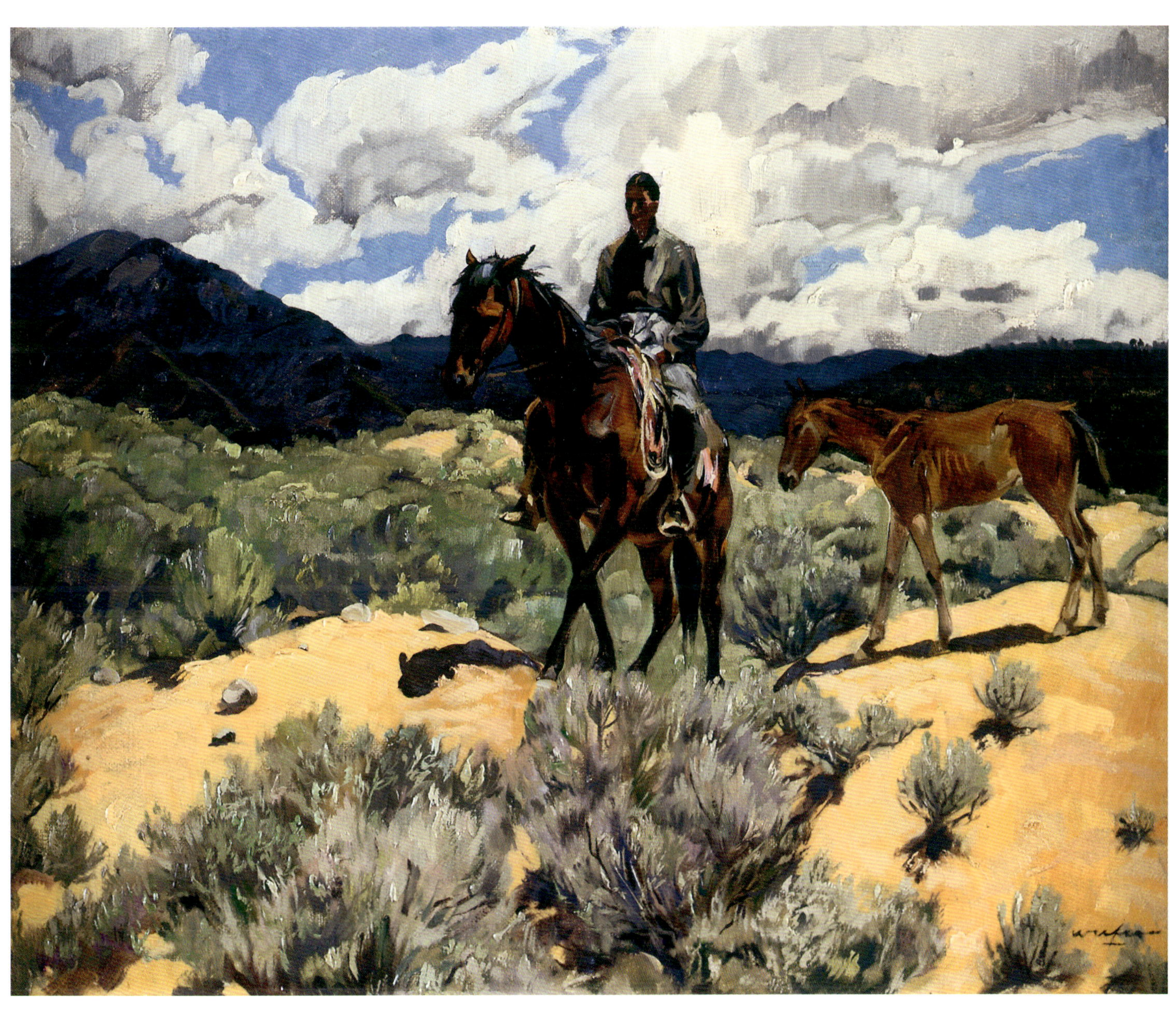

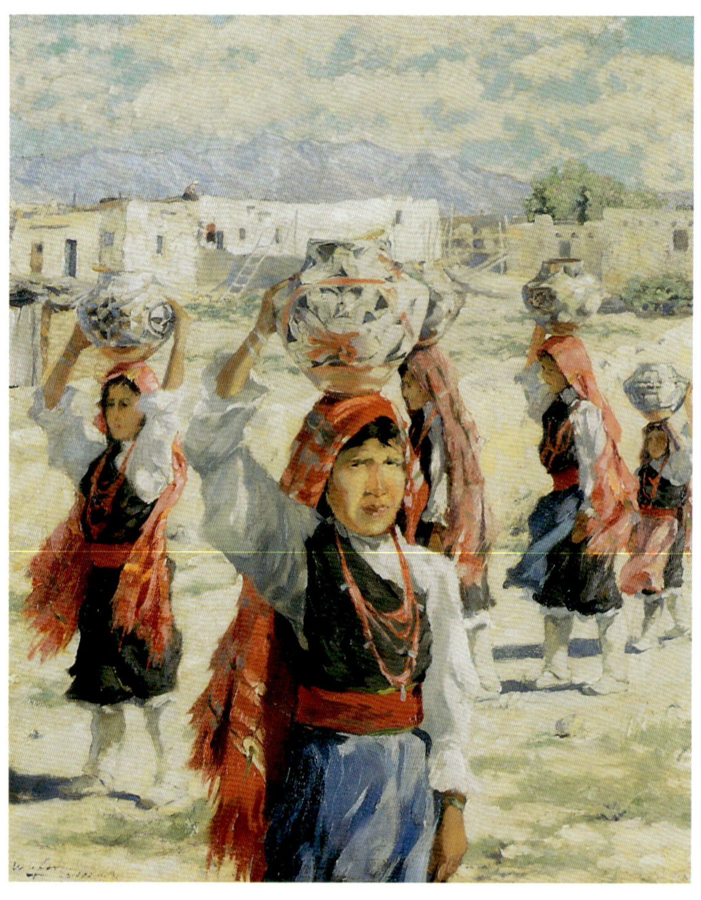

Walter Ufer
U.S., 1876–1936
Girls of Isleta, n.d., oil on canvas, 30 × 25 in.
Gift, Priscilla C. and Joseph N. Tate Collection, 2004

erased the pencil to make for a cleaner canvas, and painted by starting at the top of the canvas and working his way down to the bottom. "Treat things as a whole," he often said. Figure and ground were treated as one. "The horse becomes a part of the mesa and takes on the colors of the mesa," he explained.

Indian on Horseback with Colt shows strong sunlight almost directly overhead, which indicates that it is midday. (Eastern critics, unfamiliar with the intense light of New Mexico, sometimes questioned Ufer's fidelity to nature.) There are no traditional framing devices such as trees, and the foreground tilts forward, giving a sense of the land's undulations. The Indian on horseback is Jim Mirabal, who was Ufer's favorite model and who was, somewhat patronizingly, called "Ufer's Jim." Ufer cared financially for the Mirabal family, even when he had to borrow money to do so, and shortly before Mirabal died in his nineties in 1976, he said of Ufer, "We were like brothers."

46 E. Martin Hennings

U.S., 1886–1956

Heading for the Pueblo, n.d.
Oil on canvas
25 × 30 in.
Gift, Priscilla C. and Joseph N. Tate Collection, 2004

The son of northern German immigrants, E. Martin Hennings grew up in Chicago. He graduated from the Art Institute of Chicago in 1904, after which he worked as an illustrator. In 1912, he traveled to Munich to study under Franz von Stuck and others at the Royal Academy, and he remained in Germany—where he met fellow students and future Taos artists Walter Ufer and Victor Higgins—until World War I forced him to return to the United States.

In 1917, former Chicago mayor Carter Harrison Jr. and his associates sponsored Hennings's first trip to Taos in exchange for paintings by the artist. Hennings established permanent residence in Taos in 1921, and during the following decade, he received much critical recognition. In 1924, he became a member of the Taos Society of Artists.

Mabel Dodge Luhan was correct in calling Hennings "a true pastoral painter." The pastoral ideal is a bountiful natural world, full of leisure, in contrast to the city. Hennings typically depicted American Indians on horseback, traveling through a landscape of sagebrush or aspen, as in *Heading for the Pueblo.* The painting could be considered a pastoral vision of northern New Mexico; the Indians are in harmony with nature. (Pastorals partake of a long tradition—in poetry dating back to antiquity, with works such as Theocritus's *Idylls* and Virgil's *Eclogues,* and in painting dating back to Venetian art of the early sixteenth century and Claude Lorrain's landscapes of the seventeenth century.)

Henning's paintings are often described as "quiet," like the artist. Hennings himself believed in a correlation between temperament and the artist's style: "[The artist's] personal style is governed by his own temperament, rather than by a style molded through the intellect."

It has been suggested that Hennings was influenced by the *Jugendstil* style that he encountered in Munich. (*Jugendstil,* promoted by Franz von Stuck, is the German version of Art Nouveau.) This influence may be seen in the sinuous, interlaced aspen of *Afternoon Ride* in the museum's Fleischaker Collection.

Although primarily a painter, Hennings created lithographs in the 1920s, including one based on his *Drummer Boy,* a painting in the Thams Collection that depicts Frank Samora, one of Hennings's favorite models, who, like many of the Taos Indian models, also helped around the house. (Samora was married to Crucita, who is depicted in Hennings's *Juanita,* also in the Thams Collection. Crucita was a favorite model of Joseph Henry Sharp.)

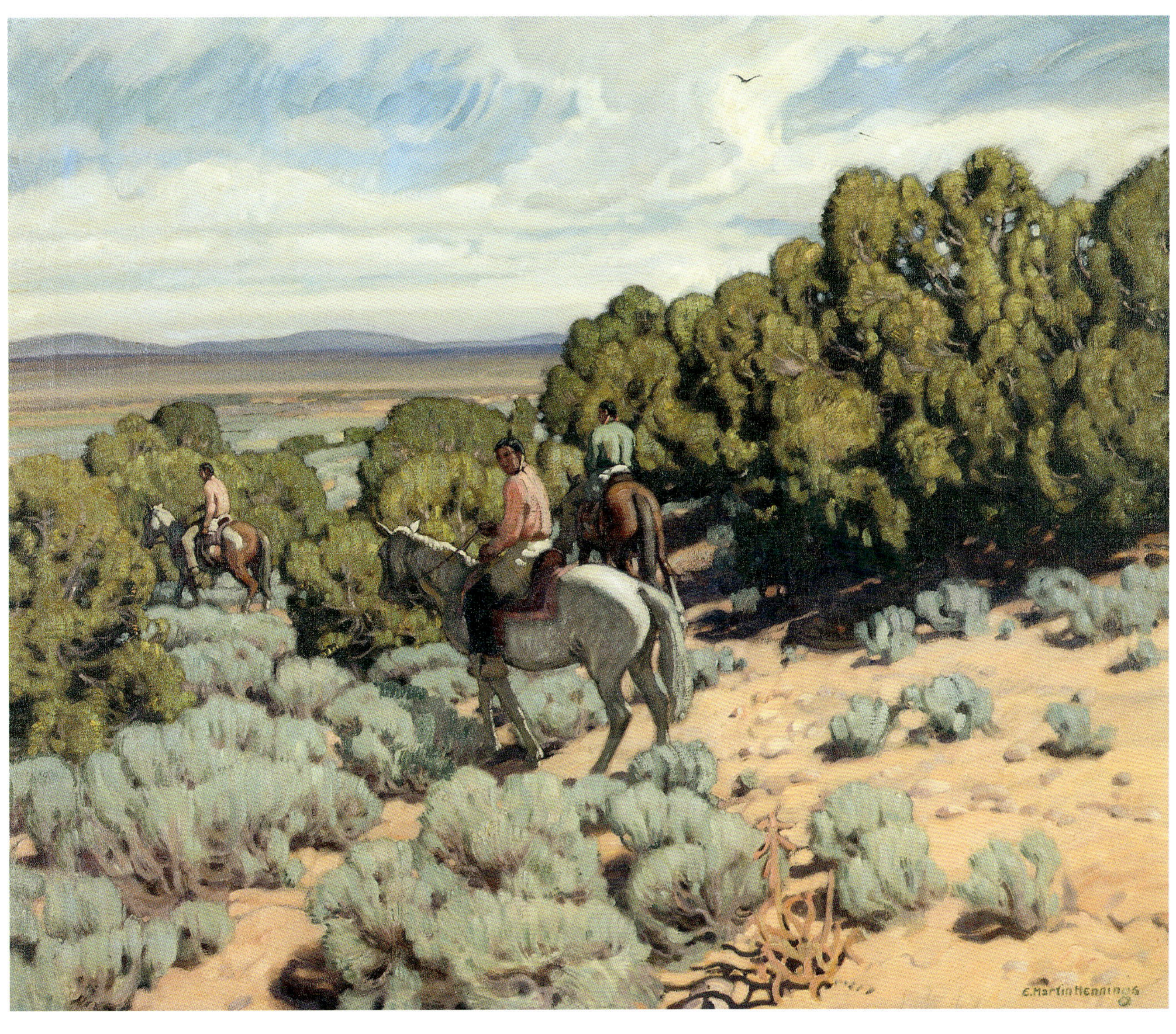
E. Martin Hennings

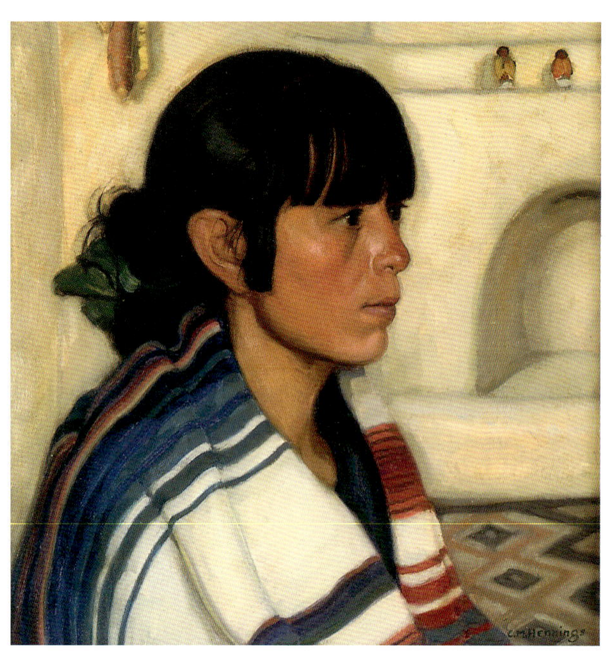

E. Martin Hennings
U.S., 1886–1956
Juanita, n.d., oil on canvas, 14 × 14 in. Gift of William H. Thams in memory of Roxanne P. Thams, 2003

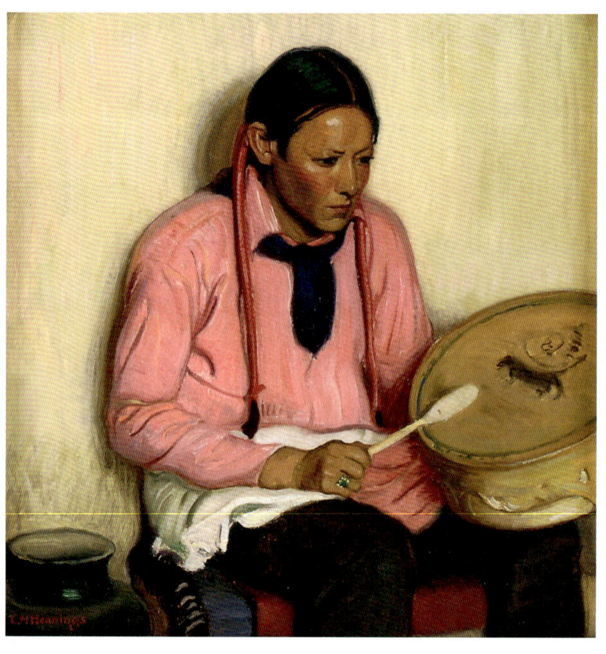

E. Martin Hennings
U.S., 1886–1956
Drummer Boy, c. 1925, oil on canvas, 14 × 14 in. Gift of William H. Thams in memory of Roxanne P. Thams, 2003

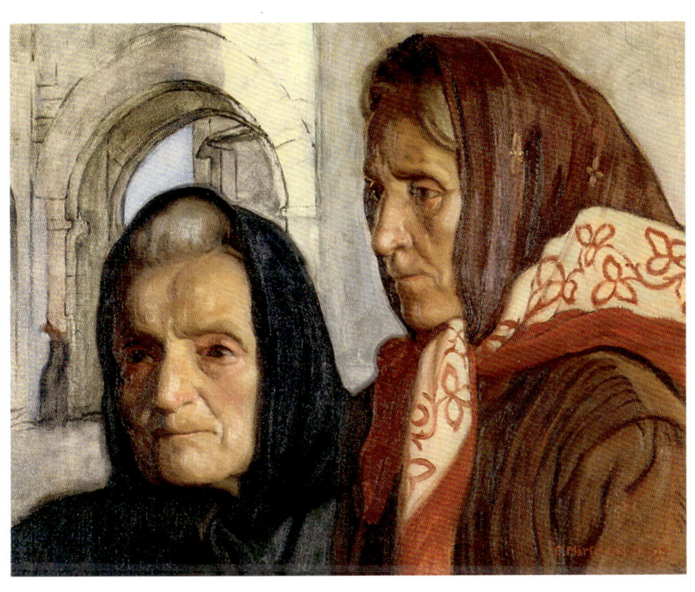

E. Martin Hennings
U.S., 1886–1956
Two Women, n.d., oil on canvas, 16 × 20 in.
Gift, Priscilla C. and Joseph N. Tate Collection, 2004

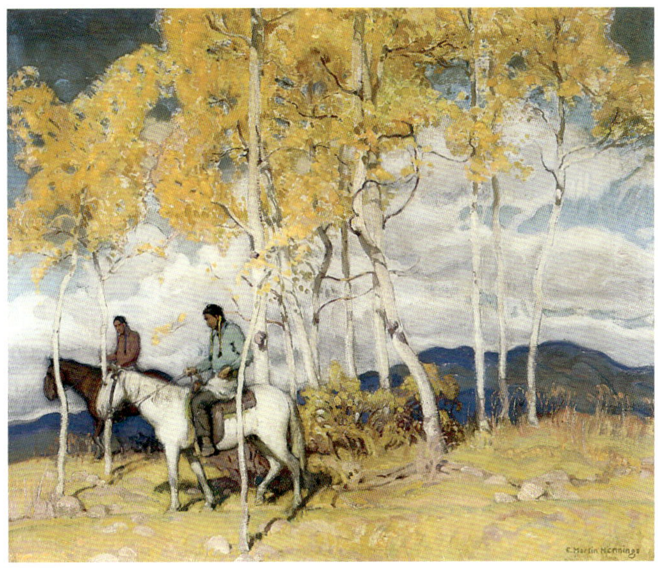

E. Martin Hennings
U.S., 1886–1956
Afternoon Ride, n.d., oil on panel, 20 × 24 in.
Purchase, Richard H. and Adeline J. Fleischaker Collection, 1996

47 Kenneth Adams

U.S., 1897–1966

French Landscape, 1927
Oil on canvas
21 × 25½ in.
Gift of William H. Thams in memory of Roxanne P. Thams, 2003

Kenneth Adams is often thought of as a bridge between the traditional Taos founders and the more Modern second-generation Taos artists. Adams grew up in Topeka, Kansas, and studied at the Art Institute of Chicago in 1916–17, before serving in the army in World War I. He then studied at the Art Students League in New York and the Art Students League Summer School in Woodstock, New York, where he met his mentor, the Modernist Andrew Dasburg (see cat. no. 50). From 1921 until 1923, Adams lived in Paris and elsewhere in Europe, and he was deeply inspired, as Dasburg had been, by the art of Paul Cézanne.

In 1924, Adams traveled to Santa Fe, where Dasburg was then based. When Adams could not find a place to stay in Santa Fe, he continued north to Taos with a letter of introduction from Dasburg to Walter Ufer, who would become Adams's close friend. In 1926, Adams became the last and youngest artist to be elected to the Taos Society of Artists, which dissolved the following year.

Influenced by the art of the Mexican muralist Diego Rivera, Adams painted murals in the 1930s for the Works Progress Administration (W.P.A.) in post offices in Kansas and New Mexico. (Rivera's influence can be seen in a lithograph, in the museum's collection, of a heroicized miner viewed from behind.) The Carnegie Corporation then sponsored Adams as an artist-in-residence at the University of New Mexico, where he also painted murals and remained to teach from 1942 until 1963.

Adams created *French Landscape* in southern France, Cézanne's locale. During Adams's European sojourn of the early 1920s, he spent several months painting in southern France with his artist friends Ward Lockwood and Alexander Warshawsky. In *French Landscape*, a bank of cypresses towers on the canvas's right side, and clouds billow on the left. Contrasting with the surrounding greens and shaded foreground, the sunny pink house in the distance enlivens the composition and establishes depth. The painting emphasizes light and naturalism.

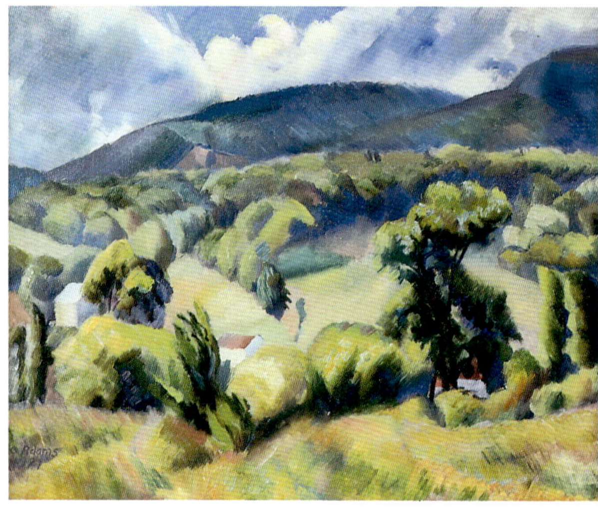

Kenneth Adams
U.S., 1897–1966
Landscape, 1921, oil on canvas, 16 × 20 in.
Gift, Priscilla C. and Joseph N. Tate Collection, 2004

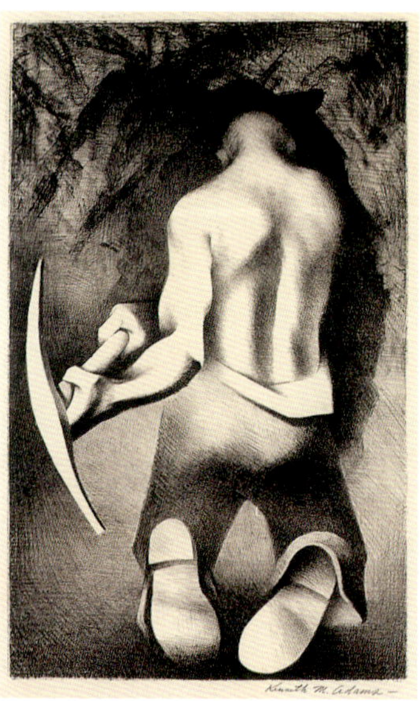

Kenneth Adams
U.S., 1897–1966
Miner, n.d., lithograph, 15 × 10 in.
Museum purchase, 1939

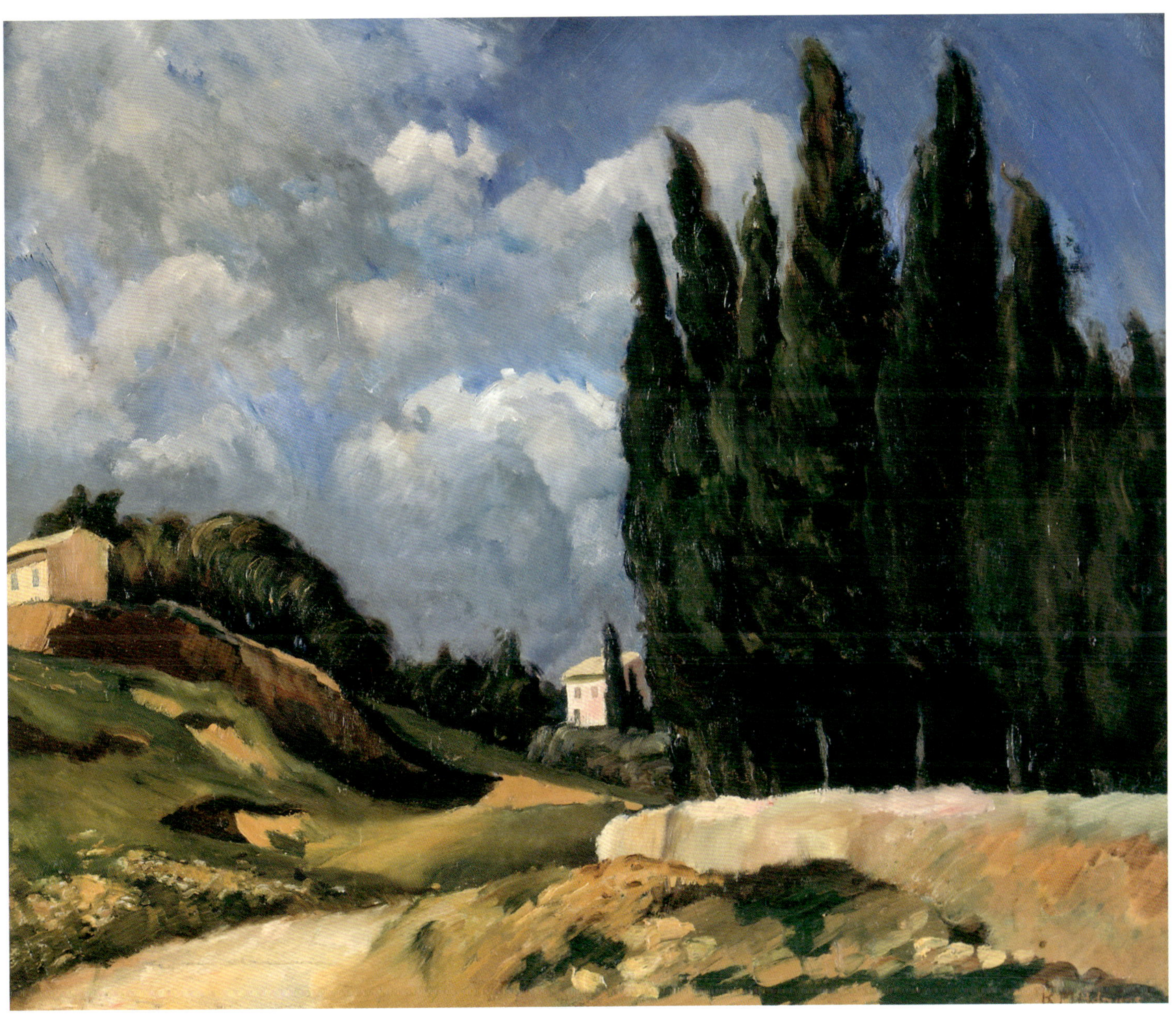

48 Irving K. Manoir

U.S., 1891–1982

Aspen and Snow, 1923
Oil on canvas
36 × 41 in.
Gift of William H. Thams in memory of Roxanne P. Thams, 2003

Irving K. Manoir was born in Chicago and studied at the Art Institute of Chicago as well as in France, Germany, and Spain. From 1916 to 1918 and from 1933 until 1937, he served on the faculty of the Art Institute of Chicago, which in 1926 gave him a solo show. In 1939, he settled in southern California.

As they had done earlier for artists E. Martin Hennings, Victor Higgins, and Walter Ufer, former Chicago mayor Carter Harrison Jr. and his associates, including Oscar Mayer, sponsored Manoir's trip to Taos in 1923–24. During the late fall of 1923, Manoir painted *Aspen and Snow,* also known as *Fairy Tale Land of New Mexico.*

Aspen and Snow depicts Glorietta, a stream and sacred grove of cottonwoods above the Taos Pueblo. Anglos were permitted to attend ceremonies there until one of them started a forest fire later in the 1920s. The painting was exhibited widely during the 1920s, including at the Art Institute of Chicago and Pennsylvania Academy of the Fine Arts, both of which reproduced it in their catalogues. *Aspen and Snow* won several awards and received extravagant acclaim.

Toward the end of his life, Manoir declared that *Aspen and Snow* was his "fondest work of that early period," and that the painting's beauty derived in large part from the principles of dynamic symmetry. Developed by the Yale art historian Jay Hambidge from his study of Greek temples, dynamic symmetry is an aesthetic theory of harmonious proportions and geometry related to the Golden Section. Hambidge popularized his theory in *The Elements of Dynamic Symmetry,* which captivated many American artists during the 1920s. Manoir himself was an instructor of dynamic symmetry in 1920–21 at the Chicago Academy of Fine Arts.

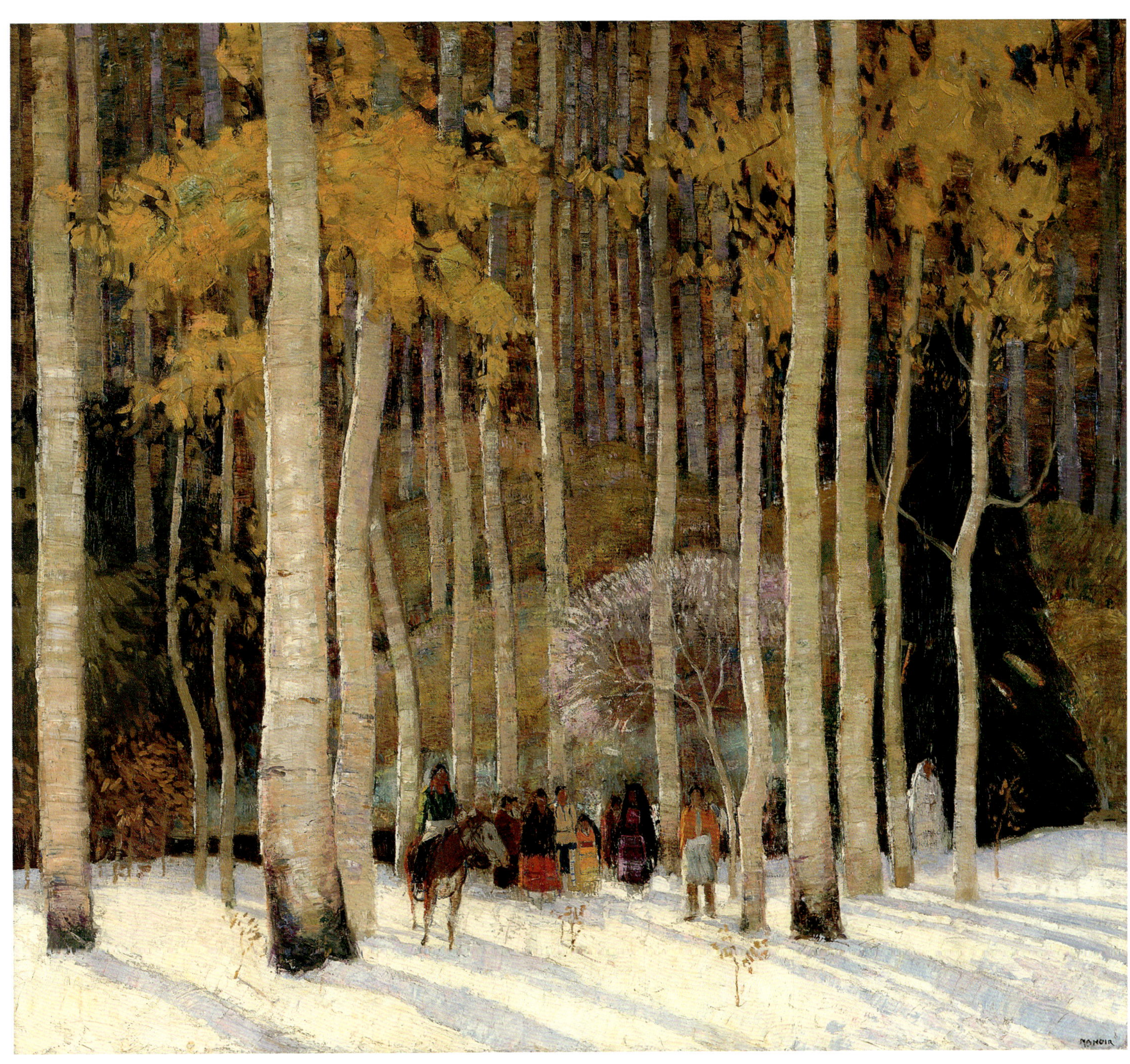

49 LaVerne Nelson Black

U.S., 1887–1938

The Trading Post, n.d.
Oil on canvas
10 × 18¾ in.
Gift of William H. Thams in memory of Roxanne P. Thams, 2003

Born in the Kickapoo River Valley of Wisconsin, near the Kickapoo Indian reservation, LaVerne Nelson Black drew horses and American Indians as a child. His family moved to Chicago in 1906, and he entered the Chicago Academy of Fine Arts, where he won a scholarship during his second year. After finishing his schooling in 1908, he became an illustrator for newspapers in Chicago and New York and gained recognition for his bronze sculptures of Western subjects, which were the first since Frederic Remington's to be sold at Tiffany's. From 1908 until 1925, Black spent summers painting in the West.

In 1925, failing health required Black to move to a drier climate, and together with his wife and two children, he settled in Taos, where he painted the Taos Pueblo, gatherings of Indians, and the Sangre de Cristo Mountains, all of which are seen in *The Trading Post*. Black painted with bold brushstrokes, often using a palette knife and avoiding extraneous detail. He preferred to work outdoors.

The Trading Post depicts a frieze of Indians and a covered wagon against adobe buildings, with trees and the Sangre de Cristo Mountains beyond. The circular wagon wheels are prominent, while the rectangular hitching post in the painting's lower right echoes the shape of the canvas, anchors the composition, and establishes depth.

Due to continued poor health, Black moved in 1937 to the warmer climate of Phoenix, where the Works Progress Administration (W.P.A.) commissioned him and Oscar E. Berninghaus to paint murals in the Phoenix Post Office. Shortly after completing the project in the spring of 1938, Black died, most likely from paint poisoning in his unventilated studio.

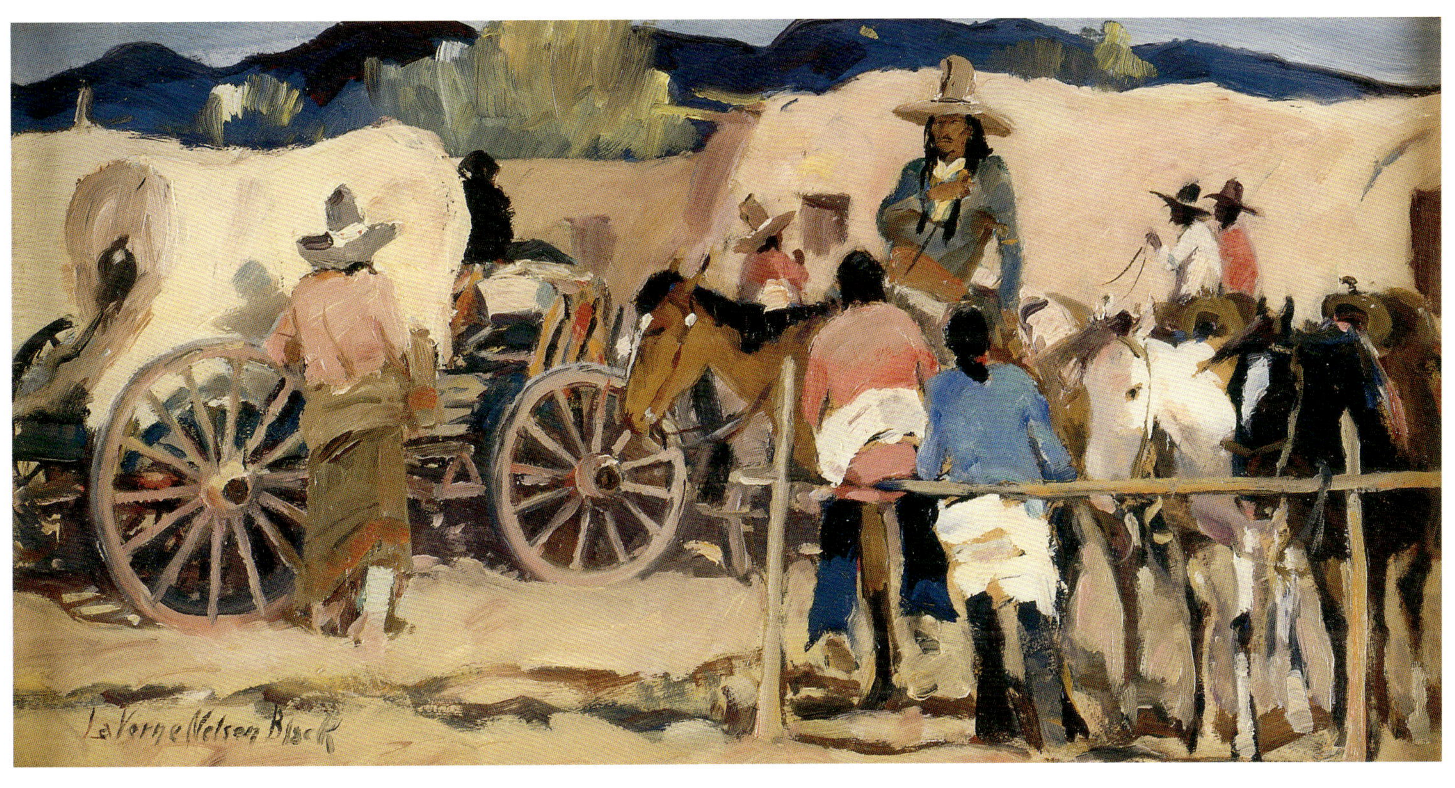
LaVerne Nelson Black

50 Andrew Dasburg

U.S., b. France, 1887–1979

Taxco, 1932
Watercolor on paper
14 × 20¾ in.
Purchase, Richard H. and Adeline J. Fleischaker Collection, 1996

Andrew Dasburg, who would become the leader of the Taos Modernists, was born in Paris but moved to New York with his widowed mother when he was five. They lived in the Hell's Kitchen section of the city, and his mother worked as a seamstress of stage costumes. He studied at the Art Students League starting in 1902 and took night classes with Robert Henri at the New York School of Arts in 1907. In 1909, he traveled to Paris, where he met Gertrude Stein and her brother, Leo, who introduced the young artist to Pablo Picasso and Henri Matisse. Dasburg also met the art dealer Ambroise Vollard, who represented Picasso, Matisse, and Paul Cézanne. Cézanne, who had recently died, would have the greatest impact on Dasburg's work. Dasburg returned to the United States in 1910, settling in the art colony of Woodstock, New York, where he painted and taught art. In 1913, he exhibited four works in the landmark Armory Show and showed near-abstract paintings in another exhibition.

Also in 1913, the artist met the bohemian patroness Mabel Dodge, who presided over a salon of artists and writers and who would become a close, lifelong friend. In 1918, Dasburg, who had been living in Dodge's New York apartment, traveled to Taos and became the first of her many guests in New Mexico. From 1918 on, he spent a portion of each year in Taos and the rest in Woodstock or New York City. In 1923, he became a part-time resident of Santa Fe.

In the summers of 1929 and 1930, Dasburg spent much time with John Marin in Taos, as guests of Mabel Dodge, who through a fourth marriage had become Mabel Dodge Luhan. Marin's frequent use of watercolor as a medium (see cat. no. 63) encouraged Dasburg to use watercolor, too, as in *Taxco.*

Dasburg painted *Taxco* in Mexico in 1932 while on a Guggenheim Fellowship to study the work of the Mexican muralists. After arriving in Mexico City, he continued south to Taxco, where he stayed with Mabel Dodge Luhan's son, John Evans, who had a house there. Taxco was a remote, picturesque mountain village that had been an important silver mining center in the eighteenth century but that the twentieth century seemed to have forgotten until the completion of a road from Taxco to Cuernavaca in 1931. A number of artists traveled to Taxco after Mexican muralist David Alfaro Siqueiros was sentenced to internal exile in the town from 1930 through 1932 for his role in unionizing miners in Jalisco.

In *Taxco,* Dasburg depicted in a Cubist manner the angular rhythms and geometric structure he felt underlay a scene of adobes on a hillside in the Mexican town. Dasburg had written about such Cubist art, which developed out of Cézanne's style, in an essay of 1923:

> *In one of his letters, Cézanne writes: "I see the planes criss-crossing and overlapping and the lines sometimes seem to fall"—a sentence vividly descriptive of the early work of the Cubists and bearing within it the germ of Cubism. . . .*
>
> *Cubism is a geometry of rhythm and an architecture of matter. Two considerations are fundamental to the understanding of rhythm. One is the force of gravity, the other, the upward impulse in living things. All matter shows the effect of one or both of these conditions.*

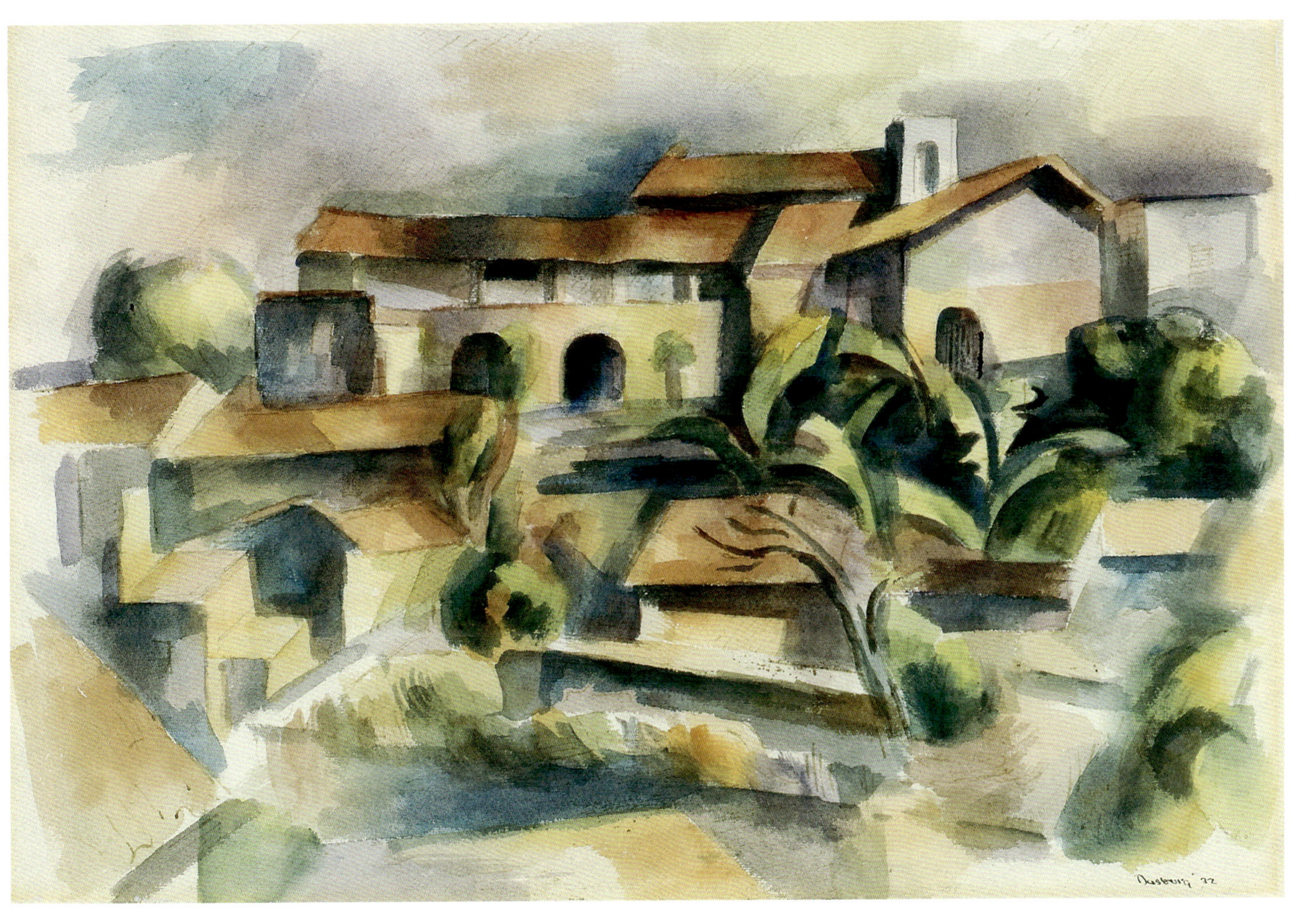

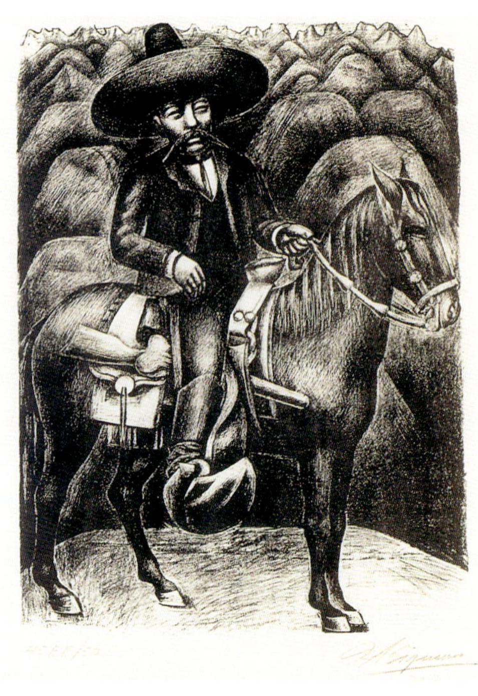

David Alfaro Siqueiros
Mexico, 1896–1974
Zapata, 1930, lithograph, edition: 45/50,
20¼ × 15⅛ in. Gift of Charles McKinney, 1968

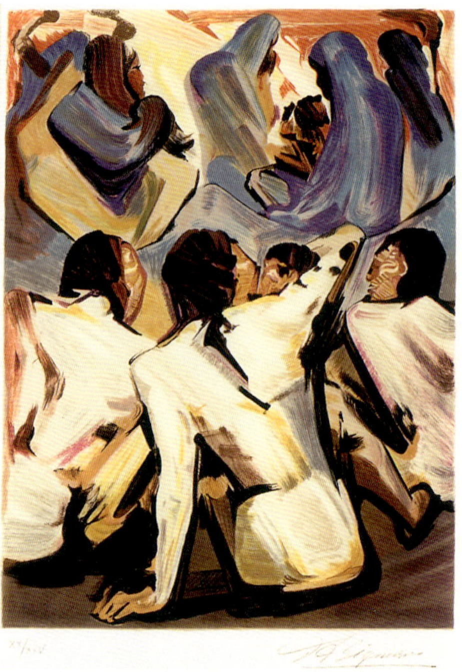

David Alfaro Siqueiros
Mexico, 1896–1974
Women of Mezquital (Mujeres del Mezquital),
1968, lithograph, edition: 20/25, 21¼ × 15⅞ in.
Gift of J. Donald Walp, 2002

In Mexico, Dasburg renewed his friendship with the Modernist Marsden Hartley, who was also on a Guggenheim Fellowship, but a shadow was cast by the suicide of Hartley's close friend, the poet Hart Crane. (In 1932, Crane, too, was a Guggenheim Fellow in Mexico, where he intended to write an epic poem. Instead, Crane felt depleted, and while returning by boat to the United States on April 26, 1932, he leaped overboard.) Dasburg's Guggenheim Fellowship was to fund a year in Mexico, but during his stay, his second wife filed for divorce in Santa Fe. Because of depression and practical concerns relating to the divorce, Dasburg abandoned his fellowship after three months and returned to Santa Fe.

In 1933, Dasburg established permanent residence in Taos, where he attempted to paint the Southwest—including landscapes, still lifes, and portraits—as Cézanne had painted the Provence region in France. Also in 1933, Dasburg married Marina Wister, the daughter of Owen Wister, author of *The Virginian*.

51 Nicolai Fechin

U.S., b. Russia, 1881–1955

Indian Girl with Pottery, n.d.
Oil on canvas
20 × 16 in.
Gift of William H. Thams in memory of Roxanne P. Thams, 2003

Nicolai Fechin was born in Arzamas, Russia, which was a prosperous trading town on the Volga River. At age four, he contracted meningitis, and his miraculous recovery involved a priest moving a revered icon over Fechin's inert body. Fechin later claimed that the illness had long-standing aftereffects: "I grew up thin, high-strung, and overimaginative. I became too sensitive and shy." His father was a woodcarver and icon-maker, and as a child, Fechin, who liked to draw, helped his father design icons and carve.

After his father deserted the family, Fechin studied at the Kazan School of Art, where he received widespread recognition. He continued his studies at the leading Russian art school, the Imperial Academy of St. Petersburg, where he was the outstanding pupil of the famed Russian painter Ilya Repin. Pursuing a typical academic education, Fechin concentrated on drawing. He won the Prix de Rome in 1901, which enabled him to travel through Europe. He then taught at the Kazan School of Art for thirteen years and married the director's daughter. (A painting of her, *Spring in the Steppe,* made in 1913, the year they married, is in the Fleischaker Collection.) Fechin achieved success, exhibiting and finding patrons in Europe and the United States.

The Bolshevik Revolution of 1917 ended Fechin's prosperity. The Modernists took over and closed the Russian art academies. Fechin's associations with Czarist Russia made him a tainted artist. After a difficult period and with the help of an American collector from Pittsburgh, Fechin, his wife, and their daughter immigrated to the United States in 1923. He set up a successful studio in New York, painted numerous portraits, received several major awards, and had a solo show at the Art Institute of Chicago.

But Fechin grew tired of city life. He first traveled through the Southwest during a trip to California. In 1927, he settled in Taos, where art patroness Mabel Dodge Luhan offered him a studio and where he remained for the next eight years. He painted the Indians of the Taos Pueblo, as in *Indian Girl with Pottery,* and the landscape around Taos. He also built in Taos an adobe home and carved its wood interior in the manner of Russian wood-carvers. After his divorce, Fechin moved to California, where he lived in Santa Monica for the rest of his life, except for trips to Mexico and Bali.

Fechin created some of his greatest works, including *Indian Girl with Pottery* and the museum's *Girl in a Purple Dress,* in Taos. Taos reminded him of the Russian Caucasus, and the American Indians recalled the nomadic Mongols and other ethnic tribes in Russia. Even in California, he would often paint Taos subjects from memory. His paintings, like *Indian Girl with Pottery,* are characterized by brilliant color and an expressionistic, painterly bravura, with a foundation of virtuoso draftsmanship.

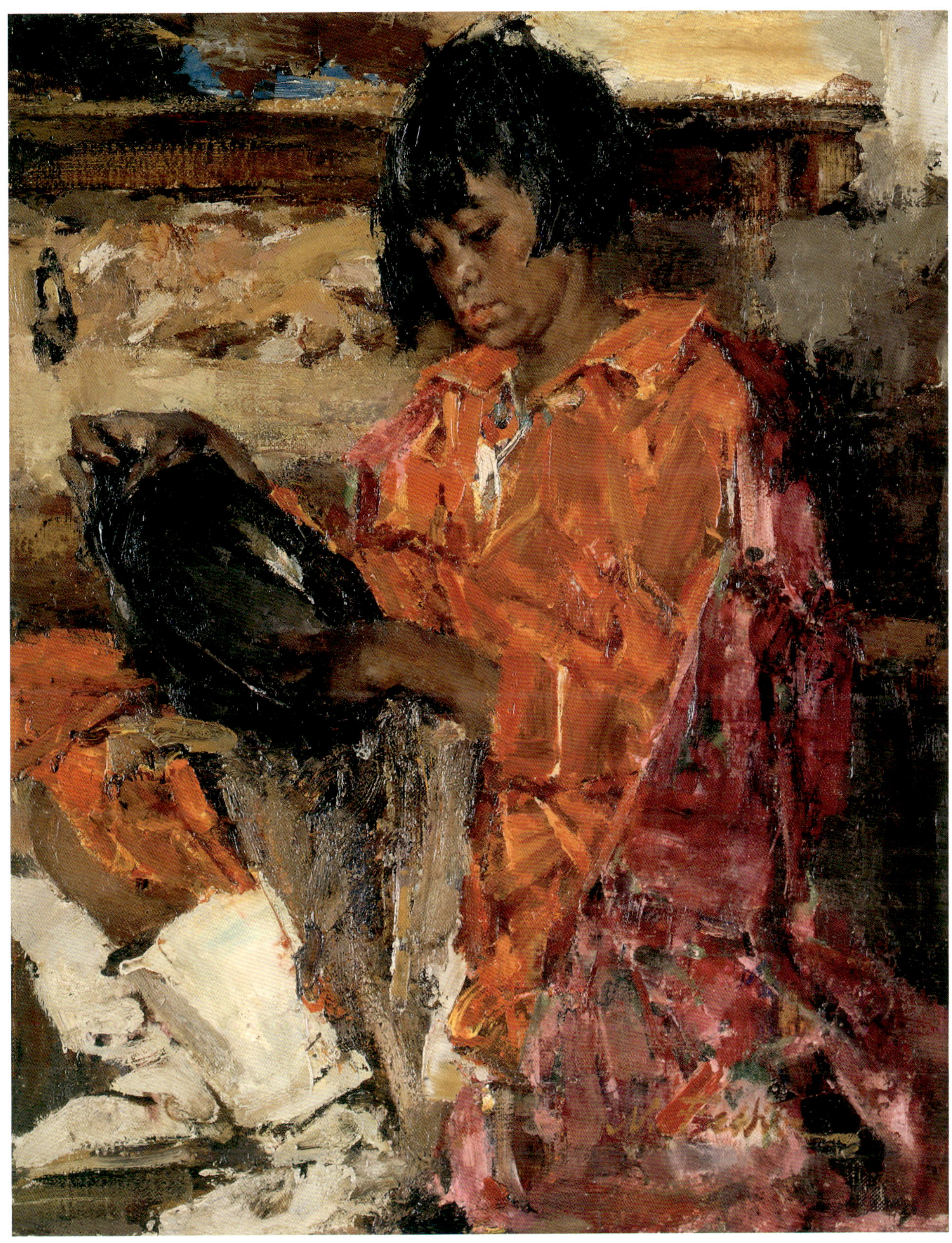

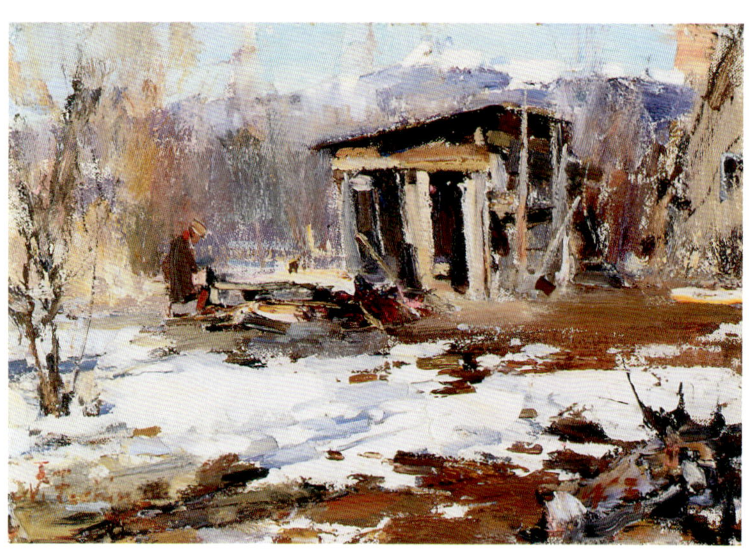

Nicolai Fechin
U.S., b. Russia, 1881–1955
The Broken Shed, n.d., oil on canvas,
11 × 16 in. Purchase, Richard H. and
Adeline J. Fleischaker Collection, 1996

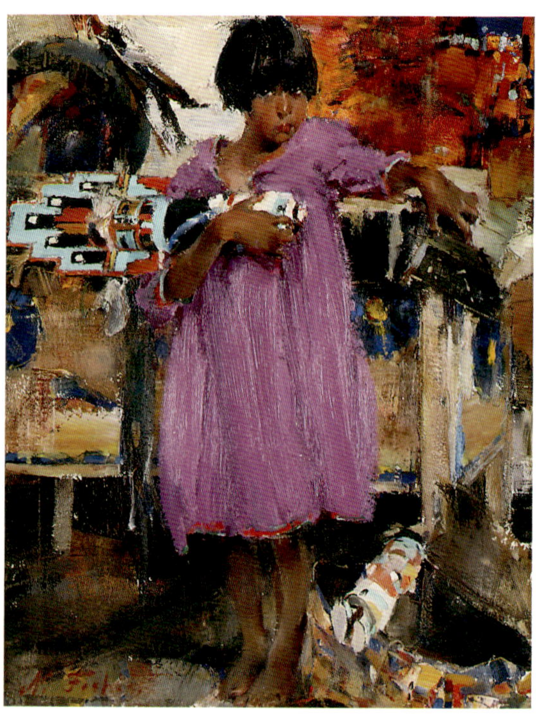

Nicolai Fechin
U.S., b. Russia, 1881–1955
Girl in a Purple Dress, n.d., oil on canvas,
20 × 16 in. Gift of William H. Thams in
memory of Roxanne P. Thams, 2003

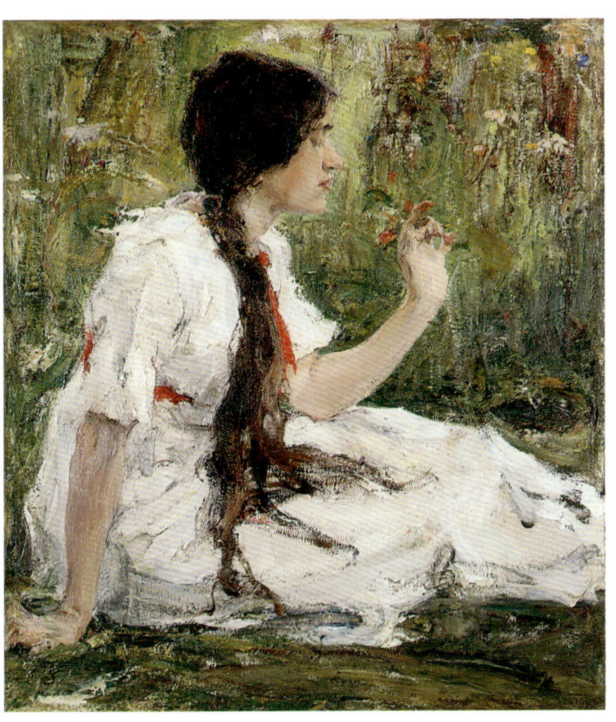

Nicolai Fechin
U.S., b. Russia, 1881–1955
Spring in the Steppe, 1913, oil on canvas, 34 × 31½ in. Purchase, Richard H. and Adeline J. Fleischaker Collection, 1996

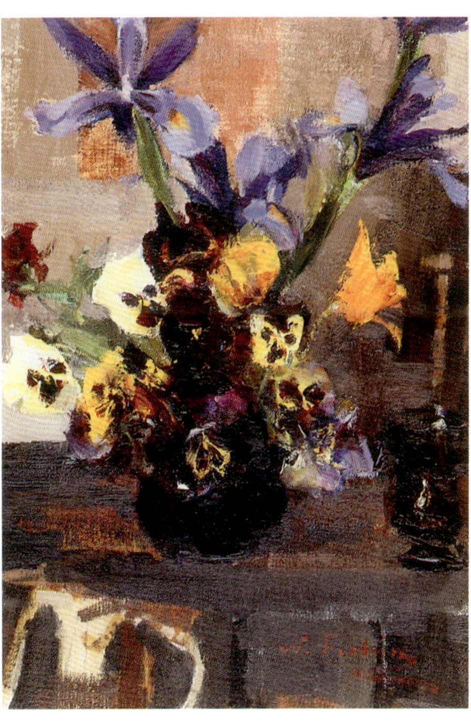

Nicolai Fechin
U.S., b. Russia, 1881–1955
Pansies, 1926–34, oil on canvas, 20 × 14 in. Purchase, Richard H. and Adeline J. Fleischaker Collection, 1996

52 Leon Gaspard

U.S., b. Russia, 1882–1964

Pearl River at Canton, 1926
Oil on board
20 × 22¼ in.
Gift of William H. Thams in memory of Roxanne P. Thams, 2003

Leon Gaspard grew up in Vitebsk, Belarus, west of Moscow, on the Dvina River. (Marc Chagall, a younger student in art school, was also from Vitebsk.) Gaspard's father was an army officer, and his mother an award-winning pianist. As a child, Gaspard played the violin, but he also loved to draw. At age seventeen, he left Russia to train at the Académie Julian in Paris.

While in France, Gaspard married an American and served in the French Aviation Corps during World War I. A great storyteller, he often told of how, during the war, he had jumped from a crashing airplane without a parachute, suffering severe head injuries. In 1916, he moved to the United States with his American wife. Doctors advised Gaspard to live in a dry climate, so the couple spent a few months in Taos; in 1918, they settled permanently in Taos, where Gaspard built a house that was an eclectic blend of Russian and adobe styles.

The museum owns seventeen paintings and pastels by Gaspard, including major works from all phases of his career. He led a life of adventure, traveling extensively through Asia and North Africa; the museum has a number of paintings from these trips, including *Pearl River at Canton.*

Like most of Gaspard's works, *Pearl River at Canton* is painterly, displaying brilliant color and broad brushstrokes. The composition is Chinese-inspired, with a high horizon line, the figures and boats pushed to the outer edges, and the negative space of the river occupying the painting's center. The rich colors of the moonlit scene—the browns and blues surrounding the turquoise of the river—recall James Abbott McNeill Whistler's paintings of night views (*Nocturnes*).

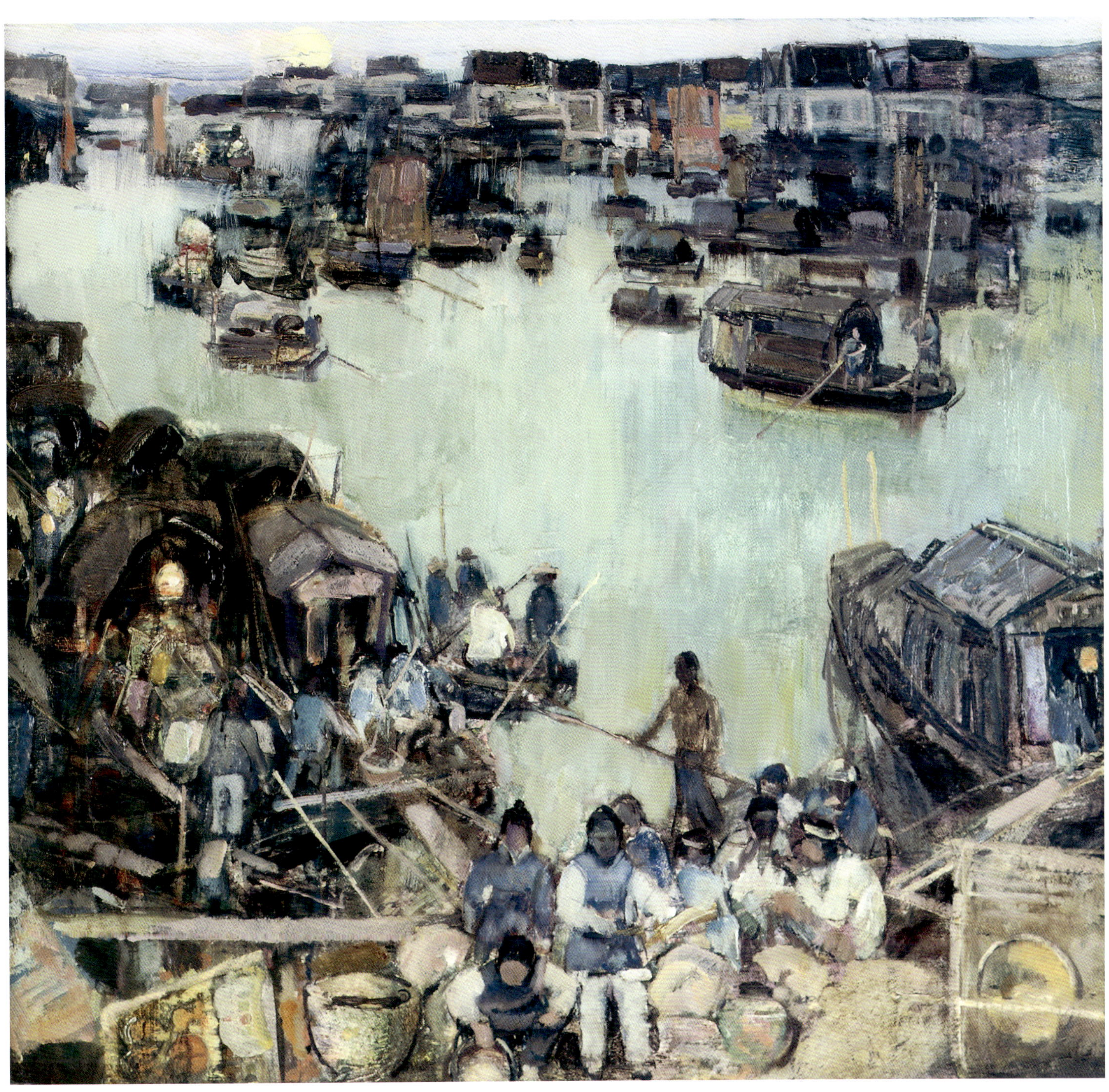

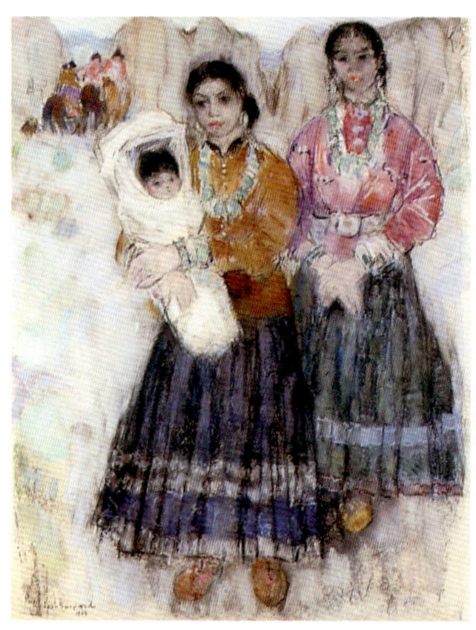

Leon Gaspard
U.S., b. Russia, 1882–1964
Navajo Women, 1954, oil and pastel on paper, 27 × 21 in. Purchase, Richard H. and Adeline J. Fleischaker Collection, 1996

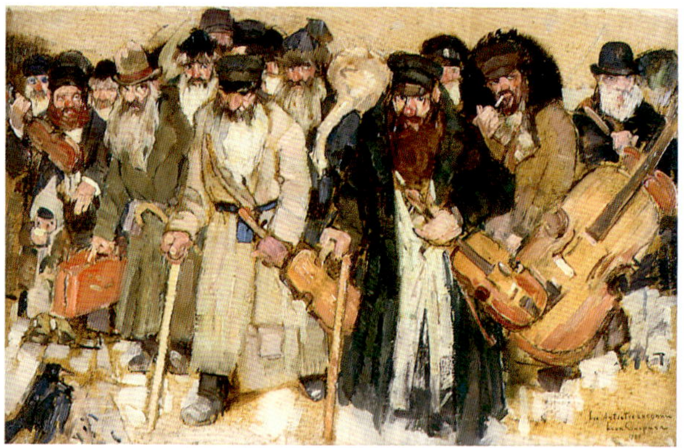

Leon Gaspard
U.S., b. Russia, 1882–1964
The Unknown Artists (Les Artistes inconnus), 1928, oil on silk on board, 12⅜ × 19⅞ in. Gift of William H. Thams in memory of Roxanne P. Thams, 2003

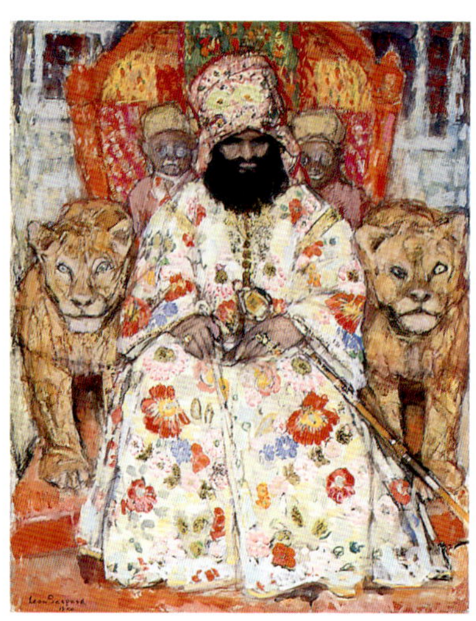

Leon Gaspard
U.S., b. Russia, 1882–1964
King Solomon, 1940, oil, gouache, and gold leaf on paper, 30 × 24 in. Purchase, Richard H. and Adeline J. Fleischaker Collection, 1996

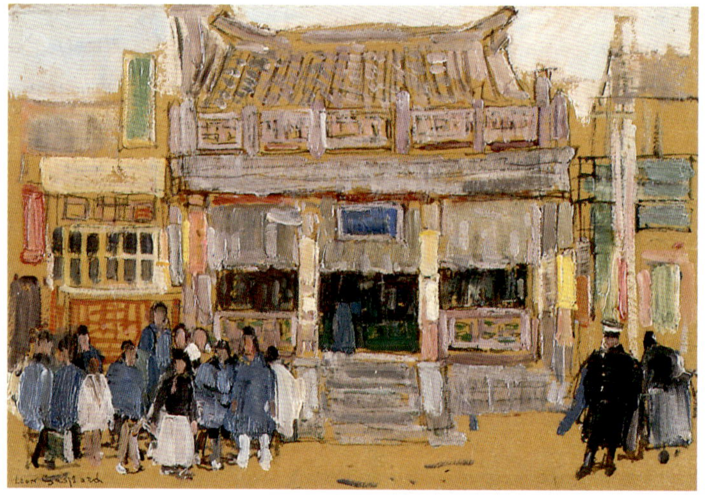

Leon Gaspard
U.S., b. Russia, 1882–1964
Silk Shop, Chinese Scene, n.d., oil on rice paper on board, 7½ × 10 in. Gift of William H. Thams in memory of Roxanne P. Thams, 2003

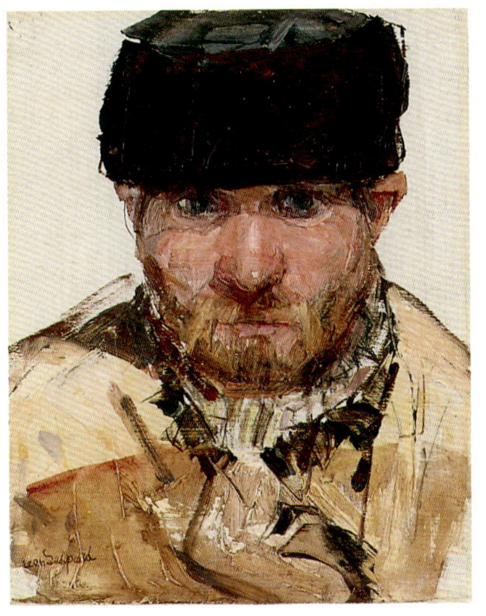

Leon Gaspard
U.S., b. Russia, 1882–1964
Russian Type in Fur Hat, n.d., oil on silk, 7½ × 6 in. Gift of William H. Thams in memory of Roxanne P. Thams, 2003

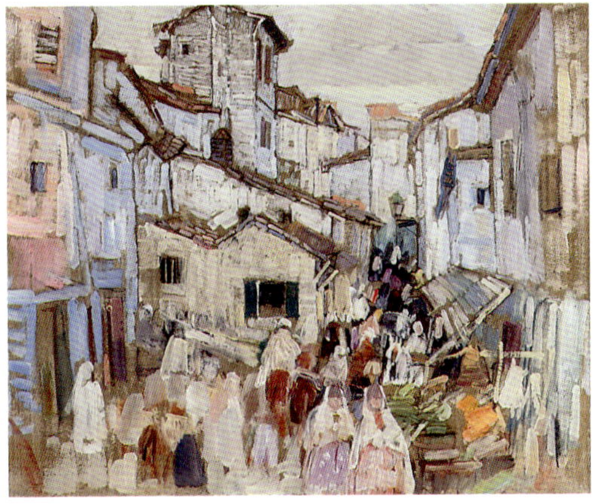

Leon Gaspard
U.S., b. Russia, 1882–1964
Moroccan Market Scene, n.d., oil on silk on board, 12 × 15 in. Purchase, Richard H. and Adeline J. Fleischaker Collection, 1996

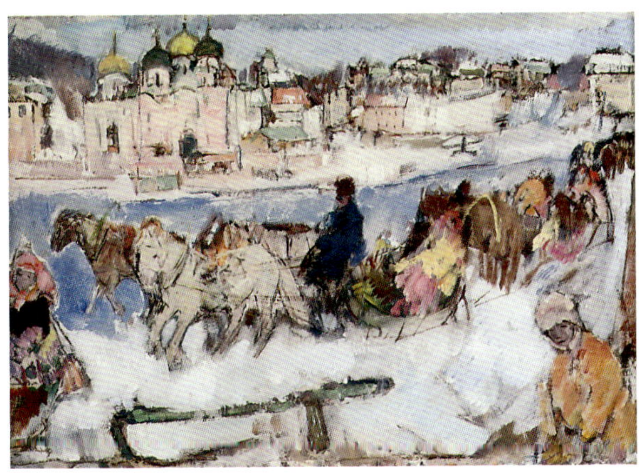

Leon Gaspard
U.S., b. Russia, 1882–1964
Vitebsk on the Dvina, n.d., oil on board, 18 × 26 in. Gift of William H. Thams in memory of Roxanne P. Thams, 2003

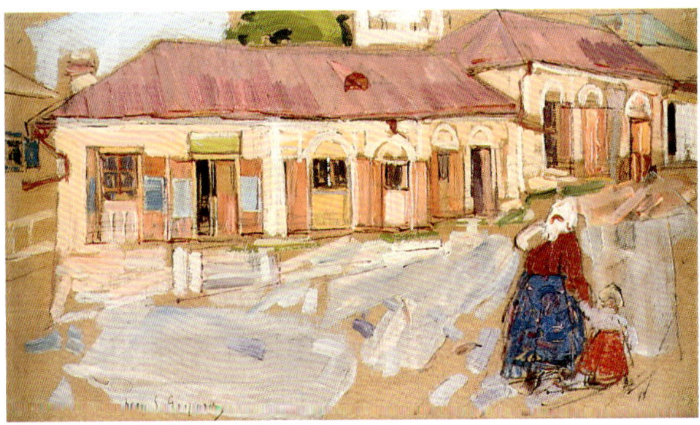

Leon Gaspard
U.S., b. Russia, 1882–1964
Russian Street Scene, 1905, oil on silk on panel, 5½ × 9¾ in. Gift of William H. Thams in memory of Roxanne P. Thams, 2003

53 John Sloan

U.S., 1871–1951

Road to Chimayó, 1926
Oil on canvas
16 × 20 in.
Purchase, Richard H. and Adeline J. Fleischaker Collection, 1996

In *Road to Chimayó,* a solitary traveler on horseback is seen from behind. He anchors the composition, gives scale, and leads the viewer's eye along the road into the distant mountains toward the village of Chimayó, which is located twenty-four miles northeast of Santa Fe, along the "High Road" to Taos. (Chimayó is famous for its miraculous healing waters, around which the Sanctuario de Chimayó, a picturesque adobe church often painted by artists, was built in the early nineteenth century. Even today, thousands of pilgrims visit the shrine annually, especially on Easter weekends.)

Considered a major figure in American art, John Sloan was born in Lock Haven, Pennsylvania. He took night classes at the Pennsylvania Academy of the Fine Arts while working as an illustrator for the *Philadelphia Inquirer.* The artist Robert Henri, whom Sloan had met in the 1890s, encouraged Sloan to paint in oils, and in 1904, Sloan moved to New York to join the Henri-led group of artists called The Eight, who were later also known as the Ashcan School because of their dark palette and their depictions of gritty urban life. Sloan participated in The Eight's historic exhibition of 1908 and in the famous Armory Show of 1913, which introduced Modernism to the American public. Stylistically, Sloan's art was at the vanguard only during the period of The Eight, but he continued to support new art movements. He never traveled abroad.

At the urging of Robert Henri, Sloan visited Santa Fe in the summer of 1919. Sloan subsequently spent every summer in Santa Fe until his death. In Santa Fe, he became the leader of the burgeoning art community and painted landscapes, American Indian rituals, and scenes of Santa Fe's daily life and environs.

Like many of the artists in Taos and Santa Fe, Sloan believed that the Southwest was the most fertile ground for American art, in part because of the precedent of American Indian art. He said, "If American art develops anywhere I think it will be out here in this pre-historic environment." Back East, Sloan promoted and organized American Indian art exhibitions.

About painting landscapes such as *Road to Chimayó,* Sloan wrote:

> *I like to paint the landscape in the Southwest because of the fine geometrical formations and the handsome color. Study of the desert forms, so severe and clear in that atmosphere, helped me to work out principles of plastic design. . . . I like the color out there. . . . Because the air is so clear you feel the reality of the things in the distance.*

Compositionally, *Road to Chimayó,* with its lone figure on horseback traveling through a landscape, is similar to the best known of Sloan's paintings of New Mexico, *Chama Running Red,* a larger canvas painted a year later and now in the Anschutz Collection in Denver.

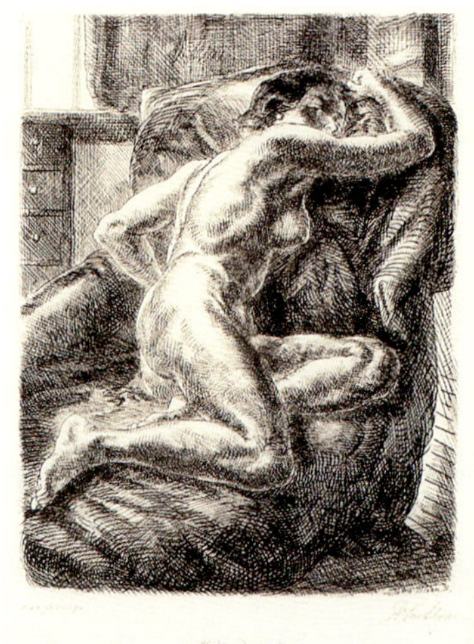

John Sloan
U.S., 1871–1951
Nude on Draped Chair, 1931, etching on paper, edition of 100, 6⅞ × 5½ in.
Gift of Leo Askew, 1962

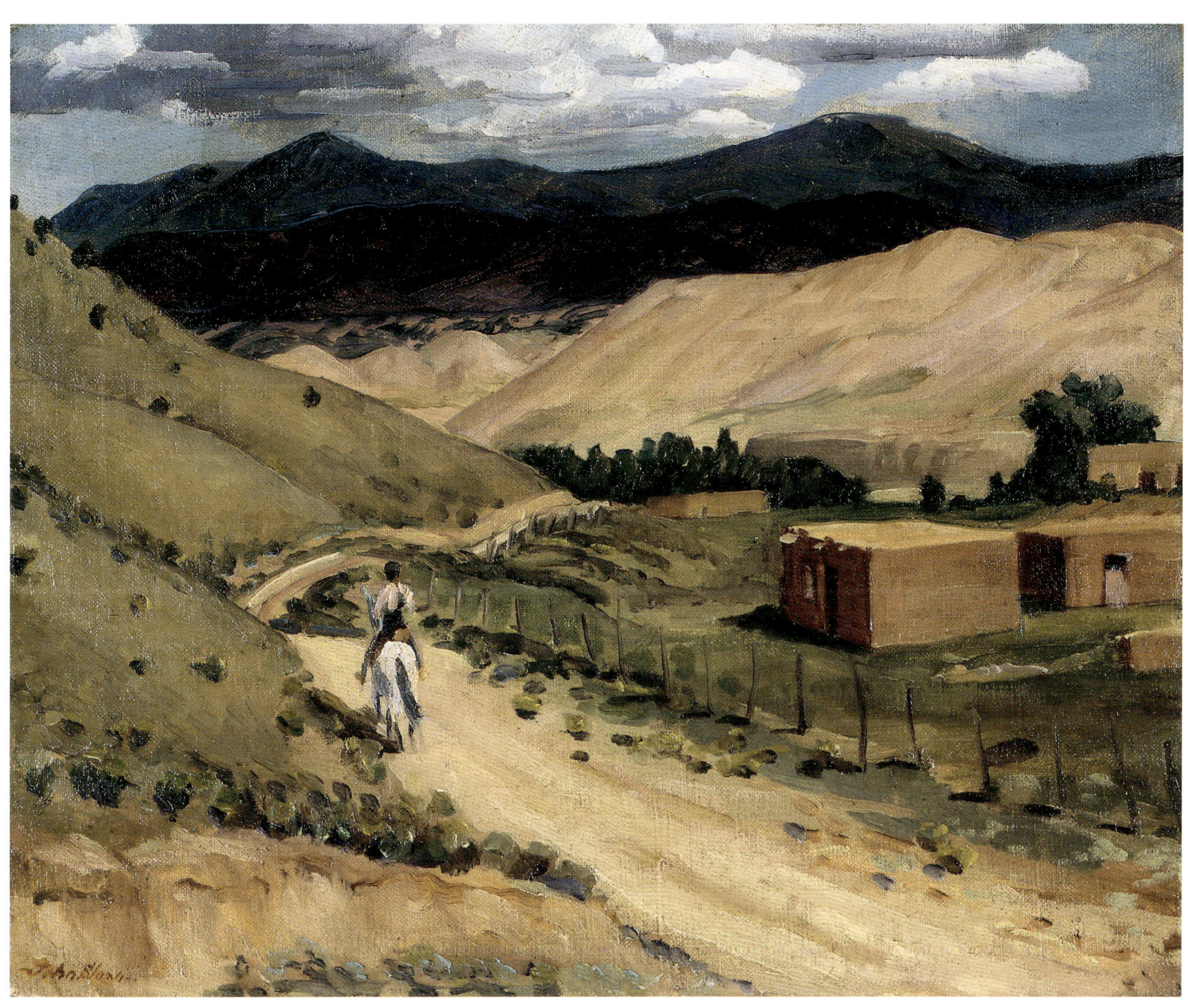

54 William Penhallow Henderson

U.S., 1877–1943

Road to Taos at the Rio Grande, n.d.
Oil on canvas
32 × 40 in.
Purchase, Richard H. and Adeline J. Fleischaker Collection, 1996

In *Road to Taos at the Rio Grande,* William Penhallow Henderson applied a Post-Impressionist style to his Southwestern subject, with an emphasis on rugged form rendered in unbroken, vivid, expressive color. In the foreground of the painting, travelers in a covered wagon rest among trees that frame the composition. In the lighter-toned middleground, a cow grazes and the river cuts the canvas horizontally, while in the background, a steep, angular, luminous mountain rises. The middleground and background are strongly distinguished from the narrow, raised foreground, so that the foreground resembles a stage set with a painted backdrop.

The artist grew up in Massachusetts, Texas, and Kansas, the son of a sea captain who was an amateur painter. Henderson trained at the Massachusetts Normal Art School and the School of the Boston Museum of Fine Arts. Starting in 1902, he traveled for two years in Europe, where he was drawn to the great colorists of the past, such as the painter Diego Velázquez. In 1904, Henderson moved to Chicago, where he taught art and married Alice Corbin, a writer and the editor of *Poetry* magazine.

Alice's tuberculosis prompted the couple to move to Santa Fe in 1916 to seek treatment in a sanitorium. Henderson became an integral member of the Santa Fe art colony as it developed after World War I. In addition to painting in oils and pastels and illustrating books such as his wife's well-known *Brothers of Light: The Penitentes of the Southwest* (1937), Henderson handcrafted Spanish Colonial–style furniture, designed stage sets, and was the architect of Santa Fe's Wheelwright Museum of the American Indian.

Although Henderson had been greatly inspired by the painter James Abbott McNeill Whistler earlier in his career, in Santa Fe, probably under the influence of B. J. O. Nordfeldt (see cat. no. 55), he turned to Paul Cézanne (see cat. no. 18) as a model. Other sources of inspiration were Asian philosophy and art, especially Japanese prints, with their flat, nonrepresentational color.

The river in *Road to Taos at the Rio Grande* flows from Colorado through New Mexico and on to form the border between Mexico and Texas. A few miles to the west of Taos, north of the location depicted in this painting, the fast-moving river slices through a plateau, forming a deep and dizzying canyon.

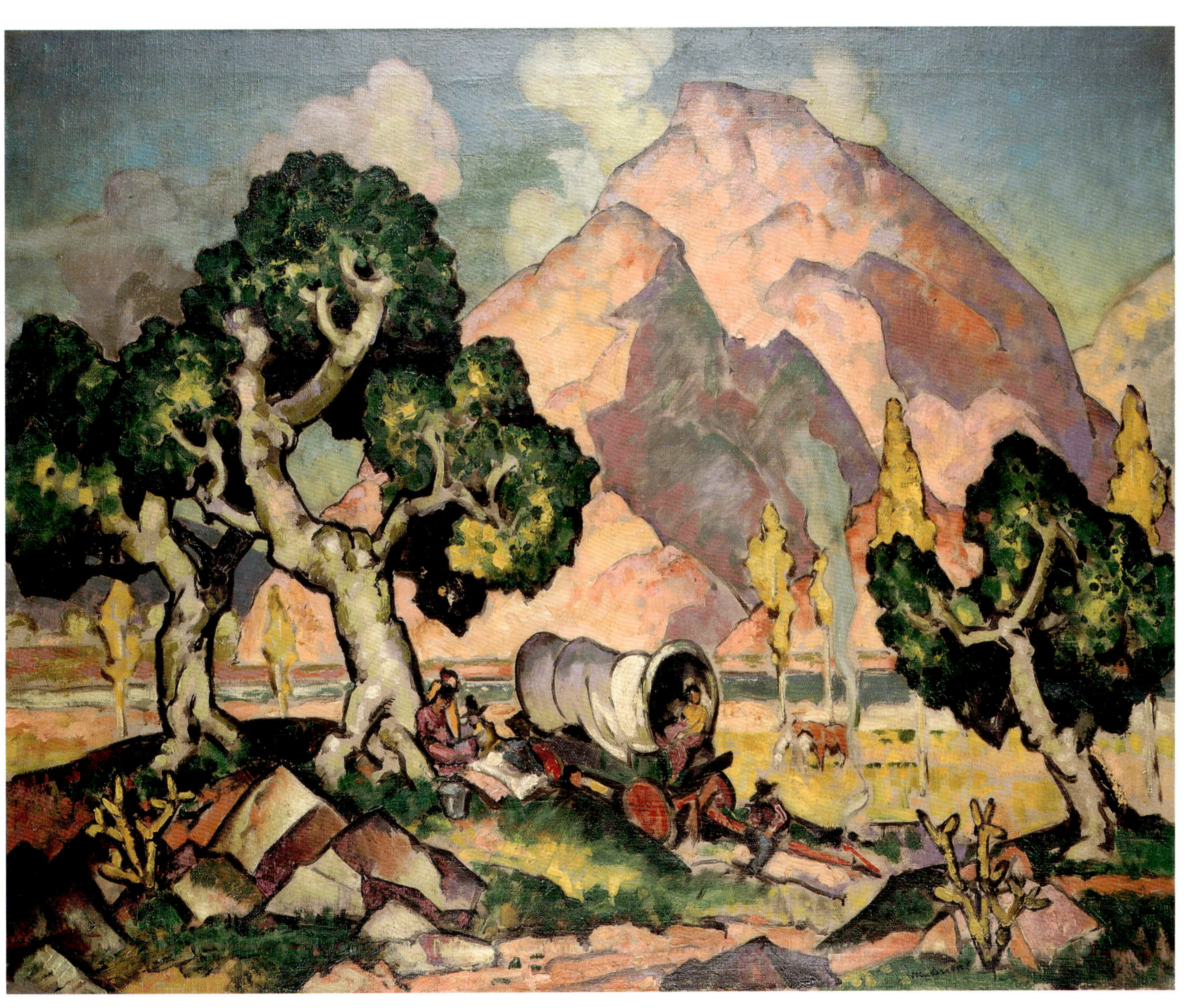

55 B. J. O. Nordfeldt

U.S., b. Sweden, 1878–1955

Thunder Dance, 1928
Oil on canvas
34 × 43 in.
Gift of Oscar B. Jacobson, 1966

Born in Sweden, B. J. O. Nordfeldt immigrated in 1891 to Chicago, where he studied at the Art Institute. After moving to New York, he received a commission to paint the International Harvester Company's murals at the 1900 Paris Exposition. Between 1903 and the outbreak of World War I in 1914, he divided his time between the United States and Europe and studied briefly at the Académie Julian in Paris. In Europe, Nordfeldt was influenced by the color in Henri Matisse's work, the expressiveness in Vincent van Gogh's, and above all, the structure in Paul Cézanne's.

Nordfeldt met artist William Penhallow Henderson when both were camouflage artists in California during World War I. Henderson, who had moved to Santa Fe in 1916, persuaded Nordfeldt to visit New Mexico in 1918. Nordfeldt was attracted by the ruggedness of the Southwest and its simplicity, dramatic landscape, and diverse cultures. The following year, the artist moved to Santa Fe, where he lived until 1937, except for time spent in Wichita and Minneapolis during the Great Depression. In 1920, Nordfeldt organized, as a counterpart to the Taos Society of Artists, the Santa Fe Art Club, along with Gustave Baumann, Randall Davey, Raymond Jonson, and John Sloan, to sponsor joint exhibitions of their work around the country.

Nordfeldt was an outstanding etcher, but he became best known for his Modernist still lifes and Southwestern paintings, such as *Thunder Dance.* One of Nordfeldt's greatest works, *Thunder Dance* depicts a tribal dance at Taos Pueblo. A frieze of dancers forms the foreground of the painting, and a mesa framed by adobe buildings fills the background. Nordfeldt often watched American Indian ceremonies, but no one was allowed to sketch or photograph the rituals, so he would return to his studio to paint them from memory. In *Thunder Dance,* he is more interested in depicting the rhythm and raw spirit of the dance than in observed reality.

As Cézanne had done in his paintings, Nordfeldt carefully constructed *Thunder Dance* one broad brushstroke at a time. The visibility of the brushstrokes emphasizes the two-dimensional surface of the canvas and creates a tension between the flatness of the canvas and the painting's illusion of depth, volume, and mass.

Nordfeldt gave *Thunder Dance* to Oscar B. Jacobson, the founding director of the University of Oklahoma's art museum and a fellow Swede. Jacobson donated the painting to the museum in 1966, shortly before his death.

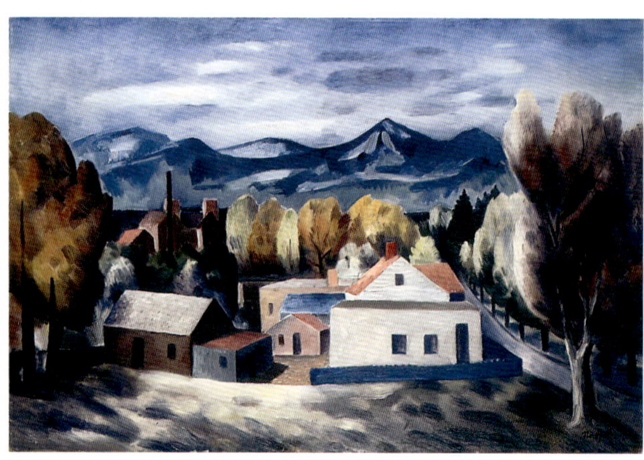

B. J. O. Nordfeldt
U.S., b. Sweden, 1878–1955
Santa Fe Landscape, 1934, oil on canvas, 24 × 36 in. Purchase, Richard H. and Adeline J. Fleischaker Collection, 1996

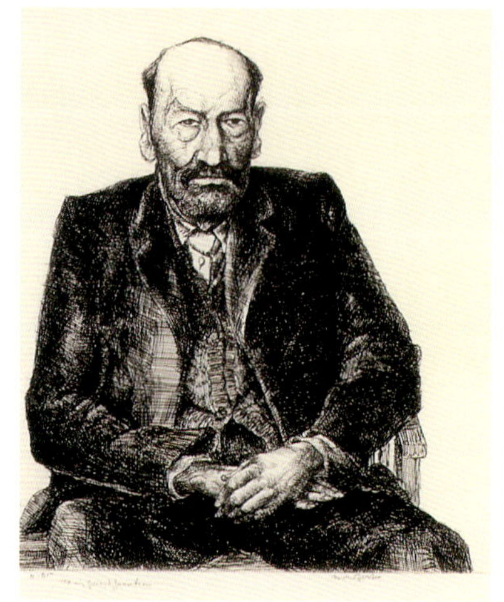

B. J. O. Nordfeldt
U.S., b. Sweden, 1878–1955
Portrait of Old Man, 1921, etching, 8¼ × 7⅜ in. Gift of Oscar B. Jacobson Estate, 1981

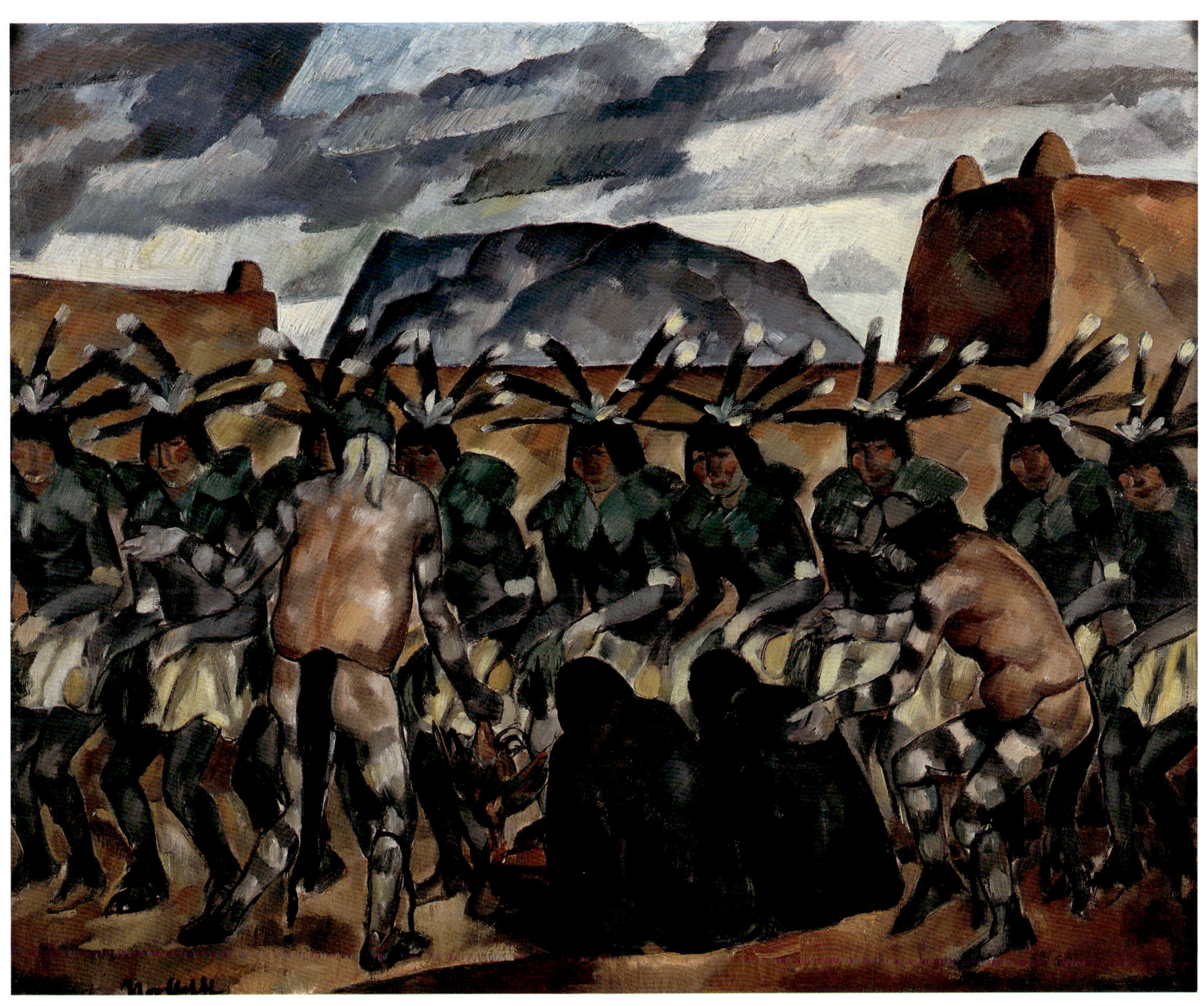

56 Jozef Bakos

U.S., 1891–1977

Still Life, c. 1922
Oil on canvas
26 × 34 in.
University purchase, before 1933

The son of Polish immigrants to Buffalo, New York, Jozef Bakos attended night classes at the Art School of the Albright Knox Gallery starting in 1912. After graduating in 1917, he studied privately with painter John E. Thompson but could not afford to travel to Europe, as was customary for artists at that time. Thompson, who had been to Paris and visited the salon of Gertrude Stein, exposed Bakos to Modernism, especially the work of Paul Cézanne.

Bakos first headed west in 1918, when he followed Thompson to Colorado. In 1920, Bakos traveled to Santa Fe to visit Walter Mruk, an artist friend from Buffalo, and in 1921, Bakos moved permanently to Santa Fe. To make money, he worked briefly with Mruk as a forest ranger in what is now the Bandelier National Monument, north of Santa Fe. Bakos later supported himself by carving Spanish Colonial–style furniture, including the headboards on the beds of Santa Fe's La Fonda Hotel.

In 1921, Bakos became a founding member of Los Cinco Pintores (The Five Painters), a group of avant-garde artists who painted the life, cultures, and landscapes of New Mexico. All under thirty and trained exclusively in the United States, Los Cinco Pintores included Bakos, Mruk, Willard Nash, William Shuster, and Fremont Ellis. Shortly after the group's foundation, Bakos articulated its populist leanings:

> *The group proposes a novel though practical plan to bring art to the public. Its concept is that art is universal, that it sings to the peasant laborer as well as to the connoisseur.*
>
> *The group will endeavor to reach out to the factory, the mine, the hospital, as well as the gallery, and it aims to awaken the workers to a keener realization and appreciation of beauty. . . . One of the first steps will be to arrange an exhibition to be sent to the larger factories and mills of industrial centers to be . . . exhibited to working men and women in the very environment in which they work.*

After failing in their attempt to exhibit in a prison, Los Cinco Pintores had an inaugural show at the Museum of Fine Arts in Santa Fe in late 1921. The following year, they arranged a traveling exhibition of their work, which opened at the University of Oklahoma, continued to venues in Kansas, and closed in Oklahoma City. Los Cinco Pintores remained intact until 1926.

In 1923, the Taos Society of Artists rejected Bakos and William Penhallow Henderson for membership because some considered the Santa Feans too Modernist. This created a rift in the Taos Society. Subsequently, artists from both Taos and Santa Fe who were sympathetic to Modernism founded a new group called the New Mexico Painters. The New Mexico Painters included Frank G. Applegate, Gustave Baumann, Ernest L. Blumenschein, Andrew Dasburg, Randall Davey, Victor Higgins, B. J. O. Nordfeldt, John Sloan, Theodore van Soelen, and Walter Ufer, as well as Henderson and Bakos.

Beginning in the 1920s, Bakos received much recognition and showed in exhibitions nationwide. In 1929, he married an Italian

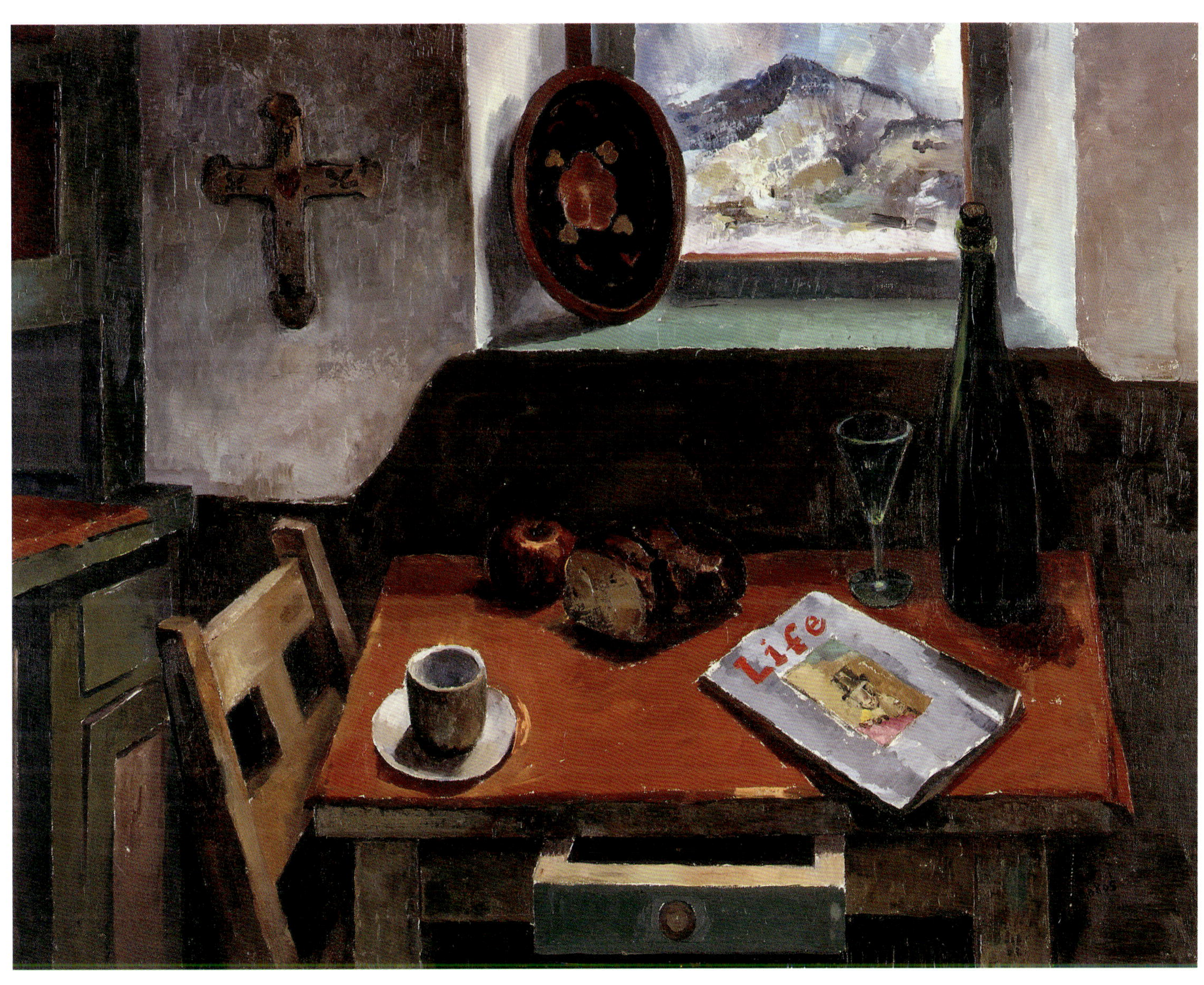
Life

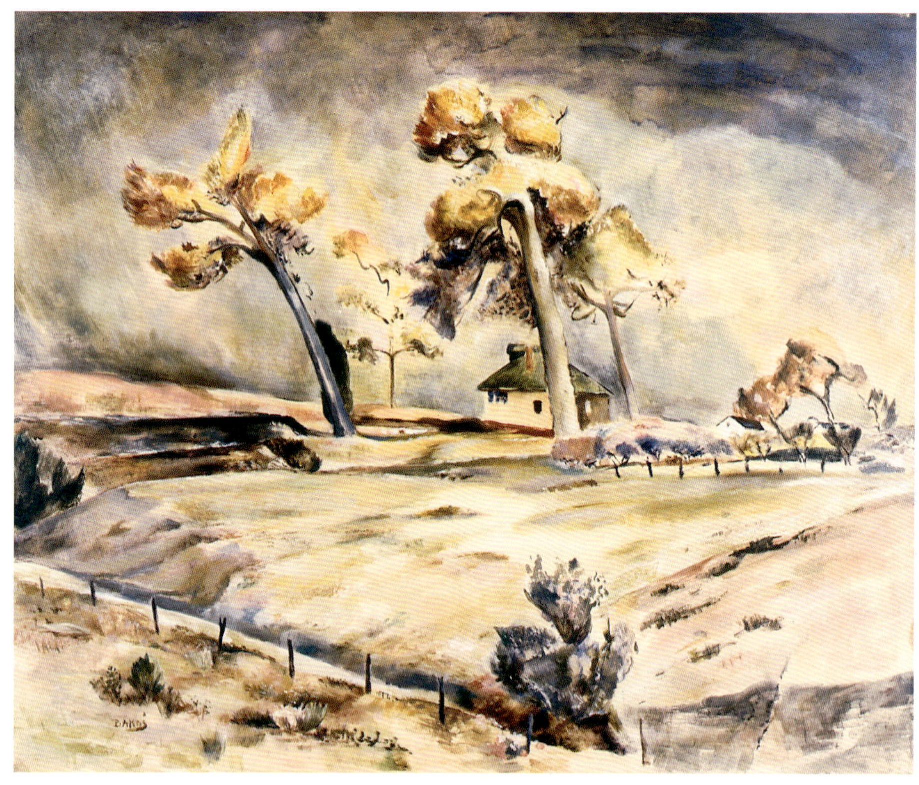

Jozef Bakos
U.S., 1891–1977
Cienega, 1942, tempera on panel,
28 × 34 in. W.P.A. Collection, 1943

countess who had studied as a concert pianist in Berlin; they entertained many artists and writers in their home, including the photographer Ansel Adams (see cat. no. 67), who had originally trained as a musician. Bakos taught art at Santa Fe High School for more than thirty years.

Still Life depicts the kitchen in Bakos's house on Camino del Monte Sol, with a view through the window of Sun Mountain. (In the fall of 1921, Los Cinco Pintores had built adobe homes for themselves on the outskirts of Santa Fe, along Camino del Monte Sol.)

Still Life could be considered an homage to Cézanne. In New Mexico, while under the influence of Cézanne followers Nordfeldt and Dasburg, Bakos drew inspiration from the French painter. Sun Mountain recalls Cézanne's countless images of Mont Sainte-Victoire, while the wooden table, with its top tilted forward, echoes similar tables in Cézanne's *Cardplayers,* a version of which is in the Barnes Collection in Pennsylvania. The open drawer in *Still Life* is like those in the *House of Cards* paintings by one of Cézanne's forebears, the eighteenth-century French painter Jean-Baptiste-Siméon Chardin.

In *Still Life,* Bakos explores the relationship of painting to life. He examines the interplay between the two-dimensional canvas and the illusion of three-dimensional space. For example, the window refers to the concept of a painting as a window, with the illusional three-dimensional space beyond the flat plane of the picture's surface correlating to an actual three-dimensional space beyond a windowpane. The open drawer, which seems to project out of the painting, creates an illusion of depth while serving to unite the viewer's actual space with the make-believe space of the painting. *Life* magazine, with its title in prominent red letters, alludes to a traditional painting's attempt to depict a life or world—in this case, the painter's own life, since it shows his kitchen. "Life" may also be a pun on the subject matter of the painting, a still life.

A variant of *Still Life,* called *My Kitchen* (1922), is in the Anschutz Collection in Denver. The major difference between the two paintings is the magazine title, which in *My Kitchen* is an illegible blur.

Still Life was one of the first paintings to enter the collection of the University of Oklahoma's art museum.

57 Birger Sandzén

U.S., b. Sweden, 1871–1954

Western Kansas, n.d.
Oil on canvas
16 × 24 in.
Museum purchase, 1961

Birger Sandzén was born in Blidsberg, Sweden, in 1871, the son of a Lutheran minister. In Sweden, Sandzén graduated from Skara College and attended Lund University. Once he decided to become a professional artist, he studied art for two years in Stockholm. Sandzén then traveled to Paris, where he met many American artists.

At age twenty-three, Sandzén came to America, intending to travel for two years through the United States and Mexico. He planned to fund the trip by teaching at Bethany College in Lindsborg, Kansas, which he had learned about from a book by Dr. Carl Aaron Swensson, a fellow Swede who had founded the college on the Great Plains in 1881. Sandzén liked the United States so much that he decided to live there permanently, making occasional visits to Europe and Mexico. He spent most of his time in Lindsborg, including fifty-two years at Bethany College, where he taught art history and studio art.

In the United States, Sandzén became known nationally, exhibiting in New York and elsewhere. He was a frequent visitor to Taos and Santa Fe, and in 1922, he was made an associate member of the Taos Society of Artists.

With a populist bent, Sandzén promoted art throughout the Great Plains region. He is especially appreciated at the University of Oklahoma as the mentor and friend of Oscar B. Jacobson, the long-serving director of the university's School of Art and the museum's founding director. Jacobson had attended Bethany College before studying art at Yale University. At Bethany College, Sandzén also taught Swedish-born Samuel Holmberg, who was the founding director of the University of Oklahoma's School of Art and whom Jacobson succeeded.

Primarily known for his landscapes, Sandzén was a great admirer of Modern French art, Asian art, and the stories of Hans Christian Andersen. *Western Kansas* typifies Sandzén's style: the controlled, constructive brushstrokes pay homage to Paul Cézanne, while the brilliant, expressionistic color veers to the nonnaturalistic and shows the influence of Vincent van Gogh and the Fauves.

Sandzén was an outstanding printmaker as well as painter. The museum owns twenty-three of his lithographs and woodcuts.

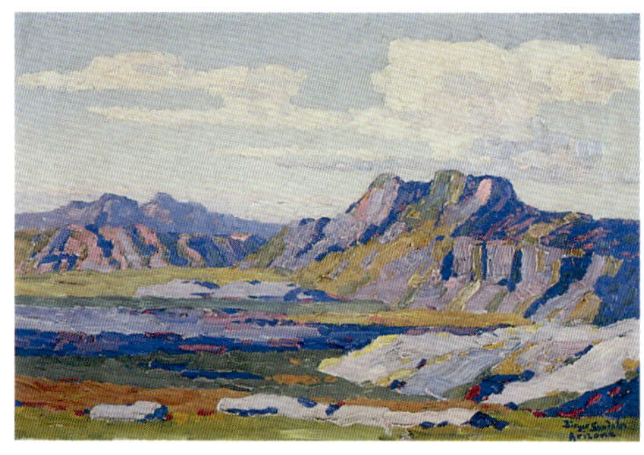

Birger Sandzén
U.S., b. Sweden, 1871–1954
In the Painted Desert, Arizona, n.d., oil on canvas, 16 × 24 in. Gift of the Oscar B. Jacobson Estate, 1977

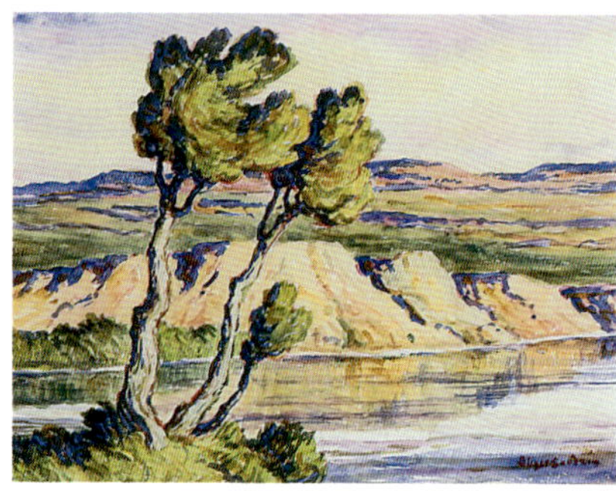

Birger Sandzén
U.S., b. Sweden, 1871–1954
Kansas Creek, n.d., watercolor on paper, 14 × 18¾ in. Museum purchase, 1942

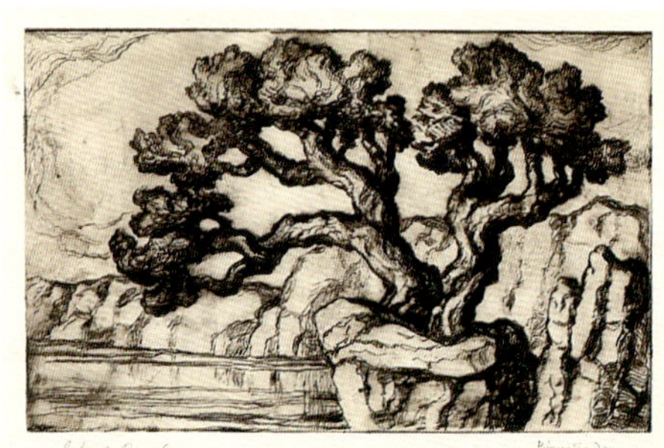

Birger Sandzén
U.S., b. Sweden, 1871–1954
Colorado River Cedars, 1933, drypoint on paper, edition: 6/35, 6⅞ × 11 in. Gift of the Oscar B. Jacobson Estate, 1976

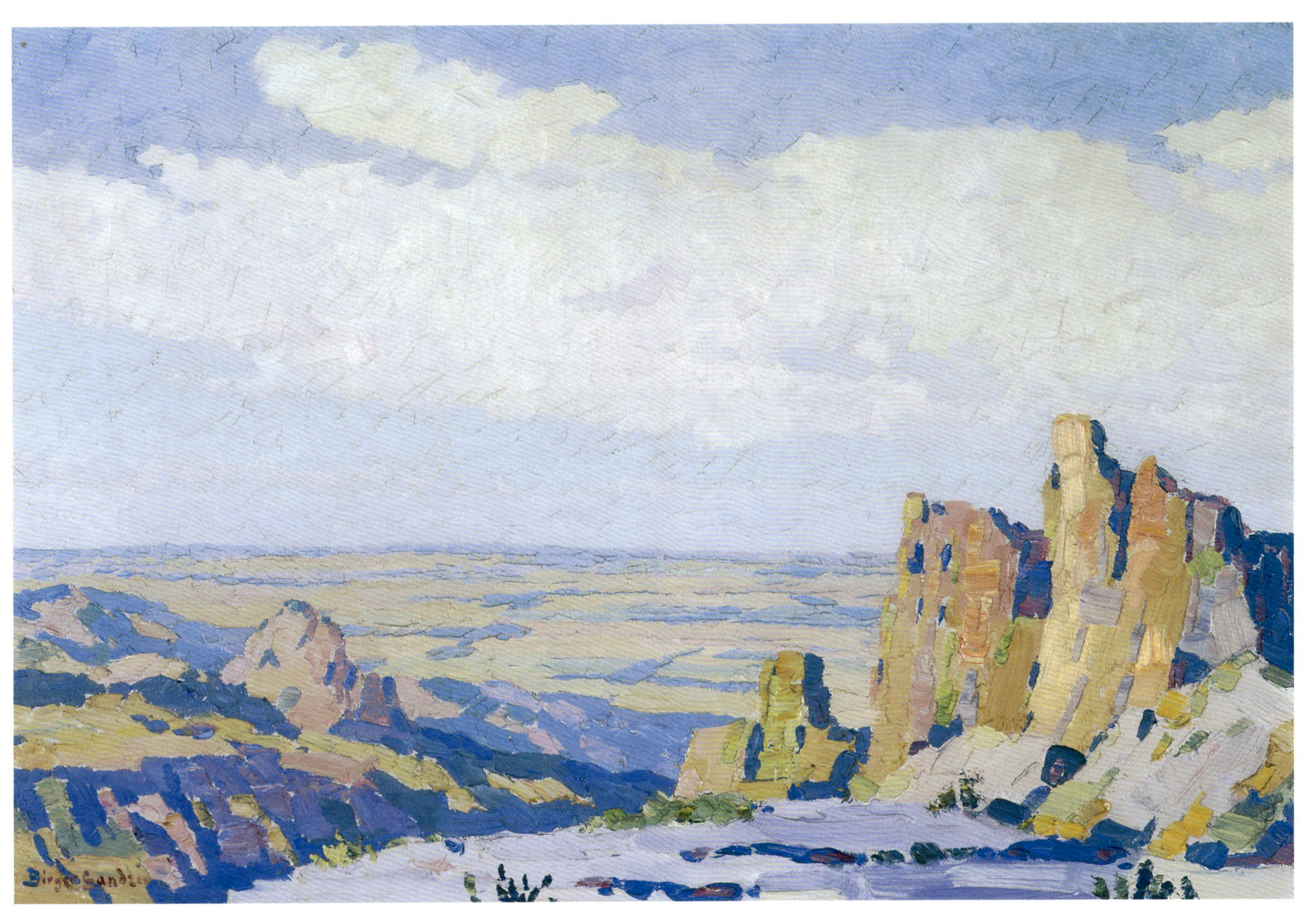

58 Carl Oscar Borg

U.S., b. Sweden, 1879–1947

Walpi, n.d.
Tempera on paper
5 × 6¾ in.
Gift of J. Donald Walp, 2003

Carl Oscar Borg was born in Sweden into a poor family. As a child, he copied pictures from books and at age fifteen apprenticed to a house painter. A few years later, he sailed for England, where he became an assistant to the portrait and marine artist George Johansen. Borg continued to the United States and worked as a house, sign, and furniture painter in Canada, New York, and Philadelphia. In 1903, he sailed to California as a seaman on the freighter SS *Arizona*. Jumping ship at San Francisco with no money to pay train fare, he walked 450 miles along the railroad tracks to Los Angeles.

Borg soon became involved with the Garvanza circle of artists, writers, anthropologists, and other intellectuals. This Los Angeles–area group believed that European-based American culture had become materialistic and decadent. The Garvanza circle hoped to revitalize American culture with the influence of American Indians, who emphasized spirituality and harmony with nature. Borg adhered to the group's thinking and chose to make the Hopi and Navajo Indians of the Southwest the primary theme of his art.

Having been essentially self-taught as an artist, Borg refined his technical skills through his friendship with the painter William Wendt. Phoebe Apperson Hearst, the mother of William Randolph Hearst and a patron of the artist Joseph Henry Sharp, sponsored Borg's return to Europe for additional study in Paris and Rome.

While living in California, Borg achieved commercial success and critical recognition. In Los Angeles in 1905, he had the first of many solo exhibitions. He also became a pioneer in the film industry—he painted early sets and was the first art director of any Hollywood studio. Borg taught at the California Art Institute and the Santa Barbara School of Arts.

From his home base in California, Borg traveled throughout the Southwest. He also traveled to Central America and back to Europe. He was visiting Sweden when World War II broke out in 1939, and was forced to remain in Sweden until the end of the war, when he returned to California. Two years later, in 1947, he died in Santa Barbara, and his family scattered his ashes over the Grand Canyon, a frequent subject of his art.

Multistoried Walpi is a pueblo dramatically perched high atop a mesa in northeastern Arizona. Hopi Indians, fearing Spanish retaliation for the Pueblo Revolt of 1680, founded the village around 1700. The inhabitants have gradually deserted Walpi for another village at the mesa's foot and have left picturesque remains, such as those depicted in the present work.

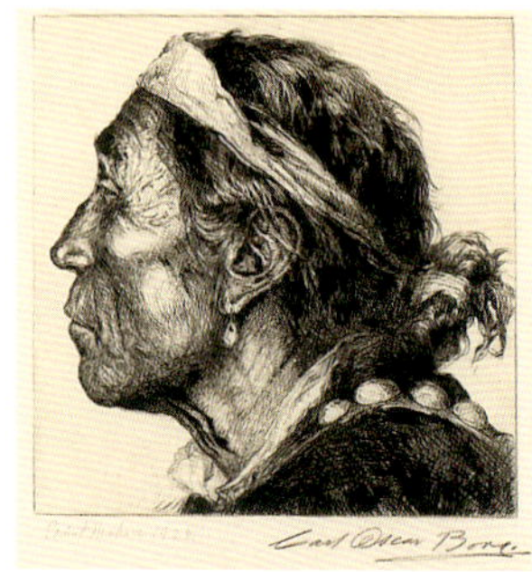

Carl Oscar Borg
U.S., b. Sweden, 1879–1947
The Navajo, 1928, drypoint etching, 6 × 6 in.
Gift of J. Donald Walp, 2003

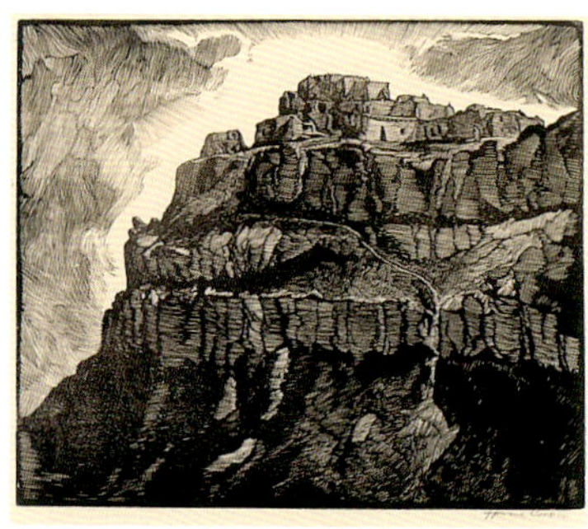

Howard Cook
U.S., 1901–1980
Walpi, 1927, woodcut, 10¼ × 12¼ in.
Gift of J. Donald Walp, 2003

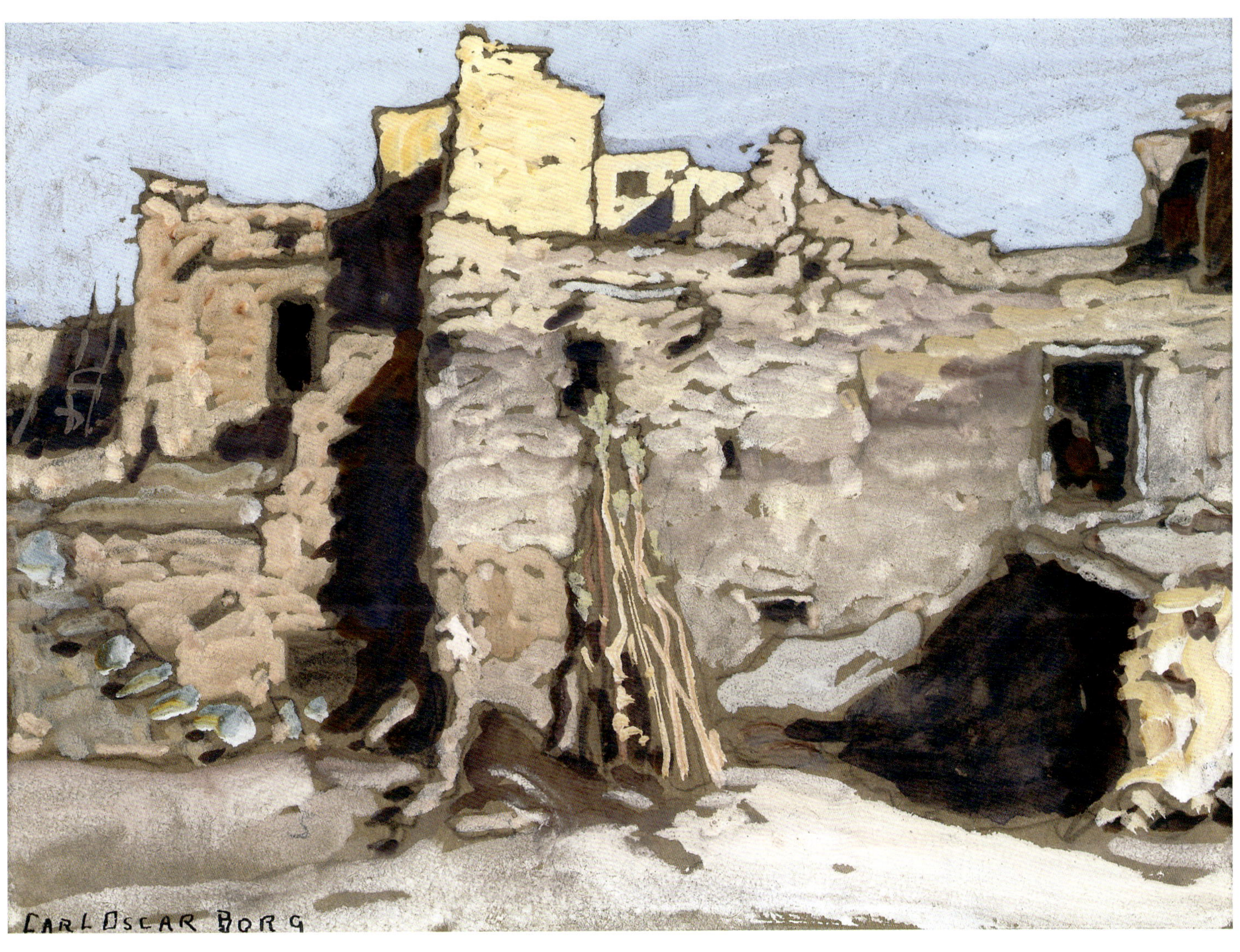
CARL OSCAR BORG

59 Maynard Dixon

U.S., 1875–1946

Volcanic Hills, 1934
Oil on canvas board
16 × 20 in.
Gift of Mr. and Mrs. Jon R. Stuart, Tulsa, 1999

With a distinctive Modernist vision, Maynard Dixon captured the solitude and stark grandeur of the American West. Born into a ranching family in Fresno, California, he decided early in life to become an illustrator of the Old West. He demonstrated great artistic promise when young but received only brief formal art training, in San Francisco. He found work as an illustrator for San Francisco newspapers and for books by authors such as Jack London, John Muir, O. Henry, and Clarence Mulford (who created the character Hopalong Cassidy).

A visit to Arizona and New Mexico in 1900 whetted Dixon's appetite for roaming the West. He joined another emerging Western artist, Edward Borein, on a trip through several Western states. Back in California, Dixon continued to illustrate Western books and magazines, although by the 1910s, he was growing tired of portraying the West in the immensely popular, romanticized fashion of the day.

The 1915 World's Fair, held in San Francisco, included art exhibitions that exposed the West Coast art community to Impressionism and various Modernist movements, such as Fauvism. After seeing the shows, Dixon began experimenting with Impressionism and Post-Impressionism while continuing to pursue a career in commercial art, particularly poster design.

During the 1920s, Dixon increasingly applied to his art a Modernist emphasis on the simplified, abstract elements of painting. For the rest of his career, he remained interested in Modernism, although he dismissed the notion that Modernism was the only legitimate style for his time.

During the Great Depression, Dixon and his wife, the celebrated photographer Dorothea Lange, focused their art on social and political issues. (In this period, Lange produced works such as *Migrant Mother* [1936], a photograph that depicts a poor Oklahoma woman surrounded by her children and that would become one of the most iconic images of the twentieth century.)

Volcanic Hills dates from the Depression era. In 1934, the federal government commissioned Dixon to document the construction of the Boulder Dam on the Colorado River in southern Nevada. While at the dam, Dixon wandered into the surrounding mountains, where he painted *Volcanic Hills,* a quick, outdoor sketch, probably executed at a single sitting. With broad, sweeping brushstrokes, Dixon depicted what he called the "immensity of the landscape" around the dam. He inscribed the painting to "old Snakebit Bob," his affectionate name for his wife.

Dixon and Lange divorced in 1935, and in 1937, he married Edith Hamlin. In 1939, the couple moved from San Francisco to Mount Carmel, Utah. They spent winter months in Tucson, Arizona, where Dixon died in 1946.

Palm Springs (1925), by Alson Skinner Clark, a contemporary of Dixon, is another museum painting by a California artist of the first half of the twentieth century.

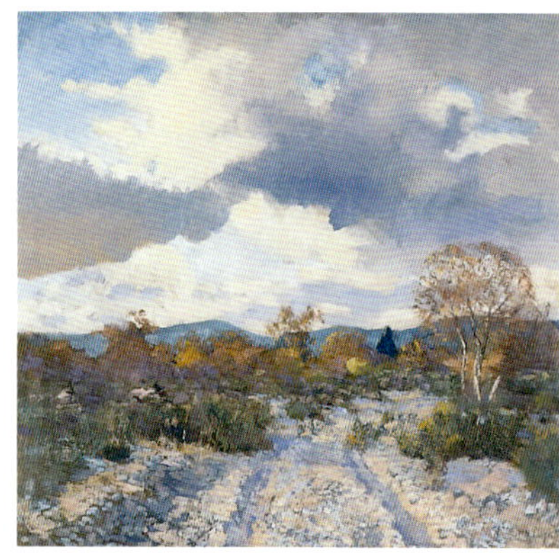

Alson Skinner Clark
U.S., 1876–1949
Palm Springs, c. 1925, oil on canvas, 30¼ × 31¾ in. Gift of Mr. and Mrs. Jon R. Stuart, Tulsa, 1999

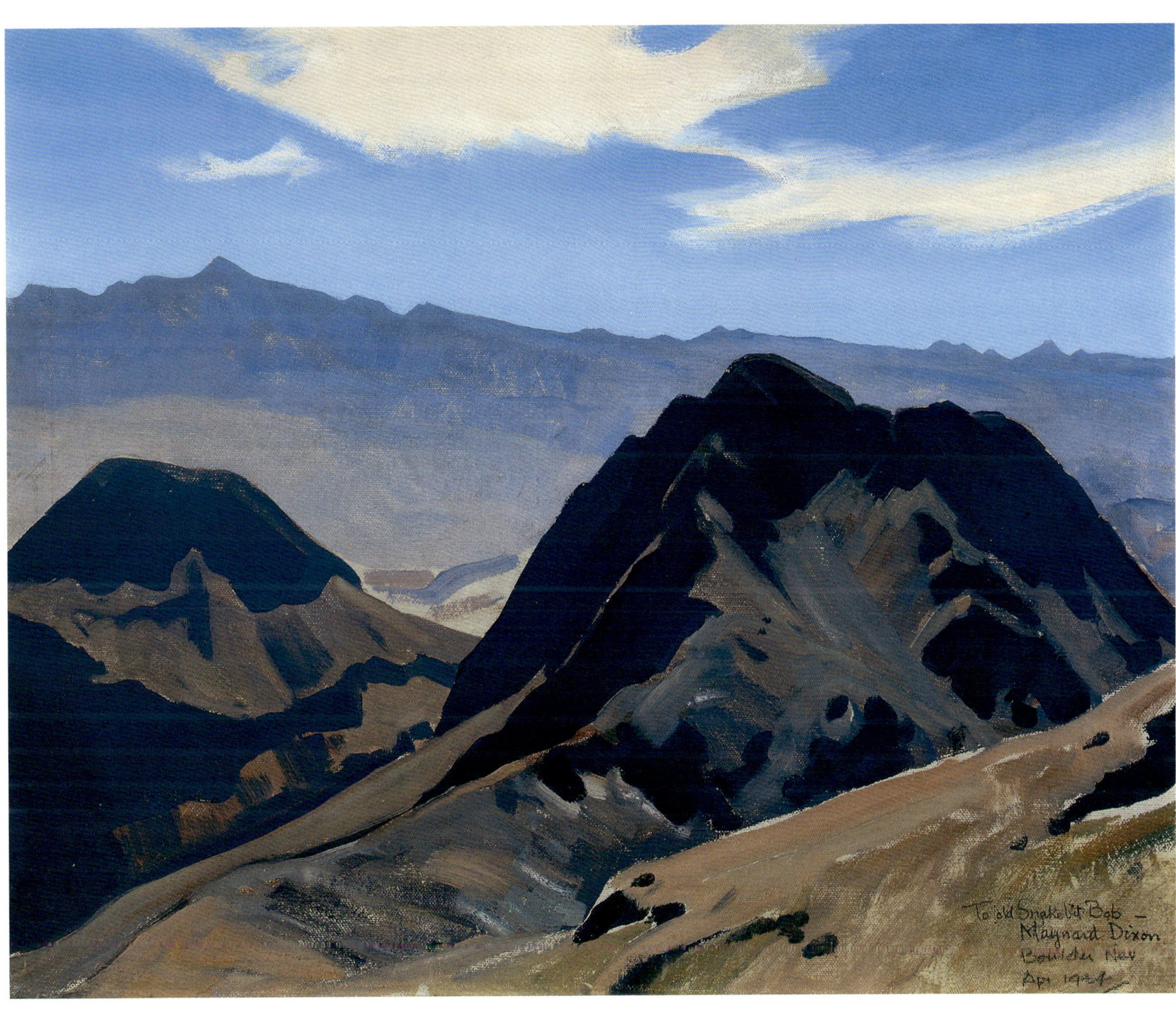
To old Snake Pit Bob —
Maynard Dixon
Boulder Nev

60 Maria Martinez and Popovi Da

U.S., San Ildefonso Pueblo,
c. 1887–1980 and 1923–1971

Pot, n.d.
Ceramic
H. 7¼ in.
Gift, R. E. Mansfield Collection, 2003

The matriarch of Pueblo pottery and perhaps the best known of all American Indian artists, Maria Martinez lived most of her life at San Ildefonso Pueblo, north of Santa Fe. Her aunt and grandmother taught her how to make pottery.

Throughout her career, Maria collaborated with others—first with her husband, Julian, who died in 1943; then with her daughter-in-law, Santana, between 1943 and 1956; and finally with her son, Popovi Da, from 1956 until his death in 1971. Typically, Maria would prepare the clay and shape and fire the wares, while the others painted decorations.

In 1904, Maria and Julian married and spent the summer demonstrating pottery-making at the World's Fair in St. Louis. Their early pottery was polychrome. A few years later, Maria examined prehistoric pottery at excavations of ancient pueblos near San Ildefonso. She realized that the prehistoric potters used a finer clay and burnished their wares with polishing stones; she also determined that the all-black color of many pots resulted from exposure to more smoke during the firing process. Maria incorporated these discoveries into her work. Around 1918, Julian developed the black-on-black technique, in which he applied matte designs onto burnished wares.

Like other Pueblo potters, who were usually women, Maria began each piece with a prayer to Mother Earth, whom she asked for clay. Maria used a combination of red clay and blue sand mixed in equal amounts, with a small amount of water added. She also added temper, a material that prevented the pot from cracking when fired. She kneaded the clay, set it aside for a day, and kneaded it again. Clay flattened into a pancake shape formed the base of the pot. Maria then built up the walls of the pot with coils of clay, after which she smoothed and shaped the pot with pieces of gourd. (She did not use a potter's wheel.) After partially drying the pot in the sun, she scraped it to smooth irregularities and refine the shape. Maria then covered the pot with slip, a thin liquid clay, which she burnished with a polishing stone.

Julian, Santana, or Popovi Da decorated the pottery with an additional slip applied with a yucca-plant brush softened at one end. Prehistoric designs inspired the decorations, which often included eagle feathers or an *avanyu,* a horned water serpent.

Maria fired pots, a delicate process, only three or four times per year, and only on days with little wind. Instead of a kiln, she used an open fire on the ground. She placed the pots upside down over a fire made with cedar wood and cow manure. The pots, which had a high content of iron and carbon, turned black in the smoke. After firing, the burnished areas of the pot were glossy, and the slip-painted decorations were matte.

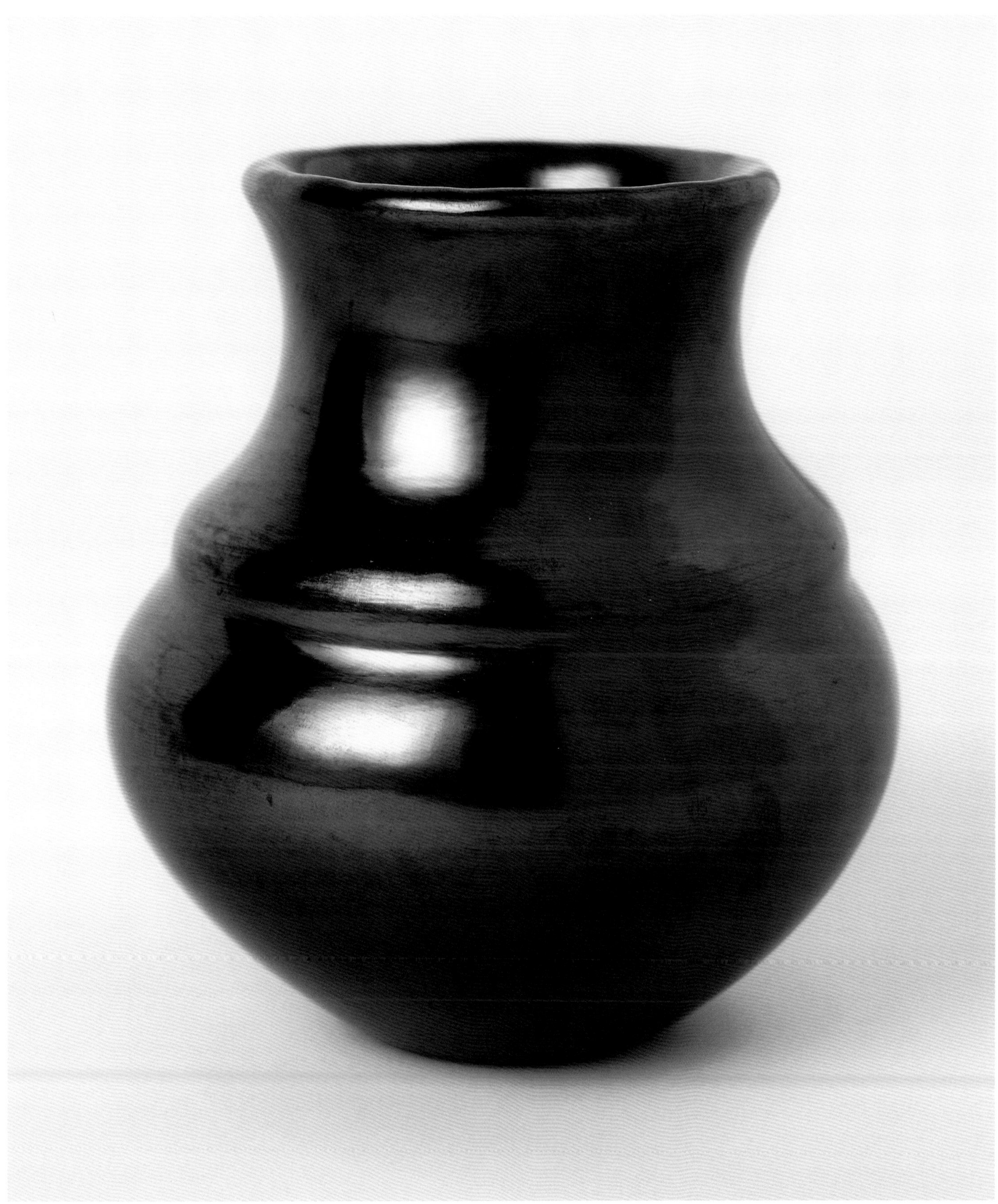

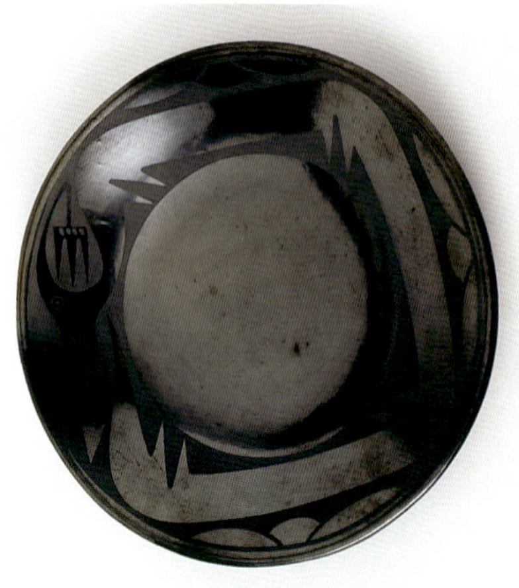

Maria Martinez and Popovi Da
U.S., San Ildefonso Pueblo,
c. 1887–1980 and 1923–1971
Plate with Avanyu Design, n.d., ceramic,
DIAM. 11½ in. Gift, R. E. Mansfield
Collection, 2003

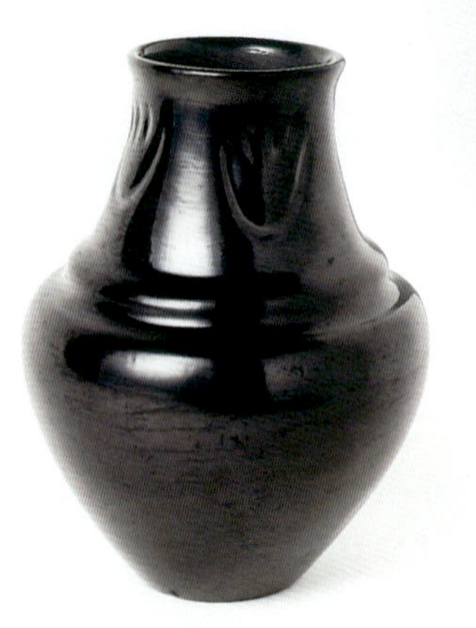

Margaret Tafoya
U.S., Santa Clara Pueblo, 1904–2001
Bear Claw Pot, n.d., ceramic, H. 17 in.
Gift, R. E. Mansfield Collection, 2003

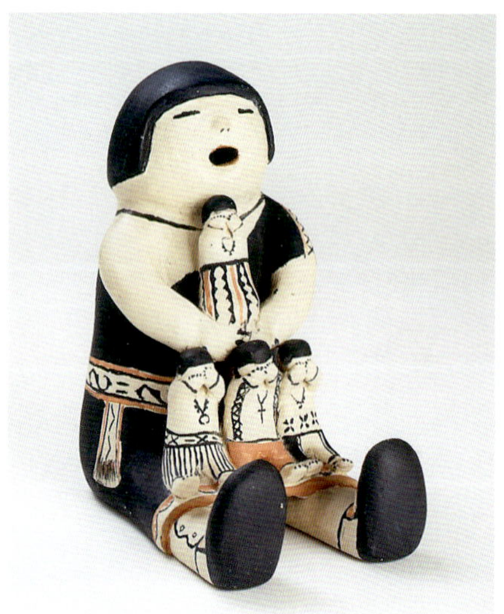

Helen Cordero
U.S., Cochiti, 1915–1994
Storyteller, c. 1980, earthenware,
H. 10⅛ in. Purchase, Richard H. and
Adeline J. Fleischaker Collection, 1996

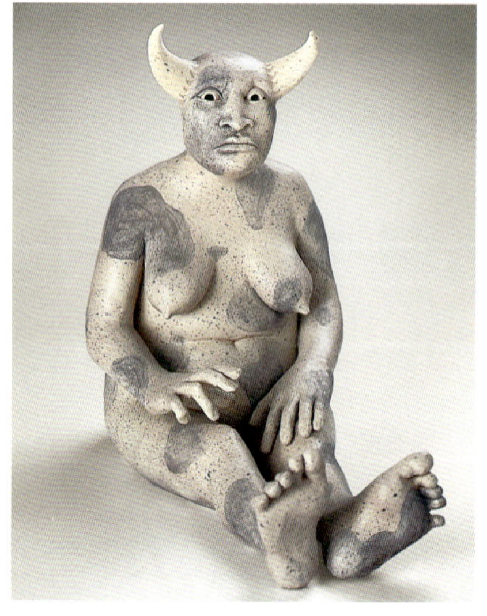

Roxanne Swentzell
U.S., Santa Clara Pueblo, b. 1962
The Cow Woman Isn't Amused, 1993,
earthenware, H. 19½ in. Gift, R. E. Mansfield
Collection, 2003

The present pot is a masterpiece created by Maria with the assistance of her son, Popovi Da. It has an exceptionally high-gloss, silvery burnish called gunmetal finish. The pot was left undecorated to accentuate its form and sheen.

The 2003 donation of the R. E. Mansfield Collection gave the Fred Jones Jr. Museum of Art an extraordinary representation of Pueblo pottery. The collection is encyclopedic and includes important examples by every major American Indian potter, from early figures to contemporary artists such as Roxanne Swentzell, whose work straddles the line between pottery and sculpture with a dose of humor. The museum owns over twenty works by Maria Martinez.

61 Monroe Tsatoke

U.S., Kiowa, 1904–1937

Dancer, 1929
Tempera on paper
10 × 7 in.
University purchase, c. 1929

Monroe Tsatoke was a member of the Kiowa Five group, which initially also included Spencer Asah (1905–1954), Jack Hokeah (1902–1973), Stephen Mopope (1898–1874), and Lois Smoky (1907–1981). When, between 1927 and 1929, these artists studied at the University of Oklahoma's School of Art, they became, so far as is known, the first American Indians to receive art training at an academic institution.

Three of the Kiowa Five—Asah, Hokeah, and Mopope—studied in 1914 at St. Patrick's Mission School in Anadarko, Oklahoma. Susie Peters, a field matron for the Kiowa agency, recognized these artists' skills, as well as the talents of Tsatoke, Smoky, and James Auchiah (1906–1974). (Auchiah later replaced Smoky as the fifth Kiowa art student when Smoky, the only woman of the group, left the University of Oklahoma after just a few months.) Peters provided art materials and in 1918 organized additional art lessons.

Years later, Peters arranged for her protégés to enroll at the University of Oklahoma. In 1927, Asah, Hokeah, Mopope, Smoky, and Tsatoke entered the university as special students who took only art classes. Oscar B. Jacobson, director of the university's School of Art, became their mentor. According to Jacobson, leaving the reservation to come to the University of Oklahoma was a momentous experience for the Kiowa artists, who seemed "shy and silent." Jacobson gave them their own painting room and taught them with the assistance of Edith Mahier. Funding for the Kiowa art students came from Ponca City oilman Louis Haines "Lew" Wentz. (Wentz's later gift of Asian art to the university led to the founding of the art museum.)

For centuries, the Kiowa had created pictographic images on buffalo hides used for robes, shields, and tepee coverings. The two-dimensional representations depicted men, horses, and various events, such as battles. In the nineteenth century, the Kiowa began to use as art materials pencils, crayons, and ledger books made available through contact with whites. In Kiowa culture, only men portrayed figures, while women depicted geometric abstractions. (In representing people, the female artist Smoky went against custom.)

At the University of Oklahoma, Jacobson encouraged his Kiowa students to produce work inspired, in both style and subject matter, by their heritage. The artists painted nostalgic themes relating to their culture, with figures in traditional dress and attention to historical accuracy. They often depicted ceremonial dances, a subject they knew well since they were themselves dancers. In their works, usually in tempera on paper, the artists emphasized flat, decorative qualities through color and line. They made no attempt to create an illusion of three-dimensionality and did not model their figures with light and shade.

The Traditional-style painting of the Kiowa Five and later Oklahoma Indian artists relates to that of Dorothy Dunn's New Mexico Studio. (For more on the Traditional style and Dorothy Dunn, see Allan Houser, *Apache Family,* cat. no. 62.)

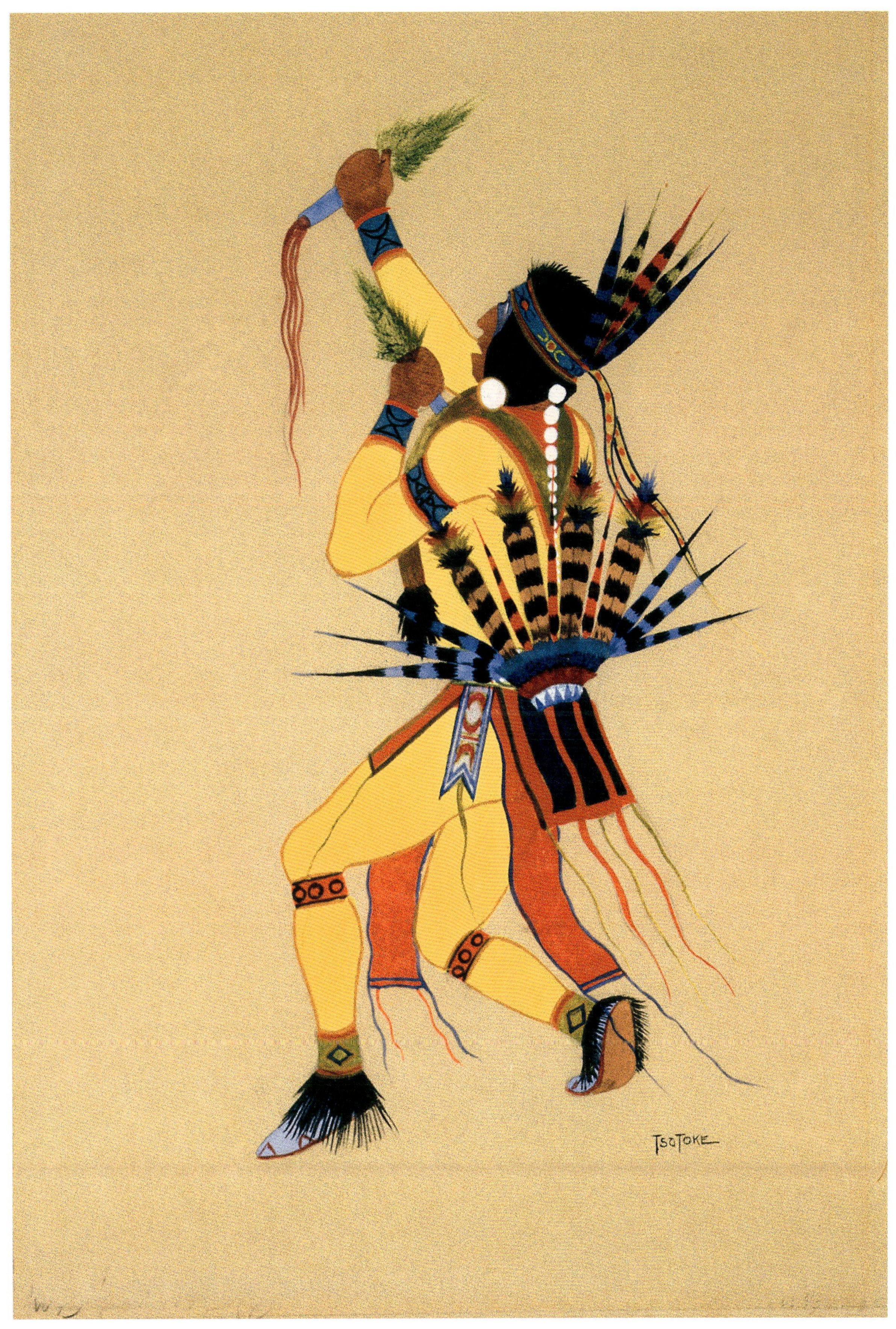
TSATOKE

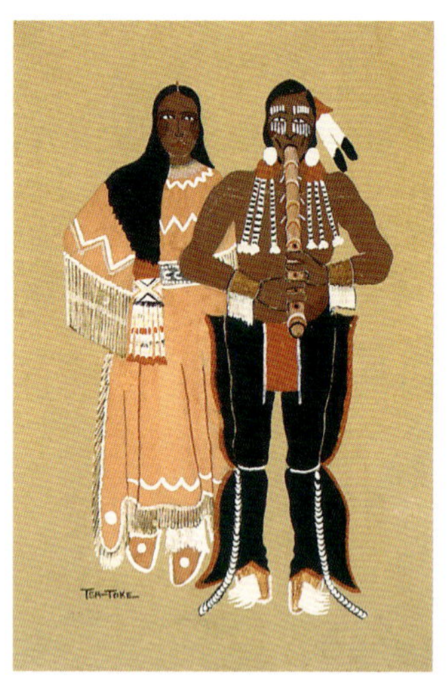

Monroe Tsatoke
U.S., Kiowa, 1904–1937
Love Call, 1929, tempera on paper, 10 × 6¾ in. Gift of Russ and Kathy Walker, 1995

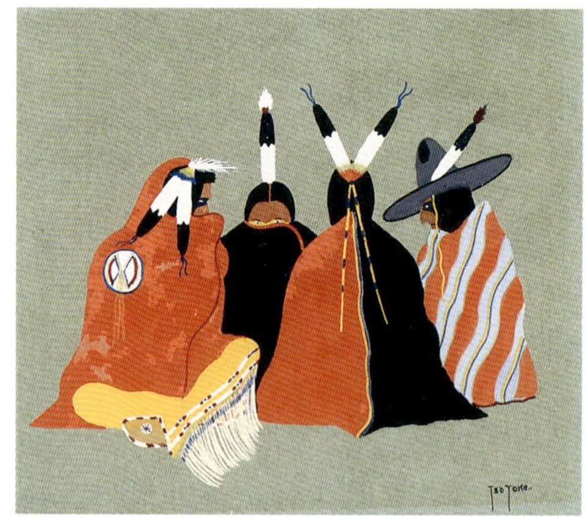

Monroe Tsatoke
U.S., Kiowa, 1904–1937
Kiowa Making Medicine, 1929, tempera on paper, 6 × 8 in. Museum purchase, 1936

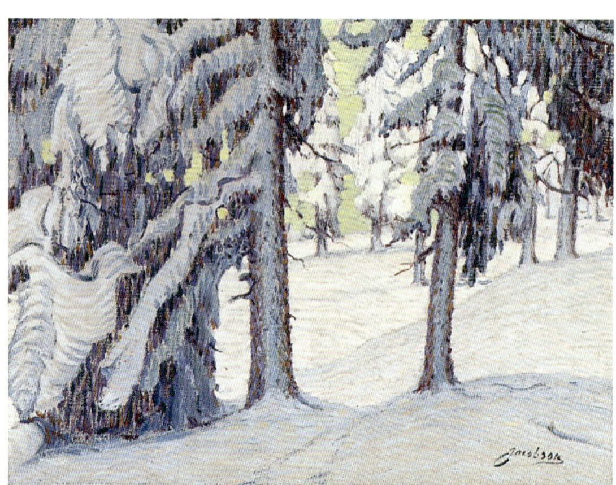

Oscar B. Jacobson
U.S., b. Sweden, 1882–1966
Winter Forest in Sweden, 1919–20, oil on canvas, 28⅛ × 36 in. Gift of Hal Johnson, 1983

Jacobson organized a promotional Kiowa Five show that traveled to San Francisco, Seattle, New York, and Cleveland. In 1928, an exhibition of the Kiowa Five's work appeared at the International Folk Art Congress in Prague and met with great success. In 1929, a portfolio of prints after their work was published in France as *Kiowa Art*.

According to Jacobson, Tsatoke was the leader and spokesperson for the Kiowa Five. The *Kiowa Art* portfolio featured a painting by Tsatoke on its cover. (This painting, *Love Call,* is now in the museum's collection.) Tsatoke was born near Saddle Mountain, Oklahoma, the son of Hunting Horse, who had been a warrior and had served as a scout to General Custer. Before coming to the University of Oklahoma, Tsatoke had also studied at Bacone College (in Muskogee, Oklahoma), worked as a farmer, married, and had children. He was a chief singer at Kiowa dances.

After leaving the University of Oklahoma in 1929, Tsatoke painted murals from 1934 until 1937 for the Oklahoma Historical Society. In 1937, at age thirty-three, he died of tuberculosis. Jacobson wrote of Tsatoke: "There was always something in him detached and profoundly spiritual. It was as if obscurely knowing that his days here were numbered, he already walked in the company of the gods and heard the music of the spheres. This quality is felt in all his works, and he ranks as one of the greatest Indian painters."

62 Allan Houser

U.S., Chiricahua Apache, 1914–1994

Apache Family, 1938
Tempera on paper
12 × 15½ in.
Museum purchase, 1948

Allan Houser was born in Apache, Oklahoma, shortly after his parents were released from Fort Sill, where they had been prisoners-of-war with their relative Geronimo, for whom Houser's father served as interpreter. During Houser's childhood on a farm, his parents told him stories of their tribal customs and people, which would later provide inspiration for his art. Like other members of his family, Houser anglicized his difficult-to-pronounce Apache name, Haozous, which means "pulling roots" in Apache.

Houser was interested in drawing from an early age. At twenty, in response to a newspaper advertisement, he moved to Santa Fe to enroll at The Studio of the Santa Fe Indian School, which was the first art school for American Indians. From 1934 until 1938, the year he made *Apache Family,* Houser studied painting at The Studio under the white director Dorothy Dunn, who had trained at the Art Institute of Chicago.

Dunn advocated a type of American Indian painting now labeled the Traditional style, characterized by flat figures demarcated by strong outlines against a neutral background. The subject matter of the Traditional style was exclusively American Indian life and culture. While Dunn believed that she was promoting a specifically Indian art, her teaching became controversial for being too restrictive and for imposing her European-inspired ideas on the students. Nevertheless, The Studio produced some of the most important figures in twentieth-century American Indian art, including Harrison Begay, Pop Chalee, Oscar Howe, Gerald Nailor, Quincy Tahoma, Andrew Tsinajinnie, and Pablita Velarde. (The museum's founding director, Oscar B. Jacobson, acquired works by all of these artists, including Houser's *Apache Family.*)

Houser became Dunn's most famous student. He received much recognition, starting with a 1936 award for the best student work at the Santa Fe Indian School. After he left The Studio, the U.S. Department of the Interior commissioned him to paint murals in its building in Washington, D.C. (The resulting murals include horses and American Indian men and women similar to those in *Apache Family.*) He taught at the Institute of American Indian Arts, the successor of the Santa Fe Indian School, from 1962 until 1975. In 1992, he became the first American Indian to be awarded the National Medal of the Arts, presented at the White House by the president.

Today, Houser is best known as the preeminent American Indian sculptor, but his first important sculpture, a memorial to American Indians who had died in World War II, was not created until 1948, ten years after he painted *Apache Family.* Houser eventually produced around seven hundred sculptures, including works that depict American Indian life and some that draw inspiration from modern sculptors, such as Henry Moore and Barbara Hepworth. Six Houser sculptures, including large ones installed outdoors on the University of Oklahoma's

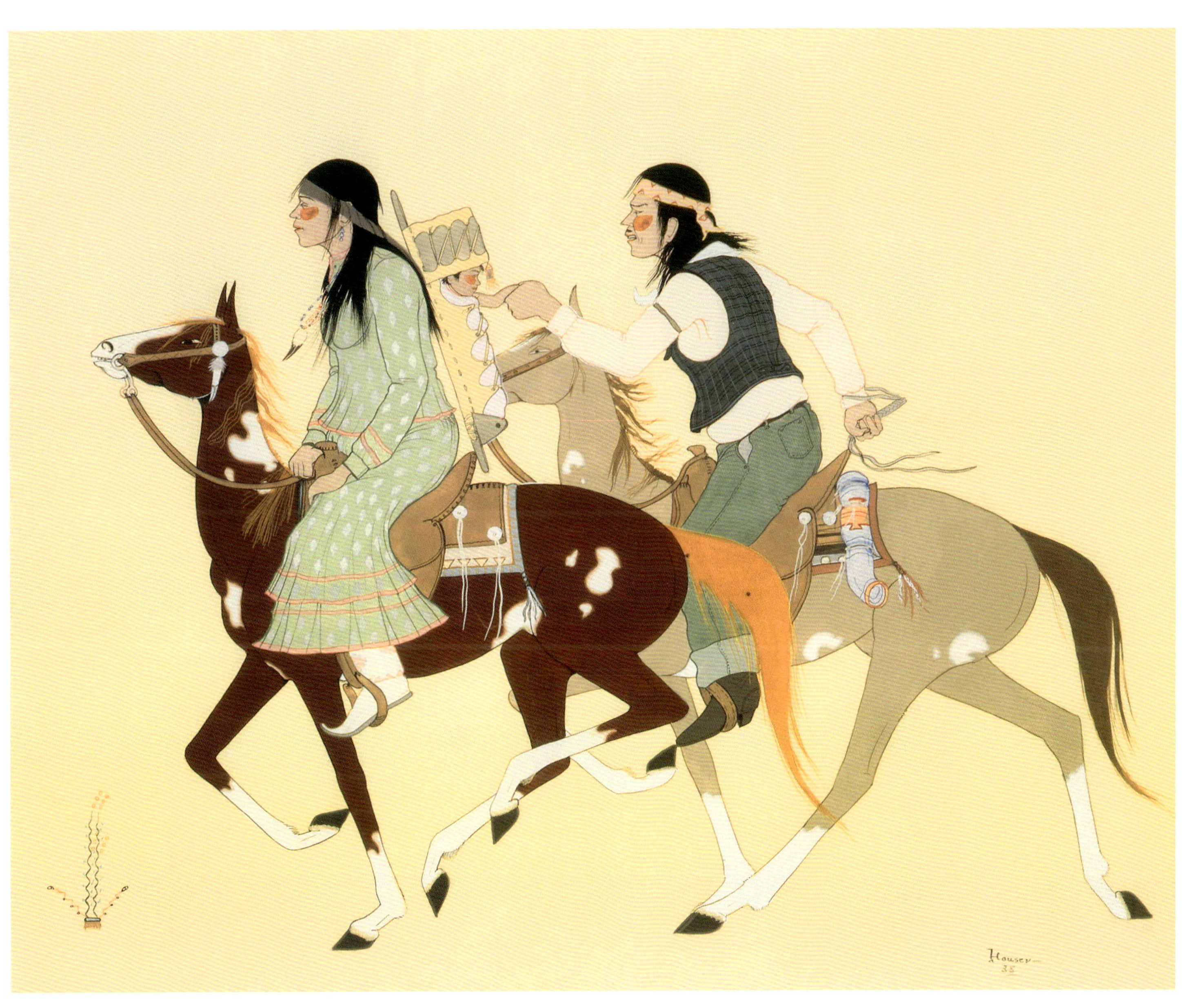

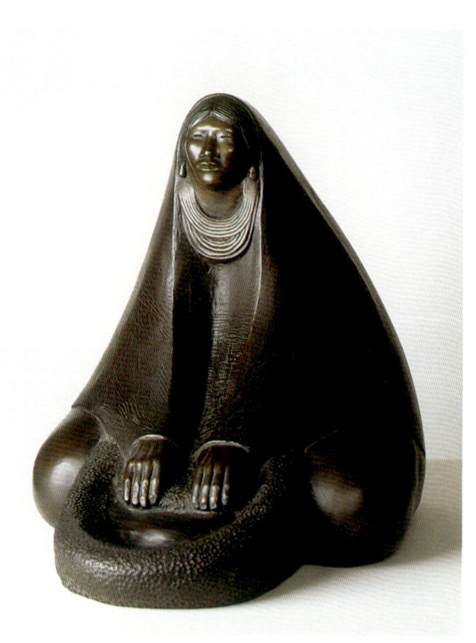

Allan Houser
U.S., Chiricahua Apache, 1914–1994
Corn Grinder, 1982, bronze, edition: 2/8, 23 × 19 × 25 in. Purchase, Richard H. and Adeline J. Fleischaker Collection, 1996

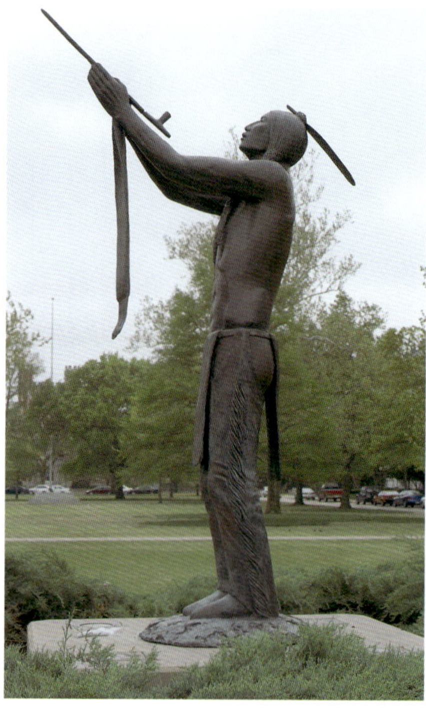

Allan Houser
U.S., Chiricahua Apache, 1914–1994
May We Have Peace, 1992, bronze, edition: 3/8, H. 11½ ft. Gift of the student body and other donors, 1995

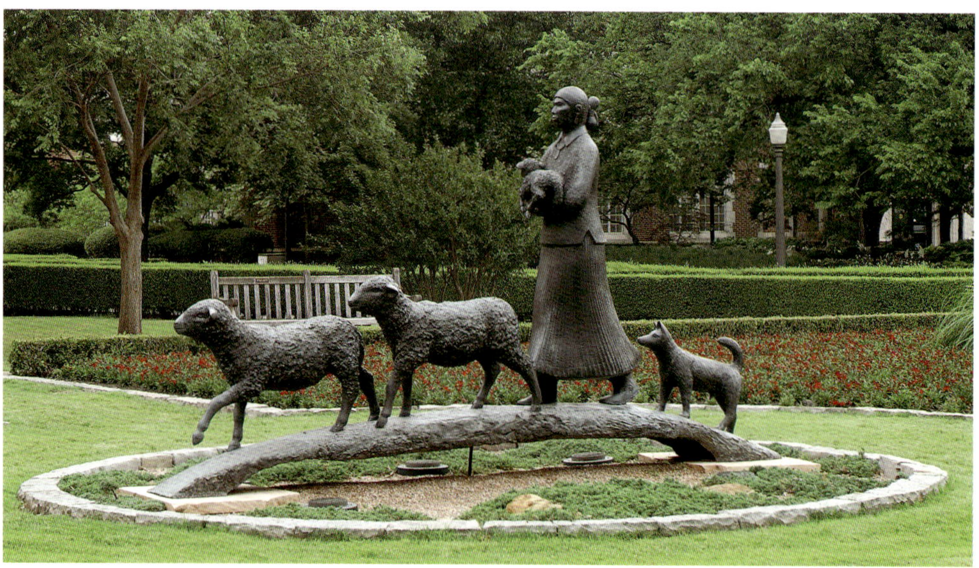

Allan Houser
U.S., Chiricahua Apache, 1914–1994
Homeward Bound, 1989, bronze, edition: 2/6, 7¼ × 12¾ ft. Gift of alumni Earl and Fran Ziegler, 1994

campus, complement the seven Houser paintings and drawings in the museum's collection.

Apache Family shows not only an Apache family but also the family in general. The mother and father are portrayed as equals, with the mother even riding slightly ahead of the father. The father's loving gesture of holding the infant's hand emphasizes the family unit and the role of the father in parenting. Although painted in the flat style taught by Dorothy Dunn, *Apache Family* anticipates Houser's mastery of three-dimensional form and volume, as evident in the mother's patterned dress.

Houser believed that even when an American Indian work of art does not overtly depict Indian themes, the work is still influenced by Indian culture. In a 1975 interview, he said:

> *I think that something always comes through . . . and that's the fact that Indian people still have this very deep feeling and they still have traditional backgrounds. Certainly some of the old ways are gone but to a very great extent the old ways are still important. Maybe they are even more important to us today because we realize how much has been lost.*

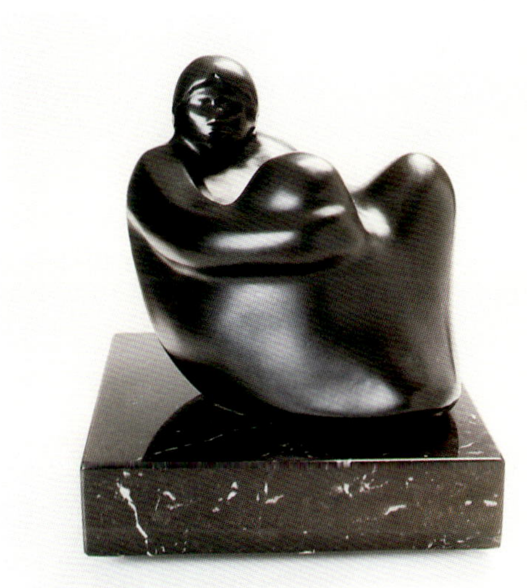

Allan Houser
U.S., Chiricahua Apache, 1914–1994
Respite (Seated Woman), 1985, bronze, edition: 16/100, H. 7½ in. Purchase, Richard H. and Adeline J. Fleischaker Collection, 1996

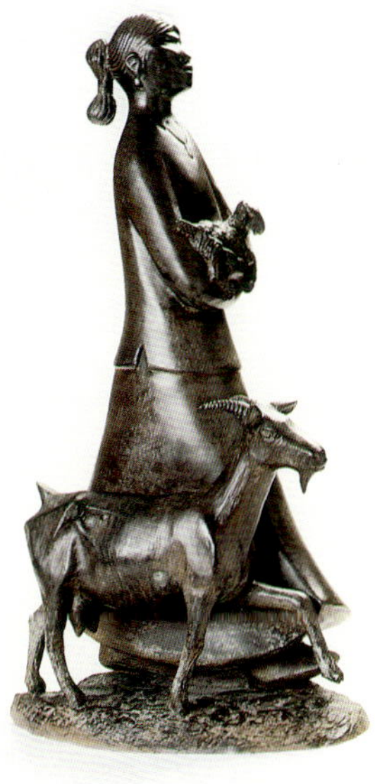

Allan Houser
U.S., Chiricahua Apache, 1914–1994
Tending the Flock, 1984, bronze, edition: 2/20, H. 26½ in. Purchase, Richard H. and Adeline J. Fleischaker Collection, 1996

63 John Marin

U.S., 1870–1953

Stevens Institute, 1925
Watercolor on paper
15 × 18¾ in.
Gift of Mr. and Mrs. W. P. Buckthal, 1993

This watercolor depicts the Stevens Institute of Technology in Hoboken, New Jersey. John Marin, born in nearby Rutherford, entered the school in the fall of 1886, when Stevens Institute offered only a degree in mechanical engineering, but he attended for just one term. After working as a draftsman and an architect for several years, he studied at the Pennsylvania Academy of the Fine Arts from 1899 to 1901, and then at the Art Students League in New York.

Beginning in 1905, Marin lived in Europe for five years. He trained briefly at the Académie Julian in Paris and traveled throughout the continent. During his first years in Europe, Marin produced etchings of picturesque sites.

Marin returned to the United States in 1911 and settled in New York. He initially worked in an Impressionist style, but gradually embraced Modernism and included Cubist fragmentation and Expressionistic distortion in his works. In New York, he became a central figure in the avant-garde circle of the art dealer, impresario, and photographer Alfred Stieglitz, whom Marin had met in Paris in 1909.

Marin's images of New York are definitive Modernist views of the city. Marin is also known for his landscapes, painted during his many travels throughout Canada, the Northeast, and the Southwest, and for his seascapes, painted during summers in Maine.

Marin received much recognition through most of his career, and in 1936, he became one of the first Americans to receive a retrospective at New York's Museum of Modern Art. Although he also painted in oils, especially later in his career, he was renowned for his use of watercolor.

In the watercolor *Stevens Institute,* Marin was looking back on his life. A few years before creating this work, Marin had published a brief memoir called *Notes (Autobiographical),* in which he stated that he "went to—not through" the Stevens Institute: "The main thing I got there was mathematics for . . . which I am duly grateful as I am now an adept at subtraction." The featured Cubist watercolor shows the Stevens Institute's red brick buildings fragmented into sharp, energetic lines and geometric shapes.

Other Marin watercolors in the museum's collection include two seascapes and a painting of the town of Suffern, New York.

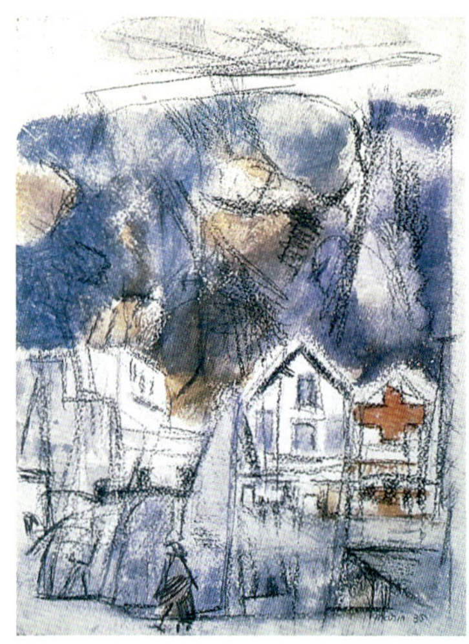

John Marin
U.S., 1870–1953
Suffern, New York, 1935, watercolor on paper, 17¼ × 13 in. Gift of Mr. and Mrs. W. P. Buckthal, 1993

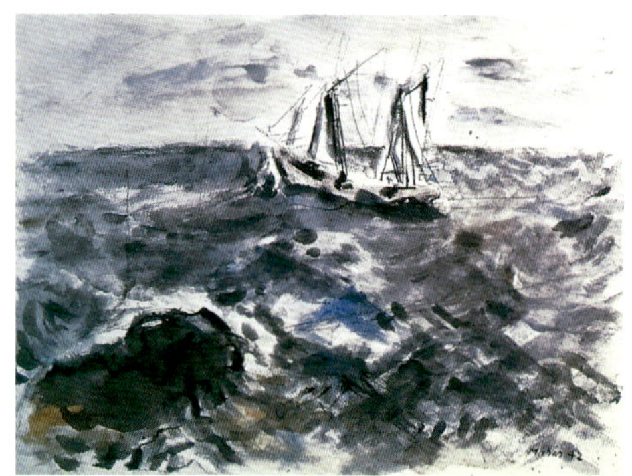

John Marin
U.S., 1870–1953
Sea Fantasy No. III, 1942, watercolor on paper, 16¾ × 22⅜ in. Gift of Mr. and Mrs. W. P. Buckthal, 1993

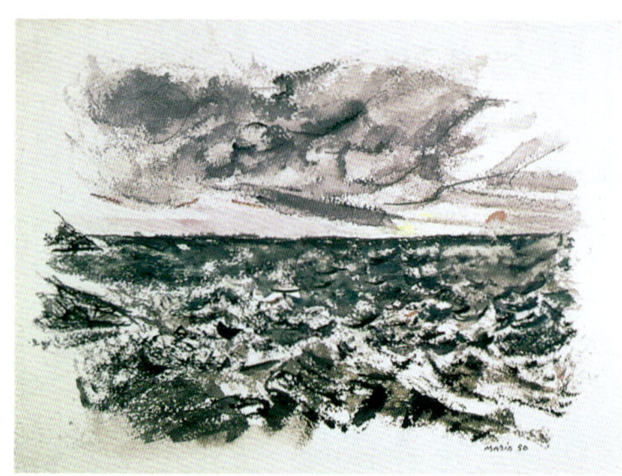

John Marin
U.S., 1870–1953
Seascape, 1950, watercolor on paper, 15⅜ × 20⅞ in. Gift of Mr. and Mrs. W. P. Buckthal, 1993

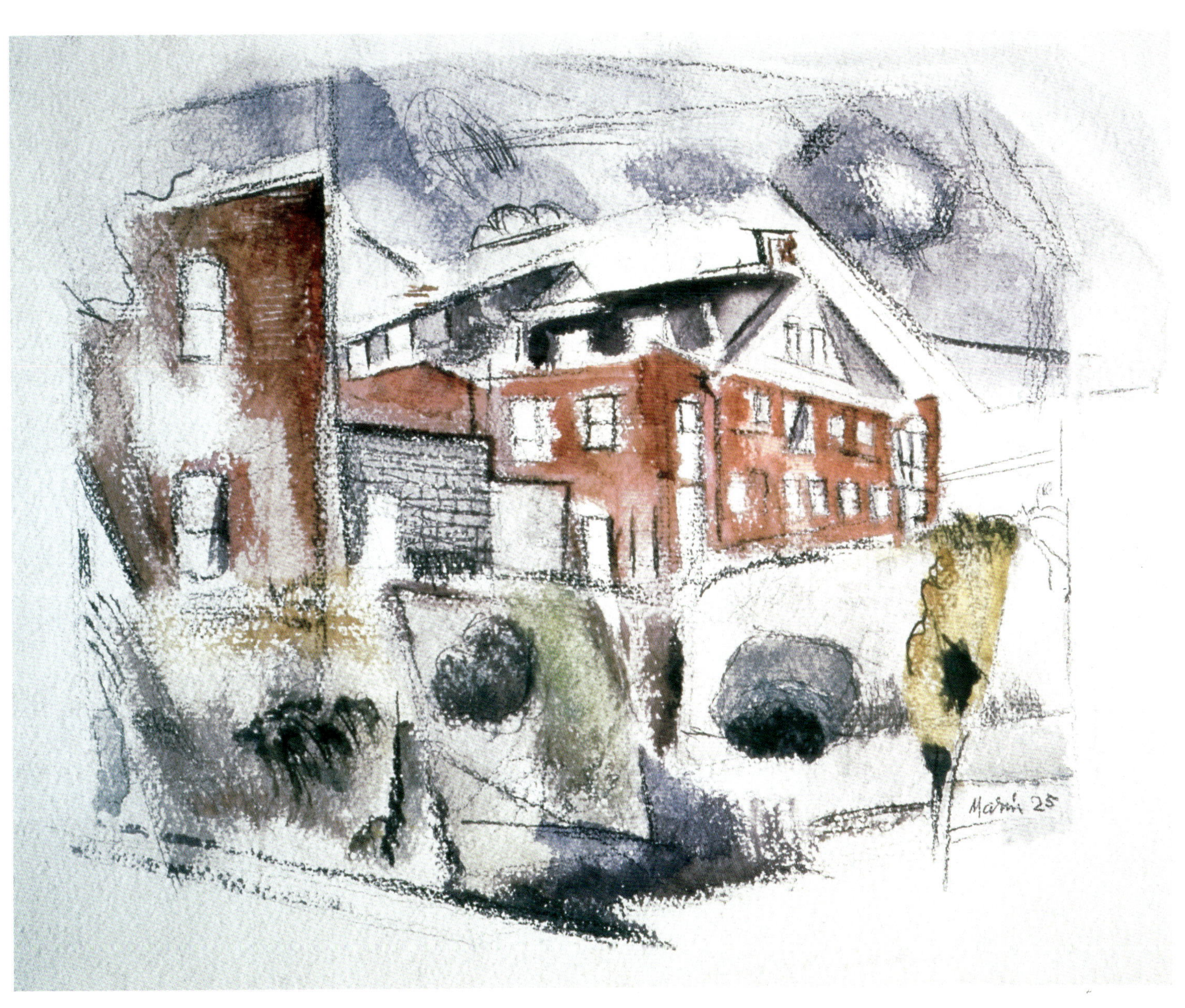
Marin 25

64 Max Weber

U.S., b. Russia, 1881–1961

Two Vases, 1944–45
Oil on panel
39¼ × 31¾ in.
Purchase, U.S. State Department Collection, 1948

A pioneering figure in the introduction of European Modernism to the United States, Max Weber was born in Bialystok, Russia (now Poland), a textile manufacturing center. His earliest memories were of his grandfather mixing dyes, which fostered in the future painter an interest in art. In 1891, Weber immigrated with his Orthodox Jewish family to New York, where he studied from 1898 to 1900 at the Pratt Institute, under Arthur Wesley Dow, the artist and art theorist who was inspired by Japanese aesthetics and who influenced Georgia O'Keeffe. From 1905 until 1908, Weber lived in Paris, where he met members of the avant-garde, visited the salon of Gertrude Stein, and attended the Académie Julian and the informal academy of Henri Matisse. Weber saw African and non-Western art in Paris museums and studied the Old Masters during his travels throughout Europe.

After returning to New York, Weber painted still lifes and nudes in landscapes in the manner of Matisse and Pablo Picasso. The art dealer and photographer Alfred Stieglitz held Weber exhibitions at his famous 291 gallery. Also at 291, Weber organized the first solo show in the United States of his friend, the French painter Henri Rousseau. Weber published two volumes of poetry and, in 1916, *Essays on Art,* a book that emphasized an intuitive and spiritual approach to the creation of art. In the decades after World War I, his paintings became more lyrical and expressionistic, as seen in *Two Vases.*

Two Vases depicts thin vases with long-stemmed flowers. Parallel vertical lines, offset by curving lines, frame and echo the forms of the vases; the curving lines perhaps even reflect the shape of the table on which the vases sit. Planes of rich blue on the canvas's right and lower sides establish the dominant hue, while accents of yellow, green, and red enliven the painting. In *Two Vases,* Weber uses both saturated, atmospheric color and cubistic, fragmented forms.

Weber produced Modernist prints and sculpture in addition to paintings. In 1930, he became the first American accorded a retrospective at the recently founded Museum of Modern Art in New York.

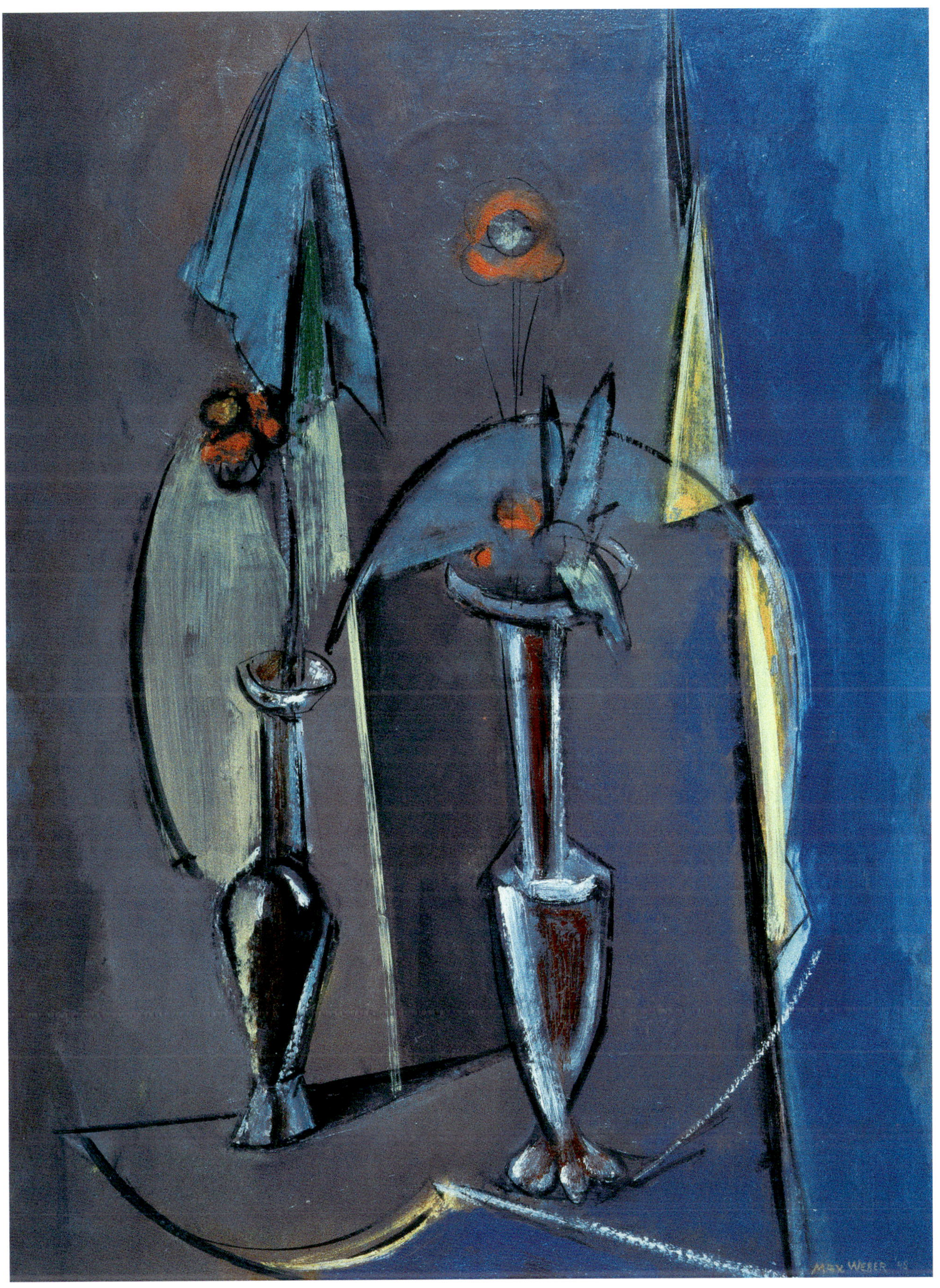
MAX WEBER '45

65 Georgia O'Keeffe

U.S., 1887–1986

Cos Cob, 1926
Oil on canvas
16 × 12 in.
Purchase, U.S. State Department Collection, 1948

Cos Cob is typical of Georgia O'Keeffe's best-known works: isolated, cropped, up-close images of flowers and plants, rendered in a simplified manner. These works date primarily from the 1920s, when O'Keeffe achieved recognition as one of America's most important artists. The present painting depicts a skunk cabbage from an early spring garden and is from a series of skunk cabbage paintings from the 1920s. This is one of the more literal, less abstracted representations, with two upright green leaves resembling hands in prayer, and a glimpse of purple leaves in the lower left.

The title *Cos Cob,* inscribed by O'Keeffe on the painting's back, refers to a section of Greenwich, Connecticut, which O'Keeffe visited. From 1890 until 1920, Cos Cob had been an art colony for American Impressionists, including Childe Hassam (see cat. no. 31). During that time, the town was changing from a small farming and fishing community to the rich New York suburb that it remains today.

O'Keeffe grew up on a farm in Sun Prairie, Wisconsin, and decided to become an artist at age twelve. She attended the School of the Art Institute of Chicago from 1905 to 1906, after which she moved to New York to enroll at the Art Students League from 1907 until 1908. In New York, she studied with William Merritt Chase. From 1908 until 1910, she worked as a commercial artist in Chicago.

The year 1912 marked a turning point in O'Keeffe's art. During the summer of that year, she enrolled in an art class at the University of Virginia, and her instructor introduced her to the unconventional teachings of Arthur Wesley Dow, who emphasized an artist's self-expression rather than imitative realism. Dow drew inspiration from Japanese prints and Symbolist ideas about visual music. While taking classes with Dow in New York in 1914, O'Keeffe familiarized herself with the latest trends in European Modernism.

In 1915, while teaching art in South Carolina, O'Keeffe attempted to practice Dow's teachings in a revolutionary series of large, abstract charcoal drawings of organic forms, which prefigured her later work. A friend showed these works to the art dealer Alfred Stieglitz, who exhibited them at his pioneering gallery 291 in 1916. The following year, Stieglitz gave O'Keeffe a solo show. Stieglitz and O'Keeffe married in 1924, and he regularly exhibited her work in his gallery until his death in 1946.

Stieglitz was a photographer and, through his gallery and his journal, *Camera Work,* a promoter of photography as a fine art. O'Keeffe often posed for him and for other photographers, a practice that has made her own strong features as recognizable and iconic in American art as her paintings. Photography also had an impact on O'Keeffe's work, as evident in her cropped images and magnified details.

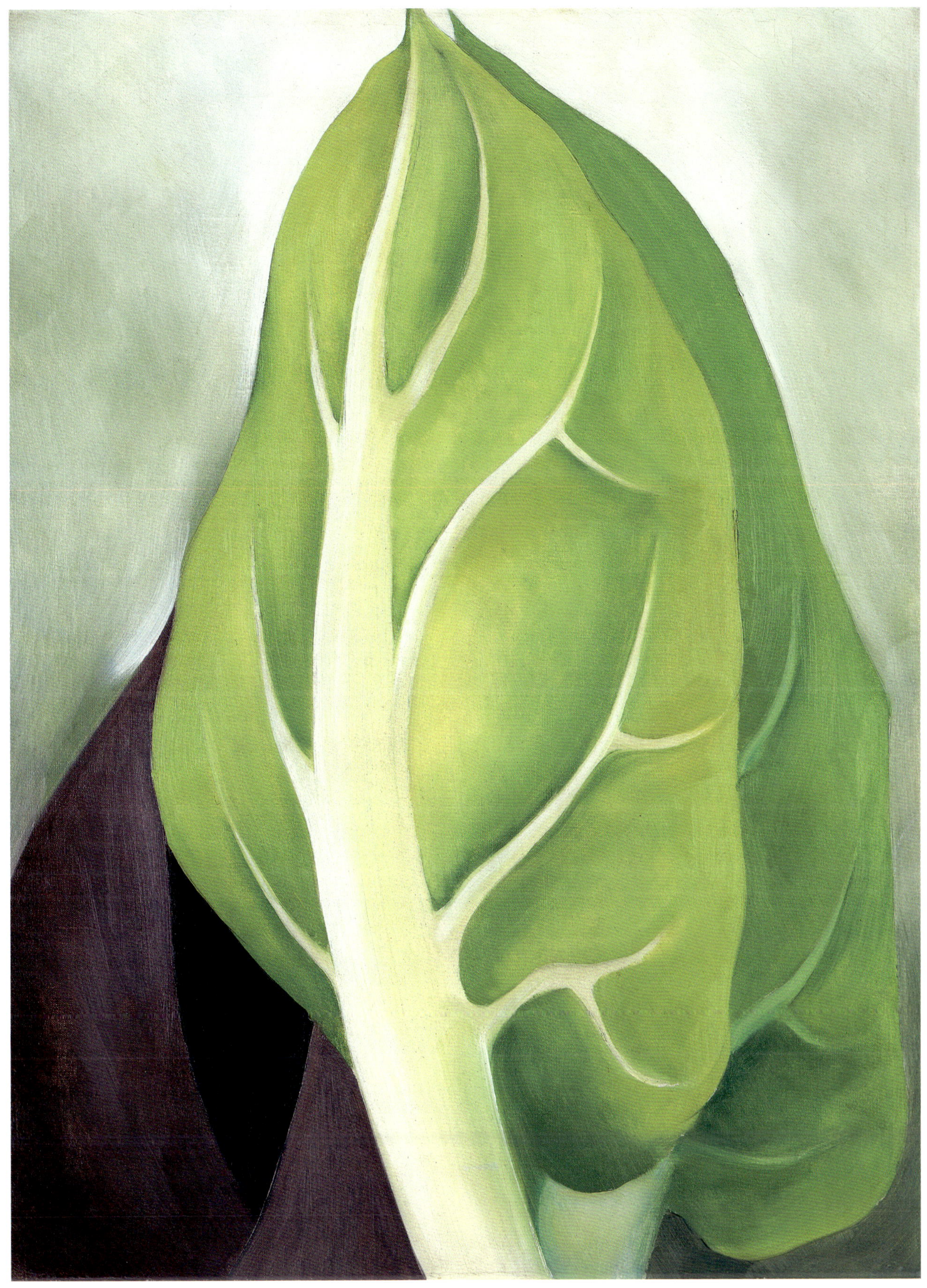

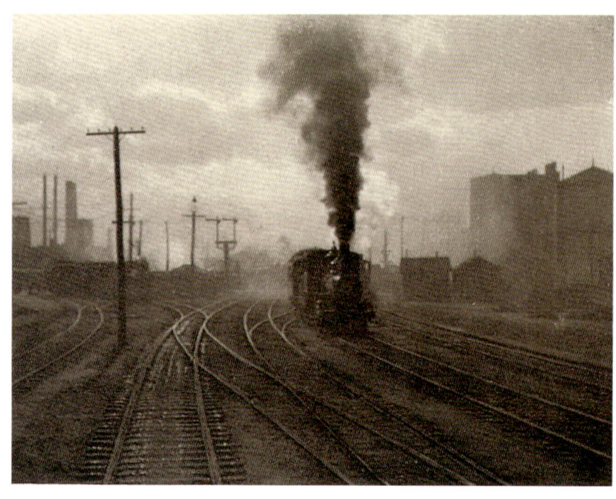

Alfred Stieglitz
U.S., 1864–1946
The Hand of Man, c. 1911, photogravure,
6 3/8 × 8 1/2 in. Museum purchase, 1978

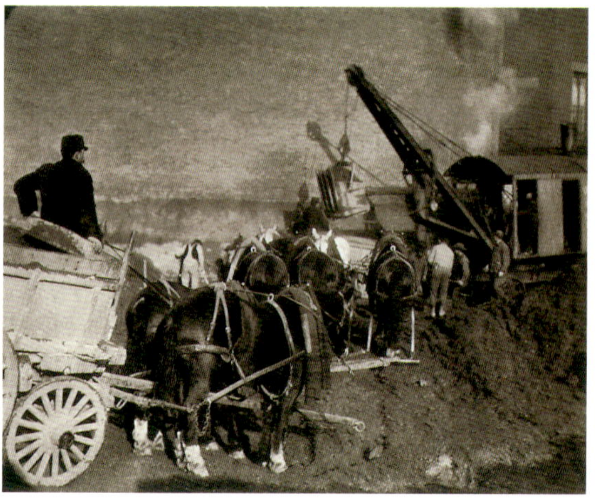

Alfred Stieglitz
U.S., 1864–1946
Excavating New York, 1911, photogravure,
5 × 6 3/16 in. Museum purchase, 1978

When O'Keeffe painted *Cos Cob,* she and Stieglitz were splitting their time between the Shelton Hotel in midtown Manhattan, from which she painted city scenes, and his family's summer home on Lake George in upstate New York. In 1929, O'Keeffe visited her friend Mabel Dodge Luhan in Taos, and she immediately felt that in New Mexico she had found her spiritual home. Henceforth, she spent most summers painting in New Mexico. She preferred greater isolation than she could find in Taos, so in 1949, after her husband's death, she settled in the village of Abiquiu.

66 Edward Weston

U.S., 1886–1958

Artichoke, Halved, 1930
Gelatin silver print
Edition: 17/50
7½ × 9½ in.
Museum purchase, 1937

One of the most important American photographers, Edward Weston grew up in the suburbs of Chicago. He became an amateur photographer after his father gave him a camera in 1902. Working as a portrait photographer, Weston moved to Los Angeles in 1906 but returned to Chicago to attend the Illinois College of Photography from 1908 until 1911.

Between 1911 and 1922, Weston ran a successful portrait studio in Tropico, California, near Los Angeles. During this period, he made Pictorialist photographs. (Pictorialism was a photographic style that emulated paintings and presented artfully arranged images in soft focus.) To keep up with his booming business, he invited photographer Margrethe Mather to become a partner in the studio. They worked closely, and Mather's enthusiasm for Asian art influenced Weston's compositions.

The Panama-Pacific International Exposition, held in San Francisco in 1915, exposed Weston to Modernist painting. His friend, the intellectual Dutch photographer Johan Hagemeyer, told Weston about Alfred Stieglitz's 291 gallery in New York, which Hagemeyer had visited in 1916, thus further stimulating Weston's interest in Modernism.

The year 1922 proved a turning point in Weston's career. He traveled to New York, where he met Stieglitz, Paul Strand, and Charles Sheeler. While visiting his sister in Ohio, Weston abandoned Pictorialism to take sharp-focused, Precisionist-inspired photographs of the ARMCO Steelworks. (Precisionism, associated with Modernism, often depicted industrial images in rectilinear forms. For more on Precisionism, see cat. no. 74.)

From 1923 until 1926, Weston lived in Mexico with Tina Modotti, his favorite model and a significant photographer in her own right. Weston befriended leading figures in Mexican art, such as Diego Rivera and David Alfaro Siqueiros. His photographs taken in Mexico include nudes of Modotti; candid, heroic portraits of writers, artists, and other intellectuals; and porcelain toilet bowls shot with Formalist perfection.

In 1926, Weston and Modotti returned to California. The following year, Weston met Henrietta Shore, a well-traveled artist who painted shells and botanical imagery in an abstracted, Precisionist style, with erotic overtones. Initially inspired by Shore and a Georgia O'Keeffe painting that Stieglitz had shown him years earlier, Weston produced between 1927 and 1930 a series of close-up photographs of isolated, common objects, such as shells, kitchen utensils, fruits, and vegetables, depicted in sharp focus and with intensity.

Artichoke, Halved is a classic example from the series of close-ups. In his own words, Weston aimed in these photographs to record "the life within the outer form. . . . To see the *Thing Itself* is essential: the quintessence revealed direct without the fog of impressionism. . . . This then: to photograph a rock, have it look like a rock, but be *more* than a rock."

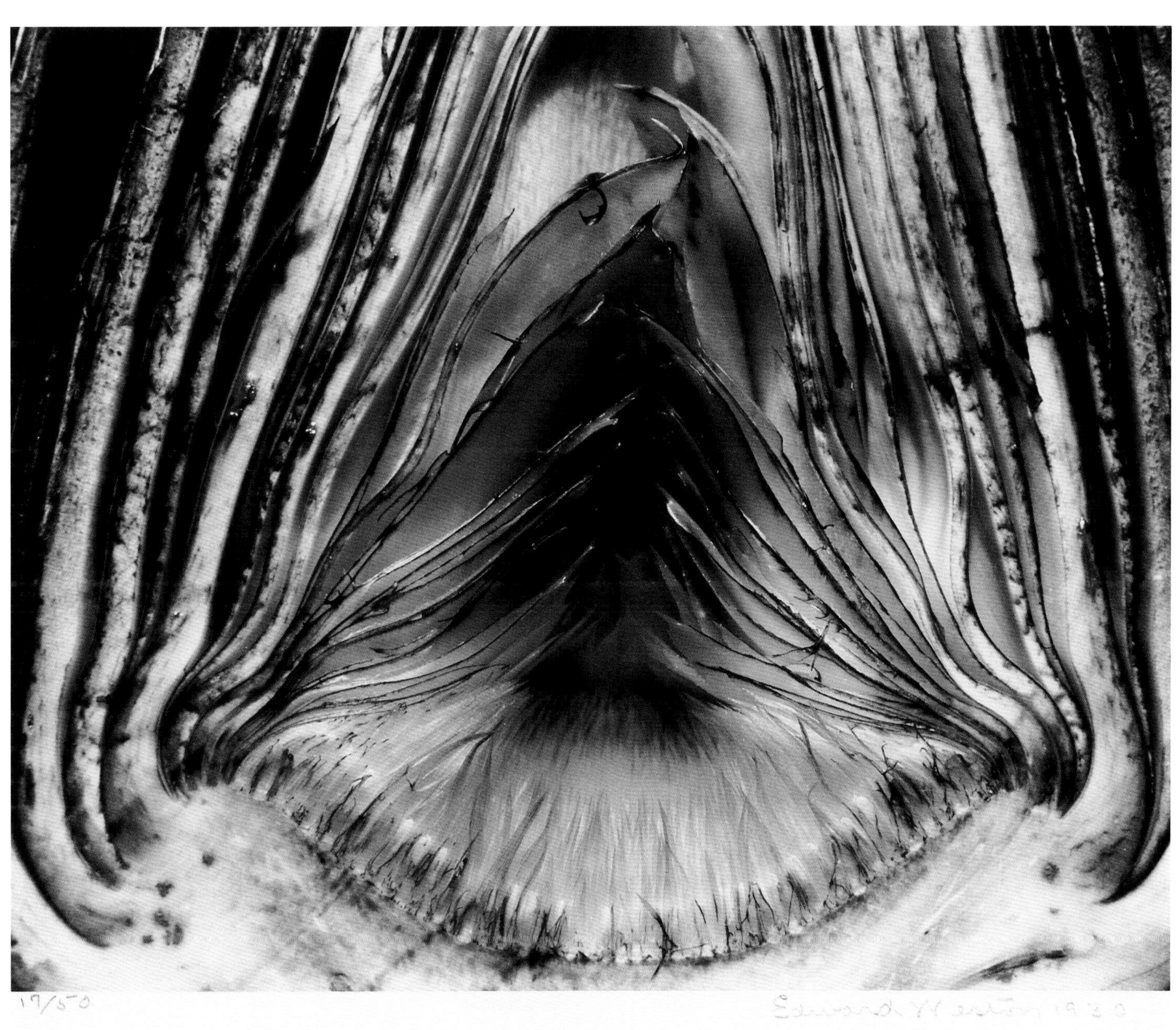
17/50
Edward Weston 1930

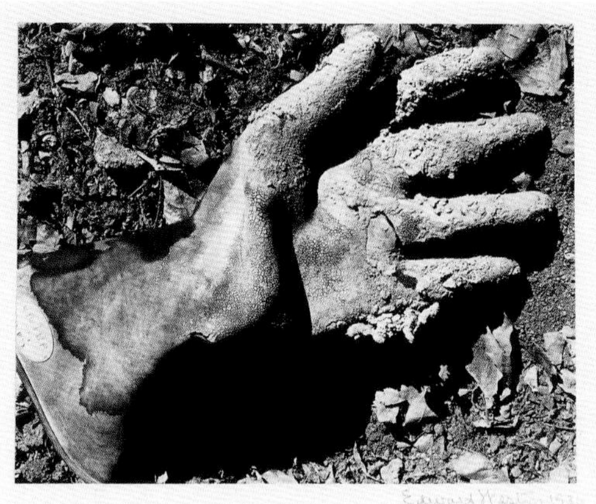

Edward Weston
U.S., 1886–1958
Cement Workers Glove, 1936, gelatin silver print, $7\frac{1}{2} \times 9\frac{1}{2}$ in. Museum purchase, 1937

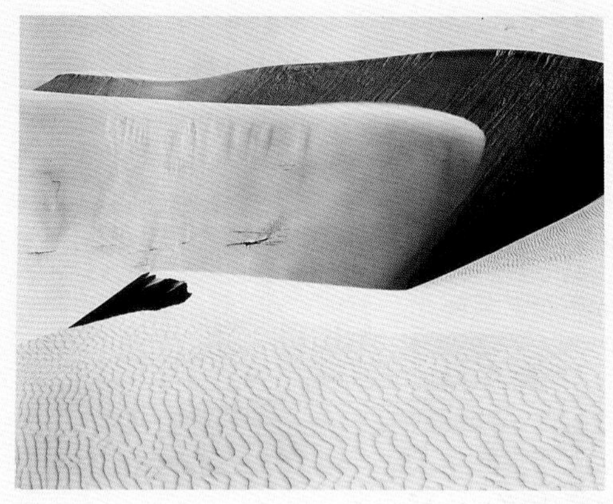

Edward Weston
U.S., 1886–1958
White Dunes, Oceano, California, 1936, gelatin silver print, $7\frac{1}{2} \times 9\frac{1}{2}$ in. Museum purchase, 1937

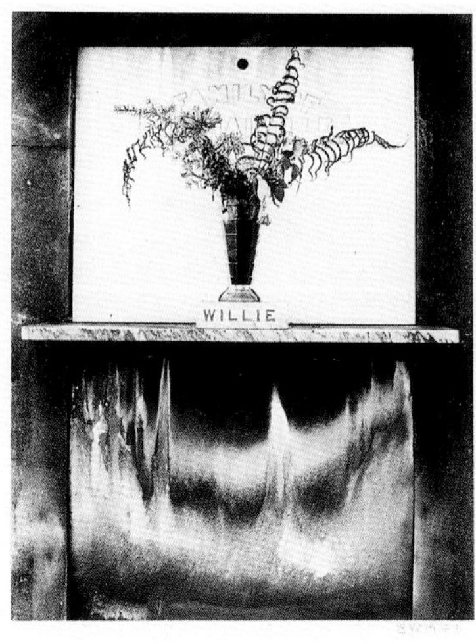

Edward Weston
U.S., 1886–1958
St. Roche Cemetery–New Orleans, 1941, gelatin silver print, $7\frac{1}{2} \times 9\frac{1}{2}$ in. Museum purchase, 1950s

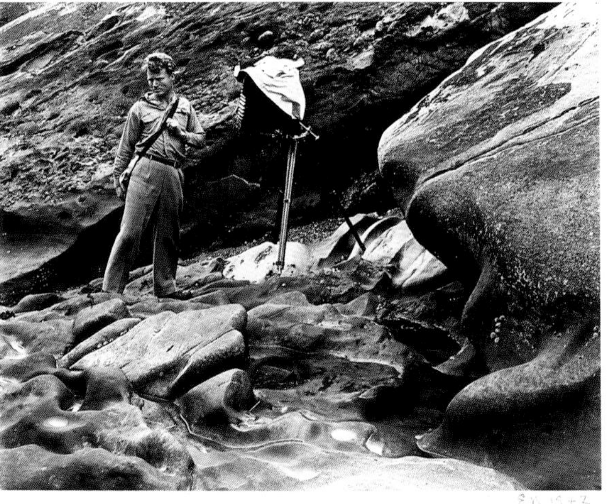

Edward Weston
U.S., 1886–1958
Brett–Pt. Lobos, 1942, gelatin silver print, $7\frac{1}{2} \times 9\frac{1}{2}$ in. Museum purchase, 1950s

Weston printed *Artichoke, Halved* from a large negative. For greater detail, tonal contrast, and clarity, he used large-format negatives to produce photographs as contact prints on glossy paper. He refused to enlarge negatives or manipulate an image.

In 1928, Weston moved to San Francisco with his second son, photographer Brett Weston. The following year, they moved to Carmel, where Weston lived for the rest of his life. He often photographed Point Lobos, a nearby nature preserve on the coast, and sand dunes on California beaches.

With the photographer Edward Steichen, Weston organized the American section of the landmark 1929 exhibition "Film und Foto" in Stuttgart, Germany. In 1932, he became a founding member of F.64, a group of California "straight" photographers who opposed Pictorialism. (Straight photography advocated shooting directly and in sharp focus what the photographer saw, without manipulation of the image.)

Weston was the first photographer to receive a Guggenheim Fellowship, awarded to him in 1937 to document the American West. (In the early 1940s, he also photographed the East Coast and the South.) In 1948, two years after the Museum of Modern Art in New York gave Weston a retrospective, Parkinson's disease effectively ended his career.

For the University of Oklahoma's fledgling art museum, Oscar B. Jacobson acquired *Artichoke, Halved* in 1937 from the photographer himself.

67 Ansel Adams

U.S., 1902–1984

Aspens, New Mexico, 1958
Gelatin silver print
10 1/16 × 13 3/8 in.
Purchased with funds from the National Endowment for the Arts, 1974

Ansel Adams, America's best-known landscape photographer, captured the power, grace, and majesty of nature. He was born in San Francisco. When he was fourteen, his parents gave him a Kodak Box Brownie camera to use when they were vacationing in Yosemite National Park, and he soon took a part-time job at a photo-finishing business. In addition to being a photographer, Adams was a musician, and he supported himself until 1930 by teaching piano.

From 1920 until 1927, Adams served as curator of LeConte Memorial Lodge, the Sierra Club's headquarters in Yosemite. In this position, he led weekly hikes and photographed the scenery as a visual diary. In 1927, he made one of his most famous images, *Monolith, the Face of Half Dome, Yosemite National Park*. That same year, Adams published the first of many portfolios of photographs. His first illustrated book, *Taos Pueblo,* appeared in 1930.

After meeting the photographer Paul Strand in New Mexico in 1930, Adams decided to pursue photography full-time. He rejected textured printing paper, a legacy of Pictorialism, for the glossy printing paper favored by "straight" photographers such as Edward Weston. (For more on Pictorialism and straight photography, see cat. no. 66.)

In 1932, Adams joined Weston to become a founding member of F.64, a group of San Francisco Bay–area photographers who promoted straight, unmanipulated, detailed photography. (Other F.64 founding members represented in the museum's collection include Imogen Cunningham and Alma Lavenson.) The following year in New York, Adams met Alfred Stieglitz, who gave Adams an exhibition at his gallery, An American Place, in 1936.

Adams frequently experimented with technique and achieved astounding technical mastery over his medium. Beginning in 1935, he published several technical manuals.

Aspens, New Mexico exemplifies Adams's ability to depict nuances of light and atmosphere. The photograph captures the crisp air and clear light of an aspen forest in northern New Mexico.

Adams helped to establish the Department of Photography at New York's Museum of Modern Art in 1940, and he co-curated its first exhibition. He also founded the Department of Photography at the California School of Fine Arts (now the San Francisco Art Institute), in 1946.

Adams's photographs have been used to promote environmental and conservation causes.

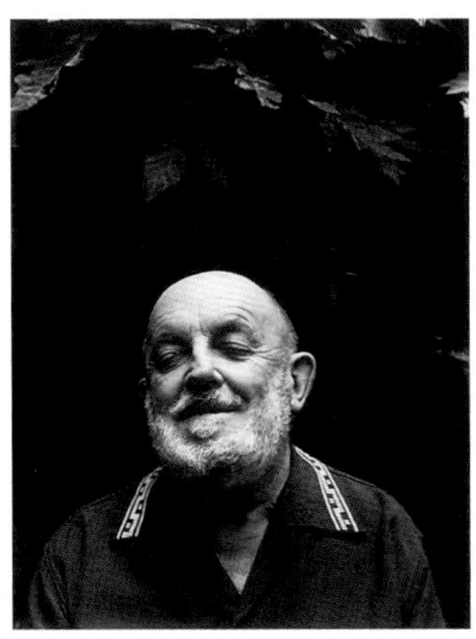

Judy Dater
U.S., b. 1941
Ansel Adams, 1977, gelatin silver print, 13 1/2 × 10 1/4 in. Museum purchase, 1982

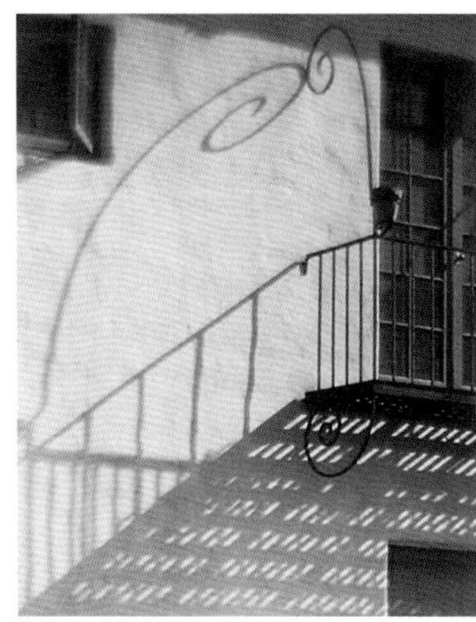

Alma Lavenson
U.S. 1897–1989
From Balcony, 1929, gelatin silver print, 10 7/8 × 8 7/8 in. Fred Jones Memorial Fund Purchase, 1982

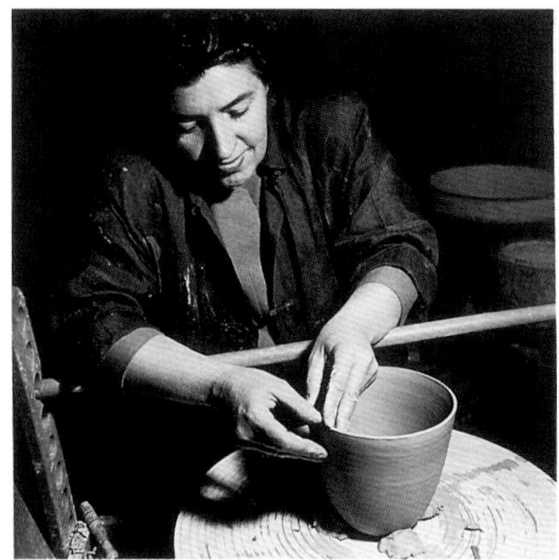

Imogen Cunningham
U.S., 1883–1976
Portrait of Laura Andreson, n.d., gelatin silver print, 7 3/4 × 7 11/16 in. Gift of Laura Andreson, 1984

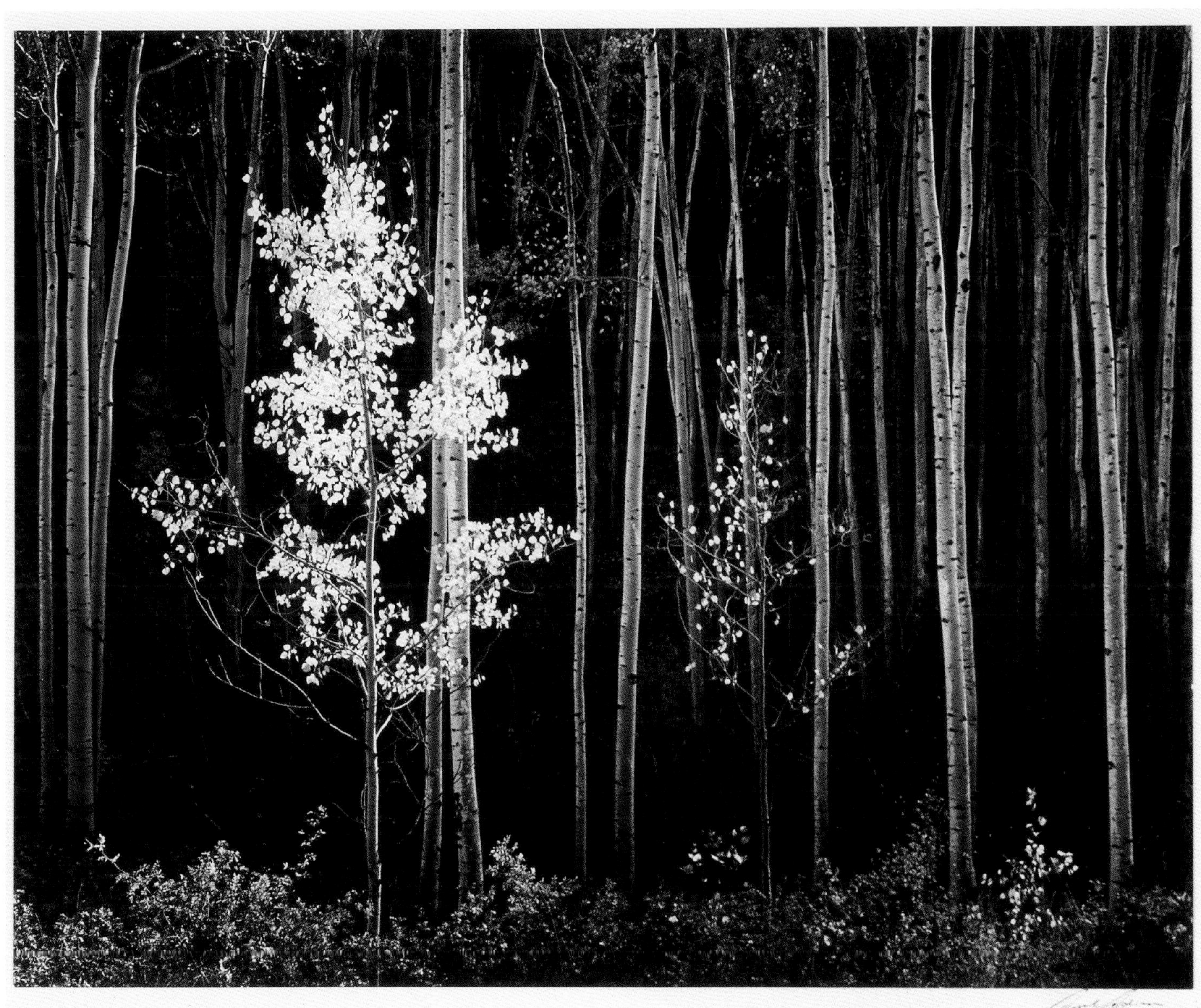

68 Thomas Hart Benton

U.S., 1889–1975

Study for "The Sheepherder," 1958–60
Graphite and watercolor on paper
10 × 13½ in.
Purchase, Richard H. and Adeline J. Fleischaker Collection, 1996

When Thomas Hart Benton, Grant Wood, John Steuart Curry, and other lesser-known "American-scene" artists exhibited at the Kansas City Art Institute in 1933, during the Depression, *Time* magazine christened them the Regionalists and named their movement Regionalism. The organizer of the exhibition stated in *Art Digest* that these Midwestern painters represented "real American art . . . which . . . springs from American soil and seeks to interpret American life." He attacked European Modernism as decadent and posited the art in his show as opposite to Modernism. *Time* publisher Henry Luce decided to promote the Kansas City exhibition artists as restorers of authentic culture for honest, hardworking Americans. Benton, considered the leader of the Regionalists, appeared in a self-portrait on the 1934 Christmas issue cover of *Time.*

Benton was born in Neosho, Missouri, the son of a U.S. congressman and grandnephew of a senator. He trained first at the Corcoran Gallery School in Washington, D.C., and then at the Art Institute of Chicago. In 1908, he moved to Paris for three years, to study independently and at the Académie Julian. Ironically for an artist who would later attack Modernism, he was drawn to the art of Paul Cézanne (see cat. no. 18) and befriended the American Modernists John Marin (see cat. no. 63) and Stanton MacDonald-Wright. Back in the United States, Benton even painted abstractions in New York, where he lived from 1912 until 1935.

While in New York, after World War I, Benton renounced Modernism for being too removed from reality. Inspired by Michelangelo, El Greco, and others, Benton developed a distinctive muscular, convulsive style, which he thought was quintessentially American. Benton taught at the Art Students League, where—again ironically—he would become the teacher of the future Abstract Expressionist Jackson Pollock.

Influenced by the Mexican muralist Diego Rivera, Benton began to paint ambitious and sometimes controversial mural cycles in the early 1930s. He painted his most important mural, *The Social History of the State of Missouri,* for the State Capitol of Missouri, after he angrily moved back to the Midwest in 1935, when he felt rejected by the New York art world. He lived and painted in the Midwest for the rest of his life.

The featured work is a study for a late landscape called *The Sheepherder,* now in a private collection. Benton produced the study during his summer travels; the hills are Wyoming's Grand Teton Mountains. Unlike this watercolor, the final painting includes a figure on horseback tending sheep, which gives the canvas its name. The study and painting capture the dynamic energy typical of Benton's art.

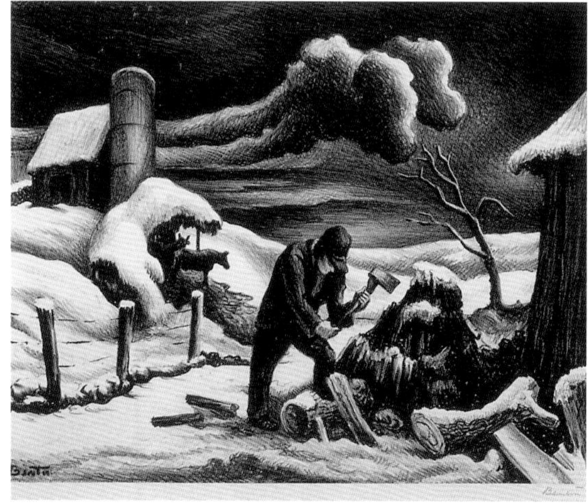

Thomas Hart Benton
U.S., 1889–1975
Woodpile, 1939, lithograph, edition of 250, 9 × 11 in. Museum purchase, 1940

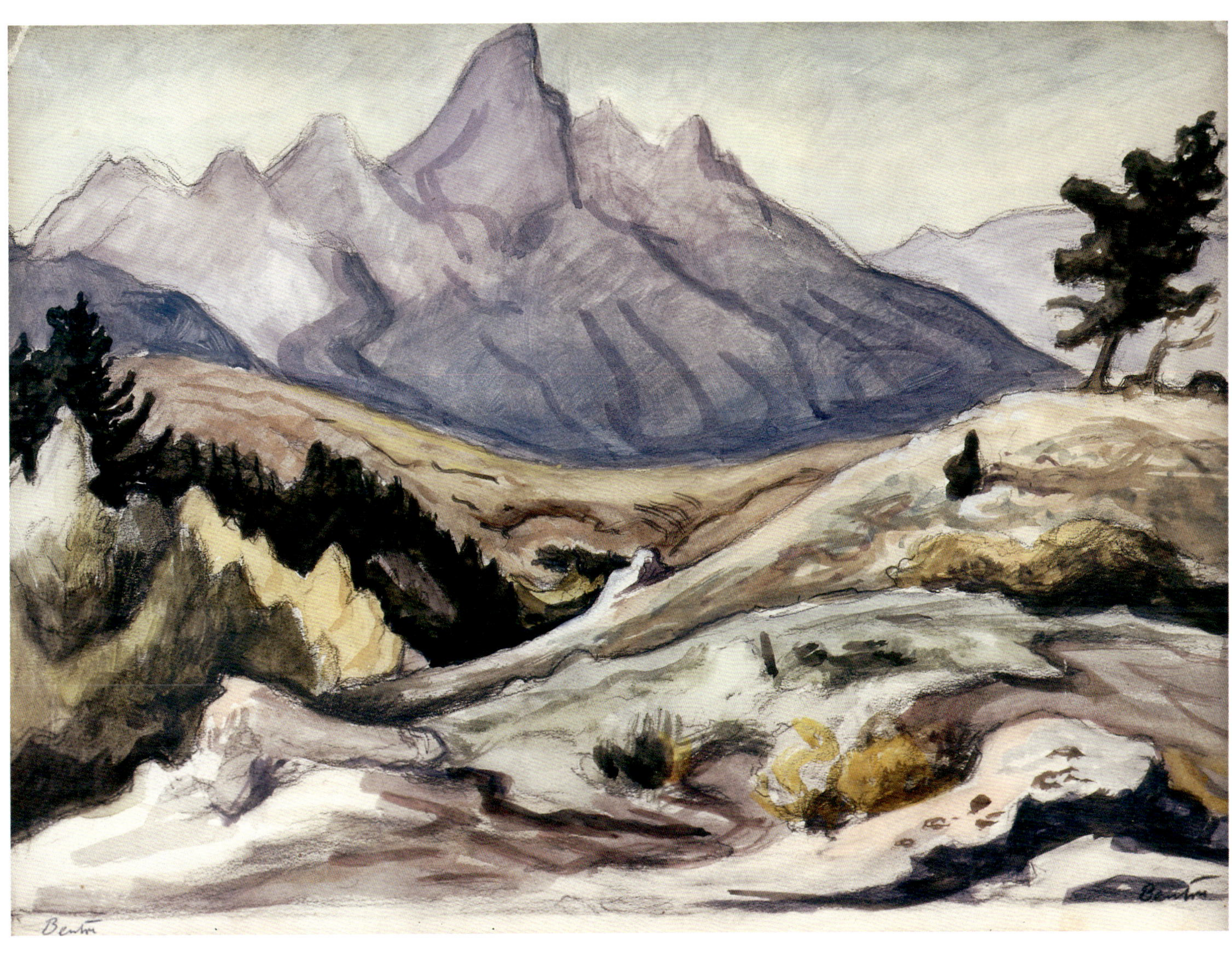

69 Berenice Abbott

U.S., 1898–1991

New York at Night (Westside Looking North from the Upper Thirties), 1933
Gelatin silver print
$9\frac{5}{16} \times 7\frac{1}{2}$ in.
Purchased with funds from the Charles Merrill Trust and the National Endowment for the Arts, 1973

Among the most significant American photographers, Berenice Abbott was born in Springfield, Ohio. After a term at Ohio State University, she moved to New York to enroll at the Columbia University School of Journalism, but decided instead to study sculpture independently. She associated with New York's Greenwich Village bohemia and met Man Ray and Marcel Duchamp. In 1921, she moved to Paris to attend the Académie de la Grande Chaumière, and in 1923, she traveled to Berlin to study at the Kunstschule.

Abbott became a photographer when she returned to Paris to work as Man Ray's darkroom assistant from 1924 until 1926. In 1926, she had her first solo exhibition, in a Paris gallery, where she exhibited portraits of artists, writers, and other intellectuals. That same year, she set up her own successful portrait studio in Paris. Her photographs appeared in French *Vogue* and other publications.

Abbott embraced "straight" photography, which called for the photographer to shoot in sharp focus undoctored images of what he or she saw. She dismissed the artifice and soft focus of Pictorialism. (For more on straight photography and Pictorialism, see cat. no. 66.)

In 1929, Abbott left Paris for New York. The architectural and other changes to New York since she had last been there astonished her, and she began to document the city. Unlike the documentary photographer W. Eugene Smith (see cat. no. 79), she took a detached approach to her work. In 1939, she published *Changing New York,* which included photographs she had made for the Federal Arts Project of the Works Progress Administration (W.P.A.). She published *Greenwich Village Today and Yesterday* in 1949. While photographing these documentary series of New York, she continued to produce portraits, such as the museum's *Portrait of Edward Hopper* (see cat. no. 70).

Abbott modeled her documentaries of New York after the French photographer Eugène Atget's photographs of a changing Paris's depopulated streets, buildings, and shop fronts. Atget's photographs documenting Paris had greatly impressed her when she had first seen them in Man Ray's studio in 1925. Abbott met Atget just before he died in 1927; upon his death, she bought all of his remaining prints and negatives, which were eventually acquired by New York's Museum of Modern Art. She made prints from Atget's negatives.

Between 1933 and 1958, Abbott taught at the New School for Social Research in Greenwich Village, and from 1947 until 1958, she ran her own business, the House of Photography. This venture sold the many inventions she made in photography and related areas, such as lighting, but the business was a financial failure. Abbott continued to make documentary series and photographs illustrating scientific principles. In 1956, she bought a house in Maine, and she moved there permanently in 1966.

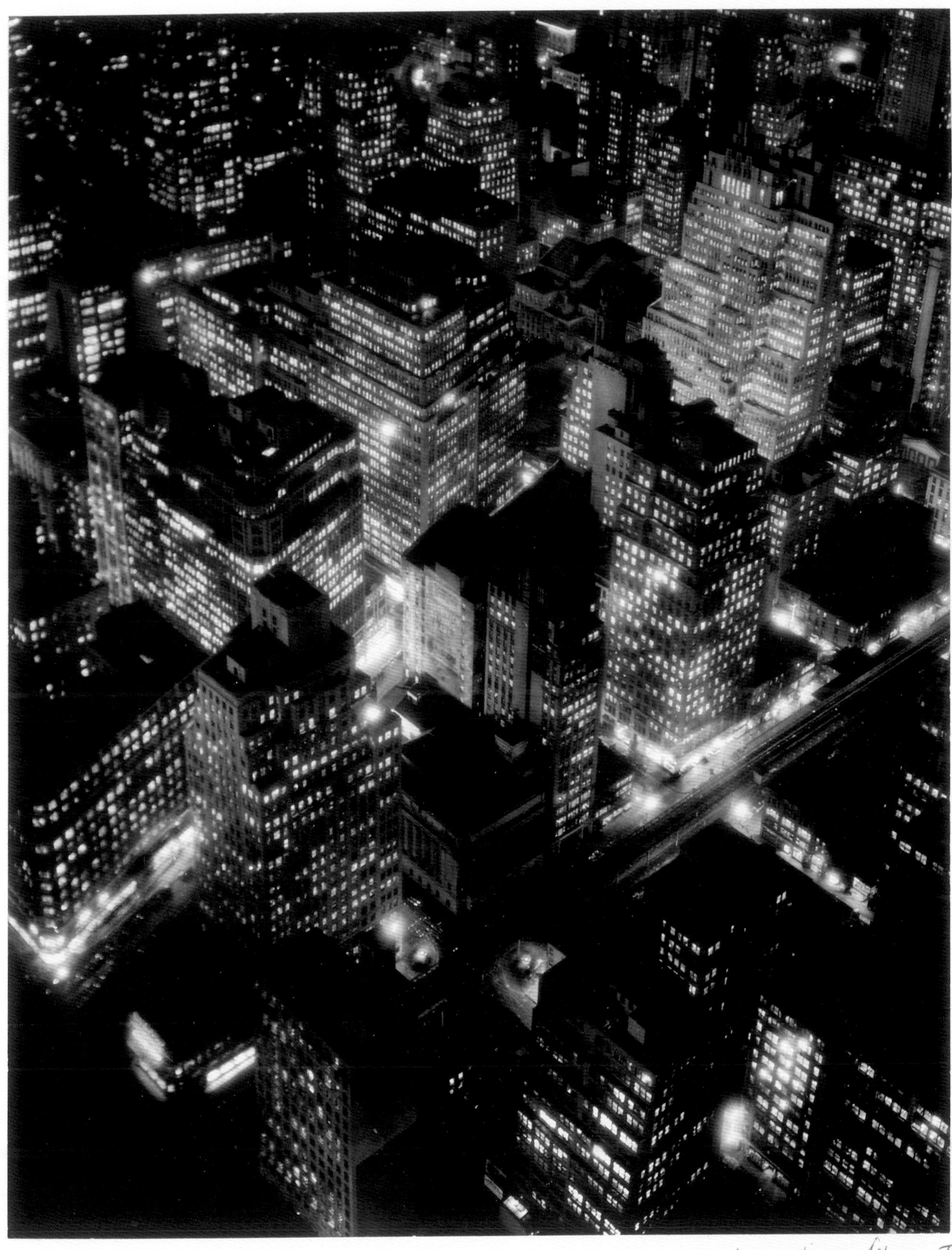

BERENICE ABBOTT

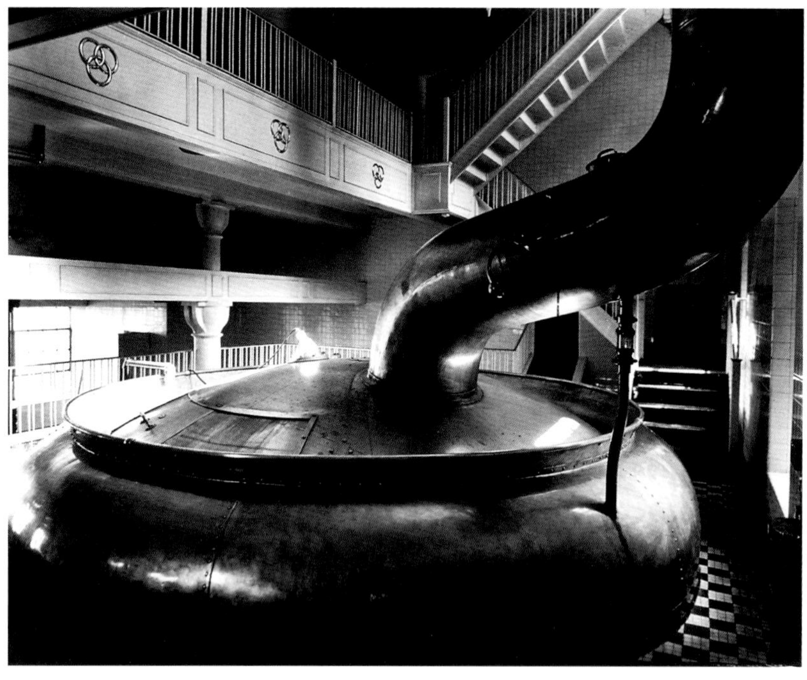

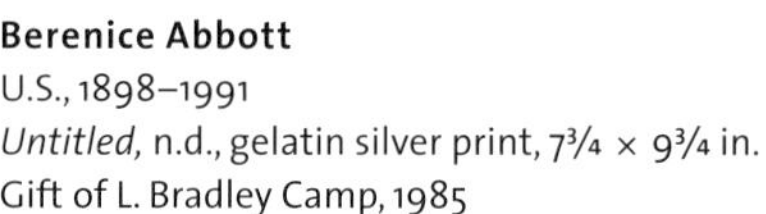

Berenice Abbott
U.S., 1898–1991
Untitled, n.d., gelatin silver print, $7\frac{3}{4} \times 9\frac{3}{4}$ in.
Gift of L. Bradley Camp, 1985

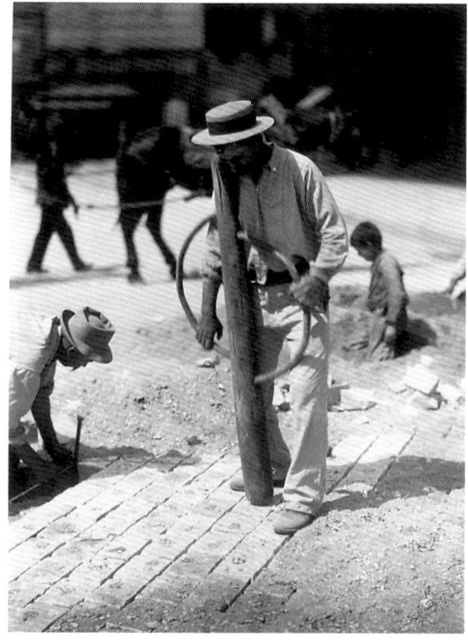

Eugène Atget
France, 1857–1927
Street Paver, 1910, gelatin silver print,
$9 \times 6\frac{11}{16}$ in. Museum purchase, 1975

One of Abbott's most famous images, *New York at Night* required much planning. She knew that to take such a night shot of the city with the office lights on, she would have to expose the film for fifteen minutes. She also knew that people turned off their lights when they went home around five o'clock. She calculated that her only chance of getting the shot would be on the short day of December 20, which would give her enough dark time before 5:00 P.M. for the long exposure. Abbott had to take the photograph from a window, because a rooftop would have been too windy, causing a blurry image from the long exposure. She had difficulty receiving permission from the building superintendent to use the selected window, because, as she wrote, "They always thought you wanted to commit suicide. . . . They usually had to be bribed."

The museum owns twenty-six photographs by Abbott and two Abbott prints from Atget negatives.

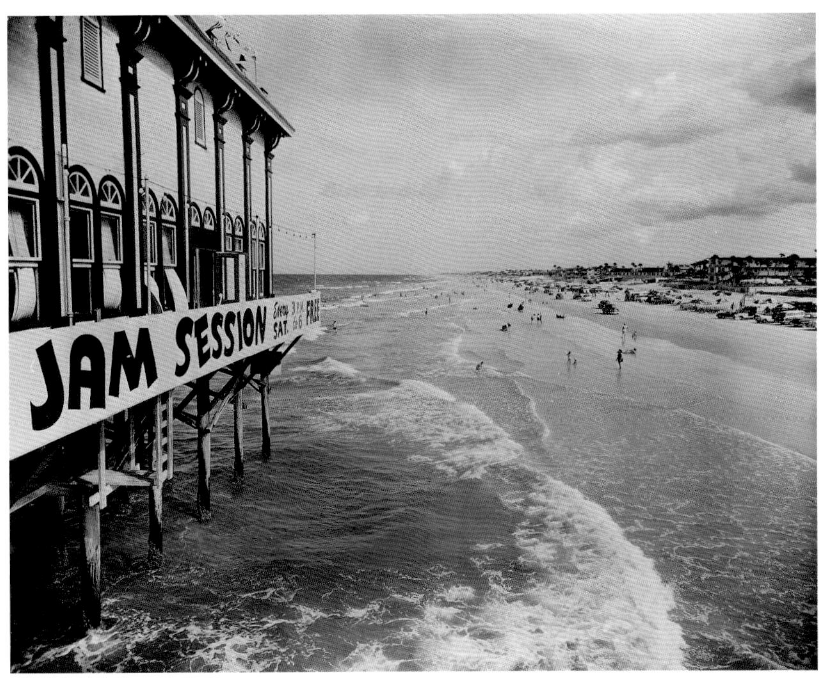

Berenice Abbott
U.S., 1898–1991
Beach from Boardwalk, Daytona Beach, Florida, 1954, gelatin silver print, 7⅞ × 9⅞ in. Gift of L. Bradley Camp, 1985

70 Edward Hopper

U.S., 1882–1967

House in Provincetown, 1930
Watercolor on paper
20¼ × 25½ in.
Purchase, U.S. State Department Collection, 1948

Edward Hopper was born in Nyack, on the Hudson River in New York. Between 1899 and 1900, he trained at the Correspondence School of Illustrating in New York City, and in 1900, he enrolled in the New York School of Art, where he soon began to study drawing and painting with, among others, William Merritt Chase, Robert Henri, and John Sloan.

Hopper left for Europe in the fall of 1906 and traveled for almost a year, touring museums, studying the Old Masters, and painting outdoors. He returned to Europe again in 1909 and 1910.

Back in New York, Hopper worked as an illustrator and produced etchings, for which he became well known. In 1913, he settled in Washington Square in Greenwich Village. He spent summers in New England, in places such as Gloucester, Massachusetts, and the coast of Maine. He exhibited and sold a painting at the famous Armory Show of 1913, but did not sell another painting for a decade. Hopper exhibited sixteen paintings in a solo show at the Whitney Studio Club in 1920, but they went largely unnoticed, and nothing sold.

His work as an illustrator aside, Hopper first gained recognition for his watercolors, not his oils. Jo Nivison, whom he had met while they were both art students and whom he would marry in 1924, convinced him to use watercolor in Gloucester during the summer of 1923. He liked the results. His watercolor exhibition at the Brooklyn Museum in the fall of 1923 was a critical success. In November 1924, he first showed in a commercial gallery, exhibiting only watercolors. The show received rave reviews and everything sold. For the rest of his life, Hopper remained a successful artist, who was hailed as an American Realist. Major exhibitions included a show at the Museum of Modern Art in New York in 1933 and at the Whitney Museum of American Art in 1950. In 1956, *Time* magazine featured him on its cover.

The year 1930 was important for Hopper. In January, the Museum of Modern Art accepted the gift of *House by the Railroad,* which became the first painting to enter its permanent collection. The same year, Hopper painted one of his best-known works, *Early Sunday Morning,* which depicts an empty street of shops in New York. The painting entered the collection of the Whitney Museum of American Art that same year.

Also in 1930, the Hoppers rented a cottage and spent their first summer on Cape Cod in Truro, south of Provincetown. (They would build a cottage in Truro in 1934.) The rented cottage was on a bluff, from which Provincetown could be seen in the distance across the bay. (Provincetown, at the tip of Cape Cod in Massachusetts, had been an important fishing and whaling center in the nineteenth century. By

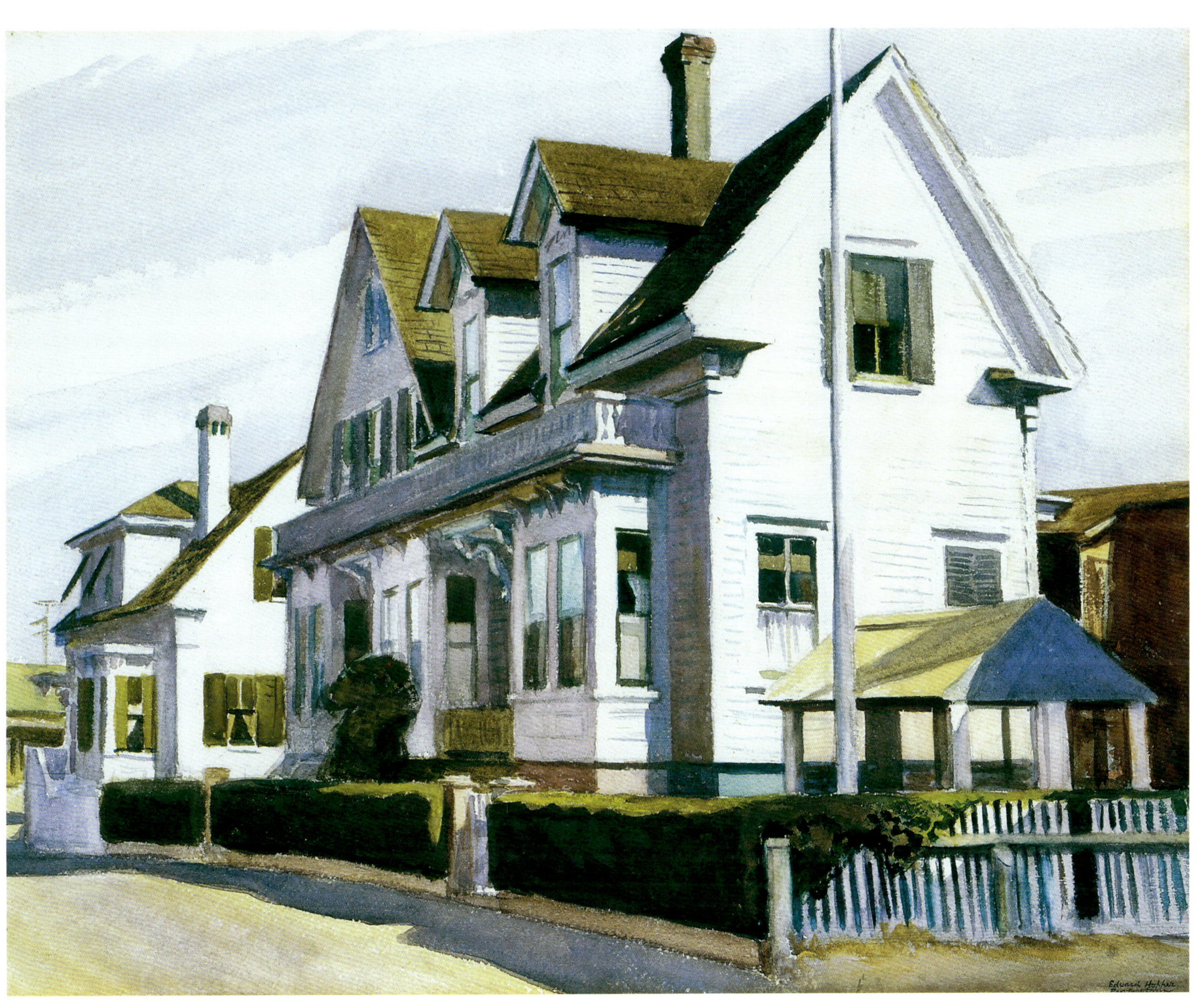

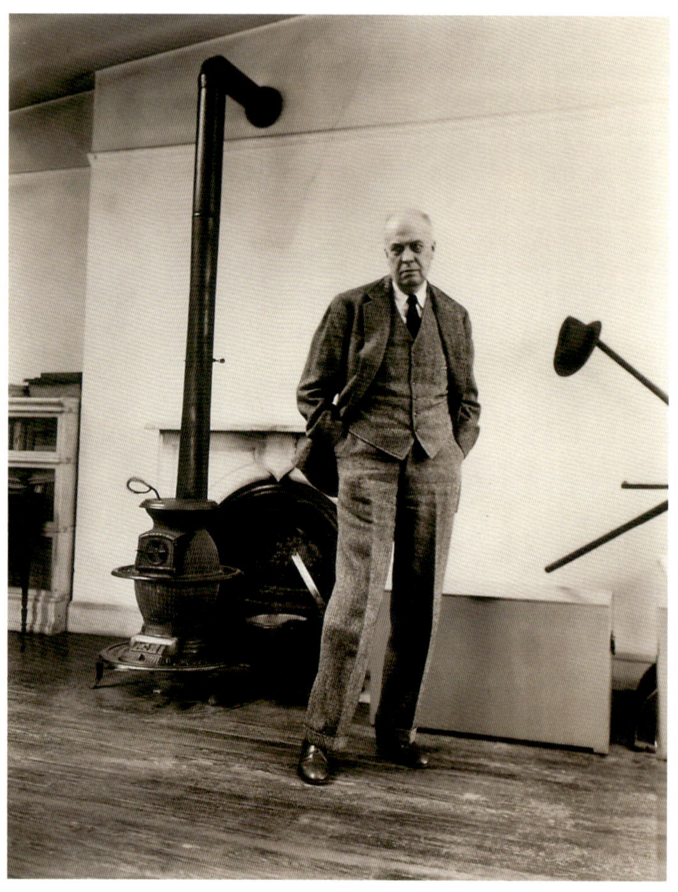

Berenice Abbott
U.S., 1898–1991
Portrait of Edward Hopper, 1947, gelatin silver print, 9⅞ × 7⅞ in. Purchased with funds from Jerome Westheimer and the National Endowment for the Arts, 1986

the early twentieth century, the town's principal income came from the artists' colony and the tourists who flocked to the town during the summer.) Hopper produced a number of watercolors in the summer of 1930: several of Truro, one of Wellfleet, and two of Provincetown, including the present work. During the early 1930s, Hopper found Cape Cod a fertile setting for subject matter, but later he traveled farther afield.

Hopper and his wife recorded the name and date of the present work—*House in Provincetown,* summer of 1930—in the ledger that they kept when each work was sold. The ledger describes the painting as "House in Provincetown. White house with 3 gables, front in strong shadow. Balcony along 2nd story front. Little pavillion in yard at side, front of picture. Hedge along front of house."

In *House in Provincetown,* Hopper made use of the white paper on which the watercolor was painted. He achieved a sunny brightness in some areas of the watercolor by leaving the paper unpainted; this technique is seen in the side of the house facing the viewer.

Unlike his oils, Hopper's watercolors usually show unpeopled buildings. The watercolors do not convey the alienation and emotional tension of the oils, especially the oils from the late 1930s on. This difference between the oils and watercolors may be because Hopper produced the watercolors outdoors during his travels, painting houses and buildings in the light and atmosphere in which he saw them. In contrast, he created the oils back home in the studio, deliberately composing them to maximize emotional nuance.

71 Stuart Davis

U.S., 1894–1964

Waterfront, 1935
Oil on panel
20 × 30 in.
W.P.A. Collection, 1942

One of the most important American artists of the twentieth century, Stuart Davis was born in Philadelphia. His mother was a sculptor, and his father was the art editor of a Philadelphia newspaper that employed a number of artists associated with Robert Henri, the leader of the Ashcan School. (For more on the Ashcan School, see cat. no. 53.) Davis studied under Henri in New York at the Art Students League from 1909 until 1912.

Davis's early works are in the manner of Henri's Ashcan School; he painted New York streets, saloons, and theaters in dark, earthy colors. In 1913, Davis exhibited five watercolors in the Armory Show, the famous exhibition that introduced European avant-garde art to America. One of the youngest exhibitors, he found European Modernist works to be a revelation. After the Armory Show, he began to paint in styles derived from Post-Impressionism, Fauvism, and Cubism.

Davis's mature style emerged in the 1920s, when, anticipating Pop Art by forty years, he depicted American consumer products such as packs of cigarettes (for example, *Lucky Strike* [1921]) and a popular mouthwash (*Odol* [1924]). Davis painted these works in a Cubist manner and incorporated words in the compositions. With their sharp-edged forms and visual puns, the paintings also related to the Precisionism of Charles Demuth and others. (For more on Precisionism, see cat. no. 74.) In the later 1920s, Davis produced abstract still-life compositions of objects such as eggbeaters. The extroverted Davis loved jazz, which he likened to abstract art.

Davis was an ardent political leftist. During the 1910s and 1920s, his illustrations appeared in magazines such as *The Masses*. During the 1930s, when Davis was America's foremost Modernist, he was an artists' advocate, serving as president of the Artists' Union and in 1936 as editor of its journal, *Art Front*.

Initially on the recommendation of John Sloan, Davis spent most summers between 1915 and 1934 on the coast of Massachusetts, in Gloucester, a fishing town that had long attracted artists. (For more on the Gloucester art colony, see cat. no. 31.) He painted numerous views of the town. In his first years in Gloucester, Davis painted outdoors and familiarized himself with the environs. Later, he sketched outdoors with a fountain pen and painted in his studio compositions based on the syntheses of various scenes from his sketchbook.

Waterfront, created in 1935 for the Federal Arts Project of the Works Progress Administration (W.P.A.), depicts Gloucester. The painting is a composite of Gloucester views—overlapping planes are playfully connected to a beacon with mooring rope. In *Waterfront*, Davis explored color and spatial relationships. The plane nearest the beacon shows a wooden pier, a boat on the water, and fishing huts beyond. Superimposed on this plane to the left is a red sail loft with a yellow-hinged blue door. Below the sail loft is a view of a wharf and Gloucester's harbor, with a fisherman in a small boat, and blue hills beyond. The beacon with attached pulleys stands in isolation from the scenes to the left. All of the painting's images float against a white ground.

The museum owns another painting of Gloucester by Stuart Davis, *Shapes of Landscape Space* (1939), a gouache-on-paper work that is an abstract depiction of the harbor.

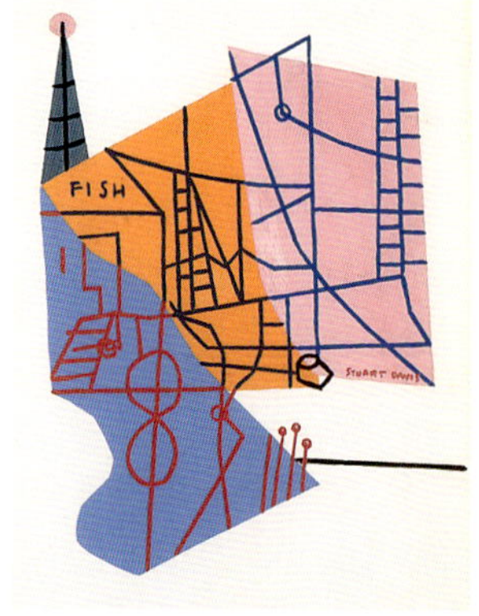

Stuart Davis
U.S., 1894–1964
Shapes of Landscape Space, 1939, gouache on paper, 15 × 11½ in. Purchase, U.S. State Department Collection, 1948

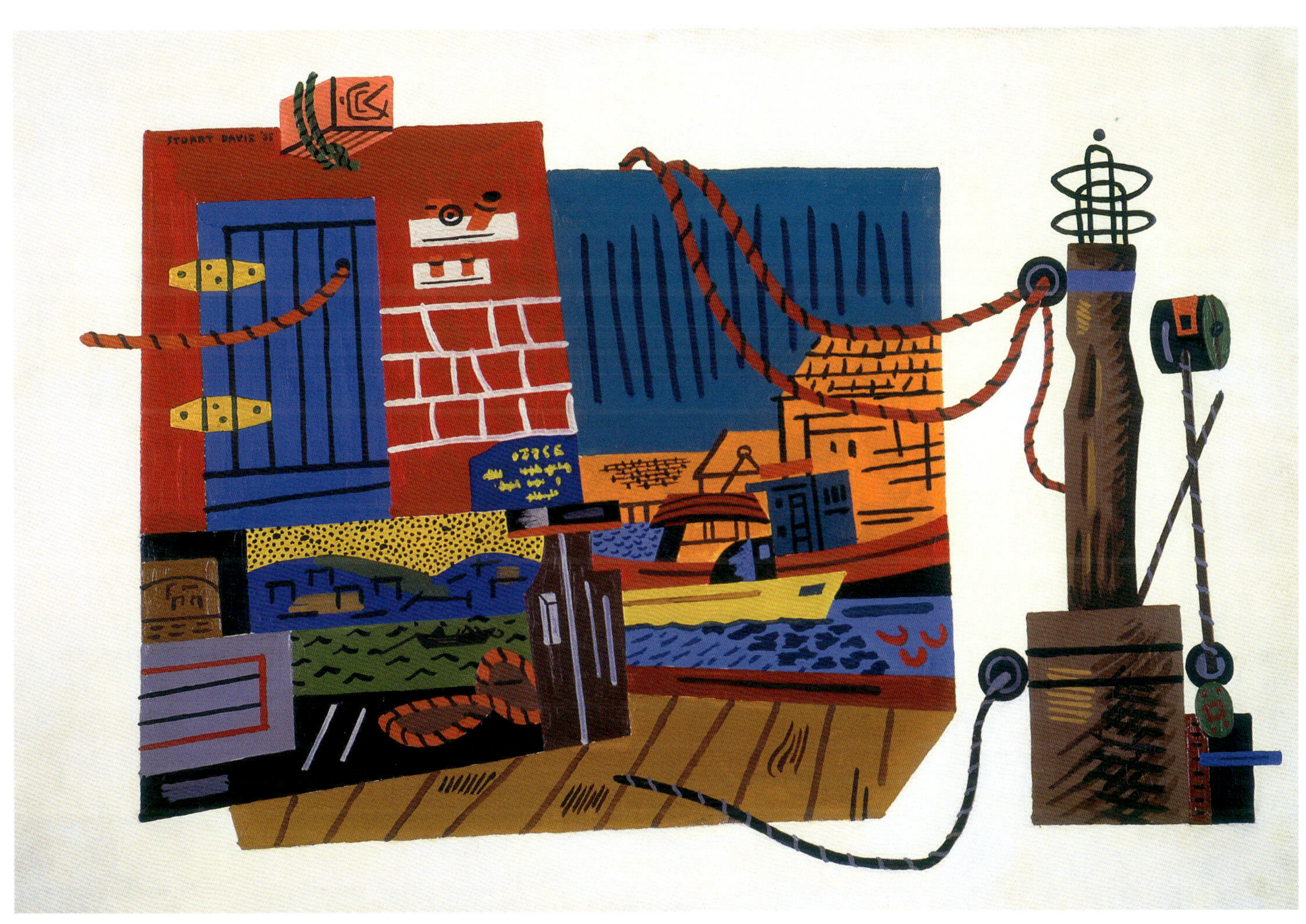
STUART DAVIS

72 Olinka Hrdy

U.S., 1902–1987

Studies for Riverside Studio Murals, 1928–29
Watercolor on paper
Top sheets 18 × 4½ in.; center sheet 23¾ × 10½ in.; bottom sheets 18⅝ × 4½ in.
Gift of the artist, 1966

Olinka Hrdy was born in a sod hut in Prague, Oklahoma. Her father was a Czech immigrant and her mother a native Iowan of Czech and American Indian descent. After her parents divorced and her father left home, when Hrdy was sixteen, she had to plow fields when she was not in school.

Hrdy enrolled at the University of Oklahoma in 1923. She worked her way through college in part by painting murals in a Norman restaurant and by painting a set of twenty panels in the dining room of the women's dormitories. She majored in art. Her teachers Oscar Jacobson and Edith Mahier—who also taught the Kiowa Five artists (see cat. no. 61) during Hrdy's final year at the university—considered her one of their most gifted students.

In an article about Hrdy published in the university's *Sooner Magazine,* Jeanne d'Ucel, Oscar Jacobson's French wife, described the student Hrdy as obsessive about her art and possessing an innate feeling for color. D'Ucel noted that the dreamy, introspective Hrdy gradually made many friends and became a favorite of campus poets, who would gather around her easel.

Before Hrdy graduated in 1928, she met the legendary maverick architect Bruce Goff, who saw Hrdy's murals in the women's dormitories. Recognizing a talented, kindred spirit, he asked to meet the artist and immediately offered her a job painting murals in a building he was designing in Tulsa.

Hrdy moved to Tulsa in the fall of 1928 to paint murals for the still-extant Riverside Studio that Goff had designed for music teacher Patti Adams Shriner. On the stair landing in the recital hall's foyer, Hrdy painted a central panel surrounded by eight canvases measuring sixteen by five feet. Near their tops, these tall, vertical paintings bent ninety degrees onto the ceiling. Goff designed the Riverside Studio to be an architectural expression of music, and Hrdy's paintings were abstract visualizations of music. The magazine *Western Architect* described them as "among the first adventures in abstract decoration in America." These paintings would have been remarkable anywhere in the world at that time; that they were painted by a young artist who had never left Oklahoma was extraordinary.

The Art Deco–like murals are now lost, but the studies that Hrdy presented for Shriner's approval survive in the museum's collection. The central decoration depicts the *Symphony of the Arts (Painting, Architecture, Music, and Dance).* The paintings flanking *Symphony of the Arts* represent various types of music: modern American, vocal, piano, and string appear here from top left to right, and symphonic, primitive, choral, and future apppear from bottom left to right.

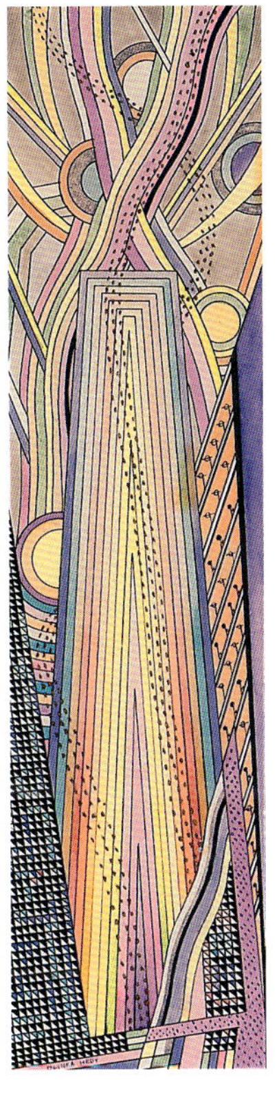
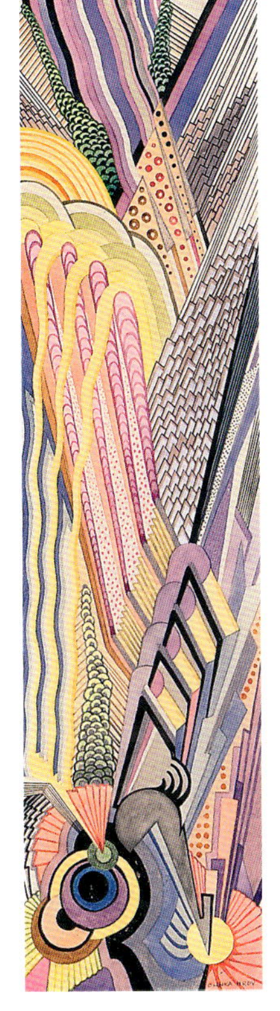
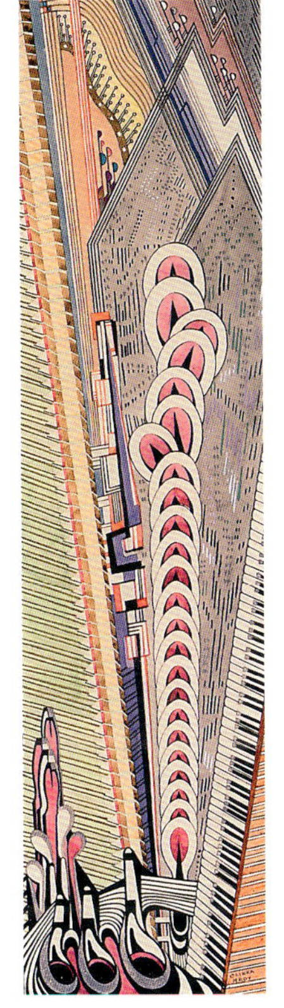
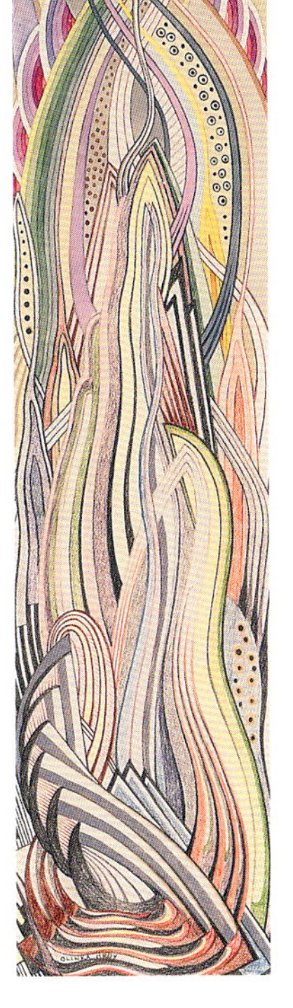
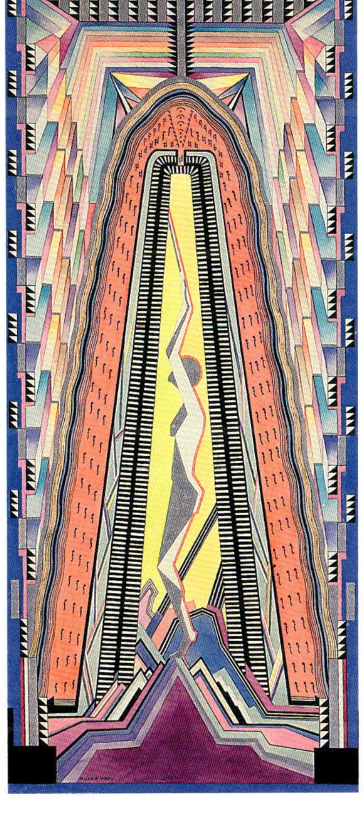
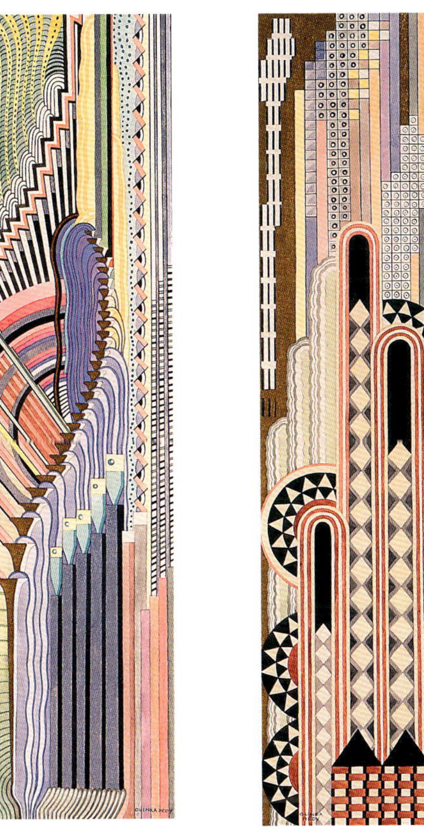
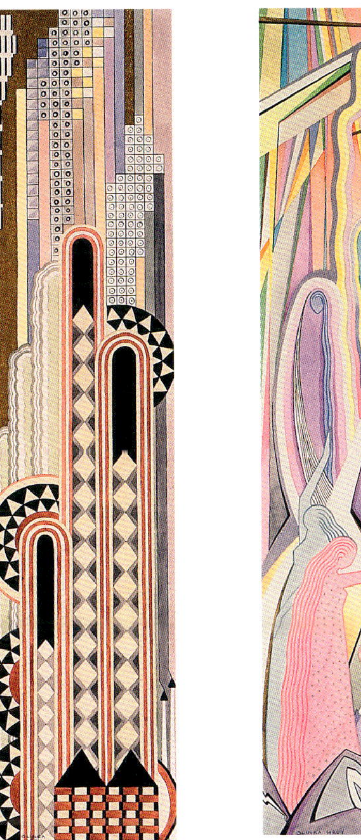
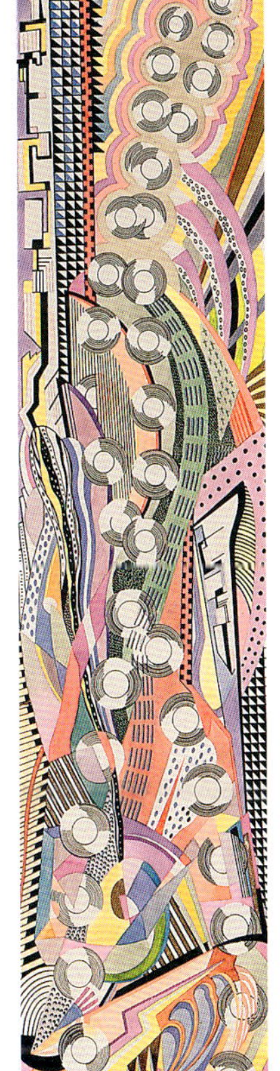

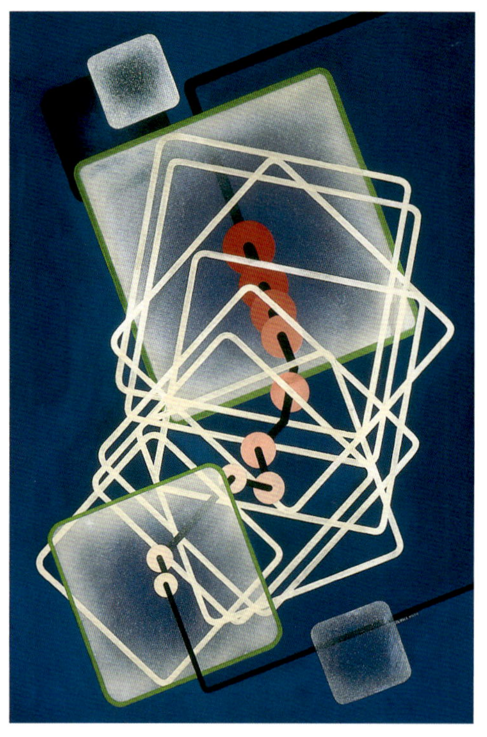

Olinka Hrdy
U.S., 1902–1987
Games, 1936, oil on canvas, 36 × 24 in.
Gift of the artist, 1966

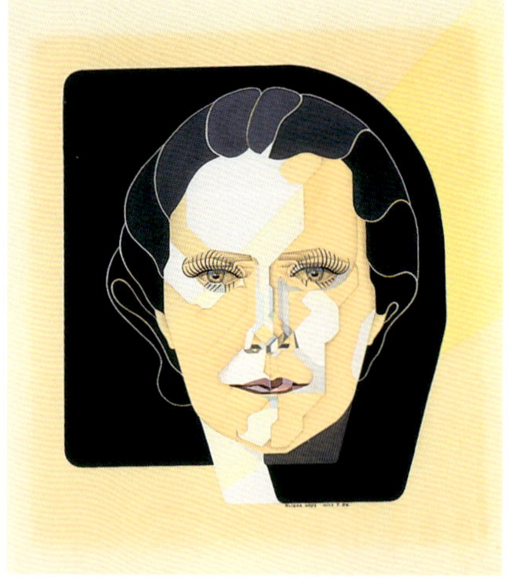

Olinka Hrdy
U.S., 1902–1987
Self Portrait, July 7, 1934, tempera on paper,
13 × 12 in. Gift of the artist, 1966

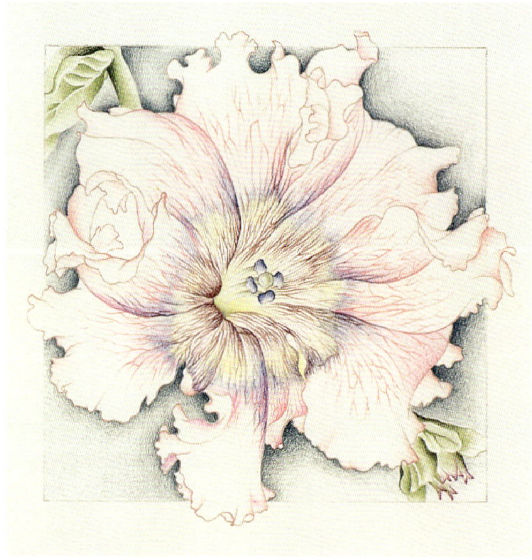

Olinka Hrdy
U.S., 1902–1987
Untitled, n.d., color pencil, 12¾ × 12 in.
Gift of the artist, 1966

In a 1965 interview, Hrdy, looking at photographs of the murals in the Riverside Studio, described how some of these paintings depicted the types of music. She said that the vocal-music panel showed "the round sounds that people make and then the little staccato-like sounds and those that pour out." The piano-music panel showed "the foot pedals and the hammers here with one hammer hitting a string here and causing this terrific vibration there." She continued:

> *How unafraid I was of color. . . .[These are] modern discs and electrical music of the future. . . . This was the primitive music panel, Indian, African, Tom Tom rhythmic beats. . . . It has a simplicity to it that the others don't have. You can see here how strong it is because it's done in black and gold and Indian red. And then these very light little block-like design[s]—you see even there that looks [like] Frank Lloyd Wright. I didn't know Mr. Wright but Bruce [Goff] was gradually introducing me to his work.*

Even though she had approved the presentation drawings, Shriner became irate when she saw the bright colors Hrdy was using. Goff interceded, and the panels were painted as Hrdy had designed them. Hrdy later worked with Goff on a number of other projects.

In the 1930s, Hrdy left Tulsa for New York, and then moved to Wisconsin to become the manager of Frank Lloyd Wright's Taliesin East in Spring Green, where she also taught creative design. Wright greatly admired her work. Around 1936, she moved to California, where she continued to paint murals, illustrated children's books, produced art for advertising, and worked in industrial design. In the 1960s, she was the chief designer for the state of California.

Other works given by Hrdy to the museum include abstractions from the 1930s as well as portraits, flowers, and landscapes.

73 George L. K. Morris

U.S., 1905–1975

New England Church, 1935–46
Oil on canvas
36⅛ × 30 in.
Purchase, U.S. State Department Collection, 1948

George L. K. Morris was one of the four Park Avenue Cubists, so-called for their wealth and addresses. He grew up in New York and graduated from the Groton School in Massachusetts and Yale University. He studied in New York at the Art Students League, under John Sloan, and in Paris at the Académie Moderne, under Fernand Léger and Amédée Ozenfant. In Paris, he also met Pablo Picasso and Georges Braque, who greatly influenced his work.

The other Park Avenue Cubists included Morris's wife, Suzy Frelinghuysen (both a painter and an opera singer); Woolworth heir Charles G. Shaw; and Morris's cousin, Albert E. Gallatin, who was a major art collector. The group based its art on the Cubists of the School of Paris, such as Léger, Juan Gris, and Cubism creators Braque and Picasso. Unlike Social Realist artists, such as Ben Shahn and Jack Levine, or Regionalist artists, such as Thomas Hart Benton, the Park Avenue Cubists divorced art from politics and focused on aesthetic issues. During the 1930s and 1940s, Morris, Frelinghuysen, Shaw, and Gallatin became important promoters of Modernism in New York; they joined the American Abstract Artists, a group that supported abstraction and that Morris helped found. (When Dutch artist Piet Mondrian moved to New York in 1940, he also joined the American Abstract Artists.)

Although the Park Avenue Cubists were talented and serious about their art, other artists and critics often dismissed them as rich dilettantes. During the 1930s and 1940s, many attacked the Park Avenue Cubists as too derivative of earlier European Cubism. The Social Realists denounced the Modernism of the Park Avenue Cubists and posited that art should focus on the class struggle, while the Regionalists believed that American art should portray an authentic America. Today, the Park Avenue Cubists have undergone a reappraisal, receiving critical recognition.

Morris began *New England Church* the year he married Frelinghuysen. The work represents a well-known American vernacular subject matter—the New England church—interpreted in a Cubist manner. Morris knew rural New England well, since he and his wife divided their time among homes in New York, Paris, and the Massachusetts Berkshires. In the painting, Morris breaks down the structure of a church into constituent angular forms and geometries. A cross appears in the lower center, with, on either side, spoked half-circles that could be either wagon wheels or the oculi in the steeple. On the left and bottom edges of the canvas, Morris painted wood, complete with grain. (Simulated wood often appears in the Cubist works of Picasso and Braque.) This "wood" could represent a church pew or the materials of an old barn. The tic-tac-toe game in the painting's center right adds a note of playfulness and might have been drawn on a church pew by children bored by a sermon. Following the teachings of Léger, Morris creates a nonhierarchical, allover composition, in which every square inch of the canvas is treated with equal importance.

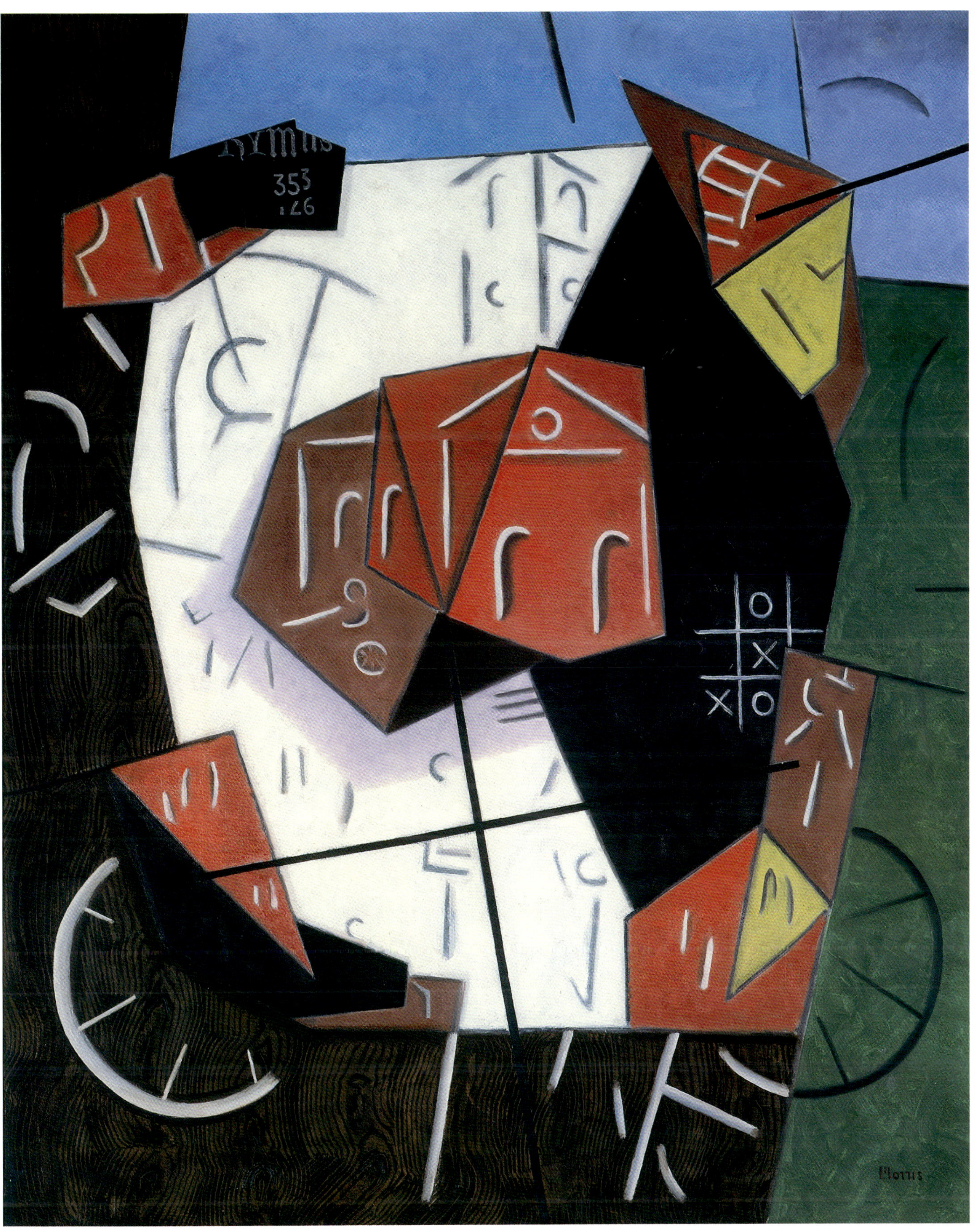
HYMNS
353
126
Morris

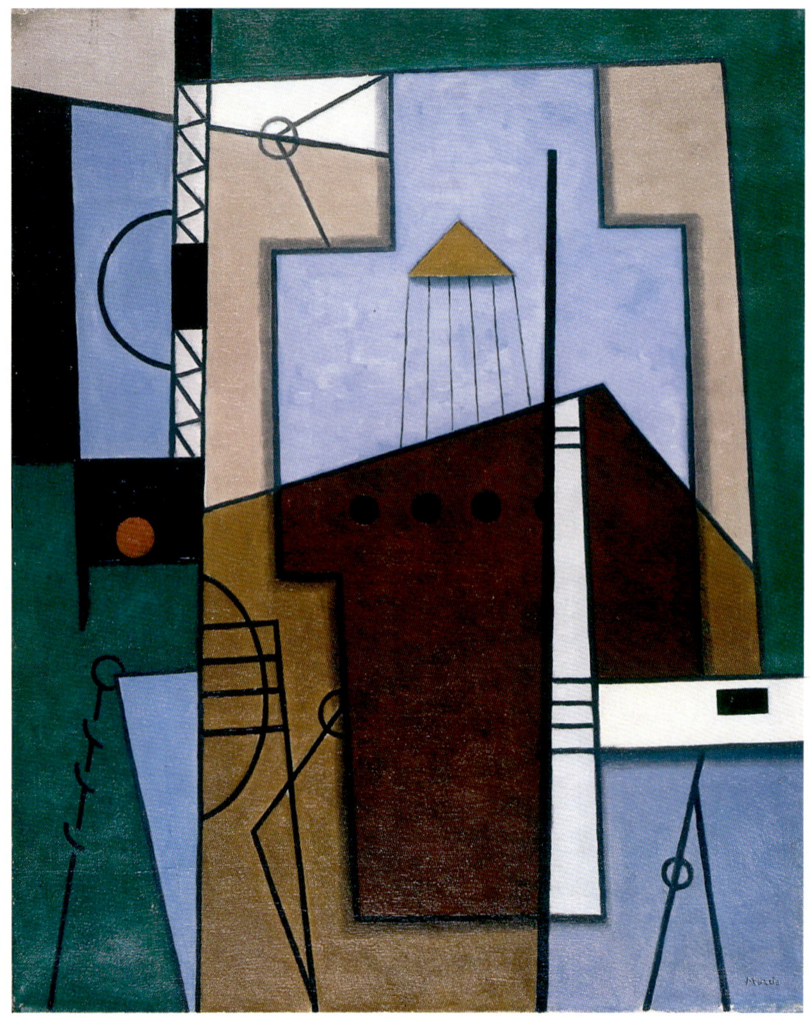

George L. K. Morris
U.S., 1905–1975
Shipbuilding Construction, 1944–45,
oil on canvas, 22 × 18 in. Purchase,
U.S. State Department Collection, 1948

Art critic Arthur Danto has written about *New England Church:*

Morris's paintings feel as if he was trying to depict the images left on the retina by the way the eye performs saccades from point to point of the visual field. The wheel segments in his 1935 New England Church *imply that one is riding past a church that one has to synthesize in order to recover its identity. The rest of the painting shows syncopated glimpses of a church through fragments of its architectural parts, distributed across the canvas. Instead of reconstructing the visual world, as the classical Cubists did, he is trying to show the process through which we construct the world visually and cinematically.*

In addition to painting, Morris financed the transition of the *Partisan Review* from a publication of the American Communist Party to a leading literary journal, of which he was an editor and the first art critic. (The influential art critic Clement Greenberg succeeded Morris as the *Partisan Review*'s art critic.)

The Modernist Frelinghuysen-Morris House and Studio, which was the artists' country home in Lenox, Massachusetts, is now open to the public. It contains murals painted by Morris and Frelinghuysen, and works from their collection of French Cubist paintings. The Frelinghuysen-Morris House and Studio was the first International-style house in New England.

74 Ralston Crawford

U.S., b. Canada, 1906–1978

Wing Fabrication, 1946
Oil on canvas
30⅛ × 25⅛ in.
Purchase, U.S. State Department Collection, 1948

The son of a ship captain on the Great Lakes, Ralston Crawford was himself an avid sailor. He was born in St. Catherines, Ontario, and moved to Buffalo, New York, at age four with his family. He studied at the Otis Art Institute in Los Angeles from 1926 until 1927 and worked briefly as an illustrator in Walt Disney's studio before moving to Philadelphia to study from 1927 to 1930 at the Pennsylvania Academy of the Fine Arts and the Barnes Foundation. He then traveled to Paris, where he studied from 1932 until 1933 at the Académie Colarossi and the Académie Scandinave.

After Crawford's return to the United States, he became identified as a younger member of the group of artists now known as the Precisionists, which included Charles Sheeler and Charles Demuth. The Precisionists, who worked mainly during the 1920s and 1930s, celebrated the machine age as distinctly American, and some of them, including Crawford, held Utopian beliefs that technology would eventually solve social problems. The Precisionists often portrayed architecture and industrial machinery and emphasized order, clarity, and simplified geometries; in their works, the artists used sharp focus, strong lines, flat planes of color, and an impersonal handling of paint. They were originally known as the "New Classicists" and the "Immaculate School"; the label "Precisionists" began to be used in the 1960s.

Crawford painted *Wing Fabrication* shortly after the end of World War II, during which he served in the U.S. Army's Weather Division, where he made weather maps to guide bomber pilots. The painting depicts military constructions in a schematic manner. Like many of Crawford's works, the composition may have initially been inspired by a photograph, the components of which the artist abstracted.

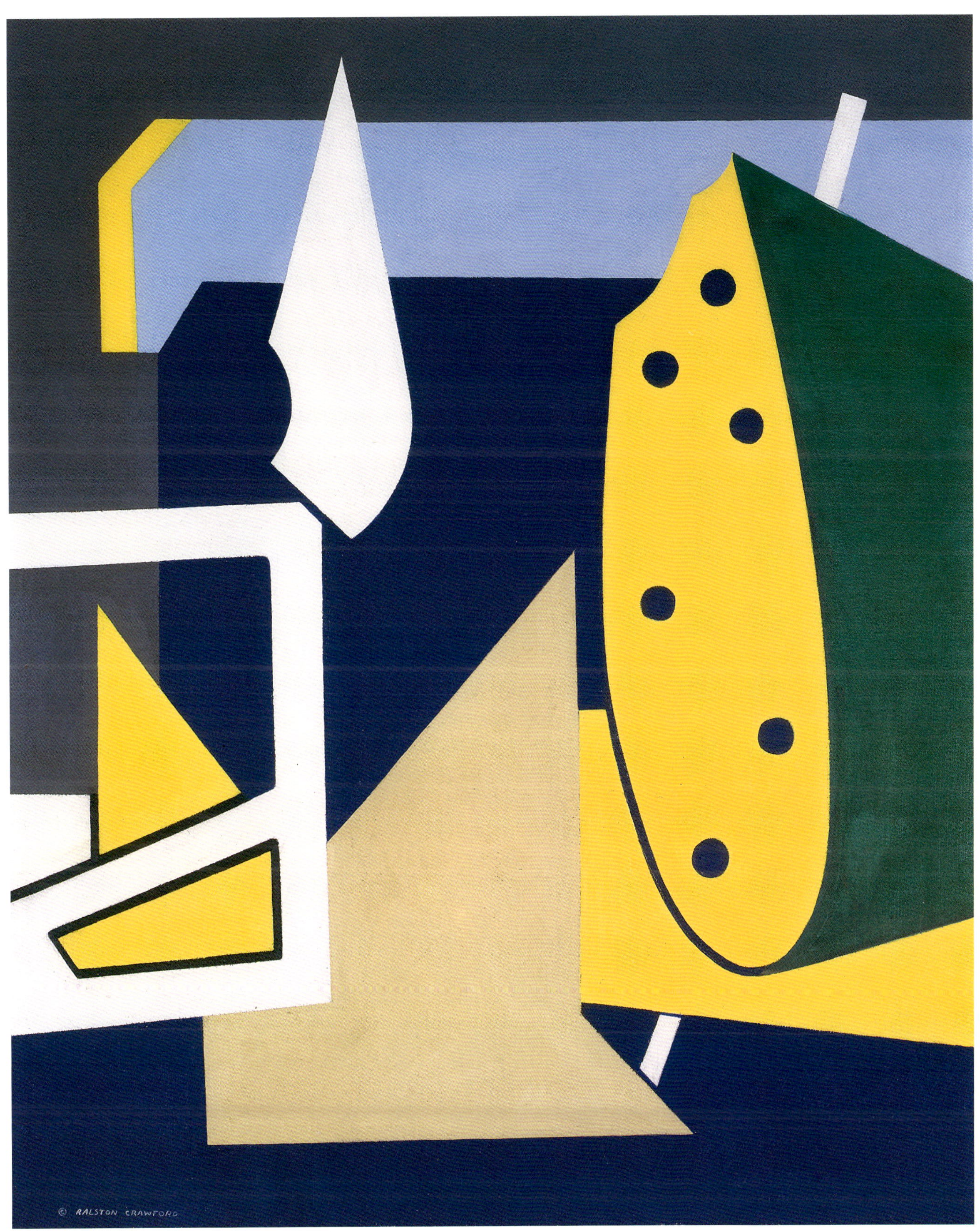
© RALSTON CRAWFORD

75 Romare Bearden

U.S., 1914–1988

At Five in the Afternoon, 1946
Oil on board
29½ × 37½ in.
Purchase, U.S. State Department Collection, 1948

Best known for his later works, photocollages that depict the African American experience, Romare Bearden is one of the most celebrated African American artists. He was born in North Carolina but moved north with his family to Harlem, in New York City. As a child, Bearden met many major figures of the 1920s Harlem Renaissance, since his parents entertained the likes of jazz great Duke Ellington and writers W. E. B. Du Bois and Langston Hughes.

After beginning an education in medicine, Bearden decided to become an artist. He studied art at Boston University, New York University, and New York's Art Students League, where he worked with the German political satirist George Grosz. Both European and African art greatly influenced Bearden's work. Following World War II, during which he served in the segregated U.S. Army in Europe, Bearden's work bore the imprint of European Modernists, such as Pablo Picasso, whose influence is evident in *At Five in the Afternoon.* (Like Bearden, Picasso drew inspiration from African art.) Bearden's friendship with the artist Stuart Davis (see cat. no. 71) led him to explore links between jazz and the visual arts.

Bearden had his first solo exhibition outside of Harlem in Washington, D.C., in 1944 and 1945; major New York art dealers represented him after 1945. In addition to producing art, he wrote prodigiously: numerous essays, poems, reviews, song lyrics, and books on art theory and African American art. Until the 1960s, he could not afford to devote himself full-time to art and held a day job with the New York City Department of Social Services.

At Five in the Afternoon was inspired by the Spanish poet Federico García Lorca's poem "Lament for Ignacio Sanchez Mejias," about the death of the celebrated bullfighter. A bull had gored Mejias at five in the afternoon on August 11, 1934; the phrase "at five in the afternoon" appears refrainlike in Lorca's poem. Mejias and Lorca had been close friends. Called the "Toreador-Poet," Mejias was a famously brave bullfighter, writer, and lover of the arts. When he was killed, he had come out of retirement at age forty-three for a few more fights. Lorca—who celebrated Spanish folk culture and considered the bullfight, like the flamenco dance, an authentic, archaic Andalusian custom—wrote the poem the following month. Lorca himself was murdered two years later, in 1936, at age thirty-eight, during the Spanish Civil War. Lorca's death came to symbolize tyranny and oppression, and so "Lament for Ignacio Sanchez Mejias" came to be read as a lament not only for Mejias but also for Lorca and for Spain itself, which was then under the dictator Francisco Franco, who had banned Lorca's poetry.

Bearden painted *At Five in the Afternoon* ten years after Lorca's death. (Bearden had actually met Lorca when the poet visited the United States in 1929 and 1930.) The work is one in a series of paintings and watercolors that Bearden produced in 1946 in response to Lorca's poem. The composition was inspired by Picasso's 1934 painting

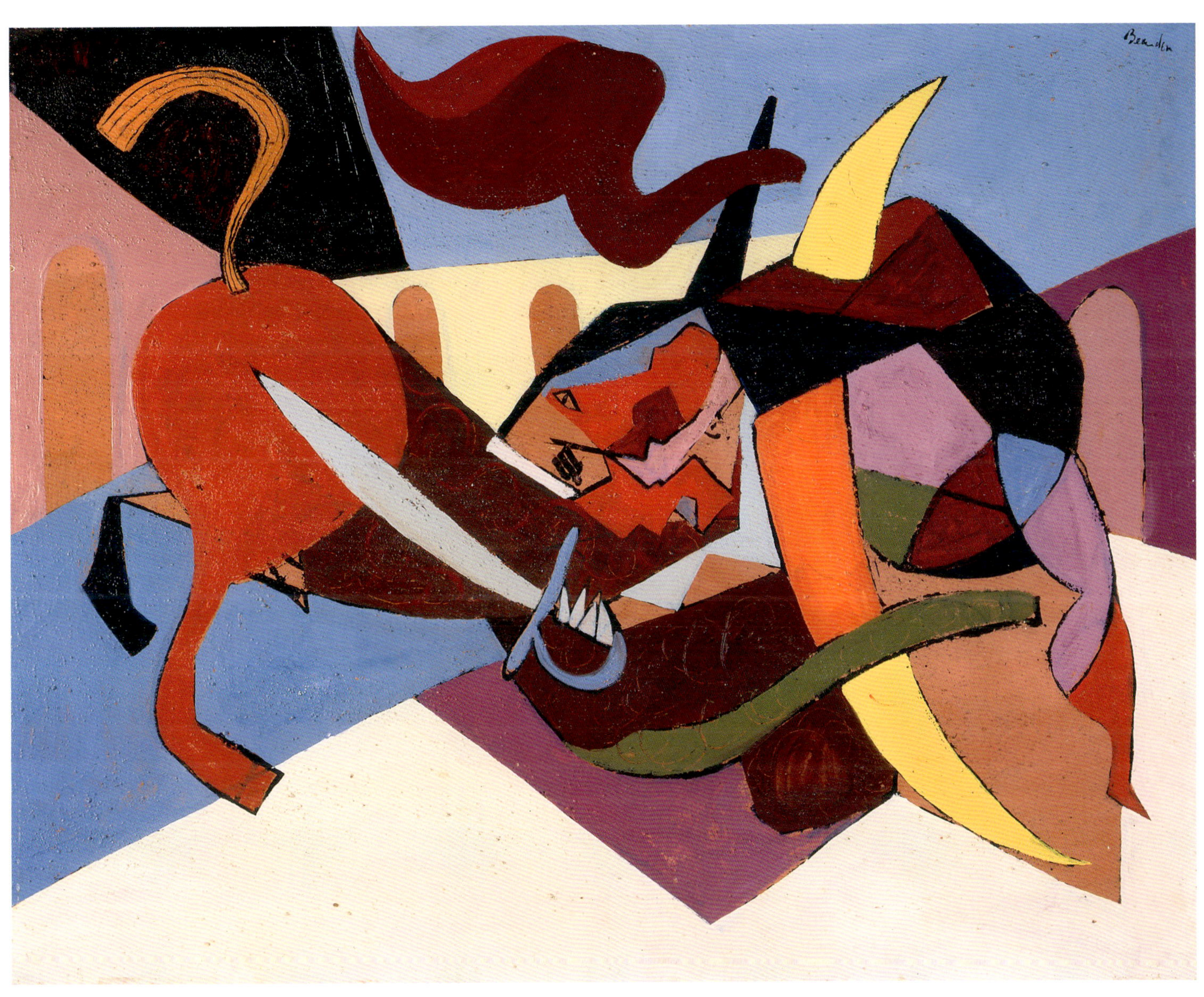

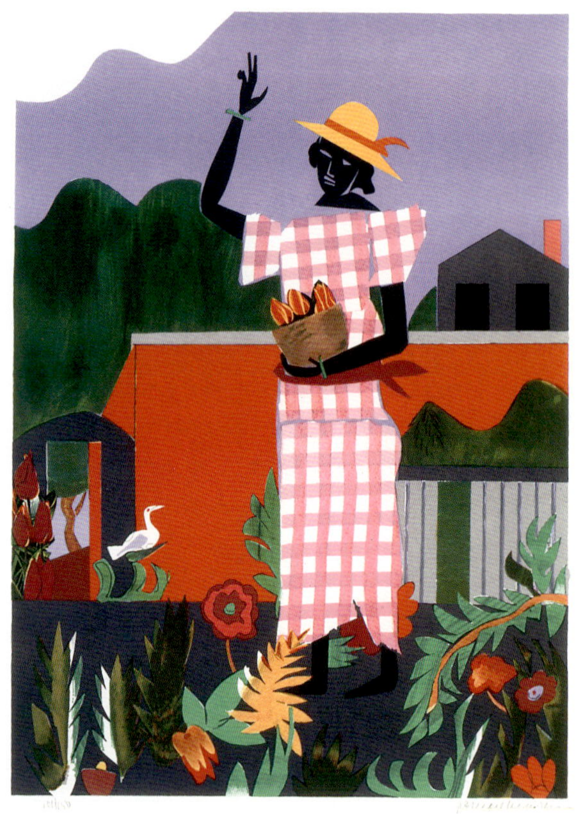

Romare Bearden
U.S., 1914–1988
In the Garden, from *American Portfolio,* 1980,
lithograph, edition: 101/150, 28⅞ × 21$^{1}/_{16}$ in.
Gift of Donald and Sharon DeCastle and
London Arts Group, 1980

Bullfight, in the Phillips Collection, Washington, D.C. *At Five in the Afternoon* depicts the clash of man and beast in a sport that ritualizes death. The picture includes no spectators—only the man and the animal, united in one clash of energy, brought together in the lines of an "X" crossing the canvas. The man has just been gored, but the prominent unsheathed blue sword against the bull's body reminds the viewer that the bull could just as easily have been killed. The bullfighter is graceful, a quality evident in his leg, on the painting's right side.

Ralph Ellison, the renowned African American writer from Oklahoma, became acquainted with Bearden's work in the 1930s. Later, Ellison wrote of Bearden's 1946 series based on Lorca:

> *I recall that . . . under the dual influences of Hemingway and the poetic tragedy of Federico Garcia Lorca, Bearden created a voluminous series of drawings and paintings inspired by Lorca's "Lament for Ignacion* [sic] *Sanchez Mejias." He had become interested in myth and ritual as potent forms for ordering human experience, and it would seem that by stepping back from the immediacy of the Harlem experience—which he knew both from boyhood and as a social worker—he was freed to give expression to the essentially poetic side of his vision. The products of that period were marked by a palette which in contrast with the somber colors of the earlier work and despite the tragic theme with its underlying allusions to Christian rite and mystery, was brightly sensual.*

76 William Gropper

U.S., 1897–1977

They Fought to the Last Man, c. 1945
Oil on canvas
30 × 40½ in.
Purchase, U.S. State Department Collection, 1948

William Gropper considered himself a social commentator in the tradition of Francisco Goya. Gropper grew up in the tenements on New York's Lower East Side and dropped out of school at age fourteen to work with his parents in sweatshops. From an early age, he drew. By 1912, he had saved enough money to study in Harlem at the Ferrer School, an experimental institution that stressed individuality and freedom and was affiliated with anarchist movements. A fellow student was the future renowned photographer and artist Man Ray. Gropper also studied briefly at the National Academy of Design before enrolling at the New York School of Fine and Applied Art.

After a series of odd jobs, Gropper began to work as a cartoonist for the *New York Tribune* in 1919. During the following decade, he became known for his political satires attacking establishment figures such as J. P. Morgan, William Randolph Hearst, U.S. Senator Huey Long, and Japan's Emperor Hirohito. The cartoons appeared in the *New York Tribune* as well as in magazines such as *The New Yorker* and *Vanity Fair* and leftist publications such as *The New Masses* and *The Sunday Worker.*

Gropper began to paint in the early 1920s. His subjects derived from a social consciousness, while his style often reflected the works of masters he had seen in museums, such as Goya and Théodore Géricault. Although he was already celebrated as a political satirist, Gropper did not have his first exhibition of paintings until 1936; critics hailed the show. In 1937, the Metropolitan Museum of Art and the Museum of Modern Art acquired paintings by Gropper, and he received a Guggenheim Fellowship funding travel to Oklahoma and the Texas Panhandle, where he painted human suffering during the Dust Bowl. He also used the trip to gather material for a mural depicting the building of the Boulder Dam, which Maynard Dixon had painted two years earlier (see cat. no. 59). In 1938, New York's A.C.A. Gallery, which specialized in Social Realism, held the first of many Gropper exhibitions.

Between 1948 and 1950, Gropper and his wife traveled in eastern Europe and Russia. In Breslau, Poland, they attended the Wroclaw Congress of Intellectuals for Peace. In the early 1950s, Gropper became one of the first to be targeted on Senator Joseph McCarthy's blacklist, and the State Department banned the artist's booklet of drawings, called *American Folklore,* in all libraries that it sponsored abroad. Although being blacklisted hurt Gropper's career, at least in the short run, he continued to exhibit for the rest of his life.

Gropper often painted themes relating to the Spanish Civil War. *They Fought to the Last Man* could depict a scene from that conflict, but it is also an indictment of the futility and ravages of war in general. (The painting's message would have been especially potent immediately after World War II.) Two men struggle against each other atop a hill littered with white-shirted, slaughtered men, their affiliations in the combat irrelevant in the face of death. Like *Prey,* a Gropper watercolor in the museum's collection, *They Fought to the Last Man* owes both thematic and stylistic debts to Goya. Compositionally, it also resembles Géricault's *Raft of the Medusa.*

During the 1940s, *They Fought to the Last Man* was one of the most expensive paintings in the U.S. State Department Collection, valued even higher than works by Edward Hopper and Georgia O'Keeffe.

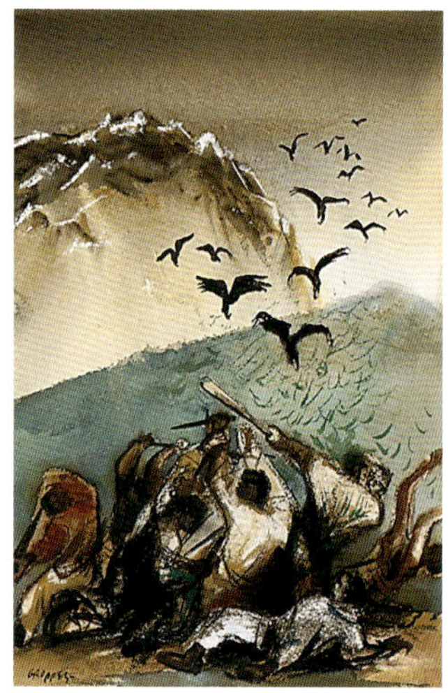

William Gropper
U.S., 1897–1977
Prey, n.d., oil on canvas, 22¼ × 15 in. Purchase, U.S. State Department Collection, 1948

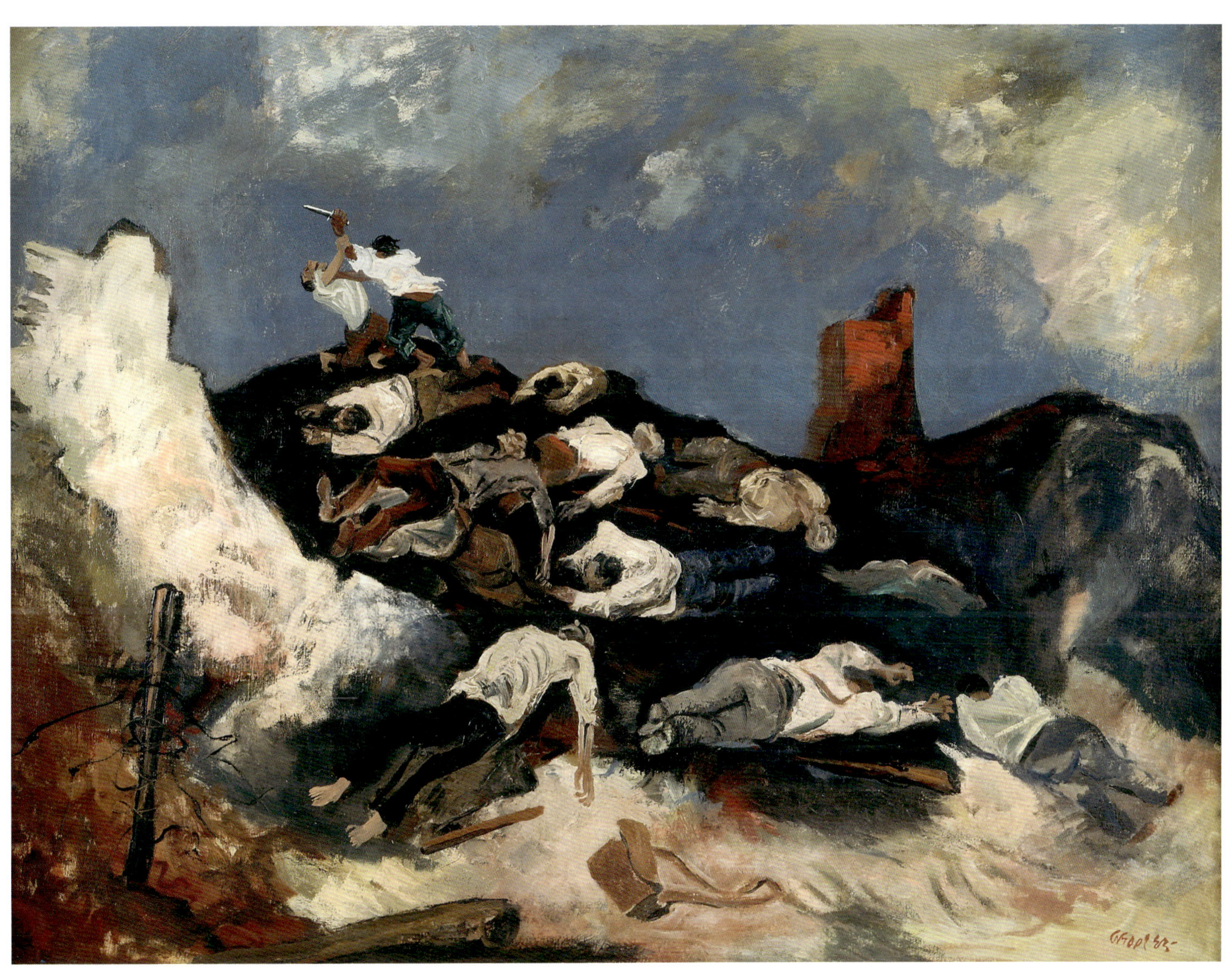

77 Jack Levine

U.S., b. 1915

The White Horse, 1946
Oil on canvas
30 × 36 in.
Purchase, U.S. State Department Collection, 1948

The brilliant draftsman and Social Realist Jack Levine was born in Boston and raised in a tough South End neighborhood populated mostly by immigrants. In his teens, he took art classes at the Museum of Fine Arts in Boston, the Roxbury Community Center, and Harvard University. The Fogg Art Museum at Harvard gave Levine his first exhibition, a show of drawings, when he was only seventeen.

During the 1930s, the Federal Arts Project of the Works Progress Administration (W.P.A.) employed Levine in Boston. He became widely recognized for his painting *The Feast of Pure Reason* (1937), a satirical social commentary showing the collusion of a politician, a businessman, and a policeman. In the late 1930s, Levine started to exaggerate and distort his figures to maximize the satire or, as in *The White Horse,* the poignancy in his art. By the time of his first solo exhibition in New York in 1939, he was a leading American Social Realist, along with Ben Shahn (see cat. no. 80).

Levine served in the U.S. Army during World War II. In 1947, he traveled to Europe, where he studied El Greco and other Old Masters, whom he preferred to twentieth-century artists.

The White Horse is one of the first works Levine painted after World War II. The canvas shows a scrawny, overworked animal that seems ready for the glue factory. Levine exaggerated the size of the horse's head and neck to emphasize the burden that the horse must endure. The horse trudges along against the backdrop of the city's squalor.

Levine often depicted white horses. A horse—not distorted—even appears in a drawing created in 1931, when the artist was just sixteen.

The Passing Scene (1941), at the Museum of Modern Art, New York, shows a white horse like the one in the present work. Levine wrote about the horses in the two paintings:

> *[In* The Passing Scene, *there is an] old horse, which I always saw as a beautiful, tender symbol—a white horse. . . .* The White Horse *was a reprise of the background from* The Passing Scene, *done four years before. You see, I hadn't really painted in three and a half years, and it was a matter of sounding certain notes again.*

Levine also made prints. The museum owns an etching depicting a horse similar to the one in the present painting.

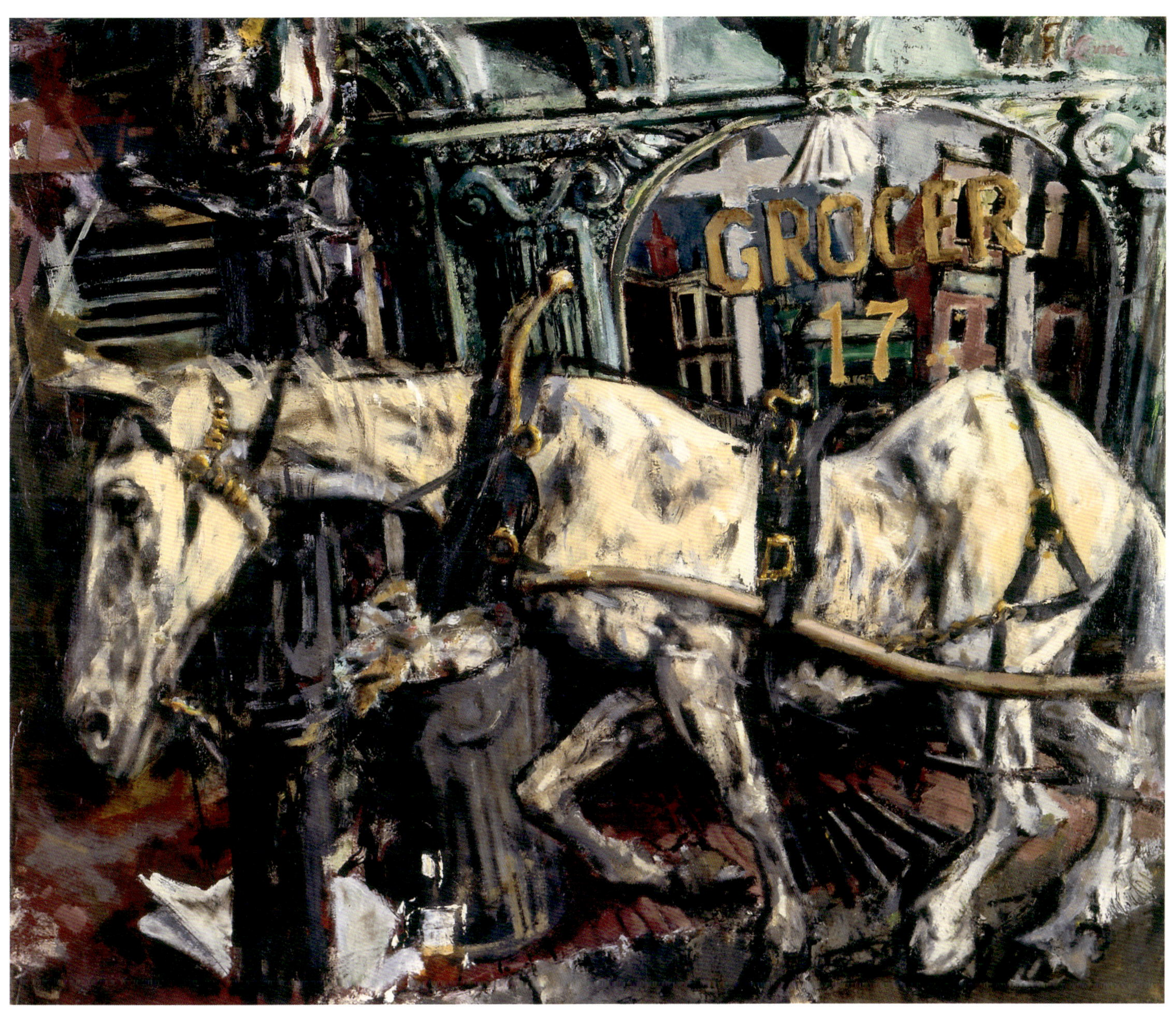
GROCER
17

78 Joseph Hirsch

U.S., 1910–1981

Street Scene, 1938
Oil on canvas
22 × 24 in.
W.P.A. Collection, 1942

Born in Philadelphia, the son of a surgeon who was a music patron, Joseph Hirsch showed an early talent for drawing. He received a scholarship to the Philadelphia College of Art and later studied under George Luks, who had been a member of the Ashcan School. (For more on the Ashcan School, see cat. no. 53.) Like the Ashcan artists, Hirsch depicted everyday urban scenes. He painted socially charged subjects and became associated with the Social Realists, such as Jack Levine (see cat. no. 77) and Ben Shahn (see cat. no. 80).

In 1934, Hirsch received national recognition with a painting that won prizes at the Pennsylvania Academy of the Fine Arts and the National Academy of Design in New York. The Federal Arts Project of the Works Progress Administration (W.P.A.) then hired him to paint murals in several Philadelphia buildings. After his first exhibition, at Philadelphia's A.C.A. Gallery in 1937, he showed at numerous museums and galleries throughout the United States, even though, especially later, he was a representational artist in an age of abstraction. He taught for many years at the Art Students League in New York.

Hirsch created *Street Scene* when he worked for the W.P.A. during the Depression. The painting depicts with humanity four unemployed men hunched over and huddled together, warming themselves over a grate on an icy day. The figure on the left wears a sandwich board; during the 1930s, businesses often paid the unemployed to wear such signs for advertising.

On the goals of his art, Hirsch commented: "Does not any genuine personal expression, by its very nature, seek to propagandize? In my painting I want to castigate the things I hate and paint monuments to what I feel is noble." He often focused his attention on the common, left-behind man, as when, in 1949, he portrayed Willy Loman for the original poster of Arthur Miller's play *Death of a Salesman.*

Sauna, a Hirsch drawing in the museum's collection, also reveals the artist as a master at depicting the human figure. The drawing otherwise contrasts with *Street Scene:* whereas the painting depicts clothed, downtrodden men in the freezing cold, the drawing shows nude women relaxing in a warm steam room.

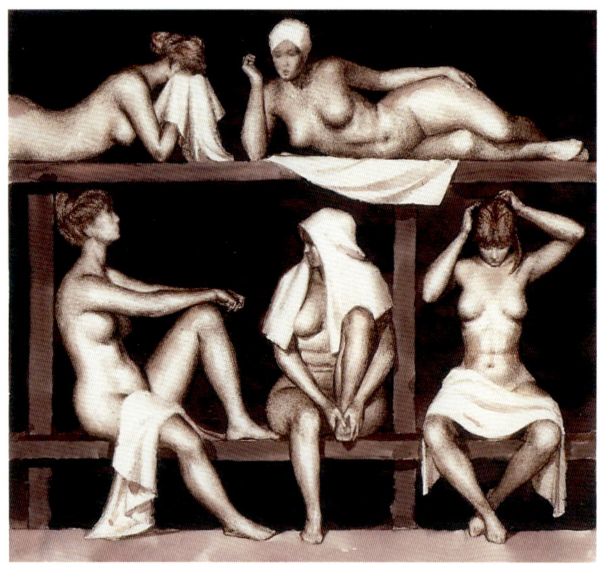

Joseph Hirsch
U.S., 1910–1981
Sauna, 1973, ink, 15½ × 17 in. Purchased with funds from Jerome Westheimer and the National Endowment for the Arts, 1975

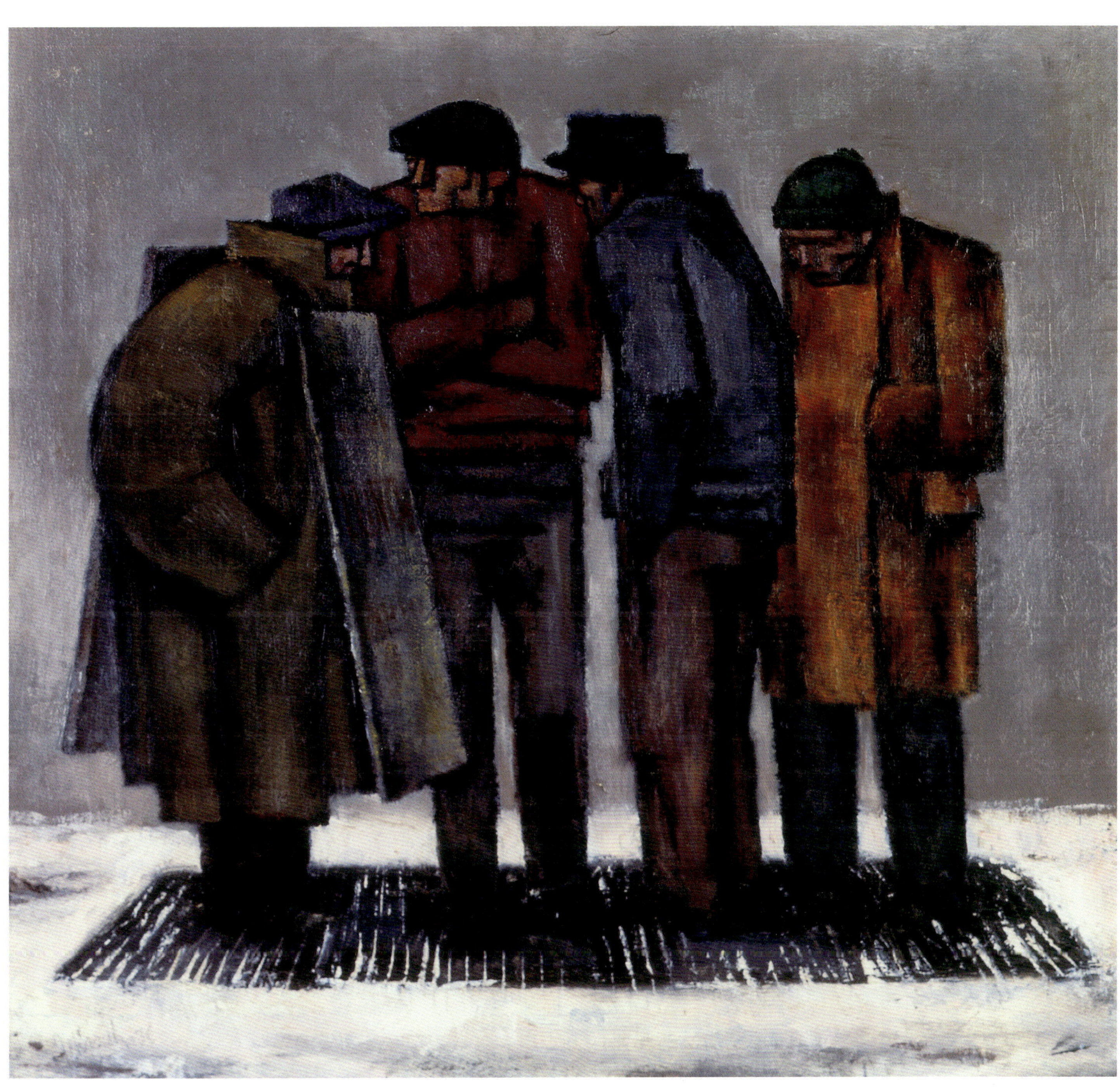

79 W. Eugene Smith

U.S., 1918–1978

Untitled, from South Seas series, 1944
Gelatin silver print
9½ × 13½ in.
Gift, Ellen and Richard L. Sandor
Collection in memory of Wanda Shi, 1997

W. Eugene Smith was one of the most important photojournalists of the twentieth century and a master of the socially aware photo-essay. He was born in Wichita, Kansas, and photographed sporting events at his high school. He studied photography briefly at the University of Notre Dame between 1936 and 1937. When he moved to New York to become a freelance press photographer, his work appeared almost immediately in major publications such as *Newsweek.* While covering World War II, he rose to prominence on the staff of *Life* magazine, and in 1949, he became president of the Photo League, a liberal organization comprised primarily of documentary photographers. He resigned from *Life* in 1954, citing lack of control over the publication of his photographs. For the rest of his career, Smith produced numerous photo-essays.

Smith used photography to focus on social problems and other human issues. Hoping to influence viewers' attitudes for the betterment of the world, he sometimes restaged events to maximize their drama or pathos. He made an effort to get to know the people he photographed.

During World War II, Smith earned the trust of American soldiers, who granted him greater access than they did most other photographers. While covering the Pacific theater, Smith took the present photograph on the island of Funa Futi, which the United States used as a base to counter Japanese advances into the Gilbert Islands. On the photograph's reverse, Smith wrote with irony in pencil: "To the so called romantic life of the South Sea Natives has been added the facts of civilized warfare. Here a little child of a peaceful little village at Funa Futi has a wonderful little hole to play by & in.—A sand-bagged fox hole. Photo made Jan. 21, '44."

The museum owns twenty-seven vintage photographs by Smith.

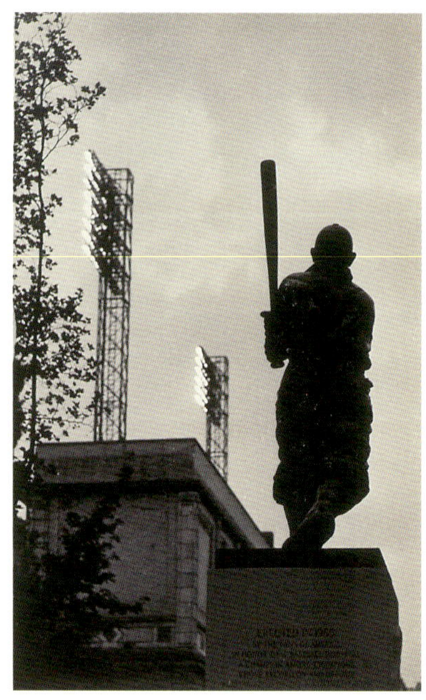

W. Eugene Smith
U.S., 1918–1978
Untitled, from *Pittsburgh* essay (statue of baseball player Honus Wagner outside Forbes Field), 1958, gelatin silver print, 13½ × 8½ in. Gift of L. Bradley Camp, 1985

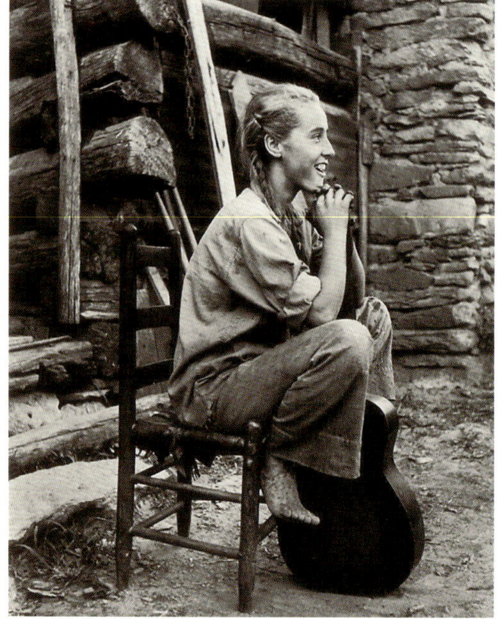

W. Eugene Smith
U.S., 1918–1978
Untitled, from *Folk Singers* essay, 1947, gelatin silver print, 13½ × 10¾ in.
Gift of L. Bradley Camp, 1985

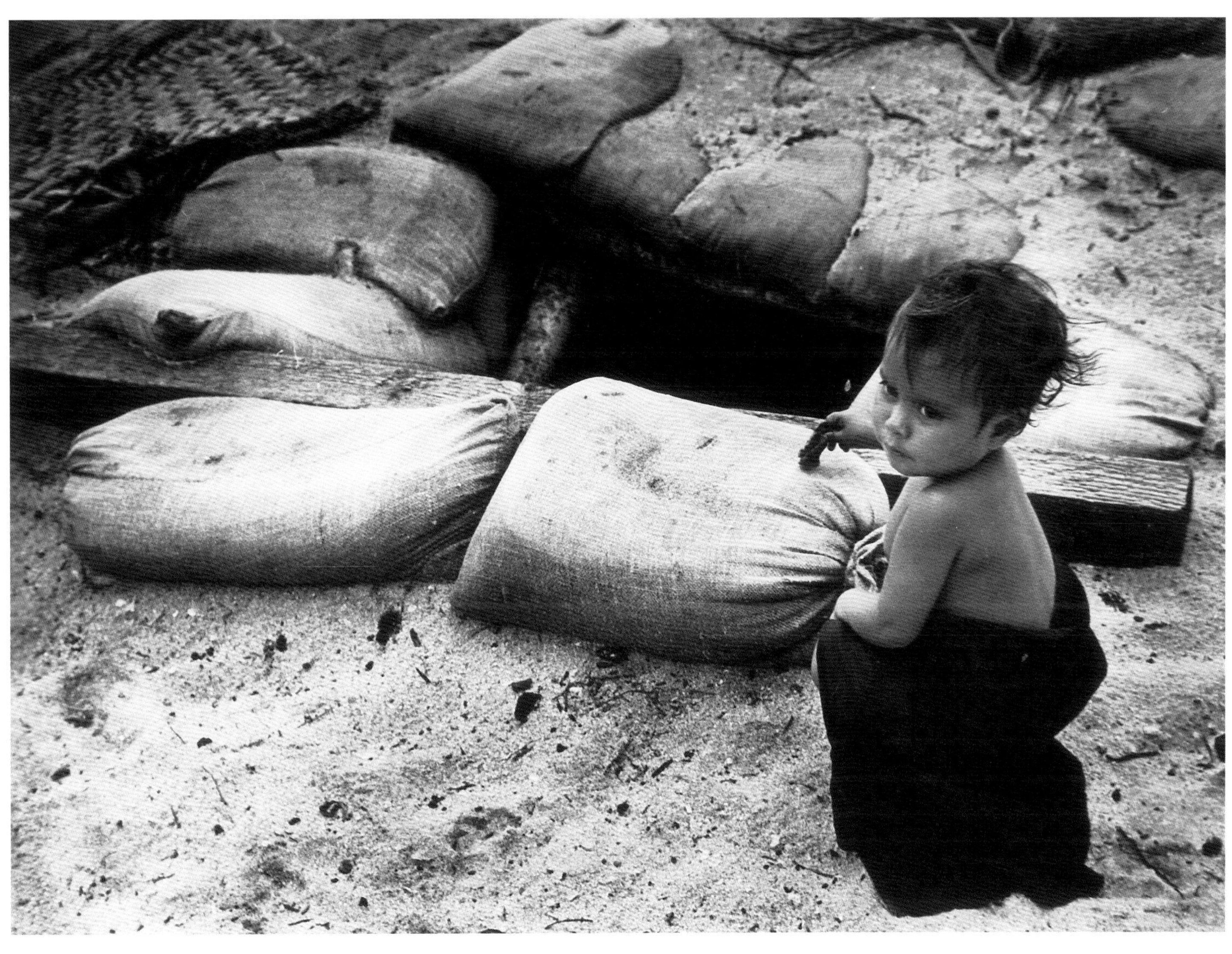

80 Ben Shahn

U.S., 1898–1969

Renascence, 1946
Gouache on Whatman hotpressed board
21⅞ × 30 in.
Purchase, U.S. State Department
Collection, 1948

A leading Social Realist, Ben Shahn emigrated from Lithuania to New York with his family of Jewish craftsmen in 1906. During his teens, he apprenticed to a lithographer while attending high school at night. In 1916, he took a life-drawing class at the Art Students League. He then studied biology at New York University and City College, before enrolling at the National Academy of Design to become an artist.

In 1924 and 1925, Shahn and his wife traveled to Europe and North Africa. While in Europe, he studied both Old Masters and Modernists such as Henri Matisse, Raoul Dufy, Pablo Picasso, and Paul Klee. Upon returning to the United States, the Shahns moved to Brooklyn Heights and began spending summers in the art colony of Truro, Massachusetts, where Shahn painted beach scenes and landscapes.

In the late 1920s, Shahn returned to Europe and North Africa, and he exhibited paintings of Tunisia in his first solo exhibition, held in New York in 1930. In 1932, he achieved recognition when he exhibited a series of linear, gouache paintings called *The Passion of Sacco and Vanzetti,* which depicted the trials and executions of two immigrant anarchists. The case had rallied left-leaning intellectuals in the 1920s. During the Depression, Shahn continued to produce politically committed paintings and murals, and he assisted Diego Rivera with the Rockefeller Center murals that were removed after Rivera included a portrait of Lenin. Shahn worked for the Federal Arts Project of the Works Progress Administration (W.P.A.), and the Farm Security Administration hired him to document the difficult lives and working conditions of American farmworkers.

As the Charles Eliot Norton Chair of Poetry at Harvard University in 1956, Shahn lectured on his philosophy of art and realism. These lectures were published the following year in the highly influential book, *The Shape of Content.*

Painted immediately after World War II, *Renascence,* whose title means "rebirth," represents the hope for regeneration after the ravages of war. Emblems of fertility and renewal include the thicket of spring grain (a product of nature) and the phallic column (a product of civilization). A heap of tangled metal in the background represents the urban landscape's recent devastation and recalls images of Hiroshima's ruins, which newspapers reproduced widely at the time.

A close friend of the photographer Walker Evans, Ben Shahn himself photographed Depression-era New York and sometimes used his own photographs as source material for his paintings. *Renascence* utilizes a Shahn photograph from around 1931–32, which depicts a group of girls standing in front of a brick wall on New York's Lower East Side. In *Renascence,* the bush, roughened wall, and figure of the girl in a coat and beret all derive from Shahn's photograph.

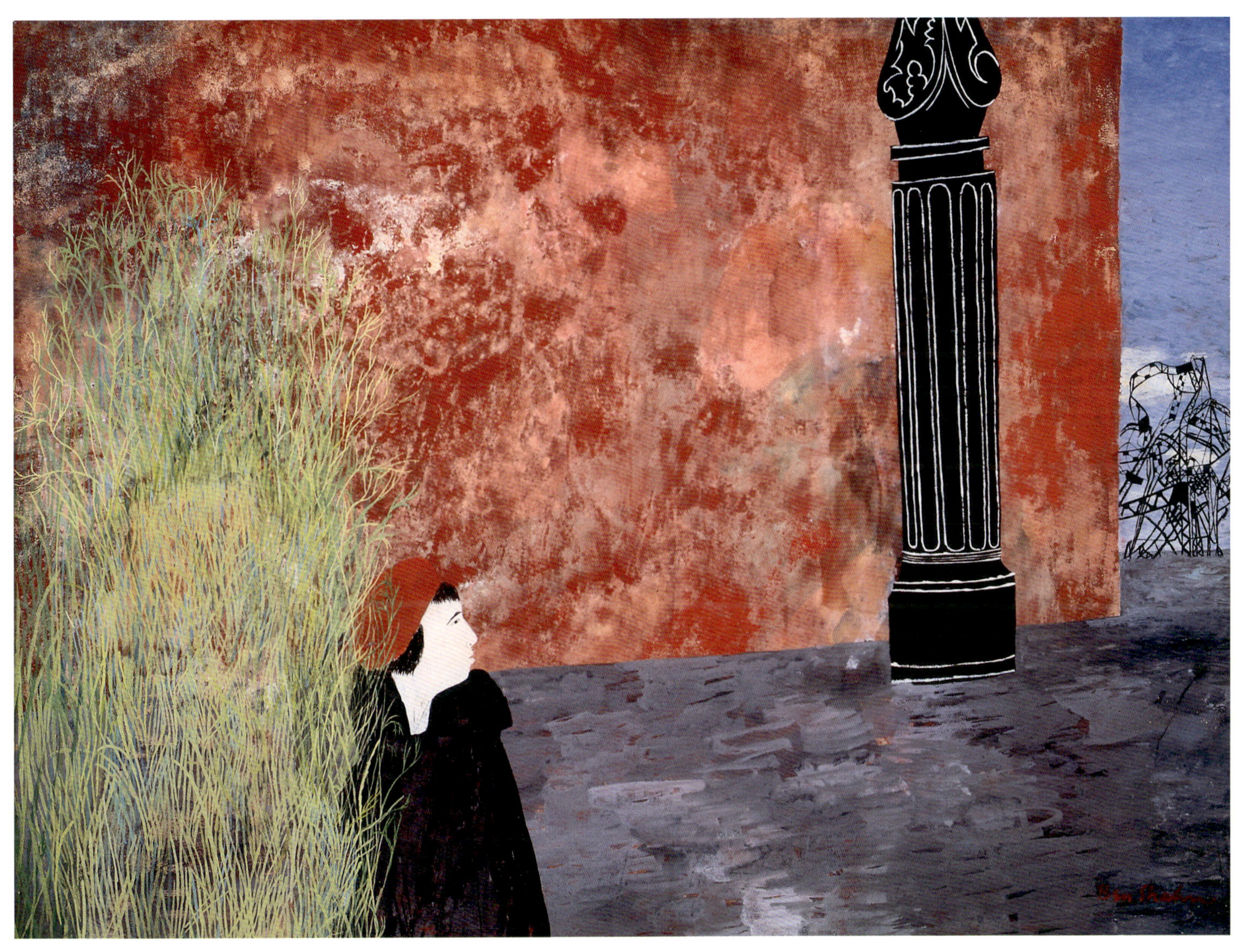

81 William Baziotes

U.S., 1912–1963

Flower Head, c. 1945
Oil on canvas
$36\frac{1}{8} \times 41\frac{7}{8}$ in.
Purchase, U.S. State Department Collection, 1948

The son of Greek immigrants, William Baziotes was born in Pittsburgh and grew up in Reading, Pennsylvania. His father's failed business plunged the family into poverty. As a young teen, Baziotes visited seamy gambling dens and brothels; these experiences may have later contributed to the sense of menace in his paintings. After studying in New York at the National Academy of Design from 1933 until 1936, he worked for the Federal Arts Project of the Works Progress Administration (W.P.A.) as a teacher at the Queens Museum. He taught at the Brooklyn Museum Art School from 1949 until 1952 and then moved to New York City's Hunter College, where he taught until his death.

Pablo Picasso and Joan Miró—whose works were exhibited at the Museum of Modern Art in New York in 1939 and 1941, respectively—greatly influenced Baziotes. He was also drawn to the exiled European and Latin American Surrealists who had converged on New York during World War II. The Surrealists led Baziotes to explore fantasy, strong emotions, and the darker sides of the mind through experimentation with automatism, a practice in which the artist created works spontaneously to release the subconscious. Although not practicing a pure form of automatism, Baziotes used its principles and began each work by doodling on the canvas and painting with no preconceptions about the outcome.

Baziotes befriended artists involved with automatism, such as Robert Motherwell and Jackson Pollock, who would later help form the Abstract Expressionist movement, with which Baziotes became associated. Peggy Guggenheim's Art of This Century, the gallery most linked with Abstract Expressionism during its early years, gave Baziotes his first solo exhibition.

As the 1940s progressed, Baziotes's paintings became less threatening and violent and more graceful and monumental, with forms filling the entire canvas, as in *Flower Head.* These works have ethereal veils of translucent paint that resemble stained glass, an effect no doubt inspired by Baziotes's work for a stained-glass manufacturer in the early 1930s.

The mysterious, dreamy depths of the underwater world fascinated Baziotes, as they had other artists linked with Surrealism. In addition to being possibly viewed as a mirror of the subconscious mind, *Flower Head* could be seen as a sea anemone.

Baziotes was long captivated by the nineteenth-century French poet Charles Baudelaire, and some of Baziotes's paintings, such as *The Balcony* (1944), derive their titles from Baudelaire poems. The title *Flower Head,* which Baziotes inscribed on the painting's back, may refer to Baudelaire's famous volume of poetry *The Flowers of Evil.*

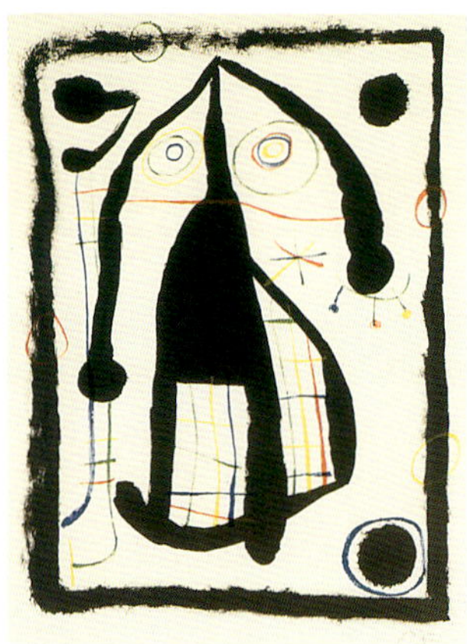

Joan Miró
Spain, 1893–1983
Figure (The Stranger) [Personnage (L'Etrangère)], n.d., lithograph, edition: 40/75, $24\frac{1}{2} \times 18\frac{3}{4}$ in. Museum purchase, 1962

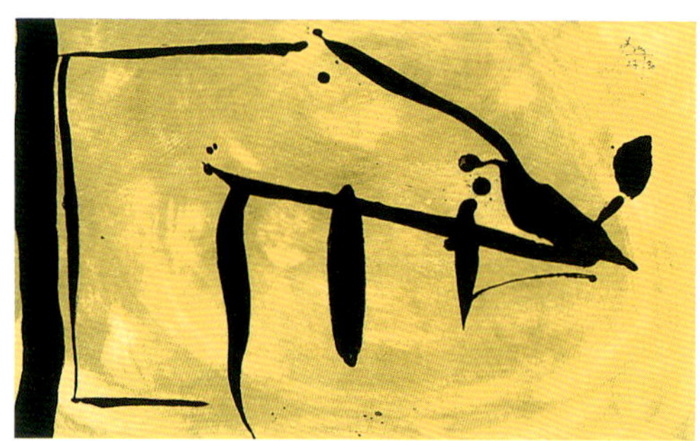

Robert Motherwell
U.S., 1915–1991
Springtime Dissonance, 1979–80, aquatint and etching, edition: 37/50, 20 × 28 in. Gift of J. Donald Walp, 1993

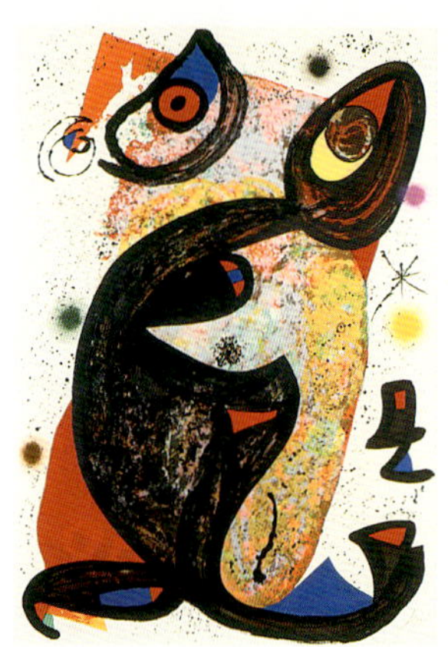

Joan Miró
Spain, 1893–1983
Onesime, 1976, lithograph, edition: 24/50, $35\frac{1}{2} \times 24\frac{1}{2}$ in. Gift of Mr. and Mrs. Richard Dunn, 1978

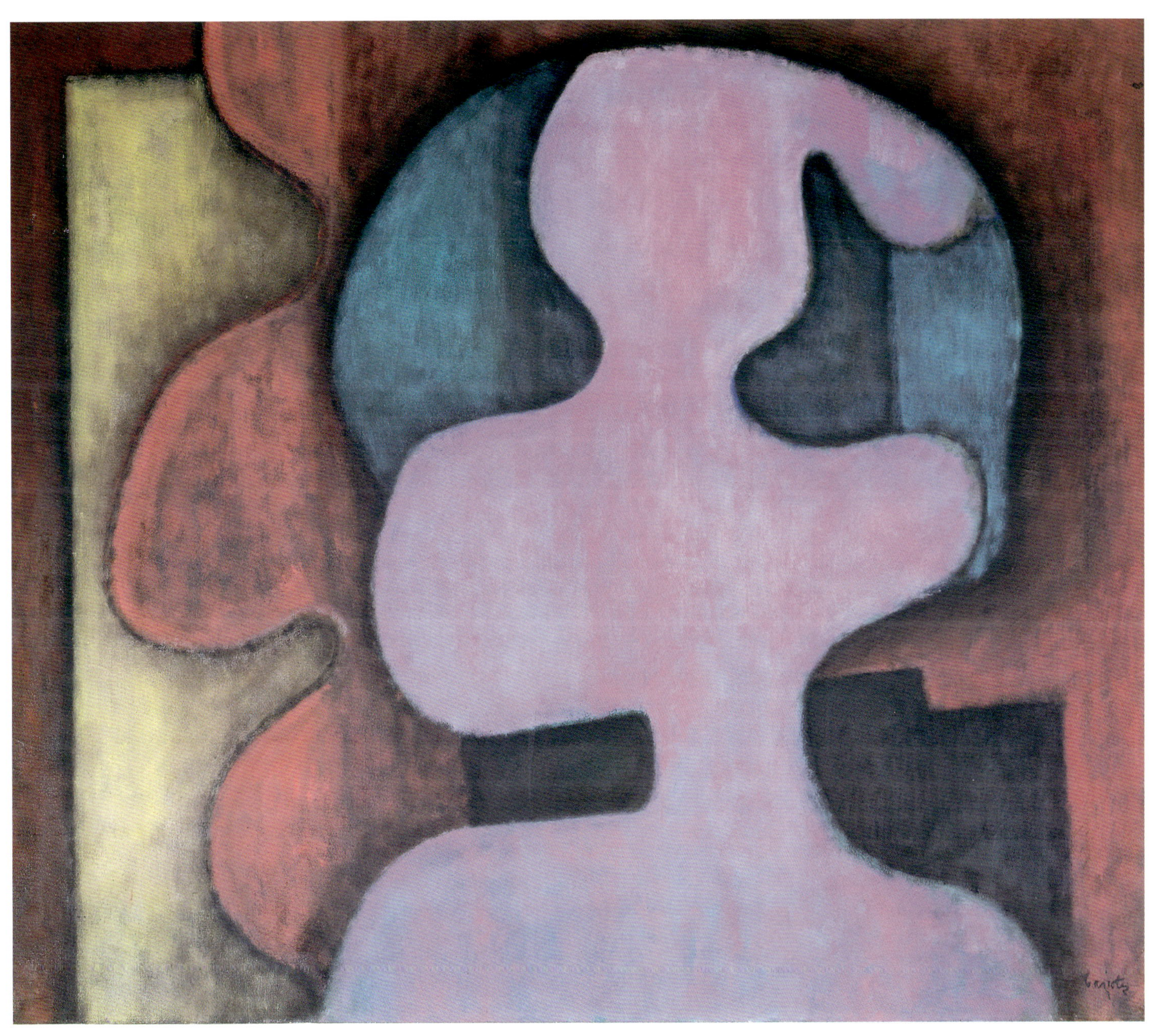

82 Adolph Gottlieb

U.S., 1903–1974

Night Passage, 1946
Gouache on paper
39 × 32 in.
Purchase, U.S. State Department Collection, 1948

Like William Baziotes (see cat. no. 81) and other painters associated with Abstract Expressionism, the New York–born artist Adolph Gottlieb adopted the ideas espoused by European Surrealists exiled in New York during World War II. He believed, as they did, that art should reveal the subconscious and depict archetypal myths.

Gottlieb studied during the early 1920s in New York at the Art Students League, under Robert Henri and John Sloan (see cat. no. 53). Gottlieb then traveled to Germany and France, where he attended the Académie de la Grande Chaumière in Paris. He returned to New York to continue his studies at the Parsons School of Design and Cooper Union. After his first solo show in 1930, the artist exhibited regularly. From 1937 until 1939, he worked for the Federal Arts Project of the Works Progress Administration (W.P.A.) and lived in the Arizona desert, where he painted cacti and desert landscapes.

In 1941 in New York, Gottlieb began creating "pictographs," such as the present work, which were inspired by American Indian rock art as well as the art of the ancient cultures of Africa, Oceania, Europe, and the Middle East. The pictographs showed archetypal, totemic symbols in grids. The signs looked as if they were derived from ancient cultures, but Gottlieb, who professed to speak a universal language, was careful to invent them. If he discovered that his signs resembled forms from a specific culture, he would not use them. Gottlieb likened his grid paintings to Italian medieval altarpieces and fresco cycles, in which scenes are at once isolated yet part of a greater whole.

Many of Gottlieb's pictographs, such as *Night Passage,* suggest nocturnal journeys that correspond to journeys into the dark reaches of the subconscious mind. These journeys are often sea voyages, as indicated by the fishlike form in *Night Passage.* A painting after *Night Passage—Night Voyage—*is at the Hirshhorn Museum in Washington, D.C.

During the early 1950s, Gottlieb turned away from pictographs and started a series of Imaginary Landscapes.

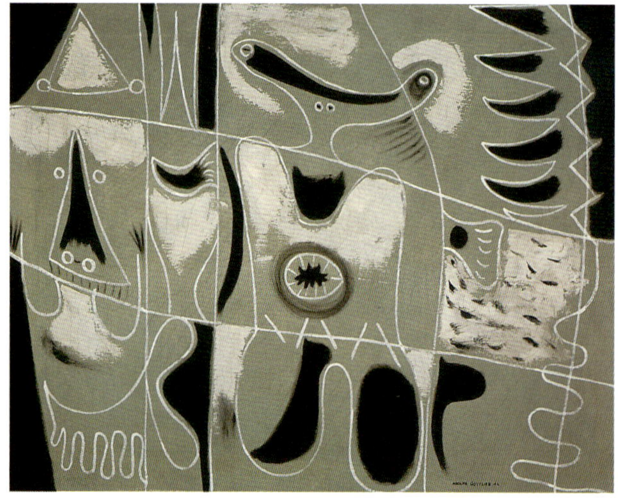

Adolph Gottlieb
U.S., 1903–1974
The Couple, 1946, oil on canvas, 24½ × 31 in.
Purchase, U.S. State Department Collection, 1948

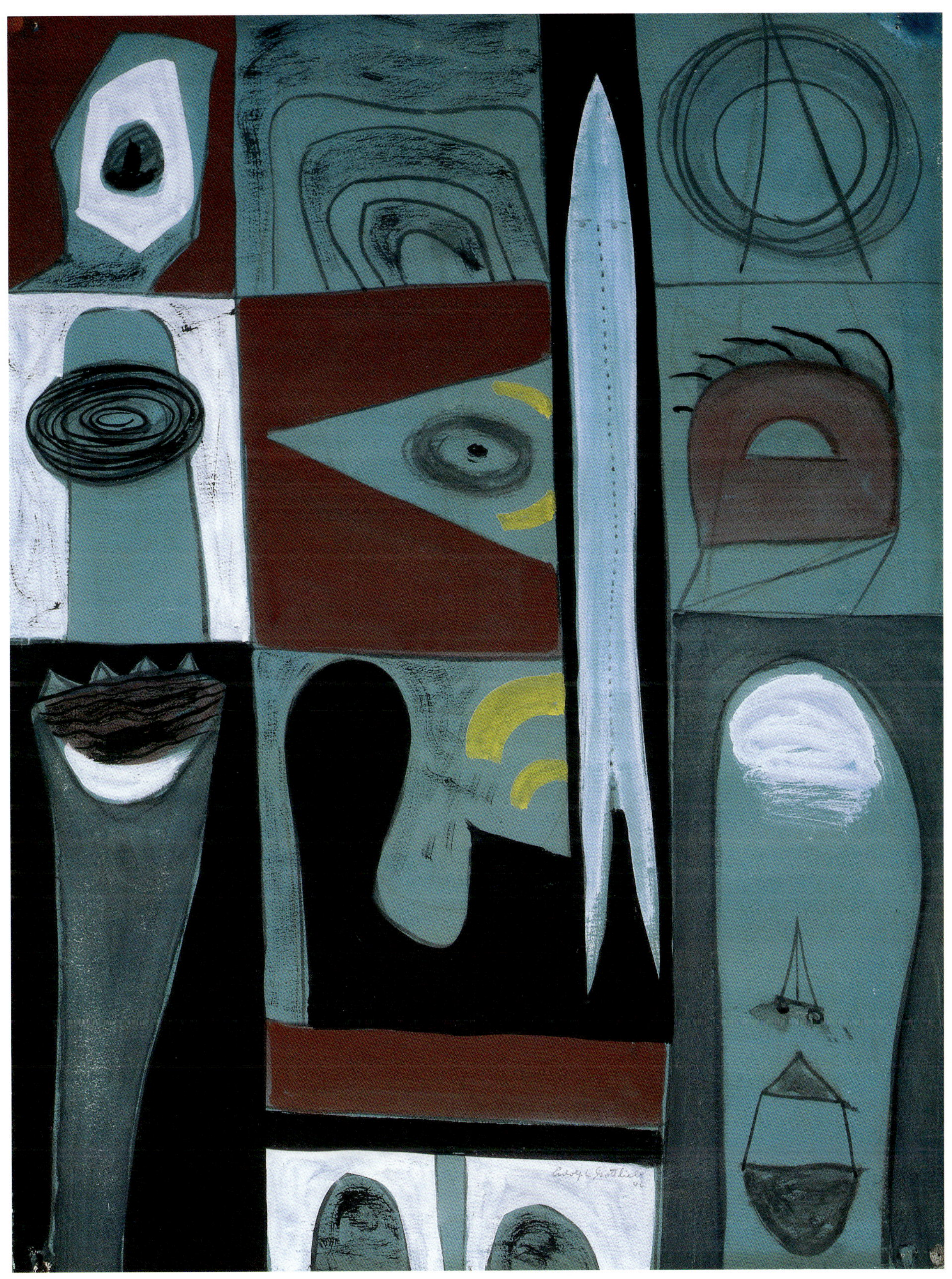

83 Sam Francis

U.S., 1923–1994

Untitled, 1983
Acrylic on rice paper
72 × 37¼ in.
Gift of Jerome M. and Wanda Otey Westheimer, 1999

Untitled typifies Francis's vibrant work: fluid drips and pools of saturated colors circulate loosely—in this instance, in an upright, elongated, pointed oval. This archetypal form recalls the mandorla, a mystical symbol of purity.

Francis was born in San Mateo, California. He began his college education at the University of California, Berkeley, intending to study medicine. While serving in the U.S. Army Air Corps during World War II, he developed spinal tuberculosis after injuring his back in a crash landing in the Arizona desert. During his years of convalescence, he began to paint as a distraction. In 1947, he studied with David Park, a San Francisco Bay–area figurative artist. Francis returned to Berkeley to focus on art and art history, earning a bachelor of arts degree in 1949 and a master of arts degree in 1950. After working in the manner of Abstract Expressionists such as Jackson Pollock, Francis developed his own distinctive style in 1949 and 1950.

Francis moved to Paris in 1950 to study art on the G.I. Bill. He worked in Fernand Léger's studio and received widespread recognition after his first solo show in Paris, in 1952.

In Paris, Francis's exposure to the color- and light-filled paintings of Claude Monet, Henri Matisse, and Pierre Bonnard reinforced the artist's California predisposition to sensuous color and light. Meanwhile, his interest in Japanese art, which he encountered during a 1957 trip to Asia, fueled a preoccupation with simplicity and white negative space. Francis settled in Santa Monica, California, in 1962.

A philosophical painter, Francis was profoundly influenced by Zen Buddhism and, like artists such as William Baziotes (see cat. no. 81) and Adolph Gottlieb (see cat. no. 82), by the Swiss psychologist Carl Jung's notions of the subconscious. Francis saw his paintings as embodying the four ancient elements of earth, water, air, and fire, with the paint representing earth and water, the white canvas or paper representing air, and the bursts and motion of color representing fire. The artist wrote, "To consciously live in chaos is to live within perfection."

Critics have identified Francis's art with Abstract Expressionism and other movements, but his work—as the artist himself wanted—defies such classification.

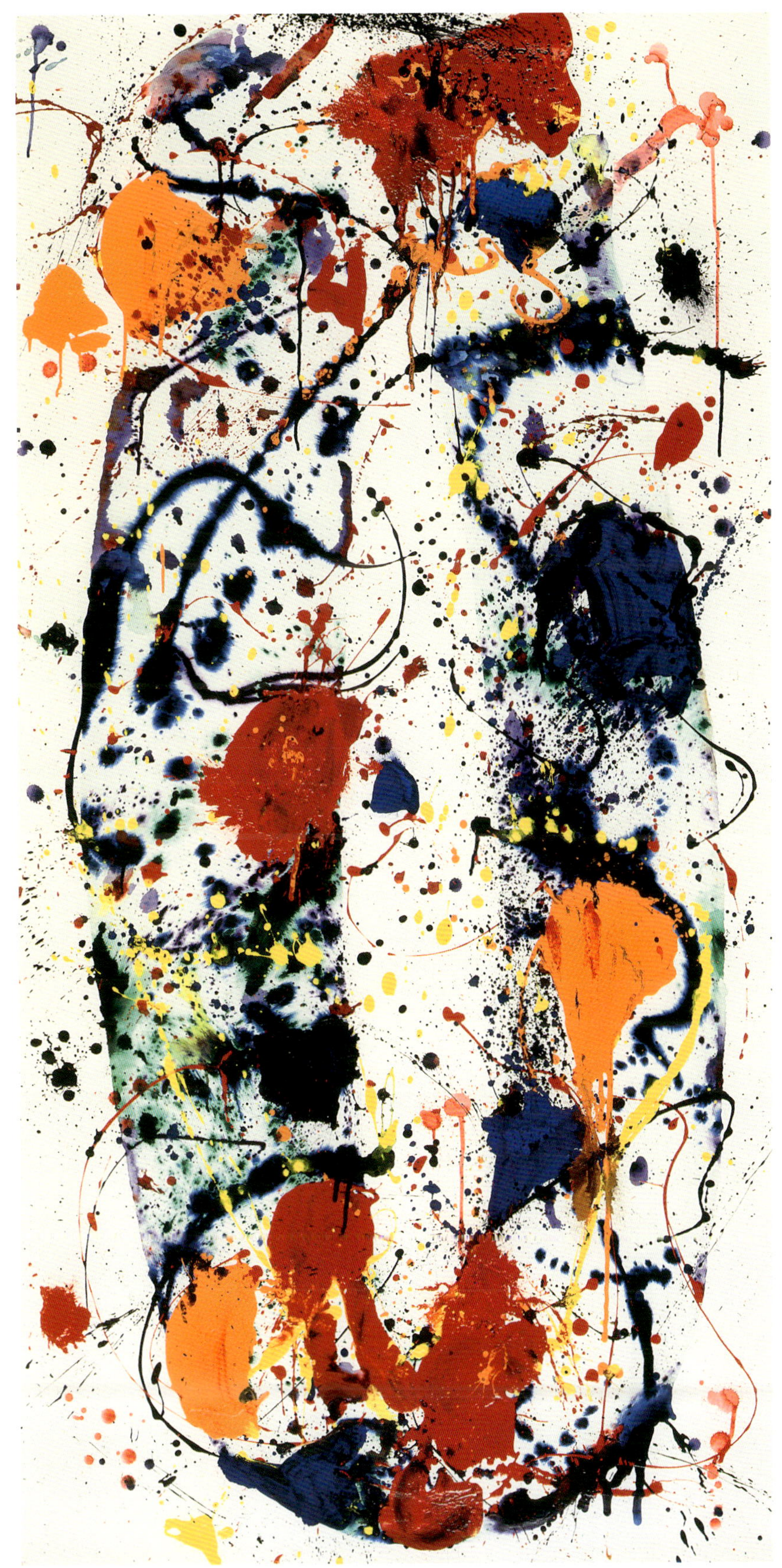

84 Leon Polk Smith

U.S., 1906–1996

Red-Black, 1958
Oil on paper
DIAM. 25½ in.
Gift of the American Academy and Institute of Arts and Letters and the Hassam and Speicher Purchase Fund, 1989

Known for his influential, Minimalist geometric abstractions, Leon Polk Smith was born of part-Cherokee parents and raised in Oklahoma, on farms near Chickasha and Ada. His art was inspired by both European Modernism and the American Indian culture of his upbringing, but he maintained a distance from art movements or groups and preferred his work not to be defined by race: "I do not make any art but my own art, and I wouldn't want to be lined up with other painters simply on the basis of race any more than I would agree, if I were female, to be exhibited with other female artists."

Smith graduated from Oklahoma State College (now East Central University), intending to become a teacher. In 1936, he moved to New York to study at the Teachers College of Columbia University, and in 1938, he received a master of fine arts degree. In 1939, he traveled through Europe. During the early 1940s, he supported himself through full-time teaching in Georgia and Delaware, and became controversial at both places for his advocacy of civil rights and racial integration. Between 1949 and 1958, he taught at New York University, Rollins College in Florida, and Mills College in California.

Smith's early works were American Scene paintings that drew from his experiences in Oklahoma and New York and showed the influence of Surrealism. In 1936, he saw European Modernist paintings—including works by Jean Arp, Constantin Brancusi, and most significantly, Piet Mondrian—in the collection of the Park Avenue Cubist Albert E. Gallatin, which was exhibited at New York University's Gallery of Living Art. (For more on the Park Avenue Cubists, see cat. no. 73.) The art of Brancusi and Mondrian led Smith to produce nonobjective (abstract) art in the 1940s.

In 1945, Mondrian became the preeminent influence on Smith's work. Smith admired the interchangeability of form and space in Mondrian's art, and this interchangeability became a key issue in Smith's own paintings. In *Red-Black*, for example, the eye reads the blacks as voids and the reds as solids, and then the reverse—the blacks as solids and the reds as voids.

Mondrian's style, called Neoplasticism, featured right-angled grids of lines and rectangles. (For more on Mondrian and Neoplasticism, see cat. no. 27.) Smith's early abstractions were in the vein of Mondrian's Neoplasticism, but Smith eventually broke free of the strictly rectilinear format prescribed by Mondrian. Smith described this move beyond Neoplasticism:

> *What I was searching for through the forties was a way to express Mondrian's findings with curvilinear forms as well as straight-line forms. This catalogue of athletic equipment had no photographic illustrations; they were all line drawings. And the tennis ball has one sort of pattern on it. It's close to the pattern of the baseball. I kept that catalogue on my desk and would go back to it every day or so. I thought, "What in the hell am I doing with this thing?"... [and] a little voice inside*

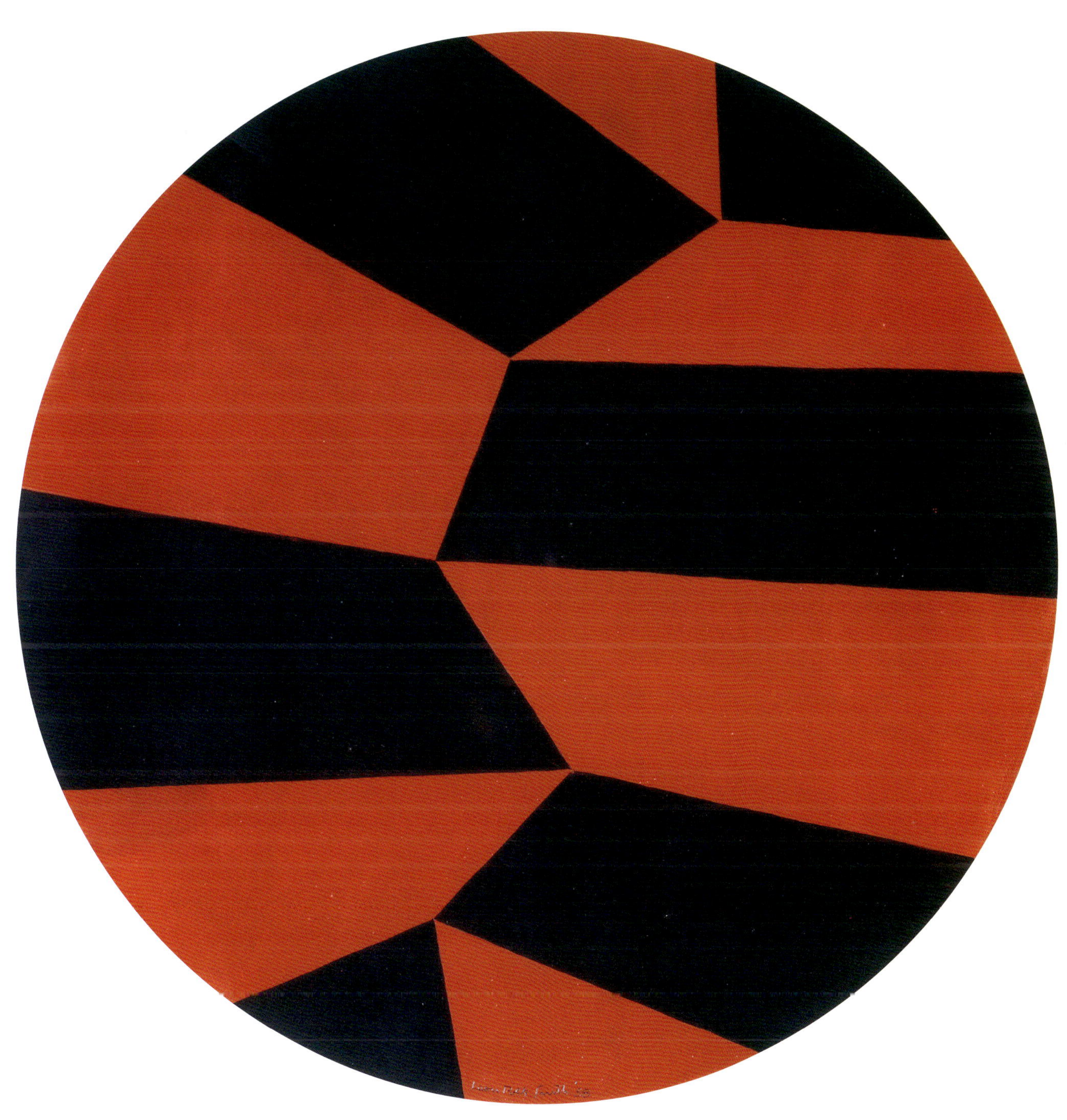

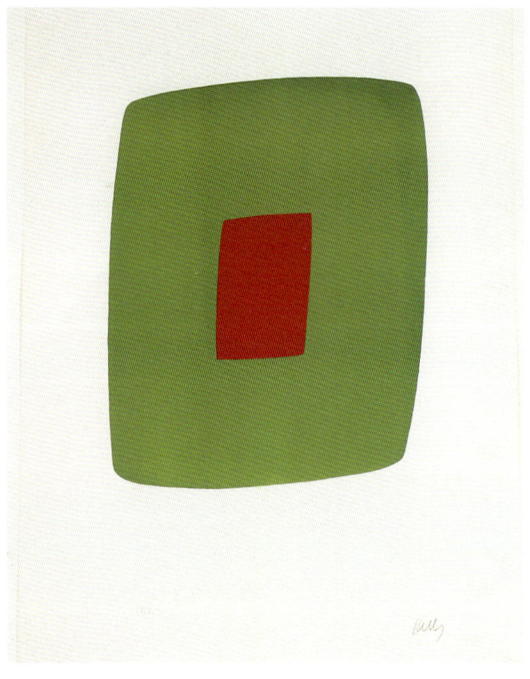

Ellsworth Kelly
U.S., b. 1923
Green with Red (Vert avec rouge), series VI, no. 8, 1964, lithograph on Rives paper, edition: 58/75, 35¼ × 23½ in. Museum purchase, 1969

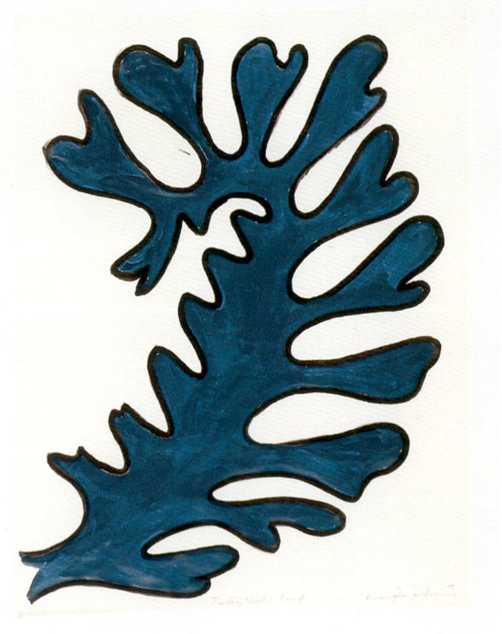

Leon Polk Smith
U.S., 1906–1996
Dusty Miller Leaf, n.d., watercolor on paper, 17¾ × 14 in. Gift of a friend of the museum, 1996

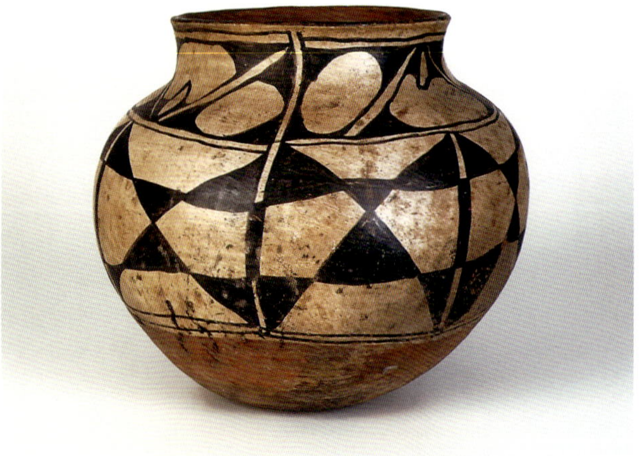

Unknown
Santa Domingo Pueblo
Storage Jar, c. 1900–1925, earthenware, H. 13 in. Purchase, Richard H. and Adeline J. Fleischaker Collection, 1996

said, "Because that's what you are looking for." I rushed into my studio and started drawing circles and ovals and ellipses. First I used these shapes that I found on the baseball, tennis ball, football, and so forth, in order to better understand what I was experiencing, and then I thought, "Now I need to find my own shapes," and so I did.

Red-Black is in a yin-yang form, cut into bands, and is a tondo (circle painting), like many of Smith's works from the period. The painting is in two colors, which is typical of the art Smith produced from the mid-1950s on.

In addition to crediting European Modernism with having shaped his work, Smith pointed to American Indian culture as an influence: "[My] freedom of color came out of my relationship with the Indians. . . . In the Indians' philosophy, thinking, and way of talking or telling stories, so much detail was left out, so much was abstract." Red-Black recalls the designs on American Indian weavings, baskets, and pots.

During the 1950s, several artists, including Ellsworth Kelly, visited Smith's studio in New York. By the early 1960s, art critics such as Lawrence Alloway—who popularized the term "Hard-Edge"—were calling Smith a precursor of Kelly and other important Hard-Edge painters. (Hard-Edge painting was a style that emerged in the 1950s and that featured precise geometric shapes of canvas and image. Hard-Edge artists treated the picture plane as a flat surface on which they applied a limited number of solid colors.)

Smith's work appeared in a number of historic exhibitions, such as the Museum of Modern Art's "The Responsive Eye" of 1965. In 1995, the Brooklyn Museum accorded him a retrospective.

85 Barbara Hepworth

England, 1903–1975

Two Figures, 1968
Bronze
Edition: 1/7
H. (left) 7 ft. 6½ in.; H. (right) 7 ft. 11 in.
Gift of Mr. and Mrs. Max Weitzenhoffer, 1971

Two Figures is an abstract exploration of light, space, and form, and suggests two upright human bodies. The sculpture is by Barbara Hepworth, an important British Modernist and arguably the most significant female sculptor of all time. Hepworth pierced the sculpture with holes, as she often did in her work, and painted the walls of the holes blue. *Two Figures* embodies her concern for the relationship between objects and, with the piercings, between the interiors and exteriors of objects. Hepworth sometimes incised lines on her sculptures; on the back side of *Two Figures,* she incised circles. In works such as *Two Figures,* she reduced natural forms to their essences and pursued shape for its own sake.

Hepworth shared parallel careers with her friend, the sculptor Henry Moore. They both grew up in Yorkshire, England; were educated at the Leeds School of Art; won scholarships to the Royal College of Art in London; and won traveling scholarships to study in Italy after graduation. In the late 1920s, they set up studios in north London, in Hampstead, a villagelike borough that was home to London's avant-garde, including several artists from continental Europe, such as Piet Mondrian, Naum Gabo, and Laszlo Moholy-Nagy. Moreover, Hepworth and Moore were both interested in carving rather than modeling, and they were both profoundly inspired by the landscapes of their native Yorkshire.

In the late 1920s, Hepworth specialized in carving animals, especially birds. After divorcing her first husband, John Skeaping, who was an English sculptor of animals, Hepworth married the English Modernist painter Ben Nicholson in 1932. The same year, Hepworth and Nicholson traveled to France, where they visited the studios of Jean Arp, Constantin Brancusi, Georges Braque, and Pablo Picasso.

Modernism increasingly influenced Hepworth, and by the mid-1930s, her work had become abtract. At this time, she exhibited widely in avant-garde shows. She was associated with Constructivism, a movement positing that the artist should reveal the order underlying the world and that a more perfect society could be built according to this order made manifest.

Just before World War II, Hepworth began spending time with other artists in the coastal town of St. Ives, Cornwall, and she decided to move there permanently.

After World War II, she received commissions for large outdoor public sculptures, and her sculptures became more vertical. Having worked primarily in wood and stone, which she carved, Hepworth in 1956 started working in bronze. Bronze enabled her to create even larger works, such as the memorial to Dag Hammarskjöld, *Single Form,* installed in front of the United Nations in New York. Hepworth became

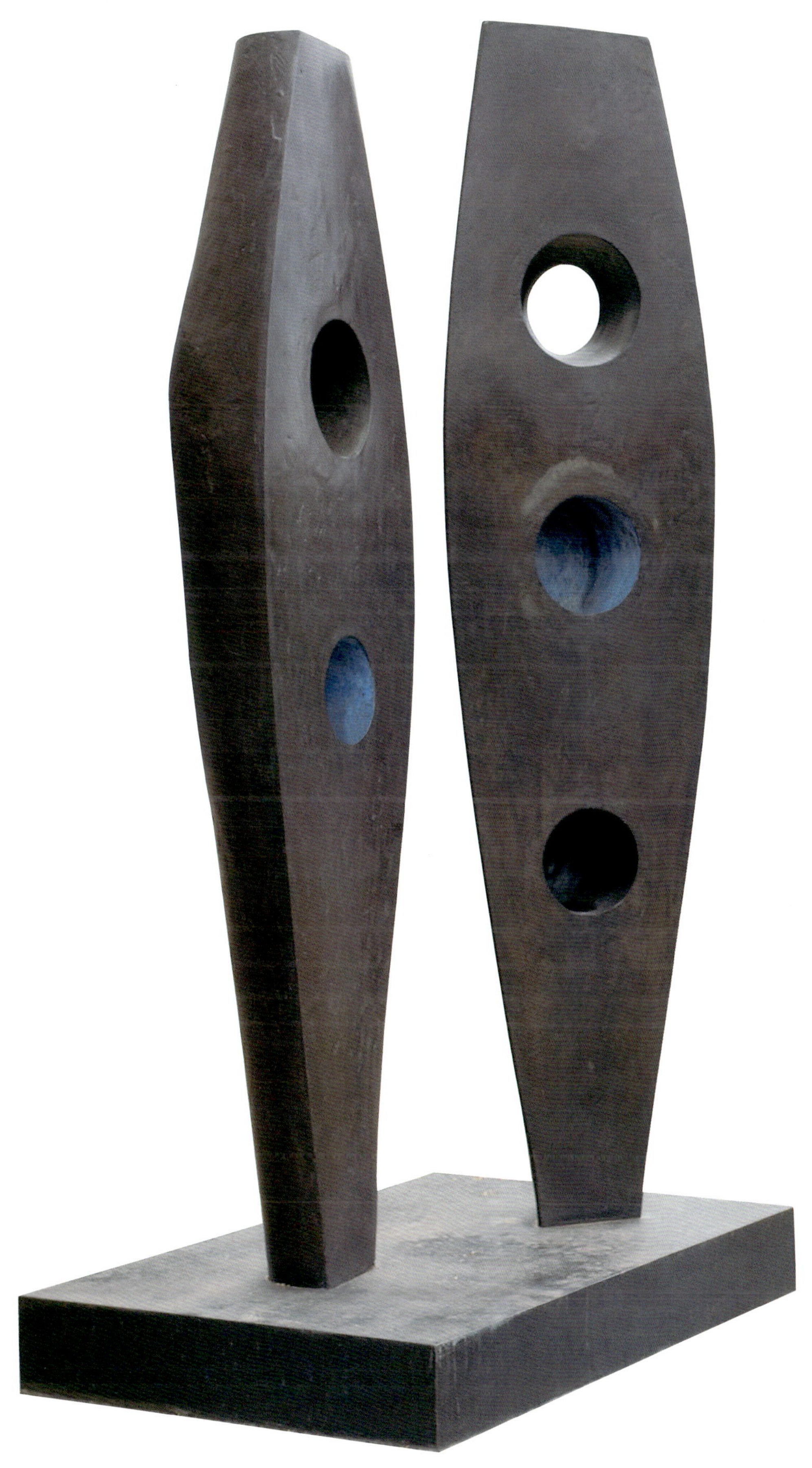

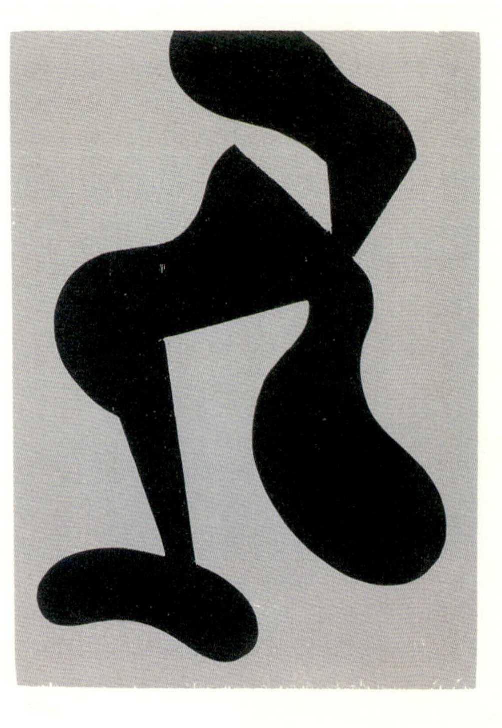

Jean Arp
France, 1886–1966
Form Heard and Seen, 1951, woodcut, edition: 58/320, 8 × 5¾ in. Museum purchase, 1963

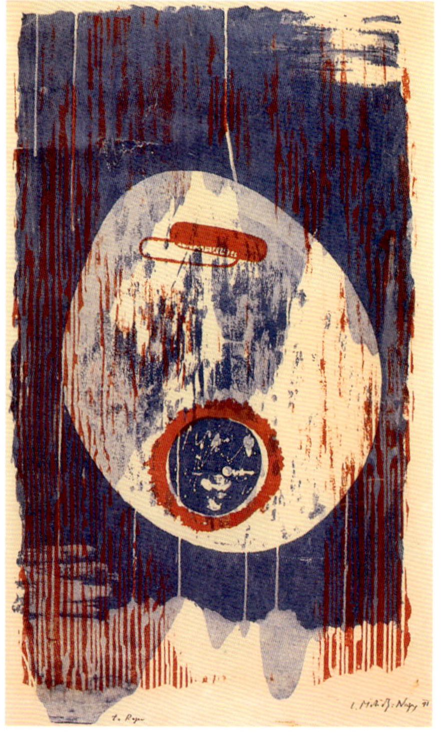

Laszlo Moholy-Nagy
U.S., b. Hungary, 1894–1946
Untitled, from Blood Cell series, 1941, screen print, 24 × 14¼ in. Museum purchase, 1968

one of the best-known sculptors in the world, and in 1965, Queen Elizabeth named her a Dame of the British Empire.

Hepworth died in a fire at her St. Ives studio in 1975. Five years later, her studio was opened to the public as a satellite of the Tate Gallery.

In words that could apply to *Two Figures,* Hepworth wrote about sculpture in her 1970 *Pictorial Autobiography:*

> *It is difficult to describe in words the meaning of forms because it is precisely this emotion which is conveyed by sculpture alone. Our sense of touch is a fundamental sensibility which comes into action at birth . . . the ability to feel weight and form and assess its significance. The forms which have had special meaning for me since childhood have been the standing form (which is the translation of my feeling towards the human being standing in landscape); the two forms (which is the tender relationship of one living thing beside another); and the closed form, such as the oval, spherical or pierced form (sometimes incorporating colour) which translates for me the association and meaning of gesture in landscape; in the repose of say a mother and child, or the feeling of the embrace of living things, either in nature or in the human spirit. In all these shapes the translation of what one feels about man and nature must be conveyed by the sculptor in terms of mass, inner tension and rhythm, scale in relation to our human size and the quality of surface which speaks through our hands and eyes. . . . [Sculpture is] a real object which relates to our human body and spirit as well as to our visual appreciation of form and colour content.*

86 Patrick Heron

England, 1920–1999

Icy Emerald Cutting into Dark Green and Blue, 1968
Watercolor on paper
30¼ × 23 in.
Gift of Max Weitzenhoffer, 1981

Patrick Heron was a leading figure in postwar British art and its staunchest advocate of color. A native of Leeds who spent part of his childhood in the seaside town of St. Ives in Cornwall, Heron decided to become an artist at an early age. His encouraging father was a textile manufacturer for whom well-known British artists made designs. Heron himself designed for the firm in the 1930s and 1940s. In the late 1930s, he studied part-time at the Slade School of Art in London.

Heron befriended many artists and writers, such as Henry Moore and T. S. Eliot, and in the 1950s, he settled in St. Ives and became associated with the artists who lived there, including Barbara Hepworth (see cat. no. 85) and Terry Frost. The St. Ives artists were known especially for abstraction informed by the appearance of the natural world. Heron's paintings of the early to mid-1950s had depicted flat, luminous still lifes and interiors inspired by Georges Braque and Henri Matisse; in St. Ives in the late 1950s, Heron produced paintings with horizontal bands of color that suggested abstracted coastal landscapes.

In the 1960s, Heron began to paint voluptuous abstractions, such as *Icy Emerald Cutting into Dark Green and Blue*, in which fields of intense, saturated colors interact and bleed into one another. He described color as the "very stuff of which sight or vision consists" and stated, "It is obvious that colour is the only direction in which paintings can travel."

The present painting, part of the museum's strong collection of British art from the 1960s and 1970s, is abstract. However, its colors and shapes evoke the boulders from Heron's garden and Cornwall's craggy coastline and inlets.

Heron was an articulate writer on art, as evident in the vivid, descriptive title *Icy Emerald Cutting into Dark Green and Blue*. During the late 1940s and 1950s, he maintained, parallel to his art, a career as an influential art critic for both British and American publications. Attacking British audiences for not yet fully appreciating the significance of artists such as Matisse, Braque, Pablo Picasso, and Pierre Bonnard, he praised British Modernist artists and became an early champion of American Abstract Expressionism.

Shortly before Heron's death, the Tate Gallery in London held an acclaimed retrospective of his work.

Terry Frost
England, 1915–2003
Four Bs and a Blue, n.d., oil on canvas, 25 × 48 in. Gift of L. Bradley Camp, 1985

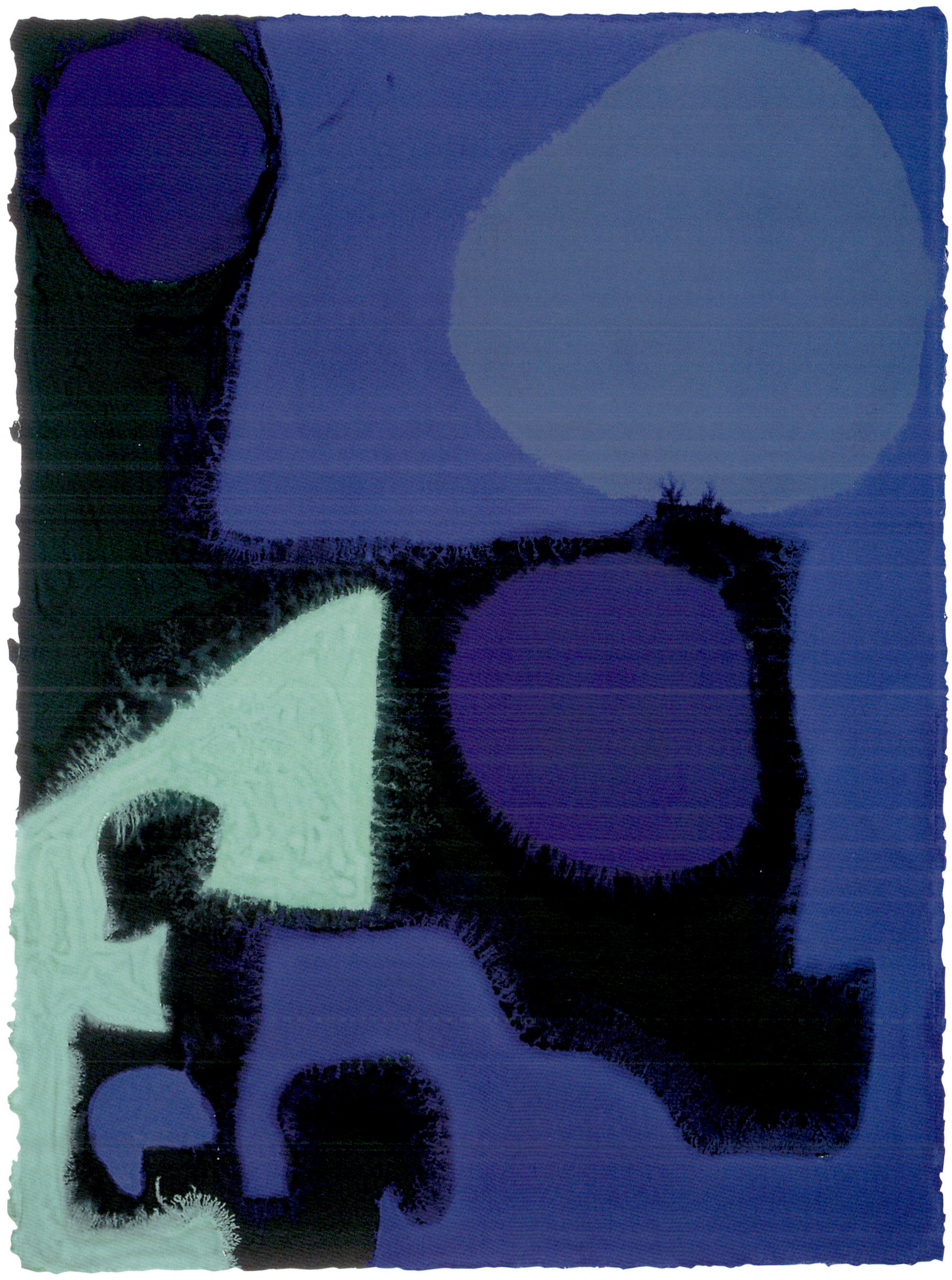

87 Alan Davie

England, b. 1920

Big Solid Sender, 1964
Oil on canvas
72 × 60 in.
Gift of Max Weitzenhoffer, 1974

Born in Grangemouth, Scotland, the son of a painter and etcher, Alan Davie studied painting at the Edinburgh College of Art from 1938 until 1940. During World War II, he wrote poetry while serving in the Royal Artillery, and between 1949 and 1953, he made gold and silver jewelry. In 1950, Davie's first major art exhibition in London brought him critical attention; commercial success followed a few years later.

Davie explores fantasy and myth in brilliantly colored paintings such as *Big Solid Sender.* He creates a unique language by using images that he invents himself together with signs derived from diverse cultures and religions; Oceanic and African cultures, Zen Buddhism, and Christianity all inform his work. In *Big Solid Sender,* a cross appears superimposed on layers of aggressive, enigmatic signs of Davie's own devising.

Davie works quickly and spontaneously. He believes in links between painting and the improvisational nature of jazz, as do other artists in this catalogue, such as Radcliffe Bailey (cat. no. 101), Romare Bearden (cat. no. 75), and Stuart Davis (cat. no. 71). (Davie even worked full-time as a jazz musician, in 1947; the artist Larry Rivers [cat. no. 88] also was a jazz musician.)

Stained glass is among the diverse influences on Davie's art. In *Big Solid Sender,* the black outlines surrounding the blocks of color perhaps correspond to the lead around the colored glass in a stained-glass window.

Davie acknowledges being inspired by other artists. He was profoundly moved by the 1945 exhibitions, held in London, of Pablo Picasso and of Paul Klee, who saw artmaking as a spiritual quest and who drew inspiration from tribal art and the art of children.

During travels through Europe between 1947 and 1949, Davie saw Peggy Guggenheim's collection in Venice, including works by Jackson Pollock. Davie became one of the first Europeans to recognize Pollock's importance. Based on Pollock's example, he began to paint on canvases laid flat on the floor and adopted expressionistic, gestural, and rapid handling of paint. Like Pollock, Davie incorporated chance into his compositions with drips and spatters of paint, as seen in *Big Solid Sender.* (Davie turns upright canvases that were painted while lying flat, so that the paint will drip.)

Davie's work has been compared to that of the CoBrA artists, such as Asger Jorn and Corneille. (The post–World War II CoBrA group took its name from the cities where the artists lived: Copenhagen, Brussels, and Amsterdam.) The CoBrA artists created abstracted but still figurative images in bold colors, and tribal, folk, and prehistoric art often inspired their work.

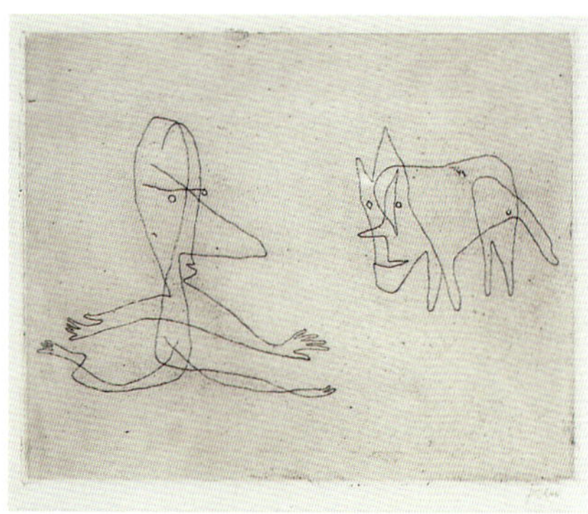

Paul Klee
Switzerland, 1879–1940
Why Does He Run?, 1932, etching, edition: 100/110, 12¼ × 15⁹⁄₁₆ in. Museum purchase, 1967

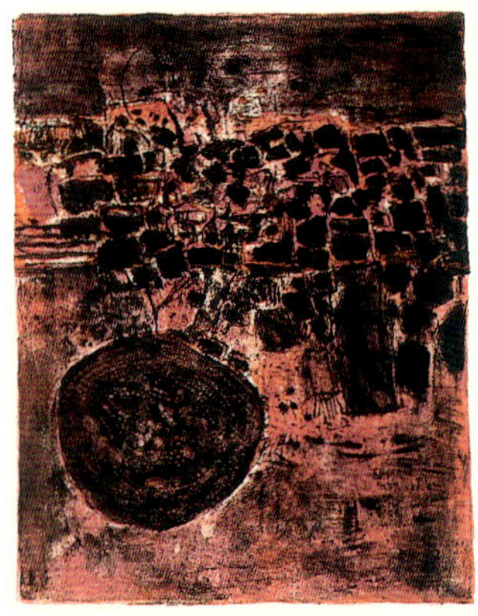

Corneille
Belgium, b. 1922
African Land (Terre Africaine), 1959, lithograph, edition: 66/100, 19½ × 15¼ in. Gift of International Graphic, 1960

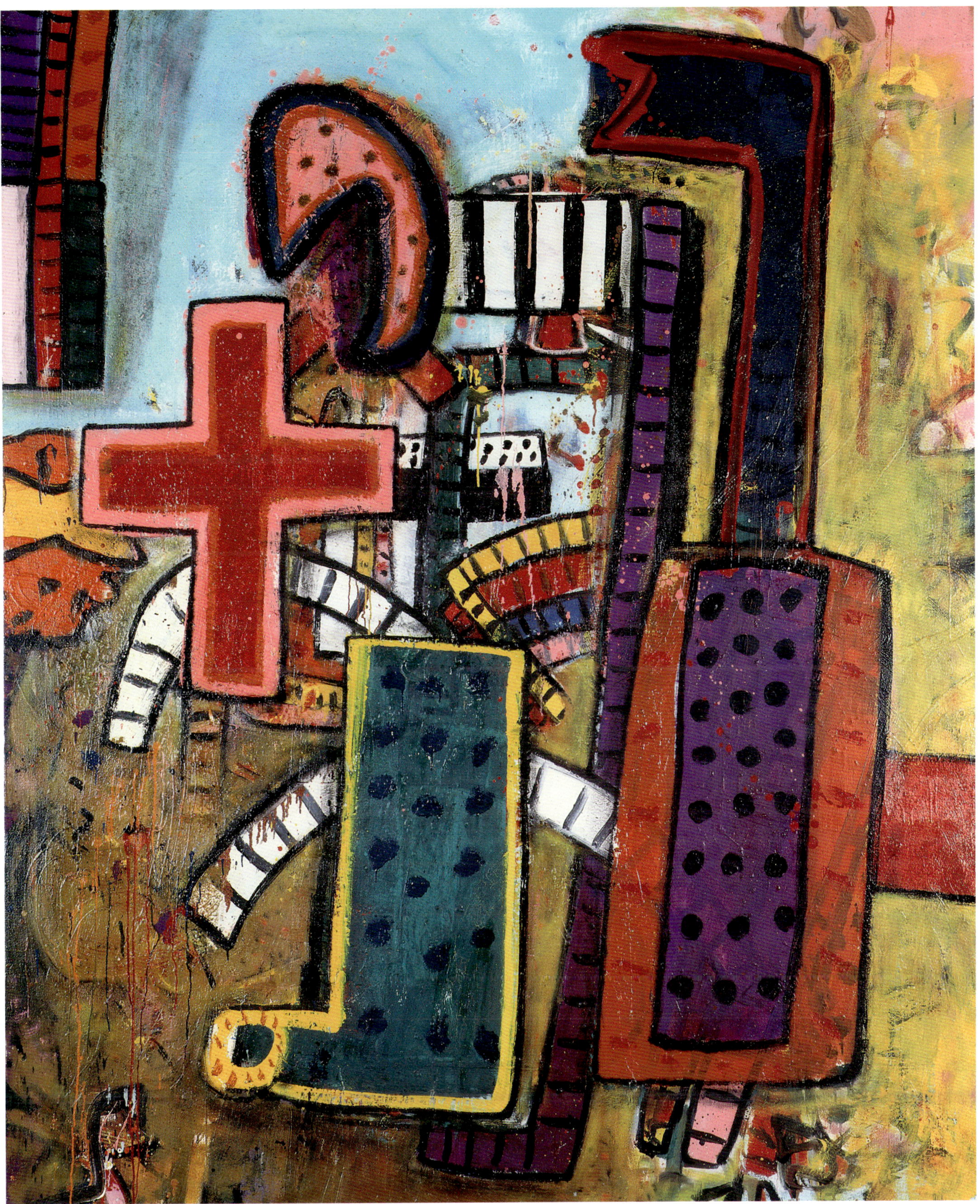

88 Larry Rivers

U.S., 1923–2002

Camels, 1962
Graphite on paper
14¾ × 12⅞ in.
Museum purchase, 1984

Larry Rivers bridged the Abstract Expressionist and Pop Art generations. He courted notoriety and was as well-known for his outrageous personality as for his art. In addition to creating art, he wrote, acted, designed stage sets, and even played in and won television game shows. An omnivorous reader, he collaborated with poets such as Allen Ginsberg and Frank O'Hara.

The son of Jewish immigrants from the Ukraine, Rivers was born Yitzroch Loiza Grossberg and grew up in the Bronx. He studied piano, and in 1940 started to work as a jazz saxophonist, changing his name when a comic introduced him and his band as "Larry Rivers and the Mudcats." Rivers enlisted in the U.S. Army Air Corps during World War II and played in the army band, but was honorably discharged for health reasons. He then studied music for a year at the Juilliard School in New York, where Miles Davis was a fellow student. After Juilliard, Rivers again worked professionally as a jazz saxophonist. A bandmate was married to the painter Jane Freilicher, who suggested that Rivers try painting. He had a natural ability and decided to become an artist foremost, although he continued playing in bands for the rest of his life.

In 1947, Freilicher and Rivers enrolled in the classes of the influential teacher-painter Hans Hofmann. Rivers continued training with Hofmann for nearly two years, but rebelled against Hofmann's insistence on abstraction. A 1948 Pierre Bonnard exhibition at the Museum of Modern Art in New York proved to Rivers that representational art could still be vital.

Rivers then spent time in Paris, studying Old Masters and nineteenth-century French art. After returning to New York, he painted *Washington Crossing the Delaware* (1953), which parodied the famous nineteenth-century painting by Emanuel Gottlieb Leutze at the Metropolitan Museum of Art. Rivers's ironic painting, which the Museum of Modern Art acquired in 1956, reintroduced wit to art at the time of Abstract Expressionism's high seriousness. Nevertheless, Rivers could also be serious and deal in his work with issues such as race or the Holocaust.

Rivers's fame and critical recognition peaked in the 1960s. During that decade, he depicted images from everyday life, as Andy Warhol did with Campbell's Soup cans. Many of Rivers's works related to tobacco; the present drawing was inspired by Camel cigarettes. *Camels* is an early rendition of a motif that Rivers would repeat for decades and that would become an icon of Pop Art.

Camels attests to Rivers's virtuosity as a draftsman. In typical fashion, Rivers revealed the process of the drawing's creation—he made no attempt to hide the revisions and erasures. These smudges imbue the work with energy.

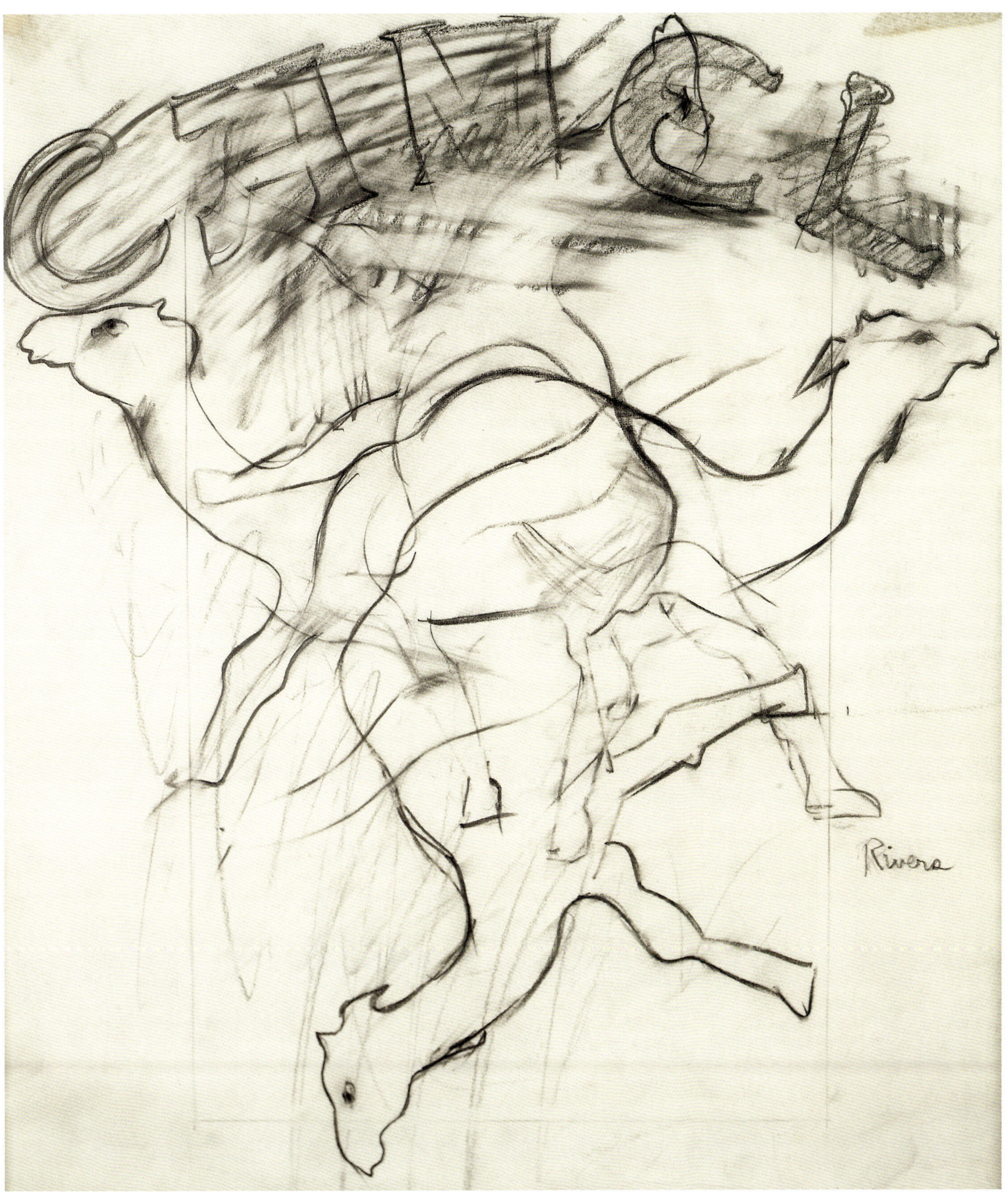
Rivera

89 Roy Lichtenstein

U.S., 1923–1997

On, 1962
Etching
Edition: 11/60
10 × 7½ in.
Museum purchase, 1965

During the 1960s, Roy Lichtenstein became one of the pioneers of Pop Art, which took subject matter from mass culture and everyday life—for example, comic strips and Campbell's Soup cans. Cool, detached, and droll, Pop Art reacted against the serious and nonrepresentational high art of Abstract Expressionism, which had dominated the art world of the 1950s.

Lichtenstein grew up in New York. While in high school, he studied at the Art Students League; later he attended the art school of Ohio State University, where he received both undergraduate and graduate degrees. During World War II, he served in Europe as a map draftsman for the army. Like Andy Warhol, he spent much of the 1950s working in commercial art and design and created displays for shop windows. Lichtenstein passed through an Abstract Expressionist phase, but around 1960, he moved away from the gestural, abstract style of Jackson Pollock and others to embrace mass culture as his subject. His paintings henceforth showed smooth, deindividualized surfaces and featured primary colors, black outlines, and painted benday dots, an overall pattern of dots that emulated, in magnified form, commercial printing.

Lichtenstein's paintings of comic strips have become icons of Pop Art. He painted the first one in 1961, after his son challenged him by pointing to a comic strip and declaring, "I bet you can't paint as good as that."

On was Lichtenstein's first Pop Art print. The print was based on a 1962 painting and was published by Milan's Galleria Schwarz in a portfolio titled *The International Avant-Garde.* The witty, irreverent print captures the optimism with which the 1960s began. Timothy Leary's famous dictum, "Turn on, tune in, and drop out," stated a few years after the print's appearance, would give *On* new shades of meaning.

Pop Art often depicts two-dimensional images; this etching, however, also plays with the illusion of depth, since the switch seems to project out of the print.

The museum owns many Pop Art prints by artists such as Warhol, Jim Dine, Claes Oldenburg, and Ed Ruscha (who grew up in Oklahoma City before moving to Los Angeles).

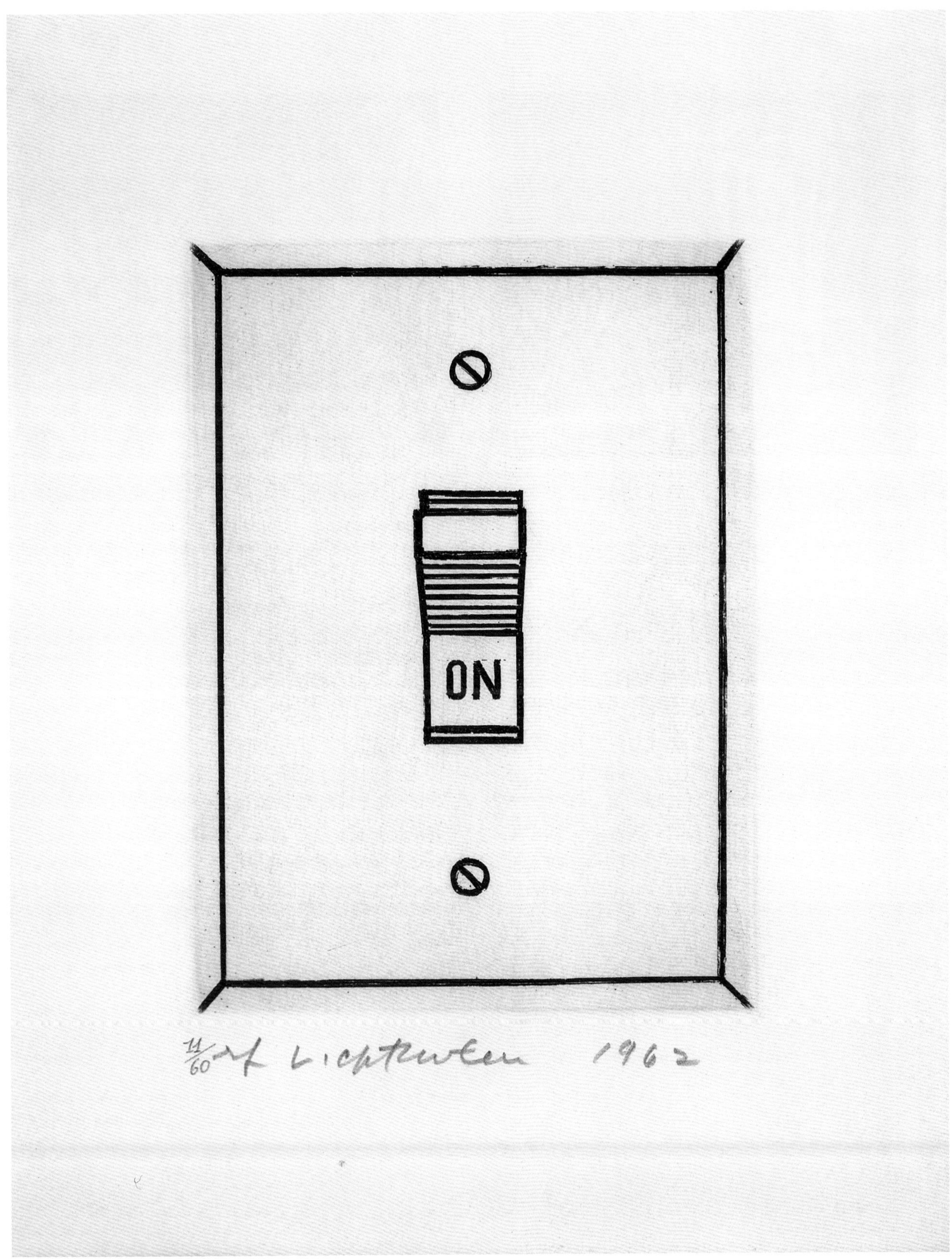
ON
11/60
1962

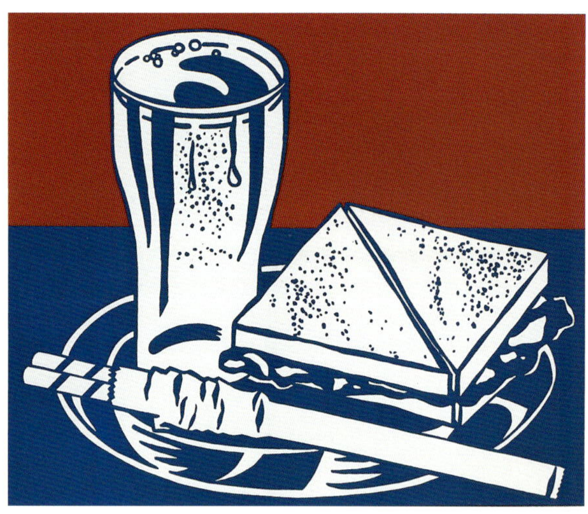

Roy Lichtenstein
U.S., 1923–1997
Sandwich and Soda, from *Ten Works by Ten Painters* portfolio, 1964, screen print, edition: 291/500, 20 × 24 in. Purchase, Alumni Development Fund, 1966

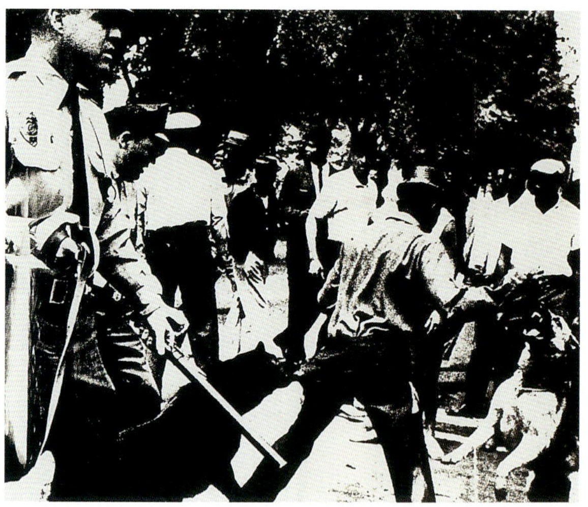

Andy Warhol
U.S., 1928–1987
Birmingham Race Riot, from *Ten Works by Ten Painters* portfolio, 1964, screen print, edition: 291/500, 20 × 24 in. Purchase, Alumni Development Fund, 1966

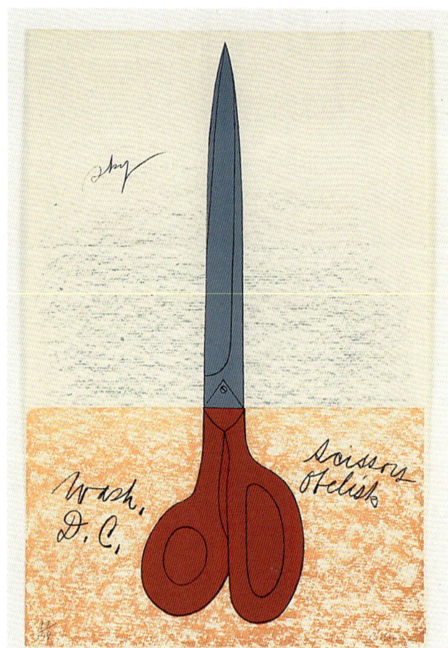

Claes Oldenburg
U.S., b. 1929
Scissors as Monument (Scissors Obelisk, Washington, D.C.), from *National Collection of Art* portfolio, 1967, lithograph, edition: 97/144, 30 × 22 in. Museum purchase, 1969

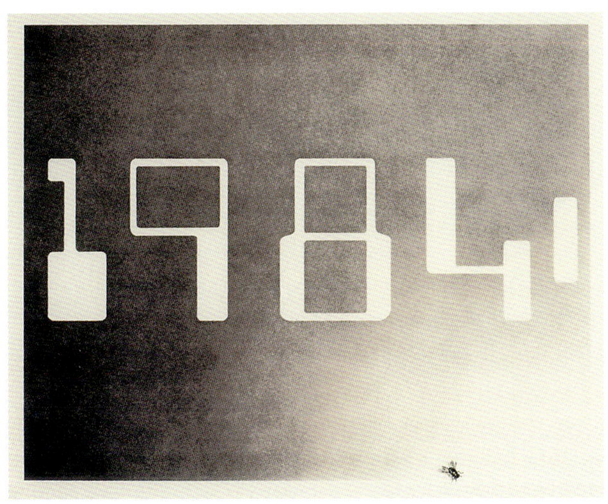

Ed Ruscha
U.S., b. 1937
1984, 1967, lithograph, edition: 26/60,
20 × 24¾ in. Museum purchase, 1969

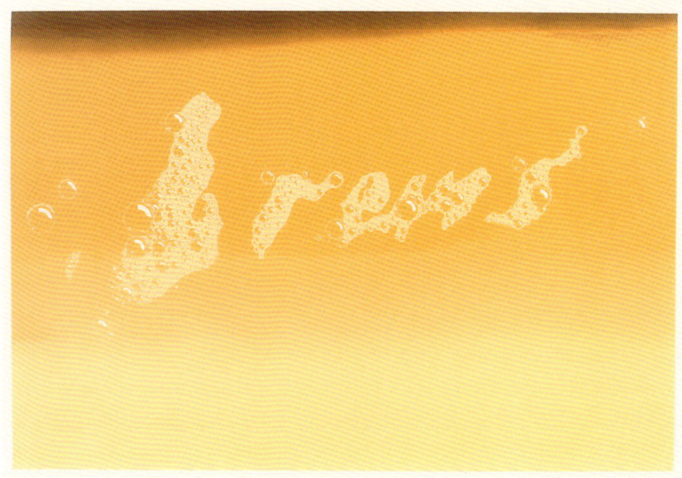

Ed Ruscha
U.S., b. 1937
Brews, 1970, screen print, edition: 51/75,
23 × 32 in. Museum purchase, 1973

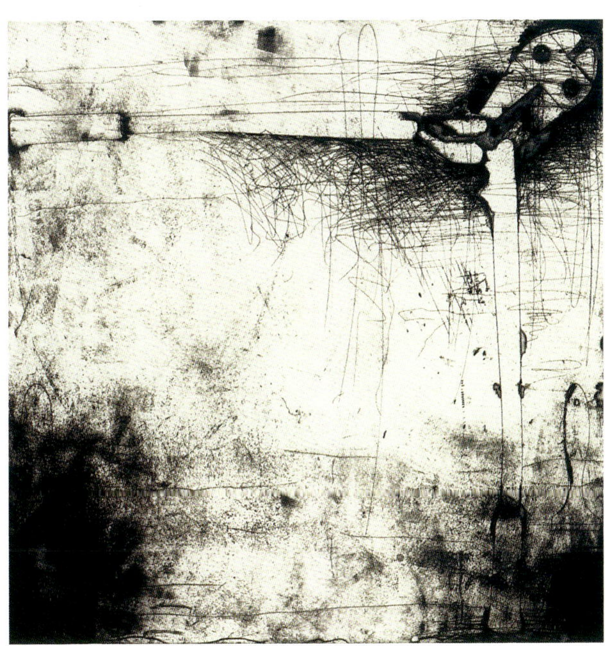

Jim Dine
U.S., b. 1935
Boltcutters, 1973, etching (2nd state),
edition: 33/45, 24¾ × 23¾ in. Museum
purchase, 1977

90 Robert Rauschenberg

U.S., b. 1925

#62 Features from "Currents," 1970
Screen print
Edition: 9/50
40 × 40 in.
Gift of Mr. and Mrs. Harold Newman, 1980

Among the most influential artists of the twentieth century, Robert Rauschenberg has famously stated that he wants to "act in the gap between [art and life]." He was born in Port Arthur, Texas, also the hometown of Janis Joplin. Early on, Rauschenberg wanted to become a preacher. In 1943, he briefly studied pharmacology at the University of Texas; he was then drafted into the navy for two years.

While stationed in California, Rauschenberg saw important art in person for the first time at the Huntington Library and Art Collections in San Marino. This encounter led to his decision to become an artist. He studied at the Kansas City Art Institute, at the Académie Julian in Paris, and at the Art Students League in New York. Until 1952, he intermittently attended Black Mountain College, the avant-garde institution in North Carolina, along with figures such as Joseph Albers, Buckminster Fuller, John Cage, and Merce Cunningham. (Rauschenberg later designed sets and costumes for and sometimes even performed with the Merce Cunningham Dance Company.)

In 1954, the extroverted Rauschenberg met the introverted Jasper Johns (see cat. no. 91); these two celebrated artists worked closely together until 1962.

Rauschenberg's early works were monochromatic paintings and conceptual pieces, such as *Erased de Kooning Drawing* (1953). In works called "combines," hybrids of painting and sculpture, he juxtaposed an assortment of found everyday objects—such as spare tires, a stuffed goat, or an old quilt—on which he then applied Abstract Expressionist–style gestural painting. With these combines, made through 1964 and inspired in part by the French artist Marcel Duchamp, Rauschenberg helped redefine what could be considered art.

Between 1962 and 1964, Rauschenberg began to incorporate newspapers into his art by using photoengraved plates based on the *New York Times* and the *New York Herald Tribune*. These works addressed visual culture and the perception of images in the contemporary world; they have been called the history paintings of the 1960s. Also in that decade, starting in 1962, Rauschenberg produced his first prints at Universal Limited Art Editions (U.L.A.E.).

The present image is from Rauschenberg's 1970 series of prints called *Currents*. Overwhelmed by current events and the tragedies of the 1960s, from the assassinations of the Kennedy brothers and Martin Luther King Jr. to the Charles Manson murders and Vietnam, Rauschenberg claimed that *Currents* was intended as "an active protest attempting to . . . communicate my response to . . . our grave times." In the series, Rauschenberg used randomly selected, unedited newspaper articles, headlines, and photographs. The title of the series referred to

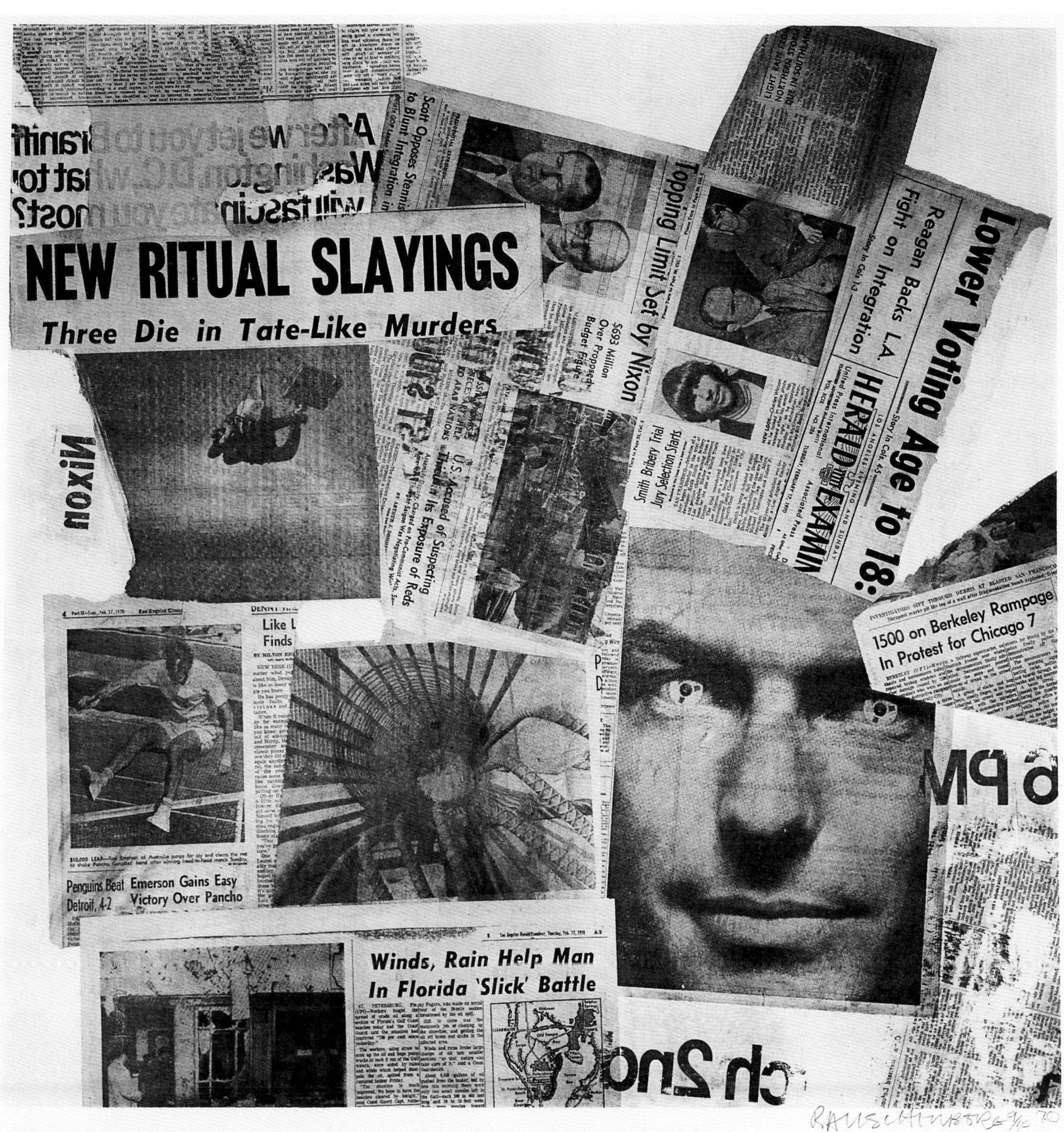

Scott Opposes Stennis
to Blunt Integration in
Topping Limit Set by Nixon
$693 Million
Over Proposed
Budget Figure
Lower Voting Age to 18:
Reagan Backs L.A.
Fight on Integration
HERALD-EXAMIN
Smith Bribery Trial
Jury Selection Starts
NEW RITUAL SLAYINGS
Three Die in Tate-Like Murders
Accused of Suspecting
Its Exposure of Reds
1500 on Berkeley Rampage
In Protest for Chicago 7
6 PM
Penguins Beat
Detroit, 4-2
Emerson Gains Easy
Victory Over Pancho
Winds, Rain Help Man
In Florida 'Slick' Battle

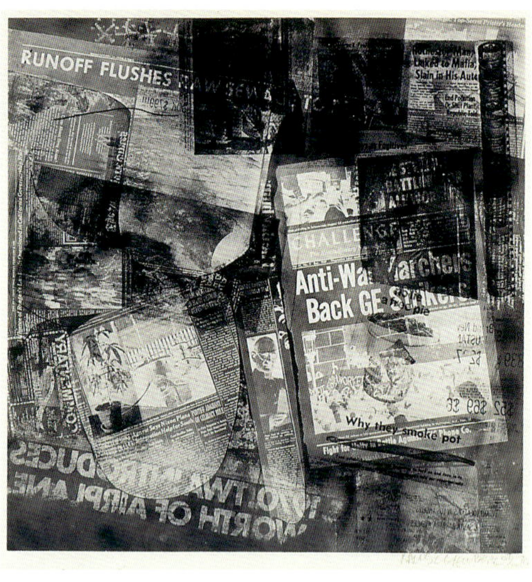

Robert Rauschenberg
U.S., b. 1925
#77 Features from "Currents," 1970, screen print, edition: 9/50, 40 × 40 in. Gift of Mr. and Mrs. Harold Newman, 1980

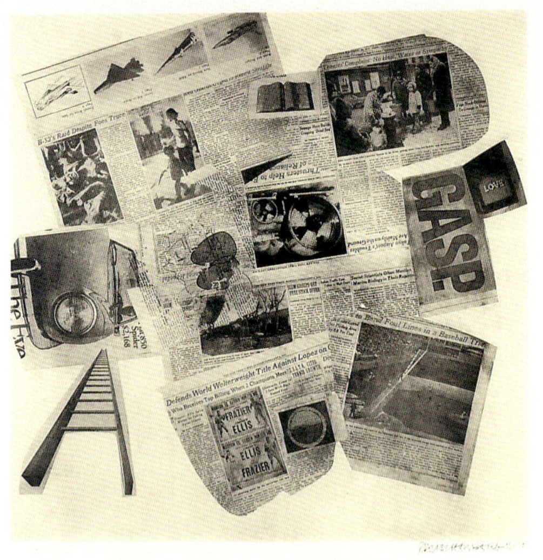

Robert Rauschenberg
U.S., b. 1925
#48 Surface Series from "Currents," 1970, screen print, edition: 9/50, 40 × 40 in. Gift of Mr. and Mrs. Harold Newman, 1980

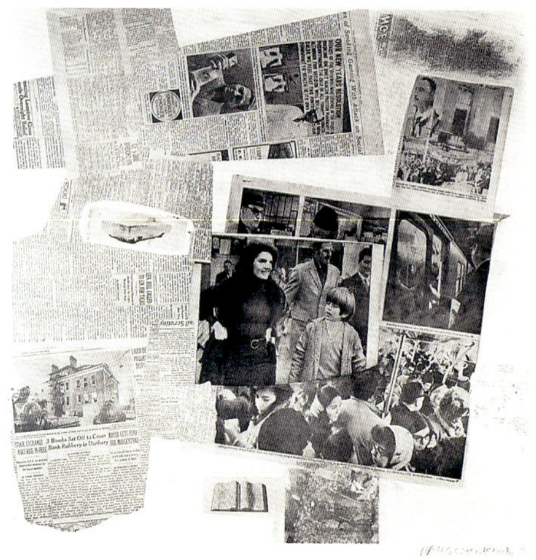

Robert Rauschenberg
U.S., b. 1925
#56 Features from "Currents," 1970, screen print, edition: 9/50, 40 × 40 in. Gift of Mr. and Mrs. Harold Newman, 1980

current events, the currents then flowing through society, and the currents of visual and information overload in which the artist felt he might drown.

The artist began *Currents* as collages of newspaper clippings from the *New York Times,* the *New York Daily News,* the *Los Angeles Times,* the *San Francisco Examiner,* and other publications of January and February 1970. He then produced a six-by-fifty-four-foot print—the largest ever made—based on the *Currents* collage. The artist exhibited the print, called *Studies for "Currents,"* in Minneapolis at Dayton's Gallery 12, which had commissioned the work, and then in Pasadena and New York.

To reach a larger audience, Rauschenberg used the images from *Studies for "Currents"* to make smaller prints assembled in two portfolios: *Features from "Currents"* and *Surface Series from "Currents."* The museum owns all forty-four screen prints from these two portfolios.

91 Jasper Johns

U.S., b. 1930

Corpse and Mirror, 1976
Lithograph
Artist's Proof, edition of 58
30¾ × 39¾ in.
Gift of Jerome Westheimer, 1985

An artist whose work is quiet, ordered, and cerebral, Jasper Johns has held a central position in American art since the 1950s. Born in Augusta, Georgia, Johns grew up in South Carolina. He is essentially self-taught as an artist, although he studied at the University of South Carolina for a year and briefly attended art school in New York.

With his friend, the artist Robert Rauschenberg (see cat. no. 90), Johns reintroduced figurative subject matter into art after Abstract Expressionism. Johns also helped lead the way to Pop Art when, during the 1950s, he depicted American flags and other everyday images in works that questioned the nature of perception and representation.

Johns created his first flag painting in 1954, and then produced paintings of two-dimensional signs, such as targets, maps, and numbers. These works both represented the sign and were the sign—at once paintings of a thing *and* the thing itself. Johns executed his images in encaustic, a difficult medium that uses wax instead of oil for binding the pigments. Encaustic yields a rich surface. In 1958, Leo Castelli, who would become a celebrated dealer, gave Johns his first solo show.

Printmaking has been a major component of Johns's work since the 1960s. Fascinated by technique, Johns has experimented with and expanded the possibilities of printmaking. In general, the themes of his prints echo those of his paintings; he explores how the same subject is rendered in different media.

The lithograph *Corpse and Mirror* is one of Johns's Crosshatch paintings and prints of 1972 to 1982. The abstract Crosshatch images have been interpreted in many ways: some critics have said that, while appearing decorative, these works are intellectual puzzles; others have claimed that Johns has encoded hidden meaning in the crosshatchings. Johns has compared his crosshatch patterns to the fingers of a hand. He has also stated, somewhat coyly: "I was riding in a car, going out to the Hamptons for the weekend, when a car came in the opposite direction. It was covered with these marks, but I only saw it for a moment—then it was gone—just a brief glimpse. But I immediately thought that I would use it for my next painting."

Johns's first *Corpse and Mirror* is a 1974 painted diptych, showing on the left panel crosshatch patterns that are doubled in a mirror image on the right panel. (Johns has used mirror images in his work since 1959.) In the present lithograph, Johns uses subtle lines where the edges of the crosshatchings meet, in order to bisect the print vertically and trisect it horizontally, thus creating six parts. In the upper-right corner of the print, as in the painting, Johns includes a large "X," which cancels the illusion that the right half is a perfect mirror image.

"Corpse" in the title refers to the Surrealist game of drawing an "exquisite corpse." In this game, artists would fold a sheet of paper so that only one portion could be seen at any given time. On each portion of the folded paper, an artist would draw, to the folded edge, part of a figure, without knowing what the other artists had drawn, and seeing only the edges of the previous artist's work. When the artists unfolded the paper, they would see a drawing composed of parts that related to one another only randomly. *Corpse and Mirror*'s vertical line and the two horizontal lines suggest the folds of paper of an exquisite corpse.

Johns printed *Corpse and Mirror* in West Islip, Long Island, at Universal Limited Art Editions (U.L.A.E.). U.L.A.E. was established by the late Tatyana Grosman, who persuaded Johns to make his first print in 1960. Oklahoman Bill Goldston, a Grosman associate, now directs the renowned print atelier.

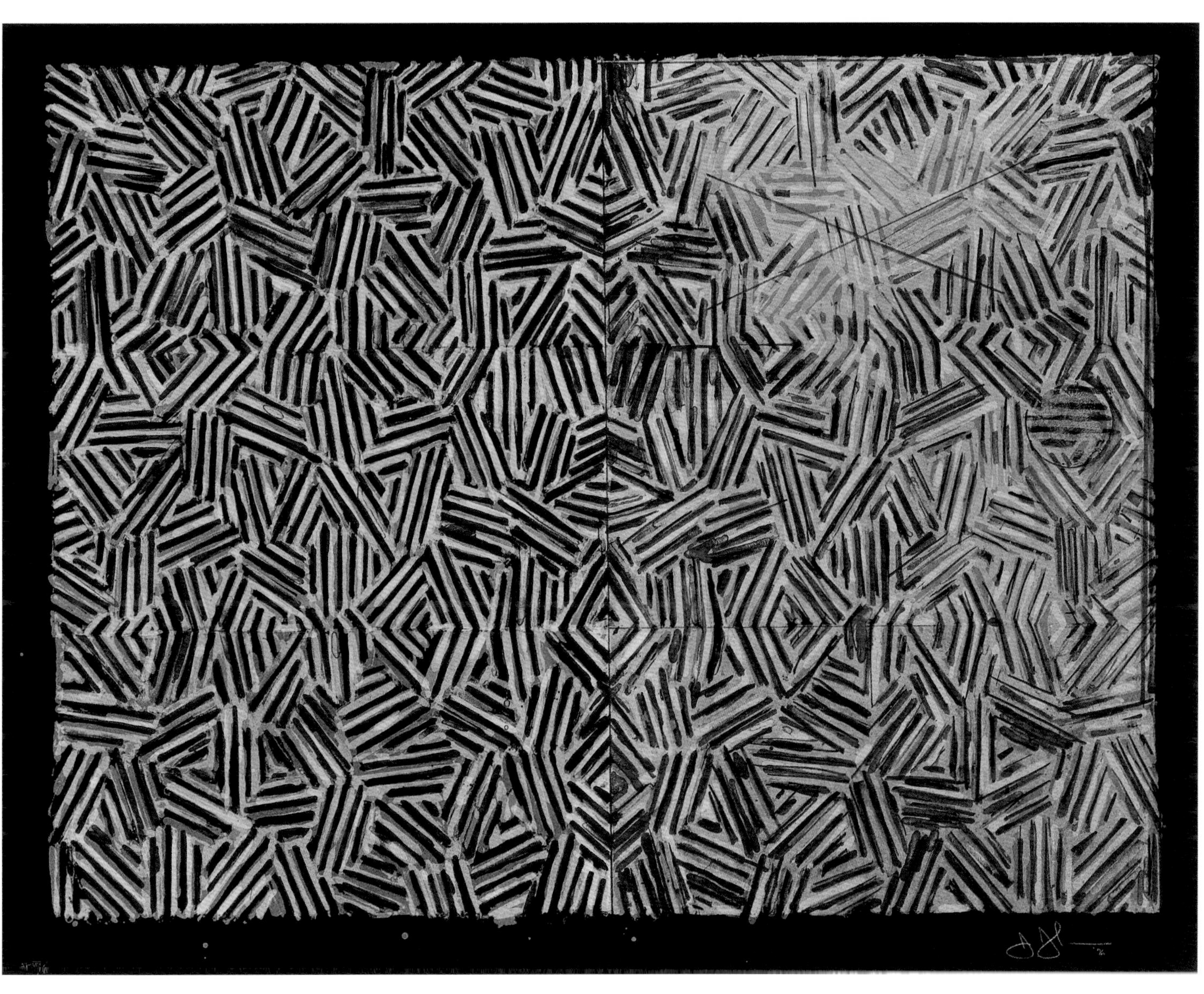

92 Robert Smithson

U.S., 1938–1973

Asphalt on Eroded Cliff, 1969
Ink and colored chalk on paper
18 × 24 in.
Museum purchase, 1973

Best known for his *Spiral Jetty*, Robert Smithson became one of the greatest exponents of Land Art before his premature death at age thirty-five. A native of New Jersey, he studied in the 1950s at the Brooklyn Museum School and the Art Students League in New York. His early works were Abstract Expressionist paintings, and his first solo exhibition was in New York in 1959. A trip to Rome in 1961 ignited Smithson's interest in religious art and history, especially of the Byzantine period; thereafter, he began to depict religious and mythological subjects in an Abstract Expressionist manner.

After his 1963 marriage to sculptor Nancy Holt, Smithson turned to sculpture and wrote extensively about art. He became acquainted with Minimalist artists, and his early sculptures showed Minimalism's influence. These sculptures often incorporated mirrors, playing on the age-old concept of art as a mirror of reality.

In 1966, Smithson began to use quarries and industrial sites in New Jersey to produce Land Art, which utilized the environment and was often outdoors. Smithson's projects grew large in scale and came to be known as Earthworks. *Spiral Jetty* (1970), his premier Earthwork, consisted of mud, rocks, and salt crystals arranged in a massive spiral that projected into Utah's Great Salt Lake. Smithson viewed the *Spiral Jetty* as partaking of a long history of large-scale works of art, such as the Egyptian pyramids or the prehistoric Great Serpent Mound in Ohio.

The drawing *Asphalt on Eroded Cliff* records the making of *Asphalt Rundown*, a project completed before Smithson began work on *Spiral Jetty*. (Smithson also filmed the creation of *Asphalt Rundown*.)

To Smithson, erosion and changes to works of art over time—what he called "entropy"—were significant. The entropic process was an important feature of the *Asphalt Rundown* project, in which Smithson unloaded a dump truck of hot asphalt down the side of an already-eroded quarry near Rome. The asphalt flowed like lava and highlighted the earlier gullies created by erosion in the quarry. The asphalt flow began from a central point and fanned out, before solidifying and stopping, in Smithson's words, "like a petrified river." Of course, the asphalt itself would become subject to entropy.

Asphalt Rundown has been compared to the drip paintings of Jackson Pollock. Both are "action" works that incorporate chance and grand gesture. Whereas Pollock used paint on canvas, Smithson, in a larger format, used asphalt on earth.

Discussing *Asphalt Rundown* in an interview, Smithson said:

> *You see, it's ultimately what's done after the truck pulls away. . . . The piece is at once solidly there, but it's subject to the elements. . . . [Y]ou have that sense of something very definitely in time, yet the moment gives you that sense of timelessness. . . .* [Asphalt Rundown *is] very thermodynamic in the sense that it's a hot material that is gradually cooling down. . . . My interest here is to root it to the contour of the land, so that it's permanently there and subject to the weathering.*

In 1973, Smithson died when his plane crashed while he was working on *Amarillo Ramp*, an Earthwork in Amarillo, Texas.

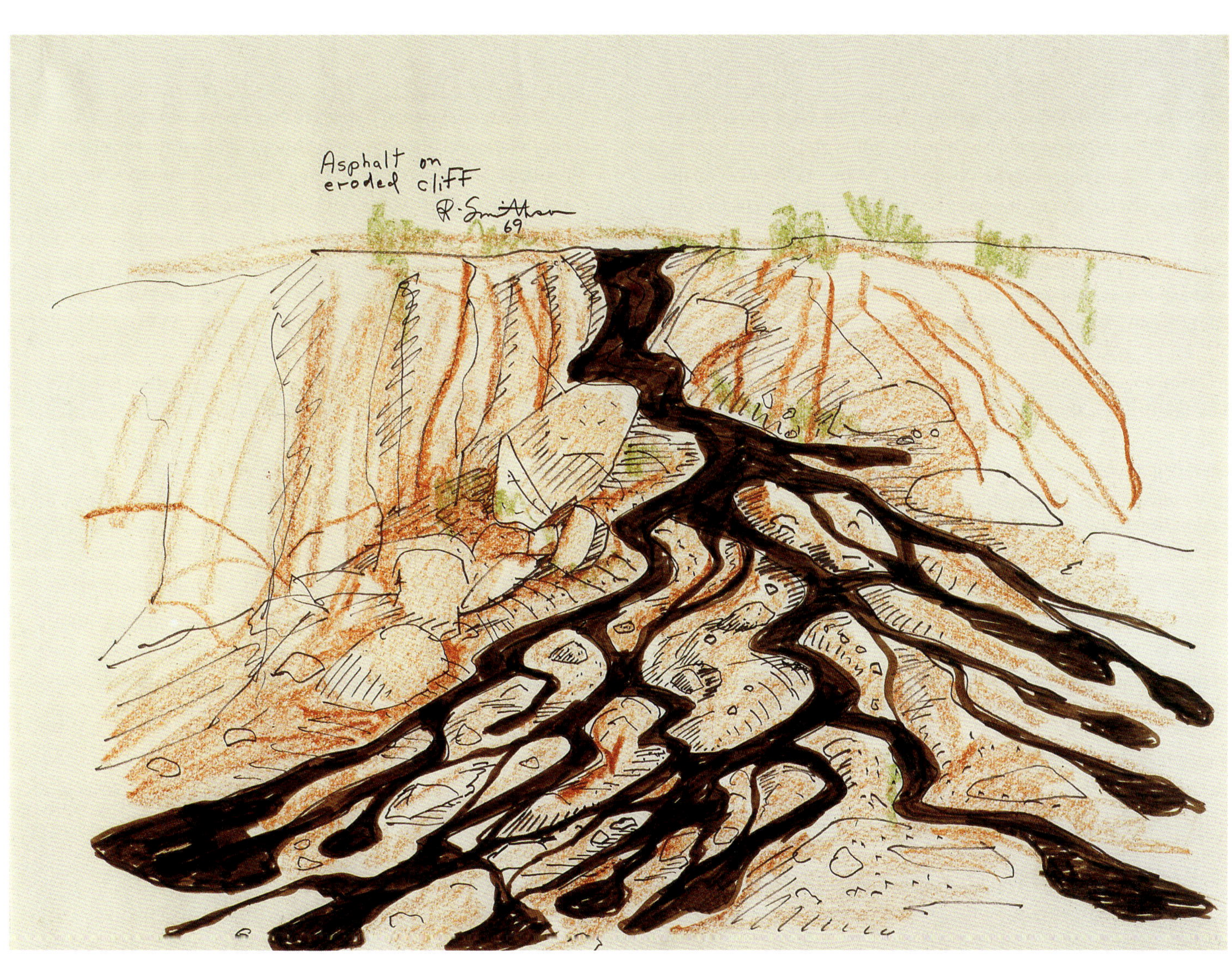
Asphalt on
eroded cliff
R. Smithson
69

Dieter Roth

Germany, 1930–1998

93a *Are You Seriously Looking for Ernestine . . . Your Tongue Sticking Out?—Yes!,* 1976
Pencil, ink, acrylic paint, glue, and collage on offset-printed card on board
15⁵⁄₁₆ × 21³⁄₁₆ in.
Gift of L. Bradley Camp, 1985

93b *Games After the Play or Before the Play,* 1976
Acrylic paint and glue on offset-printed card on board
15¼ × 21³⁄₁₆ in.
Gift of L. Bradley Camp, 1985

Dieter Roth was an influential provocateur of the avant-garde. He was born in Hanover, Germany, to a German mother and a Swiss father. During World War II, his parents sent him and his brother to live with relatives in Zurich. Roth began to draw and write poetry and, by 1946, to etch and paint. From 1947 until 1951, he apprenticed to a graphic design studio in Bern, Switzerland. At this time, he also made prints and collages. The Swiss military drafted him into service, but after Roth feigned insanity for a year, the army discharged him in 1952.

Roth opposed traditional art institutions such as museums and sought to break down the barriers between art and life. With these ideals in mind, he exhibited in a shop window in 1954 a baked sculpture made of dough, which began a career of working with unconventional, often impermanent materials, such as chocolate, cheese, and mold. As these works decomposed, they made manifest the passage of time. Also in 1954, Roth made his first film and the first of many artist's books.

From the late 1950s on, Roth lived in Reykjavík, Iceland, and Basel, Switzerland. He also spent time in London, Hamburg, and the United States, where he taught at Yale University and at the Rhode Island School of Design. Among his best-known works in the United States was an installation in Los Angeles in 1970 called *Staple Cheese: A Race,* which featured forty suitcases filled with cheese. The artist often created new identities for himself, complete with variations on his birth name, Karl-Dietrich Roth, including Dieter Roth, Diter Rot (a pun on the decomposition of many of his organic art materials), and Dieterrot.

Beginning in 1962, Roth used in his art postcards that he would manipulate with paint, collage, and other materials. The artist stated that he worked with postcards because "painting and drawing on unpainted or unmarked paper is harder to do than on paper with something already on it."

Starting around 1965, Roth created a famous series of works using a postcard of London's Piccadilly Circus, with its statue of Eros, double-decker buses, and frenetic advertising. Roth first made prints based on the Piccadilly Circus postcard. To make paintings, he mounted ninety-six of the prints on ninety-six boards and then applied to the prints a variety of materials such as paint and glue. Roth published reproductions of the resulting paintings, which include the present works, in a 1977 book called *96 Piccadillies.*

In the humorously titled *Are You Seriously Looking for Ernestine . . . Your Tongue Sticking Out?* and *Games After the Play or Before the Play,* Roth used acrylic paint mixed with glue. He intended this medium to deteriorate over time, but it has proved remarkably stable.

Roth often collaborated with other artists. For instance, in 1976, the year Roth made the present works, he and the English artist Richard Hamilton organized an exhibition—with characteristic wit—for people and dogs. For the show, Roth and Hamilton reworked one another's art. At canine level, they hung pictures dealing with sausage—a theme that would appeal to dogs—while at human-eye level, they hung works of interest to people. The exhibition opened in Spain and traveled to six museums and galleries. As Roth and Hamilton prepared the exhibition, they also made a record of songs, featuring solos performed by a dog, with Roth and Hamilton taking turns providing the accompaniment.

In 2004, the Museum of Modern Art in New York held a Dieter Roth retrospective.

In addition to the present works, the museum owns six artist's books by Roth. They all contain original drawings, including what he called "two-handed" and "speedy" drawings and "stupidograms."

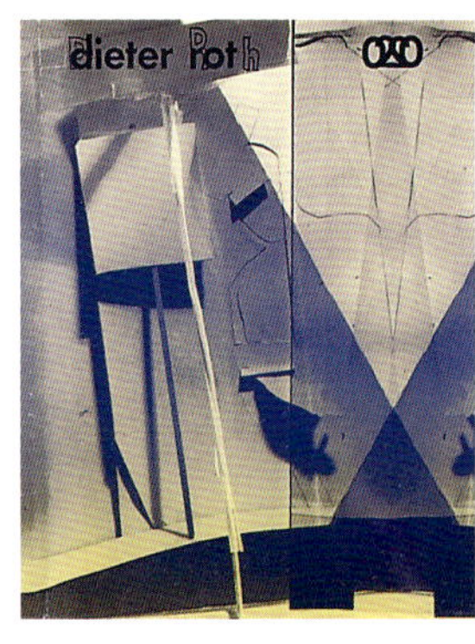

Dieter Roth
Germany, 1930–1998
Collected works vol. 20: books and graphics [part 1] from the years 1947 to 1971, special deluxe edition (Stuttgart: Edition hansjörg mayer), 1972, edition: 200, 9¹⁄₁₆ × 6¹¹⁄₁₆ in.
Gift of Donald Phillips, 1980

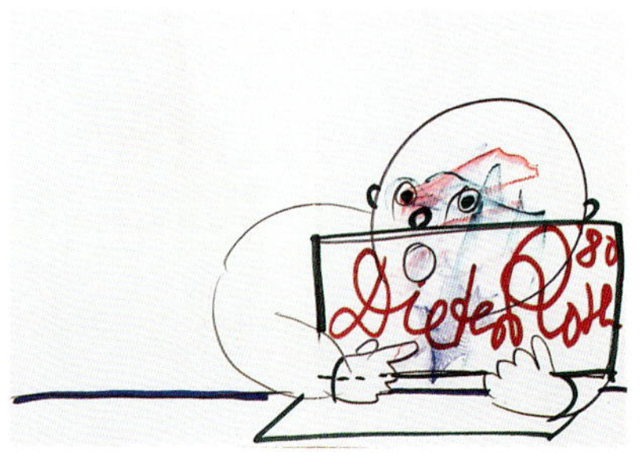

Dieter Roth
Germany, 1930–1998
Speedy Selfportrait as Printer, 1980, graphite and ink, 9 × 13 in.
Gift of Donald Phillips, 1980

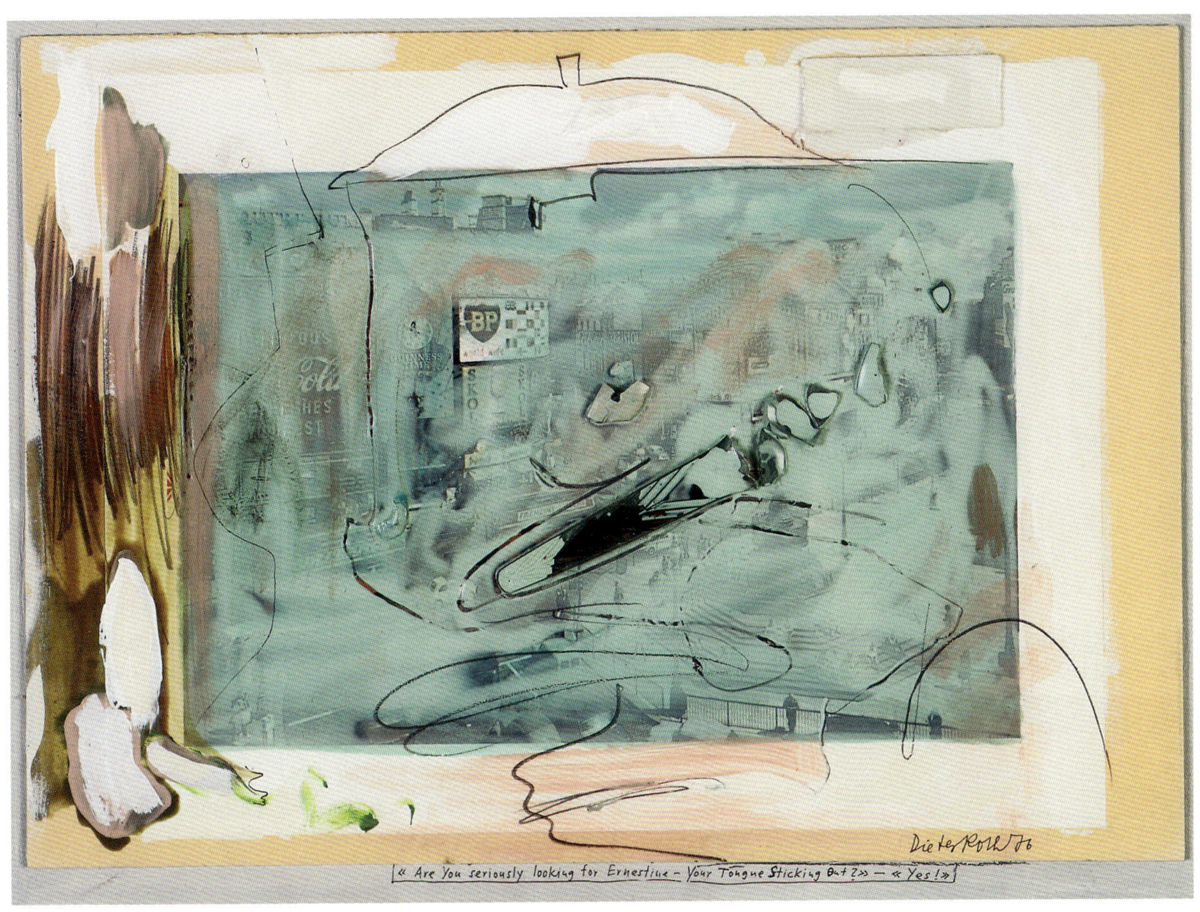
Dieter Roth 76
« Are You seriously looking for Ernestine – Your Tongue Sticking Out ?» – « Yes ! »

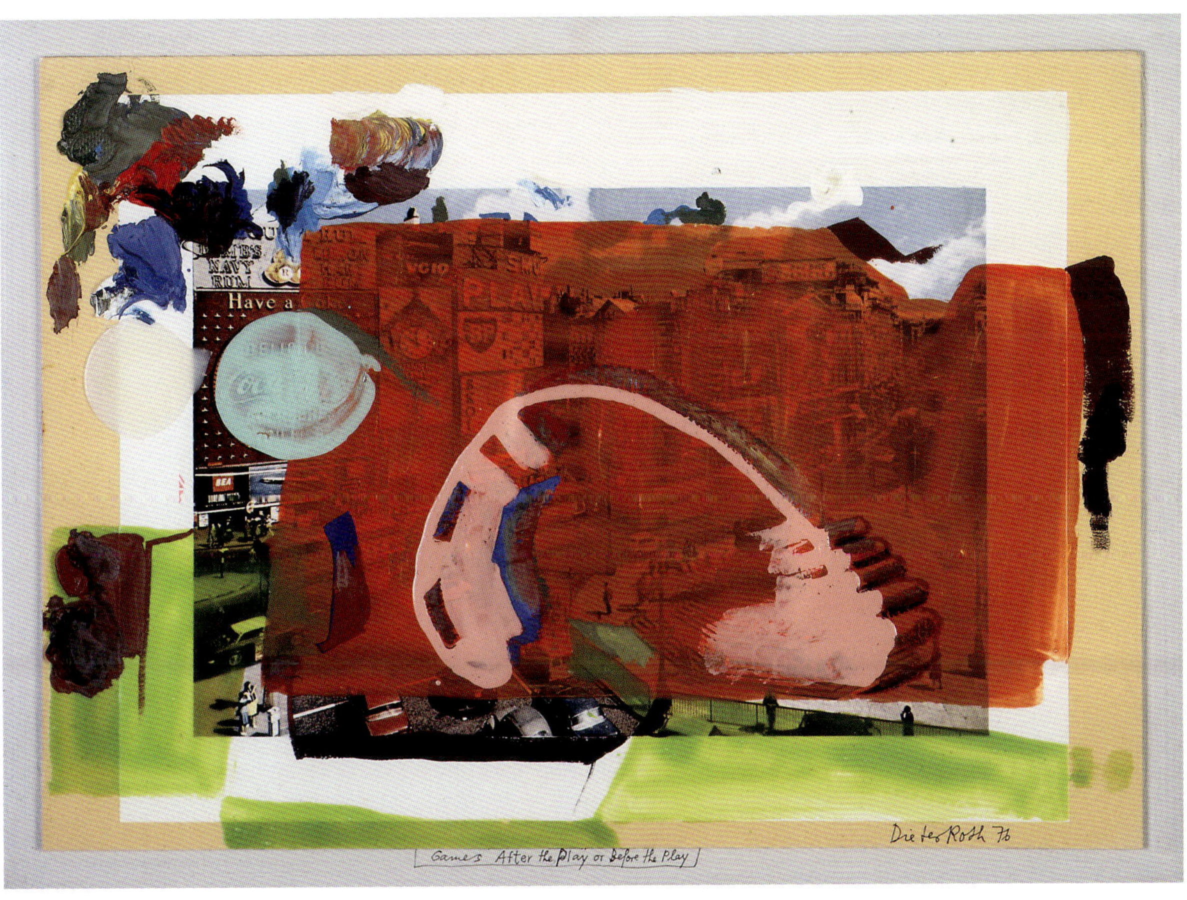
Dieter Roth 76
Games After the Play or Before the Play

94 Norval Morrisseau

Canada, Ojibwa, b. 1931

Storyteller of the Ages, 1970
Acrylic on canvas
50 × 58 in.
Gift, R. E. Mansfield Collection, 2003

> *I am a Shaman-artist. My paintings are also icons; that is to say, they are images which help focus on spiritual powers generated by traditional belief and wisdom. . . .*
>
> *Since the coming of the white man, we have fallen very low, forgetting our ancient legends and ancestral beliefs. The time has come for us all to write and to record the story of our people.*

The Ojibwa painter Norval Morrisseau is Canada's best-known Native artist. His work focuses on reclaiming and preserving his endangered Ojibwa heritage. He grew up in a period following decades of government-sponsored forced assimilation that had weakened ties between the Native generations and disrupted the passing of oral tradition. With a sense of urgency, Morrisseau, whose Native name is Copper Thunderbird, began to collect stories from northern Ontario. These tales became a primary source for his later art and appeared in his 1965 book *Legends of My People, the Great Ojibway.*

Morrisseau developed his immediately recognizable style as a means of visualizing storytelling and oral tradition. His art draws on ancient pictographs carved on rocks in the Great Lakes Woodland region and images that shamans of the Midewiwin (medicine) society incised on birchbark scrolls. Catholic sources also inform his iconography. His paintings have strong, black outlines enclosing planes of brilliant color that the artist views as having healing power.

A descendant of generations of shamans, Morrisseau considers himself a shaman-artist whose work draws inspiration from travels to what he calls the House of Invention. (In 1976, he joined the Eckankar religion, a mystical cult of soul travel.) In the present painting, Morrisseau's own features appear in the profile of the storyteller. This storyteller figure is also a fish, reflecting the shamanistic experience of self-transformation.

Morrisseau was born at Sandy Lake Reserve, near Thunder Lake, Ontario. He is largely a self-taught artist who began to paint when recovering from tuberculosis. His first solo exhibition, held in Toronto in 1962, was an instant success and inaugurated the Woodland school of painting, which features art by Morrisseau and his many followers. Morrisseau was elected to the Canadian Royal Academy of Art in 1970, the year he painted *Storyteller of the Ages.* He has received honorary doctorates and exhibited internationally. The National Gallery of Canada is currently organizing for 2006 a Morrisseau exhibition that will be the first retrospective the museum has ever accorded a Native artist.

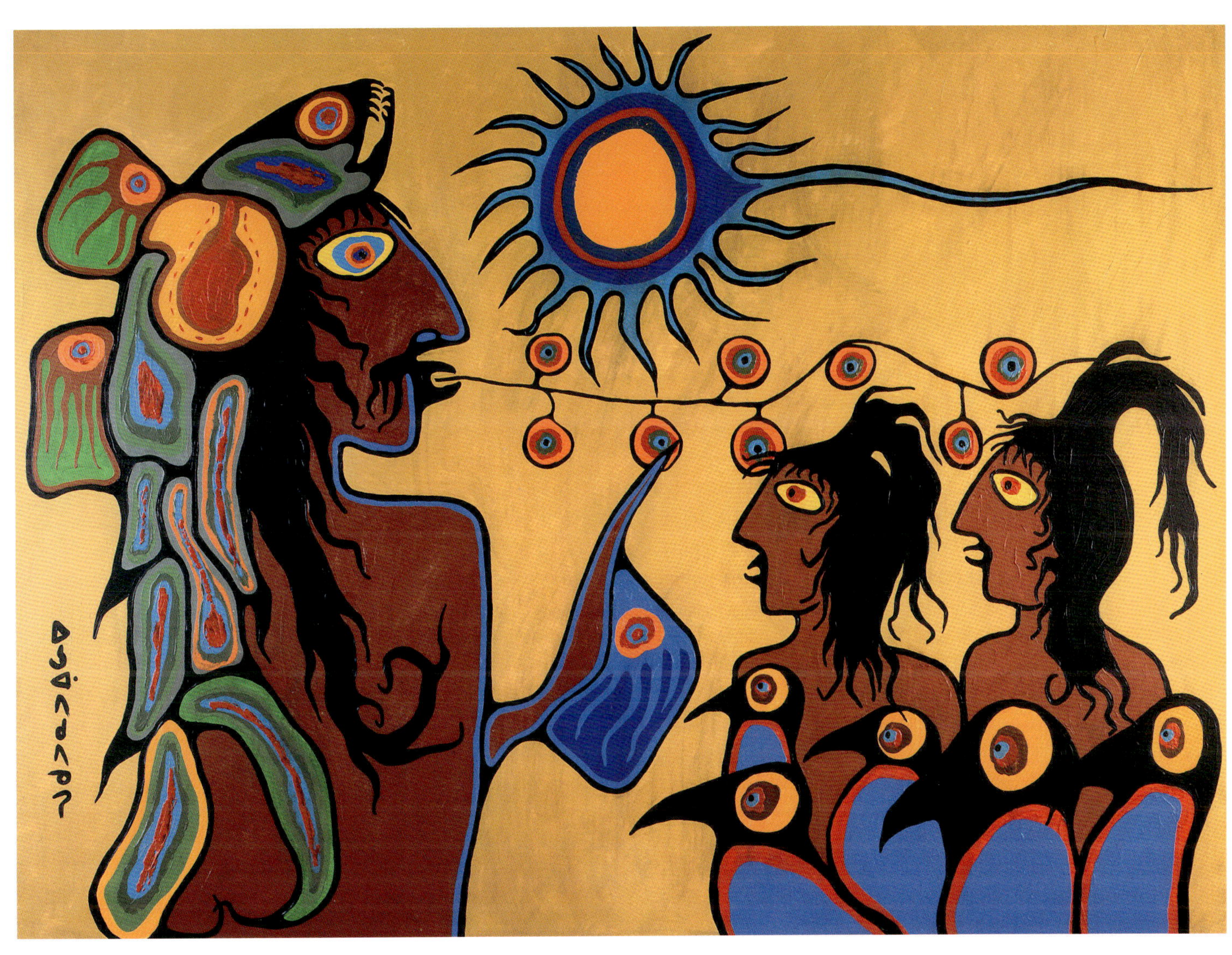

95 Fritz Scholder

U.S., b. 1937

Overexposed Indian, 1977
Acrylic on canvas
40 × 30 in.
Purchase, Richard H. and Adeline J. Fleischaker Collection, 1996

A major figure in contemporary American Indian art since the 1960s, Fritz Scholder was born in Breckenridge, Minnesota. His grandmother was from the Luiseño Indian tribe of southern California, although the artist does not label himself American Indian. His father was a school administrator for the U.S. Bureau of Indian Affairs, and the family moved frequently throughout the West and Midwest. In high school, Scholder studied art in South Dakota under the Sioux Modernist Oscar Howe, who had received a master of fine arts degree from the University of Oklahoma and who convinced Scholder to pursue a career in art. Scholder graduated with a bachelor of fine arts degree from California State University, Sacramento, and earned a master of fine arts degree from the University of Arizona in 1964. After Arizona, Scholder moved to Santa Fe where he taught at the Institute of American Indian Art until 1969.

Scholder first painted abstract works but received widespread recognition in 1967 when he began his figurative, irreverent, controversial Indians series, which challenged romantic Indian stereotypes while depicting the ironies and paradoxes of Indian life in the twentieth century. For instance, one well-known painting from the series portrays a buffalo dancer at rest who is eating an ice cream cone, and other works portray Indians cloaked in the American flag. Stylistically, the boldly colored paintings of the series, like Scholder's more recent work, hover between Abstract Expressionism and Pop Art. Scholder's paintings also show a debt to the expressionistic paintings of the British artist Francis Bacon. In both subject matter and style, the Indians series opened the door for contemporary American Indian art.

Overexposed Indian is from Scholder's Indians series. It shows a lone American Indian on horseback, seen from behind, in a bleak, snowy landscape under a cold blue sky. The Indian wears a brilliant, patterned shawl and holds a medicine staff that projects forward. (Medicine staffs are sticks decorated with various body parts of an animal; the staffs embody special powers for protection and healing.)

The title *Overexposed Indian* refers to the state of the Indian in the painting's wintry landscape; his medicine staff offers little protection. More generally, the title may refer to the overexposure and exploitation of American Indian culture by non-Indians.

In 1972, the Smithsonian Institution's American Art Museum mounted the exhibition "Two American Painters: Fritz Scholder and T.C. Cannon," which featured the work of Scholder and his talented former student, who died young in a car accident. Since the Smithsonian show, Scholder has exhibited worldwide and received numerous awards.

Scholder settled in Scottsdale, Arizona, in 1972. In addition to painting, the artist produces books, prints, photographs, collages, and sculpture. He served as a distinguished visiting artist at the University of Oklahoma in 2002. The museum owns nine works by Scholder.

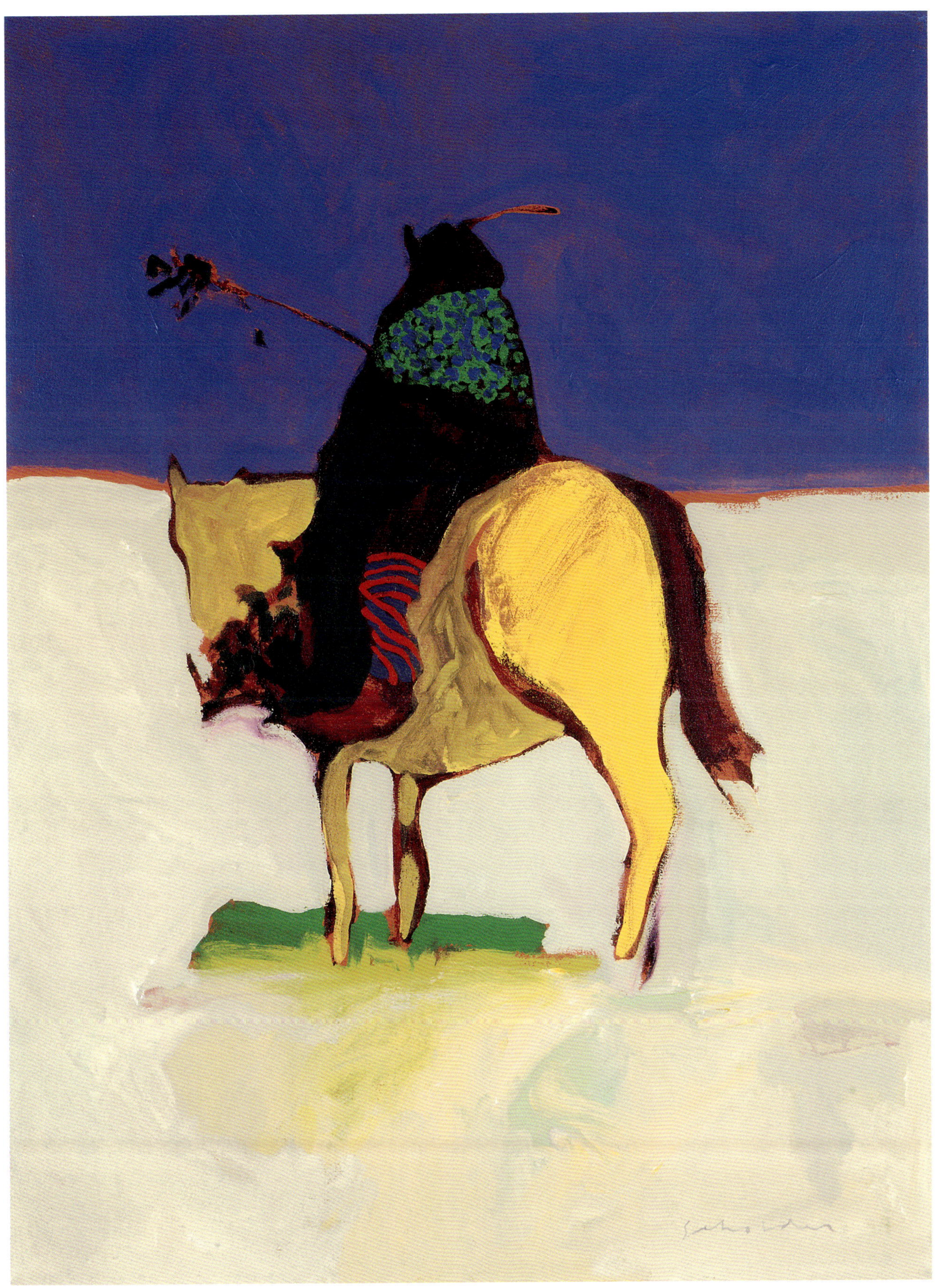

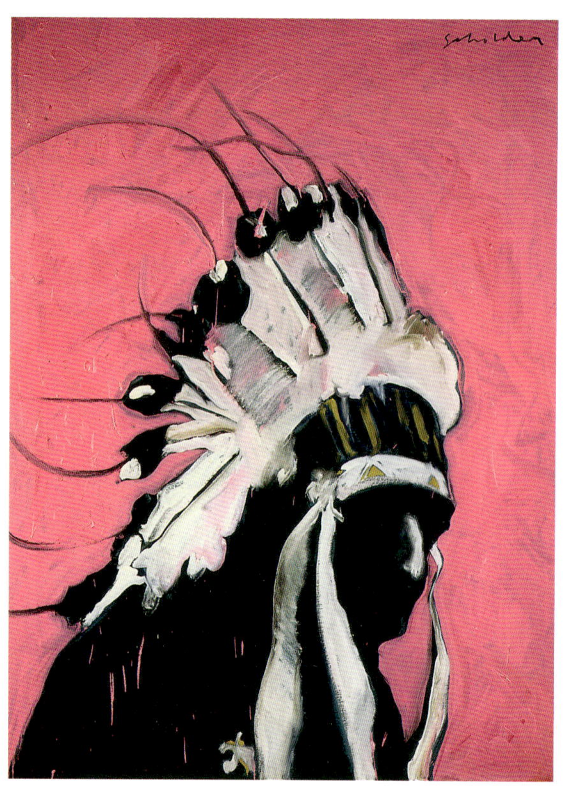

Fritz Scholder
U.S., b. 1937
American Indian, n.d., oil on canvas, 40 × 30 in. Purchase, Richard H. and Adeline J. Fleischaker Collection, 1996

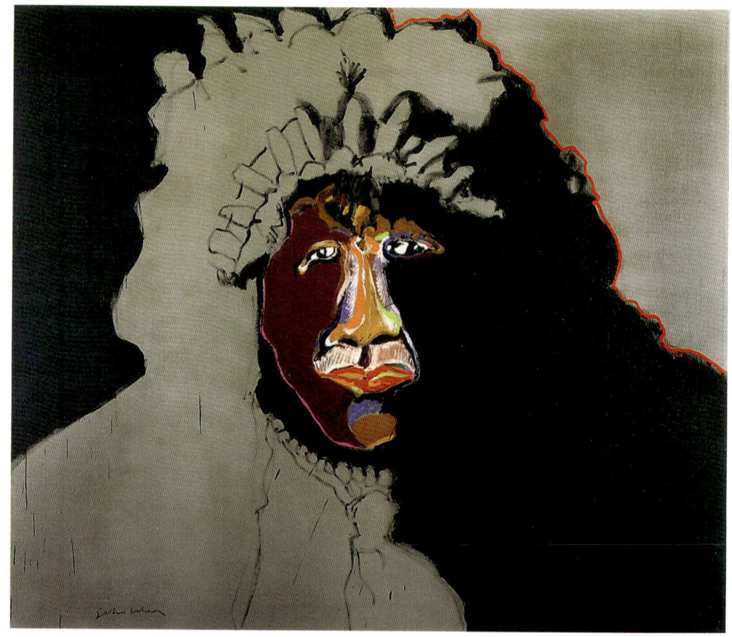

Fritz Scholder
U.S., b. 1937
Indian with Tear, n.d., acrylic on canvas, 68 × 80 in. Gift of Joanna Champlin, 1997

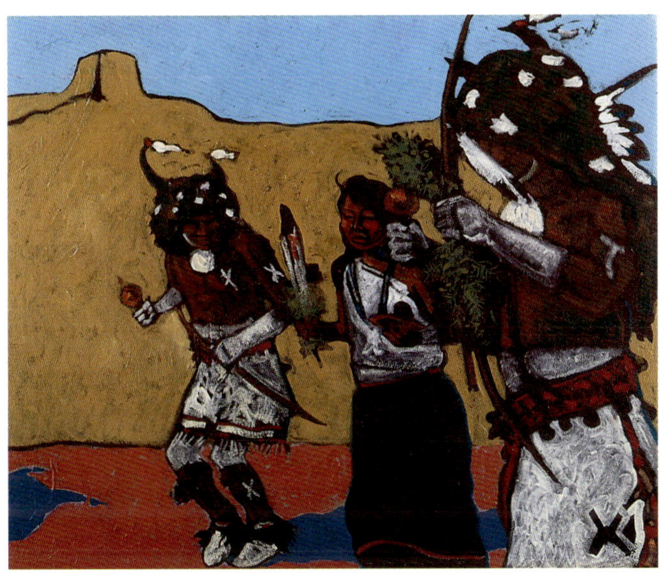

T. C. Cannon
U.S., Kiowa/Caddo, 1946–1978
Buffalo Dancers, n.d., oil on canvas,
20 × 24 in. Purchase, Richard H. and
Adeline J. Fleischaker Collection, 1996

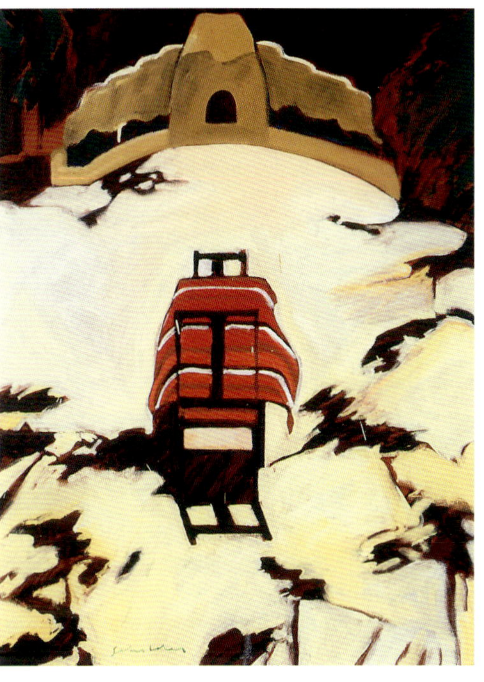

Fritz Scholder
U.S., b. 1937
Galisteo, Patio II, 1979, oil on canvas,
40 × 30 in. Purchase, Richard H. and
Adeline J. Fleischaker Collection, 1996

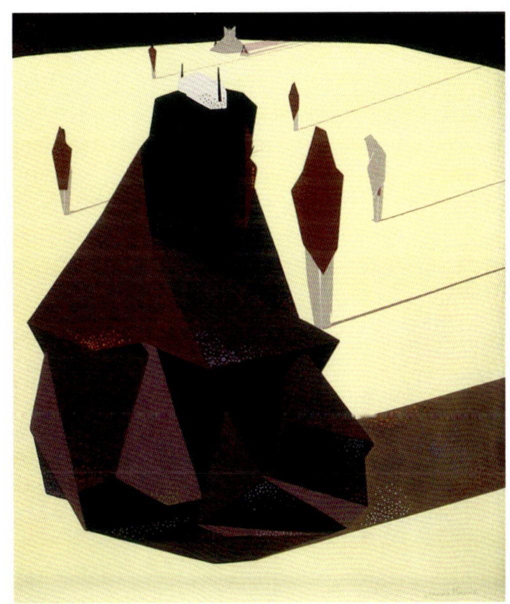

Oscar Howe
U.S., Yanktonai Sioux, 1915–1983
Woman Buffalo Dancer, n.d., tempera on
paper, 17½ × 15½ in. Gift of Gertrude
Phillips, 1978

96 Luis Jiménez

U.S., b. 1940

Mustang (Mesteño), 1997
Fiberglass
H. 8 ft.
Gift of Jerome M. and Wanda Otey Westheimer, 1998

Luis Jiménez's art celebrates and is inspired by his Chicano roots. In treating Hispanic themes, Jiménez addresses sterotypes head on. Both in medium and in subject matter, his work emphasizes popular culture and questions the nature of "high art." Jiménez typically uses fiberglass as his medium for sculpture, since he appreciates that fiberglass is a common material, used in the everyday world for cars, motorcycles, and surfboards. A more traditional sculpture material, such as marble, would separate the art from life, he maintains. He prefers his sculptures to be installed in outdoor public spaces in order for the art to be seen by as broad an audience as possible. With subjects and materials from daily life, Jiménez's works relate to Pop Art, but his art does not fit neatly into any category.

Jiménez grew up in El Paso, Texas. He received a bachelor of arts degree in art and architecture from the University of Texas at Austin in 1964, studied in Mexico City, and then moved to New York, where he became an assistant to the sculptor Seymour Lipton. In 1969, Jiménez created his first fiberglass sculpture. In the early 1970s, he returned to the Southwest, and he now lives in Hondo, New Mexico. He teaches at the University of Houston and has been a visiting artist at the Oklahoma Arts Institute.

Jiménez has received widespread national recognition. One of his fiberglass sculptures stands on Pennsylvania Avenue in Washington, D.C., as a signature work of the Smithsonian American Art Museum. The Denver International Airport has commissioned a large-scale, thirty-foot version of *Mustang*.

The artist modeled *Mustang* after his own Appaloosa stallion. Emblems around the base of the sculpture tell the story of the horse in North America. (A prehistoric species of horse became extinct in America; later, Europeans brought the horse to the United States from Mexico.) The emblems include horseshoes, Spanish and Texas spurs, barbed wire, a Mexican bit, arrowheads referring to American Indians using horses to hunt bison, and fossilized remains of the small, prehistoric horse ancestor that once roamed the Southwest. Yucca plants locate the mustang in the Southwest.

The fiberglass gives *Mustang* a glossy sheen. Since it can be painted, this medium also allows Jiménez to combine painting and sculpture. The artist often incorporates electric lights in his sculptures; in *Mustang*, the eyes are red light bulbs. When young, Jiménez had worked in his father's neon-sign shop—this perhaps sparked the artist's interest in such lighting.

Though contemporary, Jiménez's work looks back to masters from the past. In preparation for *Mustang*, the artist studied and sketched the depiction of horses in the sculptures of the Parthenon. Jiménez's work is often inspired by the seventeenth-century Baroque sculptor Gianlorenzo Bernini, and *Mustang*, like several other Jiménez sculptures, displays the fiery energy of the Baroque.

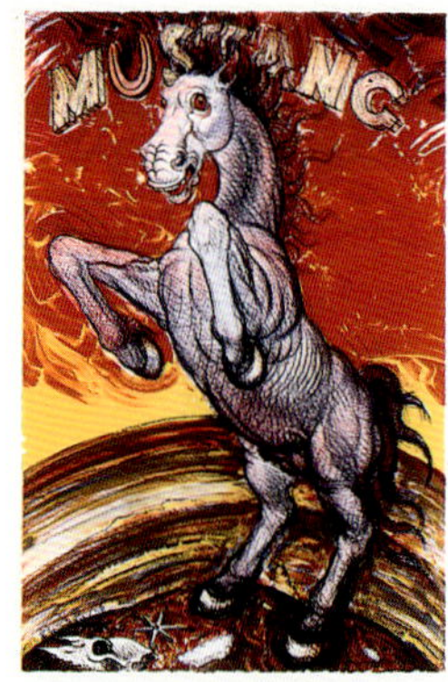

Luis Jiménez
U.S., b. 1940
Mustang, 1997, lithograph, edition: 48/50, 40¾ × 29¾ in. Fred Jones Jr. Museum of Art Association Purchase, 1999

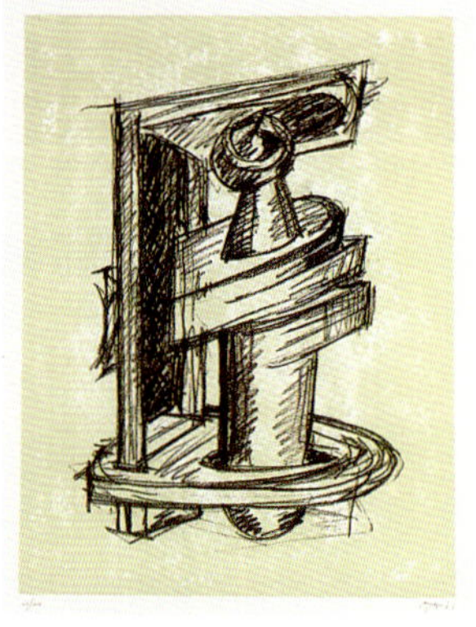

Seymour Lipton
U.S., 1903–1986
Study for Sculpture, 1969, lithograph, edition: 20/100, 22¼ × 16¾ in. Gift of Edward J. Safdie, 1981

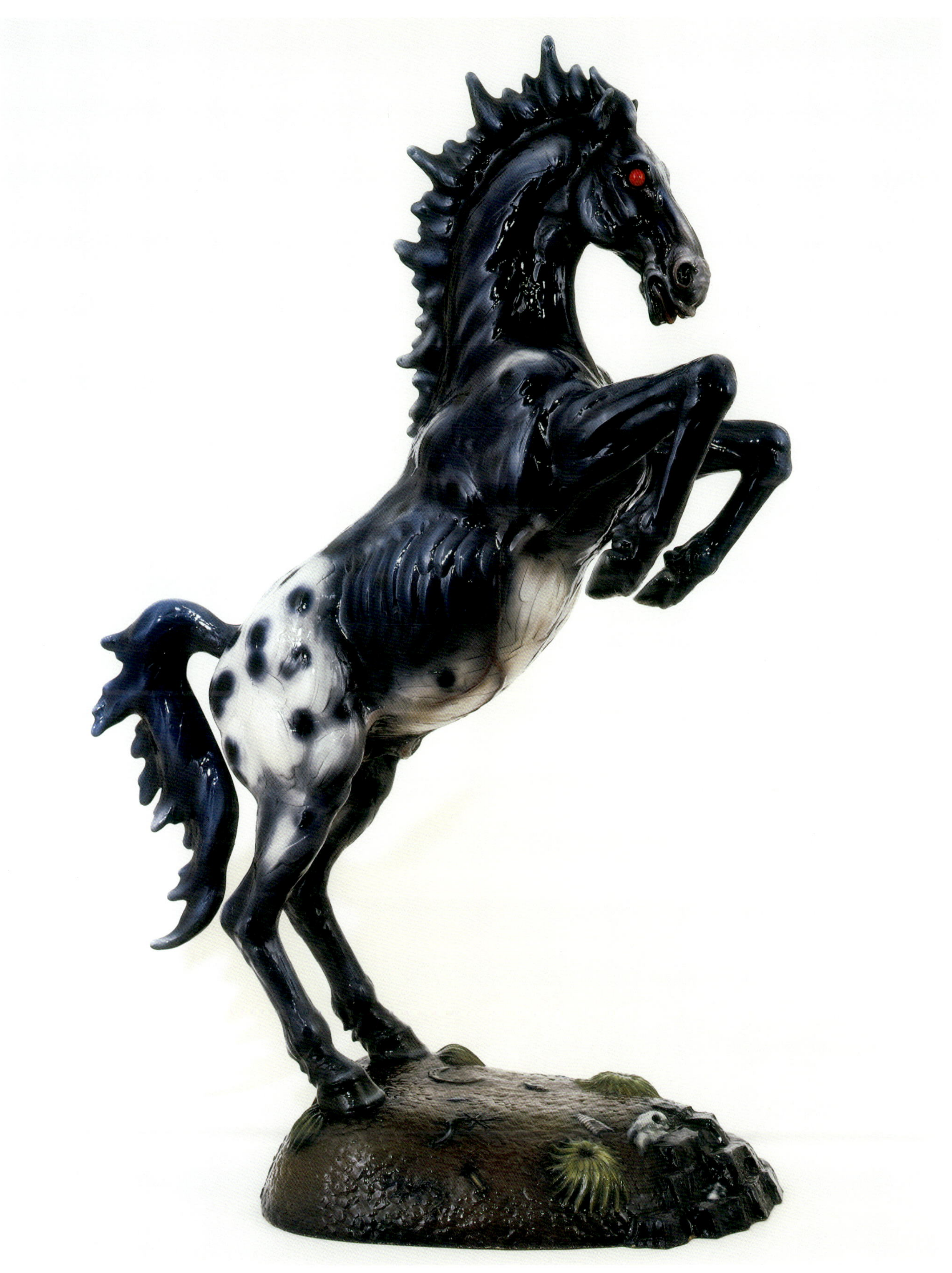

97 Jesús Moroles

U.S., b. 1950

Interlocking Triptych, 1993
Granite
H. 14 ft.
Gift of the Jerome Westheimer Family, 1994

Jesús Moroles is a Mexican American sculptor who was born in Corpus Christi, Texas, and grew up in Dallas. Moroles was always interested in art and already in eighth grade exhibited watercolors. He served in the air force during the Vietnam War and then studied art at North Texas State University in Denton, from which he graduated in 1978. As an undergraduate, he began working in granite and met the sculptor Luis Jiménez (see cat. no. 96), who was a visiting artist at the school. Moroles subsequently spent a year working as an apprentice in Jiménez's studio, followed by a year in Pietrasanta, Italy, near the Carrara quarries, where Michelangelo had selected his marble during the Renaissance.

In the Carrara quarries, Moroles observed footsteps worn into the marble over generations; this led him to state that he wanted his art to show man and nature working in unison. However, Moroles decided that instead of marble, he preferred working with granite, a much tougher, harder stone.

In 1989, Moroles moved to Rockport, Texas, near Corpus Christi, and established a studio for cutting stone with diamond-edged electric saws. The studio eventually employed many people, including several members of the artist's family. In 1996, the sculptor founded the Moroles Cultural Center in Cerrillos, New Mexico. More recently, he opened an additional studio in Barcelona, Spain.

Moroles received early recognition. During the 1980s, he made large-scale works such as a twenty-two-foot sculpture fountain for the Albuquerque Museum of Art; an installation of forty-five sculptural elements and fountains for the Birmingham Botanical Gardens; and a sculpture for a plaza in Manhattan on Fifty-third Street, across from the Museum of Modern Art.

The Fred Jones Jr. Museum of Art commissioned *Interlocking Triptych.* For the sculpture, Moroles selected stone from Granite, Oklahoma. The triptych (a three-part work of art) features both rough stone and smooth, polished stone in a harmonious interwoven form that suggests an embrace. The massive outdoor sculpture recalls ancient monuments of the Maya and Aztec cultures.

Moroles visits quarries all over the world to select stone, but he does not visualize the sculpture until he is working the stone in his studio. Echoing Michelangelo, Moroles claims that each stone has its own nature, and that the job of the sculptor is to release what the stone wants to be.

In addition to Michelangelo, artists who have inspired Moroles include the Modernists Constantin Brancusi, with his emphasis on simplicity, and Isamu Noguchi, in his search for *shibui,* the austere, understated beauty that the Japanese regard as the aesthetic ideal.

Other prominent Texan sculptors represented in the museum's collection include Luis Jiménez and James Surls.

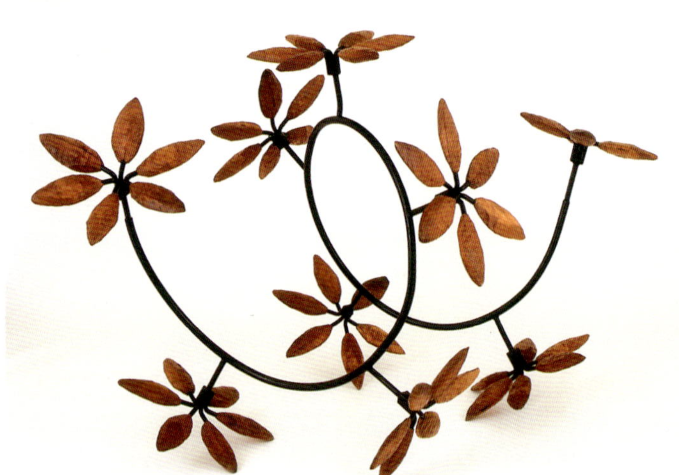

James Surls
U.S., b. 1943
Walking Series: 3-6-8, 1986, wood (walnut) and steel, 50 × 84 × 56 in. Gift of Jack Bryan and Judith Warkentin Bryan, 1994

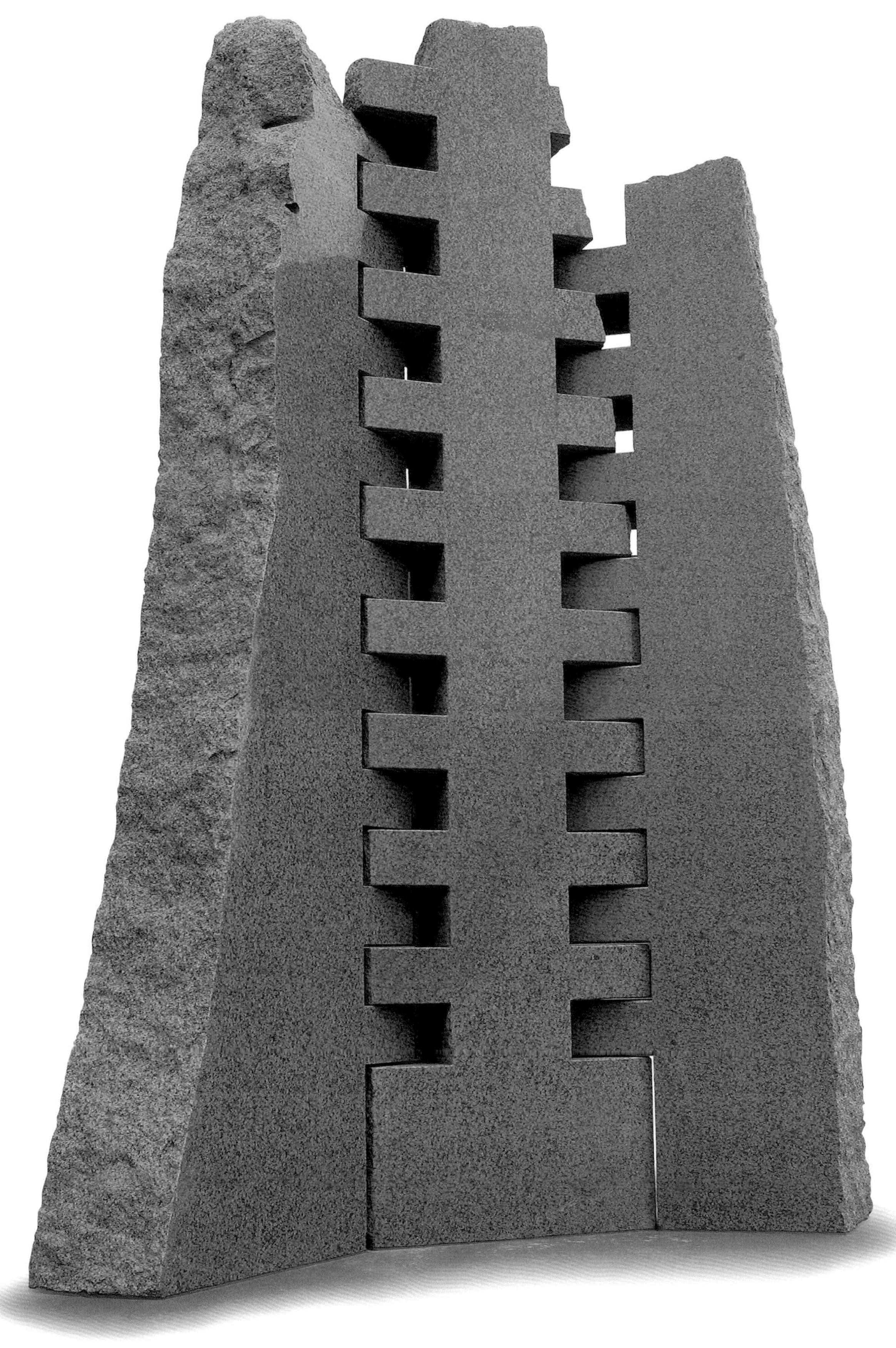

98 Joe Andoe

U.S., b. 1955

Untitled, 1994
Oil on canvas
70 × 84 in.
Gift of the artist, 1994

Donald Judd's definition of American art has been aptly applied to the paintings of Joe Andoe: "American art was born not out of a struggle against European art, but rather out of the vastness and uninterrupted space of the American landscape." Andoe's works often depict subjects inspired by Oklahoma. His serene, wistful paintings feature horses, deer, dogs, flowers, buffaloes, and landscapes with wide horizons.

A typical Andoe painting, *Untitled* presents a traditional subject matter in a modern style. The horse—depicted for centuries by cultures worldwide—appears here on a monochromatic canvas. Andoe has commented on his fondness for horses: "With a horse, you have a generic, beautiful instrument to elaborate on. Of all the images I use, I rarely paint anything manmade. I like the idea of timelessness and economy." In *Untitled,* the horse stands quietly in a painting of Minimalist austerity, but whereas the Minimalists tried to hide the hand and presence of the artist, Andoe inscribes his signature as a major formal component of the painting's composition.

Andoe is known for his unusual technique. He primes a canvas with white gesso and then covers the canvas with a thick layer of paint of a single color, such as black, brown, or red. Before the paint dries, he uses a rag to wipe it away, in order to create the image. He sometimes adds paint with his fingers, but never uses a brush. His distinctive technique requires him to work quickly, because the picture must be completed before the paint dries. The resulting image is in effect created out of the light emanating from the white gesso beneath the painted surface. Most painting is additive—the artist adds layers of paint to a canvas; Andoe's style, in which the image is "carved" out of the paint, is akin to sculpture.

Born in Tulsa, Oklahoma, Andoe first enrolled as an agricultural business major at Tulsa Junior College, and later studied art under Eugene Bavinger at the University of Oklahoma, where he received a bachelor of fine arts degree in 1979 and a master of fine arts degree in 1981. In 1983, he moved to New York, where he struggled to make ends meet. He gave up painting for a while, but in November 1987, Thomas Ammann, a prominent Swiss dealer and collector, saw Andoe's work in the back room of a gallery and was greatly impressed. Ammann then visited the artist's studio and bought nine works, making Andoe an overnight success. Andoe has since had numerous international solo shows. His paintings hang in museums such as the Metropolitan Museum of Art and the Museum of Modern Art in New York.

Of his art, Andoe has said: "I want these paintings to be like the images we perceive on the backs of our eyelids . . . which means I want them to be something we feel as well as see."

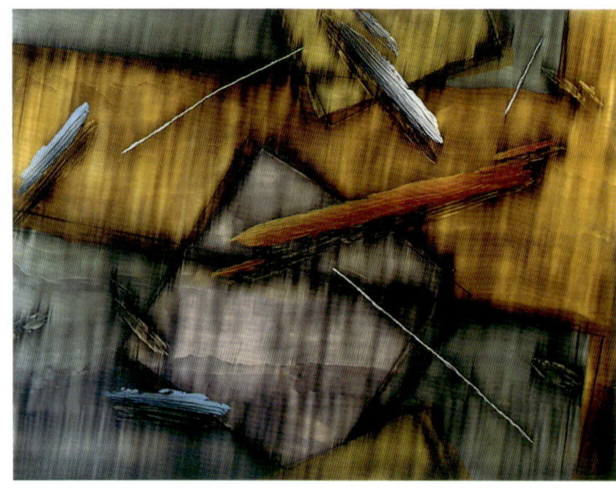

Eugene Bavinger
U.S., 1919–1997
Intermediate Force, 1981, acrylic on canvas, 54 × 72 in. Gift of Nancy Bavinger, 1998

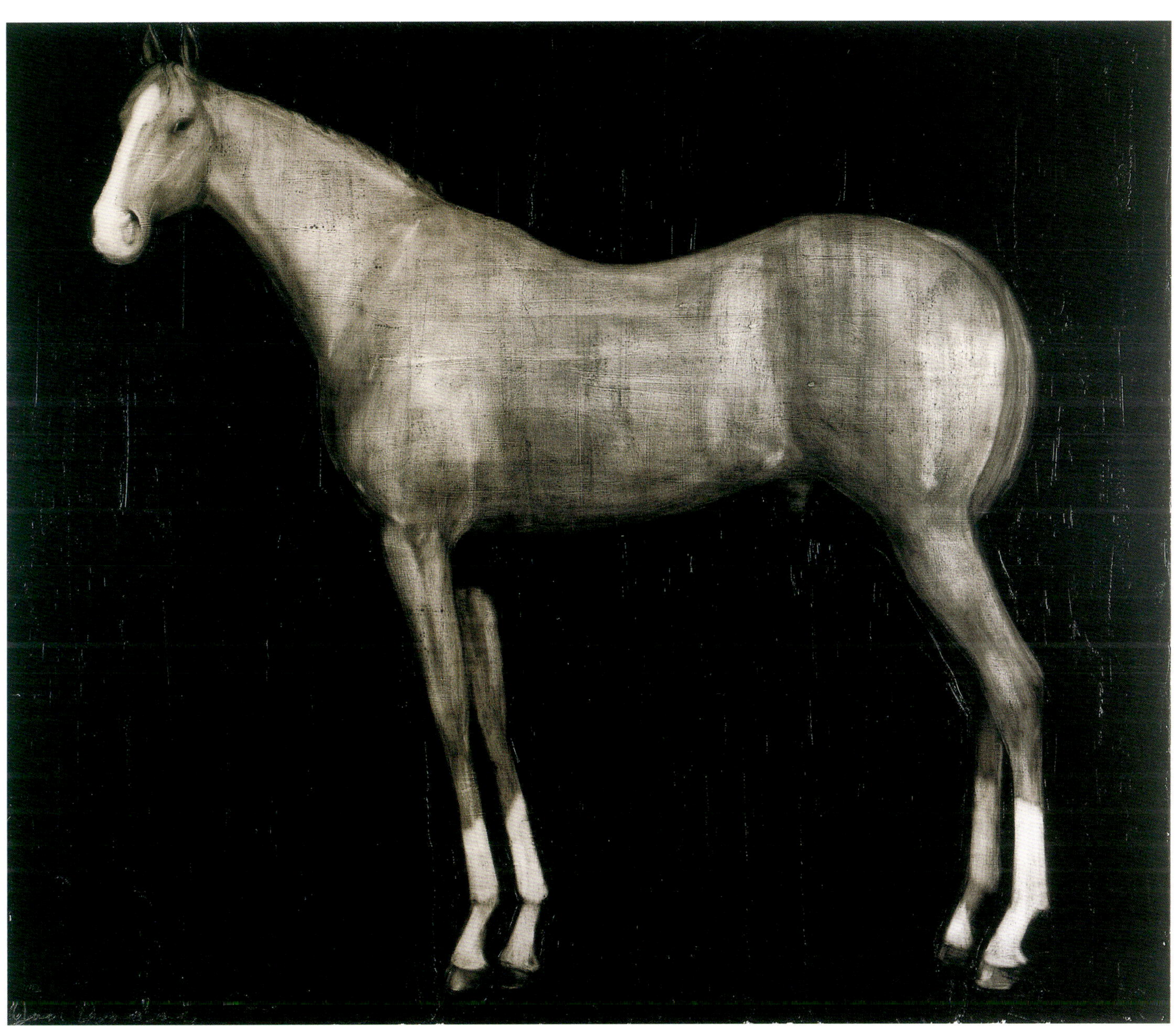

99 Ed Paschke and $(art)^n$ Laboratory

(Paschke) U.S., b. 1939

No Fumare, Per Favore (No Smoking, Please), 1997
Vintage PHSCologram
Edition: Artist's Proof, edition of 6
40½ × 30½ × 3½ in.
Gift, Ellen and Richard L. Sandor Collection, 2000

Ed Paschke was born in Chicago, the son of an artist, and trained at the School of the Art Institute of Chicago. In the 1960s, Paschke was associated with a group of young artists and students at the Art Institute who became known as the Chicago Imagists. They used a polished painting technique, yet displayed the rawness of Outsider Art (art by self-taught artists outside society's mainstream, including folk art and the art of the insane). The Chicago Imagists often derived their subject matter from the mass media. Paschke's art dealt with issues such as fame, notoriety, and the lurid. (The Fred Jones Jr. Museum's other works by Chicago Imagists include a painting by Roger Brown.)

$(art)^n$ Laboratory is a "marriage of art and science," according to its founder and director, Ellen Sandor, an Art Institute of Chicago–trained sculptor. Housed at the Northwestern University Research Park, the Laboratory specializes in three-dimensional, virtual reality works called PHSColograms, which incorporate aspects of painting, photography, sculpture, film, and computer graphics. Sandor and teammates Stephan Meyers and Janine Fron invited Paschke to work with them on the present image.

No Fumare, Per Favore, which means "No smoking, please" in Italian, was Paschke's first collaboration with the Laboratory. Based on a 1979 painting by Paschke, *No Fumare, Per Favore* began as an artwork that Paschke created on a computer by using an electronic tablet. Every stroke that the artist made with a stylus on the tablet appeared on the computer screen.

The artwork created on the computer generated the PHSCologram, a large-scale film transparency that was then mounted in a light box. The PHSCologram comprises sixty-five separate images. These images, superimposed on one another, are digital photographs of the computer artwork taken from slightly different points of view. Only one image filters to the eye from any one perspective, but as the viewer of the PHSCologram moves, additional digital images become visible, resulting in the illusion of depth and motion.

Ed Paschke has said about PHSColograms: "The other side of the painter's picture plane has never been this alive—this is the most exciting form of collaboration . . . you have a synthesis of ideas and technology."

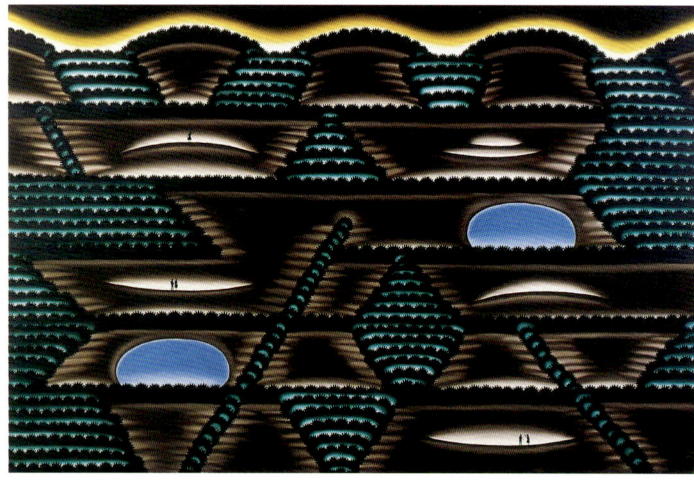

Roger Brown
U.S., 1941–1997
Fishing in a Land, Abstract, 1976, acrylic on canvas, 48 × 72 in. Gift of the Ellen and Richard L. Sandor Collection, 2000

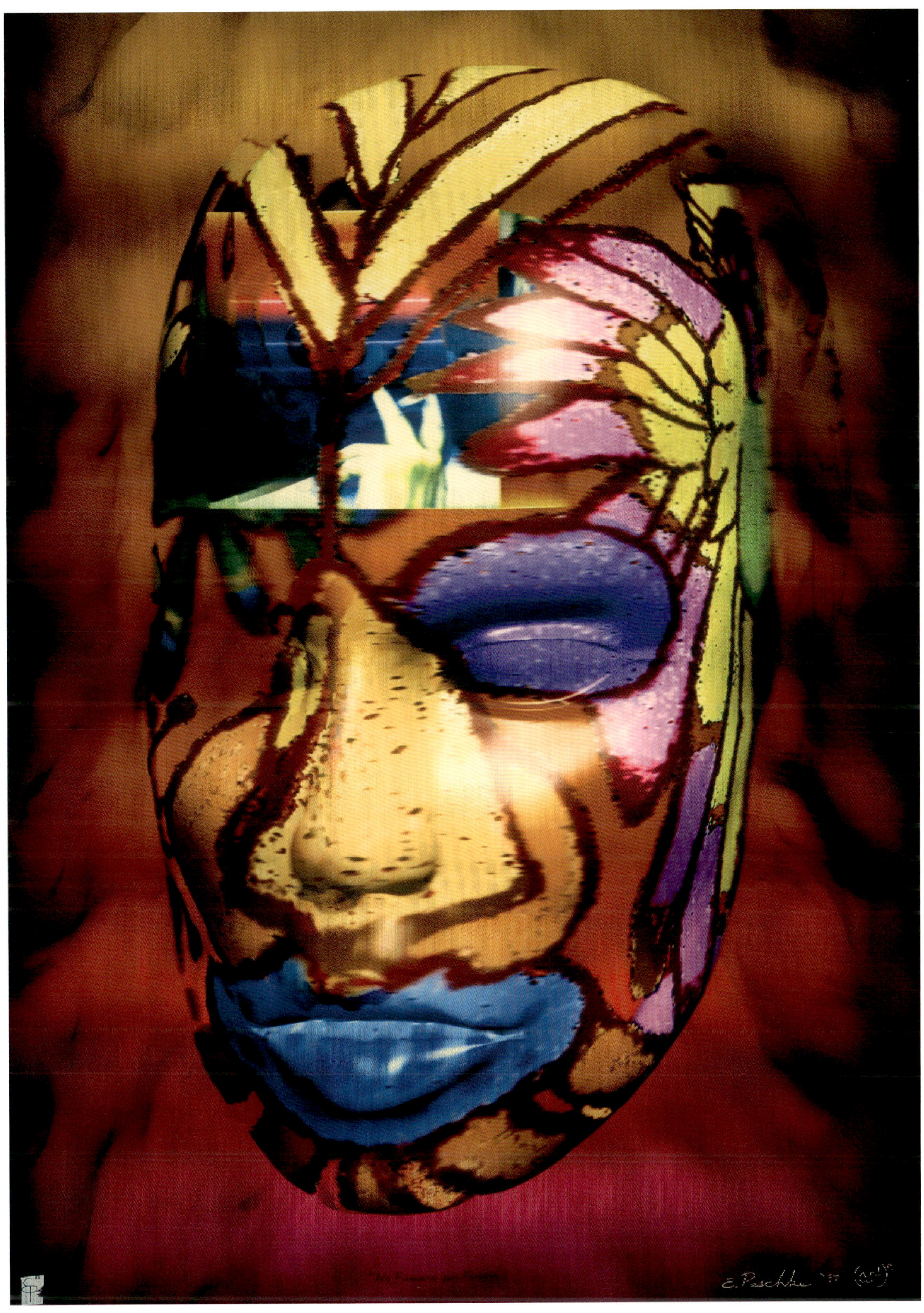
E. Paschke '97

100 Kiki Smith

U.S., b. Germany, 1954

Las Animas, 1997
Photogravure
Edition: 17/47
60 × 49¼ in.
Gift of Jerome M. and Wanda Otey Westheimer, 1999

Kiki Smith is best known for works that focus on the human—especially female—body in a manner that is clinical yet spiritual. She views the body as fragmented, imperfect, and subject to death and decay but still beautiful and powerful.

Smith was born in Nuremberg, Germany, to American parents—sculptor Tony Smith and the actress and opera singer Jane Lawrence. Kiki Smith grew up in New Jersey, surrounded by artists who gathered at her home. Between 1974 and 1975, she attended the Hartford Art School, where she focused on crafts. She decided to become an artist in 1976. In 1979–80, using *Gray's Anatomy* as a reference, she created her first works dealing with the body. She fortified her knowledge of anatomy by working as an emergency medical technician in 1985. Since her first solo show at a gallery in New York in 1988, she has received worldwide acclaim and exhibited at major institutions, such as New York's Museum of Modern Art.

Smith's Catholic roots play an important role in her art. The self-portrait *Las Animas* suggests a reliquary, what Smith has called a "chop shop of bodies," in which meaning and special powers are attributed to the body parts of saints. As a child, she was fascinated by the lives of the saints, including her namesake, St. Chiara—"Kiki" is a nickname. St. Chiara took a vow of poverty and cut off her hair as a sign of devotion. Hair, associated in our culture with both attraction and repulsion, features prominently in several Smith prints, including *Las Animas*.

A guiding principle throughout Smith's art is St. Thomas Aquinas's notion that the human soul is united with the body to constitute human life. Smith, who believes that body and soul have been separated in the modern world, seeks in her art to mend the division. She indirectly alludes to Aquinas in the title of the present self-portrait, *Las Animas,* meaning "the souls" in Spanish.

Smith has spoken about being obsessed with the notion of Frankenstein's monster, of a body being pieced together from disparate parts—a concept made real in our age of organ transplants. She likens the fragmentation of Frankenstein's monster to the ruptures of modern life, which were expressed in Cubist art nearly a century ago. Like Frankenstein with his monster, Smith seeks in her art to hold the pieces together; nevertheless, she states that she wants to let the sutures show. Smith claims that Frankenstein's monster also holds the promise of revivification and resurrection.

Illness and death have long been a presence in the artist's life. Her sister, Bebe, died of AIDS in 1988, and throughout Smith's childhood, her father was ill, several times close to dying. Her father called Smith a banshee, which in Gaelic folklore is a female spirit who foretold death in the family by wailing across the moors. The central images of Smith in *Las Animas* suggest a banshee. (These central images also bring to mind shamanistic ecstasy, through which a person becomes one with the universe.) Tony Smith died in 1980; to come to terms with his death, Kiki created *Hand in Jar,* a sculpture that suspends a found latex hand in an algae-filled jar of water. The disembodied hands in *Las Animas* recall this seminal work.

Smith often anthropomorphizes animals and gives humans animal attributes. In addition to a shaman and a banshee, Smith resembles a wild animal in the central images of *Las Animas*.

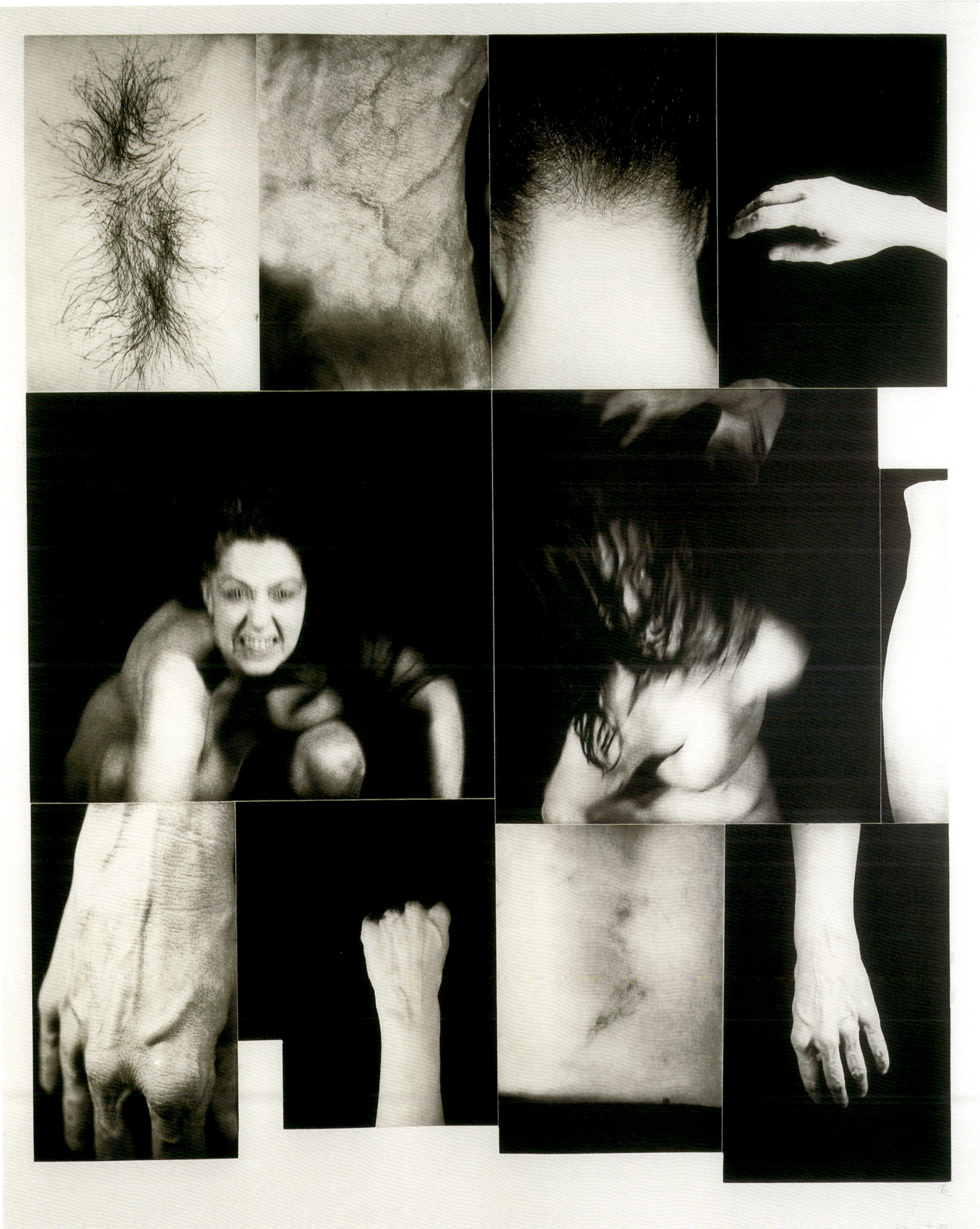

101 Radcliffe Bailey

U.S., b. 1968

Destination Unknown, 1999
Acrylic, photograph, oil stick, spray paint, resin, and collage on paper
80½ × 60 in.
Gift of Nanci and Stephen Chazen/Unus Foundation in celebration of the diversity, spirit, and vision of the University of Oklahoma, 2002

Radcliffe Bailey addresses African American history in works created from layers of paint, words, collage, and photographs. He buries some images under others, like lost memories, thus producing a historical web. Commenting on his creative process, Bailey has said: "By weaving together aesthetics derived from the Congo, Nigeria . . . the Caribbean, and the African American roots culture, I attempt . . . visual and spiritual exploration. I would draw comparisons to a jazz musician's search for a certain sound, riff, or rhythm, through the acts of improvisation."

Often, Bailey will invite jazz musicians into his studio to perform while he is painting so that they can "improvise" together. In drawing inspiration from jazz, the artist is not unlike others in this catalogue —for example, Romare Bearden (cat. no. 75), Alan Davie (cat. no. 87), Stuart Davis (cat. no. 71), and Larry Rivers (cat. no. 88). Bailey has based many paintings on specific jazz masters, such as Charles Mingus or Thelonius Monk, but he credits as having the most influence on his work another great improviser of modern jazz—Sun Ra.

Bailey has said:

> *I keep returning to musicians like Sun Ra because he would play from many different periods. He would fuse music together in such a way where you could not read the particular parts—the past became a music of today or tomorrow.*

According to Bailey, Sun Ra

> *fuses different sounds from different time periods . . . with different African instruments. I look at him as a big influence, especially how he moved, and his attitude toward space.*

Sun Ra (1914–1993), a "free jazz" musician, was born in Birmingham, Alabama, but insisted that he was an extraterrestrial from the planet Saturn. He claimed that he and his band, the Intergalactic Research Arkestra, were on a spiritual quest through their music to bring positive energy to the universe.

Destination Unknown references Sun Ra in several collaged photographs of dark skies brightened by bursts of light nebulae. The name of the planet Venus in the painting's upper left also recalls the "intergalactic" Sun Ra. Venus, of course, is the planet of love, so the name could also refer to women and perhaps even to Africa. The inscription "Saturn" points directly to Sun Ra, and the shape on which "Saturn" is inscribed resembles both a tobacco leaf, recalling plantations on which African Americans worked, and a paddle for a boat, alluding to journeys—perhaps an escape of a slave by rowboat, or possibly the Middle Passage from Africa to the New World.

For Bailey, the journey is important—the journey through time, life, and history. The name *Destination Unknown* is telling, as are the railroad tracks that crisscross the painting. The tracks and unknown destination could refer to the Middle Passage, to the "underground railroad" that led the slaves to freedom, to the African American Great Migration north, or to the Bailey family's move back to the South in 1973. The tracks could also be an homage to Bailey's father, a train engineer.

Radcliffe Bailey inherited from his grandmother around four hundred photographs and tintypes from a family album. He often incorporates in his works these pictures of relatives or other vintage photographs and tintypes of African Americans. He usually selects the photograph near the end of the painting process, after he has

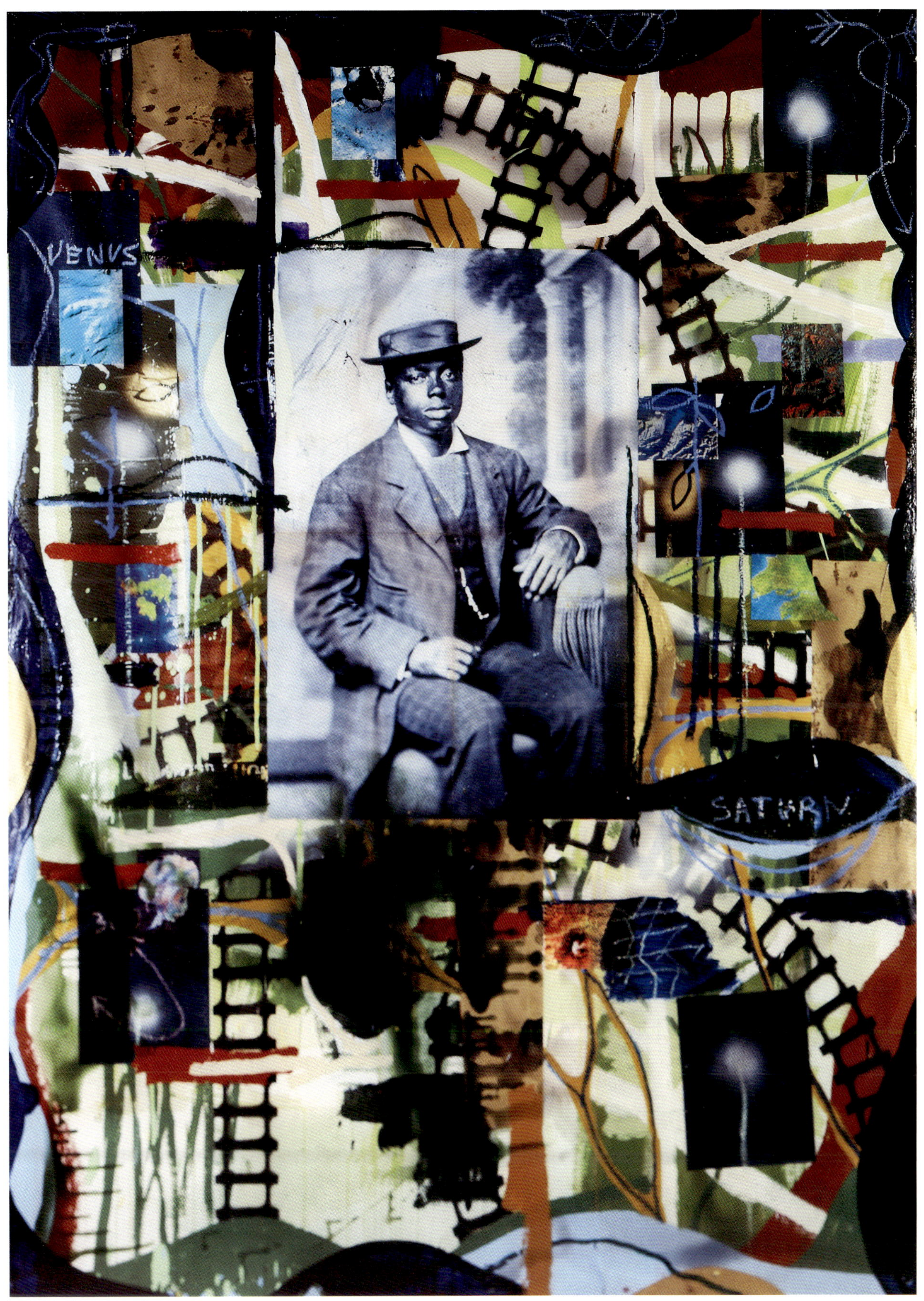
VENUS
SATURN

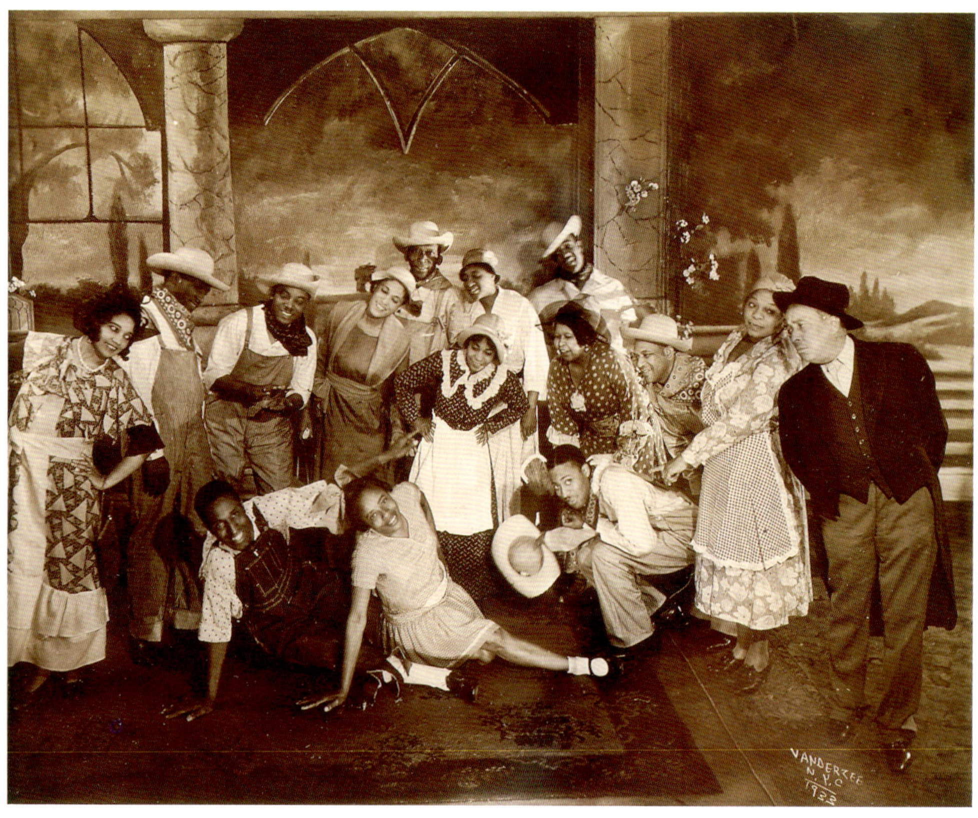

James Van Der Zee
U.S., 1886–1983
Dress Rehearsal I, 1928, sepia tone print,
8 × 9¾ in. Gift, Ellen and Richard L. Sandor
Collection in honor of Molly Shi Boren, 1999

applied layer upon layer of images. In *Destination Unknown,* the photograph is a reproduction of a nineteenth-century tintype, and it shows a figure sitting in front of a studio backdrop painted with classical columns, which allude to Western, white culture.

With its iconlike photograph placed at the center of the composition, Bailey's painting recalls altarpieces. *Destination Unknown* is covered in resin and sprinkled with glitter, which gives the surface a glistening appearance that changes with the light and reinforces the shrinelike quality.

Bailey was born in Bridgeton, a rural town in New Jersey. His family moved south to Atlanta in 1973, in reverse of the typical pattern of African American migration from the South to the North. He earned a bachelor of fine arts degree in 1991 from the Atlanta College of Art and has received much acclaim since. Among the artists he recognizes as having influenced him are the African Americans Romare Bearden, who also used collage in his work, and the photographer James Van Der Zee.

Bailey has called himself "the person who tells the story"—the story of his family, his race, and his humanity. He has said:

> *I . . . believe that the ancestors dance in us daily. They dance and sing and whisper, hoping that we will hear them, and see them and dream them back into relevant being. It is my belief that all true artists reach a point when their art becomes . . . a ritual of healing and transcendence.*

Notes

36 "They are impressionists in the sense": Ruth Berson, *The New Painting: Impressionism 1874–1886. Documentation. Volume I. Reviews.* (San Francisco: Fine Arts Museum, 1996), p. 17.

40 "the dancer has been for me no more than a pretext": Our translation, from the quotation in Ambroise Vollard, *Degas (1834–1917)* (Paris: Les Editions G. Crés et Cie, 1924), pp. 109–10.

46 "that he could have taught stones": As quoted in John Rewald, *The History of Impressionism,* rev. ed. (New York: Museum of Modern Art, 1961), p. 406.

46 "sensations": As quoted in Joachim Pissarro, *Camille Pissarro* (New York: Harry N. Abrams, 1993), p. 16.

49 "To seek a modern synthesis of methods": As quoted in Ralph E. Shikes and Paula Harper, *Pissarro: His Life and Work* (New York: Horizon Press, 1980), p. 223.

50 "painter of apples": As quoted in Françoise Cachin et al., *Cézanne* (Philadelphia: Philadelphia Museum of Art, 1996), p. 35.

54 "The likeness was so marked": As quoted in Archibald Standish Hartrick, *A Painter's Pilgrimage through Fifty Years* (Cambridge, England: The University Press, 1939), pp. 50–51.

56 "made a foolish mistake": *The Complete Letters of Vincent van Gogh* (Boston: New York Graphic Society, 1978), vol. 2: 540.

56 "very nervous": Ibid., vol. 2: 547.

56 "How often I think of Reid": Ibid., vol. 3: 188.

60 "something solid and enduring": As quoted in Lionello Venturi, *Cézanne* (New York: Rizzoli, 1978), p. 118.

68 "a corner of nature seen through a temperament": Emile Zola, *Salons* (Geneva: E. Droz, 1959), p. 73.

68 "the adventures of the optic nerve": Bonnard's diary entry for February 17, 1934, as quoted in Sasha M. Newman, ed., *Bonnard: The Late Paintings* (New York: Thames and Hudson, 1984), p. 29.

70 "Around 1905–1906, I was painting": As quoted in Dora Perez-Tibi, *Dufy* (New York: Harry N. Abrams, 1989), pp. 22–23.

76 "What I dream of is an art of balance": As quoted in Jack D. Flam, *Matisse on Art* (London: Phaidon Press Limited, 1973), p. 38.

104 "struck an artistic bonanza": As quoted in Denny Carter, *Henry Farny* (New York: Watson-Guptill Publications, 1978), p. 21.

104 "[Farny] draws Indians": Ibid., p. 21.

104 "The plains, the buttes": Ibid., p. 21.

108 "My entire horizon had now been revamped": As quoted in June DuBois, *W. R. Leigh* (Kansas City: The Lowell Press, 1977), p. 56.

110 "I was always interested": As quoted in Patricia Jane Broder, *Taos: A Painter's Dream* (Boston: New York Graphic Society, 1980), p. 38.

114 "At four p.m. on the third of September": As quoted in Laura M. Bickerstaff, *Pioneer Artists of Taos,* rev. ed. (Denver: Old West Publishing Company, 1983), pp. 30–31.

118 "an old Apache nearly ninety": As quoted in ibid., p. 56.

118 "meaning 'less two'": Phillips letter to Blumenschein, in Julie Schimmel and Robert Rankin White, *Bert Geer and The Taos Art Colony* (Albuquerque: University of New Mexico Press, 1994), p. 299.

120 "became infected with the Taos germ": As quoted in Bickerstaff, *Pioneer Artists,* p. 87.

120 "a distinctive art, something definitely American": As quoted in ibid., p. 98.

125 Source for Virginia Couse Leavitt's statement: Virginia Couse Leavitt, *Eanger Irving Couse: Image Maker for America* (Albuquerque: The Albuquerque Museum, 1991), p. 166.

126 "The west has passed": As quoted in Bickerstaff, *Pioneer Artists,* pp. 106–7.

126 "[Taos was] remote from commercialism": As quoted in Dean A. Porter, Teresa Hayes Ebie, and Suzan Campbell, *Taos Artists and Their Patrons 1898–1950* (Notre Dame, Ind.: The Snite Museum of Art, University of Notre Dame, 1999), pp. 43–44.

130 "God's country!" As quoted in Broder, *Taos: A Painter's Dream,* p. 212.

130 "I believe that if America gets a National Art": Ibid., p. 222.

130 "It seems to me that abundant artistic material": As quoted in Porter, Ebie, and Campbell, *Taos Artists and Their Patrons,* p. 91.

130 "Studio work dulls the mind": As quoted in Van Deren Coke, *Taos and Santa Fe: The Artist's Environment 1882–1942* (Albuquerque: The University of New Mexico Press, 1963), p. 24.

133 "Treat things as a whole" and "The horse becomes a part of the mesa": As quoted in Broder, *Taos: A Painter's Dream,* p. 225.

133 "We were like brothers": As quoted in Mary Carroll Nelson, *The Legendary Artists of Taos,* p. 79.

134 "a true pastoral painter": Mabel Dodge Luhan, *Taos and Its Artists* (New York: Duell, Sloan, and Pearce, 1947), p. 37.

134 "[The artist's] personal style is governed": Robert Rankin White, *The Lithographs and Etchings of E. Martin Hennings* (Santa Fe: Museum of New Mexico Press, 1978), unpaginated.

140 "fondest work of that early period": From an unpublished, unpaginated letter from Manoir to Robert Rice, c. 1979. Fred Jones Jr. Museum of Art Curatorial Files.

144–47 "In one of his letters": As quoted in Van Deren Coke, *Andrew Dasburg* (Albuquerque: University of New Mexico Press, 1979), pp. 58–59.

148 "I grew up thin": As quoted in Harold McCracken, *Nicolai Fechin* (New York: The Hammer Galleries and The Ram Press, 1961), p. 6.

156 "If American art develops": As quoted in Sharyn Rohlfsen Udall, *Modernist Painting in New Mexico 1913–1935* (Albuquerque: University of New Mexico Press, 1984), p. 152.

156 "I like to paint the landscape in the Southwest": Ibid., p. 153.

162 "The group proposes": As quoted by Stanley L. Cuba in the essay "The Art of Józef Bakos," in *Józef Bakos: An Early Modernist (1891–1977)*, exhibition catalogue (Santa Fe: Museum of Fine Arts, Museum of New Mexico, 1988), unpaginated.

170 "immensity of the landscape": As quoted in Ada Hanifin, "Artist Paints Boulder Scene," *San Francisco Examiner*, May 18, 1934.

176 "shy and silent": Oscar B. Jacobson, "Monroe Tsa-to-ke (Hunting Horse) Kiowa 1904–1937," unpublished manuscript from the O. B. Jacobson Files, Western History Collections, University of Oklahoma.

179 "There was always something in him detached": Ibid.

183 "I think that something always comes through": Interview printed in Jamake Highwater, *Song from the Earth: American Indian Painting* (Boston: New York Graphic Society, 1976), p. 146.

184 "went to—not through": As quoted in Ruth E. Fine, *John Marin* (Washington, D.C.: National Gallery of Art; New York: Abbeville Press, 1990), p. 25.

192 "the life within the outer form": Entry for April 24, 1930, in Nancy Newhall, ed., *The Daybooks of Edward Weston*, vol. 2, *California* (Newhall, N.Y.: Horizon Press, 1966), p. 154.

198 "real American art": As quoted in Robert Hughes, *American Visions: The Epic History of Art in America* (New York: Alfred A. Knopf, 1997), p. 438.

203 "They always thought you wanted to commit suicide": Berenice Abbott, "Commentary," in Hank O'Neal, *Berenice Abbott: American Photographer* (New York: McGraw-Hill, 1982), p. 4.

210 Jeanne d'Ucel article on Hrdy: "Olinka Hrdy: Her Genius Wins Applause in the Art World through Modern Masterpieces," in *Sooner Magazine* (July 1929), pp. 344–45, 368, 370.

210 "among the first adventures": "Riverside Hall, Tulsa, Oklahoma," in *The Western Architect* (December 1929), p. 220.

210–13 Hrdy description of murals: From "Oral History Interview with Olinka Hrdy," interview with Betty Hoag (Los Angeles, March 13, 1965), in Smithsonian Archives of American Art, Washington, D.C. (Interview available on the Archives Web site.)

217 "Morris's paintings feel as if". Arthur C. Danto, "The 'Indivisible Four,'" *The Nation* 276, no. 8 (March 3, 2003), p. 41.

223 "I recall that . . . under the dual influences": As quoted in Ralph Ellison, *Romare Bearden: Paintings and Projections* (Albany: The Art Gallery of the State University of New York at Albany, 1968), unpaginated.

226 "[In *The Passing Scene*, there is an] old horse": Jack Levine, "Commentary," in Stephen Robert Frankel, ed., *Jack Levine* (New York: Rizzoli, 1989), pp. 36, 38.

228 "Does not any genuine personal expression": As quoted in Dorothy C. Miller, ed., *Americans 1942, 18 Artists from 9 States* (New York: Museum of Modern Art, 1942), p. 60.

238 "To consciously live in chaos": As quoted in Donald Kuspit, Robert Shapazian, and Michael Zakian, *Sam Francis: Elements and Archetypes* (Madrid: Fundación Caja de Madrid, 1997), p. 192.

240 "I do not make any art but my own art": As quoted by Jamake Highwater, "Controversy in Native American Art," in Edwin L. Wade, ed., *The Arts of the North American Indian: Native Traditions in Evolution* (New York: Hudson Hills Press, 1986), p. 240.

240–43 "What I was searching for": Brooke Kamin Rapaport, "An Interview with Leon Polk Smith," in Leon Polk Smith, *American Painter*, exhibition catalogue (Brooklyn: The Brooklyn Museum, 1996), pp. 20–21.

243 "[My] freedom of color": Ibid., p. 19.

247 "It is difficult to describe": Barbara Hepworth, *A Pictorial Autobiography*, rev. ed. (London: The Tate Gallery, 1978), p. 53.

248 "very stuff of which sight or vision consists": As quoted in Colin Naylor and Genesis P-Orridge, *Contemporary Artists* (London: St. James Press; New York: St. Martin's Press, 1977), p. 403.

248 "It is obvious that colour is the only direction": Ibid., p. 403.

254 "I bet you can't paint as good as that": As quoted in Edward Lucie-Smith, *Lives of the Great Twentieth Century Artists* (London: Weidenfeld & Nicolson, 1986), p. 341.

258 "act in the gap between [art and life]": As quoted in Dorothy C. Miller, ed., *Sixteen Americans* (New York: Museum of Modern Art, 1959), p. 58.

258 "an active protest": As quoted in Roni Feinstein, "Rauschenberg: Solutions for a Small Planet," *Art in America* 86, no. 2 (February 1998), p. 73.

262 "I was riding in a car": As quoted in Michael Crichton, *Jasper Johns* (New York: Harry N. Abrams, 1977), p. 59.

264 "like a petrified river": As quoted in Eugenie Tsai, *Robert Smithson Unearthed: Drawings, Collages, Writings* (New York: Columbia University Press, 1991), p. 111.

264 "You see, it's ultimately what's done": Ibid., pp. 110–11, 119.

266 "painting and drawing": As quoted in Theodora Vischer and Bernadette Walter, eds., *Roth Time: A Dieter Roth Retrospective* (New York: Museum of Modern Art; Baden, Germany: Lars Müller Publishers, 2003), p. 122.

268 "I am a Shaman-artist": As quoted in Norval Morrisseau and Donald Robinson, *Norval Morrisseau: Travels to the House of Invention* (Toronto: Key Porter Books Ltd., 1997), pp. 98, 100.

278 "American art was born": As quoted in Karen Emenhiser, "Highway Minimalism," in Joe Andoe and Karen Emenhiser, *Joe Andoe—What You See*, exhibition catalogue (Buffalo, N.Y.: University of Buffalo Art Gallery, 2000). Reproduced on Joe Andoe's Web site: *www.joeandoe.com/essays/highway.htm*.

278 "With a horse, you have a generic": Interview with Rich Fisher, Studio Tulsa, KWGS 89.5 FM, National Public Radio, November 3, 1997. Transcript available on Joe Andoe's Web site: *www.joeandoe.com/essays/interview.htm*.

278 "I want these paintings to be like the images": As quoted in John Villani, "Going Beneath the Surface," *The Santa Fe New Mexican* (October 1, 1993), p. 48.

280 "marriage of art and science": As quoted in Abigail Foerstner, "Spatial Effects: Ed Paschke + $(\text{Art})^n$ = The Future," *North Shore Magazine* (March 1998). Reproduced on Ed Paschke's Web site: *www.edpaschke.com/ns398.html*.

280 "The other side of the painter's picture plane": As quoted on Ed Paschke's Web site: *www.edpaschke.com/scolo.html*.

282 "chop shop of bodies": From a 1997 interview with David Frankel, in Helaine Posner, *Kiki Smith* (Boston: Bulfinch Press, 1998), p. 38.

284 "By weaving together aesthetics": As quoted by David Moos in "Painting and the Abstract Truth: The Art of Radcliffe Bailey," in *Radcliffe Bailey: The Magic City* (Birmingham, Ala.: Birmingham Museum of Art, 2001), p. 18.

284 "I keep returning to musicians like Sun Ra": "Conversations between Radcliffe Bailey, David Moos, and Manuel Jordán," ibid., p. 87.

284 "fuses different sounds from different time periods": As quoted by Terrie Sultan in "Rhapsody in Orange," ibid., p. 26.

287 "the person who tells the story": As quoted by David Moos in "Painting and the Abstract Truth: The Art of Radcliffe Bailey," ibid., p. 22.

287 "I . . . believe that the ancestors dance in us daily": As quoted by David Moos in ibid., p. 17.

Index of Artists

Page references to illustrations appear in **bold** type.

Abbott, Berenice, 200–203, **201, 202, 203, 206**
Adams, Ansel, 165, 196–97, **197**
Adams, Kenneth, 138–39, **138, 139**
Andoe, Joe, 278–79, **279**
Arp, Jean, 240, 244, **246**
(art)^n Laboratory, 280–81, **281**
Atget, Eugène, 200, 202, **202**

Bailey, Radcliffe, 250, 284–87, **285**
Bakos, Jozef, 60, 162–65, **163, 164**
Bavinger, Eugene, 278, **278**
Baziotes, William, 13, 234–35, **235**, 236, 238
Bearden, Romare, 13, 220–23, **221, 222**, 250, 284, 287
Benton, Thomas Hart, 198–99, **198, 199**, 214
Berninghaus, Oscar E., 120–21, **120, 121**
Bierstadt, Albert, 88–89, **88, 89**, 93
Black, LaVerne Nelson, 142–43, **143**
Blumenschein, Ernest L., 14, 110, 114–17, **115, 116**, 118, 120, 122, 126, 162
Bonnard, Pierre, 66, 68–69, **69**, 96, 238, 248, 252
Borg, Carl Oscar, 168–69, **168, 169**
Boudin, Eugène, 34–35, **35**, 70
Brown, Roger, 280, **280**

Cannon, T. C., 270, **273**
Cassatt, Mary, 42, 44–45, **45**, 46
Cézanne, Paul, 13, 46, 50, 52, 60–61, **61**, 74, 80, 83, 96, 128, 138, 144, 147, 158, 160, 162, 165, 166, 198
Clark, Alson Skinner, 170, **170**
Cook, Howard, **168**
Copley, John Singleton, 86–87, **87**
Cordero, Helen, **174**
Corneille, 250, **250**
Corot, Jean-Baptiste-Camille, 32–33, **32, 33**
Couse, E. Irving, 14, 110, 120, 122–25, **122, 123, 124**
Crawford, Ralston, 218–19, **219**
Cunningham, Imogen, 196, **196**

Da, Popovi, 172–75, **173, 174**
Dasburg, Andrew, 60, 138, 144–47, **145**, 162, 165
Dater, Judy, **196**
Davie, Alan, 15, 250–51, **251**, 284
Davis, Stuart, 11, 94, 208–9, **208, 209**, 220, 250, 284
Degas, Edgar, 36, 40–41, **41**, 42, 44
Dine, Jim, 254, **257**
Dixon, Maynard, 170–71, **171**, 224
Dufy, Raoul, 58, 70–73, **71, 72**, 232
Dunton, W. H., 120, 126–27, **126, 127**

Fakeye family, 28–29, **29**
Farny, Henry, 104–5, **105**, 110
Fechin, Nicolai, 14, 148–51, **149, 150, 151**
Forain, Jean-Louis, 42–43, **43**
Francis, Sam, 14, 238–39, **239**
Frost, Terry, 248, **248**

Gaspard, Leon, 14, 152–55, **153, 154, 155**
Gauguin, Paul, 46, 52–53, **53**, 56, 66, 70, 83
Good, Leonard, **11**
Gottlieb, Adolph, 13, 236–37, **236, 237**, 238
Gropper, William, 224–25, **224, 225**
Guillaumin, Armand, 40, 46, 50–51, **51**, 60

Hassam, Childe, 94–95, **94, 95**, 188
Henderson, William Penhallow, 158–59, **159**, 160, 162
Hennings, E. Martin, 14, 128, 134–37, **135, 136, 137**, 140
Hepworth, Barbara, 15, 180, 244–47, **245**, 248
Heron, Patrick, 15, 248–49, **249**
Higgins, Victor, 60, 128–29, **128, 129**, 134, 140, 162
Hirsch, Joseph, 228–29, **228, 229**
Hopper, Edward, 13, 94, 96, 200, 204–7, **205, 206**
Houser, Allan, 176, 180–83, **181, 182, 183**
Howe, Oscar, 180, 270, **273**
Hrdy, Olinka, 210–13, **211, 212**

Jackson, William Henry, **92**, 93
Jacobsen, Hugh Newell, 8, 15–17, **16**
Jacobson, Oscar B., 11–13, **11**, 14, 98, 160, 166, 176–79, **178**, 180, 195, 210
Jiménez, Luis, 14, 274–75, **274, 275**, 276
Johns, Jasper, 258, 262–63, **263**

Kadishman, Menashe, 15, **17**
Kelly, Ellsworth, **242**, 243
Kertész, André, 14, 84–85, **84, 85**
Klee, Paul, 232, 250, **250**

Lavenson, Alma, 196, **196**
Leigh, William Robinson, 108–9, **108, 109**
Levine, Jack, 13, 214, 226–27, **227**, 228
Lichtenstein, Roy, 254–57, **255, 256**
Lipton, Seymour, 274, **274**

Manoir, Irving K., 4, 128, 140–41, **141**
Marin, John, 14, 144, 184–85, **184, 185**, 198
Martinez, Maria, 172–75, **173, 174**
Matisse, Henri, 13, 62, 70, 74, 76–79, **77, 78**, 144, 160, 186, 232, 238, 248
Miró, Joan, 234, **234**
Moholy-Nagy, Laszlo, 244, **246**
Monet, Claude, 32, 34, 36–37, **37**, 38, 46, 50, 52, 58, 70, 238
Moran, Thomas, 90–93, **91, 92**
Moroles, Jesús, 276–77, **277**
Morris, George L. K., 13, 214–17, **215, 216**
Morrisseau, Norval, 268–69, **269**
Moscow School, **30**
Motherwell, Robert, 234, **234**

Nordfeldt, B. J. O., **10**, 13, 60, 158, 160–61, **160, 161**, 162, 165

O'Keeffe, Georgia, **2**, 13, 186, 188–91, **189**, 192, 224
Oldenburg, Claes, 254, **256**

Paschke, Ed, 280–81, **281**
Phillips, Bert Geer, 14, 110, 114–17, 118–19, **118, 119**, 120, 122

Picasso, Pablo, 60, 68, 76, 80–83, **81, 82,** 144, 186, 214, 220–23, 232, 234, 244, 248, 250
Pissarro, Camille, 32, 36, 40, 46–49, **47, 48,** 50, 52, 58, 60, 70, 76
Prendergast, Maurice B., 14, 94, 96–97, **97**

Rauschenberg, Robert, 258–61, **259, 260,** 262
Redon, Odilon, 62–63, **62, 63**
Renoir, Pierre-Auguste, 13, 36, 38–39, **38, 39,** 40, 46, 70, 74, 83
Rivers, Larry, 250, 252–53, **253,** 284
Roth, Dieter, 266–67, **266, 267**
Ruscha, Ed, 254, **257**

Sandzén, Birger, 13, 166–67, **166, 167**
Scholder, Fritz, 270–73, **271, 272, 273**
Schreyvogel, Charles, 106–7, **107**
Shahn, Ben, 13, 214, 226, 228, 232–33, **233**
Sharp, Joseph Henry, 14, 110–13, **111, 112, 113,** 114, 118, 120, 122, 134, 168
Signac, Paul, **18–19,** 46–49, 50, 58–59, **59,** 70, 76, 96
Siqueiros, David Alfaro, 144, **146,** 192
Sloan, John, 156–57, **156, 157,** 160, 162, 204, 208, 214, 236
Smith, Kiki, 282–83, **283**
Smith, Leon Polk, 240–43, **241, 242**
Smith, W. Eugene, 14, 200, 230–31, **230, 231**
Smithson, Robert, 264–65, **265**
Stieglitz, Alfred, 184, 186, 188–91, **190,** 192, 196
Surls, James, 276, **276**
Swentzell, Roxanne, **174,** 175

Tafoya, Margaret, **174**
Toulouse-Lautrec, Henri de, 56, 60, 64–65, **64, 65**
Tsatoke, Monroe, 176–79, **177, 178**

Ufer, Walter, 128, 130–33, **131, 132,** 134, 138, 140, 162
Unknown (China), 24–25, **24, 25**
Unknown (Greece), 30–31, **30, 31**
Unknown (India, Gandhara), 20–23, **21, 22, 23**
Unknown (Navajo), 98–101, **99, 100, 101**
Unknown (Papago/Tohono O'odham), **102**
Unknown (Persia), 26–27, **26, 27**
Unknown (Pomo, California), **102**
Unknown (Santa Domingo Pueblo), **242**
Unknown (Western Apache), 102–3, **103**
Unknown (Yokuts, California), **102**
Unknown (Yoruba, Nigeria), **28**

Van Der Zee, James, 14, **286,** 287
Van Gogh, Vincent, 50, 52, 54–57, **55,** 64, 70, 74, 83, 160, 166
Vlaminck, Maurice de, 60, 70, 74–75, **74, 75,** 76
Vuillard, Edouard, 60, 66–67, **66, 67,** 96

Warhol, Andy, 252, 254, **256**
Weber, Max, 13, 186–87, **187**
Weston, Edward, 11, 192–95, **193, 194,** 196

Credits

All art objects were photography by Konrad Eek, Norman, Oklahoma, with the exception of: p. 17 (top right) by Jim Meeks, Oklahoma City; pp. 103, 109, 111, 116 (top right), 137 (right), 145, 151 (left), 154 (bottom left), 157, 159, 160 (left), 271, and 273 (top left) by Joseph Mills, Oklahoma City; pp. 43, 59, 69, and 95 by David Wharton, Fort Worth, Texas.

Every effort has been made to locate and contact the copyright holders of the objects herein illustrated. If omissions are noted, please contact the publisher; corrections will be made in subsequent printings.

Berenice Abbott © Berenice Abbott / Commerce Graphics, Ltd, New York, NY
Ansel Adams © 1981 Center for Creative Photography, Arizona Board of Regents
Joe Andoe © Joe Andoe
Jean Arp © 2004 Artist Rights Society (ARS), New York / VG Bild-Kunst, Bonn
Radcliffe Bailey © 2004 Radcliffe Bailey
Eugene Bavinger © Estate of Eugene Bavinger
William Baziotes © Estate of William Baziotes
Romare Bearden © Romare Bearden Foundation/Licensed by VAGA, New York, NY
Thomas Hart Benton © T.H. Benton and R.P. Benton Testamentary Trusts / UMB Bank Trustee / Licensed by VAGA, New York, NY
Pierre Bonnard © 2004 Artist Rights Society (ARS), New York / ADAGP, Paris
Roger Brown © The School of the Art Institute of Chicago and the Brown Family
T.C. Cannon © Estate of T.C. Cannon, Joyce Cannon Yi, Executor
Corneille © 2004 Artist Rights Society (ARS), New York / ADAGP, Paris
Ralston Crawford © Estate of Ralston Crawford
Imogen Cunningham © Imogen Cunningham Trust
Judy Dater © Judy Dater
Alan Davie © Alan Davie
Stuart Davis © Estate of Stuart Davis / Licensed by VAGA, New York, NY
Jim Dine © 2004 Jim Dine / Artist Rights Society (ARS), New York
Sam Francis © 2004 Samuel L. Francis Foundation, Los Angeles / Artist Rights Society (ARS), New York
Terry Frost © Estate of Sir Terry Frost
Leonard Good © Estate of Leonard Good
Adolph Gottlieb © Adolph and Esther Gottlieb Foundation / Licensed by VAGA, New York, NY
William Gropper © Estate of William Gropper
Barbara Hepworth © Bowness, Hepworth Estate
Patrick Heron © 2004 Artist Rights Society (ARS), New York / DACS, London
Joseph Hirsch © Estate of Joseph Hirsch
Allan Houser © Mrs. Anna Marie Houser / The Allan Houser Foundation
Oscar Howe © Adelheid Howe, 1983
Luis Jiménez © 2004 Luis Jiménez / Artist Rights Society (ARS), New York
Jasper Johns © Jasper Johns / Licensed by VAGA, New York, NY
Ellsworth Kelly © Ellsworth Kelly
Paul Klee © 2004 Artist Rights Society (ARS), New York / VG Bild-Kunst, Bonn
Jack Levine © Jack Levine / Licensed by VAGA, New York, NY
Roy Lichtenstein © Estate of Roy Lichtenstein
Seymour Lipton © Estate of Seymour Lipton
John Marin © 2004 Estate of John Marin / Artist Rights Society (ARS), New York
Henri Matisse © 2004 Succession H. Matisse, Paris / Artist Rights Society (ARS), New York
Joan Miró © 2004 Succession Miró / Artist Rights Society (ARS), New York / ADAGP, Paris
Laszlo Moholy-Nagy © 2004 Artist Rights Society (ARS), New York / VG Bild-Kunst, Bonn
Jesús Moroles © 2004 Jesús Moroles
George L.K. Morris © 2004 Frelinghuysen Morris House & Studio
Norval Morrisseau © 2004 Norval Morrisseau. All rights reserved. Courtesy of Kinsman Robinson Galleries
Robert Motherwell © Dedalus Foundation, Inc. / Licensed by VAGA, New York, NY
Georgia O'Keeffe © 2004 The Georgia O'Keeffe Foundation / Artist Rights Society (ARS), New York
Claes Oldenburg © Claes Oldenburg and Coosje van Bruggen
Ed Paschke and (art)^n Laboratory artists Ellen Sandor, Stephan Meyers, and Janine Fron © Ellen Sandor, (art)^n
Pablo Picasso © 2004 Estate of Pablo Picasso / Artist Rights Society (ARS), New York
Robert Rauschenberg © Robert Rauschenberg / Licensed by VAGA, New York, NY
Larry Rivers © Estate of Larry Rivers / Licensed by VAGA, New York, NY
Dieter Roth © Dieter Roth Estate
Edward Ruscha © Ed Ruscha
Fritz Scholder © Fritz Scholder
Ben Shahn © Estate of Ben Shahn / Licensed by VAGA, New York, NY
Paul Signac © 2004 Artist Rights Society (ARS), New York/ADAGP, Paris
John Sloan © Estate of John Sloan
Kiki Smith © Kiki Smith and Universal Limited Art Editions, Inc., courtesy PaceWildenstein
Leon Polk Smith © Leon Polk Smith Foundation / Licensed by VAGA, New York, NY
Robert Smithson © Estate of Robert Smithson / Licensed by VAGA, New York, NY
James Surls © 2004 James Surls
James Van Der Zee © Estate of James Van Der Zee
Maurice de Vlaminck © 2004 Artist Rights Society (ARS), New York / ADAGP, Paris
Edouard Vuillard © 2004 Artist Rights Society (ARS), New York / ADAGP, Paris
Andy Warhol © 2004 Andy Warhol Foundation for the Visual Arts / ARS, New York
Max Weber © Estate of Max Weber
Edward Weston © 1981 Center for Creative Photography, Arizona Board of Regents